The
Mary Clare Karnick
Irish history & Culture Collection

Saint Mary's University of Minnesota

JANE OHLMEYER AND ÉAMONN Ó CIARDHA

The Irish Statute Staple Books, 1596-1687

The Irish Statute Staple Books, 1596-1687

Edited By
JANE OHLMEYER AND ÉAMONN Ó CIARDHA

Third supplement to *The Calendar of Ancient Records of Dublin*

Series editor: Mary Clark, Dublin City Archivist

Dublin Corporation 1998

Published by Dublin Corporation in the Republic of Ireland

© Dublin City Archives and the British Library
(for the Staple Manuscripts in their possession);
Jane Ohlmeyer and Éamonn Ó Ciardha
(for the introductory chapters and database).

ISBN - 0-9505301-74

Typeset in Baskerville
by Dundalgan Press, Dundalk, Co. Louth, Republic of Ireland

Printed on acid-free paper to archival standards and bound
by Dundalgan Press, Dundalk, Co. Louth, Republic of Ireland

TABLE OF CONTENTS

CONTRIBUTORS

THE EDITORS:

Jane Ohlmeyer

M.A. (Hons, St. Andrews), M.A. (University of Illinois), Ph.D.(Dubl.). Jane Ohlmeyer is a lecturer in History at the University of Aberdeen. She has authored *Civil War and Restoration in the Three Stuart Kingdoms: The career of Randal MacDonnell, marquis of Antrim* (Cambridge, 1993) and edited *Ireland from Independence to Occupation, 1641-1660* (Cambridge, 1995) and (with the late John Kenyon), *The Civil Wars. A Military History of England, Scotland and Ireland 1638-1660* (Oxford, 1998). Dr Ohlmeyer is currently writing 'War and Society in Early Modern Ireland' (Longmans, forthcoming) and a monograph on the Irish elite in the seventeenth century.

Éamonn Ó Ciardha

B.A. and M.A. (NUI). Éamonn Ó Ciardha is completing his doctoral thesis on Irish Jacobitism at Cambridge University. He has published numerous articles in Irish and English in various anthologies and scholarly journals, including ones on law and disorder in early modern Ireland, on Irish Jacobitism, and on the value of the Irish language sources. He is currently working for the Dictionary of Irish Biography.

OTHER CONTRIBUTORS:

Mary Clark

B.A. (Hons), D.A.A. (NUI). Mary Clark is the Dublin City Archivist and was a member of the inaugural National Archives Advisory Council, 1987-97. Her recent publications include *Directory of Historic Dublin Guilds (1993, with Raymond Refaussé)* and *Serving the City: the Dublin City Managers and Town Clerks, 1230-1996* (1996, with Grainne Doran).

Duncan Davidson

B.Sc (Hons. Aberdeen). Duncan Davidson recently graduated with a BSc in Computer Science from the University of Aberdeen. He is involved in various historical computing projects including the use of Geographical Information Systems, Internet and database technology and their applications in the analysis and distribution of historical data. He was responsible for the design of the database, the creation of the database installation system and the preparation of all material for publication on CD ROM. He also provided invaluable technical support throughout the project.

Bridget McCormack   B.A. Th. (Hons); M.A. (NUI). Bridget McCormack has contributed to new editions of *The Chapter Act Book of Christ Church Dublin, 1574-1634* (ed. Raymond Gillespie, 1997), *The Registers of Christ Church Cathedral, 1710-1900* (ed. Raymond Refaussé, 1998) and *The Deeds of Chrsit Church, Dublin* (ed. Raymond Refaussé, forthcoming). Her book on perceptions of St. Patrick in eighteenth century Ireland is scheduled for publication in the Maynooth Historical Studies series.

ACKNOWLEDGEMENTS

The production of this book and CD ROM has been a collaborative endeavour. The University Research Committee at the University of Aberdeen University, the British Academy and the Dublin City Archives generously paid for two research assistants, Éamonn Ó Ciardha and Bridget McCormack, to prepare the database for publication. Éamonn had the daunting task of entering all of the staple records into a relational database; while Bridget meticulously checked the Dublin entries. Without their painstaking efforts this exciting project would have foundered and I am deeply indebted to them, especially to Éamonn who served as a model research assistant during his year in Aberdeen. The Dublin City Archives funded the publication of both the book and the CD ROM. I am grateful to these bodies for their financial support and to the British Library and the Dublin City Archives for their permission to reproduce the Statute Staple records in their possession.

I would like to add a special word of thanks to the scholars who have allowed me to draw on their expertise and have offered support and encouragement throughout. My colleagues in the History Department—Frederik Pedersen, Steve Murdoch and, above all, Duncan Davidson—are developing a project on historical computing and mapping (GIS Project) and they designed the database and patiently solved numerous technical problems. Their expertise and commitment to this project was greatly appreciated, as was the skill with which Bill Naphy and Frederik Pedersen translated a number of the Latin texts. The support, advice and encouragement given by Allan Macinnes, Head of the History Department, was also greatly valued. Robert Gordon and Tanya Cresswell of Rainnea Graphics, Glenurquhart, Invernesshire, reconstructed the seal of the staple that forms the design for the CD ROM and book cover. The introductory chapters have benefited enormously from the helpful and incisive comments for improvement made by Nicholas Canny, Aidan Clarke, Rolf Loeber, John MacCafferty, Bríd McGrath, Mícheál Ó Siochrú, and Kevin Whelan. I owe a particular debt to Raymond Gillespie, who drew my attention to the Staple records in the first place, and to Mary Clark, Dublin City Archivist. The success of this project and the publication of the Staple records stem in large part from Mary's drive and enthusiasm.

On a more personal note Éamonn Ó Ciardha would like to pay tribute to the continued support of his partner, Lis Henderson. I would like to thank my au-pair, Veronica Gurycova and my family—Alex Green, Richard and Jamie Parker-Green and Shirley Ohlmeyer—for their patience and encouragement.

Jane Ohlmeyer   Aberdeen, 1 August 1998

It has been a great pleasure to work with Jane Ohlmeyer on the Irish Statute Staple Books. This project began in September 1995, when Dr. Ohlmeyer visited the Dublin City Archives to inspect the Staple Books on the recommendation of Raymond Gillespie. I had long been convinced of the importance of these source materials for the history of 17th century Ireland and had been supported in this view by a report, commissioned by Dublin Corporation from Dr. Gillespie two years previously. To my delight, Dr. Ohlmeyer's enthusiasm matched my own, and within twelve months she had secured a research grant from the University of Aberdeen which allowed Eamonn O Ciardha to begin the work of transcribing the texts belonging to the City Archives in October 1996. This task was expanded in the following year to include texts relevant to the Irish Staple in the British Library, and we are grateful to Dr. Roger Evans of the Department of Manuscripts, for allowing us to include these materials. The work of designing a database capable of holding the immense amount of information generated from the staple books fell to Duncan Davidson, Steve Murdoch and Frederik Pedersen of the University of Aberdeen, who worked throughout in close collaboration with Jane Ohlmeyer. Irish historiography owes an immense debt to Dr. Ohlmeyer for her dedication, scholarship and sheer hard work, which has resulted in the production of a splendid edition of a new and valuable resource within two years.

I am indebted for advice and assistance to Ms. Aoife Dineen, Dublin City Archives; Ms. Gráinne Doran, Mid-East Regional Archivist; Ms. Fionnuala Hanrahan, Wexford County Librarian; Dr. Charles Moreton, History of Parliament Project; Mr. Terence O'Keeffe, Assistant Law Agent, Dublin Corporation; and Dr. Raymond Refaussé, R.C.B. Library. Dr. Toby Barnard, Ms. Bernadette Cunningham, Dr. Raymond Gillespie and Dr. Rolf Loeber all provided specialist insights and support from their vast acquaintance with the history of 17th century Ireland. In addition to supplying transcripts of all the staple books, Eamonn O Ciardha, uasal, offered many insights from his detailed knowledge of Jacobite Ireland, while Ms. Bridget McCormack carefully checked the transcripts against the original documents in the City Archives and made many suggestions which have been included in the publication.

When publishing the Statute Staple Books, we decided to produce this complex work in machine-readable form and in the more usual format of a bound volume. The production of the CD-ROM was a collaborative effort between Duncan Davidson of the University of Aberdeen and Robert Gordon of Rainnea Graphics and we are indebted to them for their technical expertise. As always, Eamon Mathews and his colleagues at Dundalgan Press have produced a handsomely bound volume, the third in Dublin Corporation's series of supplements to *The Calendar of Ancient Records of Dublin*. We are also grateful to the National Archives for permission to reproduce documents in its possession.

This publication is being issued in 1998 to mark the centenary of Sir John Gilbert (1829-1898) and I am grateful for support received from

Dublin Corporation Public Libraries' Gilbert Centenary Committee. The editors have at all times been encouraged by the active support of the Dublin City Librarian, Mrs. Deirdre Ellis-King, and the Dublin City Manager, Mr. John Fitzgerald, which has enabled us to bring this project to fruition.

Mary Clark   Dublin City Archivist, 1 August 1998

FOREWORD

By the Right Honourable the Lord Mayor of Dublin,
Councillor Senator Joe Doyle

Since taking up office as Lord Mayor of Dublin earlier this month I have become aware of the many treasures which are held by the city on behalf of its people—for example, when I moved into the Mansion House, I was immediately struck by a superb stained-glass window on the staircase, the work of the noted firm of Joshua Clarke and Sons, which I intend to feature on my Christmas Card this year. I am conscious that we need to bring these treasures to the people and so I was delighted to hear about the staple books and this ambitious project to publish their contents in an accessible format, using the latest technology available on CD-ROM, as well as in the more traditional format of a printed and bound volume.

The word staple immediately brings to mind the fundamentals of life— for example, the staple means of sustenance in bread and wine. I understand that the Dublin Staple began in the Middle Ages as an agency for regulating trade in basic commodities, such as wool, leather and sheepskins and that several other places were also designated as staple towns, including Cork, Drogheda, Galway and Waterford. However, by the late 16th century, the staple had been reorganised primarily as an agency for the registration of debt and it is this activity which is recorded in the staple books which are held in the Dublin City Archives and in the British Library.

At first glance, this information may appear to be unremarkable, but as the comprehensive index shows, there is a wealth of fascinating detail hidden in the staple books, which this publication has revealed for the first time. The original documents were written during the seventeenth century in secretary hand and as you will see if you examine the photographs accompanying this publication, it is almost impossible to read the text— may I extend my compliments to the scholars who have done so on our behalf! Debtors and creditors came from every part of Ireland to register bonds in the staple towns and as a result, these documents form a truly national resource, containing some 10,000 names along with occupations and places of origin—a real bonus for family and local historians.

On behalf of Dublin Corporation, may I extend our sincere gratitude to the University of Aberdeen for agreeing to participate in this exciting project of transcribing, editing and publishing the staple books and especially for providing generous funding for the project. We are also most grateful to the British Library for allowing the staple books in their care to be transcribed and included in this publication, and to the British Academy for providing a research grant to facilitate this work. This is the third volume in the series of *Supplements to The Calendar of Ancient Records of Dublin*, which has been produced by Dublin Corporation to continue the work of Sir John Gilbert in publishing material from the Dublin City

Archives. This series of *Supplements* has been very well received, and I am certain this volume will meet with the same warm welcome accorded to its predecessors and that it will prove to be of immense assistance to all scholars with an interest in Irish history.

The Mansion House, Dublin   *31 July 1998*

LIST OF ILLUSTRATIONS AND FIGURES

CONVENTIONS AND CLASSIFICATIONS

SPELLING - NAMES: With the exception of the 'names' field in the database and the appendices published below, all surnames have been standardized according to the guidelines laid down in Edward MacLysaght, ed., *The Surnames of Ireland* (6th edition, Dublin, 1985).

SPELLING - PLACES: While the original spelling of townlands has been retained, the spelling of counties has been standardized throughout.

CURRENCIES: Unless specifically stated, amounts are given in pounds sterling.

DATES: Dates are given according to the Old (Julian) calendar. The beginning of the year is taken as 1 January rather than the 25 March.

LIST OF ABBREVIATIONS

BL	British Library, London
Add MSS	Additional Manuscripts
D.	Deed
Dc	Dublin City Archives
Dc 1-3	Staple Books 1-3
ID	Staple Database, Identification Number
HMC	*Historical Manuscripts Commission*
MS/MSS	Manuscript(s)
NA	National Archives, Dublin
NLI	National Library of Ireland
PRO	Public Record Office, London
TCD	Trinity College, Dublin

GLOSSARY OF TERMS[1]

Bill of exchange: an unconditional written order, addressed by one person to another, signed by the person giving it, requiring the person to whom it is addressed to pay, on demand or at a fixed time, a sum to a specified person.

Bond: a contract under seal to pay a sum of money or a contract under seal acknowledging a debt. In a bond for the repayment of a debt, the obligation binds the debtor to pay a sum for double the amount of the debt.

Clerk of the recognizance: the clerk who certified the debt into the Court of Chancery. When a creditor wished to proceed against a debtor whose term had expired, it was the clerk of the recognizances to whom the creditor turned. The clerk presented the original statute staple to the clerk of the crown in Chancery who then furnished the creditor with a writ of *capias and extent*. The clerk noted this in his entry book. The creditor delivered the writ to the sheriff of the county in which the debtor's lands lay. The acknowledgement of a debt contained in a recognizance of statute staple was the judgement. The sheriff seized the debtor's property and, with the aid of a jury of at least 12 men, valued it by means of an inquest and made an extent. This was attached to the writ and returned to Chancery. A writ of *liberate* was then awarded to the creditor and this instructed the sheriff to release the debtor's lands to the creditor.

Court of Chancery: principal court in England and Ireland where the law of equity was enforced.

Creditor: a person to whom a debt is owing.

Debtor: a person who owes a debt to another.

Deed of indenture: a deed made between two or more parties. Each party retained a copy and cut or indented the deed with a wavy line to correspond with the other copy.

Defeazance/indenture of defeazance: a condition annexed to a statute staple, entered into a court of record, containing certain conditions outlining a repayment schedule. If the conditions of the defeazance were performed the deed was made void.

Decree: judgement in Chancery.

---

[1] The following were consulted: E. R. Hardy Ivamy, ed., *Mozley and Whiteley's Law Dictionary* (London, 1988); John Burke, ed., *Jowitt's Dictionary of English Law* (London, 1977) and W. J. Jones, *The Elizabethan Court of Chancery* (Oxford, 1967), pp. 499-504.

Recognizance: formal acknowledgement of a debt or an obligation, usually with penalties for breach of the same.

Statute staple: a recognizance or obligation of record, entered into before the mayors and constables of staple towns. The only seal required for its validity was the seal of the staple.

Staple town: a privileged market, with a monopoly for the sale of certain goods, particularly wool. By the Statute of Staple of 1353 the mayors and constables of the staple were empowered to take and seal recognizances of debt (the statute staple). If the debtor failed to pay the mayor of the staple had the power to imprison him/her and attach his/her lands and goods. These were sold to satisfy the creditor. If the debtor resided outside the limits of the staple, the recognizance was certified into the Court of Chancery. Originally only Dublin, Waterford, Cork and Drogheda were designated staple towns but by the early seventeenth century Belfast, Carrickfergus, Derry, Galway, Kilkenny, Limerick, New Ross, Sligo, Wexford and Youghal also enjoyed the accolade.

Usury: the gain of anything in consideration of a loan beyond the principal and a specified rate of interest.[2] In 1634 in an attempt to minimize usury the Irish parliament set the interest rate at 10% and declared void any bond that reserved more than this.[3]

---

[2] For a helpful discussion of what constituted usury see E. Kerridge, *Trade and Banking in early modern England* (Manchester, 1988), p. 34 fol.

[3] 10th Charles I, session II, Chap XXII (1634) - An act against usury, *The Statutes at large passed in the parliaments held in Ireland (1310-1800)* (20 vols., Dublin, 1786-1801), II, 83-4.

CHAPTER 1:

THE IRISH STATUTE STAPLE IN THE EARLY MODERN PERIOD[1]

Apart from a few notable exceptions historians of early modern Ireland have apparently overlooked the significance of the records of the Irish statute staple.[2] George O'Brien, writing earlier this century, is the only historian to have considered the Irish staple. However his article in the first volume of *Economic History*, which examined the organisation of the staple and the Irish wool trade, failed to draw attention to the importance of the staple as a credit system. O'Brien's omission no doubt stems from his failure to consult the extant staple records housed in the Dublin City Archives and in the British Library. In fact he maintained that no record of the Irish staple had survived and misleadingly suggested that by the early 1630s the staple system in Ireland had become obsolete.[3] This was clearly not the case.

The Irish staple, which dated from the thirteenth century, was initially established to regulate the trade of basic, or staple, goods such as wool and hides which could only be sold to foreign merchants in designated 'staple' towns—originally Dublin, Waterford, Cork and Drogheda. It also provided a sure way for traders to recover their debts.[4] Throughout the seventeenth century the staple continued to do this. The Dublin staple volumes contain permits to ship staple goods, especially wool and salt hides, lists of customs dues, and disciplinary hearings of merchants and aldermen, who had

[1] I am grateful to Nicholas Canny, Aidan Clarke, Mary Clark, Raymond Gillespie, Rolf Loeber, and Éamonn Ó Ciardha for reading and commenting on an earlier draft of this chapter. Éamonn Ó Ciardha kindly brought many useful references to the Percival papers to my attention.

[2] Michael MacCarthy-Morrogh, 'Credit and Remittance: Monetary Problems in early seventeenth-century Munster' in *Irish Economic and Social History* 14 (1987), pp. 5-19. The English staple records have only received marginally more attention. The principal exception is E. E. Rich, ed., *The Staple Court Books of Bristol* (Bristol Record Society, vol. 5, Bristol, 1934) which covers the years 1509-1513 and 1595-1601. The English staple records are in PRO, Lord Chamberlain's Department 4: Office of the Clerk of the Recognizances—Rolls and Entry Books of Recognizances on Statute Staple; PRO, Chancery 152: Recognizances of Statute Staple; and PRO, Chancery 228: Petty Bag Office—Proceedings on Statute Staple. For a sobering warning about how not to use the staple records see, H. R. Trevor-Roper, 'The Elizabethan Aristocracy' in *Economic History Review*, 2nd series, 3:3 (1951), pp. 279-98.

[3] George O'Brien, 'The Irish Staple Organization in the reign of James I' in *Economic History* 1 (1926-9), p. 54.

[4] The staple was regulated by a number of important statutes: 27th Edward III, Stat 2 (1353), 23rd Henry VIII cap vi (1531), 27th Elizabeth I Cap iv (1585), 16, 17 Charles II Cap v (1664), *The Statutes at Large from Magna Carta to the end of the last Parliament, 1761* (8 vols., London, 1763), I, 275-84, II, 167-9, 636-8, III, 292-3; for further details also see W. S. Holdsworth, *A History of English Law* (17 vols., 2nd edn, London, 1965), II, 542-3. For an excellent introduction to the history of the staple see Rich, ed., *Staple Court*, pp. 4-29.

infringed staple regulations.[5] For example in 1625 Peter Wybrants of Dublin and over 100 other tradesmen and merchants were reprimanded and often fined for trading goods which had not been licensed by the mayor and constables of the staple.[6] In May 1631 the Cork corporation, unhappy with the quantity and quality of apples and pears being brought into the city, passed a bye-law requiring all people trading in the fruits to pay 'a noble' for each boat load to the mayor and constables of the staple. The profits from this were assigned to the repair and improvement of the 'quay of this city'.[7]

By the early seventeenth century the real significance of the staple lay not in the co-ordination of trade but in the regulation of debt and the creation of a sophisticated credit network. Perhaps in recognition of this the Irish staple towns expanded to include Belfast, Carrickfergus, Derry, Galway, Kilkenny, Limerick, New Ross, Sligo, Wexford, and Youghal.[8] The brethren and merchants of the staple elected—for the period of a year—a mayor, who enjoyed considerable legal powers especially in the regulation and recovery of debt, and two constables of the staple.[9] Among other things the mayors of the staple were empowered to take recognizances of debt incurred on the staple.[10] The fee for this service was clearly set out: 'The mayor and constables of the staple have for every obligation of one hundred pounds or under for every pound a half-penny and of every obligation above a hundred for every pound a farthing.'[11] The clerk of the staple then recorded these transactions in a book 'safely kept by him, taking 8 pence and no more for every entry'.[12] In theory only members of

---

[5] See Appendix IV and ID 233, 281, 290, 306, 310, 312, 330.

[6] See Appendix IV Section C [Dc f. 280r fol] for details.

[7] Richard Caulfield, ed., *The Council Book of the Corporation of the city of Cork* (Guildford, Surrey, 1876), p. 158.

[8] O'Brien, 'The Irish Staple' pp. 44-46. Belfast was designated as a staple town in 1616 yet no staple appears to have met there, Jean Agnew, *Belfast Merchant Families in the Seventeenth Century* (Dublin, 1996). New Ross became a staple town in 1621 but also appears never to have functioned as one. I am grateful to Bríd McGrath for bringing this to my attention.

[9] Details of the elections of the mayors, constables and clerks of the staple, together with the brethren or merchants of the staple, are recorded in the Dublin volumes. In every case referred to Chancery, whatever the staple, the names of the mayors and staples are also listed. See Appendix I for a complete list of the staple officials for Dublin from 1598-1687, for Drogheda (1635-1690), and for Cork (1618-1640 and 1657-1687) and partial lists for Carrickfergus, Galway, Kilkenny, Limerick, Sligo, Waterford, Wexford and Youghal. If the mayor was absent from the staple no business could be conducted on it and he was replaced. For an incomplete listing of the brethren of the Dublin staple see Appendix II.

[10] For a transcript of the oaths sworn by the mayors, constables and brethren of the staple, see Appendix III Section F.

[11] Dc 2/281r, the oath is transcribed in Appendix III Section F.

[12] Clerks charged a further two pence for every search they undertook. Clerks who failed to enter the transaction within 6 months were fined £20., *The Statutes at Large*, II, 636-8.

the staple enjoyed access to these privileges.[13] In practice the staple serviced a wide range of individuals who lent and borrowed money for a variety of reasons.

The recognizances taken by the mayors of the staple, known as statutes staple, were a form of registered bond by which the debtor(s) entered into a recognizance to pay the creditor(s) a fixed sum, at a given time, together with interest at 10%.[14] The amount of the bond was not a record of the actual loan but security for the loan and was usually double the amount of the loan.[15] Three registers, covering the years 1596-37 and 1664-78, recording the entry of bonds on the Dublin staple are extant and are housed in the Dublin City Archives.[16] These volumes are all in reasonable condition and apart from two principal exceptions (May-October 1604 and August 1615—August 1616 when no transactions were recorded) appear to be remarkably complete with transactions being regularly conducted throughout the course of the year.[17] No Dublin volumes appear to have survived for the years 1638-1663 and the records for 1604 and 1615-16 are incomplete.

If a debtor defaulted on repayment and he lived within the jurisdiction of the staple town, the mayor had the power to imprison him or to take possession of his moveable goods and his lands and to use them to repay the creditor. However in many cases, especially if the debtor lived outside the jurisdiction of the staple, the clerk of the recognizances certified the debt in to the Court of Chancery. It served as 'both a court of appeal and a "clearing house", by means of which a local court in one corner of [Ireland] could enforce a distraint on property in another part of the

[13] See Appendix III Section D1-D2. Early bonds stated that money was lent 'for wool, leather and lead bought and received' (see Section C1) and this changed to 'for wool hides and lead bought and received'.

[14] The wording of these statutes staple remained remarkably consistent. For examples see Appendix III. For an example of an English statute staple see Holdsworth, *History, III*, 672-3. For a discussion of interest rates see the glossary and. Extant bonds issued by the staple occasionally survive, often amongst estate papers. For an example of a bond contracted on the Dublin staple and the accompanying indenture of defeazance see Appendix III Section C1-C2. Another staple bond, contracted on the Dublin staple (ID 2147), between James Lowman of Kilkenny and William Bretton of Wexford, dated 29 August 1636 and recorded in Chancery on 24 January 1637 has survived among the Ormond Deeds (NLI, D. 4043). For an indenture of defeazance recorded on the Dublin staple, see NA, D. 15,248 between Robert Colvill and Hugh, earl of Mount Alexander, dated 27 November 1675. For examples of bonds issued on the Kilkenny staple see NLI, D. 4146 and D. 4140 between Ormond and Sir John Temple, 14 January 1640. For a bond contracted on the Drogheda staple see NLI, D. 3989.

[15] For specific examples see Chapter 2.

[16] What became of the registers covering the years 1637-1664 remains a mystery. It is possible that staple registers dealing with the sixteenth century have also been lost. Certainly a statute of 1531 mandated that all clerks of the staple record all bonds, as did a further act of 1581, *The Statutes at Large*, II, 167-9, 636-8. The oath sworn by the mayor and constables of the staple, included in Dc2, dates from 1554 and the reign of Mary and Philip, see Appendix III Section F1.

[17] For further details see Chapter 2.

country'.[18] After certifying the debt into Chancery, the creditor then delivered a writ to the sheriff of the county in which the debtor's lands lay (the acknowledgement of a debt contained in a recognizance of statute staple was the judgement itself).[19] The sheriff seized the debtor's goods and property (after empanelling a jury to appraise its value) and returned an inquisition into Chancery. A writ of *liberate* was then issued in Chancery to the creditor which instructed the sheriff to release the debtor's goods and lands to him in fulfillment of the debt.[20] Five registers of bonds, kept by the clerk of recognizance of the Chancery between 1618 and 1687, were bought by the British Library in the mid-nineteenth century and are housed there.[21] These Chancery volumes are particularly interesting

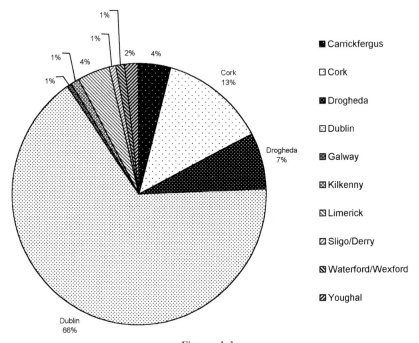

Figure 1.1:
Pie chart showing the activity of Irish Staple Towns
(recorded in the Dublin and Chancery volumes)

[18] Rich, ed., *The Staple Court*, p. 92.

[19] For an example of a bond certified into Chancery see NLI, D. 4043 between James Lowman and William Bretton, 29 August 1636.

[20] For a detailed discussion of the problems involved in interpreting the Chancery staple records see Trevor-Roper, 'The Elizabethan Aristocracy', pp. 279-98. For examples from Bristol of Chancery proceedings, see Rich, ed., *The Staple Court*, pp. 97 fol.

[21] For further details see Chapter 2. These volumes were purchased on 1 June 1854 at Sir William Betham's Sale. It is not clear how, why or when the staple volumes came into Betham's possession.

because they contain a wealth of detail on the activity of all of the Irish staple towns. As Figure 1.1 shows the greatest number of entries recorded in Chancery came from Dublin (66%), Cork (13%), Drogheda (7%), Limerick and Carrickfergus (4% each), Kilkenny and Galway (1% each) with the least coming from Londonderry (only 2 transactions or 0.15% of the total).[22]

Between them these eight volumes record 4000 individual transactions (2600 or 65% on the Dublin Staple and 1400 or 35% in the Chancery volumes). Virtually every entry lists the status or occupation of the debtor(s) and creditor(s), often with the office that they held. The address of the debtor(s) and creditor(s) was also stated, together with the date on which the transaction took place and the amount of the bond. Though this information is generally consistent between entries, the address in particular varies. For example, Chidley Coote gave his address in 1653 as 'Lanham, Essex, England' while the following year he was resident at 'Killester, Dublin'. A considerable number of individual transactions were also annotated in the margins. The Chancery volumes included lengthy memoranda and indentures of defeazance that outlined a repayment timetable and occasionally indicated why an individual wanted to borrow money in the first place. In the Dublin staple books these annotations indicated whether a case was referred to the Court of Chancery or to the local sheriff and whether the bond was cancelled and the money repaid.[23]

The important information contained in these transactions has been extracted and entered in to a relational database (see Chapter 2 for details on how the database was constructed). In all over 10,000 names—4309 creditors and 5879 debtors—were entered into the database. Predictably the same person appeared more than once and so the actual number of people using the staple was probably between 5000 and 6000 (see Chapters 3 and 4 for alphabetical listings of creditors and debtors). The names of hundreds of Irish merchants, landowners, tradesmen, aristocrats, municipal officials and government officers, and the names of scores of widows and clerics (including bishops from nearly every diocese in Ireland) were recorded. In fact the names of individuals lending and borrowing on the Irish staples read like a veritable 'Who's Who' of early modern Irish history. They included the earls of Ormond, Orrery, Antrim, Clancarthy, and Inchiquin; leading government officials—Sir John Davies, Sir William Petty, and Richard Cox; confederates—Lord Conor Maguire, Sir Phelim O'Neill, Richard Bellings, and Patrick Darcy; and the antiquarians, Mathew DeRenzy and Sir James Ware. Other interesting figures such as Valentine Greatrakes, the 'touch doctor' from County Waterford, and

---

[22] Presumably the London staple was being used as an alternative source of credit. These records are extant in Public Record Office in London. Only a few of the bonds issued by the provincial staples appear to have survived, for examples see note 14 above.

[23] For further details see Chapter 2.

Thomas Blood, who tried in 1663 to assassinate the duke of Ormond and in 1671 to steal the crown jewels, also appear.[24]

Moreover the names of these debtors and creditors embraced every ethnic and religious group living in early modern Ireland. While surnames remain only a crude guide to ethnicity, it appears that all sections of the community enjoyed access to credit particularly during the early decades of the seventeenth century. The surnames of 100 individuals who borrowed on a variety of staple towns and listed their address as County Tipperary serve as an example. Debtors with surnames associated with Old English families—Blount, Butler, Prendergast, and Tobin—borrowed throughout the course of the century; debtors with surnames associated with Gaelic Irish families—Dwyer, FitzPatrick, O'Brien, and O'Mara—borrowed more frequently before 1641 and rarely after 1660; while debtors with surnames associated with New English families—Alcock, Boate, Coleman, and Jones—borrowed more frequently after 1660 than in the pre-war years. These patterns of borrowing no doubt reflected the prevailing changes in landholding associated with the widespread mortgage of land, especially among the native Irish, and with the revolutionary land settlement of the 1650s.

The total number of transactions that were recorded in the extant staple books has been plotted on a line graph (Figure 1.2) that clearly demonstrates the relationship between staple activity and economic and political crisis. For example, the impact of harvest failure and the intermittent subsistence crises, especially of the mid-1620s and late 1630s when the availability of Irish land was at a premium, appears to result in an increase in the activity of the staple as people, deprived of their landed revenues, turned to the staple for credit. The outbreak of war after 1641 had a dramatic and devastating impact on the operation of the statute staple throughout Ireland. It provoked a major national economic crisis and fundamentally undermined the networks of trust and mutual interdependence that sustained the staple as an effective paper credit system. As a result Dublin appears to be the only city to operate a staple at all during the 1640s (though the bulk of the provincial towns continued to elect staple officials).[25] Between the outbreak of rebellion in October 1641 and the restoration of Charles II in May 1660 243 cases, involving bonds worth £173,979 were referred from the Dublin staple to Chancery (Figure 1.3). In the absence of the Dublin staple books for the years 1638-1664, it will prove impossible to determine the actual number of bonds recorded on the Dublin Staple. However during the first half of the seventeenth century nearly one-fifth of all bonds recorded on the Dublin staple proceeded to Chancery; by the later decades of the seventeenth century this figure had

---

[24] Keith Thomas, *Religion and the Decline of Magic* (London, 1991), pp. 240-2, 247, 248 and L. J. Arnold, 'Valentine Greatrakes: a seventeenth-century 'touch doctor' in *Eire-Ireland* 11:1 (1976), pp. 3-12.

[25] See Appendix I.

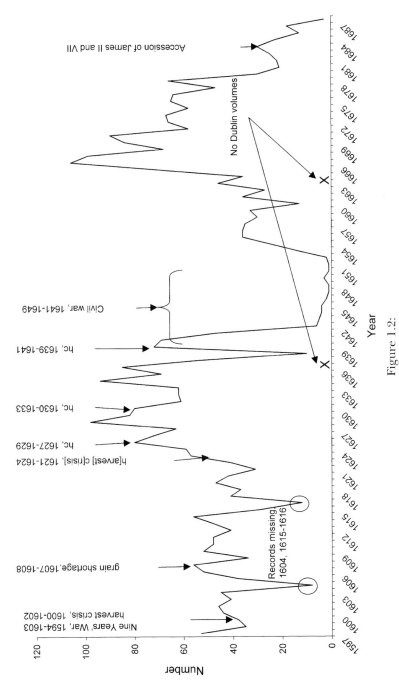

Figure 1.2:

Line graph of the total number of transactions (recorded in the Dublin and Chancery volumes)

risen to nearly one quarter (see Figure 1.10). In an attempt to determine the activity of the Dublin wartime staple this figure of 243 could probably be multiplied by a factor of between four and five. Thus between 927 and 1215 transactions could well have been recorded on the Dublin staple throughout the war and interregnum. Admittedly the lion's share of the cases taken to Chancery date from the years after 1653 when a modicum of political stability had returned to Ireland and the staples at Carrickfergus, Galway and Youghal were also operating.[26] Yet in the decade between 1642 and 1652 44 cases were referred to Chancery; perhaps as many as 220 could have been recorded on the Dublin Staple itself. The fact that the staple operated at all during the 1640s and its quick recovery during the 1650s highlights its importance as a credit network in a country where coinage was more scarce than ever before.

In social and economic terms credit was a levelling force within the community and reciprocal ties of indebtedness bound rich and poor alike irrespective of ethnicity or religion. A preliminary analysis of the staple records indicates that individuals from a wide variety of social and economic backgrounds—members of the Irish aristocracy, the gentry, merchants, soldiers, farmers, tradesmen, craftsmen, clergymen, civil and government officials, and women—made extensive use of the staple. On occasion civic bodies also used it as a means of recording an obligation. For example, in August 1611 Cork Corporation required Dominic Roche FitzWilliam and Thomas Gold and others to enter into staple bonds as security for wines and other goods. In October 1615 George Tyrry Fitz Edmond was elected mayor of Cork on the condition he paid £20 'towards the reparation of the walls'. He also promised that, in the event of his absence, to pay £10 per month to defray the costs of replacing him and entered into a staple recognizance 'to the use of the corporation'.[27] In December 1671 the bailiffs and burgesses of Charleville loaned on the Cork staple £1000 on bond to Arthur Virgin, an upholster from Cork.[28]

By far the most important creditors were members of the landed gentry (individuals who described themselves as 'knights', 'baronets', 'esquires', 'gentlemen' and 'gentlewomen'). Why did they lend money and to whom? What was the source of the cash or credit they loaned and what amounts were involved? What was the religious and ethnic origin of these landed creditors and of their debtors? To what extent did lending habits change over time? It may not be possible to answer all of these questions in full.

---

[26] By 1660 the staples were operating at Galway, Cork and Limerick, by 1661 at Kilkenny and 1662 at Drogheda. The Chancery volumes contain no reference to Sligo, Derry, Wexford and Waterford in the years after 1660. This does not mean that the staple never met. Certainly in the case of Waterford the corporation ordered in December 1662 that the court of staple should be restored to 'its antient and prestine capacity' and set appropriate fees, Seamus Pender, ed., *Council books of the Corporation of Waterford 1662-1700* (Irish Manuscripts Commission, Dublin, 1964), pp. 12, 15.

[27] Caulfield, ed., Cork, pp. 27, 59. No record of these bonds appears to have survived.

[28] ID 3791. It is not clear what the basis of the transaction was.

Figure 1.3:
Table showing staple activity, 1641-1658
(recorded in the Chancery volumes)

Year	Number of Transactions	Amount of the Bonds
From Oct. 1641	None	None
1642	6	4280
1643	5	2220
1644	4	1560
1645	4	1900
1646	2	240
1647	1	2000
1648	1	6000
1649	3	5400
1650	1	130
1651	1	200
1652	2	894
1653	14	20293
Sub Total	**44 (18%)**	**£45,117 (26%)**
1654	25	15599
1655	36	28640
1656	36	22209
1657	35	22946
1658	30	14670
1659	33	23242
Until May 1660	4	1556
Sub Total	**199 (82%)**	**£128,862 (74%)**
TOTAL	**243**	**£173,979**

However even a cursory analysis of gentry creditors suggests that they used the staple as a means of increasing their landed bases, of supplementing their incomes through money lending, and of helping out friends and kinsmen.

Certainly during the early decades of the seventeenth century Sir Philip Percival used the staple, together with other mortgage loans, to acquire and consolidate a vast estate—'stretching in an arc from Kanturk through Liscarrol to Churchtown'—in County Cork. His position as clerk of the Court of Wards and Crown feodary and escheator in Munster gave him temporary access to considerable sums of money that he invested in mortgage loans and money lending.[29] A number of these were contracted

[29] Michael MacCarthy-Morrogh, *The Munster Plantation. English Migration to Southern Ireland 1583-1641* (Oxford, 1986), pp. 164-5.

on the staple.[30] Between July 1624 and April 1636, as the Dublin staple records show, he loaned £9460 on bond to thirty individuals—mostly landed gentlemen and largely of Old English or native Irish extraction. The fact that the bulk of these hailed from every corner of Ireland— Limerick, Clare, Mayo, Dublin, Westmeath, Wexford, Queen's County, Kilkenny, Armagh, and Down—indicates that Sir Philip was engaged in money lending. Only seven debtors—MacCarthys, MacDonaghs, Barrys, Callaghans and Roches—listed their address as Cork and in all of these instances their lands passed to Sir Philip.[31]

The staple activities of Sir Gerald Lowther, who described himself as an 'esquire and chief justice of the court of common pleas', suggest that he also acted as a moneylender. Between 1628 and 1659 he lent nearly £15,000 on the staple. His debtors were geographically dispersed, residing in counties Dublin, Fermanagh, Galway, Kildare, Louth, Tyrone, Westmeath, Wexford and Queen's County. They were generally described as 'esquires' or 'gentlemen' together with two merchants and a brewer and, judging by the surname, could be classified as Old English.[32] Very occasionally the staple records contain direct references to money lending. For example in 1609 Philp Hore, a Dublin gentleman, made a series of loans to gentlemen from Wexford specifically for the use of Henry Wallop of Southampton.[33] While two years later in 1611 Bartholomew Dillon, an esquire from Meath, lent Sir William Ussher £800 in the knowledge that it was for the use of Patrick Conly, a Dublin merchant.[34]

---

[30] Percival also occasionally borrowed on the staples in both Dublin and Cork. A few references to the staple at Cork have survived amongst the Percival papers. See, for example, BL, Add 46,948 f. 68 when on 20 March 1629/30 Percival borrowed on bond £240 from James Wall of Killmallock, County Limerick.

[31] ID 1252, 1268, 1512, 2106. A staple bond for £200 between Callaghan McDonogh Carthy and Percival dated 10 May 1623 survives among the Percival papers (BL, Add MSS 47,035 f. 128) but does not appear to be recorded in the Dublin staple volumes. For details on Percival's estates and mortgages see MacCarthy-Morrogh, *The Munster Plantation*, pp. 164-7 and BL, Add MSS 47,038 ff. 8-9 where these purchases are listed. For example in April 1636 John Barry of Liscarrol borrowed £2000 on bond on the Dublin staple, ID 2109 and BL, Add MSS 47,035 f. 130. For the defeazance relating to this see Add MSS 47,035 f. 16. Even though no record appears to survive in the Dublin staple volumes, Barry also borrowed—according to extant records in the Percival papers— £2000 on a Dublin staple bond in September 1629 and a further £2000 in September 1634, BL, Add MSS 47,035 ff. 128a and 129. This only represented a fraction of what Barry owed to Percival, for examples of other deeds see BL, Add MSS 46,925 f. 137 when on 8 September 1641 Barry borrowed £3000 on bond. Presumably this was to cover Barry's debt to the Spanish ambassador, Alonso de Cárdenas. For on the same day Sir Philip stood as Barry's co-guarantor for 'the sum of £1500' which Barry had promised to Cárdenas, 'with condition for the bringing of 1000 men to Limerick, Waterford or for passage for the service of his Catholic Majesty [Philip IV] by the 25 of this instant [September]', BL, Add MSS 46,925 f. 139.

[32] See ID 1544, 1628, 1889, 1953, 2169, 2973, 2974, 2980, 2982, 2986, 2987, 2988, 3070, 3071, 3096, 3105, 3108, 3109, 3111, 3325, 3329, 3332, 3333, 3341, 3347, 3353, 3354, 3357.

[33] ID 538, 539, 540, 541, 542, 551.

[34] ID 662.

Other gentry creditors appear to be using the staple as a means of helping out friends and kinsmen who, for whatever reason, proved unable to borrow themselves. In an attempt to relieve the financial distress of their nephew and preserve the good name of the family, John Percival's uncles—Sirs William Ussher and Paul Davies—lent him £2000 on bond in 1654 and a further £420 in 1662.[35] The same appears to hold true for Chidley Coote of Killester in Dublin, who over a period of 25 years lent over £8000 on the Dublin staple. Nearly 80% of this was disbursed during the 1650s and the majority of his creditors were his kinsmen—Sir Charles Coote, later earl of Mountrath, and his son from Roscommon, and Thomas Coote from county Antrim. In the case of Sir Charles it appears that Chidley lent him money so that he could in turn satisfy his creditors. For example in 1653, Sir Charles, immediately after borrowing £4000 on bond from Chidley, lent the same amount to Sir Lucas Dillon. The following year Chidley lent Sir Charles £200 and the latter then lent £200 to Robert Presby, a Waterford merchant, to whom he presumably owed money. The staple thus served as a means of recording the payment of an outstanding obligation.[36] In the case of a debt owed to Sir John Temple the staple served a similar function. A bond, dated 14 January 1640, contracted on the Kilkenny staple for £4440 was accompanied by an indenture of defeazance which recited a transaction made on 4 January whereby Temple loaned Ormond £4440 on an unsecured bond.[37] Marriage portions were accounted for in a similar fashion. For instance, in November 1675 Wiiliam Lestrange, the groom's father, became indebted to Mary Peisley, the bride's mother, for a bond of £2000. An accompanying indenture of defeazance recited the marriage contract agreed between the two families.[38] Unfortunately in the majority of cases no specific reference is made to the marriage portion. It is not clear whether the transaction between William Savage of Kildare to Henry Sankey related to the union of Savage and Sankey's daughter. However given the fact that both the wedding and the staple transaction occurred on the same day—20 February 1658—it seems likely.[39]

---

[35] See ID 2991 and 3431 and BL Add MSS 46,938 fos. 14, 15. In April 1652 John lamented to Sir Paul Davies 'Oh, Sir, I see a deluge of misery overflowing me, a gap a breaking for all my creditors to come in on me... What will the world think, when it shall be known that so great a personal estate was left (which belonged not to me nor any but the creditors) and no one debt satisfied?', *Historical Manuscripts Commission. Report on the Manuscripts of the Earl of Egmont* (2 vols., London, 1905), II, 509-10. Between 1624 and 1636 John's father, Sir Philip, had lent considerable amounts on the staple, occasionally with Usher and Davies acting as co-lenders (ID 1918, 1920). They were also involved in other transactions with Sir Philip see BL Add Mss 46,922 ff. 80, 96, 46,924 ff. 4, 121 and 46,941B f. 98.

[36] Also see ID 1911 and 1912, 2317 and 2318, 2509 and 2510.

[37] NLI, D. 4140, D. 4141 and D. 4146.

[38] ID 2640.

[39] ID 3313. I am grateful to Aidan Clarke for bringing this to my attention.

Interestingly the lending habits of the gentry appear to change over the course of the century.[40] During the early decades of the seventeenth century gentry creditors originated from virtually every county in Ireland and from all ethnic and religious groups. Over time the number of native gentry creditors decreased sharply throughout the country, but especially in the western seaboard counties and in Counties Wicklow, Carlow, Waterford, Tipperary and Kilkenny. After 1660 the greatest number of gentry creditors were to be found in counties Antrim, Down, Meath, Kildare, King's County, Limerick, Cork and, above all, Dublin. These individuals appear to have included substantial numbers of Protestant entrepreneurs and speculators who had acquired lands during the 1650s, together with a considerable number of recent settlers. For example, even though the same individuals appeared more than once, the increase in the number of gentry creditors in county Antrim—from 2 in the pre-war years to 41 after 1660—is particularly striking.

The Colvills serve as an excellent example of a gentry family that made extensive use of the staple during the later seventeenth century. Alexander and Robert Colvill, prominent local officials and landowners with estates in counties Antrim and Down, were eager to build up their estates by lending money to individuals who, desperate for cash, had no alternative but to mortgage their lands.[41] Over a period of 25 years (1655-1685) father and son, using the staples in Dublin and Carrickfergus, lent at least £46,000 on bond (since most of these transactions were recorded in the Chancery volumes the total amount that they lent probably greatly exceeded this figure).[42] With only one exception, they lent to local men, often of considerable importance: Sir John Clotworthy, later Lord Massareene; Arthur Chichester, earl of Donegal; Sir George Rawdon; and Hugh Montgomery, earl of Mount Alexander (he borrowed c. £15,500 in a single year, 1675, see plate 3).[43] Their other debtors included planters, many of whom had settled in East Ulster during the early seventeenth century (John Edmunston, John Shaw and the Rowleys of Londonderry) or served as army officers during the 1640s and 1650s (John Galland). In only one instance, that of the

---

[40] These changes over time can be easily mapped by linking the database to Geographic Information System (GIS) programme.

[41] Alexander described himself as a 'doctor of theology' and Robert as an 'esquire'.

[42] For details of other unsecured transactions involving Alexander see NA, C. 3471 note 1 (involving Hercules Longford) and notes 14 and 36 (involving Arthur Hill). NA, C. 3471 note 30 recites a bond for £1200 (for £600) dated 12 January 1661 between Alexander and William Adair. When Adair died his wife remarried Archibald Edmonstone and Colvill pursued them for the debt. In 1663 Edmonstone had borrowed £600 on bond from Alexander (ID 3765) and it is not clear if this staple transaction related to Adair's debt.

[43] A few staple deeds relating to some of these transactions have survived. For example, an indenture of defeazance lists the lands that Hugh, earl of Mount Alexander, offered as security to Robert Colvill on a bond of £3000 and dated 27 November 1675 (NA, D.15,248). Also see NA, D.15,245. Mount Alexander apparently defaulted on his repayment and the bond was registered into Chancery on 5 February 1676 (ID 3210). In 1673 Mount Alexander also borrowed money from Colvill, NA, C. 3471 note 32.

O'Haras of Cregbilly, with whom they intermarried, did the Colvills lend to native Catholic families.[44] The absence of native debtors is striking and this no doubt reflects the changing nature of land ownership in East Ulster during the later decades of the seventeenth century, rather than a sectarian mentality among these enterprising esquires.[45]

Merchants and civic patricians also served as important sources of credit. Between 1597 and December 1679, 104 aldermen, from Cork, Galway, Limerick, Drogheda and, above all, Dublin, lent on bond £191,602 (only 44 borrowed money).[46] The lending patterns of these aldermen, who

[44] See ID 2257, 2641, 2644, 2645, 2665, 3035, 3036, 3037, 3120, 3144, 3154, 3156, 3158, 3203, 3206, 3210, 3225, 3437, 3520, 3521, 3536, 3565, 3566, 3577, 3765, 3766, 3767, 3890, 3905. In January 1675 Robert married Honora O'Hara of Cregbilly, NA, C. 3471 note 12.

[45] The Colvills were very willing to lend money, though not apparently on the staple, to Catholics, such as the earl of Antrim, Jane Ohlmeyer, *Civil War and Restoration in the Three Stuart Kingdoms* (Cambridge, 1993), pp. 254, 275.

[46] Of the 101 aldermen that form the basis for Colm Lennon's study of Dublin patricians in the sixteenth and early seventeenth centuries, 52 lent and occasionally borrowed on the staple. Names of creditors and debtors in the database were compared against Appendix II; Prosopography of the bench of aldermen of Dublin, 1550-1620 in Colm Lennon, *The Lords of Dublin in the Age of Reformation* (Dublin, 1989), pp. 223-276. The following appear as creditors and occasionally debtors (indicated in italics): John Arthur ID 303, 307; Edward Ball ID 249, 763, *1054, 1280*; Nicholas Ball ID 2, 10, 14, 15; Robert Ball ID 283, 1715; Richard Barry ID 819, 935, 990, 1008, 1216, 11296, 434, 1518; James Bellew ID 196; John Bennes ID 282; Thomas Bishop ID 516, 579, 581, 587; Sir William Bishop ID 769?, 915, 1105, 1110, 1111, 1113; Sir Richard Bolton ID 492, 640, 644, 686, 644, 693; Thomas Brandon ID 93?; John Brice ID 106; Sir Richard Browne ID 522, 1453; Sir James Carroll ID 192, 387, 794, 843, *1203, 1371, 1847*; Thomas Carroll ID 177, 452, 488, 611, 764, 765; Michael Chamberlain ID 256, 313, 326, 438, 569, 572, *324, 423, 457, 573, 664*; Philip Conran ID 52, 179, 253, 255, 279, 298, 299, 392, 510, 512, 532, 561, 568, 574, 642, 694, 696, 749; John Cusack ID 47, 149, 290, 291, 338, 373, 393, 464, 529, 598, 667, 759, *574, 772, 973*; Walter Cusack ID 1284; Peter Dermott ID 216; George Devenish ID 767, 1143, 1253, 1341; John Dowd ID 733, 736, 740, 741, 774, 776, 1391, 1653, 1893, 1944, 1963, 2002, 2043, 2067, 2074, 2123, 742; Thady Duff ID 536, 653, 664, 665, 673, 700, 799, 1181, 1359, 1421, 1576, 1615, 1627, 1629, 1643; John Elliott ID 288, 718, *278, 865*; Richard Fagan ID 181, 247, 480, 573; John FitzSimon ID *536, 653, 575, 700*; Sir Thomas FitzWilliam ID *517, 559, 612, 666, 1046, 1047, 1327, 1351, 1382, 1391, 1411, 1423, 1450, 1455, 1470, 1476, 1574*; John Fo[r]ster ID 46, 75, 87, 114, 163, 164, 265, 267, 316, 323, 593, 666; Richard Fo[r]ster ID 382, 960; Patrick Fox ID 32, 42, 129, 173, 273, 287, 321, 322, 398, 490, 521; John Goodwin[g] ID 21, 26, 191, 262, 284, 548, *1061*; Patrick Gough ID 353, 854, 886, 1235, 1319, 1437; William Gough ID 172, 193, 331; Mathew Handcock ID 98, 519, *661*; James Jans ID 103; Robert Kennedy ID 72, 85, 187, 239, 333, 440, 509, 726, 1041, 1316, 1997, 2822, 2824, *1129*; Edmund Malone ID 320, 937, 998, 1098, 1106, 1130, 1168, 1207, 1286, 1345, 1406, 1453, 1534, 1600; John Morphy ID 27, 152; Alexander Palles ID 125, 141, 178, 200, 286; Robert Panting ID 49, 73, 94, 115, 118, 142, 145, 146, 150, 151, 176; Thomas Plunkett ID 315, 318, 326, 442, 461, 471, 474, 533, 864, 888, 898, 922, 952, 973, 1023, 1054, 1058, 1091, 1208, 1237, 1362, 1366, 1390; Edmund Purcell ID 58, 201, 458, 499; Sir William Sarsfield ID 734, *888*; Christopher Sedgrave ID 695; Walter Sedgrave ID 852; John Shelton ID 133, 403; Francis Taylor ID 248, 404; Sir John Tyrell ID 51; John Ussher ID 39, 40, *41*; Nicholas Weston ID 90, 230, *351, 400*; Richard Wiggett ID 282; Gerald Young ID 3, 20, 74, 116, 157; 160; 161; 166; 170; 171; 254; 260; 271; 292; 294; 421; 437; 459; 479; 494; 497; 505; 507; 523; 524; 527; 619; 645; 660; 708. Despite the number of aldermen from Dublin appearing as debtors and creditors, no reference is made in Lennon, *Lords*, to the staple volumes.

appear to have had ready access to sources of cash, of credit, and of possibly goods, need to be systematically analysed. Consider for instance Edmund Malone, a staunch Catholic of Westmeath gentry stock, who loaned between 1603 and 1629 £6575 on bond (often in sizeable amounts) on the Dublin staple. His debtors included other Dublin aldermen, merchants, farmers and gentlemen from Kildare, Dublin, Meath and Louth. Similarly Gerald Young, a Protestant Dublin alderman, proved an important source of credit for tradesmen, farmers and lesser members of the gentry, particularly from his native County Kildare. Between 1597 and 1612 he entered into 30 transactions on the Dublin staple, lending relatively small amounts of money (the total value of the bonds amounted only to £3176). Malone and Young, together with many other aldermen, appear to have served as vital sources of credit for farmers and small landholders as well as tradesmen throughout Ireland. The same held true for merchants. Of the 780 creditors who gave their occupation as 'merchant', 62% originated in Dublin (roughly 7% came from Drogheda, Cork, and London). They included the Allens, Arthurs, Brices, Dowds, Flemings, Frenchs, Kennedys, Mapas, Purcells, and Usshers.[47] With a little effort it will prove relatively straightforward to reconstruct the financial fortunes of these merchant families, to untangle the webs of indebtedness in which they enmeshed themselves, and to determine whether they used the statute staple as a means of acquiring landed estates.[48]

Significantly these merchants and aldermen also served as brethren, constables and merchants of the staple and took advantage of their favoured position to lend—and occasionally borrow—money. For example, between 1598 and 1687, of the 100 mayors of the Dublin staple 32 appear in the database as creditors, 12 as both creditors and debtors, and 8 as debtors. For instance, the Dublin alderman, Gerald Young (discussed

[47] Agnew, *Belfast Merchant Families* serves as a model for any study of merchants in Dublin or any provincial town. Despite the fact that Belfast merchants—John Curry, Hugh Eccles, Thomas Knox and George MacCartney—made extensive use of both the Dublin and Carrickfergus staples during the later seventeenth century (ID 3039, 3256, 3291, 3808, 3906, 3977), the importance of the staple as a credit network is not discussed by Agnew. A random search of the surviving Chester port book for 1634 revealed that scores of Dublin merchants were intimately involved in trade with Chester, presumably many borrowed on the staple to finance their commercial activities while others invested their profits by lending on the staple. The Dublin creditors who also appear in 1634 Chester port book (PRO, E[xchequer] 190/1353/1) include Lawrence Allen, Robert and Thomas Arthur, John Ash, John Ball, Peter Bath, David Begg, Edward Brangan, Walter Brett, Arthur Champion, James Devenish, Bartholomew Drope, John Hill, Walter Kennedy, Christopher Mapas, Peter Quinn, John and Walter Stanley, Richard Warburton, and Edmund Warren. I am grateful to Éamonn Ó Ciardha for bringing these names to my attention.

[48] The staple as such did not exist in Scotland but merchants, in particular, used secured bonds as a means of acquiring and consolidating their landed interests, see J. J. Brown, 'The social, political and economic influence of the Edinburgh merchant elite 1600-1638' (unpublished Ph.D. thesis, Edinburgh, 1985), chapters 5- 6 and T. C. Smout, 'The Glasgow merchant community in the seventeenth century' in *Scottish Historical Review* 48 (1968), pp. 53-71.

PLATE 1:

The circular seal measured nearly two inches in diameter and bore a shield with the royal arms: the fleurs de lille of France and the three lions of England. The legend reads *Sigllum Stapule Civitas Dublinie* (Seal of the Staple of the City of Dublin). It would have been attached to all deeds issued by the Dublin staple. Presumably the other staple towns had their own distinctive staple seals. No seal of the staple appears to have survived and the Dublin one photographed by W. G. Strickland for the *Journal of the Royal Society of Antiquaries* vol. 53 (1923), on which this reconstruction is based, has been mislaid.

(Redrawn by Robert Gordon, Rainnea Graphics)

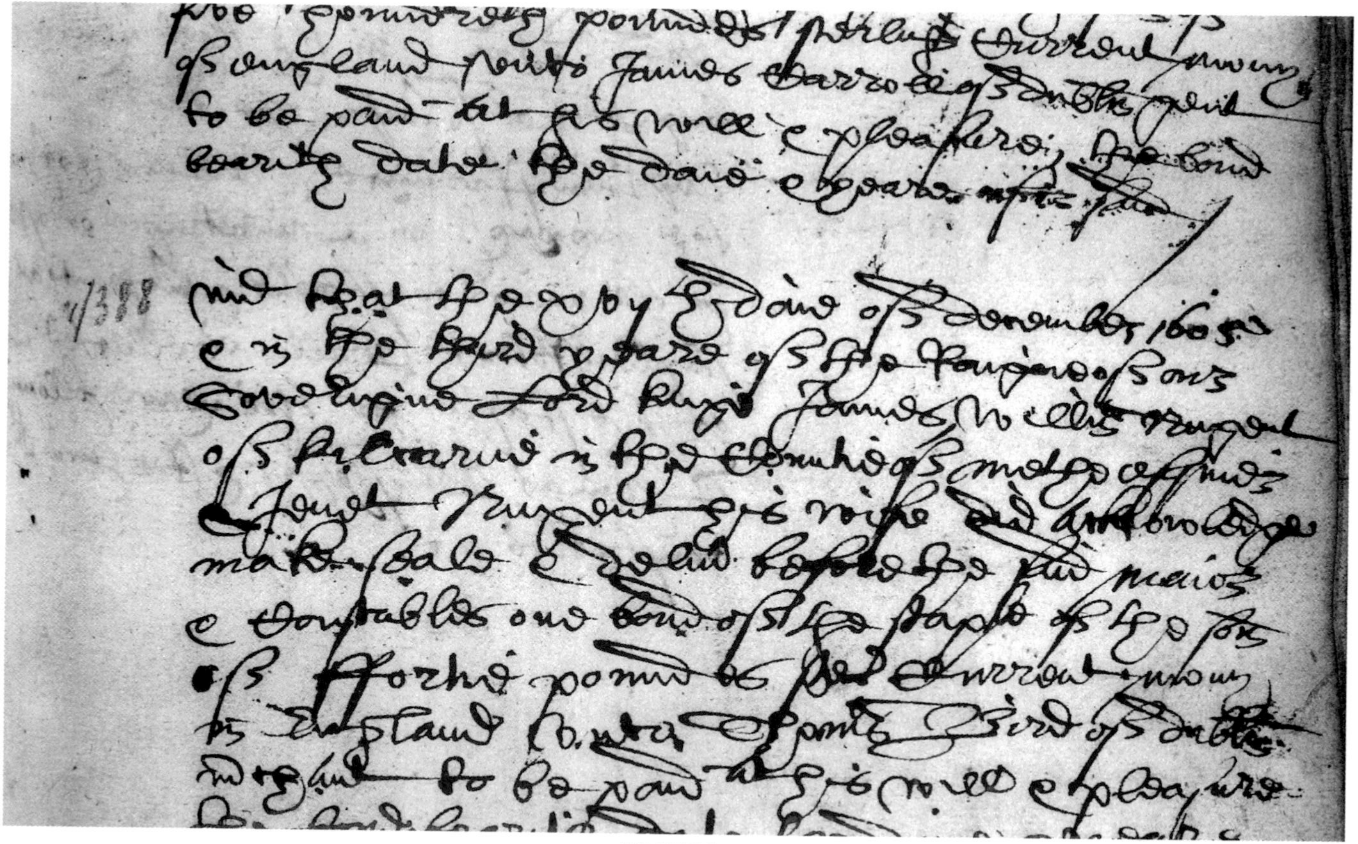

PLATE 2:

Dublin City Archives: Staple Book 1, entry 388: Bond: William Nugent of Kilcarne, Co. Meath and his wife Janet to Thomas Bird of Dublin, merchant. £40 sterling, 17 Dec 1605

[Photo by David Davison]

above), served as mayor of the city between 1599 and 1600 and mayor of the staple the following year. The lending habits of the Dublin alderman Richard Tighe, who served as mayor of the Dublin staple on 5 occasions (1652-4, 1655-6, and 1660-2), proved particularly extensive. Between February 1656 and October 1670 he lent £14,374 on bond to 22 individuals (15 landed gentlemen, 3 tradesmen, 2 knights, an alderman, and one merchant) who originated largely from Dublin and the Pale.[49] It seems likely that these two patricians were investing the profits from their municipal office by lending on the staple. No doubt further research will show the extent to which this municipal oligarchy used the staple as a means of enriching themselves. Recent research on Scottish merchants and civic officials, particularly from Edinburgh, Glasgow and Aberdeen, highlights the critical role they played as moneylenders during the early seventeenth-century. In a fascinating study of Edinburgh's patricians James Brown argues that by 1638 the wealthiest merchants were involved in money lending. There was no precise Scottish equivalent to the staple[50] and instead 'a complicated system of borrowing—requiring both sureties and co-guarantors, allowing for transferable and heritable bonds—had been developed and were part of the day-to-day business practices of the elite'. These merchants became important sources of credit for clients throughout Scotland, Ireland, England and on the continent.[51]

A number of prominent clergymen appear as creditors and could well have been acting as moneylenders. Presumably the ubiquitous Alexander Colvill used his clerical connections and income to consolidate his fortune (he was ordained as a deacon in 1622, the vicar of Carmony in 1626 and the prebend at Carmony and Carncastle in 1628).[52] In the 1680s the Leslie brothers, sons of Dr Leslie, bishop of Clogher, loaned considerable amounts. Charles, who trained as a lawyer before taking holy orders in 1680 (he later became chancellor of the diocese of Connor), loaned £5000 on bond to George Cunningham of Longford. His brother John, dean of

---

[49] For details see Appendix I note 151.

[50] There was, however, a similar procedure whereby parties to an instrument of debt registered it in the Books of Council and Session in Edinburgh or in the local sheriff court books. This gave the creditor access to do summary diligence on the obligation without any further requirement to issue proceedings. I am grateful to Alex Green for bringing this to my attention.

[51] Brown, 'Edinburgh merchants', p. 236. Also see James Brown, 'Merchant princes and mercantile investment in early seventeenth century Scotland' in M. Lynch, ed., *The early modern town in Scotland* (Wolfeboro, New Hampshire, 1987), pp. 125-46. In contrast the more conservatively minded Aberdeen patricians limited their services to the city and surrounding hinterland, Duncan MacNiven, 'Merchant and trader in early seventeenth century Aberdeen' (unpublished M.Litt. thesis, Aberdeen, 1977), pp. 231-37.

[52] Henry Cotton, *Fasti ecclesiae Hibernicae* (6 vols., Dublin, 1848-1878), III, 261. On a smaller scale Thomas Howell, used his connections with Christ Church Cathedral, to supplement his income by lending cash, see Raymond Gillespie, *Thomas Howell and his friends: Serving Christ Church Cathedral, Dublin, 1570-1700* (Dublin, 1997), pp. 8-9. Howell does not appear on the database but one of his creditors, Robert Sweet (ID 1166, 1281, 1356, 1598, 1626), and one of his debtors, Anthony Stoughton (ID 1920, 1921, 2151) do.

Dromore, loaned £800 on bond to Andrew Lindsay of County Monaghan where the family enjoyed an extensive patrimony.[53] Michael Boyle, bishop of Dublin and, after 1678, archbishop of Armagh is probably the best example of an ecclesiastical entrepreneur. Thanks to his church revenues and political office (he became Chancellor of Ireland in 1665), he accumulated considerable wealth and invested a substantial portion of this on the staples at Cork and Dublin. Between 1666 and 1686 he loaned over £14,000 on bond to members of the Dublin, Monaghan, Cork, and Tipperary gentry. Since most of these transactions were recorded in the Chancery volumes, these probably only represent a fraction of the total amounts he loaned, particularly on the Cork staple.[54] These clerics would have enjoyed access to income from tithes and church lands and the staple offered them a secure and lucrative return on their investment and protection from being accused of practising usury.

Certainly, from the perspective of the creditor—whatever their status or occupation—the staple provided reasonable security for any loan in that the bond the debtor signed usually amounted to twice the amount of the actual debt while the debtor's lands served as ultimate collateral. Moreover the staple offered the creditor easy access to the law in the event that the debtor defaulted. The reluctance of English moneylenders to accept Irish land as collateral also ensured that these entrepreneurs enjoyed a captive market and received a return of 10% on their investment.[55] Given that interest rates of between 30% to 40% were not unusual in the early seventeenth century (especially in the 1640s), this stable rate of interest, though high by English standards, also appealed to debtors.[56]

With the principal exception of the 1640s, debtors and creditors travelled from every county in Ireland to use the Dublin staple.

Nearly 3000 individuals lent money on the Dublin staple (Figure 1.4); 82% of these creditors originated in Leinster (60% listed their address as Dublin); the remaining 18% originated from every other county in Ireland (4% from Munster, 3% from Connacht and 5% from Ulster) and from England and Scotland (4%). Roughly 4100 individuals borrowed money on the Dublin staple (Figure 1.5): 76% originated in Leinster (27% listed their address as Dublin); 8% in Ulster; and 7% each in Munster and Connacht. These figures highlight the importance of Dublin as a commercial centre not simply as a source of credit for people resident in Ireland but for

---

[53] Cotton, *Fasti*, III, 359. See ID 3928, 2468, 3730.

[54] Cotton, *Fasti*, I, 228, 295, 310, 332; III, 23, 95. ID 2305, 2593, 3133, 3571, 3573, 3584, 3647, 3650, 3661, 4019, 4035.

[55] In England interest rates dropped from 10% to 8% (1625) and from 8% to 6% (1651), but in Ireland they remained at 10% for the course of the seventeenth century which, according to William Petty, was 'a great hinderance to trade', Sir William Petty, *The Political Anatomy of Ireland*, ed., John Donovan (Shannon, 1970), p. 75.

[56] Raymond Gillespie, *The Transformation of the Irish Economy 1550-1700* (Dundalk, 1991), p. 56. In Munster they ranged from 5% to 30%, MacCarthy-Morrogh, 'Credit and Remittance', pp. 5-6

debtors from England and Scotland. For instance, between 1619 and 1685 6 Scots borrowed £5510 on bond on the Dublin staple, invariably from kinsmen who had been involved with the Ulster plantation.[57] A further eight debtors gave an English address.

Figure 1.4:
Table showing the geographical origin of creditors lending on the Dublin staple, 1597-1637 and 1665-1678 (recorded in the Dublin volumes)

PROVINCE	TOTAL#	AS%		
LEINSTER	2431	82%	Dublin	1771 (60%)
ULSTER	147	5%	Armagh	46 (2%)
MUNSTER	106	4%	Cork	40 (1%)
CONNACHT	100	3%	Galway	37 (1%)
ENG. & SCOT.	121	4%	London	
NS	58	2%		
TOTAL	2963	100%		

Figure 1.5:
Table showing the geographical origin of debtors borrowing on the Dublin staple, 1597-1637 and 1665-1678 (recorded in the Dublin volumes)

PROVINCE	TOTAL#	AS%		
LEINSTER	3129	76%	Dublin	1109 (27%)
ULSTER	337	8%	Armagh/Down	59 each (1%)
MUNSTER	296	7%	Cork	99 (2%)
CONNACHT	275	7%	Mayo	80 (2%)
ENG. & SCOT.	21	1%		
NS	50	1%		
TOTAL	4108	100%		

The willingness of debtors to travel to Dublin also provides an interesting insight into the mobility of the population. Individuals living in County Tipperary, for instance, enjoyed—depending on which part of the county they resided in—relatively easy access to the staples at Limerick, Cork, Youghal, Waterford and Kilkenny.[58] Yet the bulk (73%), usually members of the gentry, opted to borrow in Dublin, often from other Tipperary landowners. One gentleman, James Coleman, even trekked to Drogheda to secure £200 on bond from Nicholas Phelps, a local landowner.[59]

---

[57] ID 976, 1270, 1271, 1272, 1273, 1274, 1329, 1510, 4030.

[58] Seven per cent travelled to Kilkenny, 6% to Youghal, 5% to Cork, 5% to Limerick, and 3% to Waterford.

[59] ID 3590.

How much were these debtors actually borrowing? The total value of bonds recorded on the Dublin staple amounted to nearly £1.5 million. The average bond was for £560 and the largest bond recorded on the Dublin staple was for £10,640. The amounts of money borrowed on the Dublin staple almost quadrupled between 1597 and 1636 (see Figure 1.10). In the years after the restoration the amounts transacted remained fairly constant, though the average size of individual bonds increased significantly from £455 to £1029. The total value of bonds recorded in the Chancery volumes amounted to £1.2 million. The largest bond recorded in Chancery was for £20,000 and the average size of individual bonds was roughly £900. However only a few individuals borrowed or lent large sums of money. An analysis of bonds worth between £5000 and £20,000 revealed that 31 members of the gentry (including 2 women), 9 peers (including one woman), one alderman and one merchant borrowed these considerable sums; while 35 members of the gentry (including 2 women), 4 peers (including one woman), and 2 officials (an alderman and mayor) lent them. Bonds of between £1000 and £5000 proved more common, but the value of the majority of bonds did not exceed £500. For example, widows, largely of Old English provenance, tended to lend small amounts of money (bonds under £500) to a large number of individuals, many of whom might be considered 'good risks' (Figure 1.6).

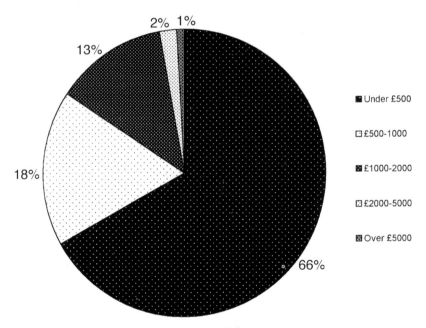

Figure 1.6:
Pie chart of amounts lent by widows on the staple
(recorded in the Dublin and Chancery volumes)

Since land effectively acted as security for those lending on the staple, the amounts of money borrowed on the Dublin staple were plotted against provincial county acreages (Figure 1.7). In Leinster, the smallest province in Ireland, £426 was borrowed per 1000 arable acres; in Ulster £87 per 1000 arable acres; in Connacht £95 per 1000 arable acres; and in Munster, the largest province, £40 per 1000 arable acres (Figure 1.8). The findings for individual counties followed the provincial pattern. Understandably the figure for Dublin was the highest (£3017/1000 arable acres) while Limerick was the lowest (£23/1000 arable acres). Even though the total value of bonds secured on lands in Cork was considerable (£48,268) the vast acreage of the county meant that the amount per acre was fairly low (£37/1000 arable acres) whereas similar amounts secured on lands in smaller counties yield much higher ratios. For example, the total value of bonds secured on land in Sligo amounted to £52,148 (almost the same as Cork) while the amount borrowed per 1000 arable acres was £179. These figures extracted from the Dublin volumes can be compared against those recorded in the Chancery volumes.

The average for Leinster remained the highest, £210 per 1000 arable acres, followed by Munster with a remarkable £122 per 1000 arable acres, by Ulster with £70 per 1000 arable acres and finally by Connacht with £69 per 1000 arable acres (Figure 1.9). In a number of instances—that of Antrim, Derry, Clare, Cork, Limerick, Roscommon, Tipperary, and Waterford—the amounts borrowed per thousand acres exceeded the figures taken from the Dublin volumes. The figures for all of the Munster counties (except Kerry) are greater and in the cases of Cork and Limerick the contrast is striking (in both instances they represent nearly a seven-fold increase). This no doubt reflected the vibrancy of the local staples particularly in Cork and Limerick.[60] Unfortunately no staple books appear to have survived for the staple towns outside Dublin but these Chancery figures could represent only 20%-25% of the total business conducted on provincial staples. If this was indeed the case the amount of business transacted on the staples outside Dublin, especially Cork and Limerick, could have been very considerable indeed. Michael MacCarthy-Morrogh's analysis of the Chancery volumes for Munster between 1639 and 1641 supports this. He concluded that 'credit was open to all sections of the community—and that the lack of capital investment was not entirely because of the difficulties of transferring money into and out of Munster'.[61]

This appears to be the case not simply for Munster but for all of Ireland and people from a wide variety of social, economic, ethnic and religious backgrounds borrowed—often very heavily—on the staple. Just as

[60] A few references to the staple at Cork have survived amongst the Percival papers. See, for example, BL, Add MSS 46,948 f. 68 when on 20 March 1629/30 Percival borrowed on bond £240 from James Wall of Killmallock, County Limerick, BL, Add MSS 47,035 f. 49 for a staple bond of 10 September 1621, BL, Add MSS 47,035 f. 127 for a staple bond of 17 March 1620/1.

[61] MacCarthy-Morrogh, 'Credit and Remittance', p. 18. He appears to have overlooked the material relating to Munster in the Dublin staple volumes.

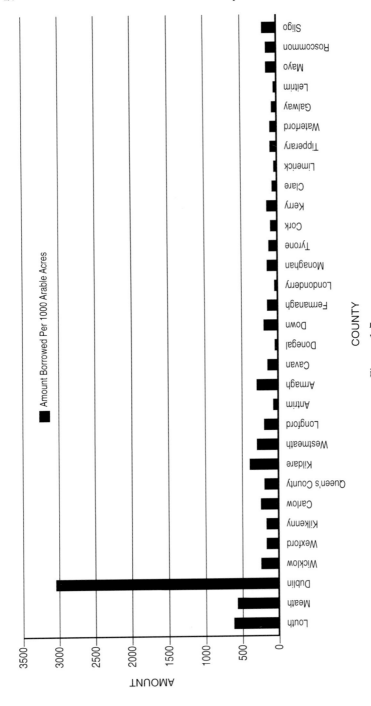

COUNTY

Figure 1.7:

Bar graph showing the amounts borrowed per 1000 arable acres (recorded on the Dublin volumes)

Figure 1.8:
Table of amounts borrowed per 1000 arable acres
(recorded on the Dublin volumes)

Province	County	Total £	Arable Acres	£/1000 Arable
Leinster	Louth	113977	178972	637
Leinster	Meath	325050	547391	594
Leinster	Dublin	591481	196063	3017
Leinster	Wicklow	55703	280393	199
Leinster	Wexford	47758	510702	94
Leinster	Kilkenny	45743	470102	97
Leinster	Carlow	42086	184059	229
Leinster	Queen's County	60770	342422	177
Leinster	Kildare	138867	356787	389
Leinster	Westmeath	97394	365218	267
Leinster	Longford	26213	191823	137
TOTAL		**£1,545,042**	**3,623,932**	**£426**
Ulster	Antrim	18260	503288	36
Ulster	Armagh	69784	265243	263
Ulster	Cavan	29421	375473	78
Ulster	Donegal	11780	393191	30
Ulster	Down	69673	514180	136
Ulster	Fermanagh	25930	289228	90
Ulster	Londonderry	7600	318282	24
Ulster	Monaghan	30334	285885	106
Ulster	Tyrone	33020	450286	73
TOTAL		**£295,802**	**3,395,056**	**£87**
Munster	Cork	48268	1308882	37
Munster	Kerry	22290	414614	54
Munster	Clare	14467	455009	32
Munster	Limerick	11971	526876	23
Munster	Tipperary	35715	843887	42
Munster	Waterford	13762	325345	42
TOTAL		**£146,473**	**3,874,613**	**£40**
Connacht	Galway	27511	742805	37
Connacht	Leitrim	6048	249350	24
Connacht	Mayo	67376	497587	135
Connacht	Roscommon	58846	440522	134
Connacht	Sligo	52148	290696	179
TOTAL		**£211,929**	**2,220,960**	**£95**

Figure 1.9:
Table of amounts borrowed per 1000 arable acres
(recorded on the Chancery volumes)

Province	County	Total £	Arable Acres	£/1000 Arable
Leinster	Louth	64307	178972	359
Leinster	Meath	81073	547391	148
Leinster	Dublin	317335	196063	1619
Leinster	Wicklow	6410	280393	23
Leinster	Wexford	31478	510702	62
Leinster	Kilkenny	45606	470102	97
Leinster	Carlow	17762	184059	97
Leinster	Queen's County	50262	342422	147
Leinster	Kildare	109730	356787	308
Leinster	Westmeath	23454	365218	64
Leinster	Longford	14227	191823	74
TOTAL		**£761644**	**3,623,932**	**£210**
Ulster	Antrim	45112	503288	90
Ulster	Armagh	31659	265243	119
Ulster	Cavan	5800	375473	15
Ulster	Donegal	4752	393191	13
Ulster	Down	62826	514180	122
Ulster	Fermanagh	21002	289228	73
Ulster	Londonderry	15667	318282	49
Ulster	Monaghan	21238	285885	74
Ulster	Tyrone	29450	450286	65
TOTAL		**£237506**	**3,395,056**	**£70**
Munster	Cork	300518	1308882	230
Munster	Kerry	1820	414614	4
Munster	Clare	28140	455009	62
Munster	Limerick	80682	526876	153
Munster	Tipperary	39982	843887	47
Munster	Waterford	21482	325345	66
TOTAL		**£472624**	**3,874,613**	**£122**
Connacht	Galway	17666	742805	24
Connacht	Leitrim	3190	249350	13
Connacht	Mayo	34881	497587	70
Connacht	Roscommon	80754	440522	183
Connacht	Sligo	15918	290696	55
TOTAL		**£152409**	**2,220,960**	**£69**

the bulk of creditors originated from amongst the landed classes, the majority of debtors described themselves as 'knights', 'esquires' and 'gentlemen'. Peers particularly featured as debtors, along with merchants and tradesmen. Unfortunately these debtors rarely divulged the nature of their obligation—whether it was for a loan, a land sale, a mortgage, or commercial agreement. Why, for example, did Richard Barry, second earl of Barrymore, borrow at least £35,000 on bond on the staple between 1656 and 1684?[62] In the absence of evidence it is only possible to speculate. Certainly the seventeenth century was an age of conspicuous consumption and loans contracted on the staple, especially by members of the elite, presumably enabled people to finance their debts, to dress in the latest fashions, and to educate their children. For instance, in May 1665 Richard Lambert, earl of Cavan, borrowed £10,000 on bond from Sir James Ware for the schooling and education of his son and heir Charles.[63] Borrowing on the staple may well have resulted in lands becoming mortgaged but this in itself could prove an indispensable tool of prudent estate management whereby land was converted into consumable wealth without selling it.[64] The cash it generated could allow landowners to improve their estates and to build greater and grander houses. Certainly a frenzy of building gripped the Irish landed classes during the early seventeenth century and it may prove possible to determine if there was a correlation between borrowing on the staple and building. A deposition, dating from 1619, in English Chancery records related how the second earl of Castlehaven had mortgaged a considerable portion of his Irish patrimony in order to finance £3000 worth of 'building'.[65] Dermot MacCarthy, an esquire from North Cork, appears to have sunk into debt thanks to his determination to remodel his mansion house at Kanturk.[66] The reasons why merchants and tradesmen borrowed also remain unknown but presumably these loans

---

[62] The bulk of these were recorded in the Chancery volumes and therefore probably only represent a fraction of the total amount which he borrowed in the staples at Dublin, Youghal and, above all, Cork. His creditors largely hailed from Cork (a few others from Tipperary, Limerick, Waterford and England) and described themselves as 'gentlemen', 'esquires' and 'merchants'. The Townsends, a Cork merchant family, lent him £7600 on bonds while Richard Peard, a soldier turned gentleman, lent him a further £7700. By the 1670s Barrymore appeared unable to borrow at all unless others—his kinsmen, his son, the Townsends or the Peards (the latter also ranked among his creditors)—co-signed the bond.

[63] ID 2232.

[64] Robert Allen, 'The price of freehold land and the interest rate in the 17th and 18th centuries' in *Economic History Review*, 2nd series, 41:1 (1988), p. 49. Admittedly mortgage procedure in Ireland, 'whereby the transaction amounted to a sale with the option of repurchase', was more antiquated than in England, MacCarthy-Morrogh, 'Credit and Remittance', p. 7.

[65] John Ainsworth, 'Some abstracts of Chancery suits relating to Ireland' in *Journal of the Royal Society of Antiquaries of Ireland*, 9 (1939), p. 39.

[66] MacCarthy-Morrogh, *The Munster Plantation*, pp.166-7. For the debts MacCarthy contracted on the Dublin staple see ID 835, 1189.

solved short-term cash flow crises, financed other debts, and funded commercial enterprise.

While the staple records can illuminate patterns of borrowing and lending especially for individuals whose personal and estate archives have not survived, they do, of course, have their limitations. To fully understand the nature of indebtedness in seventeenth century Ireland, especially what motivated debtors and creditors, the staple records must be interrogated alongside other relevant sources.[67] Qualitative evidence—letters and above all diaries—provide valuable insights. The earl of Cork's diary, for example, bristled with references to his debtors whether they were his tenants, business associates or kinsmen. Many of the '1641 depositions' included long lists of debts often amounting to thousands of pounds and Raymond Gillespie and Nicholas Canny have convincingly argued that they provide a fascinating insight to the importance of money lending and indebtedness at a local level in the pre-war years.[68] McCarthy-Morrogh's analysis of the depositions relating to Munster indicated that merchants, gentlemen and clergymen appear 'claiming debts, at a rough average of £500 each'. He concluded that, in Munster at any rate, 'there was an acceptance perforce of long-term debts with accounts being settled at infrequent intervals'.[69] A few depositions even contain direct references to the staple. For example Mathew Drope, a merchant from Dublin, claimed that he had due to him in 1641 'from such as he conceived to be solvent in the Kingdom of Ireland, upon judgements, statute staples, by specialities and by book eleven thousand pounds of principal money, one thousand pounds interest, and three hundred pounds costs in suits of law'.[70] While it will prove impossible to verify many of the claims made by desperate deponents, a systematic search of other records of debt might corroborate a proportion of them, indicate to what extent they have been inflated, and provide an excellent insight into the borrowing patterns of ordinary people and the activities of small scale moneylenders.

[67] I am currently working on a monograph entitled 'The Irish Elite in the seventeenth century: an aristocratic culture of survival?'. Much of the information on the earls of Cork, Ormond and Antrim derives from this research.

[68] See for examples Nicholas Canny, 'What really happened in 1641' in Jane Ohlmeyer, ed., *Ireland from independence to occupation, 1641-1660* (Cambridge, 1995), pp. 32-3 and 'The 1641 Depositions as a source for the writing of Social History: County Cork as a Case Study' in Patrick O'Flanagan and Cornelius G. Buttimer, eds., *Cork. History and Society* (Dublin, 1993), especially pp. 251, 265-67. Raymond Gillespie, 'The murder of Arthur Champion and the 1641 rising in Fermanagh' in *Clogher Record* 14 (1993), pp. 52-66. Arthur Champion appeared as a creditor in the staple volumes (ID 2747, 2098), as did his widow, Alice Allen (ID 2332, 2261).

[69] MacCarthy-Morrogh, 'Credit and Remittance', p. 10.

[70] TCD, MS 810 f. 231. I am grateful to Nicholas Canny for bringing this reference to my attention. Mathew Drope's name is not recorded in the database but a Bartholomew Drope, a Dublin merchant, appears. Between June 1641 and December 1642 he lent £1280 on bond to William Brownlow, Robert Caulfield, and Rory Maguire, see ID 2939, 2955, 2956.

Sadly the archives of Irish local and central courts have almost all perished.[71] There are, of course, exceptions. For instance, a few records from the Dublin Tholsell Court relating to the recovery of debts under twenty shillings have survived, as have the bail books for the Tholsell Court and from these it would be possible to see who was imprisoned for debt.[72] Larger debts were pursued in the Courts of Common Pleas, Exchequer, King's Bench and Chancery.[73] Creditors who held estates in England may also have appealed to the English courts, the archives of which remain intact.[74] The majority, however, would have sought justice in the Irish courts where many of the records have perished. However early twentieth century transcripts of the Chancery decree rolls (which deal largely with debts and mortgages) are extant in the National Archives in Dublin.[75] The records of the Commissioners of the Court of Claims have also survived and contain numerous references to debts, including ones contracted on the staple.[76] These are particularly useful since they indicated what lands stood as security for the bond. For example when William Bewley of Louth defaulted on his repayment of two staple bonds for £840 (dating from 1639 and 1641) Thomas and Ignatius Peppard of Drogheda pursued this in Chancery in 1644 and were awarded 'one stone house with divers

---

[71] For an excellent introduction see T. C. Barnard, 'Lawyers and the law in later seventeenth-century Ireland' in *Irish Historical Studies*, 28: 111 (1993), pp. 256-82.

[72] See Dublin City Archives C1/J/1 and C1/J/4.

[73] For example an indenture of defeazance in the Dublin staple noted that Sir George Hamilton's creditors were also suing him in the court of common pleas (ID 2451). For cases referred to the Castle Chambre see TCD, MS 852 and *HMC Egmont*, I, 1-60. I am grateful to Professor John Crawford for bringing these references to my attention.

[74] Ainsworth, 'Some abstracts of Chancery suits' offers a very cursory introduction to this neglected source. Also see T. Blake Butler, 'Chancery Bills 1610-1634' in *Journal of the Butler Society*, 3 (1991), pp. 380-85. It is not clear whether the bills transcribed in this article derive from the Court of Chancery in London or Dublin.

[75] For a guide to the legal records that survived the disaster of 1922 see *The Fifty-fifth report of the deputy keeper of the Public Records. . .* (Dublin, 1928), pp. 111-24 and *The Fifty-sixth report of the deputy keeper of the Public Records. . .* (Dublin, 1931), pp. 203-309. For transcripts of the Chancery decree books see NA, RC 6/1—RC6/2 and for the Chancery rolls of Charles II see NA, 2/448/21. The individual(s) who transcribed the decrees suggested that they included all relevant Chancery decrees. However the decrees relating to the staple do not appear to have been transcribed. For lists of plaintiffs and defendants whose case was heard in Chancery see NA, 2/446/20-21. For transcripts of the Exchequer papers see Equity Exchequer Orders, 1604-1673 in NA, 2/446/5/137 and 2/446/6/138 and the incomplete repertory to memoranda rolls NA, 2/446/6/138 (James I and Charles I) and 2/446/7/139 (Charles II). The Entry Books of the Recognizances in the Irish Court of Chancery, 1570-1634, are in BL, Add MSS 19,837-19,842, unfortunately they do not indicate the nature of the law suit or whether it related to the staple. Also see references to the Colvills in notes 42 and 43 above.

[76] For general references to debt see Geraldine Talon, 'Act of Settlement 1662. Court of Claims' (Irish Manuscripts Commission, forthcoming), pp. 23, 33, 40, 52, 57, 53, 60, 66, 69, 71, 84, 106, 131, 148, 302, 150, 155, 167, 172, 175, 180, 182, 188, 200, 204, 224, 227, 244, 248, 257, 263, 277, 284, 286, 287, 295, 298, 304-5, 306, 327, 346, 395, 483 (references to page proofs, compiled in 1986).

tenements' and over 900 acres of land in County Louth.[77] Other cases presented to the commissioners of the Court of Claims proved more complex. For instance Thomas Dowd of Dublin claimed that Thomas Keppock of Louth had mortgaged his lands in the parish of Atherdy to his father (John) 'long before the wars. . . for £600 and a statute staple of £1000', as had Gerrald Cowly of Ardee. Many of these transactions were indeed recorded in the staple books. In April 1634 Thomas Keppock and Richard Taaffe of County Louth borrowed £400 on bond from John Dowd, a Dublin alderman (the case was referred to Chancery in May 1664), the following April he borrowed a further £200, and in October 1635 an additional £200 (other bonds may well have been recorded in the Dublin staple in the years after 1638 of which no record survives). In return for this cash Keppock mortgaged seven townlands 'the mill and weirs; the dwelling house and garden... fourteen houses... in the town and parish of Atherdy'.[78] In July 1633 Gerrald Cowly of Ardee borrowed £200 from John Dowd and the following July borrowed a further £200. He mortgaged lands in two parishes and a stone house 'for £120, and a statute staple'.[79]

Other creditors appealed for satisfaction of their debts to the lord deputy or, during the 1650s, to the commissioners in Dublin, or directly to the English Parliament and the English Council of State.[80] For instance, in November 1652 the commissioners in Dublin ordered that Sarah Barker should receive £100 that her mother, Constance, loaned in August 1629 to Christopher Barnewall, his son, Robert, and his brother, Robert, on a staple bond.[81] In April 1650 the Council of State agreed that Colonel Arthur Hill should receive compensation for money he had loaned on the staple to the earl of Antrim 'out of the sequestration of the estates in Ireland liable to the said statute staple, with interest'.[82] No other record of the debt, for £5566 and dating from 1639, has survived presumably because it was contracted on the Dublin staple (the entry books for these years

---

[77] Tallon, 'Court of Claims', p. 483, ID 2949, 2950.

[78] Tallon, 'Court of Claims', p. 131. For Thomas Keppock see ID 1944, 1964, 2042, 2043 and 2067.

[79] Talon, 'Court of Claims', p. 132. For Cowly see ID 1137, 1728, 1893, 1963.

[80] For petitions addressed to Wentworth see Sheffield City Library, Wentworth Woodhouse Muniments, Strafford Papers 24-25/351-427, NA, 2/459/23 (for 1638), BL, Harl[eain] MSS 4297 (for 1633-4), BL, Harl MSS 430 (for 1637-8). For petitions addressed to Ormond, 1649-51, see Bodleain Library, Carte Mss 155. These petitions tend to refer to unsecured bonds often for relatively small amounts. Further research will reveal if any were secured by statute staple. Petitions to the House of Lords were included among the 'Main Papers' and are summarized in HMC, *Fifth Report* (London, 1876) and *Seventh Report* (London, 1879).

[81] BL, Egerton MSS 1762 f. 50r. I am grateful to David Menarry for bringing this reference to my attention. For the original staple record see ID 1635: Constance Barker, widow, of Dublin lent £200 on bond, to Christopher Barnewall, esquire of Louth, his son Robert and his brother Robert.

[82] *Calendar of State Papers Domestic 1650* (London, 1876), p. 101 and PRO, State Papers, 28/350/7, f. 31.

appear to be missing) and never certified into Chancery (where the entry books for these years are extant).[83]

Finally, estate records—where they survive—serve as an invaluable source for the study of debt since they often include lists of debts, promissory notes, different types of bonds, and details of mortgages. In addition to correspondence dealing with their financial activities, the Percival papers, housed in the British Library, contain numerous deeds, mortgages, promissory notes and bonds (including those transacted on the staple). A detailed examination of these, in conjunction with the staple records, the 1641 depositions and extant court proceedings, will provide a unique insight into the lending and borrowing habits of an important and influential Protestant gentry family living in Munster.[84] The lease books for the Brownlow family refer to mortgages that encumbered their county Armagh estates throughout the later seventeenth century. Some of these could have stemmed from money that Sir William borrowed on the Dublin staple.[85] Between February 1624 and December 1642 Sir William, occasionally with his brother John, signed bonds for £10,968 with a variety of Dublin merchants and landowners. Though some of these debts may well have been repaid a considerable number were not and were referred to the Court of Chancery.[86]

The extant rentals of the 'upstart' earl of Cork's estates offer a fascinating financial profile of one of Ireland's leading creditors.[87] Without doubt income from land provided Cork's most important source of revenue; but the income Cork derived from lending money represented a regular and important source of revenue.[88] In fact Cork's reputation for usury was so great that one commentator saw the serious fire of 1622 as God's punish-

[83] In February 1639 Hill lent, together with Edward Bolton, £1000 on bond to Sir Phelim O'Neill, a kinsman of Antrim's. The bond was later referred to Chancery, see ID 2819.

[84] BL, Add MSS 46,920A-46,926, 46,936B, 46,949, 47,035, and 47,038 for the estate papers of Sir Philip (1628-46) and BL, Add MSS 46,937-46,939, 46,946A, 46,949-46,951A for his son John. A selection of these papers has been printed in *HMC Egmont*, 2 vols.

[85] Raymond Gillespie, ed., *Settlement and Survival on an Ulster estate. The Brownlow Leasebook 1667-1711* (Belfast, 1988), pp. li, 3-4.

[86] Brownlow's creditors included Baron Mountnorris and Randal Aldersey of Meath, see note 108 below. Also see ID 1205, 1898, 1908, 1909, 1918, 1957, 1973, 2083, 2956.

[87] Cork owned land in Counties Cork, Waterford, Limerick, Tipperary, Kerry, Meath, Leix, Offaly, Clare, Roscommon, Mayo, Sligo, Dublin, Kildare, Wicklow and Wexford together with a manor in Dorset.

[88] Cork's bi-annual rental for the first half of 1637 amounted to over £10,000 and in his diary he thanked the Lord for this 'great bounty' and implored God to 'encrease them with his blessing, and with all happiness and prosperety as given us by his divyne hand', A. B. Grosart, *Lismore papers* (5 vols., np, 1886), 1st series, IV, 128. I am grateful to Nicholas Canny for allowing me to see Chapter 6 on 'The British Presence in Wentworth's Ireland' from his forthcoming monograph, *Ireland in the English Colonial System, 1580-1650* (Oxford University Press). The onset of war reduced his annual rental to roughly £300 in 1642, Raymond Gillespie, 'The Irish Economy at War' in Ohlmeyer, ed., *Ireland*, pp. 165-6.

ment on the city for the sin.[89] It appears that between 1637 and his death in 1643 Cork lent in the region of £60,000 (only £4000 of which had been repaid by 1641). First, he disbursed large sums to his children and immediate family (usually he gifted the money to them; if not, he rarely charged them interest or required collateral). Second, he lent cash—secured largely by mortgage—to local figures, his tenants, and to a host of Irish knights and peers (including Lords Muskerry, Kilmallock, FitzWilliam, Dowcra, Lambert and Roscommon). The majority of his debtors defaulted on their payments, enabling Cork to expand and consolidate his estates, largely—though not exclusively—at the expense of the native Irish who became lease holders rather than land owners. Finally, using secured bonds, promissory notes and bills of exchange, he loaned money to London and Dublin officials and merchants (such as William Perkins, the London tailor, or Thomas Watson, a Dublin alderman). In return he expected speedy repayment and charged interest rates of between 8% and 10%. Despite the fact that Cork made considerable amounts from money lending, only a very small proportion of his debts were recorded on the Cork or Dublin staples. Between 1632 and 1635, he lent nearly £10,000 on bond, the bulk of it to native Irish landowners from Limerick, Tipperary and Clare. It would seem that this money was never repaid and presumably the lands of these men then passed to the earl.[90]

When Cork does appear in the staple records it is invariably as a creditor no doubt eager to extend his already enormous territorial base.[91] In contrast the twelfth earl and first marquis of Ormond featured as a debtor. Between 1635 and 1640 Ormond borrowed at least £14,000 on bond on the Kilkenny and Dublin staples.[92] He also mortgaged tracts of land and borrowed heavily on bonds unsecured by the staple.[93] The need to recompense the guardian of his bride (Elizabeth Preston, daughter and sole heir of the earl of Desmond) with £15,000 severely strained Ormond's already limited resources and by 1642 he feared his interest payments would soon exceed his debts.[94] The outbreak of war exacerbated the situation. Yet even during the 1640s Ormond continued to borrow heavily. Unwilling or unable to borrow on the staple Ormond, as the hundreds of

---

[89] Cited in MacCarthy-Morrogh, 'Credit and Remittance', p. 19.

[90] ID 1810, 1853, 1919, 1938, 2115. Also see MacCarthy-Morrogh, *The Munster Plantation*, pp. 35-6, 79, 81, 146-8, 164, 166, 182-3, 248-52, 281.

[91] In March 1597 he borrowed on bond £350 on the Dublin staple, ID 13, 17.

[92] The fact that his clients and kinsmen co-signed these bonds suggests that his creditors—the most important being Thomas and James Bourke of Limerick—considered him a poor risk. See ID 2729, 2831 and 2061. A further bond transacted on the Kilkenny staple between Ormond and Sir John Temple for £4400 on 14 January 1639 survives among the Ormond deeds (NLI, D.4141 and D. 4146).

[93] Literally hundreds of bonds and promissory notes have survived amongst the Ormond deeds in the NLI. Also see a list of his debts in July 1641 in *HMC Egmont*, I, 140, 325 and BL, Add MSS 46,932 f. 108 and 46,928 f. 14.

[94] Thomas Carte, *History of the Life of James, first duke of Ormond* (2nd edn., 6 vols., Oxford, 1851), V, 358.

deeds in the National Library of Ireland show, instead mortgaged vast tracts of his extensive estates in Counties Kilkenny, Tipperary, Mayo and Galway to the tune of £20,000.[95] During his exile in 1650s his impoverished wife again resorted to borrowing on the Dublin staple and between 1658 and 1659 Sir Gerald Lowther (to whom her husband was already indebted) and others lent her £1800 on bond.[96] These debts, contracted on the staple, represent only a fraction of the total amounts borrowed by the earl and his wife throughout the seventeenth century.

The same held true for Randal MacDonnell, second earl and first marquis of Antrim. Despite the fact that he desperately needed cash, Antrim, who enjoyed an annual income of roughly £20,000 and owned a vast estate of c.340,000 acres in Ulster together with property in England, appears to have rarely used the staple as a source of credit.[97] Instead the bulk of Antrim's debts took the form of tradesmen's bills, bonds and mortgages. For instance it appears that by 1638 there was hardly a leading merchant or tradesman in London and Dublin to whom Antrim did *not* owe money.[98] In addition he borrowed nearly £30,000 on bond from family members, tenants, friends, fellow courtiers and royal servants. When this did not suffice, Antrim mortgaged English property belonging to himself and his wife, the duchess of Buckingham, together with one of his four Ulster baronies. In short the staple records paint a very misleading picture of Antrim's finances. The fact that he appears to have used the staple only occasionally could indicate that the English money market satisfied his needs or that his credit rating was so low that no one wanted to lend him money. Certainly early in 1639 the Irish lord deputy delighted in letting it be known that the earl had failed to scrape £300 together in Dublin 'to stay a seisure which in default was ready to issue against his land'.[99]

Clearly for any credit system to work effectively mutual trust between creditor and debtor was essential. To maintain their good reputation many debtors fulfilled their financial obligations on time. As Figure 1.10 shows in a significant number of instances a debtor recorded the payment of a debt and had the bond declared void—14% (306) of bonds concluded between 1597 and 1637 were apparently satisfied and this number rose to 25% between 1665 and 1678 (Figures 1.10 and 1.11). Other debts would have been cancelled without leaving any trace allowing the debtor to maintain his/her credit worthiness and to continue borrowing on the staple.

---

[95] Carte, *Ormond*, IV, 407 asserted that he raised £40,000. The extant Ormond deeds do not support this.

[96] For example in June 1640 Ormond borrowed £1000 on bond from Lowther, BL, Add MSS 46,924 f. 63, 46,933 ff. 47-8 and 46,936B f. 107.

[97] He used the staple occasionally, see ID 2907 and notes 82 and 83 above.

[98] His creditors included three individual goldsmiths, five jewelers, three merchants, four widows, the court painter (Anthony Van Dyck), two physicians, and a veritable array of haberdashers, linen drapers, mercers, milliners, seamstresses, seamsters, shoemakers, stocking sellers, tailors, upholsterers and woolen drapers, Ohlmeyer, *Civil War*, pp. 62-3.

[99] Quoted in Ohlmeyer, *Civil War*, p. 67.

Figure 1.10:
Table showing the bonds cancelled and certificates issued to Chancery and to the
Sheriff (recorded in the Dublin volumes)

Mss	Total number of bonds	Bonds cancelled as per agreement	Value of bonds cancelled	Total value of bonds	Certificates issued to Chancery	Bonds cancelled after certificate issued to Chancery	Writs issued to sheriff
Dc1,	815	98	£33,537	£282,560	116	14	14
1597-1615		(12%)	(12%)		(14%)	(2%)	(2%)
Dc2,	1318	208	£120,259	£715,958	275	31	16
1615-1637		(16%)	(17%)		(21%)	(2%)	(1%)
Dc3,	480	122	£129,317	£508,099	106	54	None
1665-1678		(25%)	(25%)		(22%)	(11%)	

Other debtors did not fulfill their obligations forcing the creditor to
resort to litigation, which appears to have been both reasonably efficient
and relatively cheap.[100] In May 1630 an irate Sir Philip Percival secured 'an
extent against' Callaghan O'Callaghan, an 'esquire' from Cork, and his
guarantors (Baron Dunboyne and Maurice Roche) for money (£600 on
bond) he had loaned him on the Dublin staple two years previously. He
noted caustically 'Mr O'Callaghan, has been too long deluded for ready
money lent out of purse, of which he has never yet paid one penny
principal or rent' and demanded that his castle and lands be seized.[101]
Percvial was not alone in pursuing tardy creditors. As Figure 1.10 shows,
between 1597 and 1637 the clerks of the Dublin staple issued 391/2133
(18%) certificates to Chancery; while between 1665 and 1678 they issued
106/480 (22%) certificates to Chancery (Figure 1.10). In other words 18%,
or nearly one fifth, of all transactions recorded in the Dublin staple books,
proceeded to the Court of Chancery during the first half of the seventeenth century; while nearly one quarter were pursued in Chancery in the
later decades of the seventeenth century. In 99 cases the instigation of
court proceedings prompted tardy debtors into paying or drawing up
repayment schedules.

---

[100] For example, in fifteenth-century Waterford, the costs of an action came to four
shillings and eight pence, Rich, ed., *Staple Court*, p. 55.
[101] ID 1512 and *HMC Egmont*, I, 63-4.

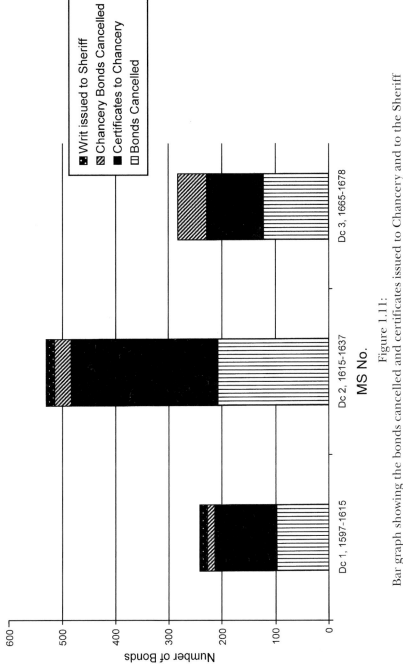

Figure 1.11:

Bar graph showing the bonds cancelled and certificates issued to Chancery and to the Sheriff

(recorded in the Dublin volumes)

Despite attempts to improve the procedures whereby debts could be recouped and legal loopholes eliminated, recovering money became complicated if the creditor or debtor died, as many did, before the debt could be repaid or if the creditor assigned the bond to someone else.[102] Consider the example of Thomas Begg, a Dublin merchant, who in June 1632 lent Edward Brandon from Dundalk £300 on bond. Begg then assigned the bond to Patrick Mapas, an alderman from Dublin. It was therefore Mapas and his heirs who pursued Brandon for the debt (a certificate was issued on this to Chancery in April 1634, in October 1638, and in December 1663).[103] Matters became more complicated still if debts were assigned to others, if the debtor or creditor had been on the losing side during the 1640s and if the estates of debtors had been confiscated.[104] In 1663 the commissioners of the Court of Claims heard how in December 1634 James Netterville of Wicklow lent £2000 on bond to Conor Maguire, one of the leaders of the 1641 rebellion. Maguire defaulted on his payment and the case made its way to Chancery in January 1639 and again in 1661 before proceeding to the Court of Claims two years later. Remarkably the debt, contracted nearly 50 years previously, was finally settled in March 1682.[105] The frustrated creditors of the other great leader of the 1641 rising, Sir Phelim O'Neill, proved less successful.[106] Between 1631 and 1639 Sir Phelim borrowed at least £8600 on bond from Dublin and Armagh 'esquires' (including the unfortunate William Caulfield, baron of Charlemont). Apart from one bond (for £400), none of Sir Phelim's

---

[102] 10th Charles I, session III, Chap VII (1634)—'An act for contention of debts upon execution' noted how creditors, who lent on the staple, had received satisfaction by the seizure of goods and lands. Some of these lands had been taken away from the creditors before the debt had been recovered. If this happened in the future the creditor had the right to resort again to law and secure a writ of *scire facias*, valid for 40 days, and thereby to recover the residue of the debt, *The Statutes at large*, II, 106-7. Also see 10th Charles I, session III, Chap VIII (1634)—'An act for to avoyde unnecessary delays of execution' and 10th Charles I, session III, Chap IX (1634)—'An act for relief of creditors against such persons as dye in execution', *The Statutes at large*, II, 107-9. 16, 17 Charles II Cap v (1664)—'An act to prevent delays in extending statutes. . .' was an attempt to improve the procedure by which a creditor, who had lent money on the staple, could assert his rights, *The Statutes at Large*, III, 292-3

[103] Tallon, 'Court of Claims', p. 155 and ID 1838. A staple bond, contracted on the Dublin staple (ID 2147), between James Lowman of Kilkenny and William Bretton of Wexford, dated 29 August 1636, and recorded in Chancery on 24 January 1637 has survived among the Ormond deeds (NLI, D. 4043). Presumably Lowman passed the bond for £100 on to Ormond.

[104] The assignment of bonds proved fairly common. For example Lord Inchiquin promised to pay Percival's outstanding debt of to Lord Ranelagh, 11 April 1640, BL, Add MSS 46,924 f. 10. A staple bond, contracted by James Barry on the Cork staple, for £400 dated 10 September 1621 was assigned by James Wall to Percival 29 June 1630 , BL, Add MSS 47,035 f. 49.

[105] ID 2008.

[106] ID 1818.

creditors appear to have been repaid and they pursued him in Chancery.[107] It is not clear whether any received satisfaction except perhaps Sir Robert Parkhurst and John Stowell (the executor for Randal Aldersey), who in 1665 were allowed to recoup monies lent to men, including O'Neill, whose estates had been confiscated.[108] The staple records thus provide a rare insight into the complex processes of the resolution of economic disputes in seventeenth-century Ireland and, perhaps, pave the way for a wider study of the role the courts played in Irish economic life.[109]

This brief introduction to the staple records has raised many more questions than it has answered. Much about the staple remains unknown and the precise mechanics of borrowing are often difficult to determine. Despite this the staple records are an invaluable—if often incomplete— guide to indebtedness and the social and economic history of seventeenth-century Ireland. In an economy where capital and coinage were particularly scarce, the staple served a very important function as a national paper credit system, albeit one centered on Dublin, which was accessible to men and women from a wide range of social and economic backgrounds.[110] However only by constructing 'webs of indebtedness' and by untangling the patronage networks in which they were embedded, especially at a local level, will the enormously complex credit systems operating in early modern Ireland and the land transfers—usually in the form of mortgages—which often accompanied them be fully understood.[111] Given the number of people involved in these credit networks this

---

[107] Sir Phelim O'Neill, leader of the Irish rebellion, mortgaged land in County Tyrone to cover debts in excess of £12,000. Little wonder, perhaps, that one of his creditors, Mr Fullerton of Loughgall, to whom Sir Phelim owed £600 'upon mortgages', was one of the first to be murdered in the rebellion, Jerrold Casway, 'Two Phelim O'Neills' in *Seanchas Ardmhacha*, 11:2 (1985), p. 340.

[108] *Calendar of State Papers relating to Ireland 1647-1660* (London, 1903), p. 561. Between February 1623 and July 1637 12 transactions involving Aldersey (and bonds worth £10,094) were recorded in the Dublin staple books. Five of these transactions (with bonds totalling £8974) were referred to the Court of Chancery. For entries relating to money lent by Aldersey see ID 1138, 1585, 1775, 1852, 1878, 1901, 1967, 1973, 2022, 2062, 2197, 2208. Sir Robert Parkhurst also lent considerable sums (the bonds total £3163) on the Dublin staple between June 1625 and June 1668, see ID 1290, 1536, 1951, 2054, 2087, 2119, 2116, 2140, 2400. Also see NA, RC 6/2 p. 354, 19 June 1624: Parkhurst sued Lord Ibrackan in Chancery for £200 plus interest.

[109] For fascinating insights on this topic in an English context see Craig Muldrew, 'Credit and the courts: debt litigation in a seventeenth century urban community' in *Economic History Review* 46: 1 (1993), pp. 23-38 and 'The culture of reconciliation: community and the settlement of economic disputes in early modern England' in *Historical Journal* 39:4 (1996), pp. 915-42.

[110] This conclusion appears to contradict recent assertions that Ireland did not have a 'well-developed credit system', Gillespie, *Transformation of the Irish Economy*, p. 53, also p. 38. Also Raymond Gillespie, 'Peter French's petition for an Irish mint' in *Irish Historical Studies*, 25:100 (1987), p. 416.

[111] Kevin McKenny has entered much of the material relating to these land transfers into a database that will be published by the Irish Manuscripts Commission.

will no doubt prove a lengthy task and one that will require historians, genealogists, and scholars interested in local and urban history to work together very closely.

Even though the staple continued to function well into the eighteenth century, it ceased after 1690 to play such an important role in the economic life of early modern Ireland.[112] Why? On the one hand, the political turmoil that beset Ireland in general and local government in particular after 1685 combined with the onset of war after 1688 and further upheavals in land ownership created a commercial crisis akin to that of the 1640s. This economic, tenurial, and political instability totally undermined the mutual trust and economic interdependence that sustained the operation of the staple as a national paper credit network. On the other, the emergence of a reasonably well-defined banking system in Dublin during the early decades of the eighteenth century (the first Irish banking act was passed in 1709, followed ten years later by calls for the establishment of a national bank) effectively rendered the staple redundant.[113] However the fact that it did not survive into the eighteenth century should in no way detract from its significance. In terms of the financial and commercial history of Ireland the staple helped to facilitate the transition from a largely redistributive economic order that was starved of specie to a more recognizably modern commercial economy.

These commercial changes, in turn, underpinned attempts by central government to 'civilize' Ireland and to overturn the traditional 'fighting and feasting' culture that sustained native society. These staple records thus offer an opportunity to analyze the torturous processes inherent in colonization at a grass roots level. Certainly Irish chieftains quickly realized that in order to survive and succeed in this 'civilizing' English world and to be considered 'worthy subjects', they had no alternative but to exploit the economic advantages of the English system of landlord-tenant relations and of a commercial economy. Many reorganised their estates accordingly.[114] Yet as a result of this, combined with increased conspicuous expenditure (on building, furniture, clothing, education, legal expenses, living at court and marriage) many sank deeply into debt and a considerable number mortgaged their estates, often to Protestant entrepreneurs.

---

[112] No transaction appears to have occurred on the Dublin staple after June 1687, on the Cork staple after February 1687, on the Limerick staple after August 1685, on the Youghal staple after May 1684 and on the Carrickfergus staple after September 1682. A fourth staple book (Dc 4), not included in the database, has also survived. This recorded the minutes of the annual meetings of the mayor, constables and brethren of the staple for the election of the mayor and constables. It also contains pleadings from merchants applying for admission as brethren and covers the years 1713-1753.

[113] Louis Cullen, 'Economic development, 1691-1750' in T. W. Moody and W. E. Vaughan, ed., *A New History of Ireland* vol. IV. *Eighteenth-Century Ireland 1691-1800* (Oxford, 1986), pp. 152-8.

[114] For a specific example see Ohlmeyer, *Civil War*, pp. 32-42. For Scotland see Allan I. Macinnes, *Clanship, Commerce and the house of Stuart, 1603-1788* (Edinburgh, 1996).

Did these financial and economic pressures prove, especially in the long-term, more potent agents of change in these outlying areas than political or polemical initiatives? One government official, writing in the early seventeenth century, predicted that they would and maintained that 'the love of [money] will sooner effect civility than any other persuasion whatsoever'.[115] If this was indeed the case the staple records will help to demonstrate that the colonisation of seventeenth-century Ireland was a messy, haphazard process that defies any simplistic explanation.

[115] *Calendar of State Papers Ireland 1611-14*, pp. 501-2.

CHAPTER 2:

CONSTRUCTING THE DATABASE[1]

'Inadequate data [does] not become scientific information simply by virtue of being processed through a computer'.[2] The late Christina Larner's cautionary 'health warning' originally aimed at overzealous scholars of seventeenth century witchcraft applies equally to the staple records that have been entered into this database. Bearing this caveat in mind, this database nevertheless offers historians, genealogists, and other interested scholars easy access to repetitive dry, legal records that were previously very difficult to interrogate and interpret. Moreover it brings together for the first time all of the surviving records which relate to the Irish staple in the early modern period.

DESIGNING THE DATABASE:

Two principal objectives determined the design and construction of the database. First and foremost, the integrity of the original manuscripts had to be preserved while, at the same time, facilitating rigorous interrogation of the staple data. Second, the database had to be easy to use and sufficiently flexible to distinguish easily between the staple books housed in the Dublin City Archives and the Chancery staple volumes housed in the British Library.

In an attempt to achieve these aims a number of compromises had to be made. The database is not a verbatim reproduction of the staple volumes. The entries in the original staple volumes are largely formulaic and very repetitive (for an example see Plate 2).[3] Therefore important information, which was remarkably consistent between entries, regarding the transactions recorded in the staple volumes and the debtor(s) and creditor(s) involved has been extracted and entered into carefully selected 'field' entries in the database. To achieve consistency in and between these field entries, figures have been rounded off; dates have been modernised; the spelling of names, counties and occupations have been standardised; punctuation has been used very sparingly; data in a number of fields has been rather arbitrarily grouped and sub-classified; and lengthy comments (whether in the margin or in the accompanying indentures of defeazance) have been summarised.[4] Finally, the debtor(s) and creditors(s) must be

---

[1] I am grateful to Éamonn Ó Ciardha for his help in writing this chapter.

[2] Christina Larner, ed., *Witchcraft and Religion. The Politics of Popular Belief* (Oxford, 1984), p. 26. I am grateful to Kenneth Nicholls for bringing this reference to my attention.

[3] See Appendix III.

[4] Discussed in detail below.

interrogated separately and the only means of viewing them simultaneously is by using the 'main form' rather than the more flexible 'query' search.[5] While the database will never serve as a substitute for consulting the original staple volumes whether in Dublin or London, it does however bring together—for the first time—all of the early modern Irish staple books. Moreover it enables interested scholars to access easily and to inter-rogate rigorously a wealth of information which has been shamelessly overlooked for far too long.

The availability of Microsoft Access, combined with the fact that a number of our colleagues within the Department of History enjoyed technical expertise in working with Access, are the principal reasons why it was selected. The complex task of designing the database was left to the computing experts—Frederik Pedersen, Steve Murdoch and, above all, Duncan Davidson. After lengthy periods of consultation and experimenta-tion they designed a relational database that preserved the integrity of the original manuscripts and was flexible (see Figure 2.1). This relational database involved breaking data down into specific fields and allows for the cross-referencing of any field in the main form with any field in either the debtor or creditor subforms. As a result the data can be easily and efficient-ly extracted and manipulated which—in the words of the great English demographic historian, E. A. Wrigley—'gives greater depth and fuller dimension to pictures of the past that would otherwise be flat and lack perspective'.[6]

FIELD NAMES:

IDENT NUMBER (numeric field)
Every transaction has a unique identification number that never changes. The statutes staple in the Dublin volumes also bear this identification number; the originals in the British Library volumes do not and should be identified by the Manuscript and folio number in the MS number field.

MS NUMBER (textual field)
The archive, volume and folio number of the original entry was recorded in this field. As far as possible the folio numbers correspond to the pagina-tion in the original volumes. A few folios in the Dublin volumes were unfoliated and so a folio number has been inserted and pencilled on to the original volumes (for example the folio in between Dc 1 f. 47 and f. 48 is blank and has been marked f. 47a). The 'recto' and 'verso' have been indicated in the Dublin volumes with 'r' and 'v'. These annotations have been added in pencil to the original staple books housed in the Dublin City Archives.

---

[5] Discussed in *Using the Database*, Section III.
[6] E. A. Wrigley, ed., *Identifying people in the past* (London, 1973), p. 5.

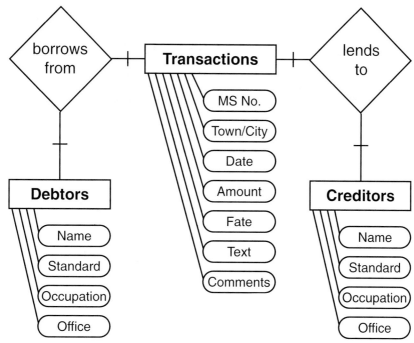

Figure 2.1:
A model of the relational database designed for the staple project[7]

Dublin City Archives: Three registers, 1596-37 and 1664-78, recording the entry of bonds on the Dublin staple are extant and are housed in the Dublin City Archives (referred to in the database as Dc1, Dc2 and Dc3). These volumes are all in reasonable physical condition and apart from two principal exceptions (May-October 1604 and August 1615—August 1616 when no transactions appear to have been entered) are remarkably complete with transactions being regularly conducted throughout the course of the year. Please note that the transactions are not entered in chronological order. The clerk of the staple would have carried these volumes around with him which explains why they, especially volume 2, are rather curled up.

---

[7] Duncan Davidson kindly drew this diagram.

For examples of other databases used to interrogate historical data see Charles Harvey and Jon Press, *Databases in Historical Research* (London, 1996). Also see Roderick Floud, *An introduction to quantitative methods for historians* (London, 1973). Steve Murdoch, 'The database in early modern Scottish history: Scandinavia and Northern Europe, 1580-1707' and Alexia Grosjean, 'Scottish-Scandinavian Seventeenth Century Naval Links: A case study for the SSNE database' in *Northern Studies. The Journal of the Scottish Society for Northern Studies* 32 (1997), pp. 83-103 and 105-123.

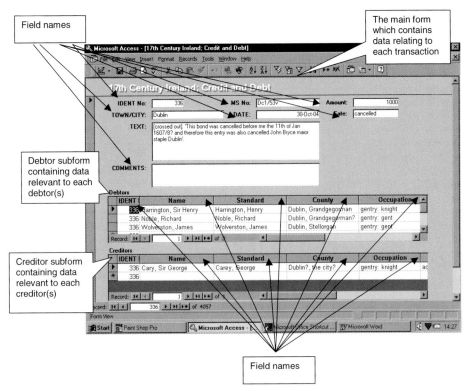

Figure 2.2:
Field names as they appear on the main form

- Dc 1 (278 folios) covers the period February 1597 to June 1630—with the exception of the first 5-6 folios which are badly damaged, the volume remains in good condition. It is in its original leather satchel binding, with a clasp leather thong and iron buckle. At least four clerks entered transactions into this volume and recorded between two and fours transactions per page.
- Dc 2 (544 folios) covers the period August 1615 to December 1666—the volume remains in reasonable condition. It is in its original leather satchel binding, with a clasp leather thong and iron buckle. This volume is particularly curled no doubt due to the fact that it was constantly carried about, and this makes it difficult to read the right-hand margin of the left page and the left-hand margin of the right page. At least four clerks entered transactions into this volume and recorded between two and four transactions per page. The supplementary material included at the back of this volume (and transcribed below in Appendix II, III, and IV) is particularly difficult to read.

- Dc 3 (382 folios) covers the period January 1665 to June 1678—the volume is in excellent condition and is the most legible of the three. It is in its original vellum binding. At least two clerks entered transactions into this volume.[8]

British Library: Five registers of bonds, kept by the clerk of recognisance of the Chancery between 1618 and 1687, were bought by the British Library in the mid-19th century and are housed there. These volumes are all in reasonable condition. Please note that the transactions are not necessarily entered in chronological order and that, with the exception of the years between 1651 and 1660, the entries are in Latin but all the indentures of defeazance are in English.[9] Individual volumes occasionally overlap but no transaction appears to be have recorded more than once. There is normally one entry per page.

- BL, Add MSS 19,843 (412 folios) covers the period October 1618 to February 1658.

- BL, Add MSS 19,844 (346 folios) covers the period May 1668 to November 1678. In some cases the left-hand page is blank and in others there are pages with no foliation.

- BL, Add MSS 15,635 (460 folios) covers the period November 1641 to December 1668.

- BL, Add MSS 15,636 (276 folios) covers the period May 1659 to March 1674.

- BL, Add MSS 15,637 (226 folios) covers the period January 1671 to June 1687.

Between them these eight volumes record c. 4,000 individual transactions (c. 2,600 or 65% on the Dublin Staple and c. 1,400 or 35% in the Chancery volumes).

AMOUNT (numeric field)
The size of the bond recorded in the staple volumes has been entered in this field. These amounts are all in pounds sterling. Occasionally it has been necessary to round off a given amount and in these instances the amount stated in the manuscript has also been entered to in the text field. In the manuscript the size of a bond was recorded in both Arabic and Roman numerals, which occasionally proved confusing.

---

[8] A fourth staple book (Dc 4), not included in the database, has also survived. This recorded the minutes of the annual meetings of the mayor, constables and brethren of the staple for the election of the mayor and constables. It also contains pleadings from merchants applying for admission as brethren and covers the years 1713-1753.

[9] Roughly fifty transactions in BL, Add MSS 19,843 (ID 2972-3119) are in English.

Field names

ID NT	DATE	Standard	Name	Occupation	Office	County	Amount	Fate	TEX	TOWN	MS
2	01-Feb-97	?	illegible	illegible		illegible				Dublin	Dc1/1r
3	03-Feb-97	?	illegible	illegible		illegible	400			Dublin	Dc1/1r
4	07-Feb-97	?	illegible	illegible		illegible	1000		[crosse	Dublin	Dc1/1r
5	10-Feb-97	Plunkett, Christ	Pluncket, C	gentry: gent		Armagh	50		DIFFICL	Dublin	Dc1/1v
5	10-Feb-97	Contant?, Dani	Contant?, D	trade: tailor		Dublin	50		DIFFICL	Dublin	Dc1/1v
6	10-Feb-97	Walsh, Theoba	Walsh, Theo	?		?			THIS EN	Dublin	Dc1/1v
6	10-Feb-97	Browne, Simon	Browne, Syr	?		?			THIS EN	Dublin	Dc1/1v
7	01-Feb-97	Bath, Thomas	Bath, Thom	gentry: gent		Dublin, I	60			Dublin	Dc1/1v
7	01-Feb-97	?	?, ?	?		?, ?	60			Dublin	Dc1/1v
8	10-Feb-97	Hetherington, F	Hethrington,	gentry: gent		Dublin, I	200			Dublin	Dc1/1v
9	18-Feb-97	Butler, Edmunc	Butler, Edm	peer: viscoun		Kilkenny	200		This Ed	Dublin	Dc1/2r
9	18-Feb-97	Butler, Richard	Butler, Rich	other: son/he		?, ?	200		This Ed	Dublin	Dc1/2r
10	27-Feb-97	Plunkett, Richa	Pluncket, R	gentry: esquir		Meath,			This ent	Dublin	Dc1/2r
11	28-Feb-97	Dickson, Patric	Dyckson, P	merchant?		Dublin?	100		This ent	Dublin	Dc1/2r
11	28-Feb-97	Duffe, ?	Duff, ?	merchant?		Dublin?	100		This ent	Dublin	Dc1/2r
12	28-Feb-97	Foster, William	Fforster, Wi	gentry: gent		Dublin, I	100			Dublin	Dc1/2r
13	03-Mar-97	Boyle, Richard	Boyle, Rich	gentry: gent		Limerick	200		[crosse	Dublin	Dc1/2v
14	23-Mar-97	Plunkett, Richa	Pluncket, R	gentry: gent		?, Bolye	300		SEE OF	Dublin	Dc1/2v
14	23-Mar-97	Plunkett, Richa	Pluncket, R	gentry: esquir		Meath, I	300		SEE OF	Dublin	Dc1/2v
15	23-Mar-97	Plunkett, Richa	Pluncket?, F	gentry: esquir		Meath, I	40		SEE OF	Dublin	Dc1/2v
16	23-Mar-97	Foster, William	Fforster, Wi	gentry: gent,		Dublin?,			William	Dublin	Dc1/2v
17	29-Mar-97	Boyle, Richard	Boyle, Rich	gentry: gent		Dublin	150	cancell	[crosse	Dublin	Dc1/3r
18	23-Apr-97	Luttrell, Henry	Luttrell, Hen		civic: cle	Kildare,	90			Dublin	Dc1/3r
19	27-Apr-97	Contant?, Nich	Contant?, N	gentry: gent?		Dublin	100			Dublin	Dc1/3r
20	17-May-97	Darcy, George	Darsye, Gec	gentry: gent		Meath, I	85	cancell	[crosse	Dublin	Dc1/3r

Record: 1 of 5936

Figure 2.3:
Field names as they appear in query 'A: Debtors master list'

Please note that the amount of the bond was not a record of the actual loan but security for the loan and was usually double the amount of the loan. For example an indenture of defeazance of June 1656 recounted how a bond for £242 was drawn up to secure a loan of £121.[10] On 25 August 1625 Constance Barker, widow, of Dublin lent £200 on bond, to Christopher Barnewall, esquire, of Louth, his son Robert, and his brother Robert. A petition, dating from 1652, confirmed that the amount actually lent was £100.[11] Unfortunately in the majority of transactions the relationship between the size of the loan and the size of the bond is not explicitly stated.

---

[10] ID 3057.

[11] ID 1635 and BL, Egerton MSS 1762 f. 50r. I am grateful to David Menarry for bringing this reference to my attention.

The size of the bond is usually given in pounds sterling but, prior to 1637, the amount of the bond was also given in Irish harps, English merks, and silver bullion.[12] In order to convert these into pounds sterling the following rates of exchange have been used:

Irish harps: 1 harp or Irish pound = 15 shillings sterling (ratio of 3:4).[13]

English merk/mark: 1 merk = two-thirds of one pound sterling.[14]

Silver: 1 pound of pure silver = 76 3/11th shillings sterling
   1 ounce of pure silver = 4.18 shillings[15]

TOWN CITY (textual field)

The town or city where the staple transaction occurred has been entered in this field. All transactions entered on the Dublin volumes occurred on the Dublin staple. The transactions entered in the Chancery volumes were transacted on a variety of staples. The greatest number of entries recorded in Chancery came from Dublin (66%); Cork (13%); Drogheda (7%); Limerick and Carrickfergus (4% each); Youghal (2%); Galway and Kilkenny (1% each); with the least coming from Londonderry, Sligo, Waterford and Wexford. In the Chancery volumes the name of the city or town is always given in the top left-hand corner, together with the names of the mayor and constables of the staple (see Appendix I).

DATE (numeric field)

The date when the transaction was recorded in the staple volume appears in this field. Debtors and creditors were obliged to record their transaction with the staple clerk within six months of it having taken place. As a result this is the date on which the clerk of the staple recorded the transaction and not necessarily the date on which the transaction actually occurred. The beginning of each year is taken as 1 January rather than 25 March. The date in the 'text' field is the date on which the entry was entered in the office of the clerk of recognisance in the Court of Chancery. The date,

---

[12] Raymond Gillespie, 'Peter French's petition for an Irish mint' in *Irish Historical Studies*, 25: 100 (1987), p. 416. For details see Michael Dolley, 'The Irish coinage' in T. W. Moody, F. X. Martin and F. J. Byrne, eds, *A New History of Ireland III Early Modern Ireland, 1534-1691* (Oxford, 1978). 'Sterling circulated in Ireland at one-third above its face value when computed in the Irish money of account', MacCarthy-Morrogh, 'Credit and Remittance', p. 7. Though it does not appear to be used in staple transactions foreign coin, especially Spanish silver and Portuguese gold, also circulated, *Calendar of State Papers relating to Ireland, 1625-32*, pp. 645-6.

[13] See for examples ID 331, 334, 338, 350, 434, 440, 455, 463, 473.

[14] See for examples ID 23, 98, 143, 443, 843. I am grateful to Bob Tyson for his guidance on prevailing rates of exchange.

[15] Estimating the value of silver is problematic since it is not clear how pure this silver was and these exchange rates must be regarded as an approximation. This rate of exchange has been taken from T. S. Ashton, *An economic history of England: the eighteenth century* (London, 1955), p. 168. In 1612 one ounce of English silver, being 11 ounces fine, was valued at 5 shillings James F. Larkin and Paul L. Hughes, eds., *Stuart Royal Proclamations* vol. 1 *Royal Proclamations of King James I 1603-1625* (London, 1973), p. 281. For examples see the following records: ID 319, 320, 323, 324, 325, 326, 332.

given in both Roman and Arabic numerals, occasionally proved very difficult to read and if in doubt about any date please consult the original.[16] The regnal years (including those for Oliver Cromwell) are often given alongside the calendar year.[17]

FATE (textual field)
The clerk who entered the transaction into the staple volumes recorded the 'fate' of a transaction in over 1200 instances. In other words the 'fate' of nearly a third of the total number of transactions is known. The bulk of these were recorded in the Dublin staple volumes.[18] This information has also been entered into the 'text' field. The following abbreviations have been used:

- **Cancelled:** A debtor was not obliged to indicate whether the debt was repaid. However in many cases a debtor recorded the payment of a debt, especially in the Dublin volumes, and had the bond declared void or had the original entry crossed out. In other instances a receipt of repayment was inserted into the staple volume.[19] Other bonds were cancelled after they had been referred to the sheriff or the Court of Chancery (see below). Many debts would have been cancelled without leaving any trace.

- **Chancery:** Certificates issued into the Court of Chancery by the clerks of the Dublin staple.

- **Chancery/cancelled:** The bond was cancelled after the case had been referred to Chancery.

- **Chancery/defeazance:** After the case had been referred to Chancery the debtor and creditor formulated a repayment schedule.

- **Court for the Administration of Justice:** Between 1654 and 1655 6 cases, recorded in Dublin volumes, were referred to the Court for the Administration of Justice.

- **Court of Claims:** During the early 1660s two cases (recorded in the Dublin volumes) were referred from Chancery to the Court of the Commissioners of the Court of Claims.[20]

- **Defeazance:** A repayment schedule was negotiated between the debtor and creditor. The clerk of the Dublin staple usually entered the indenture of defeazance when he recorded the original statue staple.

---

[16] For instance '4' was sometimes written as 'iv' and at other times as 'iiii'.

[17] For references to His Highness Oliver Cromwell or Richard Cromwell see ID 3329, 3332, 3333, and 3341. For an excellent guide to interpreting regnal dates see C. R. Cheney, ed., *Handbook of dates* (London, 1978).

[18] See Figures 1.10 and 1.11 above for details on the fate of the transactions entered into the Dublin volumes.

[19] See for examples ID 1445, 2119, 2146, and 2197.

[20] For full details on the Court of Claims see Geraldine Tallon, 'Act of Settlement, 1662. Court of Claims' (Irish Manuscripts Commission, forthcoming).

- **Sheriff:** A writ was issued to the sheriff.
- **Sheriff/cancelled:** The bond was cancelled after a writ had been issued to the sheriff.

TEXT (textual field)

A considerable number of individual transactions were annotated in the margins or included lengthy indentures of defeazance. This additional material has been summarized and recorded in the text field. In particular the Chancery and the third Dublin volume contain lengthy memoranda and indentures of defeazance, which bristle with legal jargon.[21] These usually come immediately after the related transaction and when this is not the case the relevant folio number is given.

A sizeable number of indentures of defeazance included information relating to the repayment of the debt[22], the interest payable[23], the place (Strongbow's Tomb in Christchurch, the Three Cranes, Damaske St., the Custom's-House Gate proved particularly popular[24]) and day and time of repayment.[25] Some were very complex deeds involving individuals (other creditors, heirs, widows, minors, kinsmen, and executors) who had not borrowed on the staple but who had an interest in debtor's lands.[26] Other indentures of defeazance, especially those dating from the post Restoration years, included extensive lists of the lands, mills, tenements, and orchards owned by an individual debtor.[27] Fascinating details regarding marriage portions, wills, and descriptions of moveable assets were also recorded in a few instances.[28] Occasionally an indenture of defeazance indicated why an individual wanted to borrow money in the first place. For example, in May 1665 Richard Lambert, earl of Cavan, borrowed £10,000 on bond from Sir James Ware for the schooling and education of his son and heir Charles.[29]

---

[21] Dc1 and Dc2 contain no indentures of defeazance. Bridget McCormack transcribed the indentures of defeazance contained in Dc3 in full. Time constraints made it impossible to transcribe in full the lengthy indentures of defeazance in the BL Chancery volumes and the original volumes should be consulted for full details.

[22] Occasionally (ID 2324) the creditor requested that the repayment was to be made in pure silver and gold, and not in copper or other mixed or base coin; or in kind (such as sheep in the case of ID 2322).

[23] This was invariably 10% and is clearly specified in many defeazances. See for examples ID 2339, 2414, 2417, 2651, 2654.

[24] See for examples ID 2336 and 3062. Occasionally provision was made to repay debts in England. See for example ID 2464 where the creditor requested that payments be made in the chapter house of the Cathedral or minister of St. Peter's in the city of York.

[25] Feast days—such as Annunciation of the Blessed Virgin, Nativity of St. John, Feast of St. Michael the Archangel and the feast of the birth of our Lord—proved particularly popular for repayment of debt. See for example ID 3050.

[26] See for example ID 2510.

[27] See for examples ID 2566, 2581, 2625, 2702, 2703.

[28] See for examples ID 2640, 2563, and 2665.

[29] See for example ID 2232.

Others referred to the ways in which major political events, such as the outbreak of the Anglo-Dutch war, might impact on repayment schedules.[30]

In the Dublin staple books these annotations indicated whether a case was referred to the Court of Chancery or to the local sheriff and whether the bond was cancelled and the money repaid.[31] Given the miscellaneous nature of the data entered into the 'text' field it is the most difficult field to interrogate easily. In an attempt to circumvent this, the fate of individual transactions has also been entered into the 'fate' field (see above).

Some Dublin and all Chancery transactions were endorsed with a copy of the signature of the debtor(s) and if he/she could not write their mark (usually a cross) was recorded. This has been entered into this field, together with the names of any additional witnesses, public notaries, and clerks.[32] Crude drawings of seals also pepper the volumes. Whether the ability to sign one's name offers a crude insight into literacy levels remains an area of intense debate amongst historians. However it may prove fruitful to relate the occupation or social status of a debtor or creditor and his/her ability to sign his/her name. A random analysis of merchants, women, and farmers who borrowed on the staple between 1636 and 1685, and had their case referred to Chancery, indicated that all of the merchants (58) signed their names, the vast majority (33/36) of women signed their names while only 2 (out of 10) farmers signed their name.

The names of the mayor and constables of the staple were also usually recorded and these have been extracted and are listed in Appendix I. The date when the transaction was recorded in the staple volume has been entered in the 'date' field (see above). The date in the 'text' field is the date in which the clerk of recognisance in the Court of Chancery recorded the transaction.

COMMENTS (textual field)
This field has been left blank so that an individual user can annotate the database accordingly. For details see *Using the Database.*

CREDITOR/DEBTOR IDENT NUMBER (numeric field)
This corresponds to the identity number of the transaction (discussed above).

CREDITOR/DEBTOR NAME (textual field)
The name(s) of each creditor/debtor as it appears in the original staple book has been entered into this field. Christian and surnames have been left the way they appear in the original in an attempt to retain the integrity

---

[30] See for example ID 2322.

[31] See for examples ID 1445, 2119, 2146, 2197.

[32] On occasion the clerk of the staple was unable to sign his name and in the case of Mathew Kingselagh (Kinsella) this may well have reflected the fact that he was probably an Irish-speaker, see ID 3912 and 3913.

PLATE 3:

National Archives: D.15248 A staple indenture of defeazance between Robert Colvill and Earl of Mount Alexander for £3000. It was transacted on the Dublin staple on 27 Nov 1675

[Photograph: Lorcan Farrell]

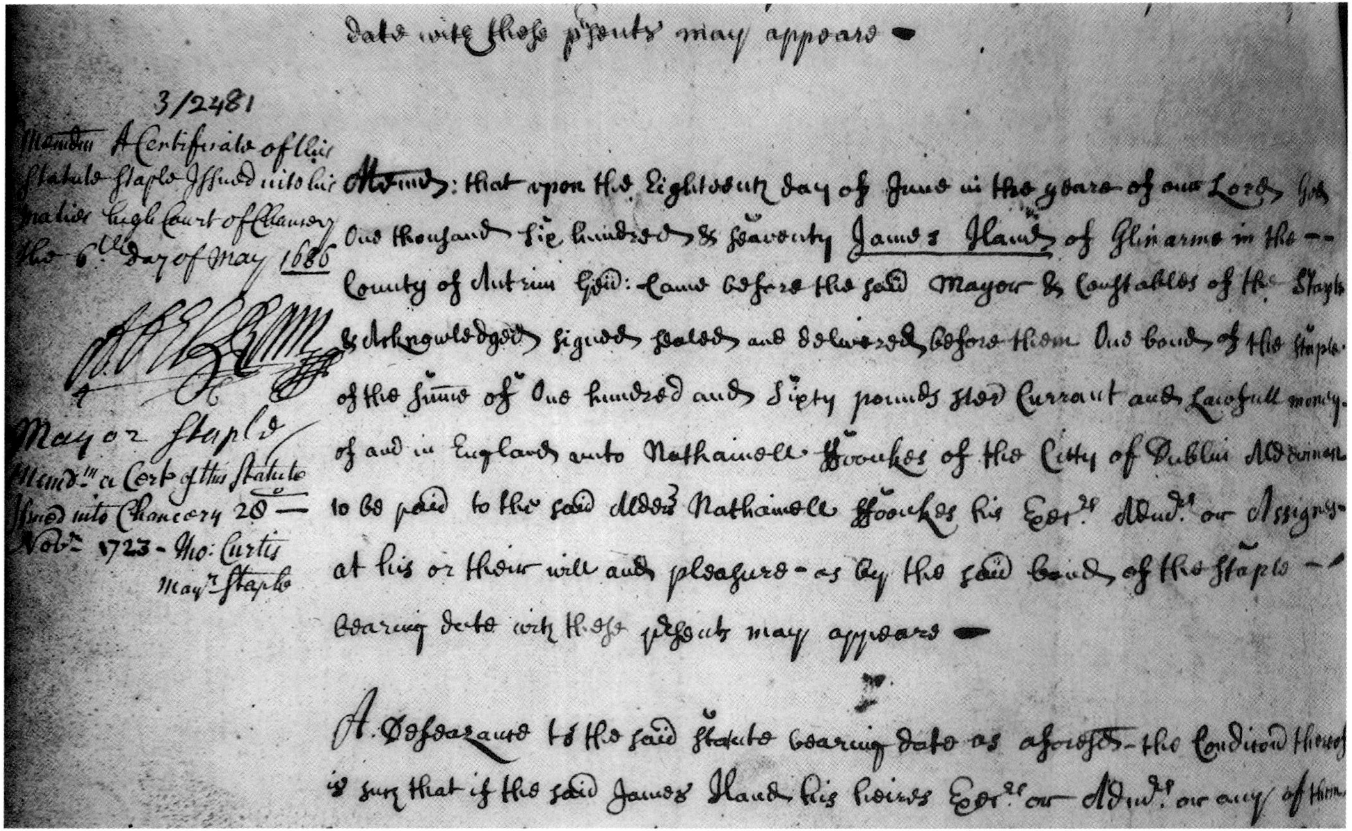

date with these p[re]sents may appeare

3/2481

Memdm A Certificate of this Statute Staple Issued into his Ma[jes]ties high Court of Chancery the 6th Day of May 1686

Mayor Staple

Memd. a Cert of this Statute Issued into Chancery 20 Nov. 1723 - Tho: Curtis May[o]r Staple

Memd: that upon the Eighteenth day of June in the yeare of our Lord God One thousand six hundred & seaventy James Hand of Glinarme in the County of Antrim Gent: came before the said Mayor & Constables of the Staple & Acknowledged signed sealed and delivered before them One bond of the Staple of the summe of One hundred and Sixty pounds ster Currant and Lawfull money of and in England unto Nathaniell ffoukes of the City of Dublin Alderman to be paid to the said Aldn Nathaniell ffoukes his Exrs Admrs or Assignes at his or their will and pleasure - as by the said bond of the Staple bearing date with these p[re]sents may appeare

A Defeazance to the said Statute bearing date as aforesd - the Condition thereof is such that if the said James Hand his heires Exrs or Admrs or any of them

PLATE 4:

Dublin City Archives: Staple Book 3, entry 2481: Bond: James Hand of Glinarme, Co. Antrim to Nathaniel Foulkes of Dublin City: £160 sterling. 18 June 1670. With memo entry certificate into Chancery.

[Photo by David Davison]

of the manuscript and because variations of spelling will be of interest to local historians and genealogists. The Chancery volumes contain a transcript of the signature of the debtor(s) or a copy of his/her mark. This information has been entered into the 'text' field (see above). In all over 10,000 names are listed—4309 creditors and 5879 debtors. Predictably the same person appears more than once and so the actual number of people using the staple was probably between 5000 and 6000. Given the vast numbers involved no attempt has been made to identify these individuals from other sources.[33]

Occasionally it proved difficult to read a name and this has been indicated with a question mark (?). When a Latin version of a name was given the case has not been changed. When an individual held a title the surname was not usually stated. For example, Richard Barry, baron of Santry, is listed in the manuscript as 'Richard, lord Santry' but in the name field as 'Barry, Richard'.[34] His title, baron of Santry, is recorded in the 'occupation/ status' field. In a similar vein the bishops tended to use the name of their bishopric, rather than their surname. For example, Michael

---

[33] The sources here are endless. For major figures see E. B. Fryde, D. E. Greenway, S. Porter and I. Roy, eds., *The Handbook of British Chronology* (3rd edn., London, 1986); T. W. Moody, F. X. Martin and F. J. Byrne, eds., *A New History of Ireland Vol. IX Maps, Genealogies, Lists. A companion to Irish History* (Oxford, 1984), *The Dictionary of National Biography and The Dictionary of Irish Biography* (Cambridge, forthcoming, 2000). For the peers see G. E. C[okayne], *Complete peerage of England, Scotland, Ireland, Great Britain and the United Kingdom* (8 vols., London, 1887-98; revised edn., 14 vols., 1910-59) and J. Lodge, *The peerage of Ireland; or a genealogical history of the present nobility of that kingdom. . .* (4 vols., Dublin, 1754). Also see Peter Townend, ed., *Burke's Peerage, Baronetage and Knightage* (2 vols., London, 1970) and J. O'Hart, *Irish and Anglo-Irish gentry when Cromwell came to Ireland* (Dublin, 1884; later edn 1892). For clergymen see Henry Cotton, *Fastic ecclesiae Hibernicae: the succession of the prelates and members of the ecclesiastical bodies in Ireland* (6 vols., Dublin, 1845-78). For the civic officials and local merchants in Dublin see J. T. Gilbert, ed., *Calendar of the ancient records of Dublin. . .* (17 vols., Dublin, 1889-1916) and Colm Lennon, *The Lords of Dublin in the Age of Reformation* (Dublin, 1989); for Belfast merchants see Jean Agnew, *Belfast Merchant Families in the Seventeenth Century* (Dublin, 1996) and other local histories (listed in the select bibliography). The Exchequer Port Books in the PRO also provide a wealth of information on individual merchants. For Members of Parliament see Bríd McGrath, 'The membership of the Irish House of Commons 1613-1615' (TCD, M. Litt. Thesis, 1986) and 'A biographical dictionary of the Irish House of Commons 1640-1641' (TCD, Ph.D. Thesis, 1998). For Catholic lawyers see Donal Cregan, 'Irish Catholic admissions to the English Inns of Court, 1558-1625' in *Irish Jurist* (summer, 1970), pp. 95-114 and 'Irish Recusant lawyers in politics in the reign of James I' in *Irish Jurist* (winter, 1970), pp. 306-320. Many of the local histories listed in the bibliography also contain a mine of information on individual families, as do extant Church records, see James G. Ryan, *Irish Church Records. Their history, availability and use in family and local history research* (Dublin, 1992). For the London merchants and alderman involved in the Irish staple see 'A supplement to the London inhabitants list of 1695 compiled by staff at Guildhall Library' in *Guildhall Studies in London History*, 11:2 (1976), pp. 77-104, 136-57 and A. E. Beavan, *The Aldermen of the city of London* (2 vols., London, 1913).

[34] See ID 3979.

Boyle, bishop of Dublin and later archbishop of Armagh, styled himself simply as 'bishop of Dublin'.[35] In the database his surname has been recorded in the 'name' field and his bishopric in the 'office' field.

CREDITOR/DEBTOR STANDARD (textual field)

The spelling of names (both Christian and surnames) varies enormously between transactions and the standardised version has been entered into this field. This is exacerbated by the fact that a large proportion of names listed in the British Library volumes have been translated into Latin. In order to interrogate them effectively names have been standardised, where possible, according to the versions given in Edward MacLysaght, ed., *The surnames of Ireland* (6th edition, Dublin 1985). Thus O'Birne and Birne have been standardised as 'Byrne'; 'Carthie', 'MacCartie', 'Carty', and 'McKartie' have been standardised as 'MacCarthy'; 'Pluncket', 'Plunckett' or 'Plunket' have been standardised as 'Plunkett'; and 'O'Neale', 'O'Neyle', 'O'Neile', 'Neale' and 'Neel' have been standardised as 'O'Neill'; and so on. If in doubt about the way a name has been standardised consult the 'name' field and/or the original entry. For an alphabetical listing of the names of creditors and debtors see Chapters 3 and 4.

CREDITOR/DEBTOR COUNTY (textual field)

Nearly every transaction recorded the address of each creditor(s) or debtor(s). The name of the county, which has been modernised, is given first followed by the name of the townland, town or city that has not been standardised.[36] Where it was given, the definite article (from the Irish) has been retained (for example, the Navan or the Cavan).[37] When the townland or county was not stated but could be identified from another

---

[35] See ID 3661, 4019, 4035.

[36] Laois has been left as Queen's County and Offaly as King's County. Eastmeath has been entered as Meath. Those interested in identifying individual townlands should begin by consulting *General Alphabetical Index to the Townlands and Towns, parishes, and baronies of Ireland* (Dublin, 1861; reprinted Baltimore Maryland, 1984), S. Pender, *A census of Ireland circa 1659* (Irish Manuscripts Commission, 1939), Y. M. Goblet, ed., *Index of Parishes and Townlands of Ireland from seventeenth century maps* (Irish Manuscripts Commission, 1932), and *An index to Griffith's Valuation* which is now available on CD ROM (Baltimore, 1998). Further invaluable information can be gleaned from the 'Civil Survey' (1654-6) and the Books of Survey and Distribution. The Irish Manuscripts Commission has published many of these volumes. Hearth Money Rolls, where they survive, are also worthy of consultation. A number of these have been printed. See for example, S. T. Carleton, *Heads and Hearths. The Hearth Money Rolls and Poll Tax Returns for County Antrim 1660-69* (Belfast, 1991), 'Hearth money roll for Dublin' in *Kildare Archaeological Journal* 10:9 (1930-33). For a complete listing see Richard Hayes, ed., *Sources for the History of Irish Civilization. Articles in Irish Periodicals* (Boston, 1977), vol. 7, p. 234. Many of the local histories listed in the bibliography also contain a wealth of information on individual townlands and regions.

[37] The spelling of various townlands provides an insight into who were Irish speakers. See J. H. Andrews, '"More suitable to the English tongue": the cartography of Celtic place-names' in *Ulster Local Studies*, 14:2 (1992), pp. 7-21.

entry it has been included followed by a question mark. For example, in a significant number of instances, especially in the case of the clergy and peers, no address was listed. To minimise the number of 'NS' (not stated) entries appearing in the database, these addresses have been included wherever possible but have also been indicated with a question mark (?).[38]

Though this data was generally consistent between entries, the address occasionally varied. For example Chidley Coote gave his address in 1653 as 'Lanham, Essex, England' while the following year he was resident at 'Killester, Dublin'.[39] Occasionally it proved difficult to read a name, especially of townlands, and this is indicated with a question mark (?).

CREDITOR/DEBTOR OCCUPATION/STATUS (textual field)

Nearly every record listed the occupation or status of each creditor/debtor and this is recorded in this field. To aid interrogation these have been crudely sub-classified under the following: peers, gentry, professionals, merchants, tradesmen, soldiers, farmers and other. However there are inevitable problems of overlap between these groups.[40] For instance, where do individuals who described themselves in the original manuscript as 'doctors of divinity' or 'doctors of theology' belong? For example, Alexander Colvill, described himself as a 'doctor of theology' and was ordained as a deacon in 1622, the vicar of Carmony in 1626 and the prebend at Carmony and Carncastle in 1628.[41] Others held similar qualifications but do not appear to have enjoyed ecclesiastical office and could be more accurately styled as members of the gentry. The same applied to men who described themselves as 'doctors of law' and 'doctors of physic'. Presumably they worked as lawyers or doctors. If they did not they could also be more accurately styled as members of the gentry. In the database these individuals have always been grouped according to their own description of their status or occupation. Thus in the specific cases of doctors of divinity, of theology, of law and of physic they have been classified under 'professional' and if they held an office this has been entered in the 'office' field.

Since all of the female debtors and creditors have been separately grouped in the 'office' field, they have been classified here according to the status or occupation of their husband or father. Similarly those individuals who described themselves as 'son', as 'son and heir', or as 'brother' have been classified according to the occupation or status of their father or elder brother. Where the occupation of a father, husband or brother remains unknown they have been sub-classified as 'other', together with individuals who listed their occupation/status as 'citizen' and 'executor'.

[38] Since the same person often appears more than once, his/her address could often be determined with reference to another entry.

[39] See ID 2976, 3003, and 3005.

[40] Bríd McGrath and Raymond Gillespie provided invaluable advice about how best to classify these groups and the many pitfalls involved.

[41] Cotton, *Fasti*, III, 261.

Within these sub-classifications the occupation or status of the individual is given as it was in the original manuscript but the spelling has been modernised and Latin words have been translated. However in the particular cases of 'clerico', 'clericu', 'clericum' it was not always clear whether individual concerned was a 'clerk' or a 'cleric' and some of these entries may prove incorrect.

The following occupations, together with the sub-classifications appear:

PEERS:
Baron
Countess
Earl
Viscount

GENTRY:
Baronet
Esquire
Gent[leman]
Knight
Dame

PROF[ESSIONAL]:
Doctor of Divinity
Doctor of Law
Doctor of Physic
Doctor of Theology
Surgeon
Archdeacon
Bishop
Deacon
Dean
Parson

MERCHANT:

TRADE:
Apothecary
Baker
Barber-surgeon
Brewer
Butcher
Carpenter
Carrier
Chandler

Chapman
Clothier
Coach-maker
Draper
Factor
Felt-maker
Fish-monger
Fisherman
Gardener
Goldsmith
Grocer
Haberdasher
Hatband-maker
Hogler/hegler?
Hosier
Innkeeper
Ironmonger
Jeweller
Leather-dresser
Maltster
Mariner
Mercer
Miller
Saddler
Scrivenor
Shoemaker
Skinner
Smith
Soap-boiler
Tailor
Tallow chandler
Tanner
Upholsterer

SOLDIER:
Captain

Colonel
Commissary
Ensign
Lieutenant
Lieutenant-Colonel
Major
Provost Marshall

FARMER:
Cottier
Farmer
Freeholder
Husbandman

OTHER:
Citizen
Executor
*Brother
*Daughter
(Son and heir
*Widow
*Wife

* When the occupation or status of the husband or father of these individuals can be determined, they are classified under these rather than 'other'.

CREDITOR/DEBTOR OFFICE HELD (textual field)

A significant number of debtors and creditors held an administrative, legal or ecclesiastical office that was recorded in the original manuscript often alongside their occupation or status. To aid interrogation these offices have been crudely sub-classified under the following: administrative, legal, civic and clerical. In a significant number of cases individuals do not indicate the office they held and therefore this listing remains incomplete. For example, not all of the Dublin aldermen discussed Colm Lennon, *The Lords of Dublin in the Age of Reformation* (Dublin, 1989) who used the Dublin staple described themselves as 'alderman'.[42] For the sake of convenience, women, who appear in the original manuscripts in a variety of guises, have also been grouped in this field.

ADMIN[ISTRATIVE OFFICE]:
Baron of the Exchequer
Chancellor of the Exchequer
Comptroller
Lord Deputy
Lord Justice
Lord Lieutenant
Lord President
Lord Treasurer
Privy Councillor
Secretary of State
Ulster knight-at-arms

LEGAL [OFFICE]:
Attorney-General
Chief Justice
Court Magistrate
Lord Chancellor
Master of the Rolls
Sergeant-at-arms
Sergeant-at-law
Solicitor General

[42] For example Sir Thomas FitzWilliam was an alderman but listed his occupation/status as a 'knight' see ID 517, 559, 612, 666, 1046, 1047, 1327, 1351, 1382, 1391, 1411, 1423, 1450, 1455, 1470, 1476, 1574 and Colm Lennon, *The Lords of Dublin in the Age of Reformation* (Dublin, 1989), pp. 250-1 or Patrick Fox who listed his occupation as 'gentleman' ID 32, 42, 129, 173, 273, 287, 321, 322, 398, 490, 521 and Lennon, *Lords*, p. 252.

CIVIC [OFFICE]:
Alderman (Dublin unless
otherwise stated)
Bailiff
Burgess
Clerk
Mayor
Recorder
Waterbailiff

CLERICAL [OFFICE]:
Archbishop
Archdeacon

Bishop
Deacon
Dean

WOMAN:
Countess
Dame
Gentlewoman
Lady
Sister
Widow
Wife

ELECTION OF MAYOR AND CONSTABLES

Details of the annual election of the mayor and constables of the Dublin staple have been included in the database. Each election, which occurred on St. Paul's Day (25 January), has been assigned an identity number and the names of the officials elected have been entered in the 'text' field. Occasionally an election took place during the course of the year usually because an official was absent, died or refused to take the oath of supremacy.[43] Details on the appointment of the clerk of the staple have also been entered.[44]

Details of the elections of mayors and constables in the provincial staple towns do not appear to have survived. However the names of the mayors and constables of the staple at a given time are recorded in the Chancery volumes and have been extracted to compile an incomplete listing see Appendix I.

ILLEGIBLE, MISSING, NOT STATED AND QUESTION MARKS:

Data has been entered into the vast majority of fields. However when a word in the original could not be determined 'illegible' was entered into the appropriate field entry in the database. If a word could not be read because the original was damaged or destroyed 'missing' was entered into the appropriate field entry in the database. Occasionally a debtor or creditor failed to state their address or occupation and 'N.S.' (not stated) was entered into the appropriate field entry in the database. Question marks have been used sparingly. When these appear they either indicate that data, not given in the original (such as the address or surname of a peer or bishop), has been entered or that it was difficult to read the original.

---

[43] See for examples ID 264, 379, 909, 913, 2638, and 2721.

[44] See for example ID 658 for the appointment of Thady Duffe and ID 1257 for the election of his son, Sir Thady Duffe.

MATERIAL IN THE ORIGINAL STAPLE VOLUMES WHICH HAS NOT BEEN RECORDED IN THE DATABASE:

Regulation of trade:

The Dublin volumes include permits allowing merchants to load vessels with staple goods. Since these were interspersed amongst the staple records, and often accompanied a bond, they have been given an identity number and recorded in the 'text' box of the database. For example a series of permits dating from early 1602 (ID 233) allowed a number of Dublin aldermen and merchants to load salt hides aboard a variety of Scottish, English, Welsh, Irish, French and Flemish vessels.[45] Other material that related to the regulation of staple goods but was not associated with a particular staple bond and was recorded at the back of the Dublin volumes has been transcribed in full in Appendix IV.

Brethren of the Dublin Staple:

Lengthy lists of the brethren of the Dublin staple 1616-37 and 1664-1674 were recorded in Dc2 and Dc3 and have been transcribed in full in Appendix II.

Contemporary indexes:

The British Library volumes all contain, either at the front or back of the volume, an index of the name of the first debtor and creditor. The publication of the database renders the reproduction of these contemporary indexes unnecessary.

[45] For examples see ID 281, 290, 306, 310, 312, 330.

CHAPTER 3:

ALPHABETICAL LISTING OF CREDITORS

In all over 10,000 people—4309 creditors and 5879 debtors—recorded transactions on the Irish staple towns between 1596 and 1687. Predictably the same individual appeared more than once and so the actual number of people using the staple was probably between 5000 and 6000. Here is an alphabetical listing of the standardised names of all of the creditors that appeared in the staple records, together with their address and, where given, their occupation/status (for a full discussion see Chapter 2).[1] The date on which the transaction was recorded, the amount of the bond, the reference to the original manuscript, and the identification number (that relates to the Staple CD ROM), are also listed here.[2]

[1] Constraints of space precluded the inclusion of any details on office held. For full details see Query 'A: Creditors - master list' on the Staple CD ROM and Jane Ohlmeyer, ed., *Using the Staple Database*, Section I.

[2] For details on the staple town or city, on the fate of the transaction, and for any accompanying text see the Staple CD ROM or the original manuscripts.

Standard	County	Occupation	Date	Amount	MS No	Ident No
Acheson, Henry	Armagh, Dromlagh	gentry: esquire	18-Mar-25	553	Dc2/63r	1275
Acheson, Henry	Armagh, Dromlagh	gentry: esquire	18-Mar-25	1100	Dc2/62r	1270
Acheson, Henry	Armagh, Dromlagh	gentry: esquire	18-Mar-25	680	Dc2/62v	1271
Acheson, Henry	Armagh, Dromlagh	gentry: esquire	18-Mar-25	660	Dc2/62v	1272
Acheson, Henry	Armagh, Dromlagh	gentry: esquire	18-Mar-25	555	Dc2/62v	1273
Acheson, Henry	Armagh, Dromlagh	gentry: esquire	18-Mar-25	554	Dc2/62v	1274
Adams, Anthony	Dublin, the city	gentry: gent	26-Feb-99	60	Dc1/15v	108
Adams, Richard	England, Lancaster, Leverpoole	gentry: gent	21-Nov-32	300	Dc2/186v	1850
Adderly, Thomas	Cork, Donnderrowe	gentry: gent	19-Feb-14	240	Dc1/127r	787
Adderly, Thomas	Cork, Ballynyboy	gentry: esquire	03-May-39	240	B.L. 19, 843 f. 31	2780
Adderly, Thomas	Cork, Ballynyboy	gentry: gent, son/heir of Thom.	01-Apr-39	800	B.L. 19, 843 f. 30	2778
Adderly, Thomas	Cork, Ballynyboy	gentry: esquire	01-Apr-39	800	B.L. 19, 843 f. 30	2778
Adderly, Thomas	Cork, Downedorrowe	gentry: esquire	27-Apr-30	800	B.L. 19, 843 f. 29a	2777
Adderly, Thomas	Cork, Downedorrowe	gentry: esquire	16-Aug-20	500	B.L. 19, 843 f. 29	2776
Adderly, Thomas	Cork, Downderry	gentry: esquire	23-May-14	340	Dc1/129v	805
Adderly, Thomas	Cork, Donderry	gentry: gent	20-May-12	200	Dc1/113v	705
Adrians, Daniel	Dublin	trade: brewer	03-Jul-30	120	Dc2/153v	1714
Adrians, Daniel	Dublin, the city	gentry: gent	20-Jun-29	600	Dc2/133r	1622
Aldersey, Ann	England, Chester	other: widow	13-Feb-29	212	Dc2/125r	1586
Aldersey, Randal	Dublin, the city	gentry: esquire	07-Jul-37	2000	Dc2/267r	2197
Aldersey, Randal	Meath, the Maudlins	gentry: esquire	26-Aug-31	100	Dc2/167v	1775
Aldersey, Randal	Meath, St. Mary Magdalin	gentry: esquire	11-Feb-29	40	Dc2/124v	1585
Aldersey, Randal	Meath, Rosmyne	gentry: gent	08-Feb-23	280	Dc2/44v	1138
Aldersey, Randal	Meath, St. Mary Magdalene	gentry: esquire	09-Aug-34	4000	Dc2/217r	1973
Aldersey, Randal	Dublin	gentry: esquire	22-Nov-32	140	Dc2/187r	1852
Aldersey, Randal	Dublin, the city	gentry: esquire	16-May-33	200	Dc2/193v	1878
Aldersey, Randal	Meath, St. Mary Magdalene	gentry: esquire	21-Sep-33	140	Dc2/199v	1901
Aldersey, Randal	Dublin	gentry: esquire	21-Jul-37	200	Dc2/269r	2208
Aldersey, Randal	Meath, St. Mary Magdalene	gentry: esquire	24-Jul-34	774	Dc2/215v	1967
Aldersey, Randal	Dublin, the city	gentry: esquire	27-Jun-35	2000	Dc2/238r	2062
Aldersey, Randal	Meath, St Mary Magdalynn	gentry: esquire	10-Feb-35	200	Dc2/229r	2022
Alexander, Jeremy	Dublin, the city	gentry: esquire	21-Mar-35	2000	Dc2/231v	2031
Alexander, Jeremy	Dublin, the city	gentry: esquire	13-Dec-34	600	Dc2/226r	2009
Alexander, Jeremy	Dublin, the city	gentry: esquire	21-Feb-35	300	Dc2/230r	2025
Alexander, Jeremy	Dublin, the city	gentry: esquire	25-Nov-34	2000	Dc2/223v	1998
Alexander, Jeremy	Dublin	gentry: esquire	10-Dec-34	200	Dc2/225v	2007
Alexander, Jeremy	Dublin, the city	gentry: esquire	21-Nov-34	1000	Dc2/222v	1995
Alexander, Walter	England, London	gentry: esquire	25-Sep-22	400	Dc2/42v	1123
Allen, Alice	Louth, Dundalke	other: widow	19-Dec-65	600	Dc3/17	2261
Allen, Alice	Dublin, the city	other: widow	24-Dec-66	200	Dc3/50	2332
Allen, Edward	Kildare, Bishopscourte	gentry: gent	01-Mar-36	1000	Dc2/246v	2102
Allen, Edward	Dublin	merchant	25-Feb-98	300	Dc1/10r	71
Allen, John	Kildare, Bishopscourte	gentry: esquire	18-Nov-31	150	Dc2/171v	1788

Standard	County	Occupation	Date	Amount	MS No	Ident No
Allen, John	Kildare, Bushopscourte	gentry: esquire	26-Jan-32	200	Dc2/174r	1800
Allen, John	Kildare, Bishops Court	gentry: gent	24-Jan-18	200	Dc2/13r	932
Allen, John	Kildare, Bishops Court	gentry: gent	16-Dec-17	700	Dc2/13r	931
Allen, John	Kildare, Bishopscourte	gentry: esquire	16-Jun-32	30	Dc2/183r	1836
Allen, John	Dublin	gentry: gent	20-May-01	400	Dc1/32r	211
Allen, John	Dublin	gentry: gent	01-Oct-00	200	Dc1/26r	175
Allen, John	Kildare, Buyshoppscourt	merchant	27-Jun-27	1200	Dc2/95v	1446
Allen, John	Dublin	gentry: gent	10-Mar-98	800	Dc1/10v	77
Allen, John	Kildare, Buyshopscourte	gentry: gent	11-Jun-07	200	Dc1/78r	475
Allen, Joshua	Dublin, the city		23-Jul-67	400	Dc3/65	2369
Allen, Joshua	Dublin, the city		04-Mar-70	400	Dc3/117	2473
Allen, Joshua	Dublin, the city		04-Mar-70	400	B.L. 15, 636 f. 56a	3719
Allen, Joshua	Dublin, the city		23-Jul-67	400	B.L. 15, 635 f. 205	3619
Allen, Lawrence	Dublin?	merchant: son of Thomas Allen	09-Jul-24	300	Dc2/57r	1232
Allen, Lawrence	Dublin	merchant	15-Nov-34	300	Dc2/221v	1991
Allen, Lawrence	Dublin, the city	merchant: son of Thomas, merchant	11-Feb-25	300	Dc2/61v	1264
Allen, Lawrence	Dublin, the city	merchant: son of Thomas, merchant	29-Jan-25	300	Dc2/60v	1258
Allen, Mathew	Dublin, the city	gentry: esquire	10-Feb-36	200	Dc2/244r	2092
Allen, Patrick	Dublin, the city	gentry: gent	25-Jun-58	900	B.L. 15, 635 f. 56a	3364
Allen, Thomas	Dublin	merchant	09-Jun-20	200	Dc2/31r	1034
Allen, Thomas	Dublin, the city	merchant	24-May-25	400	Dc2/64r	1283
Allen, Thomas	Dublin, the city	merchant	29-Apr-24	300	Dc2/54v	1212
Allen, Thomas	Dublin, the city	merchant	04-Apr-26	400	Dc2/76v	1358
Allen, Thomas	Dublin, the city	merchant	02-Apr-29	1000	Dc2/127r	1595
Allen, Thomas	Dublin	merchant	04-Feb-01	200	Dc1/28v	191
Allen, Thomas	Dublin, the city	merchant	27-Apr-24	200	Dc2/54v	1210
Allen, Thomas	Dublin, the city	merchant	30-Aug-25	200	Dc2/69r	1313
Allen, Thomas	Dublin	merchant	08-Jul-09	200	Dc1/90r	563
Allen, Thomas	Dublin	merchant	26-Jun-28	200	Dc2/111v	1520
Allen, Thomas	Dublin	merchant	04-May-17	160	Dc2/8r	905
Allen, Thomas	Dublin, the city	merchant	17-Jun-29	800	Dc2/132v	1620
Allen, Thomas	Dublin	merchant	12-Jul-06	106	Dc1/70r	424
Allen, Thomas	Dublin, the city	merchant	07-Jun-30	300	Dc2/149r	1694
Allen, Thomas	Dublin	merchant	27-Jun-27	1200	Dc2/95v	1446
Allen, Thomas	Dublin, the city	merchant	10-Feb-29	240	Dc2/124r	1580
Allen, Thomas	Dublin, the city	merchant	29-Nov-24	200	Dc2/59r	1246
Allen, Thomas	Dublin	merchant	27-Nov-27	204	Dc2/101r	1468
Allen, Thomas	Dublin	merchant	05-Jul-23	120	Dc2/48v	1169
Allen, Thomas	Kildare, Kilhele	gentry: gent	07-Dec-05	500	Dc1/63v	385
Allen, Thomas	Dublin	merchant	15-Mar-27	700	Dc2/89v	1422
Allen, Thomas	Dublin	merchant	08-Jul-23	140	Dc2/49r	1172
Allen, Thomas	Dublin, the city	merchant	05-Feb-33	200	Dc2/191r	1867

Standard	County	Occupation	Date	Amount	MS No	Ident No
Allen, Thomas	Dublin, the city	merchant	13-Aug-23	150	Dc2/50v	1178
Allen, Thomas	Dublin	merchant	12-Jul-06	200	Dc1/70r	423
Allen, Thomas	Dublin, the city	merchant	29-Nov-21	300	Dc2/36v	1081
Allen, Thomas	Dublin	merchant	10-Jun-03	400	Dc1/47r	300
Allen, Thomas	Dublin, the city	merchant	01-Feb-33	600	Dc2/190v	1866
Allen, Thomas	Dublin, the city	merchant	08-Oct-29	200	Dc2/136v	1639
Allen, Thomas	Dublin, the city	merchant	01-Jul-29	120	Dc2/135r	1630
Allen, Thomas	Dublin	merchant	12-Feb-03	600	Dc1/44v	284
Allen, Thomas	Dublin, the city	merchant	17-Oct-22	200	Dc2/42v	1124
Anderson, John	England, Chester, the city	merchant	13-Nov-78	5000	B.L. 15, 637 f. 9	3863
Anderson, William	Westmeath, Kennagad	gentry: gent	30-Jan-28	2000	Dc2/103r	1480
Anderson, William	Dublin	gentry: knight	09-Jan-33	1000	Dc2/190r	1864
Anderson, William	Westmeath, Kenagad	gentry: gent	30-Jan-28	2000	Dc2/103r	1479
Anderson, William	Dublin	gentry: knight	19-Dec-29	300	Dc2/140v	1657
Anderson, William	Dublin, the city	gentry: gent	23-Dec-23	400	Dc2/52r	1194
Andrew, Charles	Dublin, the city	merchant	29-Jan-55	1200	B.L. 19, 843 f. 153	3020
Andrew, Henry	Dublin, the city	gentry: esquire	23-Dec-23	600	Dc2/52r	1193
Andrew, Thomas	Dublin, the city	trade: shoemaker	02-Oct-58	164	B.L. 15, 635 f. 36a	3327
Annesley, Arthur	Dublin, the city	gentry: esquire	08-Feb-56	1080	B.L. 19, 843 f. 173a	3059
Annesley, Arthur	Armagh?	gentry: esquire, son/heir of Francis	05-Feb-35	1400	Dc2/229r	2021
Annesley, Arthur	Dublin	gentry: esquire	05-Feb-58	100	B.L. 15, 635 f. 28a	3312
Annesley, Francis	Armagh?	peer: baron Mountnorris	11-May-30	400	Dc2/147r	1686
Annesley, Francis	Armagh?	peer: baron Mountnorris	10-Nov-31	800	Dc2/169v	1782
Annesley, Francis	Dublin	gentry: gent	17-Dec-11	500	Dc1/110v	685
Annesley, Francis		gentry: knight and baronet	10-Nov-23	600	Dc2/51r	1185
Annesley, Francis	Armagh?	peer: baron Mountnorris	12-Dec-32	500	Dc2/188v	1857
Annesley, Francis	Armagh?	peer: baron Mountnorris	13-May-33	2000	Dc2/193r	1876
Annesley, Francis	Dublin	merchant	15-Dec-14	1000	Dc1/134r	833
Annesley, Francis	Armagh?	peer: baron Mountnorris	09-Aug-33	1000	Dc2/198v	1898
Annesley, Francis	Armagh?	peer: baron Mountnorris	09-Feb-30	1200	Dc2/159v	1741
Annesley, Francis	Armagh?	peer: baron Mountnorris	27-Jun-34	3000	Dc2/213r	1957
Annesley, Francis	Armagh?	peer: baron Mountnorris	07-Feb-31	600	Dc2/159v	1740
Annesley, Francis	Armagh?	peer: baron Mountnorris	05-Feb-31	200	Dc2/159r	1739
Annesley, Francis	Armagh?	peer: baron Mountnorris	09-Jun-30	1000	Dc2/149r	1695
Annesley, Francis	Armagh?	peer: baron Mountnorris	25-Jun-30	250	Dc2/153v	1713
Annesley, Francis	Armagh?	peer: baron Mountnorris	14-Jun-30	120	Dc2/150v	1701
Annesley, Francis	Dublin	gentry: esquire	15-Dec-14	200	Dc1/134r	832
Annesley, Francis	Armagh?	peer: baron Mountnorris	05-Feb-35	1400	Dc2/229r	2021
Annesley, Francis	Armagh?	peer: baron Mountnorris	13-Jun-30	300	Dc2/150v	1700
Aphugh, Richard	Louth, Drogheda	gentry: esquire	26-Mar-39	400	B.L. 19, 843 f. 25a	2769
Archbold, Edmund	Dublin, Portmarnoke	gentry: gent	16-Jun-08	200	Dc1/83v	520
Archbold, Edmund	Dublin, Portemarnoke	gentry: gent	08-Feb-09	90	Dc1/87r	544
Archbold, James	Wicklow, Rathnecluige	gentry: gent	21-Nov-21	500	Dc2/36v	1079

Standard	County	Occupation	Date	Amount	MS No	Ident No
Archbold, James	Wicklow, Rahinecloige	gentry: gent	13-May-29	400	Dc2/128v	1603
Archbold, James	Wicklow, Rathnicluige	gentry: gent	21-Jun-31	1500	Dc2/165r	1764
Archbold, James	Wicklow, Rathneclugg	gentry: gent	09-Dec-19	200	Dc2/27v	1013
Archbold, James	Wicklow, Rathnechlogdin	gentry: gent	29-Nov-20	300	Dc2/33v	1055
Archbold, James	Wicklow, Rathnecluig	gentry: gent	14-Feb-23	240	Dc2/45r	1141
Archbold, James	Wicklow, Rathnecluigg	gentry: gent	15-Jun-24	240	Dc2/56r	1223
Archbold, John	Wicklow, Raniecluig	gentry: gent	15-Jul-25	400	Dc2/68v	1310
Archbold, Pierce	Dublin, Knockline	gentry: gent	28-Nov-34	800	Dc2/223v	1999
Archbold, Pierce	Dublin, Knocklinge	gentry: gent	27-Jan-30	300	Dc2/141r	1660
Archbold, Pierce	Dublin, Knocklinge	gentry: gent	18-Apr-31	500	Dc2/161v	1750
Archbold, Richard	Kildare?, Sellagh	gentry: gent	13-Nov-24	400	Dc2/58v	1241
Archbold, Richard	Kildare, Sillagh	gentry: gent	11-Nov-25	200	Dc2/69v	1318
Archbold, Richard	Kildare, Tymoline	gentry: gent	20-Mar-26	300	Dc2/75v	1352
Archbold, Walter	Wicklow, Rahinecluigge	gentry: gent	14-Feb-29	200	Dc2/125r	1587
Archbold, Walter	Kildare, the Nace	merchant	02-Jul-06	300	Dc1/69v	422
Archbold, Walter	Kildare, the Nace	merchant	28-Apr-02	200	Dc1/37v	244
Archbold, Walter	Kildare, Tymolyn	gentry: gent	31-Jan-25	100	Dc2/61r	1259
Archbold, Walter	Kildare, the Nace	merchant	26-Nov-05	44	Dc1/62v	380
Archbold, Walter	Kildare, the Nace	merchant	17-Jun-05	70	Dc1/60r	365
Archbold, Walter	Kildare, the Naace	gentry: gent	07-May-14	100	Dc1/129r	801
Archbold, Walter	Kildare, the Nace	gentry: esquire	21-Jun-24	300	Dc2/56v	1228
Archbold, Walter	Kildare, the Nace	merchant	20-May-13	160	Dc1/120v	750
Archbold, Walter	Kildare, the Nace	merchant	17-Dec-13	200	Dc1/125v	779
Archbold, Walter	Kildare, the Nace	merchant	17-Jun-05	50	Dc1/60r	364
Archbold, Wiliam	Kildare, Grangemillon	gentry: gent	15-Mar-19	240	Dc2/21v	978
Archbold, William	Kildare, Grandgmillon	gentry: gent	31-Dec-19	200	Dc2/28r	1016
Archbold, William	Kildare, Crookstowne	gentry: esquire	08-Feb-28	800	Dc2/103v	1483
Archbold, William	Kildare, Tinmoling	gentry: esquire	20-Nov-29	400	Dc1/138v	1646
Archbold, William	Kildare, Grangemillon	gentry: gent	12-Jun-19	1000	Dc2/23v	992
Archbold, William	Kildare, Tymmolinge	gentry: esquire	04-May-30	200	Dc2/145r	1679
Archbold, William	Kildare, Grandgmollen	gentry: gent	10-Nov-18	200	Dc2/17r	953
Archbold, William	Kildare, Tymolin	gentry: gent	04-Nov-20	2000	Dc2/32v	1047
Archbold, William	Kildare, Crockstowne	gentry: esquire	10-Feb-29	400	Dc2/124v	1583
Archbold, William	Meath, Crookestowne	gentry: esquire	09-May-28	200	Dc2/107r	1500
Archbold, William	Kildare, Grandgmillon	gentry: gent	03-Feb-19	160	Dc2/20r	971
Archbold, William	Kildare, Tymmoling	gentry: esquire	09-Nov-30	220	Dc2/155v	1722
Archbold, William	Kildare, Tymmolinge	gentry: esquire	12-Feb-30	110	Dc2/141v	1664
Archbold, William	Kildare, the Naas	gentry: gent	07-Apr-15	300	Dc1/136r	845
Archbold, William	Kildare, Cruckston	gentry: gent	18-Nov-24	400	Dc2/59r	1245
Archbold, William	Kildare, Cruckston	gentry: gent	13-Nov-24	200	Dc2/58v	1243
Archbold, William	Kildare, Cruckston	gentry: gent	01-Feb-25	200	Dc2/61r	1260
Archbold, William	Kildare, Cruckston	gentry: gent	13-Nov-24	100	Dc2/58v	1242
Archbold, William	Kildare, Cruckston	gentry: gent	21-May-25	200	Dc2/64r	1282
Archbold, William	Kildare, Crookston	gentry: gent	17-Jun-23	100	Dc2/48r	1165
Archbold, William	Kildare, Tymolin	gentry: esquire	10-Jul-39	5000	B.L. 19, 843 f. 17a	2753

Standard	County	Occupation	Date	Amount	MS No	Ident No
Archbold, William	Kildare, the Nace	gentry: gent	17-Dec-22	200	Dc2/44r	1134
Archbold, William	Kildare, Crookstowne	gentry: esquire	07-Dec-27	1000	Dc2/101v	1473
Archbold, William	Kildare, Tymoluige	gentry: gent	15-Jun-24	200	Dc2/56r	1224
Archbold, William	Kildare, Cruckston	gentry: gent	18-Nov-24	400	Dc2/58v	1244
Archbold, William	Kildare, Tymolinge	gentry: esquire	23-Nov-35	200	Dc2/240r	2072
Archbold, William	Kildare, Timoline	gentry: esquire	16-Nov-37	400	Dc2/271r	2217
Archbold, William	Kildare, Timolinge	gentry: esquire	16-Mar-35	200	Dc2/231r	2029
Archbold, William	Kildare, Tymmolinge	gentry: esquire	17-Nov-31	200	Dc2/170r	1785
Archbold, William	Kildare, Tymmolinge	gentry: esquire	06-Feb-32	200	Dc2/175r	1804
Archbold, William	Kildare, Tymmolinge	gentry: esquire	17-Nov-31	1000	Dc2/170v	1786
Archbold, William	Kildare, Cruckston	gentry: gent	31-Jan-22	400	Dc2/38v	1094
Archbold, William	Kildare, Grandgmillan	gentry: gent	28-Jun-17	160	Dc2/8r	906
Archbold, William	Kildare, Grandge Millon	gentry: gent	19-May-17	600	Dc2/6v	900
Archbold, William	Kildare, Tymolin	gentry: gent	25-Jun-21	200	Dc2/36r	1076
Archbold, William	Kildare, Crookstowne	gentry: gent	21-Nov-27	200	Dc2/100r	1464
Archbold, William	Kildare, Tymmolinge	gentry: esquire	12-Jun-32	1400	Dc2/182v	1834
Archbold, William	Kildare, the Naas	gentry: gent	26-Apr-21	80	Dc2/35r	1067
Archbold, William	Kildare, Cruckston	gentry: gent	31-Jan-22	270	Dc2/38v	1093
Archdale, Edward	Fermanagh, Archdall	gentry: esquire	13-May-28	200	Dc2/107v	1503
Archdeacon, John	Cork, Ballybane	gentry: gent	15-Jan-70	500	B.L. 15, 636 f 53	3715
Archdeacon, John	Cork, Ballybane	gentry: gent	15-Jan-70	500	B.L. 15, 636 f. 73a	3749
Archdeacon, William	Cork, Kilmony	gentry: gent	26-Nov-72	800	B.L. 19, 844 f. 9	3128
Archdeacon, William	Cork, Kilvony	gentry: gent	29-Oct-72	320	B.L. 19, 844 f. 8	3127
Archer, Hester	England, London	other: widow	14-Jul-66	200	Dc3/33	2296
Archer, Hester	England, London	other: widow	14-Jul-66	100	Dc3/33	2295
Archer, Hester	England, London	other: widow	14-Jul-66	200	Dc3/33	2294
Archer, Michael	Kilkenny, the city	merchant	16-Nov-18	105	Dc2/17r	955
Ardagh, Patrick	Dublin	trade: haberdasher	15-Jun-97	80	Dc1/4v	31
Ardagh, Robert	Dublin, the city	gentry: gent	22-Mar-56	120	B.L. 19, 843 f. 185	3077
Arnoldi, Edward	Dublin, the city	gentry: esquire	26-Mar-68	200	B.L. 15, 635 f. 221a	3648
Arnoldi, Edward	Dublin, the city	gentry: gent	10-Dec-68	400	Dc3/86	2417
Arnoldi, Edward	Dublin, the city	gentry: esquire	10-Dec-68	400	B.L. 15, 635 f. 229	3663
Arthur, Daniel	England, London	merchant	13-Jan-71	600	Dc3/134r	2512
Arthur, Daniel	England, London	merchant	29-May-68	700	Dc3/77	2398
Arthur, Daniel	England, London	merchant	18-Dec-67	340	Dc3/71	2384
Arthur, Daniel	England, London, the city	merchant	29-May-68	700	B.L. 15, 635 f. 218a	3642
Arthur, Daniel	England, London	merchant	18-Dec-67	340	B.L. 15, 635 f. 211a	3628
Arthur, Dymphna	Dublin, the city	other: widow	11-Mar-69	1600	Dc3/94	2430
Arthur, Dymphna	Dublin, the city	gentry: widow	10-Mar-69	1600	B.L. 15, 636 f. 40	3694
Arthur, Edward	Dublin		12-Dec-29	600	Dc2/140r	1655
Arthur, Edward	Dublin, the city		16-Feb-30	600	Dc2/142v	1668
Arthur, Edward	Dublin, the city		10-Dec-35	200	Dc2/242r	2081
Arthur, Edward	Dublin	merchant	13-May-15	1500	Dc1/137v	852
Arthur, Edward	Dublin	merchant	01-Jul-15	1000	Dc1/139v	865
Arthur, Edward	Dublin, the city	merchant	26-Nov-16	1000	Dc2/2v	881

Standard	County	Occupation	Date	Amount	MS No	Ident No
Arthur, Edward	Dublin		02-Jul-26	140	Dc2/80r	1381
Arthur, Edward	Dublin, the city	merchant	12-Nov-24	300	Dc2/58r	1240
Arthur, Edward	Dublin		28-Jun-26	300	Dc2/80r	1380
Arthur, George	Dublin	merchant	01-Jul-15	1000	Dc1/139v	865
Arthur, George	Dublin, the city	merchant	26-Nov-16	1000	Dc2/2v	881
Arthur, John	Dublin		06-Jul-03	120	Dc1/47v	303
Arthur, John	Dublin		23-Jul-03	500	Dc1/47av	307
Arthur, John	Dublin		09-Jul-07	500	Dc1/79v	485
Arthur, Robert	Dublin	merchant	28-Jul-26	100	Dc2/81v	1388
Arthur, Robert	Dublin, the city		07-Sep-34	112	Dc2/220r	1985
Arthur, Robert	Dublin, the city		05-Sep-34	120	Dc2/219r	1980
Arthur, Robert	Dublin	merchant	27-Sep-23	40	Dc2/50v	1182
Arthur, Robert	Dublin, the county	gentry: gent	02-Mar-75	3000	Dc3/166r	2628
Arthur, Robert	Dublin	merchant	08-Dec-26	800	Dc2/85v	1405
Arthur, Robert	Dublin, the city		20-Dec-33	800	Dc2/205r	1924
Arthur, Robert	Dublin, the city		20-Dec-33	1000	Dc2/205r	1923
Arthur, Robert	Dublin, the city		15-Jul-37	800	Dc2/269r	2206
Arthur, Robert	Dublin, the city	merchant	20-Jun-25	200	Dc2/66v	1297
Arthur, Robert	Dublin	merchant	27-Jan-27	200	Dc2/87v	1415
Arthur, Robert	Dublin, the city		04-Dec-30	2564	Dc2/157v	1732
Arthur, Robert	Dublin, the city		07-Jul-32	1000	Dc2/184v	1842
Arthur, Robert	Dublin	merchant	30-Jun-27	800	Dc2/96r	1447
Arthur, Robert	Dublin, the city	merchant	27-Feb-23	50	Dc2/45v	1144
Arthur, Robert	Dublin	merchant	04-Jun-25	800	Dc2/65r	1289
Arthur, Robert	Dublin, the city		19-Dec-31	2000	Dc2/173v	1798
Arthur, Robert	Dublin, the city		15-Jul-37	3150	Dc2/268v	2205
Arthur, Robert	Dublin	gentry: gent	02-Mar-75	3000	B.L. 19, 844 f. 60a	3186
Arthur, Robert	Dublin, the city	gentry: gent	10-Mar-69	1600	B.L. 15, 636 f. 40	3694
Arthur, Robert	Dublin	merchant	23-Dec-24	200	Dc2/60r	1255
Arthur, Robert	Dublin, the city		20-Jul-35	440	Dc2/239r	2065
Arthur, Robert	Dublin, the city	merchant	28-Nov-25	240	Dc2/70v	1322
Arthur, Robert	Dublin	gentry: gent	23-Feb-26	200	Dc2/74v	1347
Arthur, Robert	Dublin, the city	merchant	11-Nov-25	162	Dc2/69v	1317
Arthur, Thomas	Limerick, the city	prof: doctor of phisick	03-Dec-29	120	Dc2/139r	1651
Arthur, Thomas	Dublin, the city	prof: doctor of phisick	03-Jul-37	80	Dc2/266v	2196
Arthur, Thomas	Dublin	merchant	12-Sep-25	48	Dc2/69r	1315
Arthur, Thomas	Dublin	merchant	26-Jul-26	200	Dc2/82r	1389
Arthur, Thomas	Limerick	prof: doctor of medicine	09-Mar-39	1200	B.L. 19, 843 f. 21	2760
Arthur, Thomas	Dublin, the city	merchant	21-Feb-35	600	Dc2/229v	2024
Arthur, Thomas	Dublin, the city	merchant	28-Jul-27	100	Dc2/97v	1454
Arthur, Thomas	Dublin, the city	merchant	12-Mar-31	500	Dc2/161r	1747
Arthur, William	Dublin, the city	merchant	15-Nov-31	100	Dc2/169v	1783
Arthur, William	Dublin	merchant	05-Dec-29	200	Dc2/139v	1652
Arthur, William	Dublin, the city	merchant	04-Nov-36	2000	Dc2/256v	2152
Arthur, William	Dublin	merchant	05-Mar-27	160	Dc2/88v	1418

Standard	County	Occupation	Date	Amount	MS No	Ident No
Arthur, William	Dublin, the city	merchant	14-Nov-27	160	Dc2/99v	1463
Arthur, William	Dublin	merchant	31-Jul-28	1600	Dc2/113v	1532
Ash, Clement	Dublin, the city	gentry: gent	13-Apr-35	320	Dc2/232v	2036
Ash, Clement	Dublin, the city	gentry: gent	28-May-33	280	Dc2/195v	1885
Ash, Clement	Dublin, the city	gentry: gent	23-May-35	100	Dc2/236r	2052
Ash, Clement	Dublin	gentry: gent	11-Feb-34	200	Dc2/206v	1929
Ash, Clement	Dublin, the city	gentry: gent	16-Nov-31	80	Dc2/170r	1784
Ash, Clement	Dublin, the city	gentry: gent	25-Nov-36	1000	Dc2/257v	2158
Ash, John	Dublin, the city	merchant	01-Jun-27	200	Dc2/94v	1442
Ash, John	Dublin, the city	merchant	25-May-31	120	Dc2/164r	1760
Ash, John	Dublin, the city	merchant	18-Jul-31	300	Dc2/166v	1770
Ash, John	Dublin	merchant	12-Jul-22	200	Dc2/42r	1118
Ash, John	Dublin, the city	merchant	22-Feb-30	100	Dc2/143r	1670
Ash, John	Meath, Kilmessam	gentry: esquire	14-Feb-22	600	Dc2/39r	1097
Ash, John	Meath, Kilmessan	gentry: esquire	14-Feb-22	600	Dc2/38v	1096
Ash, Richard	Dublin	merchant	05-May-01	123	Dc1/31r	206
Ash, Richard	Dublin	merchant	06-Feb-02	60	Dc1/36r	235
Ash, Richard	Dublin	merchant	18-May-07	60	Dc1/77r	468
Ash, Thomas		gentry: knight	07-Feb-07	180	Dc1/74r	447
Ash, Thomas	Meath, Trym	gentry: knight	24-Nov-10	200	Dc1/101r	632
Ash, Thomas	Meath, Tryme	gentry: knight	08-Feb-10	400	Dc1/94r	589
Ash, Thomas	Meath, Trym	gentry: knight	29-Nov-11	200	Dc1/109v	681
Ashhurst, Henry	England, London	merchant-tailor	07-Aug-58	550	B.L. 15, 635 f. 32	3319
Aston, William	Dublin, the city	gentry: knight	21-Dec-66	100	Dc3/49	2329
Astry, Samuel	England, Clements Inn, Mdlesex	gentry: esquire	19-Oct-64	252	B.L. 15, 635 f. 147a	3514
Atkins, John	Cork, Youghall		01-Feb-84	836	B.L. 15, 637 f. 86	4003
Atkins, Suzanne	Dublin, the city	gentry: wife of Thomas	30-Apr-73	2000	Dc3/155r	2580
Atkins, Thomas	Dublin, the city	gentry: esquire	30-Apr-73	2000	Dc3/155r	2580
Atkins, Thomas	Dublin	gentry: esquire	30-Apr-73	2000	B.L. 15, 636 f. 134a	3845
Aungier, Francis	Longford?	peer: baron Longford	10-Nov-69	2000	Dc3/106	2452
Aungier, Francis	Longford?	peer: baron Longford	27-Jan-24	300	Dc2/52v	1196
Aungier, Francis	Dublin	gentry: esquire	04-Dec-35	800	Dc2/241r	2076
Aungier, Francis	Longford?	peer: baron Longford	10-Nov-69	2400	B.L. 15, 636 f. 57a	3721
Aungier, Gerald	Longford?	peer: baron Longford	22-Jun-35	1600	Dc2/237v	2060
Aylmer, Gerald	Meath, Painston	gentry: gent	02-May-15	120	Dc1/136v	848
Aylmer, Gerald	Meath, Balrath	gentry: esquire	10-Mar-37	2600	Dc2/263r	2180
Aylmer, Gerald	Meath, Balrath	gentry: esquire	26-May-23	300	Dc2/47v	1161
Aylmer, Gerald	Meath, Balrath	gentry: esquire	10-Jul-29	2000	Dc2/135r	1631
Aylmer, Thomas	Kildare, Lyons	gentry: esquire	05-Sep-65	200	Dc3/14	2251
Babe, Walter	Louth, Atherdy	gentry: gent	02-Jun-97	200	Dc1/4r	29
Babington, Richard	Tyrone, Urney	gentry: gent	06-Mar-32	500	Dc2/177v	1813
Baddely, George	Dublin	merchant	23-Jun-30	400	Dc2/153r	1712
Baggott, William	Dublin, the city	merchant	05-Jun-32	300	Dc2/182v	1833

Standard	County	Occupation	Date	Amount	MS No	Ident No
Bagnall, George	Carlow, Donlickny	gentry: esquire	05-Feb-13	1000	Dc1/118r	734
Bagnall, Walter	Carlow, Dunlickny	gentry: esquire	11-Jul-37	1000	Dc2/267v	2201
Bagshaw, Edward	Dublin, the city	gentry: knight	13-Dec-28	400	Dc2/122v	1571
Bagshaw, Edward	Dublin, the city	gentry: gent	01-Jul-19	400	Dc2/24v	997
Bailey, John	Cork, the city	trade: clothier	19-Mar-69	300	B.L. 15, 636 f. 41	3696
Bailey, John	Down, Iniscargie	gentry: esquire	03-Dec-78	1000	B.L. 15, 637 f. 3	3856
Bailiffs/Burgesses	Charleville, Cork		12-Dec-71	1000	B.L. 15, 636 f. 97a	3791
Baker, George	Dublin	gentry: gent	06-May-35	220	Dc2/235v	2045
Baker, Henry	Dublin	gentry: gent	28-Nov-28	200	Dc2/117v	1551
Baldwin, James	Cork, Garranconig	gentry: esquire	20-May-78	800	B.L. 19, 844 f. 156	3287
Baldwin, John	King's Co., Castlegeshell	gentry: esquire	28-Sep-65	70	Dc3/14	2252
Baldwin, John	King's Co., Geashell	gentry: esquire	18-Feb-69	460	Dc3/91	2426
Baldwin, John	King's Co., Geshell	gentry: esquire	24-Nov-69	80	Dc3/108	2458
Baldwin, John	Longford, Geashell	gentry: esquire	18-Feb-69	460	B.L. 15, 636 f. 43	3699
Baldwin, John	King's Co., Geshill	gentry: esquire	30-Nov-71	240	Dc3/142r	2537
Balfour, James	Armagh, Clynawly	peer: baron Clanawley	02-Mar-29	400	Dc2/125v	1589
Balfour, James	Armagh, Clanawlye	peer: baron Clanawley	02-Mar-29	2000	Dc2/125v	1588
Ball, Edward	Dublin	merchant	18-Jun-02	200	Dc1/38v	249
Ball, Edward	Dublin	merchant	08-Apr-10	80	Dc1/95r	594
Ball, Edward	Dublin	merchant	24-Jun-13	120	Dc1/123r	763
Ball, John	Dublin	merchant	04-May-12	200	Dc1/133r	702
Ball, John	Dublin	merchant	21-Feb-12	60	Dc1/112v	698
Ball, John	Dublin, the city	merchant	15-Aug-44	500	B.L. 19, 843 f. 116	2951
Ball, Nicholas	Dublin		23-Mar-97	300	Dc1/2v	14
Ball, Nicholas	Dublin		01-Feb-97		Dc1/1r	2
Ball, Nicholas	Dublin		23-Mar-97	40	Dc1/2v	15
Ball, Nicholas	Dublin		27-Feb-97		Dc1/2r	10
Ball, Richard	Dublin		23-Apr-02	1000	Dc1/37v	242
Ball, Robert	Dublin		07-Nov-17	200	Dc2/10v	918
Ball, Robert	Dublin	merchant	11-Feb-03	2000	Dc1/44v	283
Ball, Robert	Dublin, the city		05-Jul-30	200	Dc2/154r	1715
Barker, Constance	Dublin, St Mary's Abbey	other: widow	14-Jun-30	200	Dc2/151r	1702
Barker, Constance	Dublin, St. Mary's Abbey	other: widow	11-Jun-30	200	Dc2/149v	1697
Barker, Constance	Dublin, St. Mary's Abbey	other: widow	25-Aug-29	200	Dc2/136r	1635
Barker, William	England, London		29-Jul-71	446	Dc3/139r	2527
Barnes, Donal	Dublin	gentry: gent	29-Apr-05	240	Dc1/57v	353
Barnewall, Alice	Meath, Robertstown	gentry: widow	30-Apr-24	500	Dc2/54v	1211
Barnewall, Bartholomew	Louth, Rathgeskir	gentry: gent	20-May-98	320	Dc1/11r	79
Barnewall, Christopher	Dublin, the Newton nr Mounton	gentry: gent	17-May-09	400	Dc1/89r	555
Barnewall, Christopher	Dublin, Strand, neere Merrion	gentry: gent	12-Jan-99	200	Dc1/14r	99
Barnewall, Christopher	Meath?, Newton	gentry: gent	10-Feb-97		Dc1/1v	6
Barnewall, Christopher	Dublin, Newton	gentry: gent	13-May-08	400	Dc1/83r	515
Barnewall, Edward	Dublin, Barrimoore	gentry: esquire	25-Jun-28	220	Dc2/111v	1519

Standard	County	Occupation	Date	Amount	MS No	Ident No
Barnewall, Edward	Dublin, Brymoore	gentry: esquire	16-Jun-30	100	Dc2/151v	1706
Barnewall, Francis	Meath, Woodparke/					
	Biggstowne	gentry: esquire	20-May-81	800	B.L. 15, 637 f. 48a	3933
Barnewall, Francis	Meath, Begstowne	gentry: esquire	02-Feb-74	2000	Dc3/160r	2602
Barnewall, James	Dublin, Dunbroe	gentry: gent	24-Feb-36	600	Dc2/246r	2100
Barnewall, John	Meath, Rathronan	gentry: gent	04-Feb-26	200	Dc2/73r	1339
Barnewall, Margaret	Meath, Roberston	gentry: widow	17-Nov-38	150	B.L. 19, 943 f.2a	2724
Barnewall, Mathew	Dublin?	gentry: son of Richard	19-Apr-41	100	B.L. 19, 843 f. 101a	2922
Barnewall, Mathew	Meath, Arthurstowne	gentry: gent	19-Dec-72	560	Dc3/152r	2568
Barnewall, Mathew	Dublin, the city	merchant	14-Mar-66	140	Dc3/26	2279
Barnewall, Mathew	Meath, Arthurstowne	gentry: gent	19-Dec-72	560	B.L. 15, 636 f. 120	3827
Barnewall, Nicholas	Dublin, Turvie	gentry: esquire	27-Jun-40	600	B.L. 19, 843 f. 61a	2842
Barnewall, Oliver	Dublin, the city	merchant	04-Jul-34	400	Dc2/214r	1960
Barnewall, Oliver	Dublin, the city	merchant	23-May-34	200	Dc2/212r	1952
Barnewall, Patrick	Meath, Kilbrewe	gentry: gent	20-Apr-14	120	Dc1/128v	800
Barnewall, Patrick	Meath, Kilbrewe	gentry: esquire	12-Jul-33	600	Dc2/197v	1894
Barnewall, Patrick	Meath, Kilbrew	gentry: esquire	22-Jun-26	360	Dc2/79v	1378
Barnewall, Patrick	Meath, Kilbrew	gentry: esquire	22-Jun-26	360	Dc2/79r	1375
Barnewall, Patrick	Meath, Kilbrewe	gentry: esquire	10-Feb-30	400	Dc2/141v	1663
Barnewall, Patrick	Meath, Kilbrewe	gentry: esquire	07-Aug-39	100	B.L. 19, 843 f. 55	2828
Barnewall, Patrick	Meath, Kilbrue	gentry: esquire	26-Jun-24	200	Dc2/57r	1229
Barnewall, Patrick	Dublin, Grasedewe	gentry: knight	19-May-10	160	Dc1/96r	604
Barnewall, Patrick	Dublin, Shankill	gentry: esquire	25-Jun-19	300	Dc2/24r	994
Barnewall, Patrick	Meath, Kilbrue	gentry: gent	22-Jun-15	500	Dc1/138v	858
Barnewall, Patrick	Dublin, Grasedieve	gentry: knight	28-Nov-07	52	Dc1/80r	495
Barnewall, Patrick	Meath, Kilbrew	gentry: esquire	09-Feb-28	200	Dc2/104r	1484
Barnewall, Patrick	Meath, Kilbrue	gentry: esquire	11-Feb-25	200	Dc2/61v	1265
Barnewall, Richard	Dublin, Lespopple	gentry: esquire	07-May-30	600	Dc2/146v	1684
Barnewall, Robert	Meath, Robertston	gentry: esquire	21-Jun-13	100	Dc1/122v	761
Barnewall, Robert	Dublin, Newton	gentry: gent	12-Dec-27	200	Dc2/102r	1474
Barnewall, Robert	Dublin, Barbeston	gentry: gent	27-Nov-10	100	Dc1/101r	633
Barnewall, Robert	Dublin, Shankhill	gentry: gent	25-May-22	600	Dc2/40r	1107
Barnewall, Simon	Dublin	trade: sadler	28-Apr-10	160	Dc1/95v	599
Barnewall, Simon	Dublin	trade: sadler	28-Nov-08	120	Dc1/85r	530
Baron, Edward	Westmeath, Kilbeggan	gentry: gent	16-Dec-11	60	Dc1/110r	684
Barrett, John	Cork, the city	soldier: lieutenant	25-Aug-67	700	B.L. 15, 635 f. 215a	3636
Barrett, William	Mayo, Rosse	gentry: gent	21-May-10	500	Dc1/96v	607
Barrington, Alexander	Wexford	gentry: gent	15-Feb-73	300	Dc3/153v	2574
Barry, Edward	Dublin	merchant	06-Jun-06	250	Dc1/69v	420
Barry, Edward	Dublin, the city	merchant	12-Dec-32	400	Dc2/188r	1856
Barry, Edward	Dublin, the city	merchant	08-Sep-34	200	Dc2/219r	1981
Barry, James	Dublin		01-Aug-99	50	Dc1/18v	126
Barry, James	Cork, Annagh	gentry: esquire	04-Apr-36	2000	Dc2/248v	2110
Barry, John	Dublin	merchant	14-Feb-12	100	Dc1/112v	697
Barry, John	Dublin	merchant	20-Jan-13	1000	Dc1/117v	731

Standard	County	Occupation	Date	Amount	MS No	Ident No
Barry, John	Dublin, the city	merchant	23-Dec-10	400	Dc1/101v	636
Barry, Mathew	Dublin, the city	gentry: esquire	02-Aug-71	100	B.L. 15, 636 f. 89a	3778
Barry, Mathew	Dublin, the city	gentry: esquire	22-Mar-71	100	B.L. 15, 636 f. 87a	3775
Barry, Mathew	Dublin, the city	gentry: gent	06-Feb-55	1000	B.L. 19, 843 f. 156	3026
Barry, Mathew	Dublin, the city	gentry: gent	21-May-59	400	B.L. 15, 635 f. 49	3349
Barry, Mathew	Dublin, the city	gentry: gent	01-May-57	1200	B.L. 19, 843 f. 192	3091
Barry, Mathew	Dublin, the city	gentry: esquire	30-Mar-67	200	B.L. 15, 635 f. 191	3592
Barry, Mathew	Dublin, the city	gentry: esquire	02-Aug-71	100	Dc3/139v	2528
Barry, Mathew	Dublin, the city	gentry: esquire	22-Mar-71	100	Dc3/137r	2520
Barry, Mathew	Dublin, the city	gentry: esquire	30-Mar-67	200	Dc3/58	2349
Barry, Mathew	Dublin, the city	gentry: esquire, exec for Tho Bourke of Dub	29-Jul-65	500	Dc3/12	2248
Barry, Mathew	Dublin, the city	gentry: esquire	29-Jul-65	400	B.L. 15, 635 f. 158a	3534
Barry, Redmond	Cork, Rathcormack	gentry: esquire	11-Jun-72	600	B.L. 15, 636 f. 111	3812
Barry, Redmond	Cork, Rathcormuck	gentry: esquire	22-Oct-67	1200	B.L. 15, 635 f. 212a	3630
Barry, Richard	Dublin, the city	gentry: gent	02-Jun-76	200	B.L. 19, 844 f. 95	3222
Barry, Richard	Dublin, the city		11-May-19	200	Dc2/23v	990
Barry, Richard	Dublin, the city		22-Jun-30	3000	Dc2/153r	1711
Barry, Richard	Dublin, the city	gentry: esquire	13-Dec-77	800	Dc3/184r	2698
Barry, Richard	Dublin, the city	gentry: gent, exec for Tho Bourke of Dub	29-Jul-65	500	Dc3/12	2248
Barry, Richard	Dublin, the city		29-Jul-65	400	B.L. 15, 635 f. 158a	3534
Barry, Richard	Dublin, the city	gentry: gent	09-Jun-73	1600	Dc3/156v	2583
Barry, Richard	Dublin		13-Feb-18	1000	Dc2/13v	935
Barry, Richard	Dublin, the city		18-Jun-28	1000	Dc2/111r	1518
Barry, Richard	Dublin, the city	gentry: esquire	02-Dec-69	600	B.L. 15, 636 f. 49	3708
Barry, Richard	Dublin, the city		13-Jun-25	600	Dc2/66r	1296
Barry, Richard	Cork?	peer: earl of Barrymore	30-Dec-67	3544	B.L. 15, 635 f. 216	3637
Barry, Richard	Dublin, the city	gentry: esquire	02-Dec-69	600	Dc3/109	2462
Barry, Richard	Dublin, the city	gentry: gent	06-Feb-55	1000	B.L. 19, 843 f. 156	3026
Barry, Richard	Dublin, the city		01-Dec-19	1000	Dc2/26v	1008
Barry, Richard	Dublin		20-May-24	400	Dc2/55r	1216
Barry, Richard	Dublin, the city	gentry: gent	09-Jul-73	1600	B.L. 15, 636 f. 137	3850
Barry, Richard	Dublin, the city		05-Jul-30	200	Dc2/154r	1715
Barry, Richard	Cork?	peer: earl of Barrymore	12-Nov-66	1000	Dc3/41	2318
Barry, Richard	Dublin		31-May-27	1500	Dc2/93r	1434
Barry, Richard	Dublin, the city	gentry: gent	02-Jun-76	200	Dc3/175r	2660
Barry, Richard	Dublin		24-Sep-14	150	Dc1/131v	819
Barton, William	Monaghan, Carrickmacross	gentry: esquire	26-Nov-68	1000	B.L. 15, 636 f. 29a	3677
Barton, William	Monaghan, Carrickmacross	gentry: esquire	26-Nov-68	1000	Dc3/83	2414
Bassett, Sarah	Cork, the city	other: widow	12-Apr-70	1000	B.L. 15, 636 f. 58a	3723
Bastwick, John	England, London	gentry: gent	14-Dec-70	480	Dc3/132v	2508
Bath, James	Meath, Athcarne	gentry: esquire	13-Feb-33	100	Dc2/191r	1868
Bath, James	Meath, Athcarne	gentry: esquire	23-Jun-37	2060	Dc2/266r	2193
Bath, James	Meath, Athcrane	gentry: esquire	04-Feb-29	400	Dc2/123v	1577

Standard	County	Occupation	Date	Amount	MS No	Ident No
Bath, James	Meath, Athcarne	gentry: esquire	15-Feb-33	400	Dc2/191v	1869
Bath, John	Dublin, Balgryffin	gentry: esquire	20-May-14	700	Dc1/129v	804
Bath, Lucas	Dublin, Clonturke	gentry: gent	30-May-39	1000	B.L. 19, 843 f. 18	2754
Bath, Patrick	Dublin, the city	trade: tailor	21-Dec-20	260	Dc2/34r	1059
Bath, Peter	Dublin, the city	merchant	23-Nov-37	830	Dc2/272r	2220
Bath, Robert	Meath, Bewshelston	gentry: gent	07-Jun-14	300	Dc1/130r	809
Bath, Robert	Meath, Beweshelston	gentry: gent	25-Jun-14	400	Dc1/130v	810
Bath, Thomas	Dublin	gentry: gent	19-Aug-99	200	Dc1/18v	128
Bathurst, Samuel	Dublin, the city	gentry: esquire	08-Mar-61	400	B.L. 15, 635 f. 67a	3382
Beckett, Anne	Dublin, the city	gentry: widow, relict of Randal	03-Dec-74	500	B.L. 19, 844 f. 48	3171
Beckett, Anne	Dublin, the city	gentry: widow, relict of Randal	03-Dec-74	500	Dc3/163r	2618
Beckett, Randal	Dublin, the city	gentry: gent	02-Jan-55	80	B.L. 19, 843 f. 148	3010
Beckett, Randal	Dublin, the city	gentry: gent	03-Nov-54	400	B.L. 19, 843 f. 146	3006
Bee, James	Dublin	trade: goldsmith	05-Feb-17	60	Dc2/4v	890
Bee, James	Dublin	trade: goldsmith	22-Nov-99	100	Dc1/20r	135
Beecher, Edward	England, Fotheringham N'hamton	gentry: gent	26-Jul-09	200	Dc1/90v	567
Beere, William	Down, Ballimcconchy	gentry: gent	26-Jun-67	400	Dc3/64	2364
Begge, David	Dublin, the city	merchant	13-Mar-33	400	Dc2/192v	1874
Begge, David	Dublin, the city		19-Nov-35	100	Dc2/240r	2071
Begge, David	Dublin, the city		23-Nov-35	600	Dc2/240v	2073
Begge, David	Dublin, the city		20-Feb-41	621	B.L. 19, 843 f. 85a	2890
Begge, David	Dublin, the city	merchant	14-May-35	500	Dc2/235v	2049
Begge, David	Dublin, the city	merchant	15-Feb-33	450	Dc2/192r	1871
Begge, David	Dublin, the city		07-Jan-36	400	Dc2/243r	2088
Begge, David	Dublin, the city	merchant	08-Jun-31	400	Dc2/164v	1762
Begge, David	Dublin, the city		10-Feb-36	1000	Dc2/244v	2093
Begge, Thomas	Dublin, the city	merchant	21-Jun-32	300	Dc2/183v	1838
Behan, Peter	Dublin, the city	gentry: esquire	09-Mar-75	3300	Dc3/166v	2631
Behan, Peter	Dublin, the city	gentry: esquire	09-Mar-75	3300	B.L. 19, 844 f. 51	3174
Behan, Peter	Dublin, the city	gentry: esquire	29-Jul-65	400	B.L. 15, 635 f. 158a	3534
Behan, Peter	Dublin, the city	gentry: esquire	07-Aug-70	700	B.L. 15, 636 f. 90a	3780
Behan, Peter	Dublin, the city	gentry: esquire	07-Aug-71	780	Dc3/139v	2529
Behan, Peter	Dublin, the city	gentry: esquire	25-Feb-78	600	B.L. 19, 844 f. 146	3277
Behan, Peter	Dublin, the city	gentry: esquire, exec for Tho Bourke of Dub	29-Jul-65	500	Dc3/12	2248
Behan, Peter	Dublin, the city	gentry: esquire	28-Jul-82	600	B.L. 15, 637 f. 63a	3962
Behan, Peter	Dublin, the city	gentry: esquire	01-Feb-78	600	B.L. 19, 844 f. 145	3276
Behan, Peter	Dublin, the city	gentry: esquire	01-Feb-78	600	Dc3/185r	2702
Behan, Peter	Dublin, the city	gentry: esquire	25-Feb-78	600	Dc3/186v	2705
Bellew, Alison	Dublin, the city	merchant: spinster, dau of James Bellew, merch	30-Jun-36	200	Dc2/254r	2139
Bellew, Arthur	Dublin, the city	gentry: gent	16-Jun-37	150	Dc2/264v	2188

Standard	County	Occupation	Date	Amount	MS No	Ident No
Bellew, Edward	Dublin, the city	merchant	15-Jun-65	280	B.L. 15, 635 f. 154a	3528
Bellew, Edward	Dublin, the city	merchant	15-Jun-65	280	Dc3/9	2242
Bellew, Frances	Meath, Bellewstowne	gentry: widow	17-Nov-68	1600	Dc3/84	2413
Bellew, Frances	Meath, Bellewestowne	gentry: widow	17-Nov-68	1600	B.L. 15, 636 f. 27	3672
Bellew, James	Dublin, the city	merchant	21-Nov-34	200	Dc2/222r	1993
Bellew, James	Dublin		08-Mar-01	120	Dc1/29v	196
Bellew, James	Dublin, the city	merchant	27-Sep-31	200	Dc2/168v	1778
Bellew, James	Louth, Verdonstowne	gentry: gent	01-Jul-61	108	B.L. 15, 635 f. 86	3408
Bellew, James	Dublin, the city	merchant	21-Nov-34	200	B.L. 19, 843 f. 15	2748
Bellew, John	Louth, Willeston	gentry: esquire	19-Mar-39	800	B.L. 19, 843 f. 13a	2745
Bellew, John	Louth, Castletowne Bellew	gentry: knight	25-May-72	500	Dc3/146r	2552
Bellew, John	Louth, Willieston	gentry: gent	07-Dec-39	40	B.L. 19,843 f. 3a	4062
Bellew, John	Meath, Stamrue	gentry: gent	18-Feb-41	600	B.L. 19, 843 f. 102a	2924
Bellew, John	Louth, Lisanny	gentry: gent	28-Nov-32	400	Dc2/187r	1851
Bellew, Lawrence	Dublin, the city	merchant: son of James, merchant	25-Nov-36	200	Dc2/257r	2156
Bellew, Mary	Louth, Thomastowne	gentry: wife of Roger	18-Oct-63	1600	B.L. 15, 635 f. 124	3475
Bellew, Nicholas	Dublin, the city	gentry: gent	06-Apr-72	400	Dc3/145v	2550
Bellew, Nicholas	Dublin, the city	gentry: gent	06-Apr-72	400	B.L. 15, 636 f. 113a	3817
Bellew, Patrick	Louth, Verdonstowne	gentry: esquire	12-Jun-30	200	Dc2/150r	1698
Bellew, Roger	Louth, Thomastowne	gentry: gent	18-Oct-63	1600	B.L. 15, 635 f. 124	3475
Bellew, Thomas	Meath, Gaffny	gentry: esquire	01-Feb-83	230	B.L. 15, 637 f. 69	3971
Bellew, Thomas	Meath, Gafny	gentry: esquire	24-Nov-81	1200	B.L. 15, 637 f. 53a	3942
Bellings, Barnaby	Louth, Drogheda	gentry: gent	13-Feb-26	300	Dc2/73v	1342
Bennett, Henry	Cork, the city	trade: tanner	30-Jan-79	1300	B.L. 15, 637 f. 18	3878
Bennett, John	England, Chester, the city	trade: mercer	08-Dec-32	50	Dc2/187v	1854
Bennett, Robert	Dublin, the city		27-May-33	400	Dc2/195r	1884
Bennett, Thomas	Dublin, the city	trade: tanner	01-Jun-85	90	B.L. 15, 637 f. 100	4029
Bennett, Thomas	Dublin, Johnstowne	gentry: esquire	18-Apr-50	130	B.L. 19, 843 f. 125a	2970
Bennett, Thomas	Dublin, Johnstowne	gentry: esquire	23-Jun-40	264	B.L. 19, 843 f. 62	2843
Bennett, Thomas	Dublin, Johnstowne	gentry: esquire	19-Jul-40	100	B.L. 19, 843 f. 62a	2844
Bennis, John	Dublin	merchant	11-Feb-03	300	Dc1/44v	282
Benson, Hugh	England?, London?	trade: ironmonger?, factor and agent	03-Apr-06	1000	Dc1/66r	400
Benson, Hugh	England, London	trade: ironmonger	08-Mar-05	1700	Dc1/57r	351
Bent, Henry	Dublin, the city	gentry: gent	23-Feb-39	30	B.L. 19, 843 f. 45a	2809
Bent, Richard	Cork, Tushimbarcky	gentry: esquire	14-Nov-62	800	B.L. 15, 635 f. 198a	3606
Beresford, Michael	Meath, Kilrowe	gentry: gent	07-Jul-41	200	B.L. 19, 843 f. 105	2929
Beresford, Nicholas	Meath, Skurlockstowne	gentry: gent	14-May-12	240	Dc1/113v	703
Beresford, Richard	Meath, Ballybucin	gentry: esquire	24-Mar-36	600	Dc2/247v	2107
Berkeley, John		peer: baron Stratton	23-Nov-71	1680	B.L. 15, 636 f. 90	3779
Berkeley, John		peer: baron Stratton	23-Nov-71	1680	Dc3/141r	2534
Bermingham, Anne	Louth, Drogheda	gentry: widow, wife of Robert, gent	18-Apr-40	100	B.L. 19, 843 f. 55a	2829
Bermingham, Edward	Dublin, the city	gentry: gent	21-Jun-39	160	B.L. 19, 843 f. 13	2744

Standard	County	Occupation	Date	Amount	MS No	Ident No
Bermingham, John	Kildare, Rahin	gentry: gent	09-Sep-36	400	Dc2/255v	2148
Bermingham, Robert	Dublin, Ballogh	gentry: gent	31-Jan-12	400	Dc1/111v	692
Bermingham, William	Meath, Corbally	gentry: gent	25-Jun-10	40	Dc1/98v	618
Bermingham, William	Meath, Corbally	gentry: gent	24-Jun-10	100	Dc1/98v	617
Bermingham, William	Kildare, Ballerenet	gentry: gent	11-May-11	60	Dc1/104r	650
Betagh, Christopher	Cavan, Dromore	gentry: gent	05-May-26	160	Dc2/76v	1360
Betagh, Christopher	Cavan, Drommore	gentry: gent	08-Jun-22	160	Dc2/41r	1112
Betagh, William	Meath, Donowre	gentry: gent	08-Jun-33	600	Dc2/196r	1888
Betterworth, Elizabeth	Cork, Malloe	gentry: spinster?, gentlewoman	13-Feb-65	400	B.L. 15, 635 f. 148a	3516
Betterworth, Elizabeth	Cork, Maloe	gentry: spinster?, gentlewoman	13-Feb-65	400	Dc3/2	2226
Bickerton, Anne	Louth, Millstowne	other: widow	26-Nov-75	300	B.L. 19, 844 f. 79	3207
Bickerton, Anne	Louth, Milstowne	other: widow	20-Jun-77	500	Dc3/183r	2691
Bickerton, Anne	Louth, Milstowne	other: widow	20-Jun-77	500	B.L. 19, 844 f. 129	3259
Bickerton, Anne	Louth, Milestowne	other: widow	26-Nov-75	300	Dc3/170r	2642
Binglie, John	Dublin	gentry: gent	24-Dec-03	2508	Dc1/50v	324
Binglie, John	Dublin	merchant	15-Apr-02	500	Dc1/37r	241
Binglie, John	Dublin	gentry: gent	07-Apr-02	500	Dc1/37r	240
Binglie, John	Dublin	gentry: gent	23-Aug-03	240	Dc1/48r	312
Binglie, Ralph		gentry: knight	23-Apr-04	2006	Dc1/52v	332
Birch, John	Dublin, the city	merchant	15-Jul-29	100	Dc2/135v	1632
Bird, John	Dublin, Cottrelston	gentry: gent	18-Nov-08	120	Dc1/84v	526
Bird, John	Dublin, Cottroltson	gentry: gent	04-Oct-06	60	Dc1/70v	426
Bird, Richard	England, Chester	merchant	13-Feb-29	212	Dc2/125r	1586
Bird, Thomas	Dublin	merchant	17-Dec-05	40	Dc1/64r	388
Bird, Thomas	Dublin	merchant	03-Mar-11	400	Dc1/105r	656
Bird, Thomas	Dublin	merchant	01-Mar-14	200	Dc1/127v	790
Bird, Thomas	Dublin	merchant	03-Mar-13	400	Dc1/120r	747
Bishop, Francis	Dublin, the city	trade: tailor	20-Aug-59	528	B.L. 15, 635 f. 52	3355
Bishop, Roger	Dublin	gentry: gent	20-Mar-55	80	B.L. 19, 843 f. 154a	3023
Bishop, Thomas	Dublin		28-May-08	40	Dc1/83r	516
Bishop, Thomas	Dublin		21-Nov-09	105	Dc1/92v	579
Bishop, Thomas	Dublin		24-Nov-09	150	Dc1/92v	581
Bishop, Tomas	Dublin		22-Dec-09	80	Dc1/93v	587
Bishop, William	Dublin	merchant	19-Nov-13	600	Dc1/123r	769
Bishop, William	Dublin	merchant	30-Oct-17	120	Dc2/10r	915
Bishop, William	Dublin, the city		03-Jun-22	200	Dc2/40v	1111
Bishop, William	Dublin, the city		03-Jun-22	200	Dc2/40V	1110
Bishop, William	Dublin, the city		22-May-22	272	Dc2/40r	1105
Bishop, William	Dublin, the city		25-Jun-22	3000	Dc2/41r	1113
Blackboroe, Ulpian	Dublin, the city	trade: haberdasher	24-Jul-37	200	Dc2/269v	2209
Blackney, Thomas	Louth, Drogheda	merchant	05-Jul-23	114	Dc2/49r	1170
Blackwell, John	England, Surrey, Mortlock	gentry: esquire	09-Jul-61	600	B.L. 15, 634 f. 89	3414
Blackwell, John	Dublin, the city	gentry: esquire	29-Sep-63	150	B.L. 15, 635 f. 117a	3465

Standard	County	Occupation	Date	Amount	MS No	Ident No
Blackwell, John	Dublin, the city	gentry: esquire	29-Aug-63	600	B.L. 15, 635 f. 112a	3455
Blake, Andrew	Galway	merchant	12-Nov-20	600	Dc2/32v	1048
Blake, Peter	Meath, Athboy	gentry: gent	03-May-00	200	Dc1/23v	156
Blake, Robert	Galway	merchant	21-Jul-14	200	Dc1/131r	813
Blake, Robert	Galway	merchant	28-Nov-06	200	Dc1/72v	439
Blake, Robert	Galway	merchant	17-Jun-13	140	Dc1/122r	758
Blake, Robert	Galway	merchant	15-Feb-10	300	Dc1/94v	591
Blake, Robert	Galway, the town	merchant	08-May-15	60	Dc1/137r	849
Blake, Robert	Galway, the town	gentry: gent	10-May-15	100	Dc1/137r	851
Blake, Robert	Galway	merchant	21-Nov-09	500	Dc1/83r	582
Blake, Robert	Galway		12-Aug-05	2752	Dc1/61r	371
Blake, Valentine	Galway, the towne	gentry: knight and baronet	28-May-31	3000	Dc2/164v	1761
Blake, Valentine	Galway	gentry: knight and baronet	30-Nov-25	400	Dc2/71r	1325
Blaney, Thomas	England, London, the city	merchant	12-Oct-48	6000	B.L. 19, 843 f. 124	2967
Blennerhasset, John	Dublin?	gentry: knight	03-Jul-24	400	Dc2/57r	1231
Blennerhasset, Robert	Kerry, Kilorglin	gentry: gent	09-Aug-60	1000	B.L. 15, 635 f. 68	3383
Blennerhasset, Ursula	Dublin	gentry: widow	19-Jul-25	80	Dc2/68v	1311
Blennerhasset, Ursula	Dublin	gentry: widow	30-Oct-30	400	Dc2/155r	1721
Blennerhasset, Ursula	Dublin, St Patrick's Close	gentry: widow	21-Dec-24	400	Dc2/60r	1254
Blood, Edmund	Clare, Cragbrien	gentry: gent	19-Feb-17	300	Dc2/4v	892
Blount, George	Tyrone, Mountjoy	gentry: esquire	02-Jun-36	2000	Dc2/253r	2134
Blundell, Arthur	Dublin, the city	gentry: esquire	19-Jun-21	1000	Dc2/36r	1074
Blundell, George	King's Co., Edenderry	gentry: baronet	04-Dec-67	700	Dc3/70	2381
Blundell, George	King's Co., Edenderry	gentry: baronet	10-Jun-67	1000	B.L. 15, 635 f. 193	3596
Blundell, George	King's Co., Edenderry	gentry: baronet	05-Dec-67	700	B.L. 15, 635 f. 208a	3624
Blundell, George	King's Co., Edenderry	gentry: baronet	10-Jun-67	1000	Dc3/62	2358
Blundell, John	Leitrim, Leytrem	gentry: esquire	10-Jan-27	100	Dc2/87v	1413
Boate, Godfrey	Dublin, the city	gentry: esquire	30-Apr-72	400	B.L. 15, 636 f. 105a	3802
Boate, Godfrey	Dublin, the city	gentry: esquire	30-Apr-72	400	Dc3/145v	2551
Bollard, John	England, London	trade: jeweller	06-Jun-72	800	Dc3/146v	2553
Bollard, William	Cork, the city	merchant	19-Feb-87	2500	B.L. 15, 637 f. 112a	4053
Bolton, Edward		gentry: knight	19-Feb-39	1000	B.L. 19,843 f. 50a	2819
Bolton, Edward		gentry: knight	04-May-37	2000	Dc2/262r	2176
Bolton, Edward		gentry: esquire	05-Dec-33	800	Dc2/202v	1913
Bolton, Edward		gentry: knight	01-Dec-40	1500	B.L. 19, 843 f. 76	2871
Bolton, Richard	Dublin	gentry: esquire	21-Dec-11	300	Dc1/110v	686
Bolton, Richard	Dublin	gentry: esquire	31-Jan-12	3000	Dc1/111v	693
Bolton, Richard	Dublin?, the city?		21-Nov-07	300	Dc1/79ar	492
Bolton, Richard	Dublin?	gentry: esquire	30-Jan-11	70	Dc1/102v	640
Bolton, Richard	Dublin?	gentry: esquire, son of Rich, Recorder of Dublin	16-Feb-11	200	Dc1/103r	644
Bonnell, Samuel	England, Chester, the city	gentry: esquire	26-Jul-61	750	B.L. 15, 635 f. 78	3397

Standard	County	Occupation	Date	Amount	MS No	Ident No
Booth?, George	Dublin, the city	gentry: gent	13-Feb-34	1000	Dc2/207r	1931
Boothby, Thomas	England?, London?	other: exec will of John Gilbert London, grocer	15-Oct-18	120	Dc2/16v	951
Bor, Christian	England, London, the city	merchant	25-Jan-64	1000	B.L. 15, 635 f. 127	3481
Bor, Christian	Wexford, Drinogh	gentry: esquire	22-Nov-81	250	B.L. 15, 637 f. 52a	3940
Bor, Christian	England, London, the city	merchant	14-Sep-63	1000	B.L. 15, 635 f. 125	3477
Bor, Christian	Wexford, Drunock	gentry: esquire	26-Sep-74	100	B.L. 19, 844 f. 39	3163
Bor, Christian	Wexford, Drynagh	gentry: esquire	16-Feb-71	100	Dc3/135r	2515
Bor, Christian	England, London, the city	merchant	05-Oct-63	150	B.L. 15, 635 f. 121a	3470
Bor, Christian	England, London, the city	merchant	24-Jul-63	300	B.L. 15, 635 f. 123	3473
Bor, Christian	England, London, the city	merchant	06-Aug-63	600	B.L. 15, 635 f. 122a	3472
Bor, Christian	England, London, the city	merchant	07-Jun-64	300	B.L. 15, 635 f. 143	3505
Bor, Christian	England, London, the city	merchant	28-Aug-63	600	B.L. 15, 635 f. 123a	3474
Bor, Christian	Wexford, Drinagh	gentry: esquire	24-Jun-72	3000	B.L. 15, 636 f.110a	3811
Bor, Christian	Wexford, Drynoch	gentry: esquire	27-Aug-80	1000	B.L. 15, 637 f. 37	3912
Bor, Christian	England, London, the city	merchant	09-Oct-63	150	B.L. 15, 635 f. 122	3471
Bor, Christian	Wexford, Drinagh	gentry: esquire	24-Jun-72	3000	Dc3/146v	2554
Bor, Christian	Wexford, Drynagh	gentry: esquire	16-Feb-71	100	B.L. 15, 636 f. 77	3756
Bor, Gerard	Dublin, the city	gentry: esquire	14-Aug-80	200	B.L. 15, 637 f. 37a	3913
Bor, John	Dublin, the city	gentry: esquire	15-May-83	264	B.L. 15, 637 f. 71	3975
Bor, John	Dublin, the city	merchant	05-Aug-64	400	B.L. 15, 635 f. 142a	3504
Boshell, Robert	Meath	farmer	06-Feb-08	100	Dc1/81r	502
Bostock, John	England, London, the city	gentry: gent	14-Dec-70	480	B.L. 15, 636 f. 81	3763
Boswell, John	Sligo, Donecoghy	gentry: esquire	04-Aug-53	448	B.L. 19, 843 f. 134	2983
Boswell, John	Dublin, St. George's Lane	gentry: esquire, executor of will of John esq	02-Dec-56	300	B.L. 19, 843 f. 189a	3086
Bourne, John	Cork, Bandonbridge	gentry: gent	05-Jun-67	3000	B.L. 15, 635 f. 200a	3610
Bowen, Robert	Queen's Co., Ballyadams	gentry: esquire	21-May-05	4000	Dc1/59v	363
Bowerman, Henry	Cork, Coolynee	gentry: gent	24-Jul-73	754	B.L. 19, 844 f. 11	3130
Boyle, Barry	Cork, Castle Lyons	gentry: gent	09-Jul-78	500	B.L. 19, 844 f. 166	3297
Boyle, Michael		prof: bishop of Dublin	06-Nov-73	459	Dc3/158ar	2593
Boyle, Michael		prof: bishop of Dublin	23-Feb-67	4000	B.L. 15, 635 f. 187	3584
Boyle, Michael		prof: bishop of Dublin	07-Feb-68	308	B.L. 15, 635 f. 222a	3650
Boyle, Michael		prof: bishop of Dublin	25-Aug-68	200	B.L. 15, 635 f. 228	3661
Boyle, Michael		prof: dean of Cloyne	06-Dec-66	4000	B.L. 15, 635 f. 181a	3573
Boyle, Michael		prof: bishop of Dublin	25-Aug-66	170	B.L. 15, 635 f. 180a	3571
Boyle, Michael		prof: bishop of Dublin	22-Jun-68	440	B.L. 15, 635 f. 221	3647
Boyle, Michael		prof: bishop of Dublin	07-Feb-68	308	Dc3/72	2388
Boyle, Michael		prof: archbishop of Armagh	05-Feb-86	3400	B.L. 15, 637 f. 104	4035
Boyle, Michael		prof: archbishop of Armagh	19-Nov-84	424	B.L. 15, 637 f. 95	4019
Boyle, Michael		prof: bishop of Dublin	13-Aug-66	600	Dc3/36	2305
Boyle, Michael		prof: bishop of Dublin	22-Jun-68	440	Dc3/79	2406

Standard	County	Occupation	Date	Amount	MS No	Ident No
Boyle, Michael		prof: bishop of Dublin	06-Nov-73	450	B.L. 19, 844 f. 15	3133
Boyle, Michael		prof: bishop of Dublin	23-Feb-67	4000	Dc3/55	2341
Boyle, Richard	Waterford?	peer: earl of Cork	15-Apr-36	1600	Dc2/249v	2115
Boyle, Richard	Waterford, Lysmore	gentry: knight	24-May-10	300	Dc1/97r	608
Boyle, Richard	Waterford?	peer: earl of Cork	16-Dec-33	3000	Dc2/204r	1919
Boyle, Richard	Waterford, Lysmore	gentry: knight	31-Jan-07	200	Dc1/73v	445
Boyle, Richard	Waterford?	gentry: knight	16-Dec-14	100	Dc1/134r	834
Boyle, Richard	Waterford, Lismore	gentry: knight	25-Nov-03	4180	Dc1/49v	319
Boyle, Richard	Waterford?	peer: earl of Cork	03-Mar-34	3000	Dc2/208v	1938
Boyle, Richard	Waterford?	gentry: knight and baronet	23-Nov-14	300	Dc1/132v	825
Boyle, Richard	Waterford?	peer: earl of Cork	04-Dec-32	2000	Dc2/187v	1853
Boyle, Richard	Waterford, Lismore	gentry: knight	28-May-06	300	Dc1/69r	416
Boyle, Richard	Waterford, Lysmore	gentry: knight	31-May-06	1200	Dc1/69r	417
Boyle, Richard	Waterford?	peer: earl of Cork	27-Feb-32	500	Dc2/176v	1810
Boyten, Edward	Tipperary, Cashell	gentry: esquire	16-Jun-37	160	Dc2/264v	2187
Boyton, Edward	Tipperary, Cashell	gentry: esquire	17-Jun-26	400	Dc2/78r	1374
Brabazon, Edward	Meath?	peer: earl of Meath	14-Mar-66	1800	B.L. 15, 635 f. 169a	3550
Brabazon, Edward	Meath?	peer: earl of Meath	14-Mar-66	1800	Dc3/25	2278
Brabazon, Mary	Meath?	peer: countess-dowager? of Meath	22-Dec-76	4000	Dc3/181r	2681
Brabazon, Mary	Meath?	peer: countess Meath, widow	22-Dec-76	1000	B.L. 19, 844 f. 119	3248
Brabazon, William	Meath?	peer: earl of Meath, ld baron of Ardee	07-Dec-33	1500	Dc2/203r	1915
Brabazon, William	Dublin, Thomas Cowrte, the city	gentry: knight	22-Feb-17	1600	Dc2/5r	894
Brabazon, William	Dublin, Thomascowrte	gentry: knight	11-Mar-14	1600	Dc1/128r	795
Brabazon, William	Dublin, Thomascourte	gentry: knight	17-Mar-14	1000	Dc1/128v	797
Brabazon, William	Meath?	peer: earl of Meath, ld baron of Ardee	06-May-37	800	Dc2/262r	2177
Bradston, Thomas	Carlow, Morterstowne	gentry: esquire	21-Jun-83	2000	B.L. 15, 637 f. 75	3983
Bragg, William	Dublin, the city	gentry: gent	01-Apr-71	200	Dc3/137v	2521
Brandon, Margaret	Dublin	merchant: widow	08-Feb-98	30	Dc1/9r	65
Brandon, Thomas	Dublin	merchant	16-Nov-98	100	Dc1/13r	93
Branigan, Edward	Dublin, the city	merchant	10-Feb-34	700	Dc2/206r	1928
Branigan, Rose	Dublin	merchant: widow	23-Feb-31	200	Dc2/160r	1743
Braughall, Robert	Dublin, Clansillagh	gentry: gent	10-Feb-66	200	Dc3/21	2270
Bready, Sampson	Antrim, Antrim	gentry: gent	12-Dec-74	880	B.L. 19, 844 f. 45	3169
Breband, David	England, London, the city	merchant	13-Mar-32	122	Dc2/177v	1814
Brereton, Elizabeth		gentry: widow, wife of Sir John, Sergeant at lawe	17-Feb-30	4000	Dc2/142v	1667
Brereton, Henry	Kildare, Inchequire	gentry: gent	10-Sep-70	220	B.L. 15, 636 f. 69a	3741
Brereton, Henry	Kildare, Inchequire	gentry: gent	02-Jul-70	200	B.L. 15, 636 f. 70	3742
Brereton, Henry	Kildare, Inchequire	gentry: gent	03-Dec-70	800	Dc3/132v	2507

Standard	County	Occupation	Date	Amount	MS No	Ident No
Brereton, Henry	Kildare, Inchequire	gentry: gent	02-Jul-70	200	Dc3/122	2484
Brereton, Henry	Kildare, Inchiquire	gentry: gent	10-Sep-70	220	Dc3/124	2490
Brereton, Randal	England, Egham, Surrey	gentry: esquire	12-Jan-30	1000	Dc2/140v	1658
Breton, Beverley	England, South[ampton], Yateley	gentry: esquire	26-Dec-32	400	Dc2/189v	1861
Brett, Bartholomew	Louth, Drogheda	merchant	08-Feb-20	120	Dc2/28v	1020
Brett, Bartholomew	Louth, Drogheda	merchant	21-Nov-21	240	Dc2/36v	1080
Brett, Edward	Louth, Drogheda	merchant	07-Feb-05	102	Dc1/55v	345
Brett, Thomas	Dublin, the city	merchant	09-Jun-62	232	B.L. 15, 635 f. 98	3430
Brett, Walter	Dublin	merchant	20-Feb-17	60	Dc2/5r	893
Bretton, William	Wexford, Ballyneparke	gentry: gent	29-Aug-36	100	Dc2/255v	2147
Brewester, Francis	Dublin, the city		23-Jul-67	400	B.L. 15, 635 f. 205	3619
Brewester, Francis	Dublin, the city		23-Jul-67	400	Dc3/65	2369
Brian, James	Dublin, Howth town	trade: fisherman	15-Jun-29	200	Dc2/132r	1618
Brice, Christopher	Dublin	merchant	27-Nov-33	418	Dc2/201r	1908
Brice, Christopher	Dublin	merchant	27-Nov-33	350	Dc2/201v	1909
Brice, Christopher	Dublin, the city	merchant	19-Jun-29	100	Dc2/133v	1623
Brice, Christopher	Dublin, the city	merchant	02-Apr-29	500	Dc2/126v	1594
Brice, Christopher	Dublin, the city	merchant	19-Feb-24	400	Dc2/53v	1205
Brice, Christopher	Dublin, the city	merchant	28-Apr-30	200	Dc2/144v	1675
Brice, Christopher	Dublin, the city	merchant	14-Mar-29	200	Dc2/126r	1592
Brice, Christopher	Dublin	merchant	21-Jun-30	100	Dc2/152v	1709
Brice, John	Dublin	merchant	09-Feb-99	203	Dc1/15v	106
Brice, John	Dublin, the city	merchant	24-Dec-32	200	Dc2/189r	1860
Brice, Mary	King's Co., Ballitaige	other: widow	03-Feb-65	100	Dc3/2	2225
Brice, Richard	Dublin	merchant	10-Nov-12	110	Dc1/116r	722
Brice, Richard	Dublin	merchant	04-Dec-05	320	Dc1/63r	383
Brice, Richard	Dublin	merchant	18-Nov-05	140	Dc1/62r	378
Brice, Richard	King's Co., Tobberdaly	gentry: gent	05-Dec-23	240	Dc2/51v	1190
Brice, Robert	Antrim, The Glin	gentry: gent	27-Mar-56	383	B.L. 19, 843 f. 181	3069
Bridges, Nathaniel	Dublin, the city	merchant	23-Feb-70	700	Dc3/116	2470
Bridges, Nathaniel	Dublin, the city	merchant	23-Feb-70	700	B.L. 15, 636 f. 46	3704
Brierley, John	England, London	trade: fishmonger	27-Nov-18	120	Dc2/18v	960
Brightwell, Samuel	England, Lincolnes Inns	gentry: esquire	14-Jun-61	600	B.L. 15, 635 f. 71	3386
Broderick, John	Cork, Ballyanane	gentry: knight	17-Apr-75	1100	B.L. 19, 844 f. 61	3187
Broderick, John	Cork, Ballyanane	gentry: knight	10-Apr-75	1200	B.L. 19, 844 f. 60	3185
Broderick, William	Cork, Ballyanan	gentry: gent	19-Jun-76	280	B.L. 19, 844 f. 109	3236
Brookes, John	Dublin, the city	trade: vintner	28-May-68	240	Dc3/76	2397
Brookes, William	Dublin, the city	trade: brewer	09-May-63	200	B.L. 15, 635 f. 111a	3453
Brough, George	Dublin	gentry: gent	10-Jul-18	500	Dc2/15v	947
Browne, Andrew	Galway, the county of the town	merchant	08-May-32	300	Dc2/180r	1823
Browne, Anthony	Meath?, Athboy	merchant	18-Jun-07	75	Dc1/78v	478
Browne, James	Westmeath, Ranaghan	gentry: gent	10-Feb-10	300	Dc1/94r	590
Browne, James	Dublin, the city	merchant	07-May-38	200	B.L. 19, 843 f. 114a	2948

Standard	County	Occupation	Date	Amount	MS No	Ident No
Browne, John	Dublin	merchant	09-Sep-02	105	Dc1/39v	257
Browne, John	Dublin	merchant	20-Dec-04	105	Dc1/54r	340
Browne, John	Dublin	merchant	28-Jan-05	105	Dc1/55r	343
Browne, Joseph	Dublin, Balgaddy	farmer: yeoman	18-May-07	200	Dc1/76v	466
Browne, Joseph	Dublin, Balgaddie	gentry: gent	11-Feb-05	200	Dc1/56r	347
Browne, Martin	Galway, the county of the town	merchant	08-May-32	300	Dc2/180r	1823
Browne, Michael	Dublin, the city	merchant	02-Dec-30	200	Dc2/157r	1731
Browne, Michael	Dublin, the city	merchant	18-Dec-30	100	Dc2/158r	1735
Browne, Nicholas	Dublin	trade: baker	23-Sep-08	120	Dc1/84r	522
Browne, Nicholas	Dublin, the city	gentry: gent	02-Sep-28	200	Dc2/114v	1537
Browne, Richard	Dublin	merchant	23-Sep-08	120	Dc1/84r	522
Browne, Thomas	Dublin, the city	gentry: esquire	30-Dec-75	400	B.L. 19, 844 f. 81	3209
Browne, Thomas	Cork, the city	gentry: gent	12-May-69	200	B.L. 15, 636 f. 39	3692
Browne, Thomas	Dublin, the city	gentry: esquire	30-Dec-75	400	Dc3/171r	2646
Browne, Thomas	England, London	trade: mercer and citizen	09-Jul-07	704	Dc1/79v	486
Browne, William	Dublin	gentry: knight	20-Oct-06	220	Dc1/70v	427
Bryan, John	Kilkenny, Baunemore	gentry: esquire	21-Nov-34	1400	Dc2/223r	1996
Bryan, Nicholas	Dublin, Howth	trade: fisherman	01-Aug-37	200	Dc2/270r	2212
Buckerton, Anne	Louth, Milltowne	other: widow	14-Jul-80	200	B.L. 15, 637 f. 35	3909
Buckley, Margaret	Meath, Balgin	other: spinster?, daughter/heir of Thomas Buckly	07-Nov-17	120	Dc2/10v	916
Buckridge, Thomas	Dublin, the city	gentry: gent	19-May-60	500	B.L. 15, 635 f. 58a	3368
Buckston, John	England, London, the city	merchant	10-Oct-43	300	B.L. 19, 843 f. 113	2945
Bull, William	Cork, Bandonbridge	gentry: gent	05-Jun-67	3000	B.L. 15, 635 f. 200a	3610
Bunbury, Anna	Wexford, Balseskin	gentry: widow	18-Jul-83	400	B.L. 15, 637 f. 81a	3995
Bunbury, John	Wexford, Newross	gentry: gent	02-May-27	50	Dc2/91v	1429
Bunbury, John	Wexford?	gentry: gent	21-May-36	600	Dc2/252r	2128
Burdon, Bartholomew	Cork, Ballycloghy	gentry: esquire	19-May-70	540	B.L. 15, 636 f. 59	3724
Burges, William	Kilkenny, the city	gentry: gent	11-Feb-61	1000	B.L. 15, 635 f. 70	3384
Burgh, Abigail	Armagh, Drumullie	other: widow	15-Jul-59	320	B.L. 15, 635 f. 52a	3356
Burke, Cecily	Galway, Derrymaclaghna	other: spinster	07-Jul-37	2000	Dc2/267v	2199
Burke, David	Limerick, Kilbeacon	gentry: gent	08-Jul-31	2200	Dc2/166r	1767
Burke, Feagh	Galway, Glynske	gentry: esquire	17-May-14	2000	Dc1/129r	803
Burke, Giles	Galway, Derrymaclaghna		07-Jul-37	2000	Dc2/267v	2199
Burke, Henry	Dublin, the city	gentry: gent	12-May-81	800	B.L. 15, 637 f. 51	3939
Burke, James	Limerick, the city	gentry: gent	28-May-17	600	Dc2/7r	902
Burke, James	Limerick, the city	gentry: esquire	30-Apr-39	4000	B.L. 19, 843 f. 5a	2729
Burke, John	Kildare, Palmerstowne	gentry: gent, exec of Thomas Bourke, Dublin, esq.	29-Jul-65	400	B.L. 15, 635 f. 158a	3534
Burke, John	Galway?	peer: viscount Clonmorris	26-Aug-29	320	Dc2/136r	1636
Burke, John	Mayo, Touskirte	gentry: gent	02-Dec-33	1000	Dc2/202r	1911

Standard	County	Occupation	Date	Amount	MS No	Ident No
Burke, John	Kildare, Pallmerstowne	gentry: gent, exec for Tho Bourke of Dub	29-Jul-65	500	Dc3/12	2248
Burke, Margaret	Limerick?	peer: baroness-dowager Brittas	13-Sep-61	4000	B.L. 15, 635 f. 88a	3413
Burke, Mary	Dublin, the city	gentry: widow	17-Dec-33	200	Dc2/204v	1921
Burke, Oliver	Mayo, Roppacke?	gentry: esquire	25-Jun-22	3000	Dc2/41r	1113
Burke, Oliver	Mayo, Ropagh	gentry: esquire	11-Jun-25	606	Dc2/65v	1292
Burke, Oliver	Mayo, Eneskoerin	gentry: gent	21-May-10	500	Dc1/96v	605
Burke, Oliver	Mayo, Rapagh	gentry: gent	21-May-10	500	Dc1/96v	605
Burke, Thomas	Limerick, Ballingeyle	gentry: gent	10-Apr-39	1000	B.L. 19, 843 f. 4	2726
Burke, Thomas	Mayo, Balloghnaske	gentry: knight	21-May-10	500	Dc1/96v	605
Burke, Thomas	Limerick, the city	gentry: gent	06-Jun-40	4000	B.L. 19, 843 f. 56a	2831
Burke, Ulick	Galway, Downoman	gentry: gent	17-May-14	2000	Dc1/129r	802
Burrowes, Erasmus	Kildare, Grangemellane	gentry: esquire	04-Jul-39	2000	B.L. 19, 843 f. 16a	2751
Burrowes, Erasmus	Kildare, Grangemellon	gentry: esquire	16-May-39	2000	B.L. 19, 843 f. 15a	2749
Burrowes, Erasmus	Kildare, Grangemellane	gentry: esquire	16-May-39	2000	B.L. 19, 843 f. 16	2750
Burrowes, Wingfield	Kildare, Giltowne	gentry: gent	16-May-39	2000	B.L. 19, 843 f. 16	2750
Burrowes, Wingfield	Kildare, Giltowne	gentry: gent	04-Jul-39	2000	B.L. 19, 843 f. 16a	2751
Burrowes, Wingfield	Kildare, Giltowne	gentry: gent	16-May-39	2000	B.L. 19, 843 f. 15a	2749
Burt, Richard	Waterford, Tallon	merchant	01-Oct-74	1000	B.L. 19, 844 f. 37	3161
Burt, Richard	Waterford, Tallon	merchant	03-Nov-74	800	B.L. 19, 844 f. 38	3162
Burt, Richard	Waterford, Tallon	merchant	29-Aug-73	1200	B.L. 19, 844 f. 17	3135
Burton, Samuel	Clare, Buncraggy	gentry: esquire	04-Jul-85	240	B.L. 15, 637 f. 113	4055
Burton, Samuel	Clare, Buncraggy	gentry: esquire	20-Feb-66	500	Dc3/23	2275
Burton, Samuel	Clare, Boncraggie	gentry: esquire	02-Aug-66	600	Dc3/35	2300
Bushen, Philip	Tipperary, Knockgraffin	gentry: gent	02-Jun-36	600	Dc2/253r	2133
Butler, Beckingham	England, Heartford, Tewinge	gentry: esquire	05-Mar-23	4000	Dc2/45v	1146
Butler, Edmund	Kilkenny?	peer: viscount Mountgarret	14-Dec-70	5000	Dc3/133v	2510
Butler, Edward	Carlow, Tullophelim?	gentry: gent	12-Nov-40	240	B.L. 19, 843 f. 71a	2862
Butler, Edward	Carlow, Tullophelim	gentry: esquire	09-Feb-41	1200	B.L. 19, 843 f. 83a	2886
Butler, Edward	Carlow, Tulloe	gentry: esquire	13-Feb-39	240	B.L. 19, 843 f. 51	2820
Butler, Edward	Dublin, the city	gentry: esquire	14-Dec-70	5000	Dc3/133v	2510
Butler, Elizabeth	Kilkenny?	peer: wife of Edmund, viscount Mountgarrett	14-Dec-70	5000	Dc3/133v	2510
Butler, Emily	Kilkenny, the city	gentry: wife of Richard	14-Dec-70	5000	Dc3/133r	2509
Butler, James	Meath?	peer: baron Dunboyne	17-May-09	300	Dc1/88v	554
Butler, James	Meath?	peer: baron Dunboyne	27-Apr-08	500	Dc1/82r	511
Butler, James	Dublin, the city	merchant: merchant-tailor	22-Feb-82	1800	B.L. 15, 637 f. 59	3953
Butler, James	Dublin, Backlane, the city	trade: tailor	04-Jul-85	2000	B.L. 15, 637 f. 113	4056
Butler, James	Wexford, Belabarowe	gentry: esquire	06-May-07	300	Dc1/76r	462
Butler, John	Tipperary, Coulekippe	gentry: esquire	23-Nov-30	46	Dc2/156r	1726
Butler, Pierce	Tipperary, Neillestowne	gentry: esquire	23-May-06	400	Dc1/68r	412

Standard	County	Occupation	Date	Amount	MS No	Ident No
Butler, Pierce	Cork, the city	gentry: gent	28-Mar-67	600	B.L. 15, 635 f. 189	3588
Butler, Pierce	Tipperary, Lysmaluig	gentry: knight	20-May-22	200	Dc2/39v	1104
Butler, Richard	Waterford	gentry: esquire	16-May-29	1000	Dc2/129v	1607
Butler, Richard	Tipperary, Knockltopher	gentry: gent	18-Jun-24	200	Dc2/56v	1227
Butler, Richard	Kilkenny, the city	gentry: esquire	14-Dec-70	5000	Dc3/133r	2509
Butler, Richard	Tipperary, Bansiagh	gentry: knight	16-May-29	1000	Dc2/129r	1606
Butt, Ephra	Cork, Kilcolman	other: widow	21-May-68	100	B.L. 15, 635 f. 227	3659
Butt, Richard	Cork, Carker	gentry: gent	21-May-68	100	B.L. 15, 635 f. 227	3659
Butt, William	Cork, Downraile	gentry: gent	21-May-68	100	B.L. 15, 635 f. 227	3659
Buttle, George	Antrim, Glanarm	gentry: gent	07-Jan-79	560	B.L. 15, 637 f. 8	3862
Buxton, John	England, London	merchant	26-Sep-44	800	B.L. 19, 843 f. 122a	2964
Buxton, John	England, London	merchant	07-Aug-44	140	B.L. 19, 843 f. 116a	2952
Buxton, John	England, London	merchant: and citizen	25-Apr-43	320	B.L. 19, 843 f. 111a	2942
Bye, William	Dublin	trade: tanner	20-Apr-05	320	Dc1/58v	357
Byrne, Arthur	Wicklow, Ballyraunan	gentry: gent	09-Aug-31	120	Dc2/167r	1773
Byrne, Arthur	Wicklow, Kilpedder	gentry: gent	17-Apr-19	100	Dc2/22r	981
Byrne, Barnaby	Meath, Dromgill	gentry: gent	01-May-22	350	Dc2/39v	1102
Byrne, Brian	Roscommon, Mologhneshee	gentry: gent	20-Nov-11	60	Dc1/108v	675
Byrne, Carbery	Roscommon, Carrowmore	gentry: gent?	20-Nov-11	60	Dc1/108v	675
Byrne, Carbery	Roscommon, Carrowemore?	gentry: gent	28-May-13	60	Dc1/121r	752
Byrne, Cormac	Roscommon, Lackan	gentry: gent	20-Nov-11	60	Dc1/108v	674
Byrne, Daniel	Roscommon, Dromebodan	gentry: gent	14-Nov-11	50	Dc1/107v	668
Byrne, Daniel	Dublin, the city	trade: tailor	10-Oct-51	200	B.L. 19, 843 f. 127	2972
Byrne, Daniel	Dublin, the city	trade: tailor	16-Aug-55	1200	B.L. 19, 843 f. 161a	3038
Byrne, Daniel	Dublin, the city	trade: tailor	17-Aug-46	100	B.L. 19, 843 f. 122	2963
Byrne, Daniel	Dublin, the city	trade: tailor	28-Jun-54	200	B.L. 19, 843 f. 143	3000
Byrne, Donal	Roscommon, Cnocknangoowne	farmer: yeoman	15-Nov-11	100	Dc1/108r	671
Byrne, Donough	Roscommon, Downine	gentry: gent	15-Nov-10	50	Dc1/100r	627
Byrne, Donough	Roscommon, Downyn	gentry: esquire	21-Nov-11	60	Dc1/108v	676
Byrne, Donough	Roscommon, Downyn	gentry: gent	14-Nov-11	60	Dc1/107v	670
Byrne, Gillyduff	Roscommon?, Cashell	gentry: gent	20-Nov-11	60	Dc1/108v	674
Byrne, James	Roscommon, Ballaghdowe	farmer: yeoman	15-Nov-11	50	Dc1/108r	672
Byrne, Melaghlin	Roscommon, Clonfadda	gentry: gent	14-Nov-10	50	Dc1/99v	625
Byrne, Patrick	Dublin	gentry: gent	15-May-27	100	Dc2/92v	1433
Byrne, Thady	Roscommon, Ardgallagh	farmer: yeoman	15-Nov-11	50	Dc1/108r	672
Byrne, Tumultagh	Roscommon, Corrala	farmer: yeoman?	15-Nov-11	100	Dc1/108r	671
Byrne, William	Roscommon, Daingrimeghteragh	gentry: gent	13-Nov-11	60	Dc1/107v	669
Byrne, William	Roscommon, Daingrinoghter	gentry: gent	14-Nov-10	50	Dc1/100r	626
Bysse, Christopher	Dublin	gentry: esquire	30-Jun-12	60	Dc1/115	711
Bysse, Christopher	Dublin, the city	gentry: esquire	19-Jun-11	105	Dc1/104v	652
Bysse, John	Dublin	gentry: gent?	02-Sep-22	1240	Dc2/42v	1121

Standard	County	Occupation	Date	Amount	MS No	Ident No
Bysse, Margaret	Dublin	gentry: widow	03-Mar-15	600	Dc1/136r	844
Bysse, Robert	Dublin, the city	gentry: gent	22-May-30	220	Dc2/148r	1691
Bysse, Robert	Dublin, the city	gentry: esquire	18-Nov-16	100	Dc2/2r	877
Bysse, Robert	Dublin, the city	gentry: esquire	11-Jan-17	100	Dc2/3v	887
Bysse, Robert	Dublin, the city	gentry: gent	07-Jun-24	220	Dc2/55v	1220
Bysse, Robert	Dublin	gentry: esquire	01-Oct-16	100	Dc2/1v	874
Bysse, Robert	Dublin	gentry: esquire	09-Dec-16	80	Dc2/3r	882
Bysse, Robert	Dublin	gentry: gent	02-Sep-22	1240	Dc2/42v	1121
Bysse, Robert	Dublin	gentry: esquire	28-Sep-16	80	Dc2/1v	873
Caddell, John	Dublin, Moreton neere Swords	gentry: gent	24-Feb-97	100	Dc1/2r	12
Caddell, John	Dublin, Morton	gentry: gent	23-Mar-97	200	Dc1/2v	16
Caddell, John	Dublin, Mooreton by Swords	gentry: gent	01-Jul-97	200	Dc1/5r	37
Caddell, Patrick	Dublin, Surgostowne	gentry: gent	19-Dec-34	150	Dc2/227r	2013
Caddell, Richard	Wexford, Myddletowne	gentry: gent	27-Jun-21	200	Dc2/36r	1077
Caddell, Richard	Wexford, Middleton	gentry: gent	01-Dec-21	200	Dc2/37r	1085
Caddell, Robert	Dublin, the Moretowne	gentry: gent	28-May-14	400	Dc1/129v	806
Caddell, Robert	Louth, Drogheda	trade: candle maker	01-Sep-40	200	B.L. 19, 843 f. 64a	2848
Cadogan, Henry	Meath, Liscarten	gentry: gent	22-Jun-65	240	Dc3/11	2245
Cadogan, Henry	Meath, Liscarten	gentry: gent	22-Jun-65	560	Dc3/11	2246
Cadogan, Henry	Meath, Liscarten	gentry: gent	22-Jun-65	560	B.L. 15, 636 f. 85a	3771
Canning, George	Londonderry, Agevie	gentry: esquire	03-Apr-37	540	Dc2/261r	2172
Cantwell, William	Tipperary, Mocarke	gentry: esquire	26-Jun-37	400	Dc2/266r	2194
Carbery, John	Dublin	merchant	05-Dec-97	400	Dc1/8r	58
Carbery, John	Dublin, the city		16-Nov-39	600	B.L. 19, 843 f. 32	2782
Carew, Ross	Tipperary, Ballyglissin	gentry: knight	05-Mar-39	400	B.L. 19, 843 f. 20	2758
Carey, George	Dublin?	gentry: knight	30-Oct-04	1000	Dc1/53v	336
Carey, Henry	Dublin?	peer: viscount Falkland	12-Dec-29	400	Dc2/140r	1654
Carey, Patrick	Dublin, the city	gentry: esquire	03-Jun-63	660	B.L. 15, 635 f. 108	3448
Carey, Theophilus	Cork, Burdenstowne	gentry: gent	19-Mar-69	300	B.L. 15, 636 f. 41	3696
Carleton, George	Dublin, the city	gentry: gent	19-Apr-69	1200	Dc3/95	2432
Carleton, George	Dublin, the city	gentry: esquire	19-Apr-69	1200	B.L. 15, 636 f. 37	3687
Carnes, David	Dublin, the city	gentry: esquire	20-Jun-86	2300	B.L. 15, 637 f. 110	4046
Carpenter, Joshua	Dublin, the city	gentry: esquire	01-Aug-39	400	B.L. 19, 843 f. 46a	2811
Carpenter, Margaret	Queen's Co., Tynehinch	gentry: widow	05-Oct-81	600	B.L. 15, 637 f. 50a	3937
Carpenter, Philip	Queen's Co., Tynehinch	gentry: gent	05-Oct-81	700	B.L. 15, 637 f. 50a	3938
Carpenter, Philip	Dublin, the city	gentry: esquire	09-Jun-73	1600	Dc3/156v	2583
Carpenter, Philip	Dublin, the city	gentry: esquire	09-Jul-73	1600	B.L. 15, 636 f. 137	3850
Carr, William	Cork, the city	gentry: esquire	02-Nov-83	330	B.L. 15, 637 f. 85	4001
Carr, William	Cork, Charlevill	gentry: esquire	20-Dec-65	1000	B.L. 15, 635 f. 163	3541
Carr, William	Cork, Charleville	gentry: esquire	20-Dec-65	1000	Dc3/18	2262
Carr, William	Cork, the city	gentry: esquire	02-Nov-83	800	B.L. 15, 637 f. 85a	4002
Carrick, Simon	Dublin, the city	merchant	20-Jul-66	1000	Dc3/34	2299

Standard	County	Occupation	Date	Amount	MS No	Ident No
Carrick, Simon	Dublin, the city	merchant	18-May-67	500	B.L. 15, 635 f. 191a	3593
Carrick, Simon	Dublin, the city	merchant	20-Jul-66	1000	B.L. 15, 635 f. 176	3561
Carrick, Simon	Dublin, the city	merchant	18-May-67	500	Dc3/61	2355
Carrick, Simon	Dublin, the city	merchant	24-Feb-70	300	Dc3/116	2472
Carrig, William	Kerry, Glandyn	gentry: esquire	06-Sep-78	800	B.L. 15, 637 f. 10a	3866
Carroll, James	Dublin, Ffinglas	gentry: knight	11-Mar-14	2500	Dc1/128r	794
Carroll, James	Dublin	gentry: gent	14-Dec-05	500	Dc1/64r	387
Carroll, James	Dublin	gentry: gent	17-Feb-01	600	Dc1/29r	192
Carroll, Joan	Dublin, the city	other: widow	11-Nov-20	200	Dc2/32v	1049
Carroll, John		gentry: knight	12-Mar-11	1200	Dc1/105r	657
Carroll, Sarah	Dublin	other: spinster	05-Mar-34	200	Dc2/208v	1939
Carroll, Thomas	Dublin		14-Jun-10	40	Dc1/97r	611
Carroll, Thomas	Dublin	merchant	13-Feb-07	800	Dc1/74v	452
Carroll, Thomas	Dublin	merchant	27-Jul-07	300	Dc1/79ar check	488
Carroll, Thomas	Dublin		31-Aug-13	200	Dc1/123r	765
Carroll, Thomas	Dublin	trade: tailor	17-Oct-00	200	Dc1/26v	177
Carroll, Thomas	Dublin		24-Jul-13	200	Dc1/123r	764
Carteret, Francis	Wexford, late of Careclough	gentry: esquire	31-May-58	2000	B.L. 15, 635 f. 29a	3314
Cashell, John	Louth, Dundalk	merchant	20-Nov-02	300	Dc1/40v	261
Cashell, Oliver	Louth, Dundalk	gentry: gent	31-Jul-34	210	Dc2/216r	1968
Cashell, Oliver	Louth, Dundalk	gentry: gent	05-Jul-36	2000	Dc2/254v	2141
Cashell, Thomas	Dublin	gentry: gent	13-Feb-26	230	Dc2/74r	1343
Cashell, Thomas	Dublin, the city	gentry: esquire	29-May-28	200	Dc2/110v	1515
Cashell, Thomas	Dublin	gentry: esquire	02-Jul-27	310	Dc2/96r	1448
Cashell, Thomas	Dublin	gentry: gent	14-Nov-27	120	Dc2/99v	1462
Cashell, Thomas	Dublin	gentry: gent	12-Mar-25	600	Dc2/63r	1276
Cashell, Thomas	Dublin	gentry: esquire	16-May-28	200	Dc2/108v	1507
Cashell, William	Meath, Walterston	farmer: yeoman	17-May-32	200	Dc2/181r	1828
Castleton, John	Dublin, the city		08-Jun-84	90	B.L. 15, 637 f. 88a	4006
Castleton, John	Dublin, the city		12-Nov-84	1200	B.L. 15, 637 f. 94a	4018
Castleton, John	Dublin, the city		13-Feb-83	1000	B.L. 15, 637 f. 70	3973
Castleton, John	Dublin, the city	merchant	27-Nov-75	1200	B.L. 19, 844 f. 80	3208
Castleton, John	Dublin, the city	trade: ironmonger	21-Mar-78	200	Dc3/187v	2709
Castleton, John	Dublin, the city		21-May-78	2000	Dc3/188av	2713
Castleton, John	Dublin, the city	merchant	09-Mar-75	680	Dc3/166r	2630
Castleton, John	Dublin, the city	merchant	09-Mar-75	680	B.L. 19, 844 f. 57	3181
Castleton, John	Dublin, the city		06-Mar-80	1800	B.L. 15, 637 f. 31	3903
Castleton, John	Dublin, the city		21-May-78	2000	B.L. 19, 844 f. 153	3284
Castleton, John	Dublin, the city		19-Dec-83	2400	B.L. 15, 637 f. 82	3996
Castleton, John	Dublin, the city		29-Jun-82	1200	B.L. 15, 637 f. 61a	3958
Castleton, John	Dublin, the city	merchant	27-Nov-75	1200	Dc3/170r	2643
Castleton, John	Dublin, the city	trade: ironmonger	21-Mar-78	200	B.L. 19, 844 f. 152	3283
Castleton, Nathaniel	Dublin, the city	gentry: gent	22-Jun-76	1000	Dc3/178r	2669
Castleton, Nathaniel	Dublin, the city	gentry: gent	22-Jun-76	1000	B.L. 19, 844 f.106	3233

Standard	County	Occupation	Date	Amount	MS No	Ident No
Cathcart, Adam	Fermanagh, Cenchill	gentry: gent	05-Dec-34	1000	Dc2/225r	2005
Caulfield, Mary	Armagh?	peer: baroness-dowager Charlemont	20-Nov-59	2000	B.L. 15, 635 f. 54	3359
Caulfield, William	Armagh?	peer: viscount Charlemont	11-Mar-69	1600	B.L. 15, 636 f. 29	3676
Caulfield, William	Armagh?	peer: baron Charlemont	30-May-36	3000	Dc2/252v	2131
Caulfield, William	Armagh?	peer: viscount Charlemont	11-Mar-69	1600	Dc3/93	2429
Caulfield, William	Armagh?	peer: baron Charlemont	04-Dec-35	700	Dc2/241r	2077
Caulfield, William	Armagh?	peer: baron Charlemont	17-Jun-35	1200	Dc2/236v	2055
Caulfield, William	Armagh?	peer: baron Charlemont	17-Nov-34	800	Dc2/221v	1990
Cawell, John	Dublin, the city	merchant	14-Sep-14	80	Dc1/131v	818
Challoner, Margaret	Dublin	other: widow	15-Jun-11	320	Dc1/104r	651
Chamberlain, John	Dublin, the city	merchant	29-Nov-21	160	Dc2/37r	1082
Chamberlain, Michael	Dublin		27-Nov-06	500	Dc1/72r	438
Chamberlain, Michael	Dublin		13-Sep-09	126	Dc1/91v	572
Chamberlain, Michael	Dublin, the city	gentry: gent	09-Jun-68	300	Dc3/78	2402
Chamberlain, Michael	Dublin, the city	gentry: esquire	27-Feb-75	400	Dc3/165v	2626
Chamberlain, Michael	Dublin, the city	gentry: esquire	17-Feb-75	200	B.L. 19, 844 f. 52	3176
Chamberlain, Michael	Dublin		12-Aug-09	600	Dc1/91r	569
Chamberlain, Michael	Dublin, the city	gentry: esquire	27-Feb-75	400	B.L. 19, 844 f. 54	3178
Chamberlain, Michael	Dublin, the city	gentry: esquire	15-Feb-75	400	B.L. 19, 844 f. 53	3177
Chamberlain, Michael	Louth, Drogheda	merchant?: son/heir of Stephen, merchant	27-Nov-06	500	Dc1/72r	438
Chamberlain, Michael	Dublin, the city	gentry: esquire	15-Feb-75	400	Dc3/164v	2622
Chamberlain, Michael	Dublin, the city	gentry: esquire	17-Feb-75	200	Dc3/164v	2623
Chamberlain, Michael	Dublin		24-Dec-03	2508	Dc1/51r	326
Chamberlain, Michael	Dublin, the city	gentry: esquire	07-Jul-83	600	B.L. 15, 637 f. 76a	3986
Chamberlain, Michael	Dublin, the city	gentry: gent	09-Jun-68	300	B.L. 15, 635 f. 219	3643
Chamberlain, Michael	Dublin, the city	gentry: esquire	03-Dec-81	2000	B.L. 15, 637 f. 53	3941
Chamberlain, Michael	Dublin		11-Aug-03	400	Dc1/48v	313
Chamberlain, Michael	Dublin		06-Sep-02	200	Dc1/39v	256
Chamberlain, Nigel	Dublin		10-Feb-97	50	Dc1/1v	5
Chamberlain, Richard	Dublin, Kilreske	gentry: genty	19-Apr-05	400	Dc1/57v	352
Chamberlain, Robert	Dublin	merchant	20-Feb-98	120	Dc1/9v	68
Chambre, Calcott	Wicklow, Carnow	gentry: esquire	07-Dec-33	3000	Dc2/202v	1914
Chambre, Robert	Dublin, the city		25-May-76	700	Dc3/175r	2659
Chambre, Thomas	Louth, Stermonstowne		25-May-76	700	Dc3/175r	2659
Champion, Arthur	Fermanagh, Shancocke	gentry: esquire	21-Jun-39	400	B.L. 19, 843 f. 14a	2747
Champion, Arthur	Dublin, Christchurch yard	merchant	24-Feb-36	2000	Dc2/245v	2098
Cheadle, Judith	Dublin, the city	other: widow	20-Oct-57	600	B.L. 19, 843 f. 202	3110
Cheevers, Bartholomew	Louth, Drogheda	merchant	18-Aug-40	400	B.L. 19, 843 f. 66a	2852
Cheevers, John	Dublin	merchant	15-Nov-18	110	Dc2/17r	954
Cheevers, Nicholas	Meath, Gerraldston	gentry: gent	02-Mar-01	2000	Dc1/29r	194
Cheevers, Patrick	Louth, Drogheda	merchant	18-Aug-40	400	B.L. 19, 843 f. 66a	2852

Standard	County	Occupation	Date	Amount	MS No	Ident No
Cheevers, Thomas	Louth, Drogheda	merchant	30-Aug-39	200	B.L. 19, 843 f. 36a	2791
Chichester, Arthur	Tyrone, Dungannon	gentry: esquire	15-Dec-53	2000	B.L. 19, 843 f. 135a	2985
Chichester, Arthur	Donegal?	gentry: knight	02-Mar-08	2000	Dc1/81v	504
Chichester, Arthur		gentry: knight	22-May-06	600	Dc1/68r	410
Chichester, Arthur	Antrim?	peer: viscount Chichester	02-Jan-56	6000	B.L. 19, 843 f. 164	3042
Chillam, Christopher	Louth, Drogheda	merchant	11-May-19	100	Dc2/23v	991
Chillam, Christopher	Louth, Drogheda	merchant	20-May-17	50	Dc2/7r	901
Chillam, Christopher	Louth, Drogheda	merchant	27-Sep-20	120	Dc2/32v	1046
Chillam, Patrick	Louth, Drogheda	merchant	26-Jun-40	400	B.L. 19, 843 f. 59	2836
Chillam, Robert	Meath, Gafnie	gentry: gent	01-Mar-32	600	Dc2/177r	1812
Choppin, Robert	Sligo, Cottlestowne	gentry: esquire	12-Oct-66	4000	Dc3/39	2313
Choppin, Robert	Sligo, Cottlestowne	gentry: esquire	15-Jan-72	6000	B.L. 15, 636 f. 95	3787
Choppin, Robert	Sligo, Ballincottle	gentry: gent	22-Mar-66	600	Dc3/26	2281
Choppin, Robert	Sligo, Cottlestowne	gentry: esquire	15-Jan-72	6000	Dc3/143v	2542
Choppin, Robert	Sligo, Cottlestowne	gentry: esquire	03-Aug-69	700	Dc3/102	2445
Clanchy, John	Limerick, the city	merchant	09-Nov-41	1124	B.L. 15, 635 f. 140	3501
Clapham, George	Dublin, the city	gentry: gent	13-Feb-60	200	B.L. 15, 635 f. 57a	3366
Clapham, George	Dublin, the city	gentry: gent	16-Jul-59	200	B.L. 15, 635 f. 50	3351
Clapham, George	Dublin, the city	gentry: gent	29-Jul-59	200	B.L. 15, 635 f. 50a	3352
Clapham, George	Dublin, the city	gentry: gent	13-Feb-60	200	B.L. 15, 635 f. 57	3365
Clare, Robert	England, London	merchant	30-Jun-97	140	Dc1/5v	38
Clare, Robert	Dublin	gentry: gent	12-May-05	120	Dc1/59r	361
Clare, Robert	Queen's Co., Colbanno	gentry: gent	30-Jun-10	120	Dc1/99r	620
Claridge, Samuel	Dublin, the city	merchant	19-Jun-77	700	B.L. 19, 844 f. 134	3264
Claridge, Samuel	Dublin, the city	merchant	19-Jun-77	700	Dc3/182v	2690
Claridge, Samuel	Dublin, the city	merchant	23-Jan-77	300	Dc3/181v	2682
Claridge, Samuel	Dublin, the city	merchant	23-Jan-77	300	B.L. 19, 844 f. 115	3244
Clarke, Andrew	Dublin, the city	merchant	08-Feb-25	200	Dc2/61v	1263
Clarke, Andrew	Dublin, the city	merchant	22-Jun-26	200	Dc2/79v	1376
Clarke, Andrew	Dublin, the city	merchant	12-Jul-23	200	Dc2/49v	1174
Clarke, Andrew	Dublin, the city	merchant	18-Jun-24	200	Dc2/56v	1226
Clarke, Andrew	Dublin, the city	merchant	05-Jun-24	500	Dc2/55v	1218
Clarke, George	Dublin?	merchant	15-Dec-34	100	Dc2/226r	2010
Clarke, George	Dublin, the city	merchant	21-Nov-25	400	Dc2/70r	1321
Clarke, George	Dublin, the city	merchant	04-Dec-34	400	Dc2/224v	2004
Clarke, George	Dublin, the city	merchant	15-May-35	200	Dc2/235v	2050
Clarke, George	Dublin, the city	merchant	22-Dec-36	600	Dc2/259v	2165
Clarke, James	England, Surrey, Monlsey	gentry: esquire	06-Nov-58	900	B.L. 15, 635 f. 33a	3322
Clarke, John	Dublin, the bay	gentry: gent	18-Jun-36	100	Dc2/253v	2135
Clarke, John	England, Essex, Netswell	gentry: esquire	18-Jul-61	1248	B.L. 15, 635 f. 77a	3396
Clarke, Simon	Dublin, Tirrelston	farmer: yeoman	23-Mar-00	200	Dc1/22r	148
Clarke, Simon	Dublin	gentry: gent	19-Nov-31	500	Dc2/170v	1787
Clarke, Simon	Dublin, Terrelston	gentry: gent	17-Jul-99	200	Dc1/18r	122
Clarke, Simon	Dublin?, Torrelston	gentry: gent	01-May-97	120	Dc1/3v	22
Clarke, Simon	Meath, Terrelston	farmer: yeoman	06-Nov-98	200	Dc1/12v	91

Standard	County	Occupation	Date	Amount	MS No	Ident No
Clarke, Thomas	Dublin	merchant	01-May-18	60	Dc2/14v	941
Clarke, Thomas	Dublin, the city	merchant	25-Jun-22	3000	Dc2/41r	1113
Clayton, Dorothy	Cork, Courtmacsherrey	other: widow	27-Apr-82	1600	B.L. 15, 637 f. 57a	3950
Clayton, Robert	England, London	gentry: gent	02-Aug-65	680	B.L. 15, 635 f. 157a	3532
Clear, Patrick	Dublin	merchant	08-Jun-13	60	Dc1/121v	756
Clifford, Knight	Dublin, the city	gentry: gent	09-Dec-76	300	Dc3/181r	2678
Clinch, William	Dublin, Loughtowne	gentry: gent	27-Jan-65	2000	Dc3/1	2223
Clinch, William	Dublin, Loughtowne	gentry: gent	27-Jan-65	2000	B.L. 15, 635 f. 214	3633
Clint, Littleton	England, Knightwith, Wuster	gentry: esquire	27-Jan-77	6000	B.L. 19, 844 f. 128	3257
Clint, Littleton	England, Woster Kintwick	gentry: esquire	27-Jan-77	6000	Dc3/181v	2684
Clinton, Nicholas	Dublin	merchant	20-Jun-03	400	Dc1/47v	301
Clinton, Richard	Dublin	merchant	20-Jul-00	100	Dc1/25r	169
Cloone, Robert	Dublin, the city	trade: tallow chandler	20-Jun-21	200	Dc2/36r	1075
Cloone, Robert	Dublin, the city	trade: tallow chandler	29-Jun-22	600	Dc2/41v	1115
Cloone, Robert	Dublin, the city	trade: tallow chandler	15-May-26	400	Dc2/77r	1363
Clotworthy, John	Antrim?	peer: viscount Massereene	13-Dec-66	280	Dc3/48	2325
Clotworthy, Mary	Londonderry, Muigmore	other: widow, of James	11-Sep-60	400	B.L. 15, 635 f. 59	3369
Clyball, John	England, London	trade: leather-seller and citizen	09-Sep-19	1332	Dc2/25v	1001
Codington, William	Dublin, Holme Patricke	gentry: esquire	05-Dec-56	1000	B.L. 19, 843 f. 188	3083
Codington, William	Dublin, Holme Patrick	gentry: esquire	25-Sep-56	300	B.L. 19, 843 f. 188a	3084
Codington, William	Dublin, Holme Patricke	gentry: esquire	03-Jul-57	500	B.L. 19, 843 f. 194	3095
Colclough, Thomas	Wexford, Tinterne	gentry: knight	23-May-09	400	Dc1/89v	558
Cole, John	Dublin, Newland	gentry: baronet	17-Feb-71	420	Dc3/136r	2517
Cole, John	Dublin, Nuland	gentry: knight and baronet	28-Feb-63	240	B.L. 15, 635 f. 105	3442
Cole, John	Dublin, Newland	gentry: baronet	07-Oct-70	3000	Dc3/check	2494
Cole, Michael	Dublin, the city	merchant	10-May-67	500	B.L. 15, 635 f. 192	3594
Cole, Michael	Dublin, the city	merchant	30-Mar-82	900	B.L. 15, 637 f. 62	3959
Cole, Michael	Dublin, the city	merchant	10-May-67	500	Dc3/60	2354
Coleman, Robert	Meath	farmer	06-Feb-08	100	Dc1/81r	502
Colley, Gerard	Dublin, the city	trade: apothecary	30-Aug-71	200	Dc3/140r	2530
Collins, John	Dublin, the city	gentry: gent	04-Jun-59	2100	B.L. 15, 635 f. 48	3348
Collins, John	Dublin	gentry: gent	05-Apr-59	2100	B.L. 15, 635 f. 41a	3337
Colthurst, John	Cork, Coolintuburidd	gentry: gent	16-Dec-67	560	B.L. 15, 635 f. 214a	3634
Colthurst, John	Cork, Conlintubber	gentry: gent	22-Jun-68	2000	B.L. 15, 635 f. 225a	3656
Colthurst, John	Cork, Coolitubrid	gentry: gent	13-Jun-70	2000	B.L. 15, 636 f. 65	3733
Colthurst, John	Cork, Ballyally	gentry: esquire	02-Jun-85	1240	B.L. 15, 637 f. 98a	4026
Colum, Hugh	Antrim, Glanarm	gentry: gent	07-Jan-79	560	B.L. 15, 637 f. 8	3862
Colvill, Alexander	Antrim, Gallgorme	prof: doctor of theology	20-Nov-66	600	B.L. 15, 635 f. 183a	3577
Colvill, Alexander	Antrim, Gallgorme	prof: doctor of theology	28-Mar-65	30	B.L. 15, 635 f. 150a	3520
Colvill, Alexander	Antrim, Galgorme	prof: doctor of theology	20-Feb-55	2400	B.L. 19, 843 f. 161	3037
Colvill, Alexander	Antrim, Golgorme	prof: doctor of theology	17-May-55	2240	B.L. 19, 843 f. 160a	3036

Standard	County	Occupation	Date	Amount	MS No	Ident No
Colvill, Alexander	Antrim, Gallgorme	prof: doctor of theology	08-Apr-63	600	B.L. 15, 636 f. 82a	3765
Colvill, Alexander	Antrim, Galgorme	prof: doctor of theology	29-Apr-55	1000	B.L. 19, 843 f. 160	3035
Colvill, Alexander	Antrim, Gallgorme	prof: doctor of theology	21-Mar-65	315	B.L. 15, 635 f. 151	3521
Colvill, Alexander	Antrim, Gallgorme	prof: doctor of theology	02-Nov-65	200	B.L. 15, 636 f. 83a	3767
Colvill, Alexander	Antrim, Gallgorme	prof: doctor of theology	18-Sep-66	600	B.L. 15, 635 f. 178a	3566
Colvill, Alexander	Antrim, Gallgorme	prof: doctor of theology	21-Jun-64	840	B.L. 15, 636 f. 83	3766
Colvill, Robert	Antrim, Gallgorme	gentry: esquire	10-Apr-73	1300	B.L. 19, 844 f. 1	3120
Colvill, Robert	Antrim, Galtgorme	gentry: esquire	28-Feb-63	1200	B.L. 15, 635 f. 101a	3437
Colvill, Robert	Antrim, Golt Gorme	gentry: esquire	14-Jun-76	5200	Dc3/176ar	2665
Colvill, Robert	Antrim, MountColvill	gentry: esquire	22-Nov-75	10640	B.L. 19, 844 f. 75	3203
Colvill, Robert	Antrim, MountColvill	gentry: esquire	30-Nov-75	1870	B.L. 19, 844 f. 78	3206
Colvill, Robert	Antrim, Mountcolvill	gentry: esquire	30-Nov-75	1870	Dc3/170v	2645
Colvill, Robert	Antrim, Gallgorme	gentry: esquire	25-Aug-74	2000	B.L. 19, 844 f. 34	3158
Colvill, Robert	Antrim, Gillgorme	gentry: esquire	25-Nov-65	1500	Dc3/16	2257
Colvill, Robert	Antrim, Galgorme	gentry: esquire	14-Jun-76	5200	B.L. 19, 844 f. 98	3225
Colvill, Robert	Antrim, Mountcolvill	gentry: esquire	22-Nov-75	10640	Dc3/169r	2641
Colvill, Robert	Antrim, Gilgorme	gentry: esquire	25-Nov-65	1500	B.L. 15, 635 f. 159a	3536
Colvill, Robert	Antrim, Galgorme	gentry: esquire	20-Aug-74	600	B.L. 19, 844 f. 32	3156
Colvill, Robert	Antrim, Galgorme	gentry: knight	12-Apr-80	350	B.L. 15, 637 f. 32	3905
Colvill, Robert	Antrim, Gallgorme	gentry: esquire	11-Oct-66	85	B.L. 15, 635 f. 178	3565
Colvill, Robert	Antrim, Gallgorme	gentry: esquire	19-Aug-74	880	B.L. 19, 844 f. 31	3154
Colvill, Robert	Antrim, Galgorme	gentry: esquire	03-Apr-74	612	B.L. 19, 844 f. 23	3144
Colvill, Robert	Antrim, Mountcolvill	gentry: esquire	27-Nov-75	3000	B.L. 19, 844 f. 82	3210
Colvill, Robert	Down, Newtowne	gentry: knight	27-Nov-79	10000	B.L. 15, 637 f. 24a	3890
Colvill, Robert	Antrim, Mountcolvill	gentry: esquire	27-Nov-75	3000	Dc3/170v	2644
Coman, John	Westmeath, Athlone	merchant	25-Jun-22	3000	Dc2/41r	1113
Comer?, Andrew	Limerick	merchant	18-Jun-10	120	Dc1/97v	614
Comerford, George	Carlow, Wells	gentry: esquire	28-Nov-28	300	Dc2/118r	1554
Comerford, Richard	Tipperary, Crompuscashell?	gentry: gent	19-May-06	150	Dc1/67v	409
Conly, Patrick	Dublin, city	merchant	26-Apr-05	1200	Dc1/60v	368
Connelly, Lucas	Louth, Drogheda	merchant	09-Jul-84	700	B.L. 15, 637 f. 94	4017
Connery, Owen	Tyrone, Gortin	gentry: gent	26-Feb-34	200	Dc2/207v	1935
Connigan, William	Dublin	gentry: gent	25-Aug-27	120	Dc2/98v	1457
Conran, Alison	Dublin	other: widow	01-Feb-06	130	Dc1/65r	391
Conran, Bartholomew	Dublin	trade: tailor	01-Dec-19	120	Dc2/26v	1007
Conran, Philip	Dublin		03-Jun-03	500	Dc1/47r	299
Conran, Philip	Dublin		01-Jul-09	40	Dc1/89v	561
Conran, Philip	Dublin		08-Feb-12	86	Dc1/112r	694
Conran, Philip	Dublin		01-Dec-08	60	Dc1/85r	532
Conran, Philip	Dublin		12-Feb-11	400	Dc1/102v	642
Conran, Philip	Dublin		26-Apr-08	105	Dc1/82r	510
Conran, Philip	Dublin		10-May-03	520	Dc1/47r	298
Conran, Philip	Dublin		11-May-13	60	Dc1/120v	749
Conran, Philip	Dublin		10-Feb-12	60	Dc1/112r	696

Standard	County	Occupation	Date	Amount	MS No	Ident No
Conran, Philip	Dublin		24-Nov-00	100	Dc1/26v	179
Conran, Philip	Dublin		29-Jul-09	120	Dc1/90v	568
Conran, Philip	Dublin		11-May-08	70	Dc1/82v	512
Conran, Philip	Dublin		04-Feb-06	1200	Dc1/65r	392
Conran, Philip	Dublin, the city	merchant	04-Nov-25	332	Dc2/69v	1316
Conran, Philip	Dublin, the city	merchant	24-May-37	300	Dc2/264r	2185
Conran, Philip	Dublin		31-Jul-02	120	Dc1/39r	253
Conran, Philip	Dublin		28-Aug-02	120	Dc1/39v	255
Conran, Philip	Dublin		25-Nov-97	400	Dc1/7r	52
Conran, Philip	Dublin		03-Feb-03	100	Dc1/44r	279
Conran, Philip	Dublin		28-Sep-09	300	Dc1/91v	574
Conran, Thomas	Dublin, Wyanston?	gentry: gent	24-Nov-13	160	Dc1/124v	772
Conroy, Laughlin	Roscommon, Clonshy	gentry: gent	21-Nov-11	60	Dc1/109r	677
Conway, Henry	Dublin	gentry: gent	22-Nov-13	200	Dc1/124r	771
Cooke, Ann	Dublin	gentry: widow, wife of Sir Richard Cooke	01-Apr-17	280	Dc2/6r	899
Cooke, Arthur	Meath, Dunshaghlen		31-Oct-08	120	Dc1/84r	525
Cooke, Arthur	Dublin	prof: physician	12-May-99	1000	Dc1/16v	112
Cooke, Arthur	Dublin	prof: physician	15-Nov-99	1000	Dc1/19v	134
Cooke, Arthur	Dublin	prof: physician	18-Jun-99	200	Dc1/17v	119
Cooke, Arthur	Dublin	prof: physician?	18-May-97	666	Dc1/3v	23
Cooke, Arthur	Dublin	prof: physician?	02-Jul-99	200	Dc1/18r	123
Cooke, Benjamin	Dublin, the city	merchant	31-Jul-76	2000	Dc3/179v	2674
Cooke, John	Westmeath, Culletore	gentry: esquire	25-May-66	1000	Dc3/29	2288
Cooke, John	Dublin, the city	gentry: gent	08-Dec-57	106	B.L. 19, 843 f. 203	3112
Cooke, Thomas	Dublin, the city	merchant	31-Jul-76	2000	Dc3/179v	2674
Cooke, Thomas	Dublin, the city	merchant	14-Sep-66	400	Dc3/38	2310
Cooke, William	Wexford, Tomeduffe	gentry: gent	06-Dec-34	2000	Dc2/225r	2006
Cooke, William	Dublin	gentry: gent	11-Aug-37	1200	Dc2/270r	2213
Cooley, Henry	Kildare, Castel Carbry	gentry: knight	19-Dec-18	240	Dc2/19v	968
Cooley, Patrick	Dublin	merchant	12-Feb-03	200	Dc1/45r	285
Cooley, Patrick	Dublin	merchant	03-May-05	80	Dc1/58r	354
Cooley, Patrick	Dublin	merchant	17-Apr-06	1000	Dc1/66v	402
Cooley, Patrick	Dublin	merchant	08-Dec-02	40	Dc1/41v	268
Cooley, Patrick	Dublin	merchant	21-May-02	500	Dc1/38r	245
Coote, Charles	Roscommon, Castlecoote	gentry: knight and baronet	20-Apr-54	200	B.L. 19, 843 f. 137a	2989
Coote, Charles	Queen's Co., Castlecuffe	gentry: knight and baronet	19-Dec-34	600	Dc2/227r	2014
Coote, Charles	Roscommon, Castlecoote	gentry: knight and baronet	04-Aug-53	4000	B.L. 19, 843 f. 135	2984
Coote, Chidley	Dublin, Killester	gentry: esquire	29-Nov-65	390	Dc3/16	2258
Coote, Chidley	Dublin, Killester	gentry: esquire	20-Mar-55	210	B.L. 19, 843 f. 155	3024
Coote, Chidley	England, Essex, Lanham	gentry: esquire	08-Feb-53	2600	B.L. 19, 843 f. 129a	2976
Coote, Chidley	England, Essex, Lanham	gentry: esquire	13-Apr-53	400	B.L. 19, 843 f. 132	2979

Standard	County	Occupation	Date	Amount	MS No	Ident No
Coote, Chidley	Dublin, Killester	gentry: esquire	08-Dec-54	400	B.L. 19, 843 f. 147a	3009
Coote, Chidley	Dublin, Killester	gentry: esquire	06-Oct-54	660	B.L. 19, 843 f. 145a	3005
Coote, Chidley	Dublin, Killester	gentry: esquire	26-Oct-54	660	B.L. 19, 843 f. 145	3004
Coote, Chidley	Dublin, Killester	gentry: esquire	04-Oct-54	400	B.L. 19, 843 f. 144a	3003
Coote, Chidley	England, Essex, Lanham	gentry: esquire	08-Feb-53	1400	B.L. 19, 843 f. 129	2975
Coote, Chidley	Dublin, Killester	gentry: esquire	22-May-67	431	Dc3/61	2356
Coote, Chidley	Dublin, Killester	gentry: esquire	29-Nov-65	390	B.L. 15, 635 f. 160	3537
Coote, Chidley	Limerick, Kilmallock	gentry: esquire	06-Sep-78	460	B.L. 15, 637 f.10	3865
Coote, Chidley	Dublin, Killester	gentry: esquire	22-May-67	431·	B.L. 15, 635 f. 194	3598
Coote, Chidley	Dublin, Killester	gentry: esquire	10-Nov-68	600	Dc3/83	2411
Cope, Darkes	Armagh, Ballerath?	gentry: d of Ant Cope of Balrath, esquire	24-May-33	400	Dc2/194v	1881
Cope, Mary	Armagh, Ballerath	gentry: spinster?, daughter of Anthony	16-May-33	400	Dc2/193v	1877
Cope, Richard	Wexford, Banbery	gentry: esquire	17-Aug-16	400	Dc2/0v	868
Cope, Richard	England, Oxford, Bambery	gentry: esquire	15-Jun-18	600	Dc2/15r	942
Coppinger, Thomas	Cork, the city	gentry: gent	26-Oct-36	2440	B.L. 19, 843 f. 42a	2803
Coppinger, Thomas	Dublin, the city	gentry: gent	23-Jul-36	270	B.L. 19, 843 f. 41a	2801
Coppinger, Thomas	Dublin, the city	gentry: gent	23-Jul-36	800	B.L. 19, 843 f. 42	2802
Corbally, John	Dublin	merchant	23-Oct-12	250	Dc1/115v	719
Corbally, Patrick	Dublin, Cottrelston	farmer	16-May-07	20	Dc1/76v	465
Corker, Edward	Dublin, the city	gentry: gent	03-Mar-69	1200	Dc3/92	2427
Corker, Edward	Dublin, the city	gentry: esquire	12-Dec-74	1300	Dc3/163v	2619
Corker, Edward	Dublin, the city	gentry: gent	11-Mar-67	1100	B.L. 15, 635 f. 203	3615
Corker, Edward	Dublin, the city	gentry: gent	14-Mar-67	1320	B.L. 15, 635 f. 203a	3616
Corker, Edward	Dublin, the city	gentry: gent	16-Mar-67	7800	Dc3/57	2347
Corker, Edward	Dublin, the city	gentry: esquire	12-Dec-74	1300	B.L. 19, 844 f. 58a	3183
Corker, Edward	Dublin, the city	gentry: gent	14-Mar-67	1320	Dc3/57	2346
Corker, Edward	Dublin, the city	gentry: gent	11-Mar-67	2100	Dc3/56	2345
Corker, Edward	Dublin	gentry: gent	03-Mar-69	1200	B.L. 15, 636 f. 38	3690
Corkin, Mathew	Londonderry	gentry: esquire	12-Feb-86	1000	B.L. 15, 637 f. 107	4041
Corkin, Mathew	Londonderry	gentry: esquire	13-Feb-86	1000	B.L. 15, 637 f. 106a	4040
Cotter, James	Cork, Ballinsperry	gentry: esquire	09-Jun-76	1100	B.L. 19, 844 f. 99	3226
Cottingham, James	Dublin, Skinner Row	trade: goldsmith	04-Dec-71	400	Dc3/142v	2539
Cottington, Nicholas	Dublin, Holmepatrick	gentry: esquire	30-May-66	500	Dc3/30	2290
Cottrell, John	Dublin	gentry: esquire	05-Mar-10	120	Dc1/94v	592
Coughlan, Terence	Dublin	gentry: gent	26-Nov-27	160	Dc2/100v	1467
Coughlan, Terence	Dublin	gentry: gent	20-Dec-25	300	Dc2/72v	1336
Coughlan, Terence	Dublin	gentry: gent	09-Dec-25	100	Dc2/72r	1331
Coughlan, Terence	Dublin	gentry: gent	12-Dec-26	500	Dc2/86r	1408
Coughlan, Terence	Dublin	gentry: gent	12-Dec-26	500	Dc2/86v	1409
Courthop, Peter	Cork, Wallingstowne	gentry: knight	02-May-73	2600	Dc3/155v	2581
Courthop, Peter	Cork, Courtstowne	gentry: esquire	16-May-57	1200	B.L. 19, 843 f. 198	3103
Courthop, Peter	Cork, Wallinstowne	gentry: knight	02-May-73	2600	B.L. 15, 636 f. 129	3837
Cowell, Robert	Down, Lesduffe	gentry: esquire	25-Nov-14	60	Dc1/133r	827

Standard	County	Occupation	Date	Amount	MS No	Ident No
Cox, Richard	Dublin, the city	gentry: esquire	09-Nov-77	500	Dc3/183v	2696
Cox, Richard	Dublin, the city	gentry: esquire	01-May-78	1350	Dc3/188ar	2712
Cox, Richard	Cork, Bandonbridge	gentry: esquire	05-Aug-75	660	B.L. 19, 844 f. 70	3198
Cox, Richard	Dublin, the city	gentry: esquire	01-May-78	1350	Dc3/188v	2711
Cox, Richard	Dublin, the city	gentry: esquire	09-Nov-79	500	B.L. 15, 637 f. 29	3899
Cox, Richard	Dublin, the city	gentry: esquire	01-May-78	1350	B.L. 15, 637 f. 29a	3900
Cox, Richard	Cork, the city	gentry: esquire	25-Jun-83	800	B.L. 15, 637 f. 79a	3992
Cox, Richard	Dublin, the city	gentry: esquire	01-May-78	1350	B.L. 15, 637 f. 30	3901
Cox, Richard	Cork, Clonakilty	gentry: esquire	15-Jan-80	480	B.L. 15, 637 f. 26a	3894
Coyle, Simon	Dublin, the city	gentry: gent	17-Jun-31	200	Dc2/165r	1763
Coyle, Simon	Dublin	gentry: gent	09-Dec-35	240	Dc2/241v	2080
Crafton, William	Dublin, the city	gentry: esquire	25-Apr-23	660	Dc2/46v	1151
Crawford, John		prof: dean of Emile	05-Dec-34	1000	Dc2/225r	2005
Creagh, Peter	Limerick, the city	other: son of Andrew, alderman	02-May-40	600	B.L. 19, 843 f. 49a	2817
Creagh, William	Limerick	gentry: gent	24-Nov-27	100	Dc2/100r	1465
Creamer, Toby	Kilkenny, Ballefoyle	gentry: esquire	31-Jan-66	300	B.L. 15, 635 f. 164	3543
Creamer, Toby	Kilkenny, Ballyfoyle	gentry: esquire	31-Jan-66	300	Dc3/20	2268
Crean, Andrew	Sligo, Annagh	gentry: esquire	26-Jan-33	160	B.L. 19, 843 f. 9	2736
Credland, John	Dublin, Cowlocke		10-Mar-27	40	Dc2/89r	1420
Creefe, Agnes	Dublin, the city	other: spinster	19-Jun-35	20	Dc2/237v	2058
Croft, Benjamin	Cork, the city	gentry: esquire	14-Jan-59	332	B.L. 15, 635 f. 36	3326
Croft, Philip	Dublin, the city	gentry: gent	03-Nov-79	500	B.L. 15, 637 f. 22	3885
Crofton, John	Roscommon, Ballemorre	gentry: gent	26-May-01	300	Dc1/32v	214
Croly, Dominic	Dublin, the city	gentry: gent	21-Apr-40	100	B.L. 19, 843 f. 46	2810
Croly, Edmund	Louth, Drogheda	merchant	18-May-97	200	Dc1/3v	24
Croly, Matthew	Dublin, the city	trade: shoemaker	01-Feb-39	160	B.L. 19, 843 f. 91a	2902
Cronin, Patrick	Cork, the city	merchant	03-Dec-25	120	B.L. 19, 843 f. 93	2905
Crooke, Thomas	England, London	gentry: esquire	03-May-05	1000	Dc1/58r	355
Crosby, John	Dublin, the city	prof: doctor of phisick	11-Jun-73	240	Dc3/157r	2584
Crosby, John	Dublin, the city	prof: doctor of medicine	11-Jun-73	240	B.L. 15, 636 f. 134	3844
Crosby, Patrick	Queen's Co., Mareborough	gentry: gent	29-Mar-97	150	Dc1/3r	17
Crosby, Patrick	Dublin	gentry: gent	03-Dec-97	30	Dc1/9r	62
Cross, Henry	England, Devonshire, Bastable	merchant	25-Nov-11	130	Dc1/109r	679
Crowe, John	England, Northampton	gentry: esquire	30-Jun-25	200	Dc2/67v	1303
Crowe, Richard	Dublin	merchant	23-Oct-29	300	Dc2/137r	1641
Crowe, Stephen	Dublin	gentry: esquire	09-Jan-33	1000	Dc2/190r	1864
Crowe, Thomas	Dublin, the city	merchant	06-Feb-55	1000	B.L. 19, 843 f. 149a	3013
Crowe, Thomas	Dublin, the city	merchant	16-Feb-55	300	B.L. 19, 843 f. 150a	3015
Crowe, William	Dublin, the city	gentry: gent	26-Feb-99	60	Dc1/15v	108
Crowe, William	Dublin	gentry: esquire	19-Feb-21	1000	Dc2/34v	1064
Crowley, Patrick	Dublin, the city	trade: shoemaker	08-Jun-20	2000	Dc2/30v	1032
Crowley, Richard	Dublin	merchant	15-Mar-19	200	Dc2/21v	979
Cruise, James	Dublin, Westowne	gentry: gent	05-Dec-73	460	Dc3/150v	2565

Standard	County	Occupation	Date	Amount	MS No	Ident No
Cruise, James	Dublin, Westowne	gentry: gent	05-Dec-72	460	B.L. 15, 636 f. 133a	3843
Cudmore, Samuel	Dublin, the city	merchant	22-Jun-76	1000	Dc3/178r	2670
Cudmore, Samuel	Dublin, the city	merchant	22-Jun-76	1000	B.L. 19, 844 f. 101	3228
Cuffe, Robert	England, London	trade: ironmonger	29-Aug-03	200	Dc1/48v	314
Cuffe, Robert	England, London	trade: ironmonger	23-Aug-03	120	Dc1/48r	311
Cullen, Philip	Dublin, the city	gentry: gent	15-Dec-34	600	Dc2/226v	2011
Cullen, Philip	England, London	merchant	28-Sep-24	200	Dc2/58r	1239
Culme, Arthur	Cavan, Clowater	gentry: esquire	11-Jul-39	2000	B.L. 19, 843 f. 17	2752
Culme, Benjamin	Dublin?	prof: doctor of theology	18-Aug-56	500	B.L. 19, 843 f. 180	3066
Culme, Benjamin	Dublin, the city	prof: dean of St. Patrick's	19-Jun-35	400	Dc2/237v	2059
Culme, Benjamin	Dublin, St.Patrick's Street	prof: dean of St. Patrick's	20-May-29	200	Dc2/129v	1608
Culme, Benjamin	Dublin, St Patrick's	prof: dean of St. Patrick's	06-May-30	600	Dc2/145v	1681
Culme, Benjamin	Dublin, the city	prof: dean of St. Patrick's	07-Dec-35	800	Dc2/241v	2079
Culme, Hugh	Cavan, Cloghoughter	gentry: knight	24-May-26	330	Dc2/78r	1368
Culme, Philip	England, London	merchant	04-Dec-21	600	Dc2/37v	1088
Culme, Philip	England, London	merchant	18-May-25	80	Dc2/63v	1280
Culme, Robert	England, London	gentry: gent	27-Apr-33	160	Dc2/193r	1875
Cunningham, Albert	Dublin, the city	gentry: esquire	31-Jan-65	1000	Dc3/2	2224
Cunningham, Mary	Londonderry, Monymore	other: widow	13-Feb-68	300	Dc3/73	2390
Cunningham, Mary	Londonderry, Monemore	other: widow	13-Feb-68	300	B.L. 15, 635 f. 220a	3646
Curran, Nicholas	Dublin		10-Nov-97	200	Dc1/6v	48
Currathy, Teige	Queen's Co., Castlebracke	farmer: yeoman	20-Nov-16	300	Dc2/2r	878
Curry, John	Antrim, Belfast	merchant	19-Nov-55	1500	B.L. 19, 843 f. 162	3039
Curtis, Christopher	Meath, Grenok	trade: tanner	13-Jun-01	200	Dc1/32v	215
Curtis, Thomas	Meath, Grenok	trade: tanner	13-Jun-01	200	Dc1/32v	215
Cusack, Adam	Meath, Trevett	gentry: esquire	28-Jun-31	2000	Dc2/165v	1766
Cusack, Adam		gentry: son of Richard	28-Jun-26	200	Dc2/81r	1386
Cusack, Adam	Meath, Trevett	gentry: esquire	01-Mar-32	1500	Dc2/176v	1811
Cusack, James	Meath, Gerrardston	gentry: gent	21-May-10	500	Dc1/96v	606
Cusack, John	Dublin		15-Nov-04	160	Dc1/54r	338
Cusack, John	Dublin	merchant	07-Apr-03	210	Dc1/45v	290
Cusack, John	Dublin		12-Nov-11	50	Dc1/107v	667
Cusack, John	Dublin		11-May-07	200	Dc1/76r	464
Cusack, John	Dublin		06-Feb-06	100	Dc1/65r	393
Cusack, John	Dublin		25-Nov-08	400	Dc1/84v	529
Cusack, John	Dublin		18-Nov-05	107	Dc1/61v	373
Cusack, John	Dublin	merchant	08-Nov-97	41	Dc1/6v	47
Cusack, John	Dublin		17-Jun-13	240	Dc1/122r	759
Cusack, John	Dublin		24-Apr-10	200	Dc1/95v	598
Cusack, John	Dublin, the city	merchant	13-Apr-03	200	Dc1/46r	291
Cusack, John	Dublin	merchant	01-Apr-00	200	Dc1/22v	149
Cusack, Margaret	Meath, Staforstowne	gentry: wife of Robert, esquire	10-Jul-29	2000	Dc2/135r	1631
Cusack, Patrick	Meath, Douloghe	gentry: gent	12-May-06	200	Dc1/67r	406
Cusack, Richard	Meath, Lesmollin	gentry: esquire	18-May-05	1000	Dc1/59v	362

Standard	County	Occupation	Date	Amount	MS No	Ident No
Cusack, Robert	Dublin	merchant	09-Aug-97	52	Dc1/6r	45
Cusack, Robert	Meath, Gerrardston	gentry: esquire	20-May-23	500	Dc2/47r	1158
Cusack, Walter	Dublin	merchant	30-May-25	84	Dc2/64r	1284
Cussen, David	Cork, Youghal	trade: mariner	01-May-84	1000	B.L. 15, 637 f. 91a	4012
Cutt, Henry	England, London	merchant	18-Nov-06	80	Dc1/71v	432
Cutt, Henry	England, London	merchant-tailor	18-Feb-07	750	Dc1/75r	455
Cutt, William	England, London	trade: goldsmith	16-Jan-23	200	Dc2/44r	1135
Dade, John	England?, London?	other: exec will of John				
		Gilbert, London, grocer	15-Oct-18	120	Dc2/16v	951
Dallway, Robert	Antrim, Ballyhill	gentry: gent	22-Jan-66	600	B.L. 15, 635 f. 167	3547
Daly, Ambrose	Cork, the city	merchant	16-Feb-14	120	Dc1/126v	786
Daly, Ambrose	Cork, the city	merchant	03-Dec-13	276	Dc1/125r	777
Damer, Joseph	Dublin, the city	gentry: gent	14-Aug-80	1800	B.L. 15, 637 f. 39	3916
Damer, Joseph	Dublin, the city	merchant	28-May-77	800	B.L. 19, 844 f. 128a	3258
Damer, Joseph	Dublin, the city	merchant	28-May-77	800	Dc3/182v	2689
Darcy, Edmund	Westmeath, Redinniston?	gentry: gent	13-May-25	400	Dc2/63v	1279
Darcy, John	Meath, Dunmore	gentry: esquire	12-May-23	350	Dc2/46v	1154
Darcy, John	Meath, Donmowe	gentry: esquire	30-Apr-12	300	Dc1/113r	701
Darcy, Mark	Galway, Cloran	gentry: gent	29-Jan-68	600	B.L. 15, 635 f. 223	3651
Darcy, Martin	Galway, the town	gentry: esquire	14-Mar-36	400	Dc2/247r	2104
Darcy, Mary	Kildare, Rathcoffy	other: widow	23-Apr-11	500	Dc1/103v	647
Darcy, Nicholas	Meath, Platten	gentry: esquire	08-Jul-41	120	B.L. 19, 843 f. 104a	2928
Darcy, Nicholas	Meath, Platten	gentry: esquire	10-May-37	3000	Dc2/263r	2181
Dardis, Patrick	Dublin	gentry: gent	08-Jan-01	200	Dc1/28r	186
Dardis, Patrick	Dublin	gentry: gent	03-Mar-99	300	Dc1/16r	109
Dardis, Patrick	Dublin	gentry: gent	30-Apr-01	240	Dc1/31r	205
Darell, Richard	England, London	trade: hosier	10-Feb-68	1500	Dc3/73	2389
Davey, Rowse	Dublin, the city	gentry: gent	20-Oct-66	1000	B.L. 15, 635 f. 177	3563
Davey, Rowse	Dublin, the city	gentry: gent	31-May-65	200	Dc3/7	2235
Davey, Rowse	Dublin, the city	gentry: gent	20-Oct-66	1000	Dc3/39	2314
Davey, Rowse	Dublin, Chappellizard	gentry: gent	07-Sep-63	200	B.L. 15, 635 f. 117	3464
Davey, Rowse	Dublin, the city	gentry: gent	08-Apr-65	220	Dc3/3	2229
Davey, Rowse	Dublin, the city	gentry: gent	04-Nov-67	1000	B.L. 15, 635 f. 199a	3608
Davey, Rowse	Dublin, the city	gentry: gent	04-Nov-67	1000	Dc3/67	2373
Davis, Edmund	Antrim, Carrickefrgus	merchant	29-Jan-72	273	B.L. 15, 636 f. 108a	3808
Davis, John	Dublin, the city	gentry: knight	06-Dec-73	1300	Dc3/159r	2598
Davis, John		gentry: knight	18-Nov-09	600	Dc1/92r	576
Davis, John	Dublin, the city	gentry: esquire	10-Jan-87	1000	B.L. 15, 637 f. 111a	4051
Davis, Paul	Dublin, the city	gentry: esquire	18-Nov-35	1000	Dc2/240r	2070
Davis, Paul	Dublin, the city	gentry: esquire	13-Oct-31	2000	Dc2/168v	1779
Davis, Paul	Dublin, the city	gentry: esquire	20-Aug-33	1000	Dc2/199r	1899
Davis, Paul	Dublin, the city	gentry: knight	12-Jun-67	400	Dc3/63	2360
Davis, Paul	Dublin, the city	gentry: knight	12-Jul-67	400	B.L. 15, 635 f. 197a	3605
Davis, Paul	Dublin, the city	gentry: knight	18-May-54	2000	B.L. 19, 843 f. 138a	2991

Standard	County	Occupation	Date	Amount	MS No	Ident No
Davis, Paul	Dublin	gentry: esquire	23-Oct-34	1200	Dc2/219v	1983
Davis, Paul	Dublin, the city	gentry: knight	14-May-53	2000	B.L. 19, 843 f. 133	2981
Davis, Paul	Dublin .	gentry: esquire	17-Dec-33	400	Dc2/204r	1920
Davis, Paul	Dublin	gentry: esquire	12-Dec-33	800	Dc2/203r	1918
Davis, Paul	Dublin	gentry: esquire	09-Dec-33	400	Dc2/203r	1916
Davis, Paul	Dublin	gentry: knight	07-Dec-58	108	B.L. 15, 635 f. 35	3324
Davis, William	Dublin, the city	gentry: knight	13-Nov-62	420	B.L. 15, 635 f. 98a	3431
Davis, William	Dublin, the city	gentry: knight	09-May-63	240	B.L. 15, 635 f. 104a	3441
Davis, William	Dublin, the city	gentry: knight	15-Dec-69	210	Dc3/111	2464
Davis, William	Dublin, the city	gentry: gent	05-Mar-67	8000	Dc3/56	2344
Dawson, Richard	Londonderry, Castledawson	gentry: gent, son of Thomas	16-Jun-80	2000	B.L. 15, 637 f. 35a	3910
Dawson, Robert	Galway, Clonferte	prof: bishop of Clonfert	09-Dec-30	200	Dc2/157v	1733
Deane, Joseph	Dublin	gentry: esquire	21-Nov-70	2000	Dc3/131r	2502
Deane, Joseph	Dublin, the city		21-Nov-70	2000	B.L. 15, 636 f. 74a	3751
Deane, Joseph	Dublin, the city	gentry: esquire	13-May-62	1800	B.L. 15, 635 f. 95a	3425
Deane, Mathew	Cork, the city		24-Feb-79	600	B.L. 15, 637 f. 12a	3870
Deane, Mathew	Cork, the city	gentry: knight	15-Oct-86	100	B.L. 15, 637 f. 110a	4048
Deane, Mathew	Cork, the city	gentry: knight	16-Feb-82	800	B.L. 15, 637 f. 58	3951
Deane, Mathew	Cork, the city	gentry: knight	28-May-85	300	B.L. 15, 637 f. 98	4025
Deane, Mathew	Cork, the city	merchant	26-Nov-78	600	B.L. 19, 844 f. 173	3304
Deane, Mathew	Cork, the city	gentry: knight	18-Apr-85	305	B.L. 15, 367 f. 97a	4024
Deane, Mathew	Cork, the city	gentry: knight	27-Nov-86	2000	B.L. 15, 637 f. 111	4049
Deane, Robert	Cork, Ballincalla	gentry: esquire	01-Jan-39	900	B.L. 15, 637 f. 113a	4057
Deane, Thomas	Cork, the city	merchant	02-May-78	140	Dc3/188r	2710
Deane, Thomas	Cork, the city	merchant	27-Jan-77	1000	B.L. 19, 844 f. 117	3246
Deane, Thomas	Cork, the city	merchant	28-Apr-77	200	B.L. 19, 844 f. 122	3251
Deane, Thomas	Cork, the city	merchant	23-May-83	960	B.L. 15, 637 f. 78a	3990
Deane, Thomas	Cork, the city	merchant	02-May-78	240	B.L. 19, 844 f. 151	3282
Deane, Thomas	Cork, the city	merchant	23-Aug-77	240	B.L. 19, 844 f. 141	3271
Deane, Thomas	Cork, the city	merchant	23-May-83	1360	B.L. 15, 637 f. 78	3989
Dease, William	Louth, Drogheda	merchant	27-Nov-06	500	Dc1/72r	438
Dease?, Robert	Dublin, the city		25-Jun-63	800	B.L. 15, 635 f. 110	3450
Deey?, Abraham	Dublin, the city	gentry: gent	13-Dec-77	800	Dc3/184r	2698
Delabarr, John	England, London	merchant	10-Jul-20	2000	Dc2/32r	1042
Delahyde, Katherine	Louth, Drogheda	other: widow	06-Mar-41	200	B.L. 19, 843 f. 94a	2908
Delahyde, Luke	Meath, Moyglare	gentry: esquire	07-Jun-24	280	Dc2/55v	1219
Delahyde, Luke	King's Co., Castletowne	gentry: esquire	31-Jul-40	10000	B.L. 19, 843 f. 69a	2858
Delahyde, Peter	Meath, Bellandry	gentry: esquire	19-Nov-06	150	Dc1/71v	434
Delahyde, Thomas	Louth, Drogheda		01-May-41	120	B.L. 19, 843 f. 90a	2900
Delaney, Gideon	Dublin, the city	gentry: esquire	29-Sep-75	200	B.L. 19, 844 f. 72	3200
Delaney, Gideon	Dublin, the city	gentry: esquire	05-Apr-76	220	B.L. 19, 844 f. 89	3216
Delaney, Gideon	Dublin, the city	gentry: gent	19-Jun-68	200	Dc3/79	2404
Delaney, Gideon	Dublin, the city	gentry: esquire	28-Sep-75	200	Dc3/168v	2639
Delaney, Gideon	Dublin, the city	gentry: gent	10-Jul-74	480	Dc3/162r	2613

Standard	County	Occupation	Date	Amount	MS No	Ident No
Delaney, Gideon	Dublin, the city	gentry: esquire	08-Jan-69	400	B.L. 15, 636 f. 24	3666
Delaney, Gideon	Dublin, the city	gentry: gent	10-Jul-74	480	B.L. 19, 844 f. 30	3153
Delaney, Gideon	Dublin, the city	gentry: gent	19-Jun-68	200	B.L. 15, 635 f. 222	3649
Delaney, Gideon	Dublin, the city	gentry: esquire	08-Jan-69	400	Dc3/88	2421
Delaney, Gideon	Dublin, the city	gentry: esquire	05-Apr-76	220	Dc3/173r	2653
Delaney, Gideon	Dublin, the city	gentry: gent	22-Oct-69	400	Dc3/103	2449
Delaney, Henry	Cork, Gortinroe	gentry: esquire	21-Feb-39	600	B.L. 19, 843 f. 53a	2825
Dempsey, Lawrence	Dublin, the city	soldier: lieutenant-colonel, esquire	08-Feb-70	400	B.L. 15, 636 f. 53a	3716
Dempsey, Lawrence?	Dublin, the city	soldier: lieutenant-colonel	08-Feb-70	400	Dc3/113	2467
Derenzey, Mathew	Dublin	gentry: knight	19-Nov-31	200	Dc2/171v	1789
Dermott, Peter	Dublin	merchant	27-Jun-01	40	Dc1/33r	216
Desmynieres, John	Dublin, the city		14-Apr-71	3000	B.L. 15, 636 f. 78	3758
Desmynieres, John	Dublin, the city		14-Apr-71	3000	Dc3/137v	2522
Desmynieres, Peter	Dublin, the city	merchant	23-Nov-77	1600	Dc3/183v	2697
Desmynieres, Peter	Dublin, the city	merchant	23-Nov-77	1600	B.L. 19, 844 f. 142a	3273
Devenish, George	Dublin		27-Sep-13	200	Dc1/123v	767
Devenish, George	Dublin, the city	merchant	27-Feb-23	2000	Dc2/45v	1143
Devenish, George	Dublin, the city	merchant	14-Dec-22	1000	Dc2/44r	1133
Devenish, George	Dublin, the city	merchant	18-Dec-24	80	Dc2/59v	1253
Devenish, George	Dublin	merchant	04-Feb-26	180	Dc2/73v	1341
Devenish, James	Dublin, the city	merchant	10-Mar-36	100	Dc2/247r	2103
Devin, William	Dublin, the city	trade: baker	19-May-69	480	Dc3/98	2437
Devin, William	Dublin, the city	trade: baker	19-May-69	480	B.L. 15, 636 f. 43a	3700
Devisher, Samuel	England, London	merchant	30-Apr-73	2000	Dc3/155r	2580
Devisher, Susan	England, London	merchant: wife of Samuel, merchant	30-Apr-73	2000	B.L. 15, 636 f. 134a	3845
Dexter, Stephen	Mayo, Rathbrany	gentry: esquire	28-Nov-13	2000	Dc1/124r	773
Dickson, Abraham	England, Tanton, Somerset	merchant	28-Oct-76	2000	B.L. 19, 844 f. 108	3235
Dickson, Abraham	Cork, Ballybrickan	gentry: gent	05-Nov-83	1500	B.L. 15, 637 f. 80	3993
Dickson, Abraham	England, Somersett, Taunton	merchant	28-Oct-76	2000	Dc3/180r	2676
Dickson, Toby	England, London	trade: haberdasher	14-Jul-23	400	Dc2/49v	1176
Digby, Simon		prof: bishop of Limerick	29-Jan-80	400	B.L. 15, 637 f. 25	3891
Dillon, Arthur	Monaghan, Ballymacny	gentry: esquire	14-May-32	600	Dc2/180v	1825
Dillon, Arthur	Monaghan, Ballymacny	gentry: esquire	11-May-32	200	Dc2/180r	1824
Dillon, Elizabeth	Mayo, Costello-Gallen	peer: viscountess Dillon of Costello-Gallen, widow	13-Dec-80	4000	B.L. 15, 637 f. 44a	3927
Dillon, Garret	Westmeath, Lysheteillen	gentry: gent	09-Feb-14	200	Dc1/126r	783
Dillon, George	Cork, Quarterstowne	gentry: esquire	13-Jun-70	960	B.L. 15, 636 f. 64a	3732
Dillon, Gerald	Meath, Balgeth	gentry: esquire	27-Jan-03	800	Dc1/43v	278
Dillon, Henry	Meath, Kentestelson	gentry: esquire	31-Aug-05	600	Dc1/61v	374
Dillon, Henry	Meath, Moyme	gentry: gent	13-Dec-97	240	Dc1/8v	60
Dillon, Henry	Meath, Moymett	gentry: gent	30-Jun-97	400	Dc1/5v	41

Standard	County	Occupation	Date	Amount	MS No	Ident No
Dillon, Henry	Roscommon, Clonerebreckan	gentry: esquire	14-Aug-39	600	B.L. 19, 843 f. 31a	2781
Dillon, James	Dublin, Hunteston	gentry: gent	22-Mar-98	60	Dc1/10v	76
Dillon, James	Meath, Stafferston	gentry: gent	19-Apr-05	400	Dc1/57v	352
Dillon, James	Meath?, Moymott	gentry: knight	24-Dec-03	2508	Dc1/50v	325
Dillon, John	Armagh, Dromully	gentry: knight	18-Nov-20	600	Dc2/33r	1050
Dillon, Luke	Mayo, Benfadda	gentry: gent	17-May-14	2000	Dc1/129r	803
Dillon, Luke	Louth, Richardston	gentry: gent	18-Jun-97	1000	Dc1/5r	35
Dillon, Martin	Meath, Huntston	gentry: gent	19-Apr-05	400	Dc1/57v	352
Dillon, Mary	Louth, Drogheda	other: spinster	13-May-31	160	Dc2/162r	1752
Dillon, Maurice	Westmeath, Gortmore	gentry: gent	24-Sep-33	800	Dc2/199v	1902
Dillon, Patrick	Dublin, Castellknoke		18-Jun-97	1000	Dc1/5r	35
Dillon, Robert	Westmeath, Connarston	gentry: gent	25-Jul-14	400	Dc1/131r	814
Dillon, Robert	Kilkenny?	peer: baron Kilkenny West	26-Aug-40	3000	B.L. 19, 843 f. 67	2853
Dillon, Robert	Galway, Clonbrocke	gentry: gent	04-Dec-19	300	Dc2/27r	1011
Dillon, Robert	Kilkenny?	peer: baron Kilkenny West	17-May-34	3000	Dc2/211v	1950
Dillon, Robert	Westmeath, Canarstone	gentry: esquire	01-Dec-19	500	Dc2/26r	1005
Dillon, Robert	Westmeath, Cancreston	gentry: esquire	04-Dec-19	600	Dc2/27r	1010
Dillon, Robert	Galway, Clonebroke	gentry: esquire	17-Jun-10	400	Dc1/98r	616
Dillon, Theobald	Westmeath, Killenefarten	gentry: knight	28-Nov-08	500	Dc1/85r	531
Dillon, Thomas	Dublin, the city	merchant	05-Mar-23	60	Dc2/46r	1147
Dillon, Thomas	Meath, Ardnecrany	other: son/heir of Talbot	01-Dec-19	500	Dc2/26r	1006
Dillon, William	Meath, Ffitzleonston	gentry: gent	13-Jul-20	300	Dc2/32r	1043
Dillon, William	Meath, Ffleenstowne	gentry: gent	22-Jun-37	500	Dc2/265r	2189
Disbrowe, Nathaniel	Dublin, the city	gentry: esquire	31-Dec-79	2000	B.L. 15, 637 f. 24	3889
Disney, William	Louth, Stabannan	gentry: esquire	02-Sep-75	400	B.L. 19, 844 f. 76	3204
Dixon, Abraham	Cork, Ballybruckane	merchant	05-Jun-83	600	B.L. 15, 637 f. 74a	3982
Dixon, Abraham	Cork, Ballebrickane	gentry: gent	27-Jan-83	400	B.L. 15, 637 f. 70a	3974
Dixon, Andrew	Meath, Baronstowne	gentry: gent	09-May-34	400	Dc2/210r	1946
Dixon, Andrew	Scotland, Lyeth	trade: mariner	05-Aug-18	100	Dc2/16r	950
Dixon, Robert	Dublin	gentry: esquire	17-Nov-23	250	Dc2/51r	1186
Dixon, Robert	Dublin, the city	gentry: esquire	28-Nov-22	700	Dc2/43r	1127
Dixon, Robert	Meath, Castle Rickard	gentry: gent	16-Jun-57	600	B.L. 19, 843 f. 199	3104
Dixon, Robert	Dublin, the city	gentry: knight	04-May-37	2000	Dc2/262r	2176
Dixon, Robert	Dublin, the city	gentry: esquire	20-Nov-28	800	Dc2/118v	1556
Dixon, Robert	Dublin	gentry: esquire	19-Aug-34	200	Dc2/217v	1974
Dixon, Robert	Dublin, the city	gentry: esquire	25-Nov-28	200	Dc2/117r	1546
Dixon, Robert	Dublin, the city	gentry: knight	20-Dec-34	1200	Dc2/227v	2016
Dixon, Robert	Dublin, the city		10-Feb-31	500	Dc2/160v	1742
Dixon, Walter	Meath, Baronstowne?	gentry: son/heir of Andrew	09-May-34	400	Dc2/210v	1946
Dixon, William	Dublin, the city	gentry: esquire	13-Sep-55	150	B.L. 19, 843 f. 166	3046
Dixon, William	Dublin, the city	gentry: esquire	22-Apr-57	80	B.L. 19, 843 f. 190a	3088

Standard	County	Occupation	Date	Amount	MS No	Ident No
Dobson, Isaac	Dublin, Dundrum	gentry: esquire	10-Nov-71	1000	Dc3/140v	2532
Dobson, Isaac	Dublin, Dundrum	gentry: esquire	10-Nov-71	1000	B.L. 15, 636 f. 91	3781
Dobson, Isaac	Dublin, Dundrum	gentry: esquire	09-Jan-62	500	B.L. 15, 635 f. 90a	3417
Domville, Gilbert	Dublin	gentry: gent	23-Jun-18	220	Dc2/15v	945
Domville, Gilbert	Dublin	gentry: esquire	16-May-23	200	Dc2/47r	1156
Domville, Gilbert	Dublin, the city	gentry: esquire	22-Jun-29	200	Dc2/133v	1625
Domville, Gilbert	Dublin	gentry: esquire	02-Oct-27	200	Dc2/99r	1460
Domville, Gilbert	Dublin	gentry: gent	31-May-10	500	Dc1/97r	609
Domville, Gilbert	Dublin	gentry: esquire	07-Dec-27	280	Dc2/98v	1458
Domville, Gilbert	Dublin	gentry: esquire	26-Jun-34	440	Dc2/213r	1956
Domville, Gilbert	Dublin, the city	gentry: esquire	03-Mar-28	860	Dc2/105r	1490
Domville, Gilbert	Dublin, the city	gentry: esquire	04-May-37	2000	Dc2/262r	2176
Domville, Gilbert	Dublin	gentry: esquire	16-May-23	200	Dc2/47r	1157
Domville, Gilbert	Dublin	gentry: esquire	16-May-23	200	Dc2/47r	1155
Domville, Gilbert	Dublin	gentry: gent	25-Jul-18	310	Dc2/16r	948
Domville, William		gentry: knight	18-Dec-68	267	Dc3/88	2419
Domville, William	Dublin	gentry: gent, son/heir of Gilbert	01-Mar-32	1500	Dc2/176v	1811
Domville, William			22-Nov-67	400	Dc3/68	2374
Domville, William		gentry: knight	18-Aug-70	5000	Dc3/124	2489
Donaldson, John	Antrim, Gabban, Island Magee	gentry: gent	13-May-71	200	B.L. 15, 636 f. 87	3774
Donaldson, Robert	Antrim, Gabban, Island Magee	gentry: gent	26-May-79	280	B.L. 15, 637 f. 21	3884
Donbavane, Nathan	Dublin, the city	gentry: esquire	14-Jul-74	4000	Dc3/162v	2614
Dongan, Edward	Kildare, Rathangan		15-Jun-27	300	Dc2/94v	1441
Dongan, Mary	Roscommon, Clondara	gentry: widow	22-Jul-61	6000	B.L. 15, 635 f. 76a	3394
Dongan, Walter	Kildare, Possickston	gentry: gent	11-Jun-07	700	Dc1/78r	476
Dongan, Walter	Kildare, Possickston	gentry: esquire	15-Jul-11	700	Dc1/104v	654
Dongan, Walter	Kildare, Posserston	gentry: gent	22-May-06	400	Dc1/68v	413
Dongan, Walter	Kildare, Possockstowne	gentry: esquire	06-Jul-12	700	Dc1/115r	715
Dongan, Walter	Kildare, Castletownkildrough	gentry: baronet	30-Jun-25	800	Dc2/67v	1305
Dongan, William	Dublin?		23-Nov-22	600	Dc2/43r	1126
Donnellan, James	Dublin	gentry: esquire	24-Nov-31	150	Dc2/172r	1793
Dopping, Anthony	Dublin, the city	gentry: esquire	12-Dec-57	800	B.L. 19, 843 f. 204a	3115
Dopping, Anthony	Dublin	gentry: esquire	01-Mar-32	1500	Dc2/176v	1811
Dopping, Anthony	Dublin	gentry: gent	12-Jun-29	160	Dc2/132r	1617
Dormer, Francis	Wexford?, Rosse	merchant	18-Feb-97	200	Dc1/2r	9
Dowd, Charles	Dublin	merchant	30-Nov-13	60	Dc1/124v	774
Dowd, Charles	Dublin	merchant	04-Feb-13	100	Dc1/118r	733
Dowd, Charles	Dublin	merchant	15-Feb-13	50	Dc1/119r	740
Dowd, Francis	Dublin	merchant	12-Feb-13	16	Dc1/118v	737
Dowd, Francis	Dublin	merchant	15-Feb-13	50	Dc1/119r	740
Dowd, Francis	Dublin	merchant	04-Feb-13	100	Dc1/118r	733

Standard	County	Occupation	Date	Amount	MS No	Ident No
Dowd, John	Dublin, the city		30-Apr-35	200	Dc2/234r	2043
Dowd, John	Dublin, the city		09-Dec-29	200	Dc2/139v	1653
Dowd, John	Dublin, the city		06-Jul-33	200	Dc2/197v	1893
Dowd, John	Dublin		19-Feb-13	40	Dc1/119v	741
Dowd, John	Dublin		04-Feb-13	100	Dc1/118r	733
Dowd, John	Dublin		13-Sep-26	800	Dc2/82v	1391
Dowd, John	Dublin, the city		28-Nov-35	120	Dc2/240v	2074
Dowd, John	Dublin, the city		31-May-26	2000	Dc2/78v	1372
Dowd, John	Dublin		12-Feb-13	62	Dc1/118v	736
Dowd, John	Dublin		15-Feb-13	50	Dc1/119r	740
Dowd, John	Dublin, the city		17-May-36	80	Dc2/251v	2123
Dowd, John	Dublin		03-Dec-13	60	Dc1/125r	776
Dowd, John	Dublin, the city		15-Jul-34	200	Dc2/214v	1963
Dowd, John	Dublin, the city		01-Apr-34	400	Dc2/210r	1944
Dowd, John	Dublin, the city		01-Dec-34	200	Dc2/224v	2002
Dowd, John	Dublin, the city		24-Oct-35	200	Dc2/239v	2067
Dowd, John	Dublin		30-Nov-13	60	Dc1/124v	774
Dowdall, Alexander	Meath, Athboy	merchant	18-Apr-00	200	Dc1/23r	154
Dowdall, Edward	Dublin, the city	gentry: esquire	22-Jun-29	200	Dc2/133v	1625
Dowdall, Edward	Dublin	gentry: esquire	06-Jun-14	80	Dc1/130r	807
Dowdall, Edward	Meath, Monktowne	gentry: esquire	15-Jun-27	300	Dc2/94v	1441
Dowdall, Edward	Meath, Belgry	gentry: esquire	14-Jul-09	2000	Dc1/90r	564
Dowdall, Edward	Meath, Mounckton	gentry: esquire	04-May-37	2000	Dc2/262r	2176
Dowdall, Edward	Louth, Drogheda	merchant	18-Feb-25	200	Dc2/62r	1267
Dowdall, Edward	Dublin, the city	gentry: esquire	30-Jun-19	500	Dc2/24v	995
Dowdall, Edward	Meath, Rathmore	gentry: esquire	13-Feb-19	100	Dc2/21r	975
Dowdall, Edward	Meath, Rathmore	gentry: esquire	22-Feb-13	300	Dc1/119v	743
Dowdall, Edward	Meath, Athlumny	gentry: esquire	13-May-20	400	Dc2/29v	1027
Dowdall, Edward	Meath, Belgree	gentry: gent	17-Feb-09	300	Dc1/87v	546
Dowdall, Edward	Meath, Munckston	gentry: esquire	01-Mar-32	1500	Dc2/176v	1811
Dowdall, Edward	Meath, Belgrie	gentry: gent	19-May-09	400	Dc1/89r	556
Dowdall, Edward	Meath, Moncktown	gentry: esquire	07-Dec-38	600	B.L. 19, 843 f. 97a	2914
Dowdall, Edward	Meath, Munckton	gentry: esquire	24-Feb-34	700	Dc2/207v	1933
Dowdall, Edward	Meath, Athlumny	gentry: esquire	12-Feb-24	1000	Dc2/53v	1202
Dowdall, Edward	Meath, Belgry	merchant	29-Jan-11	150	Dc1/102r	638
Dowdall, Edward	Meath, Balgre	gentry: gent	07-Jul-03	700	Dc1/47v	302
Dowdall, Edward	Dublin	gentry: gent	13-Nov-14	120	Dc1/132r	822
Dowdall, Elizabeth	Meath, Monckstowne	gentry: spinster	23-Aug-66	600	B.L. 15, 635 f. 180a	3570
Dowdall, Elizabeth	Meath, Monketowne	gentry: spinster	23-Aug-66	600	Dc3/37	2307
Dowdall, Henry	Meath, Kells	merchant	22-Jan-14	80	Dc1/125v	780
Dowdall, Henry	Louth, Hagestowne	gentry: gent	15-May-28	200	Dc2/107v	1504
Dowdall, Henry	Meath, Kells	merchant	18-Jun-30	2000	Dc2/152r	1708
Dowdall, Henry	Meath, Kells	merchant	08-Feb-23	150	Dc2/44v	1137
Dowdall, Henry	Meath, Kells	merchant	19-Nov-14	80	Dc1/132v	824
Dowdall, John	Meath, Clonlyon	gentry: gent	16-Feb-36	240	Dc2/244v	2094

Standard	County	Occupation	Date	Amount	MS No	Ident No
Dowdall, Lawrence	Meath, Athlumny	gentry: gent	02-May-31	2000	Dc2/162r	1751
Dowdall, Margaret	Dublin	other: widow	22-Apr-08	200	Dc1/82r	508
Dowdall, Nicholas	Dublin	gentry: gent	06-Jun-14	80	Dc1/130r	807
Dowdall, Nicholas	Dublin	gentry: gent	11-Feb-14	200	Dc1/126v	784
Dowdall, Nicholas	Louth, Drogheda		07-May-28	180	Dc2/107r	1499
Dowdall, Richard	Dublin	gentry: gent	11-Feb-14	200	Dc1/126v	785
Dowdall, Stephen	Louth, Droheday	merchant	03-Aug-27	200	Dc2/98r	1455
Dowdall, William	Dublin	merchant	01-Mar-32	1500	Dc2/176v	1811
Dowling, Murrough	Dublin, the city	gentry: gent	12-Dec-74	1300	B.L. 19, 844 f. 58a	3183
Dowling, Murrough	Dublin, the city	gentry: gent	12-Dec-74	1300	Dc3/163v	2619
Downey, Cahir	Queen's Co., Castlebracke	merchant	20-Nov-16	300	Dc2/2r	878
Downing, Richard	Dublin	gentry: gent	23-Feb-98	60	Dc1/9v	69
Doyne, Barnaby	Queen's Co., Brittas	gentry: gent	27-Nov-17	200	Dc2/12r	925
Doyne, Barnaby	Queen's Co., Brittas	gentry: gent	27-Nov-17	400	Dc2/11v	924
Doyne, Charles	Queen's Co., Brittas	gentry: gent	11-Mar-76	500	Dc3/172v	2652
Drope, Bartholomew	Dublin, the city	merchant	14-Dec-42	80	B.L. 19, 843 f. 118a	2956
Drope, Bartholomew	Dublin, the city	merchant	10-Jun-41	200	B.L. 19, 843 f. 118	2955
Drope, Batholomew	Dublin, the city	merchant	02-Dec-42	1000	B.L. 19, 843 f. 110	2939
Drumgoole, Thomas	Dublin	trade: haberdasher	06-Jul-99	40	Dc1/17v	120
Duff, James	Wexford?, Rosse	merchant	18-Feb-97	200	Dc1/2r	9
Duff, Lawrence	Dublin, the city	gentry: gent	17-Dec-32	100	Dc2/188v	1858
Duff, Lawrence	Dublin, the city	gentry: gent	02-Aug-32	200	Dc2/185r	1843
Duff, Lawrence	Dublin, the city	trade: butcher	20-Jun-29	600	Dc2/133r	1622
Duff, Lawrence	Dublin, the city	gentry: gent	13-Jul-31	300	Dc2/166v	1769
Duff, Lawrence	Dublin	trade: butcher	26-Aug-23	300	Dc2/50r	1180
Duff, Stephen	Louth, Drogheda		28-May-23	500	Dc2/48r	1162
Duff, Stephen	Louth, Drogheda	gentry: gent	16-Nov-12	250	Dc1/116v	724
Duff, Thady	Dublin, the city	gentry: gent	23-Mar-14	60	Dc1/128v	799
Duff, Thady	Dublin, the city	gentry: knight	10-Mar-27	200	Dc2/89v	1421
Duff, Thady	Dublin	gentry: knight	29-Jun-29	2000	Dc2/134v	1629
Duff, Thady	Dublin, the city	gentry: knight	20-Nov-29	100	Dc2/137v	1643
Duff, Thady	Dublin		15-Jan-09	120	Dc1/85v	536
Duff, Thady	Dublin	gentry: gent	04-Apr-12	200	Dc1/113r	700
Duff, Thady	Dublin, the city	gentry: knight	29-Apr-26	100	Dc2/76v	1359
Duff, Thady	Dublin, the city	gentry: knight	27-Jan-29	100	Dc2/123v	1576
Duff, Thady	Dublin	gentry: gent	19-Sep-11	120	Dc1/107r	665
Duff, Thady	Dublin, the city	gentry: knight	23-Nov-29	400	Dc2/138r	1644
Duff, Thady	Dublin		27-Jun-11	120	Dc1/104v	653
Duff, Thady	Dublin		18-Sep-23	800	Dc2/50r	1181
Duff, Thady	Dublin, the city	gentry: knight	20-Jun-29	120	Dc2/134r	1627
Duff, Thady	Dublin	gentry: gent	16-Nov-11	200	Dc1/108r	673
Duff, Thady	Dublin	gentry: gent	18-Sep-11	200	Dc1/664	664
Duff, Thady	Dublin, the city	gentry: knight	12-Jun-29	400	Dc2/131v	1615
Duff, Thomas	Louth, Drogheda		12-Jul-98	300	Dc1/11v	84
Duff, Thomas	Dublin, the city	gentry: knight	28-Apr-37	1000	Dc2/261v	2175

Standard	County	Occupation	Date	Amount	MS No	Ident No
Dukes, Edward	Dublin, the city	gentry: gent	26-Aug-67	200	Dc3/66	2371
Dunbar, George	Dublin	gentry: gent	24-Dec-34	160	Dc2/228r	2018
Dunscomb, Noble?	Cork, the city	gentry: esquire	11-Mar-85	1100	B.L. 13, 637 f.97	4023
Durant, Giles	Dublin	gentry: gent	18-Jul-28	200	Dc2/113v	1531
Dwyre, Derby	Tipperary, Clonyhirma	gentry: esquire	17-May-09	1000	Dc1/88v	552
Dwyre, John	Tipperary, Downedroma	gentry: esquire	17-May-09	1000	Dc1/88v	553
Eaton, Theophilus	Dublin, the city	gentry: esquire	19-Jul-58	500	B.L. 15, 635 f. 32a	3320
Eccles, Arthur	Dublin, the city	merchant	08-Nov-65	240	Dc3/15	2254
Eccles, Hugh	Antrim, Belfast	merchant	14-May-80	5000	B.L. 15, 637 f. 33	3906
Eccleston, William	Dublin	gentry: gent	26-Feb-21	200	Dc2/34v	1065
Echlin, Henry	Dublin, the city	gentry: gent	09-May-63	190	B.L. 15, 635 f. 120a	3469
Echlin, Henry	Dublin, the city	gentry: esquire	03-Dec-78	600	B.L. 15, 637 f. 7	3860
Echlin, Robert	Tyrone, Omagh		20-Jun-78	200	Dc3/191v	2722
Echlin, Robert	Tyrone, Omagh		20-Jun-78	200	B.L. 15, 637 f. 2a	3855
Edgeworth, Francis	Dublin, the city	gentry: esquire	22-Feb-17	450	Dc2/5v	895
Edgeworth, Francis	Dublin	gentry: esquire	20-Apr-24	80	Dc2/54r	1209
Edkins, James	Dublin, the city	gentry: esquire	05-Dec-55	600	B.L. 19, 843 f. 169a	3053
Edmunds, Thomas	Dublin	gentry: esquire	10-Jun-34	400	Dc2/212v	1954
Edwards, Edward	Tyrone, Castledarge	gentry: esquire	23-May-76	3000	Dc3/173v	2656
Edwards, Margaret	Londonderry, the city	other: spinster	23-May-76	1600	Dc3/174r	2658
Eiffe, William	Meath, Raystowne	farmer	27-Jun-36	100	Dc2/253v	2136
Elliott, Alexander	Dublin, Tirenure	gentry: esquire	04-Nov-59	96	B.L. 15, 635 f. 56	3363
Elliott, John	Dublin, city		16-Mar-03	400	Dc1/45v	288
Elliott, John	Meath?, Balreske	gentry: esquire	27-Jan-03	800	Dc1/43v	277
Elliott, John	Meath, Balreaske	gentry: knight	01-Jul-15	1000	Dc1/139r	866
Elliott, John	Dublin		06-Oct-12	120	Dc1/115v	718
Elliott, John	Meath, Balreske	gentry: knight	22-Apr-11	120	Dc1/103v	646
Elliott, Thomas	Meath, Balreaske	gentry: esquire	22-Jun-15	200	Dc1/139r	863
Elliott, Thomas	Meath, Balneaske	gentry: esquire	22-Nov-16	300	Dc2/2v	879
Elliott, Thomas	Dublin, the city	gentry: esquire	04-Feb-68	300	Dc3/72	2387
Elliott, Thomas	Dublin, the city	gentry: esquire	04-Feb-68	300	B.L. 15, 635 f. 224a	3654
Ellis, Howell	Dublin, the city	gentry: gent	13-Jan-68	120	Dc3/71	2385
Ellis, Howell	Dublin	gentry: gent	01-Dec-73	700	Dc3/159r	2597
Ellis, Howell	Dublin, the city	gentry: gent	13-Jan-68	120	B.L. 15, 635 f. 212	3629
Ellis, Howell	Dublin	gentry: gent	28-Jul-68	100	B.L. 15, 635 f. 225	3655
Ellis, Howell	Dublin, the city	gentry: gent	12-Aug-64	200	B.L. 15, 635 f. 142	3503
Ellis, Howell	Dublin	gentry: gent	28-Jul-68	100	Dc3/82	2409
Ellis, Thomas	Dublin, the city	gentry: gent	20-Feb-36	200	Dc2/245v	2097
Elwood, Richard	Wexford, Enescorthy	gentry: gent	10-Nov-12	140	Dc1/116r	720
Elwood, William	Louth, Drogheda	merchant	21-Sep-78	800	B.L. 15, 637 f. 11a	3868
Emerson, Arthur	Dublin, the city	trade: brewer	19-Apr-82	3000	B.L. 15, 637 f. 55a	3946
English, Patrick	Dublin	trade: baker	31-Jul-01	400	Dc1/33v	221
Erskine, James		gentry: knight	06-Nov-23	200	Dc2/50v	1184
Esmond, Lawrence	Kildare?, Arcklo	gentry: gent	03-Jul-01	600	Dc1/33r	218

Standard	County	Occupation	Date	Amount	MS No	Ident No
Eustace, Christopher	Kildare, Cradockstowne	gentry: esquire	18-Nov-65	300	Dc3/15	2256
Eustace, Maurice	Dublin?	gentry: knight	08-Dec-40	1000	B.L. 19, 843 f. 76a	2872
Eustace, Maurice	Kildare, Carnalwey	gentry: gent	24-Sep-32	200	Dc2/186r	1847
Eustace, Nicholas	Cork	other: son/heir of John, late of Cork	20-Mar-01	100	Dc1/29v	198
Eustace, Nicholas	Kildare, Coufy	gentry: gent	07-Dec-19	120	Dc2/27r	1012
Eustace, William	Kildare, Kilgoen	gentry: gent	04-Jun-32	240	Dc2/182r	1832
Eustace, William	Kildare, Gallmorstowne	gentry: gent	26-Jul-37	1200	Dc2/270r	2211
Eustace, William	Kildare, Castlemarten	gentry: esquire	07-May-11	1000	Dc1/104r	649
Eustace, William	Kildare, Castlemarten	gentry: esquire	28-Nov-97	1000	Dc1/8r	57
Evans, Ellis	England, Fflint, Northapp Hall	gentry: esquire	16-May-64	660	B.L. 15, 635 f. 130a	3488
Evans, George	Cork, Garranboy	gentry: gent	12-Jan-69	200	B.L. 15, 636 f. 26	3670
Evans, George	Cork, Phylipstowne	gentry: esquire	30-Jul-75	6000	B.L. 19, 844 f. 73	3201
Evans, George	Cork, Gurranesboy	gentry: gent	05-Dec-67	1000	B.L. 15, 635 f. 204a	3618
Evans, George	Cork, Garreneboy	gentry: gent	17-Sep-67	1000	B.L. 15, 635 f. 202a	3614
Evans, George	Cork, Gurranebey	gentry: gent	05-Dec-67	1000	Dc3/70	2382
Evans, George	Cork, Garranboy	gentry: gent	20-Mar-63	800	B.L. 15, 635 f. 146	3511
Evans, George	Limerick, Ballygrenane	gentry: esquire	25-Feb-75	4200	Dc3/165r	2625
Evans, George	Limerick, Ballegrenane	gentry: esquire	22-Feb-75	4200	B.L. 19, 844 f. 50	3173
Evans, George	Cork, Garraneboy	gentry: gent	01-May-65	300	B.L. 15, 635 f. 194a	3599
Evans, George	Cork, Garreneboy	gentry: gent	05-Jan-65	500	B.L. 15, 635 f. 202	3613
Exham, John	Dublin, the city	gentry: esquire	03-Jun-68	200	Dc3/77	2399
Exham, John	Dublin, the city	gentry: esquire	03-Jun-68	200	B.L. 15, 635 f. 226a	3658
Exham, John	Dublin, the Inns	gentry: esquire	07-Feb-59	866	B.L. 15, 635 f. 43a	3339
Fagan, Jane		other: widow	21-Feb-28	400	Dc2/104v	1487
Fagan, Jane		other: widow	14-Feb-28	120	Dc2/104r	1486
Fagan, Jane		other: widow	20-Dec-26	400	Dc2/87r	1412
Fagan, John	Dublin	gentry: gent	01-Dec-00	500	Dc1/27r	180
Fagan, Richard	Dublin		14-Jun-02	1000	Dc1/38r	247
Fagan, Richard	Dublin		02-Dec-00	500	Dc1/27r	181
Fagan, Richard			19-Jun-07	500	Dc1/78v	480
Fagan, Richard	Dublin		23-Sep-09	400	Dc1/91v	573
Fanning?, William	England, London, city	trade: barber-surgeon	16-Jul-03	1000	Dc1/47ar	306
Farrell, Brian	Longford, Mileckan	gentry: gent	03-Dec-19	200	Dc2/26v	1009
Farrell, Donough	Longford, Mileckan	gentry: gent	03-Dec-19	200	Dc2/26v	1009
Farrell, Donough	Longford, Mileckan	gentry: gent	03-Dec-19	200	Dc2/26v	1009
Farrell, Edmund	Longford, Mileckan	gentry: gent	03-Dec-19	200	Dc2/26v	1009
Farrell, Fachtna	Longford, Mileckan	gentry: gent	03-Dec-19	200	Dc2/26v	1009
Farrell, Gerald	Longford, Newcastell	gentry: gent	27-Jul-03	1000	Dc1/47av	309
Farrell, Hubert	Longford, Pallis	gentry: gent	08-May-32	200	Dc2/179v	1822
Farrell, Hugh	Longford, Mileckan	gentry: gent	03-Dec-19	200	Dc2/26v	1009
Farrell, James	Longford, Castelruighe	gentry: gent?	27-Jul-03	1000	Dc1/47av	310
Farrell, James	Roscommon, Killmore	gentry: gent	20-Sep-69	600	B.L. 15, 636 f. 51a	3712

Standard	County	Occupation	Date	Amount	MS No	Ident No
Farrell, James	Roscommon, Killmore	gentry: gent	20-Sep-69	600	Dc3/102	2447
Farrell, John	Longford, Mileckan	gentry: gent	03-Dec-19	200	Dc2/26v	1009
Farrell, John	Longford, Ardenraghe	gentry: gent	27-Jul-03	1000	Dc1/47av	310
Farrell, John	Longford, Ardenragh	gentry: esquire	17-May-14	2000	Dc1/129r	802
Farrell, Laughlin	Longford, Mileckan	gentry: gent	03-Dec-19	200	Dc2/26v	1009
Farrell, Murrough	Longford, Mileckan	gentry: gent	03-Dec-19	200	Dc2/26v	1009
Farrell, Rose	Dublin, the city	other: spinster	20-Feb-40	100	B.L. 19, 843 f. 44	2806
Farrell, Ross	Longford, Mileckan	gentry: gent	03-Dec-19	200	Dc2/26v	1009
Farrell, Turlough	Longford, Mileckan	gentry: gent	03-Dec-19	200	Dc2/26v	1009
Farren, William	Dublin	gentry: esquire	20-Apr-55	600	B.L. 19, 843 f. 155a	3025
Fearcher, George	Fermanagh, Cleenish		22-Jun-39	441	B.L. 19, 843 f. 23	2764
Fenwick, Robert	Down, Knocknearing	gentry: esquire	10-Nov-56	110	B.L. 19, 843 f. 185a	3078
Fernely, Philip	Dublin, the city	gentry: esquire	31-May-32	1200	Dc2/181v	1830
Fernely, Philip	Dublin, the city	gentry: esquire	06-Oct-70	500	Dc3/125	2491
Field, Christopher	Dublin	merchant	22-Nov-16	500	Dc2/2v	880
Field, Christopher	Dublin, the city	merchant	14-Mar-29	200	Dc2/126r	1592
Field, Christopher	Dublin, the city	merchant	28-Apr-30	200	Dc2/144v	1675
Field, Christopher	Dublin	merchant	27-Nov-33	418	Dc2/201r	1908
Field, Christopher	Dublin	merchant	27-Nov-33	350	Dc2/201v	1909
Field, Christopher	Dublin, the city	merchant	19-Jun-29	100	Dc2/133v	1623
Field, Christopher	Dublin, the city	merchant	19-Feb-24	400	Dc2/53v	1205
Field, Christopher	Dublin, the city	merchant	02-Apr-29	500	Dc2/126v	1594
Field, Christopher	Dublin	merchant	10-Dec-16	400	Dc2/3v	885
Field, Christopher	Dublin	merchant	18-Dec-16	60	Dc2/3r	884
Field, Christopher	Dublin, the city	merchant	17-Aug-29	300	Dc2/135v	1634
Field, James	Monaghan, Coulry	gentry: esquire	15-Jun-30	1000	Dc2/151v	1704
Field, James	Monaghan, Gould Key	gentry: esquire	01-Dec-30	300	Dc2/157r	1730
Field, Mathew	Dublin	merchant	28-Nov-10	300	Dc1/101r	634
Field, Simon	Dublin, the city	gentry: gent	19-Nov-28	200	Dc2/118v	1555
Finch, Simon	Dublin, the city	gentry: esquire	05-May-56	200	B.L. 19, 843 f. 179a	3065
Finch, Simon	Dublin, the city	soldier: lieutenant-colonel	09-Nov-55	270	B.L. 19, 843 f. 167	3048
Findlay, John	Antrim, Ralow	Farmer: yeoman	05-Apr-79	440	B.L. 15, 637 f. 20a	3883
Finglas, Margaret	Kildare, Lexlyp	other: widow	02-Jun-00	1000	Dc1/24r	159
Finglas, Sebastian	Dublin, Murrogh	gentry: gent	31-Jan-31	160	Dc2/159r	1738
Finn, Melchior	Louth, Drogheda	merchant	15-Jan-08	150	Dc1/80v	500
Finn, Melchior	Louth, Drogheda	merchant	03-Jul-07	400	Dc1/79r	483
Finn, Robert	Carlow, Catherlagh	gentry: gent	04-Nov-40	200	B.L. 19, 843 f. 83	2885
Finn, William	England, London	trade: barber-surgeon	19-Jun-98	220	Dc1/11r	81
Finn, William	England, London	trade: barber-surgeon	02-Dec-97	1600	Dc1/8r	56
Fish, Edward	Wexford?	gentry: baronet	13-Jun-25	1000	Dc2/66r	1295
Fish, Mary		gentry: spinster?, daughter of Sir John	13-Jun-25	1000	Dc2/66r	1294
Fisher, Alice	Wexford, Prospecte	gentry: widow	21-Dec-32	2000	Dc2/189r	1859

Standard	County	Occupation	Date	Amount	MS No	Ident No
Fisher, Edward	Dublin, the city	gentry: knight	28-Feb-20	500	Dc2/29r	1022
Fitton, Alexander	Limerick, Glanoger	gentry: esquire	18-Nov-07	600	Dc1/79av	491
Fitzgerald, Bridget	Kildare, Carricke	other: widow	11-Jul-28	160	Dc2/112v	1527
Fitzgerald, Edmund	Meath, Tecroghan	gentry: knight	11-Feb-07	500	Dc1/74r	448
Fitzgerald, Edward	Dublin, the city	merchant	10-Jun-40	200	B.L. 19, 843 f. 67a	2854
Fitzgerald, Edward	Dublin, the city	gentry: gent	01-Jun-36	400	B.L. 19, 843 f. 38	2794
Fitzgerald, Edward	Kildare, Blackhale	gentry: gent	09-May-10	100	Dc1/96r	602
Fitzgerald, Edward	Meath?, Tercroghan	gentry: knight	29-Nov-05	500	Dc1/63r	381
Fitzgerald, Edward	Dublin, the city	gentry: gent	30-Jun-36	400	Dc2/253v	2137
Fitzgerald, Edward	Dublin, the city	gentry: gent	30-Jun-36	400	Dc2/254r	2138
Fitzgerald, Elizabeth	Kildare?	peer: countess of Kildare, widow	04-Apr-28	600	Dc2/106v	1496
Fitzgerald, Elizabeth	Kildare?	peer: countess-dowager of Kildare	17-Feb-35	1400	Dc2/229v	2023
Fitzgerald, Elizabeth	Kildare, Killmaoge?	other: widow	17-Feb-76	400	Dc3/172v	2651
Fitzgerald, Elizabeth		peer: countess of Kildare, widow	21-Jun-39	4000	B.L. 19, 843 f. 21a	2761
Fitzgerald, Elizabeth	Kildare, Killmaoge	other: widow	17-Feb-76	400	B.L. 19, 844 f. 123	3252
Fitzgerald, Garret	Kildare, Glaselie	gentry: esquire	30-Nov-28	1000	Dc2/119v	1559
Fitzgerald, Gerald	Meath, Mollenetaght?	gentry: gent	13-Jul-03	260	Dc1/47ar	305
Fitzgerald, Gerald	Waterford, Coole Ishell?	gentry: gent	14-Mar-40	800	B.L. 19, 843 f. 60	2838
Fitzgerald, Gerald	Kildare, Thomaston	gentry: gent	18-Nov-22	400	Dc2/43r	1125
Fitzgerald, Henry	Meath, Tercroghan	gentry: gent	20-May-12	200	Dc1/114r	706
Fitzgerald, Henry	King's Co., Ballicomman	gentry: gent	11-Feb-28	300	Dc2/104r	1485
Fitzgerald, James	Kildare, Osbartston	gentry: gent	10-May-09	120	Dc1/88r	550
Fitzgerald, James	Westmeath, Kilanston	gentry: esquire	03-Mar-14	1000	Dc1/127v	791
Fitzgerald, James	Westmeath, Villarston	gentry: gent	29-May-00	400	Dc1/23v	158
Fitzgerald, James	Meath, Castle Moylagh	gentry: esquire	20-May-31	2000	Dc2/163r	1756
Fitzgerald, James	Meath, Moylagh	gentry: gent	15-Jun-19	150	Dc2/24r	993
Fitzgerald, James	Kildare, Osberton	gentry: gent	27-Jun-20	120	Dc2/31v	1039
Fitzgerald, James	Kildare, Osberston	gentry: gent	03-Dec-21	200	Dc2/37v	1087
Fitzgerald, John	Kildare, Kilmaske	gentry: gent	05-Feb-13	1000	Dc1/118r	734
Fitzgerald, John	Waterford, Dromany		04-Jun-25	200	Dc2/65r	1288
Fitzgerald, John	Dublin, Ffieldston	gentry: gent	23-Mar-26	80	Dc2/76r	1355
Fitzgerald, Luke	Meath, Tecrochan	gentry: knight	25-Nov-36	1200	Dc2/258r	2160
Fitzgerald, Luke	Meath, Tycroghan	gentry: knight	05-May-29	400	Dc2/128r	1601
Fitzgerald, Luke	Meath, Tycroghan	gentry: knight	17-Apr-35	1500	Dc2/233r	2037
Fitzgerald, Luke	Meath, Tycrohan	gentry: knight	05-Dec-28	200	Dc2/121v	1567
Fitzgerald, Luke	Meath, Tecrochan	gentry: knight	03-Dec-36	1200	Dc2/259r	2163
Fitzgerald, Oliver	Dublin, Chapel Isod	gentry: gent	17-Mar-03	400	Dc1/45v	289
Fitzgerald, Richard	Dublin, the city	gentry: gent	01-Dec-28	200	Dc2/119v	1560
Fitzgerald, Richard	Westmeath, Clonmochallam	gentry: gent	10-Jul-23	200	Dc2/49r	1173
Fitzgerald, Richard	Westmeath, Clonycollan	gentry: gent	19-May-21	400	Dc2/35v	1072
Fitzgerald, Robert	Kildare, Grangemellin	gentry: esquire	02-Oct-73	2000	Dc3/158v	2592

Standard	County	Occupation	Date	Amount	MS No	Ident No
Fitzgerald, Thomas	Meath, Tigcroghan	gentry: gent	22-Nov-31	400	Dc2/171v	1791
Fitzgerald, Thomas	Cork, Rostealan	gentry: esquire	04-Dec-13	400	Dc1/125v	778
Fitzgerald, William	Meath, Rathtroken	gentry: esquire	22-May-37	800	Dc2/264r	2184
Fitzpatrick, Joan		other: widow	01-Dec-97	5000	Dc1/7v	55
Fitzsimons, Gerrald	Dublin	gentry: gent	25-Apr-27	500	Dc2/91r	1426
Fitzsimons, Nicholas	Dublin	gentry: gent	13-Dec-20	600	Dc2/33v	1056
Fitzsimons, Thomas	Dublin, the city	trade: baker	17-Feb-74	400	Dc3/160r	2603
Fitzsimons, Thomas	Dublin, the city	trade: miller	17-Feb-74	400	B.L. 19, 844 f.19	3137
Fitzwilliam, Bridget		peer: countess Tyrconnell	14-May-66	220	B.L. 15, 636 f. 58	3722
Fitzwilliam, Bridget	Dublin?	peer: lady dowager Tyrconnell	14-May-66	220	Dc3/28	2286
Fitzwilliam, Edward	Dublin, the city	merchant	21-Nov-34	200	Dc2/222v	1994
Fitzwilliam, Nicholas	Dublin, Baldongane	gentry: esquire	05-Dec-28	200	Dc2/121r	1566
Fitzwilliam, Thomas	Dublin, the city	gentry: esquire	10-Mar-74	800	Dc3/161r	2607
Flattisburne?, Christopher	Kildare, Johnston	gentry: gent	26-Jan-00	200	Dc1/20v	140
Fleming, Christopher	Meath, Clonlion	gentry: gent	20-Nov-30	500	Dc2/156r	1725
Fleming, Elizabeth	Dublin	merchant: wife of Thomas	03-Feb-98	7	Dc1/9v	67
Fleming, James	Meath, Derpatricke	gentry: gent	08-Dec-08	120	Dc1/85v	534
Fleming, James	Meath, Stephenstowne	gentry: esquire	18-Aug-28	300	Dc2/114r	1533
Fleming, James	Meath, Stephenstowne	gentry: esquire	17-Feb-32	800	Dc2/176r	1809
Fleming, James	Meath, Stephenstowne	gentry: esquire	10-Feb-29	100	Dc2/124r	1581
Fleming, James	Meath, Stephenstowne	gentry: esquire	15-Jun-30	2000	Dc2/151v	1705
Fleming, James	Meath, Stevenston	gentry: esquire	26-Nov-24	200	Dc2/59r	1248
Fleming, John	Dublin, the city	merchant	13-Mar-34	205	Dc2/209r	1941
Fleming, Randal	Meath?	peer: baron Slane	06-Oct-70	500	Dc3/125	2491
Fleming, Thomas	Dublin	merchant	20-Dec-02	60	Dc1/43r	275
Fleming, Thomas	Dublin	merchant	18-Apr-03	300	Dc1/46r	293
Fleming, Thomas	Dublin	merchant	20-Dec-02	60	Dc1/43r	274
Fleming, Thomas	Dublin	merchant	20-Dec-03	300	Dc1/51r	327
Fleming, Thomas	Dublin	merchant	04-Dec-02	240	Dc1/42r	269
Fleming, Thomas	Dublin	merchant	03-Feb-98	7	Dc1/9v	67
Fleming, Thomas	Dublin	merchant	15-Aug-98	60	Dc1/12r	88
Fleming, Thomas	Dublin	merchant	20-Jul-99	40	Dc1/18r	124
Fleming, Thomas	Dublin	merchant	10-Feb-97	200	Dc1/1v	8
Fleming, Thomas	Dublin	merchant	13-Jul-01	80	Dc1/33r	219
Fleming, Thomas	Dublin	merchant	23-Apr-99	40	Dc1/17r	117
Fleming, Thomas	Dublin	merchant	27-Nov-99	60	Dc1/20r	136
Fleming, Thomas	Dublin	merchant	20-Jun-98	80	Dc1/11v	83
Fletcher, Benjamin	Roscommon, Elphin	gentry: esquire	17-May-75	1000	Dc3/167v	2634
Flinn, Owen	Roscommon, Clounrough	gentry: gent	27-Jun-33	300	Dc2/196v	1890
Flood, William	Dublin, the city	gentry: gent	16-May-65	740	B.L. 15, 635 f. 175	3559
Flood, William	Dublin, the city	gentry: gent	16-May-65	740	Dc3/6	2233
Flower, Henry	Dublin, the city	gentry: esquire	12-May-69	800	Dc3/96	2434
Flower, Henry	Dublin	gentry: esquire	12-May-69	800	B.L. 15, 636 f. 37a	3688

Standard	County	Occupation	Date	Amount	MS No	Ident No
Flower, Henry	Meath, Gallstowne	gentry: esquire	04-May-70	800	Dc3/118	2476
Flower, Henry	Dublin, the city	gentry: esquire	26-Jul-69	300	B.L. 15, 636 f. 42a	3698
Flower, Henry	Dublin	gentry: esquire	20-Jan-59	4000	B.L. 15, 635 f. 75	3392
Flower, Henry	Meath, Gallstowne	gentry: esquire	04-May-70	800	B.L. 15, 636 f. 57	3720
Flower, Henry	Dublin	gentry: esquire	30-Aug-60	1200	B.L. 15, 635 f. 75a	3393
Flower, John	Dublin, Ffinglas	gentry: gent	17-Dec-74	1100	Dc3/164r	2620
Flower, John	Dublin, Ffinglas	gentry: gent	17-Dec-74	1100	B.L. 19, 844 f. 47	3170
Flower, William	Dublin, Finglas	gentry: knight	03-Mar-75	200	Dc3/166r	2629
Flower, William	Dublin, Ffinglas	gentry: knight	03-Mar-75	200	B.L. 19, 844 f. 62a	3190
Forbes, Arthur	Longford, Castleforbes	gentry: baronet	10-Nov-69	2400	B.L. 15, 636 f. 57a	3721
Forbes, Arthur	Longford, Castleforbes	gentry: baronet	10-Nov-69	2000	Dc3/106	2452
Ford, Edward	Dublin	gentry: gent	23-May-26	200	Dc2/78r	1367
Ford, Mathew	Dublin, the city	gentry: gent	27-Jan-20	160	Dc2/28v	1019
Ford, Mathew	Dublin, the city	gentry: gent	31-Jan-22	240	Dc2/38v	1095
Ford, Mathew	Dublin, the city	gentry: gent	13-Feb-27	2200	Dc2/88r	1416
Ford, Mathew	Dublin, the city	gentry: esquire	23-Nov-30	100	Dc2/157r	1729
Ford, Mathew	Dublin	gentry: gent	05-Jul-17	200	Dc2/8v	908
Ford, Mathew	Dublin, the city	gentry: gent	15-Jul-14	200	Dc1/131r	812
Ford, Mathew	Dublin, the city	gentry: esquire	14-Feb-32	120	Dc2/176r	1808
Ford, Mathew	Dublin	gentry: gent	04-Dec-17	200	Dc2/12v	928
Ford, Mathew	Dublin	gentry: gent	02-Dec-17	200	Dc2/12r	927
Ford, Mathew	Dublin	gentry: gent	05-Mar-14	240	Dc1/127v	792
Ford, Mathew	Dublin, the city	gentry: esquire	20-May-33	2000	Dc2/194r	1880
Ford, Nicholas	Dublin	farmer: yeoman	09-May-98	105	Dc1/11r	78
Ford, Peter	Dublin, the city	merchant	07-Sep-22	60	Dc2/42v	1122
Ford, Robert	Louth, Drogheda		28-Jan-73	150	B.L. 15, 636 f. 127	3834
Ford, Robert	Cavan, Tullevin	gentry: knight	28-Jun-31	2000	Dc2/165v	1766
Forest, John	Dublin, the city	merchant	14-Feb-57	520	B.L. 19, 843 f. 187a	3082
Fortescue, Faithful	Louth, Dromyskine	gentry: knight	07-Dec-28	240	Dc2/120r	1561
Fortescue, Faithful	Louth, Dromyske	gentry: knight	13-Feb-26	200	Dc2/74r	1344
Forth, Edward	King's Co.?	gentry: son of [2nd] of Sir Ambrose Forth	04-Feb-26	200	Dc2/73r	1338
Forth, Edward	King's Co., Corbetston	gentry: gent	15-May-26	300	Dc2/77v	1364
Foster, Alice	Kildare, Maynoth	gentry: widow	14-Jan-07	66	Dc1/73r	443
Foster, Charles	Dublin, the city		21-Mar-37	350	Dc2/261r	2171
Foster, Daniel	Dublin	gentry: gent	30-Apr-30	63	Dc2/144v	1677
Foster, George	Dublin, Ballidowde	gentry: gent	12-Dec-27	220	Dc2/102r	1475
Foster, John	Dublin		10-Aug-97	240	Dc1/6r	46
Foster, John	Dublin		18-Jun-00	440	Dc1/24v	163
Foster, John	Dublin		18-Jun-99	400	Dc1/17r	114
Foster, John	Dublin		04-Dec-02	400	Dc1/41v	267
Foster, John	Dublin		21-Sep-11	200	Dc1/107r	666
Foster, John	Dublin		03-Mar-98	300	Dc1/10v	75
Foster, John	Dublin		18-Jun-00	200	Dc1/24v	164
Foster, John	Dublin		10-Dec-03	201	Dc1/50v	323

Standard	County	Occupation	Date	Amount	MS No	Ident No
Foster, John	Dublin		24-Nov-02	300	Dc1/41r	265
Foster, John	Dublin		15-Sep-03	1000	Dc1/49r	316
Foster, John	Dublin		16-Aug-98	200	Dc1/12r	87
Foster, John	Dublin		28-Mar-10	80	Dc1/94v	593
Foster, Nicholas	Dublin	gentry: gent	31-May-10	500	Dc1/97r	610
Foster, Nicholas	Dublin	gentry: gent	19-Nov-01	500	Dc1/34v	227
Foster, Nicholas	Dublin	gentry: gent	03-Jul-07	40	Dc1/79	484
Foster, Nicholas	Dublin	gentry: gent	01-Dec-07	200	Dc1/80r	496
Foster, Nicholas	Dublin	gentry: gent	05-Apr-10	150	Dc1/95r	595
Foster, Nicholas	Dublin	gentry: gent	16-May-01	200	Dc1/31v	208
Foster, Nicholas	Dublin	gentry: gent	04-May-03	300	Dc1/46v	296
Foster, Richard	Dublin	merchant	28-Nov-05	189	Dc1/63r	382
Foster, Walter	Kildare, Maynoth	gentry: gent	18-Jun-97	150	Dc1/4v	33
Foster, Walter	Kildare, Moynoth	gentry: gent	08-Apr-01	40	Dc1/30r	199
Foster,William	Kildare, Maynoth	gentry: gent	23-Apr-97	90	Dc1/3r	18
Fottrell, James	Dublin, Grasdue	gentry: gent	22-Nov-20	200	Dc2/33r	1052
Fottrell, James	Dublin?, Fildston	gentry: gent	20-Nov-23	200	Dc2/51r	1187
Foulkes, Nathaniel	Dublin, the city		18-Jun-70	160	B.L. 15, 636 f. 69	3740
Foulkes, Nathaniel	Dublin, the city		13-Nov-69	210	B.L. 15, 636 f. 55a	3718
Foulkes, Nathaniel	Dublin, the city		13-Nov-69	210	Dc3/106	2453
Foulkes, Nathaniel	Dublin, the city		13-Feb-67	220	Dc3/53	2338
Foulkes, Nathaniel	Dublin, the city		18-Jun-70	160	Dc3/120	2481
Foulkes, Robert	Cork, Curraghnahinshy	gentry: esquire	02-Aug-78	400	B.L. 19, 844 f.172	3303
Fountain, John	Queen's Co., Kilmarter	gentry: esquire	23-Nov-33	1000	Dc2/201r	1907
Fountain, John	Queen's Co., Kilmarter	gentry: gent	17-Jun-35	960	Dc2/237r	2056
Fowles, Thomas	Dublin, the city	gentry: esquire	06-Feb-56	500	B.L. 19, 843 f. 170a	3054
Fox, Nathaniel	Longford, Rathreagh	gentry: esquire	05-Jul-34	600	Dc2/214r	1961
Fox, Patrick	Dublin	gentry: esquire	31-Oct-07	300	Dc1/79ar	490
Fox, Patrick	Dublin	gentry: gent	03-Mar-03	200	Dc1/45r	287
Fox, Patrick	Dublin	gentry: gent	18-Jun-97	331	Dc1/4v	32
Fox, Patrick	Dublin	gentry: gent	06-Jul-97	300	Dc1/5v	42
Fox, Patrick	Dublin	gentry: gent	23-Dec-03	100	Dc1/50r	322
Fox, Patrick	Dublin	gentry: gent	02-Nov-03	80	Dc1/50r	321
Fox, Patrick	Dublin	gentry: gent	23-Feb-06	300	Dc1/66r	398
Fox, Patrick	Dublin, city	gentry: esquire	06-Aug-08	120	Dc1/83v	521
Fox, Patrick	Dublin	gentry: gent	23-Dec-02	200	Dc1/42v	273
Fox, Patrick	Dublin	gentry: gent	19-Sep-00	300	Dc1/25v	173
Fox, Patrick	Dublin	gentry: gent	20-Aug-99	500	Dc1/18v	129
Foxon, Samuel	Limerick, the city	gentry: esquire	18-Oct-69	700	B.L. 15, 636 f. 52	3713
Frank, John	Meath, Tercrahan	gentry: esquire	25-May-63	1500	B.L. 15, 635 f. 119	3468
Frankland, William	Dublin, the city	gentry: esquire	03-Apr-57	140	B.L. 19, 843 f. 191a	3090
Freake, Arthur	Cork, Garrne Tames	gentry: esquire	19-Mar-69	800	B.L. 15, 636 f. 38a	3691
Freake, Pierce	Cork, Rathbarry	gentry: esquire	14-Mar-79	2000	B.L. 15, 637 f. 19	3880
Freake, Pierce	Cork, Rathbarry	gentry: esquire	27-Mar-82	720	B.L. 15, 637 f. 57	3949

Standard	County	Occupation	Date	Amount	MS No	Ident No
French, Anthony	Galway	merchant: son of Peter,				
		merchant	03-Sep-74	500	B.L. 19, 844 f. 41	3165
French, Bartholomew	Cork, St Finbarr's	merchant	13-Apr-69	400	B.L. 15, 636 f. 34a	3683
French, Edmund	Cork, parish of					
	St. Finbarry?	gentry: gent	03-Feb-41	1200	B.L. 19, 843 f. 100a	2920
French, Godfrey	Sligo, Sligo	gentry: gent	06-Jun-39	170	B.L. 19, 843 f. 10a	2739
French, Godfrey	Sligo, Sligo	gentry: gent	09-May-39	154	B.L. 19, 843 f. 8	2734
French, James	Sligo, the town	merchant	01-Jul-38	100	B.L. 19, 843 f. 9a	2737
French, James	Sligo, the town	merchant	11-Aug-38	100	B.L. 19, 843 f.10	2738
French, John	Galway	merchant	03-Aug-22	1200	Dc2/42r	1120
French, John	Galway	merchant	27-May-29	2000	Dc2/130r	1609
French, Mathew	Dublin, the city	merchant	03-Jun-74	200	Dc3/162r	2612
French, Mathew	Dublin, the city	merchant	06-Aug-72	400	B.L. 15, 636 f. 119a	3826
French, Mathew	Dublin, the city	merchant	28-Jan-78	1800	Dc3/184v	2701
French, Mathew	Dublin, the city	merchant	15-Feb-73	600	B.L. 15, 636 f. 124	3831
French, Mathew	Dublin, the city	merchant	19-Apr-81	3000	B.L. 15, 637 f. 47a	3931
French, Mathew	Dublin, the city	merchant	06-Aug-72	400	Dc3/149r	2561
French, Mathew	Dublin, the city	merchant	28-Jan-78	1800	B.L. 19, 844 f. 149	3280
French, Mathew	Dublin, the city	merchant	15-Feb-73	600	Dc3/153v	2575
French, Nicholas	Galway	merchant: son of Peter,				
		merchant	03-Sep-74	500	B.L. 19, 844 f. 41	3165
French, Patrick	Galway	merchant	28-Nov-11	100	Dc1/109v	680
French, Peter	Galway	gentry: esquire	06-Dec-12	500	Dc1/117r	727
French, Peter	Galway	merchant	19-Jul-09	440	Dc1/90r	565
French, Peter	Galway	merchant	16-Dec-99	100	Dc1/20r	137
Fyan, Edmund	Dublin, the city	merchant	27-May-37	80	Dc2/264v	2186
Fyan, Edmund	Dublin, the city	merchant	24-Dec-27	280	Dc2/102v	1477
Fyan, Richard	Dublin, the city	merchant	17-Dec-25	40	Dc2/72r	1333
Galt, John	Londonderry, Coleraine	merchant	03-Dec-79	400	B.L. 15, 637 f. 31a	3904
Galway, Edward	Cork, Lowtaghbeg	gentry: gent	29-Oct-79	800	B.L. 15, 637 f. 27	3895
Galway, Edward	Cork, Loutaghbegg	gentry: gent	02-Mar-67	800	B.L. 15, 635 f. 185	3580
Galway, Edward	Cork, Lwotaghbeg, the city	gentry: gent	18-Jan-77	880	B.L. 19, 844 f. 130	3260
Galway, Edward	Cork, Loughtabegg	gentry: gent	21-Dec-66	500	B.L. 15, 635 f. 182a	3575
Galway, Edward	Cork, Lesnekernig	gentry: gent	18-Nov-64	800	B.L. 15, 635 f. 145a	3510
Galway, Edward	Cork, Livotaghbeg	gentry: gent	09-Apr-68	300	B.L. 15, 635 f. 215	3635
Galway, Edward	Cork, Loughtabegg	gentry: gent	12-Feb-69	600	Dc3/89	2424
Galway, Edward	Cork, Lwotaghbegg	gentry: gent	03-Jan-72	600	B.L. 15, 636 f. 106a	3804
Galway, Edward	Cork, Lwotaghbeg	gentry: gent	21-Dec-71	1000	B.L. 15, 636 f. 107	3805
Galway, Edward	Cork, Lwotaghbeg	gentry: gent	21-Dec-71	1000	B.L. 15, 636 f. 107a	3806
Galway, Edward	Cork, Loughtabegg	gentry: gent	10-Feb-69	600	B.L. 15, 636 f. 27a	3673
Galway, Edward	Cork, Loutagbegg	gentry: gent	21-Dec-66	500	Dc3/48	2327
Galway, Edward	Cork, Loutaghbegg	gentry: gent	02-Mar-67	800	Dc3/56	2343
Galway, James	Cork, the city	gentry: gent	23-Oct-18	120	B.L. 19, 843 f. 4a	2727
Galway, John	Cork, the city	gentry: esquire	13-Sep-78	660	B.L. 19, 844 f. 169	3300

Standard	County	Occupation	Date	Amount	MS No	Ident No
Galway, Walter	Cork, the city	merchant	28-Jun-23	37	Dc2/48v	1167
Gamble, George	Cork, the city	merchant	07-Nov-72	160	B.L. 15, 636 f. 128	3836
Gamble, George	Cork, the city	merchant	04-May-70	120	B.L. 15, 636 f. 62	3728
Gamble, George	Cork, the city	merchant	09-Feb-69	332	B.L. 15, 636 f. 33	3681
Gamble, George	Cork, the city	merchant	04-May-70	240	B.L. 15, 636 f. 61	3727
Gandy, Henry	Dublin, the city	merchant	02-Dec-70	50	B.L. 15, 636 f. 80a	3762
Gandy, Henry	Dublin, the city	merchant	02-Dec-70	150	Dc3/132r	2506
Garnett, Matthew	Louth, Drogheda		27-Jan-36	160	B.L. 19, 843 f. 72a	2864
Gash, John	Cork, Castle Lyons	gentry: gent	09-Jul-78	500	B.L . 19, 844 f.171	3302
Gay, John	Dublin, the city	gentry: esquire	21-Feb-57	200	B.L. 19, 843 f. 187	3081
Gay, John	Dublin, the city	gentry: gent	20-Mar-71	500	Dc3/136v	2519
Gay, John	Dublin, the city	gentry: esquire	23-Jul-58	200	B.L. 15, 635 f. 34	3323
Gay, John	Dublin, the city	gentry: gent	23-Dec-65	92	Dc3/18	2263
Gay, John	Dublin, the city	gentry: gent	04-Feb-76	800	B.L. 19, 844 f. 87	3215
Gay, John	Dublin, the city	gentry: gent	19-Aug-63	200	B.L. 15, 635 f. 125a	3478
Gay, John	Dublin, the city	gentry: gent	22-Sep-63	200	B.L. 15, 635 f. 126	3479
Gay, John	Dublin, the city	gentry: esquire	24-May-58	400	B.L. 15, 635 f. 30	3315
Gay, John	Dublin, the city	gentry: gent	12-May-74	500	Dc3/161r	2609
Gay, John	Dublin, the city	gentry: esquire	24-Mar-57	200	B.L. 15, 635 f. 24a	3306
Gay, John	Dublin	gentry: esquire	21-Jul-59	200	B.L. 15, 635 f. 54a	3360
Gay, John	Dublin, the city	gentry: esquire	22-Feb-58	100	B.L. 19, 843 f. 205	3117
Gay, John	Dublin, the city	gentry: esquire	08-Jul-57	400	B.L. 19, 843 f. 195	3097
Gay, John	Dublin, the city	gentry: gent	12-May-74	500	B.L. 19, 844 f. 29	3152
Gay, John	Dublin	gentry: esquire	09-Oct-57	200	B.L. 19, 843 f. 197	3101
Gay, John	Dublin, the city	gentry: esquire	13-Feb-58	200	B.L. 19, 843 f. 204a	3116
Gay, John	Dublin, the city	gentry: esquire	07-Feb-59	200	B.L. 15, 645 f. 38	3330
Gay, John	Dublin, the city	gentry: gent	20-Mar-71	500	B.L. 15, 636 f. 85	3770
Gay, John	Dublin, the city	gentry: gent	04-Feb-76	800	Dc3/171v	2648
Gaynor, James	Westmeath, Koghennell	farmer	26-Nov-31	200	Dc2/172v	1795
Gaynor, Thady	Westmeath, Desert	farmer: yeoman	27-Apr-15	120	Dc1/136v	846
Gaynor, Thady	Westmeath, Desert	farmer: husbandman	13-Feb-13	100	Dc1/119r	738
Gaynor, Thady	Westmeath, Blackcastle	farmer: yeoman	15-Jun-24	200	Dc2/56r	1222
Gaynor, Thady	Westmeath, Blackcastle	farmer: yeoman	10-Jun-29	50	Dc2/131r	1614
Gaynor, Thady	Westmeath, Desert	farmer: husbandman	16-May-12	100	Dc1/113v	704
Geere, William	England, London, the city	gentry: esquire	06-Sep-42	2000	B.L. 19, 843 f. 108a	2936
Geere, William	England, London	gentry: esquire	06-Sep-42	200	B.L. 19, 843 f. 109	2937
Genison, William	England, London	gentry: gent	22-May-06	200	Dc1/68v	414
Geoghegan, Hugh	Westmeath, Castelton	gentry: esquire	24-Nov-18	60	Dc2/18r	958
Geoghegan, Hugh	Westmeath, Lara [Moycashell]	gentry: gent	01-Jul-12	200	Dc1/114v	713
George, Robert	Dublin, the city	prof: doctor of law	05-Dec-66	1288	B.L. 15, 636 f. 24a	3667
George, Robert	Dublin, the city	prof: doctor of law	05-Dec-66	1288	Dc2/42	2320
George, Robert	Dublin, the city	gentry: esquire	02-May-59	1200	B.L. 15, 635 f. 43	3338
Gerald, John	Dublin		11-Feb-98	200	Dc1/9v	66
Gerald, Thomas	Dublin		01-Feb-97	60	Dc1/1v	7

Standard	County	Occupation	Date	Amount	MS No	Ident No
Gerard, James	King's Co., Phillippston	merchant	03-Jul-26	200	Dc2/80v	1383
Gernon, Edward	Louth, Germonston	gentry: esquire	19-May-06	300	Dc1/67v	408
Gernon, George	Louth, Milton	gentry: esquire	01-Dec-26	250	Dc2/84r	1400
Gernon, Richard	Louth, Stabanon	gentry: gent	06-Oct-32	300	Dc2/186r	1848
Gernon, Robert	Dublin	gentry: gent	27-Apr-22	167	Dc2/39r	1101
Gernon, Roger	Dublin	merchant	01-Jun-27	60	Dc2/93v	1436
Gernon, Thomas	Louth, Mollenston	gentry: gent	02-Dec-18	200	Dc2/18v	961
Gibbons, Bridget	Dublin	other: spinster?, daughter of Margaret	12-May-35	600	B.L. 19, 843 f. 6a	2731
Gibbons, Bridget	Dublin	other: spinster?, daughter of Margaret	12-May-35	600	Dc2/235r	2048
Gibbons, Eleanor	Dublin	other: spinster?, daughter of Margarett	12-May-35	600	Dc2/235r	2048
Gibbons, Eleanor	Dublin	other: spinster?, daughter of Margaret	12-May-35	600	B.L. 19, 843 f. 6a	2731
Gibbons, Francis	Dublin	other: spinster?, daughter of Margaret	12-May-35	600	Dc2/235r	2048
Gibbons, Francis	Dublin	other: spinster?, daughter of Margaret	12-May-35	600	B.L. 19, 843 f. 6a	2731
Gibbons, John	Cork, Garrans	gentry: gent	10-Apr-86	3000	B.L. 15, 637 f. 104a	4036
Gibbons, John	Dublin, the city		24-May-33	700	Dc2/195r	1883
Gibbons, John	Dublin, the city	merchant	08-May-23	200	Dc2/46v	1153
Gibbons, John	Dublin, the city	merchant	08-Mar-19	80	Dc2/21r	977
Gibbons, John	Dublin, the city		02-Jul-28	600	Dc2/112r	1522
Gibbons, Margaret	Dublin	other: spinster?, daughter of Margaret	12-May-35	600	B.L. 19, 843 f. 6a	2731
Gibbons, Margaret	Dublin, the city	other: widow	28-Jun-38	600	B.L. 19, 843 f. 7	2732
Gibbons, Margaret	Dublin	other: widow	12-May-35	600	Dc2/235r	2048
Gibbons, Margaret	Dublin	other: widow	12-May-35	600	B.L. 19, 843 f. 6a	2731
Gibbons, Mary	Dublin	other: spinster?, daughter of Margaret	12-May-35	600	Dc2/235r	2048
Gibbons, Tibbot	Mayo, Dowlagh	gentry: gent	06-Jun-14	300	Dc1/130r	808
Gibbons, William	Dublin	gentry: gent	11-Mar-14	80	Dc1/128r	793
Gibson, John	England, London	merchant	25-Aug-25	40	Dc2/69r	1312
Gibson, Seafoule	Dublin, the city	gentry: esquire	27-Jul-55	2000	B.L. 19, 843 f. 158	3031
Gibson, Seafoule	Louth, Drogheda	gentry: esquire	04-May-70	800	Dc3/117	2475
Gibson, Seafoule	Louth, Drogheda	gentry: esquire	04-May-70	800	B.L. 15, 636 f. 68a	3739
Gifford, John	King's Co., Castlejordan		17-Jul-39	4000	B.L. 19, 843 f. 22a	2763
Gilbert, John	England, London	merchant	06-Feb-02	200	Dc1/36r	234
Gilbert, Thomas	England?, London?	other: exec will of John Gilbert, London, grocer	15-Oct-18	120	Dc2/16v	951
Gilbert, Thomas	Meath, Rahinstowne	gentry: gent	04-Mar-78	410	Dc3/187r	2707
Glyde, John	England, London	trade: skinner	22-Mar-14	186	Dc1/128v	798
Glyde, Solomon			22-Mar-14	186	Dc1/128v	798
Goddard, Bridget	Cork, the city	other: widow	17-Apr-86	330	B.L. 15, 637 f. 106	4039

Standard	County	Occupation	Date	Amount	MS No	Ident No
Goddard, Bridget	Cork, the city	other: widow	10-Apr-86	220	B.L. 15, 637 f. 105	4037
Goodman, James	Dublin, the city	gentry: esquire	13-Dec-28	400	Dc2/122v	1571
Goodman, William	Dublin, Loughlauste		17-Feb-02	20	Dc1/36r	237
Goodwin, John	Dublin	merchant	17-May-97	200	Dc1/4r	26
Goodwin, John	Dublin	merchant	18-Nov-02	200	Dc1/40v	262
Goodwin, John	Dublin	merchant	04-Feb-01	200	Dc1/28v	191
Goodwin, John	Dublin	merchant	12-Feb-03	600	Dc1/44v	284
Goodwin, John	Dublin	merchant	23-Feb-09	60	Dc1/87v	548
Goodwin, John	Dublin	merchant	07-May-97	40	Dc1/3v	21
Gookin, Anne	Cork, Courtmacsherrey	other: spinster, daughter of Dorothy	27-Apr-82	1600	B.L. 15, 637 f. 57a	3950
Gookin, Mary	Cork, Courtmacsherrey	other: spinster, daughter of Dorothy	27-Apr-82	1600	B.L. 15, 637 f. 57a	3950
Gooley, Michael	Cork, the city	gentry: esquire	25-Aug-68	300	B.L. 15, 635 f. 227a	3660
Gore, Hugh		prof: bishop of Waterford and Lismore	26-Jun-68	3000	B.L. 15, 635 f. 226	3657
Gore, Hugh		prof: bishop of Waterford and Lismore	26-Jun-68	3000	Dc3/80	2407
Gorey, Henry	Meath, Trim	merchant	07-May-18	320	Dc2/14r	938
Gormican, Henry	Carlow, Newton	gentry: gent	24-Nov-36	420	Dc2/257v	2157
Gormican, Henry	Carlow, Newton	gentry: gent	11-Nov-34	200	Dc2/220v	1987
Gormican, Henry	Carlow, Newton	gentry: gent	11-Nov-34	200	Dc2/221r	1988
Gormican, Henry	Carlow, Newton	gentry: gent	10-Feb-30	400	Dc2/142r	1666
Gormican, Thady	Carlow, Newton	gentry: gent	16-Nov-30	200	Dc2/155v	1723
Gormican, Thady	Carlow, Newtowne	gentry: esquire	27-Mar-32	200	Dc2/178r	1816
Gormican, Thady	Carlow, Newton	gentry: gent	15-Dec-25	320	Dc2/72r	1332
Gough, Christopher	Dublin	gentry: gent	25-Sep-58	170	B.L. 15, 635 f. 45a	3343
Gough, Edward	Dublin	merchant	21-May-04	300	Dc1/53r	334
Gough, Edward	Dublin, the city	merchant	30-Mar-17	200	Dc2/5v	896
Gough, Edward	Dublin		21-Jun-27	400	Dc2/95r	1444
Gough, Edward	Dublin, the city		04-Dec-28	400	Dc2/120v	1564
Gough, Edward	Dublin		30-Nov-26	200	Dc2/84r	1399
Gough, Edward	Dublin	merchant	05-Dec-17	300	Dc2/12v	929
Gough, Edward	Dublin		28-Feb-28	200	Dc2/104v	1488
Gough, Edward	Dublin, the city		26-May-28	120	Dc2/110r	1513
Gough, Edward	Dublin	merchant	10-Dec-17	200	Dc2/12v	930
Gough, Edward	Dublin		05-May-28	200	Dc2/106v	1498
Gough, Edward	Dublin	merchant	04-Jul-25	600	Dc2/68r	1308
Gough, Francis	Cork, Ballynagaule	gentry: gent	04-Apr-83	4000	B.L. 15, 637 f. 72a	3978
Gough, Patrick	Dublin		27-Sep-23	40	Dc2/50v	1182
Gough, Patrick	Dublin		08-Jun-27	1000	Dc2/93v	1437
Gough, Patrick	Dublin	gentry: gent	22-May-15	240	Dc1/137v	854
Gough, Patrick	Dublin, the city		14-Nov-25	400	Dc2/70r	1319
Gough, Patrick	Dublin	gentry: gent	21-Dec-16	100	Dc2/3v	886

Standard	County	Occupation	Date	Amount	MS No	Ident No
Gough, Patrick	Dublin, the city		27-Jul-24	200	Dc2/57v	1235
Gough, William	Dublin		06-Mar-01	60	Dc1/29r	193
Gough, William	Dublin		02-Apr-04	600	Dc1/52r	331
Gough, William	Dublin		25-Aug-00	200	Dc1/25v	172
Gould, Adam	Dublin	merchant	24-Oct-60	240	B.L. 15, 635 f. 126a	3480
Gould, David	Cork, Kinsale	merchant	21-Mar-83	2800	B.L. 15, 637 f. 71a	3976
Gould, Edward	Cork	gentry: gent	14-Nov-09	40	Dc1/92v	580
Gould, Garret	Cork, Knockraghy	gentry: gent	08-Feb-67	300	Dc3/52	2336
Gould, Garret	Cork, Knuckraghy	gentry: gent	08-Feb-67	300	B.L. 15, 635 f. 201	3611
Gould, Henry	Cork, the city	merchant	05-Nov-40	1000	B.L. 19, 843 f. 92a	2904
Gould, Henry	Cork, the city	merchant	07-Apr-39	400	B.L. 19, 843 f. 30a	2779
Gould, Ignatius	Cork, the city	merchant	23-Jan-65	600	B.L. 15, 635 f. 149a	3518
Gould, Ignatius	Cork, the city	merchant	29-Nov-79	600	B.L. 15, 637 f. 25a	3892
Gould, Ignatius	Cork, the city	merchant	13-Jul-76	260	B.L. 19, 844 f. 109a	3237
Gould, James	Cork, the city	gentry: gent	03-Feb-41	1200	B.L. 19, 843 f. 100a	2920
Gould, James	Cork, the city	gentry: gent	26-May-65	300	B.L. 15, 635 f. 152a	3524
Gould, Stephen	Cork, Kinsale	merchant	21-Mar-83	2800	B.L. 15, 637 f. 71a	3976
Goulding, Auge	Dublin, the city	gentry: gent	05-Sep-65	200	Dc3/14	2251
Goulding, Richard	Dublin, the city	merchant	03-Jan-31	160	Dc2/158v	1736
Grace, James	Dublin, the city	gentry: gent	19-Dec-34	220	B.L. 19, 843 f. 98	2915
Grace, James	Dublin, the city	gentry: gent	18-Mar-34	200	Dc2/209v	1942
Grace, James	Dublin, the city	gentry: gent	19-Dec-34	220	Dc2/226v	2012
Grace, John	Kilkenny, Courtstowne	gentry: esquire	23-Feb-70	1400	Dc3/116	2471
Grace, Sheffield	Kilkenny, Cowitstowne	gentry: esquire	13-Dec-80	4000	B.L. 15, 637 f. 44a	3927
Graham, George	Wicklow, Ballynure	gentry: gent	31-Dec-19	200	Dc2/28r	1017
Graham, William	Wicklow, Kelballyowen	gentry: esquire	04-Dec-34	400	Dc2/224v	2003
Graves, Christopher	Dublin	gentry: gent	26-Oct-26	200	Dc2/82v	1393
Graves, William	Meath, Rathmollan	gentry: gent	07-May-64	280	B.L. 15, 635 f. 148	3515
Greames, George	Wicklow, Ballinure	gentry: gent	20-Mar-26	600	Dc2/75v	1353
Greames, Robert	England?, London?	other: exec will of John Gilbert, London, grocer	15-Oct-18	120	Dc2/16v	951
Green, Elizabeth	Waterford, Killmanaheene	gentry: widow, of Godfrey, esquire	04-Apr-83	4000	B.L. 15, 637 f. 72a	3978
Green, Godfrey	Waterford, Killmaneheene	gentry: esquire	10-May-75	500	B.L. 19, 844 f. 66	3194
Greenstreet, Simon	Waterford, the county	gentry: gent	30-Nov-29	400	Dc2/139r	1650
Gregory, George	Louth, Sheepgrange	gentry: gent	16-Jun-38	200	B.L. 19, 843 f. 25	2768
Gregory, George	Louth, Sheepgrange	gentry: gent	30-Aug-39	200	B.L. 19, 843 f. 24a	2767
Gregory, Mary	Dublin, the city	other: spinster	14-Jun-76	1000	B.L. 19, 844 f. 96	3223
Gregory, Mary	Dublin, the city	other: spinster	14-Jun-76	1000	Dc3/177v	2667
Grenndich, George	Dublin	gentry: esquire	16-Sep-11	105	Dc1/106r	661
Grenndich, George	Dublin	gentry: esquire	25-Nov-10	200	Dc1/100v	630
Grenndich, George	Dublin	gentry: esquire	12-Nov-10	200	Dc1/99v	623
Grenndich, George	Dublin	gentry: esquire	29-Jan-11	250	Dc1/102r	639
Grenndich, George	Dublin	gentry: esquire	22-Nov-11	400	Dc1/109r	678
Gressingham, William	Dublin, the city	trade: courier	22-Jul-65	120	Dc3/12	2247

Standard	County	Occupation	Date	Amount	MS No	Ident No
Grey, Henry	Limerick, Tongh	gentry: esquire	23-Jul-72	1600	Dc3/148v	2560
Gribble, Nicholas	Limerick, the city	gentry: gent	24-Apr-79	600	B.L. 15, 637 f. 16a	3876
Griffith, John	Down, Cumber	gentry: gent	26-Aug-71	540	B.L. 15, 636 f. 92a	3784
Griffith, John	Down, Cumber	merchant	03-Nov-71	160	B.L. 15, 636 f. 93	3785
Grimsell, Humphry	England, Westminster, the city	trade: grocer	06-Feb-55	1400	B.L. 19, 843 f. 152	3018
Grimsell, Jean	England, Westminster, the city	trade: wife of Humphry	06-Feb-55	1400	B.L. 19, 843 f. 152	3018
Hackett, Edmund	Meath, Prieston	farmer: yeoman	16-May-35	200	Dc2/236r	2051
Hackett, James	Meath, Pristowne	gentry: gent	09-Dec-72	80	Dc3/151r	2566
Hackett, John	Wicklow, Ballynekill	gentry: esquire	16-Jan-61	600	B.L. 15, 635 f. 61a	3374
Hackett, Roger	Dublin, the city	gentry: gent	27-Jun-20	120	Dc2/31v	1038
Hackett, Roger	Dublin, the city	gentry: gent	23-Jun-20	90	Dc2/31r	1037
Hackett, Thomas	Dublin, the city	merchant	03-Jan-73	90	B.L. 15, 636 f. 123	3830
Hackett, Thomas	Dublin, the city	merchant	02-Mar-75	2500	B.L. 19, 844 f. 55	3179
Hackett, Thomas	Dublin, the city	merchant	23-Mar-66	200	Dc3/27	2282
Hackett, Thomas	Dublin, the city	merchant	02-Mar-75	2500	Dc3/165v	2627
Hackett, Thomas	Dublin, the city	merchant	10-Nov-71	3200	Dc3/140r	2531
Hackett, Thomas	Dublin, the city	merchant	12-Feb-80	3200	B.L. 15, 637 f. 27a	3896
Hackett, Thomas	Dublin, the city	merchant	30-Nov-70	2800	B.L. 15, 636 f. 76a	3755
Hackett, Thomas	Dublin, the city	merchant	30-Nov-70	2800	Dc3/132r	2504
Hackett, Thomas	Dublin, the city	merchant	21-Jan-74	800	Dc3/159v	2599
Hackett, Thomas	Dublin, the city	merchant	03-Jan-73	900	Dc3/152v	2569
Hackett, Thomas	Dublin, the city	merchant	10-Nov-71	3200	B.L. 15, 636 f. 92	3783
Hadsor, George	Louth, Drogheda	merchant	22-Dec-40	200	B.L. 19, 843 f. 79	2877
Hadsor, Richard	Louth, Kepock	gentry: esquire	13-May-08	200	Dc1/82v	513
Hall, John	Dublin, St. Patrick's Close	merchant	05-May-45	800	B.L. 19, 843 f.119	2957
Halley, Nicholas	Limerick, the city	gentry: esquire	09-Nov-39	3600	B.L. 19, 843 f. 33a	2785
Halley, Oliver	Cork, Ffernought	gentry: gent	16-Mar-28	180	B.L. 19, 843 f. 19a	2757
Halley, Oliver	Cork, Ffernought	gentry: gent	24-Mar-38	440	B.L. 19, 843 f. 19	2756
Halley, Oliver	Cork, Ffernought	gentry: gent	10-Dec-36	800	B.L. 19, 843 f. 18a	2755
Halley, William	Limerick	merchant	13-Feb-07	87	Dc1/74v	450
Hallows, John	Dublin	merchant	20-Mar-46	140	B.L. 19, 843 f. 121	2961
Hamill, Hugh	Tyrone, Strabane	gentry: esquire	23-May-76	3000	Dc3/174r	2657
Hamill, Hugh	Tyrone, Strabane	gentry: esquire	23-May-76	3000	B.L. 19, 844 f. 110	3238
Hamilton, Alexander	Dublin, the city	gentry: knight	11-Jun-47	2000	B.L. 19, 843 f. 123	2965
Hamilton, Alice	Dublin?	peer: lady Hamilton	04-Jun-41	1600	B.L. 19, 843 f. 94	2907
Hamilton, Archibald	Tyrone, Tatycosker	gentry: esquire	22-Nov-33	400	Dc2/200v	1906
Hamilton, Claude	King's Co., Blundelsbury	gentry: esquire	28-Jun-72	220	Dc3/147r	2556
Hamilton, Claude	King's Co., Blundelsbury	gentry: esquire	28-Jun-72	210	Dc3/147r	2555
Hamilton, Claude	King's Co., Liscluny	gentry: esquire	13-Jun-73	300	Dc3/157v	2585
Hamilton, Francis	Cavan, Castlekeylagh	gentry: knight	19-Jul-36	1200	Dc2/255r	2145
Hamilton, George	Tyrone, Greenlagh	gentry: knight	18-Mar-25	553	Dc2/63r	1275
Hamilton, George	Tyrone, Greenlagh	gentry: knight	18-Mar-25	555	Dc2/62v	1273

Standard	County	Occupation	Date	Amount	MS No	Ident No
Hamilton, George	Tyrone, Greenlagh	gentry: knight	18-Mar-25	680	Dc2/62v	1271
Hamilton, George	Tyrone, Greenlagh	gentry: knight	18-Mar-25	1100	Dc2/62r	1270
Hamilton, George	Tyrone, Greenlagh	gentry: knight	18-Mar-25	660	Dc2/62v	1272
Hamilton, George	Tyrone, Greenlagh	gentry: knight	18-Mar-25	554	Dc2/62v	1274
Hamilton, Hans	Armagh, Hamilton Bawn	gentry: knight	19-Jun-78	10000	Dc3/191r	2720
Hamilton, Hans	Armagh, Hamilton's Bawn	gentry: knight and baronet	19-Jun-78	10000	B.L. 15, 637 f. 2	3854
Hamilton, Hellenor	Antrim, Ballyskelly	gentry: widow, of John, esquire	10-Aug-63	1280	B.L. 15, 635 f. 171	3552
Hamilton, Henry	Kildare, Tully	gentry: esquire	05-Jun-78	4000	B.L. 19, 844 f. 157	3288
Hamilton, Henry	Kildare, Tully	gentry: esquire	29-Jan-79	600	B.L. 15, 637 f. 11	3867
Hamilton, Henry	Kildare, Tully	gentry: esquire	19-Jun-78	10000	Dc3/190v	2719
Hamilton, Henry	Kildare, Tully	gentry: esquire	19-Jun-78	10000	B.L. 19, 844 f. 162	3293
Hamilton, Henry	Kildare, Tully	gentry: esquire	05-Jun-78	4000	Dc3/189r	2715
Hamilton, Hugh	Tyrone, Loaghneneas	gentry: esquire	18-Mar-25	553	Dc2/63r	1275
Hamilton, Hugh	Tyrone, Loaghneneas	gentry: esquire	18-Mar-25	1100	Dc2/62r	1270
Hamilton, Hugh	Tyrone, Loaghneneas	gentry: esquire	18-Mar-25	680	Dc2/62v	1271
Hamilton, Hugh	Tyrone, Loaghneneas	gentry: esquire	18-Mar-25	554	Dc2/62v	1274
Hamilton, Hugh	Tyrone, Loaghnecneas	gentry: esquire	18-Mar-25	660	Dc2/62v	1272
Hamilton, Hugh	Tyrone, Loaghneneas	gentry: esquire	18-Mar-25	555	Dc2/62v	1273
Hamilton, James	Down, Newcastle	gentry: esquire	19-Jun-78	10000	Dc3/191r	2720
Hamilton, James	Down, Newcastle	gentry: esquire	19-Jun-78	10000	B.L. 15, 637 f. 2	3854
Hamilton, James	Tyrone, Ballyloghmcguffe	gentry: esquire	08-May-18	400	Dc2/14v	939
Hamilton, James	Down, Bangore	gentry: esquire	15-Jan-06	1000	Dc1/64v	389
Hamilton, James	Tyrone?	peer: viscount Clandeboy	19-Apr-27	1800	Dc2/90v	1425
Hamilton, Jane	Antrim, Ballyskelly	gentry: spinster?, daughter of John and Hellonor	10-Aug-63	1280	B.L. 15, 635 f. 171	3552
Hamilton, John	Cavan, Croonaree	gentry: esquire	18-Mar-25	554	Dc2/62v	1274
Hamilton, John	Cavan, Corronaree	gentry: esquire	18-Mar-25	660	Dc2/62v	1272
Hamilton, John	Cavan, Coronaree	gentry: esquire	18-Mar-25	555	Dc2/62v	1273
Hamilton, John	Cavan, Corronaree	gentry: esquire	18-Mar-25	1100	Dc2/62r	1270
Hamilton, John	Cavan, Corronaree	gentry: esquire	18-Mar-25	680	Dc2/62v	1271
Hamilton, John	Cavan, Coronaree	gentry: esquire	18-Mar-25	553	Dc2/63r	1275
Hamilton, Mary	Tipperary, Cashell, the city	other: widow	07-Oct-82	640	B.L. 15, 637 f. 65	3964
Hamilton, Rachel	Antrim, Ballyskelly	gentry: spinster?, daughter of John and Hellenor	10-Aug-63	1280	B.L. 15, 635 f. 171	3552
Hamilton, Robert	Scotland, Twydy	gentry: esquire	09-May-15	1000	Dc1/137r	850
Hamilton, Robert	Tipperary, Rathcoule		05-Dec-34	1000	Dc2/225r	2005
Hamilton, William	King's Co., Liscloney	gentry: gent	13-Dec-58	400	B.L. 15, 635 f. 45	3342
Hamilton, William	Down, Downe	gentry: esquire	28-Feb-66	300	B.L. 15, 635 f. 174	3557
Hamilton, William	Tyrone, Loughcurrine	gentry: esquire	23-Dec-65	600	Dc3/18	2264
Hamilton, William	Dublin, the city	gentry: esquire	17-Dec-64	1000	B.L. 15, 635 f. 151a	3522

Standard	County	Occupation	Date	Amount	MS No	Ident No
Hamilton, William	King's Co., Liscloony	gentry: esquire	22-Jun-69	400	Dc3/100	2442
Hamilton, William	Donegal, Clonly	gentry: gent	20-Feb-55	600	B.L. 19, 843 f. 154	3022
Hamilton, William	Tyrone, Calidon/Kinard	gentry: esquire	08-Nov-69	3000	Dc3/104	2451
Hamilton, William	Dublin, the city	gentry: esquire	27-Apr-65	650	B.L. 15, 635 f. 153	3525
Hamilton, William	Down, Downe	gentry: esquire	07-Dec-65	217	Dc3/17	2259
Hamilton, William	Down, Downe	gentry: esquire	28-Feb-66	300	Dc3/24	2277
Hamilton, William	Down, Downe	gentry: esquire	02-Dec-65	261	B.L. 15, 635 f. 173a	3556
Handcock, Henry	Dublin, the city	gentry: esquire	13-Sep-82	200	B.L. 15, 637 f. 62a	3960
Handcock, Mathew	Dublin	merchant	01-Dec-98	133	Dc1/14r	98
Handcock, Mathew	Dublin		13-Jun-08	120	Dc1/83v	519
Handcock, William	Westmeath, Twy	gentry: esquire	09-Jun-73	1600	Dc3/156v	2583
Handcock, William	Westmeath, Athlone	gentry: esquire	22-Jun-65	560	Dc3/11	2246
Handcock, William	Westmeath, Athlone	gentry: esquire	22-Jun-65	560	B.L. 15, 636 f. 85a	3771
Handcock, William	Westmeath, Troy?	gentry: esquire	09-Jul-73	1600	B.L. 15, 636 f. 137	3850
Handcock, William	Westmeath, Athlone	gentry: esquire	22-Jun-65	240	Dc3/11	2245
Hanlon, John	Dublin, the city	trade: navigator	07-Sep-22	60	Dc2/42v	1122
Hanlon, Redmond	Louth, Dundalk	gentry: gent	08-Jun-20	2000	Dc2/30v	1032
Hanmer, Mary	Dublin	other: widow?	05-Dec-18	200	Dc2/18v	962
Hanmer, Mary	Dublin	other: widow	04-Mar-26	400	Dc2/75r	1350
Hannan, Robert	Limerick, the city	merchant	15-Nov-82	4000	B.L. 15, 637 f. 67	3967
Hansard, Richard	Donegal, Lifford	gentry: esquire	22-Jun-78	2400	B.L. 19, 844 f. 165	3296
Hansard, Richard	Donegal, Lifford	gentry: esquire	22-Jun-78	2000	B.L. 19, 844 f. 164	3295
Hanson, John	Dublin, the city	gentry: gent	16-Apr-78	300	B.L. 19, 844 f. 155	3286
Hanson, John	Dublin, the city	gentry: gent	16-Apr-78	43	B.L. 19, 844 f. 154	3285
Hanson, Thomas	Cavan, Aghacreevy	gentry: gent	10-Nov-65	240	B.L. 15, 635 f. 158	3533
Hanson, Thomas	Cavan, Aghacreevy	gentry: gent	10-Nov-65	240	Dc3/15	2255
Harman, Nicholas	Carlow, Painston	gentry: esquire	21-May-05	4000	Dc1/59v	363
Harmer, William	Cork, Downmaghon	gentry: esquire	13-Apr-81	850	B.L. 15, 637 f. 47	3930
Harold, Patrick	Dublin	trade: butcher	29-Apr-01	40	Dc1/30v	203
Harold, Thomas	Dublin, the city	trade: sadler	21-Apr-19	40	Dc2/22r	982
Harold, Walter	Kildare, Kilbery	gentry: gent	24-Jun-00	140	Dc1/25r	167
Harrick, John	Cork, Powlenelonge	gentry: gent	14-Aug-69	800	B.L. 15, 636 f. 47a	3705
Harrington, Henry	Wicklow, Grandgeconn	gentry: gent	09-Nov-26	100	Dc2/83r	1394
Harrington, Henry	Wicklow, Grange	gentry: gent	20-Mar-26	60	Dc2/75v	1354
Harrington, Henry	Wicklow, Grangcoone	gentry: gent	29-Aug-31	100	Dc2/168r	1776
Harrison, John	Dublin, the city	gentry: gent	05-Jun-39	1000	B.L. 19, 843 f.8a	2735
Harrison, Mathew	Dublin, the city	gentry: esquire	12-Jun-67	2000	Dc3/62	2359
Harrison, Mathew	Dublin, the city	gentry: esquire	12-Jun-67	2000	B.L. 15, 635 f. 192a	3595
Harrison, Mathew	Dublin, the city	gentry: esquire	10-Jun-61	2000	B.L. 15, 635 f. 70a	3385
Harrison, Mathew	Dublin, the city	gentry: gent	24-Feb-58	800	B.L. 19, 843 f. 206	3118
Harrison, Michael	Antrim, Magherleane	gentry: esquire	13-Feb-61	620	B.L. 15, 635 f. 64a	3378
Harrison, Michael	Antrim, Lisnegarvey	gentry: esquire	19-Dec-57	400	B.L. 19, 843 f. 204	3114
Harrison, Michael	Antrim, Magherleave	gentry: esquire	01-May-57	200	B.L. 19, 843 f. 197a	3102
Harrison, Michael	Antrim, Magherileave	gentry: esquire	03-Jan-56	210	B.L. 19, 843 f. 169	3052
Harrison, Michael	Antrim, Magherleanne	gentry: esquire	07-Apr-55	500	B.L. 19, 843 f. 159a	3034

Standard	County	Occupation	Date	Amount	MS No	Ident No
Harrison, Michael	Antrim, Magheraleve	gentry: esquire	17-Jan-72	340	B.L. 15, 636 f. 102	3797
Harrison, Michael	Antrim, Magheraleve	gentry: esquire	27-Mar-82	800	B.L. 15, 637 f. 58a	3952
Harrison, Michael	Antrim, Magherileave	gentry: esquire	02-Jan-56	800	B.L. 19, 843 f. 164a	3043
Harrison, Robert	Dublin	gentry: gent	13-Mar-14	30	Dc1/128r	796
Harrold, Edmund	Dublin, Kilmakhioke	gentry: gent	19-May-06	500	Dc1/67v	407
Hart, Henry	Clare, Carriggomane?	gentry: esquire	05-Feb-39	600	B.L. 19, 843 f.2	2723
Hartshorne, Henry	Wicklow, Wickloe	merchant	14-Mar-65	260	Dc3/3	2228
Hartstonge, James	Antrim, Muckamore	trade: leather worker	10-Oct-68	99	B.L. 15, 636 f. 25	3668
Hartstonge, Standish	Limerick?		28-Sep-72	720	B.L. 15, 636 f. 116	3821
Hartstonge, Standish	Limerick?		18-Apr-77	300	B.L. 19, 844 f. 139	3269
Hartstonge, Standish	Limerick	gentry: esquire	29-Jun-70	3300	Dc3/122	2483
Hartstonge, Standish	Limerick	gentry: esquire	29-Jun-70	3300	B.L. 15, 636 f. 64	3731
Harvey, John	Donegal, Enilagh	gentry: gent	30-Apr-86	800	B.L. 15, 637 f. 109	4043
Harvey, John	Wexford, Wexford	gentry: esquire	11-Dec-80	800	B.L. 15, 637 f. 41	3920
Harvey, John	Wexford, Wexford	gentry: esquire	16-Sep-84	200	B.L. 15, 637 f. 90	4009
Hatch, John	Meath, Duleeke	gentry: gent	08-Mar-54	540	B.L. 19, 843 f. 139	2992
Hatfield, Ridley	Dublin, the city	merchant	29-May-45	100	B.L. 19, 843 f. 120a	2960
Haughton, Thomas	Dublin, the city	merchant	22-Dec-54	160	B.L. 19, 843 f. 147	3008
Hawkins, Edward	Cork, the city	trade: grocer	27-Sep-72	500	B.L. 15, 636 f. 118a	3824
Hawkins, John	Dublin, the city	gentry: esquire	02-May-65	333	Dc3/4	2231
Hawkins, John	Dublin, the city	gentry: esquire	02-May-65	333	B.L. 15, 635 f. 166a	3546
Hayward, John	Limerick, the city	gentry: gent	15-Jan-62	200	B.L. 15, 635 f. 90	3416
Henry, Robert	Antrim, Carrickfergus		05-Apr-79	440	B.L. 15, 637 f. 20a	3883
Henry, Sedgrave	Dublin, little Cabragh	gentry: gent	23-Jun-37	1200	Dc2/265v	2191
Herbert, George	King's Co., Dorrow	gentry: knight and baronet	07-Apr-36	2000	Dc2/248v	2111
Herbert, George	King's Co., Durrow	gentry: knight and baronet	07-Jul-37	3000	Dc2/267r	2198
Herbert, Henry	England, Worcester, Bridford	gentry: knight	05-Jul-70	1000	Dc3/123	2486
Herbert, John	Kildare, Coclanston	gentry: gent	23-May-15	400	Dc1/138r	855
Herbert, Thomas	Dublin, the city	gentry: esquire	09-Jul-58	420	B.L. 15, 635 f. 30a	3316
Hetherington, Robert	Dublin, Raconle	gentry: gent	16-Aug-23	60	Dc2/50r	1179
Hibbots, Thomas	Dublin	gentry: knight	31-May-32	2000	Dc2/182r	1831
Hibbots, Thomas	England, Worcester, Inckborrow	gentry: gent	04-Feb-36	3000	Dc2/244r	2091
Hibbots, Thomas	Dublin, city	gentry: esquire	18-Apr-10	400	Dc1/95r	596
Hibbots, Thomas	Dublin?	gentry: esquire	06-Aug-07	200	Dc1/79ar	489
Hibbots, Thomas	Dublin, the city	gentry: knight	04-Dec-28	400	Dc2/120v	1563
Hibbots, Thomas	Dublin	gentry: esquire	16-Mar-09	500	Dc1/88r	549
Hibbots, Thomas	Dublin?	gentry: knight	23-Mar-27	2000	Dc2/90r	1423
Hibbots, Thomas	Dublin	gentry: knight	21-Nov-29	200	Dc2/138r	1645
Hickman, Edward	Kildare, Athy	merchant	05-Mar-29	1000	Dc2/125v	1590
Higgen, Morgan	Dublin, the city	merchant	15-Apr-22	36	Dc2/39r	1099
Higgs, William	England, Stafford, Voxall	gentry: gent	30-Apr-30	80	Dc2/144v	1676

Standard	County	Occupation	Date	Amount	MS No	Ident No
Hill, Arthur	Dublin, Ffinglas	gentry: esquire	19-Feb-39	1000	B.L. 19,843 f. 50a	2819
Hill, Emery	England, Westminster, the city	gentry: gent	06-Feb-55	1400	B.L. 19, 843 f. 152	3018
Hill, James	Meath, Allenston	gentry: gent	30-Nov-10	120	Dc1/101v	635
Hill, James	Meath, Allenstowne	gentry: esquire	06-Jul-33	200	Dc2/197r	1892
Hill, John	Dublin	merchant	08-May-40	600	B.L. 19, 843 f. 61	2841
Hill, Patrick	Wicklow, Dromen	gentry: esquire	14-Jul-37	1200	Dc2/268v	2204
Hill, Thomas	Dublin	gentry: gent	24-Nov-26	1000	Dc2/83r	1396
Hill, Thomas	Dublin, the city	gentry: gent	24-Dec-39	560	B.L. 19, 843 f. 48	2814
Hill, Thomas	Dublin, the city	trade: brewer	28-Oct-31	40	Dc2/169r	1781
Hill, William	Meath, Ballibegg	gentry: knight	27-Nov-28	200	Dc2/117v	1550
Hill, William	Meath, Allenston	gentry: gent	21-Apr-08	300	Dc1/81v	506
Hilton, William	Dublin, the city	gentry: esquire	14-May-32	40	Dc2/180v	1826
Hodder, Francis	Cork, the city	merchant	03-May-59	800	B.L. 15, 636 f. 76	3754
Hodder, Margaret	Cork, Coolemore	other: widow	01-May-67	240	B.L. 15, 635 f. 210a	3626
Hodder, William	Cork, the city		07-Apr-64	1350	B.L. 15, 635 f. 129	3485
Hodson, John		prof: bishop of Elphin	25-Nov-71	500	Dc3/141v	2535
Hoey, John	Kildare, Collanstowne	gentry: knight	27-Jan-55	1200	B.L. 19, 843 f. 149	3012
Holden, Henry	England, London	merchant	09-Sep-25	360	Dc2/69r	1314
Holgate, Charity	England, London, the city	trade: widow, exec of William Holgate, haberdasher	09-Dec-79	800	B.L. 15, 637 f. 28a	3898
Hollenprist, John	Dublin, Newtown, Rathfarnam	gentry: gent	15-Dec-26	300	Dc2/86v	1410
Hollenprist, John	Dublin	gentry: gent	31-May-17	220	Dc2/7v	904
Hollywood, John	Meath, Beashelston	gentry: gent	17-Jun-24	100	Dc2/56v	1225
Hollywood, John	Meath, Bewshelstowne	gentry: gent	15-Jun-32	1200	Dc2/183r	1835
Hollywood, John	Meath, Beaushelstowne	gentry: gent	25-Apr-35	640	Dc2/333v	2039
Hollywood, John	Meath, Beashelstowne	gentry: gent	14-May-34	1600	Dc2/211r	1949
Hollywood, John	Meath, Bewshelstowne	gentry: gent	20-Jul-33	2000	Dc2/198r	1895
Hollywood, John	Meath, Birshelston	gentry: gent	06-Dec-22	200	Dc2/43v	1131
Hollywood, John	Meath, Bewshelston	gentry: gent	26-Oct-31	200	Dc2/169r	1780
Hollywood, John	Meath, Bewshelstowne	gentry: gent	22-Nov-36	600	Dc2/257r	2154
Hollywood, John	Meath, Bewshelstone	gentry: gent	14-Jun-30	200	Dc2/151r	1703
Holmes, James	Westmeath, Clonyn	gentry: gent	20-Jun-45	600	B.L. 19, 843 f. 119a	2958
Holmes, James	Westmeath, Clonyn	gentry: gent	01-Jul-45	400	B.L. 19, 843 f. 120	2959
Holmes, Peter	Dublin, the city	gentry: gent	17-Jun-67	600	Dc3/63	2361
Holmes, Peter	Dublin, the city	gentry: gent	07-Jun-67	600	B.L. 15, 635 f. 193a	3597
Holmes, Thomas	Limerick, Kilmallock	gentry: esquire	14-Jan-86	1200	B.L. 15, 637 f. 103	4034
Holt, Samuel	Dublin, the city	gentry: gent	23-Jan-63	1075	B.L. 15, 635 f. 100a	3435
Hooke, Edward	England, London	trade: grocer	23-Dec-35	96	Dc2/243r	2086
Hooke, Thomas	Dublin, the city	merchant	23-Dec-62	150	B.L. 15, 635 f. 100	3434
Hooper, Nicholas	Limerick, the city	gentry: gent	23-Feb-65	1300	Dc3/3	2227
Hope, Alexander	Westmeath, Molingar	gentry: gent	12-Jun-27	250	Dc2/94r	1439
Hope, Alexander	Westmeath, Mullengarr	gentry: gent	31-May-25	200	Dc2/64v	1285

Standard	County	Occupation	Date	Amount	MS No	Ident No
Hope, Alexander	Westmeath, Mollingare	gentry: esquire	26-Nov-31	500	Dc2/172v	1794
Hope, John	Westmeath, Skolstowne?	gentry: gent	12-Mar-62	200	B.L. 15, 635 f. 92	3418
Hope, Richard	Westmeath, Leduston	gentry: gent	20-May-37	4000	Dc2/263v	2183
Hope, Richard	Westmeath, Hopestowne	gentry: gent	26-May-28	300	Dc2/110r	1514
Hope, Richard	Westmeath, Coolenehane	gentry: gent	20-Jun-15	60	Dc1/138v	860
Hopper, Richard	England, London	gentry: gent	21-Apr-19	2000	Dc2/22r	983
Hopper, Richard	England, London	gentry: gent		2000	Dc2/25r	999
Hopper, Richard	England, St. Andrews, Midl.sex	gentry: esquire	29-Nov-26	1000	Dc2/83v	1398
Hopper, Richard	England, London	gentry: gent	23-Feb-15	666	Dc1/136r	843
Hore, Alison	Dublin, the city	other: widow	01-Sep-32	200	Dc2/185v	1845
Hore, Edward	Cork, the city	merchant	27-Sep-84	500	B.L. 15, 637 f. 93a	4016
Hore, Edward	Cork, the city	merchant	27-Sep-84	1000	B.L. 15, 637 f. 93	4015
Hore, James	Cork, Monigormy	gentry: gent	18-Jan-68	700	B.L. 15, 635 f. 213a	3632
Hore, James	Cork, Cummyn	gentry: gent	02-Apr-74	1000	B. L. 19, 844 f. 24	3145
Hore, James	Dublin, Kilsalchan	gentry: gent	07-Jul-37	200	Dc2/267v	2200
Hore, James	Dublin, Kilsalchan	gentry: gent	12-Jul-37	300	Dc2/268r	2203
Hore, Margaret	Dublin, Kilsalchan	gentry: spinster	01-Aug-31	300	Dc2/167r	1772
Hore, Margaret	Dublin, Killsaulghan?	gentry: spinster?, daughter of Philip	31-Mar-28	400	Dc2/106r	1494
Hore, Margaret	Dublin, the city	gentry: spinster	29-Aug-29	350	Dc2/136v	1637
Hore, Philip	Dublin, Kilsalchan	gentry: gent	27-May-07	300	Dc1/77v	473
Hore, Philip	Dublin, Kilsalghan	gentry: gent	13-Feb-07	105	Dc1/74r	449
Hore, Philip	Dublin, Kilsalghan	gentry: gent	31-Jan-09	160	Dc1/86v	540
Hore, Philip	Dublin, Kilsalghan	gentry: gent	15-Apr-36	1400	Dc2/249r	2114
Hore, Philip	Dublin, Kilsalghan	gentry: gent	20-Jul-09	80	Dc1/90v	566
Hore, Philip	Dublin, Kilsalchan	gentry: gent	17-Feb-07	300	Dc1/75r	454
Hore, Philip	Dublin, Killsalghan	gentry: esquire	28-Feb-28	200	Dc2/104v	1488
Hore, Philip	Dublin, Kilsalghan	gentry: gent	31-Jan-09	160	Dc1/87r	543
Hore, Philip	Dublin, Kilsalghan	gentry: gent	31-Jan-09	160	Dc1/86v	542
Hore, Philip	Dublin, Killsaulghan	gentry: gent	31-Mar-28	400	Dc2/106r	1494
Hore, Philip	Dublin, Kilsalghan	gentry: gent	31-Jan-09	160	Dc1/86v	541
Hore, Philip	Dublin, Kilsalchan	gentry: gent	16-May-09	160	Dc1/88r	551
Hore, Philip	Dublin, Kilsalghan	gentry: gent	21-Aug-09	400	Dc1/91r	570
Hore, Philip	Dublin, Kilsalchan	gentry: gent	29-Aug-05	160	Dc1/61r	372
Hore, Philip	Dublin, Killsalghan	gentry: gent	31-Jan-09	160	Dc1/86r	539
Hore, Philip	Dublin, Killsalghan	gentry: gent	31-Jan-09	160	Dc1/86r	538
Hore, Philip	Dublin	gentry: gent	02-Aug-99	140	Dc1/19r	130
Hore, Philip	Dublin	gentry: gent	15-Jan-99	800	Dc1/14r	100
Hore, Philip	Meath, Kilsalchan	gentry: gent	12-Feb-25	120	Dc2/61v	1266
Hore, Philip	Dublin	gentry: gent	28-Nov-98	800	Dc1/13v	95
Hore, Philip	Dublin, Kilsalchan	gentry: gent	11-Aug-31	400	Dc2/167v	1774
Hore, Philp	Dublin	gentry: gent	12-May-99	400	Dc1/16v	111
Horsam, John	England, Bristol, the city	merchant	05-Sep-55	1800	B.L. 19, 843 f. 165	3044
Horsfall, Ciprian	Kilkenny, Insnagen	gentry: gent	08-Feb-06	400	Dc1/65v	395

Standard	County	Occupation	Date	Amount	MS No	Ident No
Howard, John	Dublin, the city	trade: winecooper	04-Mar-74	2000	Dc3/160v	2605
Howard, John	Dublin, the city	trade: winecoop	04-Mar-74	2000	B.L. 19, 844 f. 27	3150
Howard, Nicholas	Dublin	gentry: esquire	14-Nov-12	200	Dc1/116v	723
Howard, Richard	Dublin	gentry: gent	14-Jul-00	40	Dc1/25r	168
Howard, Thomas	Dublin, the city	merchant	03-Dec-40	230	B.L. 19, 843 f. 89	2897
Howard, Thomas	England, London	gentry: esquire	13-Jul-66	1000	Dc3/31	2291
Howell, William	Cork, the city	merchant	25-Mar-72	240	B.L. 15, 636 f. 105	3801
Hubbert, Derek	Dublin	merchant: barber & strandger?	22-Feb-13	60	Dc1/120r	744
Hubbert, Derek	Dublin	merchant	09-Dec-16	120	Dc2/3r	883
Hubbert, Derek	Dublin	merchant	24-Sep-16	500	Dc2/1r	871
Hughes, John	Dublin, the city	gentry: gent	13-Jul-61	1400	B.L. 15, 635 f. 77	3395
Hughes, John	Dublin, the city	gentry: gent	27-Jul-63	430	B.L. 15, 635 f. 109a	3449
Hughes, John	Dublin, the city	gentry: esquire	17-Jun-62	800	B.L. 15, 635 f. 92a	3419
Hughes, Mary	Dublin, the city	gentry: widow, of John Hughes esquire	30-Sep-69	600	Dc3/103	2448
Hughes, Mary	Dublin, the city	gentry: widow, of John, esquire	30-Sep-69	600	B.L. 15, 636 f. 45a	3703
Hughes, Owen	England, Chester	merchant	13-Feb-29	212	Dc2/125r	1586
Hughes, Peter	Cork, Ragheroones	gentry: esquire	02-May-62	280	B.L. 15, 635 f. 207	3623
Hughes, Robert	Dublin, the city	gentry: gent	05-Jun-63	100	B.L. 15, 635 f. 106	3444
Hughes, Robert	Dublin, the city	gentry: gent	28-Jul-70	540	B.L. 15, 636 f. 66	3734
Hughes, Robert	Dublin, the city	gentry: gent	28-Jun-70	540	Dc3/121	2482
Hughes, Samuel	Dublin, the city	gentry: gent	24-Jun-76	600	B.L. 19, 844 f. 112	3240
Hughes, Samuel	Dublin, the city	gentry: gent	24-Jun-76	600	Dc3/178v	2671
Hull, Richard	Cork, Lemcon	gentry: esquire	20-Jan-70	1000	B.L. 15, 636 f. 52a	3714
Humphrey, Edward	Carlow, Oldtown	gentry: gent	01-Feb-78	1200	Dc3/185v	2703
Humphrey, Henry	Wicklow, Knockandaragh	gentry: gent	01-Feb-78	1200	Dc3/185v	2703
Humphrey, William	Dublin, the city	merchant	15-Jul-42	400	B.L. 19, 843 f. 108	2935
Hunt, Raphael	Dublin, the city		16-Aug-55	600	B.L. 19, 843 f. 163a	3041
Hurley, Thomas	Limerick, Kilmallocke	gentry: gent	13-Jul-30	200	Dc2/154r	1716
Hussey, Edward	Meath, the Rath of Kilmore	gentry: gent	11-Nov-37	300	Dc2/271r	2216
Hussey, James	Meath, the little Ardrons	gentry: gent	22-Dec-00	120	Dc1/27v	183
Hussey, John	Meath, Baltinoran?	farmer: yeoman	20-Nov-26	200	Dc2/83v	1397
Hussey, Martin	Meath, Culmollin	gentry: gent	01-Dec-13	300	Dc1/125r	775
Hussey, Martin	Meath, Culmullen	gentry: gent	24-Feb-06	200	Dc1/66r	399
Hussey, Martin	Dublin	merchant	08-Feb-03	200	Dc1/44r	281
Hussey, Martin	Dublin	merchant	18-Jun-97	200	Dc1/5r	34
Hussey, Patrick	Meath?	peer: baron Galtrim	04-Feb-26	200	Dc2/73v	1340
Hussey, Peter	Meath, Culmullen	gentry: gent	07-Nov-23	1000	Dc2/50v	4058
Hussey, Peter	Meath, Galtrim	gentry: gent	04-Feb-26	200	Dc2/73r	1339
Hussey, Peter	Dublin, Weston	gentry: esquire	21-Jan-37	600	Dc2/259v	2166
Hussey, Peter	Meath, Culmullen	gentry: gent	28-Sep-30	600	Dc2/155r	1720
Hussey, Peter	Meath, Culmullen	gentry: gent	21-Nov-23	300	Dc2/51v	1188
Hussey, Peter	Dublin, Weston	gentry: esquire	13-Mar-35	400	Dc2/230v	2028

Standard	County	Occupation	Date	Amount	MS No	Ident No
Hussey, Walter	Meath, the Rath of Kilmore	gentry: gent	11-Nov-37	300	Dc2/271r	2216
Hutchinson, Daniel	Dublin, the city		19-Dec-49	2000	B.L. 19, 843 f. 125	2969
Hutchinson, Daniel	Dublin, the city		04-Dec-55	600	B.L. 19, 843 f. 206a	3119
Hutchinson, Daniel	Dublin, the city		28-Apr-75	2800	Dc3/167r	2632
Hutchinson, Daniel	Dublin, the city		28-Apr-75	2800	B.L. 19, 844 f. 58	3182
Hutton, Robert	Louth, Drogheda	merchant	04-Jul-14	40	Dc1/130v	811
Huxley, Richard	Dublin	farmer: yeoman	30-Sep-99	900	Dc1/19v	132
Hyde, Arthur	Cork, Castlehyde	gentry: esquire	03-May-76	1000	B.L. 19, 844 f. 104	3231
Hyde, John	Dublin, the city	trade: shoemaker	03-May-73	200	Dc3/156v	2582
Ingram, Randolf	England, London, the city	trade: ironmonger	16-Oct-39	500	B.L. 19, 843 f. 41	2800
Jackson, Lodovic	Cork, Youghall	gentry: esquire	06-Feb-77	500	B.L. 19, 844 f. 120	3249
Jacob, Patrick	Dublin, Clondolcan	farmer: freeholder	15-Jul-06	100	Dc1/70r	425
Jacob, Richard	Dublin, Loughton	gentry: gent	20-Jun-27	200	Dc2/94v	1443
Jans, Edward	Dublin, the city		29-Nov-31	400	Dc2/173r	1796
Jans, Edward	Dublin	gentry: gent	12-Dec-05	108	Dc1/64r	386
Jans, Edward	Dublin		01-Mar-37	500	Dc2/260r	2168
Jans, Edward	Dublin		30-Jun-26	200	Dc2/80r	1379
Jans, Edward	Dublin, the city		08-Oct-36	1600	Dc2/256r	2150
Jans, Edward	Dublin		28-Feb-28	200	Dc2/104v	1488
Jans, James	Dublin		27-Jan-99	200	Dc1/15r	103
Jennett, John	Meath, Oldbridge	gentry: gent	27-May-75	300	B.L. 19, 844 f. 68	3196
Jennett, John	Meath, Ouldbridge	gentry: gent	20-Jul-70	200	B.L. 15, 636 f. 72a	3747
Jennett, John	Meath, Oldbridge	gentry: gent	27-Apr-81	400	B.L. 15, 637 f. 42	3922
Jennett, John	Meath, Oldbridge	gentry: gent	16-Jun-84	800	B.L. 15, 637 f. 87	4004
Jennett, John	Meath, Oldbridge	gentry: gent	17-Sep-73	220	B.L. 19, 844 f. 6	3125
Jennett, John	Meath, Oldbridge	gentry: gent	01-Jul-74	500	B.L. 19, 844 f. 35	3159
Jennett, John	Meath, Oldbridge	gentry: gent	25-Aug-75	400	B.L. 19, 844 f. 69	3197
Jennett, John	Meath, Ouldbridge	gentry: gent	19-Apr-71	600	B.L. 15, 636 f. 84	3768
Jennett, John	Meath, Olbridge	gentry: gent	07-Mar-76	700	B.L. 19, 844 f. 91	3218
Jephson, John	England, Fraile, Hampshire	gentry: John's wife	20-Nov-28	220	Dc2/116r	1543
Jephson, John	England, Fraile, Hampshire	gentry: knight	20-Nov-28	220	Dc2/116r	1543
Jervis, Humphrey	Dublin, the city	merchant	29-Jan-72	273	B.L. 15, 636 f. 108a	3808
Jervis, John	King's Co., Roscurragh	gentry: gent	02-May-68	220	Dc3/74	2393
Jervis, William	England, Mayford, Stafford	gentry: gent	27-Jan-77	6000	B.L. 19, 844 f. 128	3257
Jervis, William	England, Staford, Mayford	gentry: gent	27-Jan-77	6000	Dc3/181v	2684
Johnson, David	Dublin, the city	merchant	19-Jun-68	200	Dc3/79	2405
Johnson, Isabella	Dublin, the city	other: spinster	01-Dec-66	200	B.L. 15, 635 f. 188a	3587
Johnson, Isabella	Dublin, the city	other: spinster	21-Dec-66	200	Dc3/49	2328
Johnson, John	Dublin	gentry: gent	19-Nov-13	20	Dc1/124r	770
Johnson, John	Dublin	gentry: gent	28-May-13	40	Dc1/121r	751
Johnson, John	Dublin	gentry: gent	25-Feb-24	100	Dc2/54r	1206
Johnson, John	Dublin	gentry: gent	09-Jun-13	60	Dc1/122r	757
Johnson, John	Dublin	gentry: gent	05-Jun-13	40	Dc1/121v	754

Standard	County	Occupation	Date	Amount	MS No	Ident No
Johnson, Robert	Dublin, the city	gentry: esquire	23-May-83	2000	B.L. 15, 637 f. 73	3979
Johnson, William	Antrim, Glen	gentry: gent	29-Oct-78	1200	B.L. 15, 637 f. 5	3858
Johnson, William	Scotland, Edenburugh, the city	gentry: esquire	03-Jul-56	400	B.L. 19, 843 f. 175a	3062
Jones, Arthur	Meath?	peer: viscount Ranelagh	13-Feb-67	2300	Dc3/53	2337
Jones, Brian	Dublin, the city	gentry: gent	19-Feb-34	1254	Dc2/207r	1932
Jones, Brian	Dublin	gentry: gent	02-Sep-34	160	Dc2/218r	1977
Jones, Edward	Westmeath, Athlone	gentry: gent	11-Feb-13	240	Dc1/118v	735
Jones, Edward	Westmeath, Athlone	gentry: gent	11-Nov-13	400	Dc1/123v	768
Jones, Elizabeth	Dublin, the city	gentry: sister of viscount Ranelagh	06-Oct-70	2200	Dc3/126	2493
Jones, Eugene	Dublin, Donabrooke	gentry: gent	22-Dec-76	1000	B.L. 19, 844 f. 119	3248
Jones, Frances	Dublin, the city	gentry: spinster?, sister of viscount Ranelagh	06-Oct-70	2200	Dc3/125	2492
Jones, George	Dublin	trade: apothecary	30-Mar-17	300	Dc2/6r	897
Jones, George	Dublin	trade: apothecary	25-Jul-18	620	Dc2/16r	949
Jones, Henry	Dublin, the city, St Pat Close	gentry: esquire	04-Feb-25	200	Dc2/61r	1262
Jones, Henry	Dublin	merchant	07-May-13	140	Dc1/120v	748
Jones, Henry	Dublin, the city, St Pats Close	gentry: esquire	03-Feb-25	200	Dc2/61r	1261
Jones, Henry	Dublin	gentry: esquire	24-May-23	600	Dc2/47v	1160
Jones, Henry	Dublin, Newtowne	gentry: esquire	10-Jun-40	800	B.L. 19, 843 f. 70	2859
Jones, Henry	Dublin	gentry: esquire	17-Jul-22	280	Dc2/42r	1119
Jones, Henry	Dublin	gentry: gent	21-Jun-13	50	Dc1/122v	762
Jones, Henry		prof: dean of Ardagh	03-Dec-36	600	Dc2/258v	2161
Jones, John	Westmeath, Athlone	merchant	13-Jun-07	600	Dc1/78r	477
Jones, John	Westmeath, Athlone	merchant	06-Nov-06	100	Dc1/70v	428
Jones, John	Westmeath, Athlone	merchant	13-Nov-06	40	Dc1/71r	429
Jones, John	Westmeath, Athlone	merchant	13-Nov-06	30	Dc1/71r	430
Jones, John	Westmeath, Athlone	merchant	07-May-07	600	Dc1/76r	463
Jones, Lewis		prof: bishop of Killaloe	03-Dec-36	1000	Dc2/258v	2162
Jones, Lewis		prof: dean of St. Patrick's	24-Nov-30	100	Dc2/156v	1728
Jones, Lewis		prof: dean of St. Patrick's	23-Nov-30	220	Dc2/156v	1727
Jones, Lewis		prof: bishop of Killaloe	21-May-36	200	Dc2/252r	2127
Jones, Nicholas	Dublin, the city	gentry: gent	10-Nov-73	480	B.L. 19, 844 f. 16	3134
Jones, Nicholas	Dublin, the city	gentry: gent	26-Feb-73	400	Dc3/154v	2578
Jones, Nicholas	Dublin, the city	gentry: gent	26-Feb-73	400	B.L. 15, 636 f. 132	3841
Jones, Nicholas	Dublin, the city	gentry: gent	28-Jun-73	200	B.L. 19, 844 f. 3	3122
Jones, Nicholas	Dublin, the city	gentry: gent	22-May-75	190	Dc3/168r	2637
Jones, Nicholas	Dublin, the city	gentry: gent	31-Jan-73	200	Dc3/153r	2571
Jones, Nicholas	Dublin, the city	gentry: gent	28-Jun-80	800	B.L. 15, 637 f. 34	3908
Jones, Nicholas	Dublin, the city	gentry: gent	28-Jun-73	200	Dc3/158v	2590
Jones, Nicholas	Dublin, the city	gentry: gent	22-May-75	190	B.L. 19, 844 f. 63	3191
Jones, Nicholas	Dublin, the city	gentry: gent	10-Nov-73	480	Dc3/158ar	2594

Standard	County	Occupation	Date	Amount	MS No	Ident No
Jones, Nicholas	Kilkenny, the city	gentry: gent	28-Jun-28	200	Dc2/111v	1521
Jones, Roger	Sligo, Sligo	gentry: knight	23-May-28	300	Dc2/109r	1510
Jones, Roger	Meath?	peer: viscount Ranelagh	28-Feb-31	100	Dc2/160r	1744
Jones, Roger	Dublin, the city	gentry: gent	18-May-68	300	Dc3/76	2396
Jones, Roger	Dublin	gentry: knight	16-Feb-24	867	Dc2/53v	1204
Jones, Theophilus	Dublin, Lucan	gentry: knight	13-May-69	300	Dc3/97	2435
Jones, Thomas	Dublin, the city	gentry: esquire	22-Nov-61	200	B.L. 15, 635 f. 87	3410
Jones, Thomas	Dublin, the city	gentry: esquire	11-Jun-56	600	B.L. 19, 843 f. 175	3061
Jones, Thomas	Dublin, the city	gentry: esquire	20-Nov-57	400	B.L. 19, 843 f. 200a	3107
Jones, Thomas	Dublin, the city	gentry: esquire	01-Feb-55	400	B.L. 19, 843 f. 153a	3021
Jones, Thomas	Dublin, the city	gentry: esquire	13-Dec-54	1000	B.L. 19, 843 f. 152a	3019
Jones, William	Dublin, the city	gentry: esquire	27-Jan-77	6000	Dc3/181v	2684
Jones, William	Dublin, the city	gentry: esquire	27-Jan-77	6000	B.L. 19, 844 f. 128	3257
Joyner, Thomas	Dublin	gentry: gent	12-Dec-35	1000	Dc2/242r	2082
Juxon, Thomas	England, Surrey, Mortlake	gentry: esquire	17-Aug-61	1000	B.L. 15, 635 f. 83	3402
Kardiffe, James	Kildare, Keardiffestowne	gentry: gent	07-Dec-27	1000	Dc2/101v	1472
Kardiffe, Robert	Dublin, Donsaick	gentry: gent	14-Nov-10	400	Dc1/99v	624
Kardiffe, Robert	Dublin, Donsynck	gentry: gent	18-Sep-10	400	Dc1/99r	622
Kardiffe, Simon	Dublin	merchant	27-Jul-41	200	B.L. 19, 843 f. 106a	2932
Kardiffe, William	Meath, Castletowne-Killpatrick	gentry: gent	07-Dec-68	400	Dc3/85	2415
Kealy, James	Kilkenny, Gowran	merchant	04-Aug-41	700	B.L. 19, 843 f. 106	2931
Kealy, James	Kilkenny, Gawron	merchant	25-May-39	2200	B.L. 19, 843 f. 14	2746
Keating, Edmund	Dublin, the city	gentry: esquire	23-Jul-55	240	B.L. 19, 843 f. 158a	3032
Keating, Gerald	Kildare, Poynstersgrandge	gentry: gent	30-Jun-25	800	Dc2/67v	1305
Keating, Gerald	Kildare, Castlewarning	gentry: gent	04-Sep-30	400	Dc2/154v	1718
Keating, John	Dublin, the city	gentry: esquire	19-Jun-76	2000	B.L. 19, 844 f. 100	3227
Keating, John	Dublin, the city	gentry: esquire	19-Jun-76	2800	Dc3/178r	2668
Keating, William	Queen's Co., Castlebracke	farmer: yeoman	20-Nov-16	300	Dc2/2r	878
Keegan, John	Dublin	gentry: gent	22-Jun-26	1000	Dc2/79v	1377
Kelly, John	Dublin, the city	gentry: gent	22-Dec-49	400	B.L. 19, 843 f. 126	2971
Kelly, Nicholas	Dublin, the city		30-Jun-28	180	Dc2/112r	1524
Kelly, Nicholas	Dublin	merchant	14-Jan-25	160	Dc2/60r	1256
Kelly, Nicholas	Dublin, the city	merchant	06-Apr-20	300	Dc2/29v	1025
Kelly, Nicholas	Dublin	merchant	03-Jul-24	100	Dc2/57r	1230
Kelly, William	Kilkenny, the city	gentry: gent	07-Jul-41	240	B.L. 19, 843 f. 99a	2918
Kelly, William	Dublin	prof: physician, surgeon	12-May-97	200	Dc1/3v	25
Kennedy, Christopher	Dublin	merchant	11-Mar-37	400	Dc2/260v	2170
Kennedy, Christopher	Dublin, the city	merchant: son of Robert	04-Dec-35	200	Dc2/241r	2078
Kennedy, George	Dublin, the city	merchant: son of Robert	04-Dec-35	200	Dc2/241r	2078
Kennedy, George	Dublin, the city	merchant: son of Robert?, alderman	25-Nov-14	600	Dc1/133r	826
Kennedy, James	Dublin, the city	merchant	24-Feb-20	320	Dc2/28v	1021
Kennedy, John	Longford, Mullagh	gentry: esquire	24-Nov-34	1200	Dc2/223r	1997

Standard	County	Occupation	Date	Amount	MS No	Ident No
Kennedy, John	Dublin, the city	merchant	24-Feb-20	320	Dc2/28v	1021
Kennedy, John	Longford, Mullagh	gentry: esquire	07-Oct-26	233	Dc2/82v	1392
Kennedy, John	Dublin	merchant	11-Jul-22	120	Dc2/41v	1116
Kennedy, John	Dublin	gentry: esquire	30-Jun-25	120	Dc2/67r	1302
Kennedy, Mark	Dublin, the city	merchant: son of Robert	04-Dec-35	200	Dc2/241r	2078
Kennedy, Patrick	Dublin, the city	merchant: son of Robert, alderman	04-Dec-35	200	Dc2/241r	2078
Kennedy, Richard	Dublin, the city	gentry: gent	24-Nov-34	1200	Dc2/223r	1997
Kennedy, Robert	Dublin	merchant	03-Mar-98	170	Dc1/10r	72
Kennedy, Robert	Dublin, the city	gentry: esquire	24-Nov-34	1200	Dc2/223r	1997
Kennedy, Robert	Dublin	merchant	22-Jul-98	100	Dc1/11v	85
Kennedy, Robert	Dublin		29-Nov-12	200	Dc1/117r	726
Kennedy, Robert	Dublin, the city	gentry: esquire	04-Nov-25	332	Dc2/69v	1316
Kennedy, Robert	Dublin, the city	merchant: son/heir of Walter	27-Feb-40	1200	B.L. 19, 843 f. 52	2822
Kennedy, Robert	Dublin		18-May-04	120	Dc1/52v	333
Kennedy, Robert	Dublin, the city	merchant: son/heir of Walter	24-Apr-40	2000	B.L. 19, 843 f. 53	2824
Kennedy, Robert	Dublin		03-Dec-06	750	Dc1/72v	440
Kennedy, Robert	Dublin, the city	gentry: esquire	05-Jul-20	200	Dc2/31v	1041
Kennedy, Robert	Dublin		25-Apr-08	300	Dc1/82r	509
Kennedy, Robert	Dublin	merchant	24-Jan-01	80	Dc1/28r	187
Kennedy, Robert	Dublin	merchant	01-Mar-02	200	Dc1/36v	239
Kennedy, Silvester	Dublin, the city	gentry: gent	24-Nov-34	1200	Dc2/223r	1997
Kennedy, Walter	Dublin, the city	merchant	26-Jun-32	60	Dc2/184r	1840
Kennedy, Walter	Dublin, the city		20-Feb-40	700	B.L. 19, 843 f. 52a	2823
Kennedy, Walter	Dublin, the city		27-Feb-40	1200	B.L. 19, 843 f. 52	2822
Kennedy, Walter	Dublin, the city		24-Apr-40	2000	B.L. 19, 843 f. 53	2824
Kennedy, Walter	Dublin, the city	merchant	25-Apr-35	1600	Dc2/233v	2040
Kent, Thomas	Meath, Daneston	gentry: gent	11-Dec-00	200	Dc1/27r	182
Kerrin, Daniel	Queen's Co., Ballynekill	gentry: esquire	26-Jul-77	400	Dc3/183r	2693
Kerrin, Daniel	Queen's Co., Ballynekill	gentry: esquire	26-Jul-77	400	B.L. 19, 844 f. 138	3268
Kiernan, Christopher	Galway, the town	merchant	07-Jun-33	800	Dc2/196r	1887
Kiernan, Thomas	Dublin, Newross	gentry: gent	28-Jan-81	200	B.L. 15, 637 f. 40a	3919
Kiernan, Thomas	Dublin, the city	gentry: gent	19-Aug-81	200	B.L. 15, 637 f. 48	3932
Kinersly, Phillip	Dublin	gentry: gent	05-Apr-59	2100	B.L. 15, 635 f. 41a	3337
Kinersly, Phillip	Dublin, the city	gentry: gent	04-Jun-59	2100	B.L. 15, 635 f. 48	3348
King, Edward	Dublin, St Patrick's St	trade: chandler	13-Feb-09	40	Dc1/87r	545
King, George	Dublin, Clontarffe	gentry: esquire	12-Jun-29	800	Dc2/131v	1616
King, George	Dublin, Clontarf	gentry: esquire	03-Apr-26	1000	Dc2/76r	1357
King, George	Dublin, Clontarffe	gentry: gent	17-Feb-15	400	Dc1/135v	841
King, Henry	Dublin, the city	gentry: gent	08-Jun-39	200	B.L. 19, 843 f. 20a	2759
King, John	Dublin	gentry: gent	24-Dec-03	2508	Dc1/50v	324
King, John	Dublin	gentry: gent	12-Jul-01	300	Dc1/33v	220
King, Robert	Roscommon, Boyle	gentry: knight	30-Nov-28	1000	Dc2/119r	1557

Standard	County	Occupation	Date	Amount	MS No	Ident No
King, Robert	Roscommon, the Boyle	gentry: knight	01-Aug-33	1000	Dc2/198r	1896
King, William		gentry: knight	25-Oct-61	500	B.L. 15, 635 f. 86a	3409
Kingdon, Richard	England, Westminster	gentry: esquire	14-Nov-62	1080	B.L. 15, 635 f. 99	3432
Kirwan, Andrew	Galway, the town	merchant	05-May-19	1000	Dc2/23r	989
Kirwan, Richard	Galway	merchant	02-Jul-25	1000	Dc2/68r	1307
Kitchinman, Thomas	England, London, the city	trade: mercer	19-May-36	140	Dc2/251v	2124
Knight, Anne	Dublin, the city	gentry: widow, relict of				
		William, esquire	09-Dec-76	300	Dc3/181r	2679
Knight, Anne	Dublin, the city	other: widow	21-Jan-74	2000	Dc3/159v	2600
Knight, Francis	Mayo, Borishoole	gentry: gent	17-Jul-63	600	B.L. 15, 635 f. 107a	3447
Knight, Nicholas	Dublin, the city	gentry: esquire	15-Jun-65	70	Dc3/10	2243
Knight, Nicholas	Dublin, the city	gentry: esquire	15-Jun-65	70	B.L. 15, 635 f. 159	3535
Knight, Nicholas	Dublin, the city	gentry: esquire	01-Aug-64	400	B.L. 15, 635 f. 141a	3502
Knight, Nicholas	Dublin, the city	gentry: esquire	02-Dec-71	400	Dc3/142r	2538
Knight, William	Dublin, the city	gentry: esquire	12-Jul-56	200	B.L. 19, 843 f. 181	3068
Knight, William	Dublin, the city	gentry: esquire	13-Jan-59	250	B.L. 15, 635 f. 46	3344
Knox, Thomas	Antrim, Belfast	merchant	03-Apr-78	200	B.L. 19, 844 f. 160	3291
Knox, Thomas	Antrim, Belfast	merchant	20-Apr-77	240	B.L. 19, 844 f. 127	3256
Knox, Thomas	Antrim, Belfast	merchant	15-May-83	1200	B.L. 15, 637 f. 72	3977
Lacy, Peter	Limerick, the city	merchant	17-Jun-40	400	B.L. 19, 843 f. 69	2857
Lacy, Peter	Limerick, the city	merchant	27-Aug-40	1000	B.L. 19, 843 f. 68a	2856
Lacy, Peter	Limerick, the city	merchant	30-Jan-41	300	B.L. 19, 843 f. 86a	2892
Lambert, Elizabeth	Dublin, the city	other: widow	21-Jun-67	160	Dc3/64	2363
Lambert, Elizabeth	Dublin?	other: widow,				
		administrator of George	21-Jun-67	160	B.L. 15, 635 f. 195a	3601
Lambert, George	Dublin, the city	gentry: gent	16-Feb-66	120	Dc3/23	2274
Lambert, Hester		gentry: dame	29-Mar-23	1200	Dc2/46r	1148
Lambert, James	Cork, the city	merchant	29-Nov-23	600	Dc2/51v	1189
Lambert, Oliver		gentry: knight	03-Feb-04	666	Dc1/52r	330
Lambert, Thomas	Dublin	gentry: gent	27-Nov-97	200	Dc1/7v	53
Lamly, John	Queen's Co., Dunbrinn	gentry: gent	09-May-74	690	B.L. 19, 844 f. 31a	3155
Lamly, John	Queen's Co.	gentry: gent?	09-May-74	690	Dc3/161r	2608
Lamport, John	Wexford, Ballyshitt	farmer	15-Nov-16	240	Dc2/2r	876
Landy, Edward	Cork, Youghall	gentry: esquire	07-Feb-79	2000	B.L. 15, 637 f. 16	3875
Lane, Elizabeth	Antrim, Carrickfergus	gentry: wife of John,				
		gent	30-Oct-72	1200	B.L. 15, 636 f. 118	3823
Lane, Francis	Roscommon, Tulske	peer: countess				
		Lanesborough, widow	03-Jul-84	2000	B.L. 15, 637 f. 89a	4008
Lane, Francis	Roscommon, Tulske	peer: countess				
		Lanesborough, widow	07-Jun-84	1600	B.L. 15, 637 f. 90a	4010
Lane, Francis	Roscommon, Tulske	peer: countess				
		Lanesborough, widow	08-Jul-85	400	B.L. 15, 637 f. 99a	4028
Lane, George	Dublin, the city	gentry: knight	12-Sep-63	600	B.L. 15, 635 f. 131	3489
Lane, George	Dublin, the city	gentry: knight	13-Feb-66	600	B.L. 15, 635 f. 164a	3544

Standard	County	Occupation	Date	Amount	MS No	Ident No
Lane, George	Dublin, the city	gentry: knight	13-Feb-66	600	Dc3/21	2271
Langford, Thomas	Dublin	gentry: gent	14-Feb-15	60	Dc1/135r	839
Lattin, John	Kildare, the Nase	merchant	06-Feb-99	300	Dc1/15r	105
Lattin, John	Kildare, the Nase	merchant	31-Jan-99	300	Dc1/15r	104
Lattin, John	Kildare?, the Nase	merchant	03-Aug-99	540	Dc1/18v	127
Lawrence, Richard	Dublin, the city	gentry: esquire	17-Jan-83	2000	B.L. 15, 637 f. 73a	3980
Lawrence, Richard	Dublin, the city	merchant	05-Dec-66	500	B.L. 15, 635 f. 184	3578
Lawrence, Richard	Dublin, the city	merchant	26-Jun-73	200	Dc3/158r	2589
Lawrence, Richard	Dublin, the city	merchant	20-Jun-73	200	Dc3/158r	2588
Lawrence, Richard	Dublin, the city	merchant	05-Dec-66	500	Dc3/42	2319
Lawrence, Richard	Dublin, the city	merchant	22-Dec-66	220	Dc3/50	2331
Lawrence, Richard	Dublin, the city	gentry: esquire	16-Jan-83	2000	B.L. 15, 637 f. 60a	3956
Lawrence, Richard	Dublin, the city	merchant	22-Dec-66	220	B.L. 15, 635 f. 184a	3579
Le Power, Richard	Waterford?	peer: baron Coroghmore	16-Feb-71	200	Dc3/135v	2516
Ledbetter, Edmund	Dublin	gentry: gent	22-Feb-12	160	Dc1/112v	699
Legge, Edward	England, London	gentry: gent	13-Feb-24	120	Dc2/53v	1203
Lehunt, Richard	Tipperary, Cashell, the city	gentry: esquire	17-Sep-56	2000	B.L. 19, 843 f. 184a	3076
Leicester, John	Dublin	merchant	20-Nov-01	140	Dc1/34v	228
Leigh, Francis	Kildare, Rathhide	gentry: esquire	07-May-75	2200	Dc3/167r	2633
Leigh, Francis	Kildare, Rathbride	gentry: esquire	07-May-75	2200	B.L. 19, 844 f. 61a	3188
Leigh, Thomas	Dublin, the city	gentry: gent	28-Mar-40	1000	B.L. 19, 843 f. 49	2816
Leigh, Thomas	Dublin	gentry: gent	02-Dec-33	100	Dc2/201v	1910
Leigh, Thomas	Kildare, Killadowne	gentry: gent	20-Aug-39	1000	B.L. 19, 843 f. 35a	2789
Leigh, Thomas	Louth, Drogheda	merchant	09-Aug-62	160	B.L. 15, 635 f. 95	3424
Leighton, Jane	Dublin, the city	other: spinster	21-May-69	400	Dc3/99	2439
Lenthall, Thomas	England, London	merchant	06-Nov-58	900	B.L. 15, 635 f. 33a	3322
Lesgrandge, Thomas	Roscommon, Castlegrandge	gentry: esquire	12-Jun-24	200	Dc2/56r	1221
Leslie, Charles	Monaghan, Castlelesly	gentry: esquire	14-Jun-81	5000	B.L. 15, 637 f. 45a	3928
Leslie, John	Monaghan, Lesley		10-Feb-70	800	B.L. 15, 636 f. 63a	3730
Leslie, John	Monaghan, Castleleslie	gentry: esquire	10-Feb-70	800	Dc3/114	2468
Leslie, Robert		prof: bishop of Raphoe	15-Oct-70	2000	Dc3/129	2498
Leslie, Robert		prof: bishop of Raphoe	14-Feb-71	400	Dc3/135r	2514
Leslie, William	Antrim, Prospect	gentry: esquire	20-Nov-78	660	B.L. 15, 637 f. 9a	3864
Leventhorpe, Ralph	Dublin, St. Werburgh's parish	gentry: esquire	22-Nov-39	200	B.L. 19, 843 f. 48a	2815
Leventhorpe, Ralph	Dublin, the city	gentry: esquire	03-Mar-34	800	Dc2/208r	1936
Leventhorpe, Raphael	Dublin	gentry: gent	15-Jun-18	200	Dc2/15r	943
Leventhorpe, Rapheal	Dublin	gentry: esquire	22-Feb-26	100	Dc2/74v	1346
Leventhorpe, Stafford	England, Stevenage, Hertford		13-Dec-77	900	B.L. 19, 844 f. 143	3274
Leventhorpe, Stafford	England, Hartford, Stevenage		13-Dec-77	900	Dc3/184r	2699
Lewis, John	England, York, Ledston	gentry: knight and baronet	22-Dec-66	520	B.L. 15, 635 f. 180	3569

Standard	County	Occupation	Date	Amount	MS No	Ident No
Lewis, John	England, Ledston, Yorke	gentry: knight	22-Dec-66	520	Dc3/49	2330
Lightburne, Stafford	Meath, Littleffresans	gentry: esquire	16-Jul-68	200	Dc3/81	2408
Lillies, John	Limerick, the city	other: executor of will of				
		Henry Bindon, alderman	05-Jun-65	300	Dc3/8	2237
Lillies, Nicholas	Limerick, Disert	gentry: esquire	27-May-40	800	B.L. 19, 843 f. 70a	2860
Lindsay, Andrew	Monaghan, Clownice	gentry: esquire	31-Jan-65	1000	Dc3/2	2224
Lindsay, John	England, London, the city	gentry: esquire	09-Mar-78	2600	B.L. 19, 844 f. 148	3279
Lindsay, John	England, London	gentry: esquire	04-Mar-78	2600	Dc3/186v	2706
Lister, John	Dublin	merchant	02-May-01	74	Dc1/31r	204
Little, Thomas	Dublin	gentry: esquire	08-Apr-37	300	Dc2/261r	2173
Lloyd, Andrew	Dublin, the city	merchant	04-Jul-64	500	B.L. 15, 635 f. 172	3553
Lloyd, Andrew	Dublin, the city	merchant	27-Jul-54	600	B.L. 19, 843 f. 151	3016
Locke, Patrick	Meath, Arbracan	farmer: cottier	02-Dec-97	1500	Dc1/8v	59
Lockhart, Peter	Dublin, the city	trade: brewer	03-Apr-67	160	B.L. 15, 635 f. 186	3582
Lockhart, Peter	Dublin, the city	trade: brewer	03-Apr-67	161	Dc3/59	2351
Loftus, Adam	Dublin	gentry: knight	13-May-05	2000	Dc1/59r	360
Loftus, Adam	Dublin	gentry: knight	11-Feb-05	144	Dc1/56v	348
Loftus, Adam	King's Co.?	peer: viscount Ely	17-Dec-25	2000	Dc2/72v	1335
Loftus, Adam	Dublin, Dromnagh	gentry: knight	08-Feb-11	3000	Dc1/103r	643
Loftus, Adam	Dublin	gentry: knight	03-Mar-05	110	Dc1/57r	350
Loftus, Adam	Dublin	gentry: knight	11-May-05	2000	Dc1/59r	359
Loftus, Adam	Dublin, Rathfarnam	gentry: esquire	04-Jul-67	4000	Dc3/65	2366
Loftus, Adam	Dublin, Rathfarnam	gentry: esquire	04-Jul-67	5000	Dc3/65	2367
Loftus, Adam	Dublin, Dromnegh	gentry: knight	09-Dec-07	300	Dc1/80v	498
Loftus, Edward	Dublin	gentry: knight	28-Feb-26	2000	Dc2/75r	1349
Loftus, Edward	King's Co.?	peer:				
		viscount Loftus of Ely	29-Nov-67	264	B.L. 15, 635 f. 213	3631
Loftus, Edward	King's Co.?	peer:				
		viscount Loftus of Ely	29-Nov-67	264	Dc3/68	2376
Loftus, Francis	Dublin	gentry: gent	20-Apr-14	120	Dc1/128v	800
Loftus, Nicholas	Dublin, Rathfernam	gentry: gent	13-Dec-22	1000	Dc2/44r	1132
Loftus, Nicholas	Dublin, the city	gentry: esquire	28-Apr-49	3000	B.L. 19, 843 f. 124a	2968
Loftus, Robert	Dublin	gentry: knight	28-Feb-26	2000	Dc2/75r	1349
Loftus, Thomas	Queen's Co., Tymogho	gentry: knight	03-Feb-15	300	Dc1/135r	838
Logan, Mathew	Antrim, Whitshead	gentry: gent	13-Jun-68	320	B.L. 15, 635 f. 223a	3652
Long, Joan	Dublin	other: widow	12-Jul-02	40	Dc1/38v	251
Long, Joan	Dublin	other: widow	19-Sep-01	200	Dc1/33v	222
Long, Joan	Dublin	other: widow	20-Feb-02	200	Dc1/36r	236
Long, Richard	Kildare, Abbottstowne	farmer	16-Sep-30	300	Dc2/155r	1719
Long, Richard	Dublin	gentry: gent	20-May-01	60	Dc1/32r	210
Long, Richard	Meath, Harbertstowne	gentry: gent	14-Nov-85	600	B.L. 15, 637 f. 102a	4033
Long, Thomas	Dublin	merchant	04-Feb-01	200	Dc1/28v	191
Long, Thomas	Dublin, Abbotstowne	farmer	01-Dec-35	400	Dc2/240v	2075
Long, Thomas	Dublin	merchant	12-Feb-03	600	Dc1/44v	284
Long, Thomas	Dublin	merchant	12-May-99	200	Dc1/16r	110

Standard	County	Occupation	Date	Amount	MS No	Ident No
Long, William	Dublin	trade: tanner	04-Feb-01	200	Dc1/28v	191
Lott, John	Dublin	farmer: yeoman	16-Jun-10	250	Dc1/97v	613
Louewy?, Caleb	England, London	gentry: gent	20-Jun-54	500	B.L. 19, 843 f. 141	2996
Lovelace, Thomas	Roscommon, Ballybridge	gentry: esquire	25-Nov-71	500	Dc3/141v	2535
Lovett, Christopher	Dublin, the city		07-Oct-70	200	Dc3/127	2495
Lovett, Christopher	Dublin, the city		07-Oct-70	200	B.L. 15, 636 f. 75a	3753
Lovett, Christopher	Dublin, the city		04-Feb-73	800	B.L. 15, 636 f. 122	3829
Lovett, Christopher	Dublin, the city		04-Feb-73	800	Dc3/153r	2573
Lovett, Lawrence	England, Edthorpe, Bucks.	gentry: gent	12-Nov-74	1000	B.L. 19, 844 f. 36	3160
Lovett, Lawrence	England, Edthrop, Bucks.	gentry: gent	12-Nov-74	1000	Dc3/163r	2617
Lowther, Gerard	Dublin; the city	gentry: knight	16-Dec-57	200	B.L. 19, 843 f. 202a	3111
Lowther, Gerard	Dublin, the city	gentry: knight	14-Nov-57	200	B.L. 19, 843 f. 199a	3105
Lowther, Gerard	Dublin		04-Mar-37	400	Dc2/260v	2169
Lowther, Gerard	Dublin, the city	gentry: knight	04-Dec-57	120	B.L. 19, 843 f. 201a	3109
Lowther, Gerard	Dublin, the city	gentry: knight	05-Nov-58	800	B.L. 15, 635 f. 37a	3329
Lowther, Gerard	Dublin?, the city?	gentry: knight	02-May-59	300	B.L. 15, 635 f. 44a	3341
Lowther, Gerard	Dublin	gentry: knight	10-Jun-34	200	Dc2/212r	1953
Lowther, Gerard	Dublin	gentry: esquire	21-Nov-28	200	Dc2/116v	1544
Lowther, Gerard	Dublin, the city	gentry: knight	19-Feb-59	400	B.L. 15, 635 f. 39	3332
Lowther, Gerard	Dublin, the city	gentry: knight	07-Mar-59	600	B.L. 15, 635 f. 39a	3333
Lowther, Gerard	Dublin	gentry: knight	26-Aug-59	420	B.L. 15, 635 f. 51	3353
Lowther, Gerard	Dublin, the city	gentry: knight	14-Jun-33	200	Dc2/196v	1889
Lowther, Gerard	Dublin, the city	gentry: knight	11-Sep-56	1000	B.L. 19, 843 f. 182	3071
Lowther, Gerard	Dublin, the city	gentry: knight	13-Jun-56	200	B.L. 19, 843 f. 181a	3070
Lowther, Gerard	Dublin, the city	gentry: knight	27-Jun-57	200	B.L. 19, 843 f. 194a	3096
Lowther, Gerard	Dublin, the city	gentry: knight	04-Feb-54	2000	B.L. 19, 843 f. 136	2986
Lowther, Gerard	Dublin	gentry: knight	13-Jun-59	200	B.L. 15, 635 f. 47a	3347
Lowther, Gerard	Dublin, the city	gentry: knight	13-Apr-53	400	B.L. 19, 843 f. 132a	2980
Lowther, Gerard	Dublin, the city	gentry: knight, exec for Sir Richard Osbaldston	15-Nov-52	494	B.L. 19, 843 f. 127a	2973
Lowther, Gerard	Dublin, the city	gentry: knight	01-Dec-57	120	B.L. 19, 843 f. 201	3108
Lowther, Gerard	Dublin, the city	gentry: knight	20-Apr-54	1000	B.L. 19, 843 f. 137	2988
Lowther, Gerard	Dublin, the city	gentry: knight	03-Aug-53	345	B.L. 19, 843 f. 133a	2982
Lowther, Gerard	Dublin	gentry: esquire	23-Jun-29	2000	Dc2/134v	1628
Lowther, Gerard	Dublin, the city	gentry: knight	31-Dec-58	500	B.L. 15, 635 f. 35a	3325
Lowther, Gerard	Dublin, Ostmanstowne, suburbs	gentry: knight	19-Oct-59	1000	B.L. 15, 635 f. 53	3357
Lowther, Gerard	Dublin, the city	gentry: knight, exec for Sir Richard Osbaldston	20-Nov-52	400	B.L. 19, 843 f. 128	2974
Lowther, Gerard	Dublin, the city	gentry: knight	03-Mar-54	200	B.L. 19, 843 f. 136a	2987
Lowther, Gerard	Dublin	gentry: knight	28-Sep-59	600	B.L. 15, 635 f. 51a	3354
Luddington, Thomas	Dublin, the city	gentry: gent	17-Jul-66	50	Dc3/34	2297
Luddington, Thomas	Dublin, the city	gentry: gent	26-Apr-67	130	Dc3/60	2353
Ludlow, Stephen	Dublin, the city	gentry: esquire	10-Jun-71	200	B.L. 15, 636 f. 84a	3769
Ludlow, Stephen	Dublin, the city	gentry: esquire	16-Feb-80	418	B.L. 15, 637 f. 28	3897

Standard	County	Occupation	Date	Amount	MS No	Ident No
Ludlow, Stephen	Dublin, the city	gentry: esquire	10-Feb-76	500	B.L. 19, 844 f. 90	3217
Ludlow, Stephen	Dublin, the city	gentry: esquire	30-Dec-71	600	B.L. 15, 636 f. 94	3786
Ludlow, Stephen	Dublin, the city	gentry: esquire	17-Dec-86	1000	B.L. 15, 637 f. 113	4054
Ludlow, Stephen	Dublin, the city	gentry: esquire	15-Feb-77	300	B.L. 19, 844 f. 135	3265
Ludlow, Stephen	Dublin, the city	gentry: esquire	31-May-82	1400	B.L. 15, 637 f. 61	3957
Ludlow, Stephen	Dublin, the city	gentry: esquire	15-Feb-77	300	Dc3/182r	2686
Ludlow, Stephen	Dublin, the city	gentry: esquire	25-Jun-80	500	B.L. 15, 637 f. 33a	3907
Ludlow, Stephen	Dublin, the city	gentry: esquire	30-Dec-71	600	Dc3/143r	2541
Ludlow, Stephen	Dublin, the city	gentry: esquire	10-Feb-76	500	Dc3/172r	2649
Ludlow, Stephen	Dublin, the city	gentry: esquire	17-Jul-84	300	B.L. 15, 637 f. 92	4013
Ludlow, Stephen	Dublin, the city	gentry: esquire	10-Jun-71	200	Dc3/138r	2523
Lunn, Ellnathan?	Dublin, the city	merchant	29-Nov-84	1000	B.L. 15, 637 f. 96	4021
Luttrell, Alison	Dublin, Diswelstowne	other: widow	27-Jun-35	1600	Dc2/238r	2061
Luttrell, Edward	Kildare, Woodstock	gentry: gent	12-Aug-98	1000	Dc1/12r	86
Luttrell, Henry	Dublin	gentry: gent	08-Jul-03	200	Dc1/47ar	304
Luttrell, Thomas	Dublin, the city	gentry: esquire	14-Jul-64	200	B.L. 15, 635 f. 144a	3508
Luttrell, Thomas	Dublin, the city	gentry: esquire	28-Jun-73	400	Dc3/158v	2591
Luttrell, Thomas	Dublin, Luttrellston	gentry: esquire	02-Mar-01	2000	Dc1/29r	194
Luttrell, Thomas	Dublin, the city	gentry: esquire	28-Jun-73	400	B.L. 19, 844 f. 2	3121
Lynan, Christopher	Meath, Killmoore	gentry: gent	28-Jun-72	160	B.L. 15, 636 f. 111a	3813
Lynan, Christopher	Meath, Kilmore	gentry: gent	28-Jun-72	160	Dc3/147r	2557
Lynan, James	Dublin, the city	merchant	07-Apr-36	1000	Dc2/249r	2113
Lynan, Mary	Meath, Kilmore	gentry: wife of Christopher	28-Jun-72	160	Dc3/147r	2557
Lynan, Mary	Meath, Killmoore	gentry: wife of Christopher	28-Jun-72	160	B.L. 15, 636 f. 111a	3813
Lynan, Richard	Meath, Sommerston	gentry: gent	09-Sep-36	400	Dc2/255v	2148
Lynan, Thomas	Dublin, Houth	trade: fishmonger	02-Jun-30	1000	Dc2/148v	1692
Lynch, Christopher	Meath, Croboy	gentry: esquire	18-Nov-06	120	Dc1/71v	433
Lynch, Garret	Meath, the Knocke	gentry: esquire	29-Nov-25	700	Dc2/70v	1323
Lynch, Garret	Meath, Kilmerr	gentry: gent	29-Nov-25	600	Dc2/70v	1324
Lynch, Garret	Meath, the Knocke	gentry: esquire	05-Apr-31	930	Dc2/161v	1749
Lynch, Garret	Meath, Knocke	gentry: esquire	13-Nov-35	600	Dc2/239v	2069
Lynch, John	Galway, the towne		14-May-34	400	Dc2/211r	1948
Lyne, Peter	Dublin, the city	merchant	01-Mar-67	400	Dc3/55	2342
Lyne, Peter	Dublin, the city	merchant	28-Oct-67	720	B.L. 15, 635 f. 199	3607
Lyne, Peter	Dublin, the city	merchant	01-Mar-67	400	B.L. 15, 635 f. 190a	3591
Lyne, Peter	Dublin, the city	merchant	28-Oct-67	720	Dc3/67	2372
Lyvet, John	Waterford, the city	merchant	16-Apr-40	1400	B.L. 19, 843 f. 65a	2850
Mabbott, Gilbert	Dublin, the city	gentry: esquire	19-Feb-68	200	Dc3/74	2391
Mabbott, Gilbert	Dublin, the city	gentry: esquire	29-Nov-67	1000	Dc3/68	2375
Mabbott, Gilbert	Dublin, the city	gentry: esquire	29-Nov-67	1000	B.L. 15, 635 f. 217a	3640
Mabbott, Gilbert	Dublin, the city	gentry: esquire	29-Feb-68	200	B.L. 15, 635 f. 218	3641
MacAuley, Henry	Westmeath, Ballyloghtoe	gentry: gent	28-Jul-64	1000	B.L. 15, 635 f. 201a	3612

Standard	County	Occupation	Date	Amount	MS No	Ident No
MacCarthy, Catherine	Limerick, Longford	other: widow	26-Jul-86	1200	B.L. 15, 637 f. 111	4050
MacCarthy, Charles	Cork?	peer: viscount Muskerry	11-Apr-35	1000	Dc2/232v	2035
MacCarthy, Cormac	Cork, Blarny	gentry: esquire	23-Feb-13	300	Dc1/120r	745
MacCartney, George	Antrim, Belfast	merchant	29-Jan-72	273	B.L. 15, 636 f. 108a	3808
MacDermot, Charles	Roscommon, Meery	gentry: gent, brother of Terrence	03-Dec-40	6000	B.L. 19, 843 f. 75a	2870
MacDonnell, Randal	Antrim?	peer: earl of Antrim	10-May-27	2000	Dc2/92v	1430
MacDonnell, Randal	Antrim?	peer: earl of Antrim	11-May-27	4000	Dc2/92v	1432
MacGeneure, Teige	Westmeath, Blackcastle	gentry: gent	10-Feb-23	100	Dc2/45r	1139
MacInerney, Mahony	Clare, Ballyfallagh	gentry: gent	13-Apr-40	600	B.L. 19, 843 f. 56	2830
MacMahon, Owen	Monaghan, Drumrever	gentry: gent	27-Feb-36	3000	Dc2/246v	2101
MacManus, Brian	Antrim, Ballybegg	gentry: gent	29-Mar-78	220	B.L. 19, 844 f. 158	3289
MacManus, Cormac	Mayo, Knocknehorne	gentry: gent	04-Aug-66	300	Dc3/35	2302
Madden, John	Dublin, the city	gentry: gent	19-Feb-41	400	B.L. 19, 843 f. 86	2891
Madden, John	Dublin, the city	gentry: gent	17-Jul-39	400	B.L. 19, 843 f. 22	2762
Magee, John	Antrim, The Glin		27-Mar-56	383	B.L. 19, 843 f. 181	3069
Maguer, William	Queen's Co., Castlebracke	gentry: gent	20-Nov-16	300	Dc2/2r	878
Mahony, Terrence	Clare, Klennagh	gentry: gent	13-Apr-40	600	B.L. 19, 843 f. 56	2830
Mallady, Anthony	Meath, Robertstowne	gentry: esquire	09-Dec-76	1000	Dc3/180v	2677
Malone, Edmund	Dublin, the city		10-Jul-19	700	Dc2/25r	998
Malone, Edmund	Dublin, the city		23-Mar-23	900	Dc2/54r	1207
Malone, Edmund	Dublin	merchant	28-Nov-03	515	Dc1/50r	320
Malone, Edmund	Dublin		01-Jun-25	340	Dc2/64v	1286
Malone, Edmund	Dublin		23-Apr-18	260	Dc2/14r	937
Malone, Edmund	Dublin		21-Mar-22	200	Dc2/39r	1098
Malone, Edmund	Dublin		17-Feb-26	600	Dc2/74r	1345
Malone, Edmund	Dublin, the city		04-Dec-22	400	Dc2/43v	1130
Malone, Edmund	Dublin, the city		20-Aug-28	400	Dc2/114r	1534
Malone, Edmund	Dublin, the city		24-May-22	160	Dc2/40r	1106
Malone, Edmund	Dublin, the city		23-Apr-29	200	Dc2/128r	1600
Malone, Edmund	Dublin		09-Dec-26	400	Dc2/85v	1406
Malone, Edmund	Dublin		23-Jul-27	1300	Dc2/97v	1453
Malone, Edmund	Dublin		28-Jun-23	200	Dc2/48v	1168
Malone, Edward	Dublin		29-Mar-25	4000	Dc2/63r	1277
Malone, Joan	Dublin	merchant: widow	28-Nov-03	515	Dc1/50r	320
Malone, John	Dublin	gentry: gent, brother of Alison Russell	03-Aug-99	300	Dc1/19r	131
Malone, Simon	England, Manchester	merchant	22-May-01	120	Dc1/32r	212
Malone, Walter	Dublin	merchant	03-Aug-10	60	Dc1/99r	621
Malone, William	Meath, Lismullen	gentry: gent	22-Jan-35	800	Dc2/228v	2019
Malone, William	Meath, Lismullen	gentry: gent	13-Feb-34	240	Dc2/206v	1930
Malone, William	Dublin, the city	merchant: son of Edmund, alderman	20-Nov-20	400	Dc2/33r	1051
Malone, William	Dublin, the city	merchant: son/heir of Edmund, alderman	10-Jan-21	500	Dc2/34r	1060

Standard	County	Occupation	Date	Amount	MS No	Ident No
Mannering, Mathew	Dublin	gentry: gent	08-Feb-19	200	Dc2/20v	972
Mannering, Mathew	Dublin, the city	gentry: esquire	11-Dec-18	200	Dc2/19r	965
Manning, Charles	Fermanagh, Garrison	gentry: gent	02-Jun-36	2000	Dc2/253r	2134
Manning, Edward	England, London, the city	gentry: gent	02-Jun-36	2000	Dc2/253r	2134
Manning, Henry	Fermanagh, Drumbrocus	gentry: esquire	02-Jun-36	2000	Dc2/253r	2134
Mapas, Amy	Dublin	merchant: widow	19-Jan-21	200	Dc2/34r	1061
Mapas, Amy	Dublin	merchant: widow	19-Jun-21	200	Dc2/35v	1073
Mapas, Amy	Dublin	merchant: widow	11-Apr-21	272	Dc2/35r	1066
Mapas, Christopher	Dublin, the city	merchant	08-Feb-25	200	Dc2/61v	1263
Mapas, Christopher	Dublin, the city	merchant	30-Nov-28	200	Dc2/121r	1565
Mapas, Christopher	Dublin, the city	merchant	09-Jun-20	200	Dc2/31r	1035
Mapas, Christopher	Dublin, the city	merchant	01-Dec-27	180	Dc2/101r	1469
Mapas, Elizabeth	Dublin, the city	other: widow	22-Jun-37	300	Dc2/265r	2190
Mapas, Elizabeth	Dublin, the city	other: widow	28-Jan-36	600	Dc2/243v	2090
Mapas, Patrick	Dublin, the city		24-May-33	500	Dc2/194v	1882
Mapas, Patrick	Dublin	merchant	03-Jul-26	200	Dc2/80v	1382
Mapas, Patrick	Dublin, the city	merchant	18-Jun-24	200	Dc2/56v	1226
Mapas, Patrick	Dublin	merchant	13-May-15	1500	Dc1/137v	852
Mapas, Patrick	Dublin, the city	merchant	21-Jul-26	200	Dc2/81v	1387
Mapas, Patrick	Dublin, the city	merchant	28-Jun-27	400	Dc2/96v	1450
Mapas, Patrick	Dublin, the city	merchant	05-Jun-24	500	Dc2/55v	1218
Mapas, Patrick	Dublin, the city	merchant	03-Jun-22	200	Dc2/40V	1110
Mapas, Patrick	Dublin, the city	merchant	08-Dec-25	200	Dc2/71v	1330
Mapas, Patrick	Dublin	merchant	04-Jun-25	800	Dc2/65r	1289
Mapas, Patrick	Dublin	merchant	25-Jun-25	300	Dc2/66v	1298
Mapas, Patrick	Dublin, the city	merchant	30-Jun-25	200	Dc2/67r	1301
Mapas, Patrick	Dublin, the city		07-Nov-28	500	Dc2/115v	1541
Mapas, Patrick	Dublin, the city	merchant	22-May-22	272	Dc2/40r	1105
Mapas, Patrick	Dublin, the city	merchant	25-Jun-22	3000	Dc2/41r	1113
Mapas, Patrick	Dublin, the city		18-Jul-28	1100	Dc2/113v	1530
Mapas, Patrick	Dublin, the city	merchant	03-Jun-22	200	Dc2/40v	1111
Mapas, Patrick	Dublin, the city	merchant	04-Dec-22	200	Dc2/43v	1129
Mapas, Patrick	Dublin, the city	merchant	06-Dec-24	200	Dc2/59v	1250
Margetson, James		prof: archbishop of Armagh	03-Aug-66	1000	Dc3/35	2301
Markham, Henry	Dublin, the city	soldier: colonel	02-Nov-57	400	B.L. 19, 843 f. 203a	3113
Markham, Nathaniel	Dublin	trade: vintner	20-Jan-34	400	Dc2/205v	1925
Markham, William	Meath, Castlerikard	gentry: gent	26-Jun-54	300	B.L. 19, 843 f. 143a	3001
Marruk, John	England, London	gentry: gent	02-Aug-65	680	B.L. 15, 635 f. 157a	3532
Marsh, Francis		prof: bishop of Kilmore and Ardagh	27-Mar-79	2000	B.L. 15, 637 f. 13	3871
Marsh, Francis		prof: dean of Ardagh	25-Mar-66	3240	B.L. 15, 635 f. 172a	3554
Marsh, Francis		prof: bishop of Kilmore and Ardagh	11-Dec-76	1000	B.L. 19, 844 f. 114	3243

Standard	County	Occupation	Date	Amount	MS No	Ident No
Marsh, Francis		prof: bishop of Kilmore and Ardagh	11-Dec-76	1000	Dc3/181r	2680
Marshall, Robert	Dublin, the city	gentry: gent	09-Dec-72	500	Dc3/151v	2567
Marshall, Robert	Dublin, the city	gentry: gent	09-Dec-72	500	B.L. 15, 636 f. 119	3825
Martin, Anthony	Meath	prof: bishop Meath	05-Dec-33	800	Dc2/202v	1913
Martin, Foulke	Louth, Drogheda	gentry: esquire	01-Jul-39	160	B.L. 19, 843 f. 34a	2787
Martin, Giles	Dublin, Clantarfe	gentry: esquire	20-Feb-75	420	B.L. 15, 637 f. 91	4011
Martin, Giles	Dublin, Clantarfe	gentry: esquire	11-Feb-76	420	Dc3/172r	2650
Martin, James	Galway, Cloran		29-Jan-68	600	B.L. 15, 635 f. 223	3651
Martin, James	Clare, Bally Sallagh	merchant	28-May-41	1200	B.L. 19, 843 f. 95a	2910
Martin, John	Louth, Drogheda	gentry: esquire	30-May-36	2000	Dc2/252v	2130
Martin, John	Louth, Drogheda	gentry: esquire	31-May-36	1000	Dc2/253r	2132
Martin, William	Dublin, the city	trade: brewer	03-Aug-61	220	B.L. 15, 635 f. 80a	3400
Martin, William	Dublin, the city	trade: brewer	01-Jul-61	600	B.L. 15, 635 f. 74a	3391
Martin, William	Dublin, the city	trade: brewer	26-Nov-61	320	B.L. 15,635 f. 88	3412
Martin, William	Dublin, the city	trade: brewer	26-Nov-61	220	B.L. 15, 635 f. 87a	3411
Martin, William	Dublin, the city	trade: brewer	14-Jun-61	300	B.L. 15, 635 f. 73	3390
Martin, William	Dublin, the city	trade: brewer	12-May-55	156	B.L. 19, 843 f. 184	3075
Martin, William	Dublin	trade: brewer	20-Feb-59	1000	B.L. 15, 635 f. 40a	3335
Martin, William	Dublin, the city	trade: brewer	24-Sep-61	640	B.L. 15, 635 f. 85	3406
Martin, William	Dublin, the city	trade: brewer	16-Apr-56	216	B.L. 19, 843 f. 183a	3074
Martin, William	Dublin, the city	gentry: gent	02-Dec-70	2000	B.L. 15, 636 f. 75	3752
Martin, William	Dublin, the city	gentry: gent	02-Dec-70	2000	Dc3/132r	2505
Marwood, William	Dublin	gentry: esquire	13-May-08	320	Dc1/82v	514
Mason, William	Dublin	gentry: gent	12-Feb-21	400	Dc2/34v	1063
Mason, William	Dublin, the city	gentry: gent	16-Jun-29	120	Dc2/133r	1621
Masterson, Richard	Wexford, Kilbride	gentry: gent	16-May-79	440	B.L. 15, 637 f. 18a	3879
Masterson, Roger	Wexford, Monesceede	gentry: esquire	03-Dec-69	1460	Dc3/110	2463
Maud, Robert	Dublin, the city	gentry: esquire	07-Apr-82	4000	B.L. 15, 637 f. 59a	3954
Maule, Thomas	Dublin	gentry: esquire	16-Oct-54	650	B.L. 19, 843 f. 146a	3007
Maule, Thomas	Dublin, the city	gentry: esquire	26-Aug-40	3000	B.L. 19, 843 f. 67	2853
Maxwell, Henry	Down, Fawnabrroge		03-Dec-78	400	B.L. 15, 637 f. 7a	3861
Maxwell, John	Down, Ballyhalbart	gentry: gent	19-Feb-19	400	Dc2/21r	976
Maxwell, John	Down, Aghnidriske	gentry: gent	24-Mar-35	500	Dc2/232r	2033
Maxwell, Robert		prof: bishop of Kilmore and Ardagh	20-Sep-61	700	B.L. 15, 635 f. 84	3404
Maynard, Boyle	Cork, Curryglasse	gentry: knight	18-Jun-73	180	B.L. 15, 636 f. 135	3846
Maynard, Boyle	Cork, Curriglass	gentry: knight	18-Jun-73	180	Dc3/157v	2586
Mayo, Robert	Dublin, the city	gentry: esquire	09-Aug-36	600	Dc2/256r	2149
Meade, David	Cork	gentry: gent	30-Nov-09	20	Dc1/93r	583
Meade, David	Cork, the city	gentry: gent	15-Dec-20	200	Dc2/33v	1057
Meade, David	Cork, the city	merchant	17-May-21	400	Dc2/35v	1071
Meade, David	Limerick, Kilmallocke	other: son of Patrick, Kilmallock, burgess	06-May-40	800	B.L. 19, 843 f. 93a	2906
Meade, John	Cork, Ballyneturbrett	gentry: esquire	12-Feb-69	800	Dc3/90	2425

Standard	County	Occupation	Date	Amount	MS No	Ident No
Meade, John	Cork	gentry: esquire	20-Jun-15	500	Dc1/139r	862
Meade, John	Cork, Ballyneturberet	gentry: esquire	12-Feb-69	800	B.L. 15, 636 f. 28	3674
Meade, William	Limerick, the city		13-Feb-13	100	Dc1/119r	739
Meller, Robert	Dublin, the city	trade: apothecary	13-Sep-72	450	Dc3/149r	2562
Mercer, Robert	Dublin, the city	merchant	13-Feb-67	220	Dc3/53	2338
Meredith, Robert	Dublin, the city	gentry: knight	13-Jun-53	700	B.L. 19, 843 f. 139a	2993
Meredith, Dorothy	Dublin, the city	gentry: gentlewoman	04-Jul-70	220	B.L. 15, 636 f. 67a	3737
Meredith, Dorothy	Dublin	gentry: gentlewoman	04-Jul-70	220	Dc3/122	2485
Meredith, Mary	Dublin	gentry: gentlewoman	04-Jul-70	220	Dc3/122	2485
Meredith, Mary	Dublin, the city	gentry: gentlewoman	04-Jul-70	220	B.L. 15, 636 f. 67a	3737
Meredith, Robert	Dublin, the city	gentry: esquire	13-Dec-21	160	Dc2/37v	1089
Meredith, Robert	Dublin, the city	gentry: knight	01-Jul-53	400	B.L. 19, 843 f. 140a	2995
Meredith, Robert	Dublin, the city	gentry: knight	01-Mar-54	600	B.L. 19, 843 f. 140	2994
Meredith, William	Dublin, the city	gentry: baronet	27-Jul-61	210	B.L. 15, 635 f. 79a	3398
Meredith, William	Kildare, Greenhill	peer: baron	30-Aug-62	2500	B.L. 15, 635 f. 94	3422
Merriman, Robert	Down, Sheepland	gentry: gent	07-May-19	400	Dc2/23r	988
Meskill, Richard	Cork, the city	merchant	21-Mar-83	2800	B.L. 15, 637 f. 71a	3976
Metcalf, Henry	Dublin, the city	gentry: esquire	14-May-70	4000	Dc3/119	2478
Metcalf, Henry	Dublin	gentry: esquire	14-May-70	4000	B.L. 15, 636 f. 66a	3735
Metcalf, James	Dublin, the city	prof: doctor of phisick	28-Nov-28	240	Dc2/118r	1553
Metcalf, James	Dublin, the city	prof: doctor of phisick	09-Dec-28	100	Dc2/121v	1568
Meye?, Mathew	Dublin	merchant	26-Nov-99	500	Dc1/20v	138
Mihill, John	Wexford, Wexford	gentry: esquire	25-Mar-84	300	B.L. 15, 637 f. 84a	4000
Miles, Catherine	Dublin	gentry: spinster?, sister of John and Richard	09-Sep-36	400	Dc2/255v	2148
Miles, Edward	Dublin	gentry: gent	02-Dec-02	160	Dc1/41v	266
Miles, Edward	Dublin, the city	gentry: gent	10-Sep-19	80	Dc2/25v	1002
Miles, Elizabeth	Dublin	gentry: spinster?, sister of John and Richard	09-Sep-36	400	Dc2/255v	2148
Miles, John	Dublin	gentry: gent	09-Sep-36	400	Dc2/255v	2148
Miles, Ralph	Dublin	merchant	30-Oct-01	40	Dc1/34r	224
Miles, Raphael	Dublin	gentry: gent	21-May-18	120	Dc2/14v	940
Miles, Richard	Dublin	gentry: gent	09-Sep-36	400	Dc2/255v	2148
Miles, Robert	Dublin, the city		22-Apr-56	32	B.L. 19, 843 f. 180a	3067
Miles, Roger	Dublin	merchant	09-Jul-12	66	Dc1/115r	716
Mill, Roger	England, Southhampton	gentry: gent	02-Jun-06	120	Dc1/69r	418
Millner, Tempest	England, London	gentry: esquire	07-Aug-58	450	B.L. 15, 635 f. 31a	3318
Mills, Thomas	Cork, the city	trade: leather-dresser	04-Jan-66	308	B.L. 15, 635 f. 162a	3540
Mills, Thomas	Cork, the city	trade: leather-dresser	14-Nov-65	400	B.L. 15, 635 f. 162	3539
Mitchell, Thomas	Cork, the city	merchant	30-Dec-67	1772	B.L. 15, 635 f. 216a	3638
Mitchell, Thomas	Cork, the city	merchant	20-Jun-70	1000	B.L. 15, 636 f. 72	3746
Molloy, Walter	Dublin, the city	merchant	14-Mar-68	60	Dc3/74	2392
Molyneux, Daniel			21-May-07	300	Dc1/77r	469
Monck, Charles	Dublin	gentry: esquire	14-May-28	100	Dc2/108r	1506

Standard	County	Occupation	Date	Amount	MS No	Ident No
Monck, Charles	Dublin	gentry: esquire	01-Feb-28	400	Dc2/103v	1482
Monck, Henry	Dublin, the city	gentry: esquire	21-Mar-78	2000	Dc3/187v	2708
Monck, John	England, London	trade: clothworker and citizen	28-Sep-19	400	Dc2/25v	1003
Monckton, Nicholas	Limerick, Knockany	gentry: esquire	22-May-75	2909	Dc3/167v	2635
Monckton, Nicholas	Limerick, Knockany	gentry: esquire	22-May-75	2909	B.L. 19, 844 f. 62	3189
Monckton, Nicholas	Limerick, Awny	gentry: gent	08-Oct-66	500	B.L. 15, 635 f. 179	3567
Moneypenny, Andrew	Antrim, Conor		03-Dec-24	1000	Dc2/59r	1249
Montgomery, Catherine	Down?	peer: countess-dowager Mount Alexander	05-Jan-71	800	Dc3/134r	2511
Montgomery, Catherine	Down, the Ards	peer: countess of Mount Alexander, widow	05-Jan-71	800	B.L. 15, 637 f. 14	3873
Montgomery, Hugh	Down?	peer: viscount of the Ards	05-Dec-25	600	Dc2/71v	1329
Montgomery, Hugh	Down?	gentry: son of viscount Montgomery of the Ards	19-Apr-27	1800	Dc2/90v	1425
Montgomery, Hugh	Down?	peer: viscount Montgomery of the Ards	19-Apr-27	1800	Dc2/90v	1425
Montgomery, John	Down, Creaghbuy	gentry: gent	22-Jun-85	1000	B.L. 15, 637 f. 100a	4030
Montgomery, Robert	Fermanagh, Rusky	gentry: esquire	29-May-23	500	Dc2/48r	1163
Moore, Alice	Louth?	peer: countess-dowager Drogheda	09-Jun-76	1400	Dc3/176v	2664
Moore, Alice	Louth?	peer: countess-dowager Drogheda	09-Jun-76	2400	Dc3/176r	2663
Moore, Alice	Louth?	peer: countess Drogheda, widow	01-Jul-84	1000	B.L. 15, 637 f. 89	4007
Moore, Alice	Louth?	peer: countess Drogheda, widow	08-Feb-84	1000	B.L. 15, 637 f. 84	3999
Moore, Alison	Kildare, Der		07-Feb-24	200	Dc2/53r	1199
Moore, Andrew	Dublin, Cowlocke	farmer	13-Nov-33	300	Dc2/200v	1905
Moore, Balthazar	Meath, Athboy	gentry: gent	17-Apr-00	120	Dc1/23r	153
Moore, Bartholmew	Dublin	gentry: gent	24-Feb-14	200	Dc1/127r	788
Moore, Bartholomew	Meath, Dowanston	gentry: gent	21-Jun-32	800	Dc2/184r	1839
Moore, Bartholomew	Meath, Dowanston	gentry: gent	27-Jun-39	300	B.L. 19, 843 f. 27a	2773
Moore, Bartholomew	Meath, Dowanstowne	gentry: gent	28-Apr-35	600	Dc2/234r	2042
Moore, Eleanor	Louth, Turlogh Donnell	gentry: widow	29-May-74	800	Dc3/161v	2610
Moore, Eleanor	Louth, Turlogh Donnell	gentry: widow	01-Jun-74	1200	Dc3/161v	2611
Moore, Emanuel	Cork, Roscarbery	gentry: esquire	20-Dec-79	300	B.L. 15, 637 f. 26	3893
Moore, Gerald	Louth?	peer: viscount Drogheda	26-Apr-27	2000	Dc2/91r	1427
Moore, Henry	Louth?	peer: earl of Drogheda	10-May-81	600	B.L. 15, 637 f. 43	3924
Moore, Henry	Louth?	peer: earl of Drogheda	15-Jun-87	4000	B.L. 15, 637 f. 108	4042
Moore, John	King's Co., Croghan?	gentry: knight	08-Dec-18	120	Dc2/19r	963
Moore, John	England, London	trade: clothworker and citizen	28-Sep-19	400	Dc2/25v	1003
Moore, Marjory	Dublin, Dowlagh	farmer: wife of Thomas	13-Nov-33	300	Dc2/200v	1905

Standard	County	Occupation	Date	Amount	MS No	Ident No
Moore, Melchior	Westmeath, Cronanston	gentry: gent	06-Feb-11	200	Dc1/102v	641
Moore, Robert	Louth, Drogheda	merchant	23-Jun-30	400	Dc2/153r	1712
Moore, Roger	Kildare, Ballena	gentry: esquire	04-Dec-28	600	Dc2/120r	1562
Moore, Roger	Dublin, the city	gentry: gent	20-Aug-40	120	B.L. 19, 843 f. 121a	2962
Moore, Roger	Dublin, the city	merchant	09-Aug-67	800	B.L. 15, 635 f. 205a	3620
Moore, Roger	Dublin, the city	merchant	09-Aug-67	800	Dc3/66	2370
Moore, Thomas	Cork, the city	gentry: gent	06-Dec-66	4000	B.L. 15, 635 f. 181a	3573
Moore, Thomas	Dublin, Dowlagh	farmer	13-Nov-33	300	Dc2/200v	1905
Moore, Thomas	Louth, Turlogh Donnell	gentry: esquire	01-Jun-74	1200	Dc3/161v	2611
Moore, Thomas	Louth, Turlogh Donnell	gentry: esquire	29-May-74	800	Dc3/161v	2610
Moore, William	Roscommon, Athlone	gentry: esquire	03-Jul-56	268	B.L. 19, 843 f. 176a	3063
Moore, William	Roscommon, Athlone	gentry: esquire	06-Jul-56	242	B.L. 19, 843 f. 178	3064
Moore, William	Louth, Deanrath	gentry: gent	06-Aug-39	280	B.L. 19, 843 f. 63a	2846
Moore, William	Roscommon, Athlone	gentry: esquire	06-Jun-56	242	B.L. 19, 843 f. 171a	3056
Moore, William	Roscommon, Athlone	gentry: esquire	06-Jun-56	242	B.L. 19, 843 f. 172a	3057
Moore, William	Roscommon, Athlone	gentry: esquire	02-Jun-56	800	B.L. 19, 843 f. 173a	3058
Moore, William	Tyrone, Garvey	gentry: esquire	23-Jul-81	3000	B.L. 15, 637 f. 49a	3935
Moran, Nicholas	Westmeath, Morinston	gentry: gent	19-Nov-09	60	Dc1/92r	578
Morely, James	Dublin, the city	gentry: esquire	16-Feb-58	40	B.L. 15, 635 f. 25a	3308
Morely, James	Dublin, the city	gentry: esquire	16-Feb-58	500	B.L. 15, 635 f. 27a	3310
Morgan, Anthony	Dublin, the city	gentry: knight	09-Jul-61	300	B.L. 15, 635 f. 83a	3403
Morgan, Patrick	Meath, Ballibimne	farmer	04-Jul-28	170	Dc2/112v	1525
Morgan, Robert	Sligo, Cottleston	gentry: esquire	30-Jul-75	6000	B.L. 19, 844 f. 74	3202
Morgan, Robert	Dublin	gentry: esquire	28-May-17	400	Dc2/7v	903
Morris, Abraham	Cork, the city	merchant	04-Jun-84	1000	B.L. 15, 637 f. 92a	4014
Morrison, Richard	Wicklow, Newcastell	gentry: knight	02-Jun-15	2000	Dc1/138r	856
Morrison, Richard	Cork, Yoghall	gentry: knight	03-Dec-09	600	Dc1/93v	585
Motley, Walter	Carlow, Tullow	merchant	16-Nov-30	200	Dc2/155v	1723
Motley, Walter	Carlow, Tulliephelim	merchant	26-Oct-30	300	B.L. 19, 843 f. 11a	2741
Motley, Walter	Carlow, Tullophely	merchant	20-Apr-35	400	Dc2/233r	2038
Motley, Walter	Carlow, Tulliephelim	merchant	10-Mar-36	300	B.L. 19, 843 f.12	2742
Motley, Walter	Carlow, Tullyphelin	merchant	15-Dec-25	320	Dc2/72r	1332
Motley, Walter	Carlow, Tullocke	merchant	12-Nov-34	400	Dc2/221r	1989
Mountage, Stephen	England, London, the city	gentry: gent	13-May-62	1800	B.L. 15, 635 f. 95a	3425
Mountford, John	Cork, Kinsale	merchant	22-Apr-68	200	B.L. 15, 635 f. 228a	3662
Moyle?, Mary	Dublin, the city	other: widow	06-May-64	200	B.L. 15, 635 f. 130	3487
Mullis, Joseph	Dublin	gentry: gent	19-Dec-18	500	Dc2/19v	967
Mulryan, Mary	Tipperary, Neillestowne	gentry: widow	23-May-06	400	Dc1/68r	412
Murphy, Janet	Dublin, the city	farmer: widow	06-Feb-24	200	Dc2/53r	1200
Murphy, John	Dublin		13-Apr-00	60	Dc1/23r	152
Murphy, John	Dublin, Swords	gentry: gent	05-Sep-65	200	Dc3/14	2251
Murphy, John	Dublin		17-May-97	60	Dc1/4r	27
Murphy, Theodore	Wexford, Ballyneclash	gentry: gent	18-May-69	200	Dc3/97	2436
Murray, Henry	Monaghan, Ballymacny	gentry: esquire	14-May-32	600	Dc2/180v	1825
Murray, Henry	Monaghan, Ballymacny	gentry: gent	11-May-32	200	Dc2/180r	1824

Standard	County	Occupation	Date	Amount	MS No	Ident No
Murray, Robert	England, Westminster, the city	gentry: gent	20-Dec-58	500	B.L. 15, 635 f. 37	3328
Murrough, Donough	Cork, the city	merchant	09-Nov-40	160	B.L. 19, 843 f. 81a	2882
Murrough, Thomas	Cork, the city	merchant	25-Nov-82	600	B.L. 15, 637 f. 69a	3972
Muschamp, Denis	Dublin, the city	gentry: esquire	03-Feb-73	1000	Dc3/153r	2572
Muschamp, Denis	Dublin, the city	gentry: esquire	03-Feb-73	1000	B.L. 15, 636 f. 131	3839
Muschamp, Denis	Cork, Grange	gentry: esquire	21-Jun-70	800	B.L. 15, 636 f. 71	3744
Muschamp, Denis	Cork, Grange	gentry: esquire	21-May-68	400	B.L. 15, 635 f. 224	3653
Muschamp, Thomas	England, London	trade: grocer and citizen	23-May-56	1000	B.L. 19, 843 f. 171	3055
Muschamp, William	England, Surrey, Rowebarnes	gentry: esquire	23-May-56	1000	B.L. 19, 843 f. 171	3055
Nangle, Bartholomew	Longford, the towne	merchant	04-Feb-32	200	Dc2/174v	1802
Nangle, David	Cork, Carragoone, in Ffermoy	gentry: gent	27-Aug-79	400	B.L. 15, 637 f. 23a	3888
Nangle, Edmund	Longford, Lisduffe	gentry: gent	16-Feb-36	320	Dc2/245r	2095
Nangle, Richard	Dublin, the city	gentry: esquire	22-Feb-86	2000	B.L. 15, 637 f. 105a	4038
Nangle, Richard	Cork, Carrickona?	gentry: esquire	21-Feb-83	1800	B.L. 15, 637 f. 77	3987
Nangle, Robert	Kildare, Ballysaxe	gentry: gent	12-May-06	130	Dc1/67r	405
Nash, Maurice	Limerick, Askeaton	merchant	13-Jul-66	200	B.L. 15, 636 f. 35a	3685
Nash, Maurice	Limerick, Askeaton	merchant	13-Jul-66	200	Dc3/32	2293
Nash, Maurice	Limerick, Askeaton	merchant	13-Jul-66	200	B.L. 15, 636 f. 35	3684
Nash, Maurice	Limerick, Askeaton	merchant	13-Jul-66	200	Dc3/32	2292
Nash, Nicholas	Kilkenny, Newhouse	gentry: gent	25-May-39	2200	B.L. 19, 843 f. 14	2746
Neale, John	Tipperary, Carricke	gentry: esquire	12-Nov-66	1000	Dc3/41	2317
Neale, Stephen	Louth, Carlingford	gentry: gent	06-Aug-34	1200	Dc2/217r	1972
Nelson, Frances	Dublin	other: widow	07-Aug-33	200	Dc2/198v	1897
Nelson, Marmaduke	Queen's Co., Clarehill	gentry: esquire	13-May-28	200	Dc2/108v	1508
Netterville, James	Wicklow, Tobber	gentry: gent	02-May-35	460	Dc2/234v	2044
Netterville, James	Wicklow, Tobber	gentry: gent	12-Dec-34	2000	Dc2/225v	2008
Netterville, Luke	Dublin, Corballish	gentry: esquire	11-Jul-37	1000	Dc2/267v	2201
Netterville, Luke	Dublin, Corballyes	gentry: esquire	13-May-34	2000	Dc2/210v	1947
Netterville, Nicholas	Meath, Douth	gentry: gent	21-Feb-06	400	Dc1/65v	396
Netterville, Nicholas	Louth?	peer: viscount Nettervill	13-Jun-28	800	Dc2/111r	1517
Netterville, Nicholas	Meath, Dowth	gentry: esquire	07-Nov-17	300	Dc2/10v	917
Nettles, John	Waterford, Towrine	gentry: esquire	21-Jul-74	240	B.L. 19, 844 f. 33	3157
Nettles, John	Wexford, Towrine	gentry: esquire	17-May-74	300	B.L. 19, 844 f. 26	3148
Neville, Richard	Kildare, Maynaham	gentry: gent	23-Aug-66	560	B.L. 15, 635 f. 176a	3562
Neville, Richard	Kildare, Maynham	gentry: gent	23-Aug-66	500	Dc3/37	2306
Newcomen, Robert	Dublin, the city	gentry: knight	26-Dec-21	1500	Dc2/38r	1090
Newcomen, Thomas	Longford, Ballonamore	gentry: esquire	15-Feb-61	720	B.L. 15, 635 f. 62a	3376
Newcomen, Thomas	Dublin, Sutton	gentry: esquire	19-Apr-66	1000	Dc3/27	2283
Newcomen, Thomas	Dublin, Sutton	gentry: esquire	01-Oct-64	800	B.L. 15, 635 f. 149	3517
Newcomen, Thomas	Dublin, the city	gentry: esquire	08-Aug-63	200	B.L. 15, 635 f. 116a	3463
Newman, John	Cork, the city		09-Mar-76	300	B.L. 19, 844 f. 103	3230

Standard	County	Occupation	Date	Amount	MS No	Ident No
Newman, John	Cork, the city	merchant	22-Jan-69	1000	B.L. 15, 636 f. 28a	3675
Newman, John	Cork, the city	merchant	20-May-69	2008	B.L. 15, 636 f. 36a	3686
Newman, John	Cork, the city	merchant	29-May-67	300	B.L. 15, 635 f. 211	3627
Newman, Richard	Cork, the city	gentry: esquire	01-May-65	220	B.L. 15, 635 f. 157	3531
Newman, Richard	Cork, St Finbarr's?	gentry: esquire	20-Jan-69	220	B.L. 15, 636 f. 31	3679
Newman, Richard	Cork, the city	gentry: esquire	27-Apr-77	1160	B.L. 19, 844 f. 126	3255
Newman, Richard	Cork, the city, St Finbarr's	merchant	29-Mar-60	1400	B.L. 15, 635 f. 65	3379
Nicholas, Henry	Waterford, Kilmeadon	gentry: esquire	18-May-58	600	B.L. 15, 635 f. 25	3307
Nicholas, John	Dublin, the city	gentry: esquire	03-Apr-77	1561	B.L. 19, 844 f. 125	3254
Nicholas, John	Dublin, the city	merchant	11-May-64	280	B.L. 15, 635 f. 133	3491
Nicholas, John	Dublin, the city	gentry: esquire	03-Apr-77	1561	Dc3/182v	2687
Nicholas, John	Dublin, Lazyhill	gentry: esquire	09-Jul-67	282	B.L. 15, 635 f. 197	3604
Nicholas, John	Dublin, the city	gentry: esquire	06-Apr-77	640	B.L. 19, 844 f. 124	3253
Nicholas, John	Dublin, the city	gentry: esquire	06-Apr-77	640	Dc3/182v	2688
Nicholas, John	Dublin, the city	merchant	17-May-64	120	B.L. 15, 635 f. 133a	3492
Nicholas, John	Dublin, the city	merchant	29-Mar-64	200	B.L. 15, 635 f. 132a	3490
Nicholas, John	Dublin, Lazyhill	gentry: esquire	09-Jul-67	282	Dc3/65	2368
Nicholas, John	Londonderry, the city	merchant	18-Jun-54	1060	B.L. 15, 635 f. 62	3375
Nicholson, Gilbert	Dublin, the city	gentry: gent	29-Jan-70	200	Dc3/113	2466
Nicholson, John	Louth, Drogheda	merchant	15-Jul-72	100	B.L. 15, 636 f. 115	3820
Nicholson, Robert	Dublin	gentry: gent	21-Sep-24	100	Dc2/58r	1238
Nicholson, Robert	Dublin, the city	gentry: gent	30-Jun-20	40	Dc2/31v	1040
Nicholson, Robert	Dublin, the city	gentry: gent	24-May-22	70	Dc2/40r	1108
Nightingale, Luke	England, Berkshire, Windsor	gentry: gent	27-Oct-28	3000	Dc2/115r	1538
Noble, Mary	Dublin	gentry: wife of Richard	20-Aug-00	100	Dc1/25v	171
Noble, Richard	Dublin	gentry: gent	15-Jan-04	400	Dc1/51v	328
Noble, Richard	Dublin, Grandgorman	gentry: gent	10-Dec-04	100	Dc1/54r	339
Noble, Richard	Dublin	gentry: gent	20-Aug-00	100	Dc1/25v	171
Noble, Richard	Dublin, Grandgegorman	gentry: gent	31-Oct-04	2000	Dc1/53v	337
Noble, Richard	Dublin, Grandgegorman neere	gentry: gent	06-May-05	127	Dc1/58r	356
Noble, Richard	Dublin, Grandge Gorman	gentry: gent	15-Jul-02	200	Dc1/39r	252
Noble, Richard	Dublin, Grandge Gorman	gentry: gent	11-Apr-06	400	Dc1/66v	401
Noble, Richard	Dublin, Grandgegorman	gentry: gent	07-Jul-09	100	Dc1/90r	562
Nolan, Charles	Galway	merchant	25-Jun-22	3000	Dc2/41r	1113
Nolan, Gregory	Mayo, Ballinrobe	gentry: esquire	18-Dec-33	70	Dc2/204v	1922
Nolan, James	Dublin, the city	merchant	20-Jun-65	800	Dc3/10	2244
Nolan, James	Dublin, the city	merchant: executor of will of William Whitched	05-Aug-65	100	Dc3/13	2249
Nolan, James	Dublin, the city	merchant: administrator of Will, Hester Whitchett	31-Jan-67	400	B.L. 15, 635 f. 185a	3581
Nolan, James	Dublin, the city	merchant: administrator of Will, Hester Whitchett	22-May-67	200	B.L. 15, 635 f. 196	3602

Standard	County	Occupation	Date	Amount	MS No	Ident No
Nolan, James	Dublin, the city	merchant: administrator of William Hester Whitche	18-Jun-67	300	B.L. 15, 635 f. 196a	3603
Nolan, James	Dublin, the city	merchant: administrator	22-Jun-69	200	Dc3/99	2441
Nolan, James	Dublin, the city	merchant: administrator, William, Hester Whitchet	22-Jun-69	200	B.L. 15, 636 f. 50	3709
Nolan, James	Dublin, the city	merchant	18-Jun-67	300	Dc3/63	2362
Nolan, James	Dublin, the city	merchant: admin of Wm Whitchett	22-May-67	200	Dc3/61	2357
Nolan, James	Dublin, the city	merchant: administrator of William	19-Jul-71	200	Dc3/139r	2526
Nolan, James	Dublin, the city	merchant: administrator of Wm/Hester Whitchett	31-Jan-67	400	Dc3/51	2334
Nolan, James	Dublin, the city	merchant: administrator William, Hester Whitchet	19-Jul-71	200	B.L. 15, 636 f. 89	3777
Nolan, John	Sligo, Eskerowen	gentry: esquire	08-Jul-34	400	Dc2/214v	1962
Nolan, John	Dublin, Gallonston	gentry: esquire	08-Jun-25	320	Dc2/65v	1291
Nolan, John	Sligo, Eskerowne	gentry: esquire	02-Dec-33	1000	Dc2/202r	1912
Nolan, Nicholas	Dublin	merchant	22-Nov-69	100	B.L. 15, 636 f. 48	3706
Nolan, Nicholas	Dublin	merchant	22-Nov-69	100	Dc3/107	2456
Nolan, Nicholas	Dublin, the city	merchant	27-Nov-69	350	Dc3/108	2459
Nolan, Nicholas	Dublin, the city	merchant	27-Nov-69	350	B.L. 15, 636 f. 48a	3707
Nolan, Richard	Westmeath, Mollengarr	merchant	20-Jun-07	80	Dc1/78v	481
Nolan, Thomas	Mayo, Ballenerobe	gentry: gent	18-Feb-15	200	Dc1/135v	842
North, William	Dublin, the city	merchant	08-Aug-66	600	B.L. 15, 635 f. 183	3576
North, William	Dublin, the city	merchant	08-Aug-66	600	Dc3/36	2303
Norwood, Charles	England, Glositer, Leckinton	gentry: esquire	07-Feb-77	660	Dc3/181v	2685
Norwood, Charles	England, Leckinton, Glositer	gentry: esquire	07-Feb-77	660	B.L. 19, 844 f. 113	3241
Nottingham, Lambert	Dublin, Ballyowen	gentry: esquire	30-Mar-36	240	Dc2/248r	2108
Nottingham, Lambert	Dublin, Ballyowen	gentry: esquire	27-Dec-32	700	Dc2/189v	1862
Nottingham, Lambert	Dublin, Ballybane	gentry: gent	17-Feb-07	200	Dc1/74v	453
Nottingham, Lambert	Dublin, Deanrath	gentry: gent	17-Jun-10	200	Dc1/98r	615
Nottingham, Lambert	Dublin, Balluwey	gentry: gent	10-May-27	1000	Dc2/92r	1431
Nottingham, Lambert	Dublin, Denrath	gentry: gent	26-Feb-14	500	Dc1/127r	789
Nugent, Andrew	Westmeath, Downower	gentry: esquire	04-Jun-27	200	Dc2/93r	1435
Nugent, Andrew	Westmeath, Donower	gentry: esquire	10-Sep-27	200	Dc2/98v	1459
Nugent, Andrew	Westmeath, Donore	gentry: esquire	01-Feb-28	100	Dc2/103v	1481
Nugent, Andrew	Westmeath, Downower	gentry: esquire	12-Jun-27	250	Dc2/94r	1440
Nugent, Christopher	Westmeath?	peer: baron Delvin	22-May-02	1000	Dc1/38r	246
Nugent, Christopher	Meath, Beallina	gentry: esquire	17-May-31	300	Dc2/163r	1755
Nugent, Christopher	Dublin, Clophran, Sworde	gentry: gent	19-Dec-12	1000	Dc1/117v	730
Nugent, Christopher	King's Co., Corbetston	gentry: esquire	26-May-23	300	Dc2/47v	1161
Nugent, Christopher	Westmeath, Carpentestone	gentry: esquire	11-Nov-17	200	Dc2/11r	919

Standard	County	Occupation	Date	Amount	MS No	Ident No
Nugent, Edward	Westmeath, Rathconyll	gentry: esquire	02-Jul-12	500	Dc1/115r	714
Nugent, Edward	Westmeath, Quoine	gentry: gent	22-Nov-28	200	Dc2/116v	1545
Nugent, Edward	Westmeath, Tullyhan	gentry: gent	04-Jul-26	250	Dc2/80v	1384
Nugent, George	Westmeath, Clonen	gentry: gent	04-Jul-32	50	Dc2/184v	1841
Nugent, George	Westmeath, Clonine	gentry: gent	28-Nov-34	220	Dc2/224r	2000
Nugent, George	Westmeath, the Clonin	gentry: gent	04-Feb-32	50	Dc2/174v	1803
Nugent, James	Dublin	merchant	15-Feb-23	400	Dc2/45r	1142
Nugent, James	Kildare, Woodstock	gentry: gent	12-Aug-98	1000	Dc1/12r	86
Nugent, James	Meath, Annagh	gentry: gent	17-May-31	300	Dc2/163r	1755
Nugent, Richard	Kildare, Maynouth	gentry: gent	23-Sep-29	200	Dc2/136v	1638
Nugent, Richard	Westmeath?	peer: earl of Westmeath	21-May-23	800	Dc2/47v	1159
Nugent, Richard	Westmeath?	peer: earl of Westmeath	16-Jun-32	200	Dc2/183v	1837
Nugent, Richard	Westmeath?	peer: baron Delvin	23-May-07	80	Dc1/77v	472
Nugent, Robert	Westmeath, Rathgarrett	gentry: gent	20-May-37	4000	Dc2/263v	2183
Nugent, Robert	Westmeath, Rathgarrott	gentry: gent	16-Jun-29	120	Dc2/132v	1619
Nugent, Robert	Westmeath, Rathgerrott	gentry: gent	19-Jul-27	200	Dc2/97r	1452
Nugent, Robert	Westmeath, Taghman	gentry: baronet	01-Dec-69	200	Dc3/109	2460
Nugent, Thomas	Kildare, Donfert	gentry: esquire	16-May-29	80	Dc2/129r	1605
Nugent, Thomas	Louth, Drogheda	merchant	08-Feb-17	300	Dc2/4v	891
Nugent, Walter	Meath, Portloman	gentry: esquire	25-Aug-28	1000	Dc2/114v	1535
Nugent, Walter	Westmeath, Portlamman	gentry: esquire	16-May-28	100	Dc2/108r	1505
Nugent, William	Meath, Kilcarne	gentry: esquire	23-Aug-09	160	Dc1/91r	571
O'Brien, Barnaby	Carlow, Catherlagh	gentry: knight	12-Oct-32	500	Dc2/186v	1849
O'Brien, Barnaby	Carlow, Catherlagh	gentry: knight	18-Sep-32	1200	Dc2/185v	1846
O'Brien, Dermot	Clare?	peer: baron Inchiquin	17-Apr-22	200	Dc2/29r	1100
O'Brien, Donogh	Clare?	peer: earl of Thomond	18-May-07	440	Dc1/76v	467
O'Brien, Henry	Clare?	peer: earl of Thomond	13-Sep-73	3012	B.L. 19, 844 f. 20	3138
O'Brien, Mabel	Clare?	peer:				
		lady dowager Inchiquin	18-May-33	400	Dc2/194r	1879
O'Brien, Murrough	Clare?	peer: baron Inchiquin	06-May-41	1500	B.L. 19, 843 f. 98a	2916
O'Hara, Teige	Antrim, Crebillie	gentry: esquire	10-Aug-39	5000	B.L. 19, 843 f. 33	2784
O'Meara, Dermot	Dublin, the city	prof: doctor of phisick	27-Aug-32	600	Dc2/185r	1844
Ogden, John	Dublin	gentry: gent	09-Jul-18	105	Dc2/15v	946
Ogden, Mary	Dublin	other: widow	13-Dec-18	110	Dc2/19v	966
Ogle, Thomas	Dublin	gentry: esquire	03-Jul-34	3000	Dc2/213v	1959
Oliver, Christopher	Cork, the city	merchant	06-Dec-66	4000	B.L. 15, 635 f. 181a	3573
Orlibeare?, John	England, London, the city	merchant-tailor	12-Sep-42	600	B.L. 19, 843 f. 109a	2938
Orlibeare?, John	England, London	merchant-tailor	20-Jun-43	400	B.L. 19, 843 f. 112	2943
Ormsby, Thomas	Dublin, the city	trade: upholster	14-Feb-23	300	Dc2/45r	1140
Orpie, Thomas	Dublin	merchant	10-Dec-14	110	Dc1/133v	830
Osbaldston, William	England, York, Homnanby?	gentry: esquire	26-Jun-54	655	B.L. 19, 843 f. 142	2998
Osbaldston, William	England, York, Humnanby?	gentry: esquire	13-Aug-54	502	B.L. 19, 843 f. 144	3002
Osborne, John	Down, Killelea	gentry: esquire	03-Dec-78	400	B.L. 15, 637 f. 6	3859

Standard	County	Occupation	Date	Amount	MS No	Ident No
Osborne, Roger	Cork, Ballycrenan	gentry: esquire	09-Nov-66	1000	Dc3/40	2316
Osborne, Roger	Cork, Ballycrenan	gentry: esquire	09-Nov-66	1000	B.L. 15, 635 f. 177a	3564
Osborne, Samuel	Louth, Drogheda	merchant	17-Mar-74	200	B.L. 19, 844 f. 22a	3143
Osborne, Thomas	Dublin	gentry: gent	25-Oct-09	200	Dc1/92r	575
Otterington, John	Dublin, the city	merchant	06-Jun-76	400	Dc3/175v	2661
Otterington, John	Dublin, the city	merchant	18-Jul-66	130	Dc3/34	2298
Owen, Jones	Dublin, Donabrooke	gentry: gent	22-Dec-76	4000	Dc3/181r	2681
Packenham, Philip	Dublin, the city	gentry: gent	31-Mar-69	400	Dc3/94	2431
Pakenham, Philip	Westmeath, Mullingare	gentry: gent	21-Jan-59	840	B.L. 15, 635 f. 40	3334
Palfrey, Richard	Dublin, the city	gentry: esquire	20-Apr-67	800	Dc3/60	2352
Palfrey, Richard	Louth, Drogheda	gentry: gent	16-Jan-79	500	B.L. 15, 637 f. 12	3869
Palfrey, Richard	Dublin, the city	gentry: gent	06-Jun-79	120	B.L. 15, 637 f. 20	3882
Pallas, Alexander	Dublin		24-Oct-00	320	Dc1/26v	178
Pallas, Alexander	Dublin		16-Apr-01	120	Dc1/30r	200
Pallas, Alexander	Dublin		14-Feb-03	200	Dc1/45r	286
Pallas, Alexander	Dublin		27-Jan-00	130	Dc1/21r	141
Pallas, Alexander	Dublin		30-Jul-99	200	Dc1/18r	125
Pallas, Andrew	Dublin	gentry: gent	15-Nov-34	300	Dc2/221v	1991
Pallas, James	Dublin, the city	gentry: gent	09-Jun-62	500	B.L. 15, 635 f. 102	3438
Pallas, John	Dublin	merchant: son of Alexander, merchant	28-Jun-98	120	Dc1/11v	82
Pallas, William	Dublin, the city	gentry: gent	29-May-41	600	B.L. 19, 843 f. 92	2903
Palmer, Stephen	Meath, Ffyanston	gentry: esquire	14-Jul-25	123	Dc2/68v	1309
Palmer, Stephen	Dublin, the city	gentry: esquire	03-Dec-21	200	Dc2/37v	1086
Palpay, Richard	Dublin, the city	gentry: esquire	20-Apr-67	800	B.L. 15, 635 f. 187a	3585
Panckart?, Frederick	Dublin, the city	merchant	10-Apr-41	120	B.L. 19, 843 f. 103a	2926
Panting, Robert	Dublin		04-Apr-00	40	Dc1/22v	150
Panting, Robert	Dublin		04-Apr-00	40	Dc1/2v	151
Panting, Robert	Dublin		06-Mar-00	200	Dc1/22r	146
Panting, Robert	Dublin	merchant	16-Nov-98	120	Dc1/13r	94
Panting, Robert	Dublin	merchant	07-Mar-98	40	Dc1/10r	73
Panting, Robert	Dublin	merchant	30-Jun-99	220	Dc1/17v	118
Panting, Robert	Dublin		08-Feb-00	200	Dc1/21r	142
Panting, Robert	Dublin	merchant	18-Nov-97	120	Dc1/6v	49
Panting, Robert	Dublin	merchant	18-Jun-99	100	Dc1/117r	115
Panting, Robert	Dublin		16-Oct-00	400	Dc1/26r	176
Panting, Robert	Dublin		05-Mar-00	200	Dc1/21v	145
Park, Robert	Leitrim, Newtowne	gentry: esquire	13-May-39	200	B.L. 19, 843 f. 23a	2765
Park, Robert	Leitrim, Newtowne	gentry: esquire	10-Jan-38	80	B.L. 19, 843 f. 24	2766
Park, Robert	Sligo, Sligo	gentry: gent	23-May-28	300	Dc2/109r	1510
Park, Robert	Leitrim, Newton	gentry: gent	19-Dec-35	300	Dc2/242r	2084
Park, Thomas	Louth, Atherdee	gentry: gent	02-Jan-78	700	B.L. 19, 844 f. 144	3275
Parkhill, Richard	Fermanagh, Kilshane	farmer	19-Apr-05	400	Dc1/57v	352
Parkhurst, Robert	England, London	merchant	01-Sep-28	630	Dc2/114v	1536

Standard	County	Occupation	Date	Amount	MS No	Ident No
Parkhurst, Robert	England, London	gentry: knight	04-Jul-36	200	Dc2/254r	2140
Parkhurst, Robert	England, London		23-May-34	630	Dc2/211v	1951
Parkhurst, Robert	England, London		07-Jun-25	606	Dc2/65r	1290
Parkhurst, Robert	England, London	gentry: knight and citizen	07-May-36	40	Dc2/249v	2116
Parkhurst, Robert	England, Pirrord, Surrey	gentry: knight	04-Jun-68	400	Dc3/77	2400
Parkhurst, Robert	England, London	gentry: knight	01-Dec-35	80	Dc2/23	2087
Parkhurst, Robert	England, London	gentry: knight and citizen	11-May-36	400	Dc2/250v	2119
Parkhurst, Robert	England, London	gentry: knight and citizen	15-Jun-35	200	Dc2/236v	2054
Parrett, Joseph	Dublin, the city	gentry: gent	20-Oct-64	200	B.L. 15, 635 f. 145	3509
Parry, Henry	Dublin	gentry: gent	04-Jul-33	240	Dc2/197r	1891
Parsons, Arthur	Wexford, Tomduffe	gentry: esquire	18-May-81	20000	B.L. 15, 637 f. 44	3926
Parsons, Lawrence	England, York, Newtonhall	gentry: esquire	18-Aug-69	1000	B.L. 15, 636 f. 42	3697
Parsons, Lawrence		gentry: knight	24-Nov-26	200	Dc2/83r	1395
Parsons, Lawrence	King's Co.?	gentry: knight	28-Jun-25	400	Dc2/67r	1300
Parsons, Lawrence	England, York/Newtonhall	gentry: esquire	18-Aug-69	1000	Dc3/102	2446
Parsons, Richard	Dublin	gentry: esquire	11-May-36	2000	Dc2/250r	2118
Parsons, William	Dublin, the city	trade: felt-maker	11-Apr-35	400	Dc2/232r	2034
Parsons, William	Dublin, the city	gentry: esquire	19-Sep-16	200	Dc2/1r	870
Parsons, William	King's Co., Killtubbritt	gentry: esquire	09-Dec-85	1000	B.L. 15, 637 f. 102	4032
Paulet, Philip	England, Georeshenton, Somerset	gentry: esquire	27-Oct-28	3000	Dc2/115r	1538
Peake, Thomas	England, Lancaster, Warrington	merchant	18-Jun-63	400	B.L. 15, 635 f. 107	3446
Peard, Richard	Cork, Coole	gentry: gent	18-Jan-77	1760	B.L. 19, 844 f. 136	3266
Peard, Richard	Cork, Coole	gentry: gent	29-Oct-79	1600	B.L. 15, 637 f. 30a	3902
Peard, Richard	Cork, Coole	gentry: gent	11-Jan-84	1000	B.L. 15, 637 f. 95a	4020
Peard, Richard	Cork, Castlelyons	soldier: ensign	25-Aug-67	700	B.L. 15, 635 f. 215a	3636
Peard, Richard	Cork, Coole	soldier: ensign	10-Apr-75	2400	B.L. 19, 844 f. 65	3193
Peard, Richard	Cork, Coole	gentry: gent	29-Oct-79	1600	B.L. 15, 637 f. 36	3911
Peard, Richard	Cork, Coole	gentry: gent, son/heir of Richard.	10-Apr-75	2400	B.L. 19, 844 f. 65	3193
Peard, Richard	Cork, Coole	gentry: gent, son/heir of Richard.	22-Jun-75	400	B.L. 19, 844 f. 71	3199
Peard, Richard	Cork, Coole	soldier: ensign	22-Jun-75	400	B.L. 19, 844 f. 71	3199
Pemberton, Thomas	Dublin, the city	gentry: gent	18-May-68	300	Dc3/75	2395
Penn, William	England, Essex, Wansted	gentry: knight	26-May-70	320	B.L. 15, 636 f. 60	3725
Pennington, John	Dublin, the city	trade: brewer	08-Jul-58	400	B.L. 15, 635 f. 31	3317
Pennington, John	Dublin, the city	trade: brewer	06-May-61	600	B.L. 15, 635 f. 72a	3389
Pennington, John	Dublin, the city	trade: brewer	27-Jun-64	600	B.L. 15, 635 f. 139	3499
Pennington, John	Dublin, the city	trade: brewer	08-Aug-63	1000	B.L. 15, 635 f. 116	3462
Pennington, John	Dublin, the city	trade: shoemaker	15-Jul-41	240	B.L. 19, 843 f. 107a	2934
Pennington, John	Dublin, the city	trade: brewer	11-May-63	200	B.L. 15, 635 f. 106a	3445

Standard	County	Occupation	Date	Amount	MS No	Ident No
Pennington, John	Dublin, the city	trade: metal maker	08-May-66	1000	B.L. 15, 635 f. 173	3555
Pennington, John	Dublin, the city	trade: malster	08-May-66	1000	Dc3/28	2285
Pentheny, James	Louth, Drogheda	merchant	22-Jul-41	200	B.L. 19, 843 f. 105a	2930
Pentheny, Richard	Dublin, the city	merchant	10-Mar-35	600	Dc2/230v	2027
Pentheny, Richard	Dublin, the city	merchant	12-Jun-30	600	Dc1/150r	1699
Peppard, Agueta?	Louth, Drogheda	other: widow, wife of Thomas, alderman	22-Jan-41	100	B.L. 19, 843 f. 79a	2878
Peppard, Christopher	Louth, Drogheda	merchant	08-Jul-86	400	B.L. 15, 637 f. 110	4047
Peppard, George	Louth, Drogheda	merchant	23-Nov-40	200	B.L. 19, 843 f. 110a	2940
Peppard, George	Louth, Drogheda	merchant	15-Aug-41	100	B.L. 19, 843 f. 111	2941
Peppard, George	Louth, Drogheda	merchant	31-Oct-40	300	B.L. 19, 843 f. 80a	2880
Peppard, George	Louth, Drogheda	merchant	25-Nov-40	200	B.L. 19, 843 f. 80	2879
Peppard, George	Meath?, Sarfildstowne	gentry: gent	30-Jan-73	200	B.L. 15, 636 f. 130	3838
Peppard, Igantius	Louth, Drogheda	merchant: son of Christopher and Margaret	10-Oct-39	600	B.L. 19, 843 f. 115	2949
Peppard, Ignatius	Louth, Drogheda	other: son of Thomas, alderman	27-Mar-44	120	B.L. 19, 843 f. 113a	2946
Peppard, Lucas	Louth, Drogheda	merchant	25-Nov-40	200	B.L. 19, 843 f. 80	2879
Peppard, Lucas	Louth, Drogheda	merchant	27-Mar-44	120	B.L. 19, 843 f. 113a	2946
Peppard, Lucas	Louth, Drogheda	merchant	23-Nov-40	200	B.L. 19, 843 f. 110a	2940
Peppard, Margaret	Louth, Drogheda	merchant: widow, wife of Christpher, merchant	10-Oct-39	600	B.L. 19, 843 f. 115	2949
Peppard, Margaret	Louth, Drogheda	merchant: widow, wife of Christopher, merchant	24-Sep-41	240	B.L. 19, 843 f. 115a	2950
Peppard, Thomas	Louth, Drogheda	merchant: son of Christopher and Margaret	10-Oct-39	600	B.L. 19, 843 f. 115	2949
Percival, Anne	Dublin, the city	gentry: spinster	09-Dec-68	2000	Dc3/86	2416
Percival, Catherine	Dublin, the city	gentry: spinster	09-Dec-68	2000	Dc3/86	2416
Percival, George	Dublin, the city	gentry: esquire	02-Apr-67	600	Dc3/58	2350
Percival, George	Dublin, the city	gentry: esquire	18-Nov-72	6000	Dc3/149r	2563
Percival, Philip	Dublin, the city	gentry: esquire	16-Jul-28	300	Dc2/113r	1528
Percival, Philip	Dublin	gentry: esquire	02-Dec-25	120	Dc2/71v	1328
Percival, Philip	Dublin	gentry: esquire	09-Dec-33	400	Dc2/203r	1916
Percival, Philip	Dublin	gentry: esquire	23-May-28	600	Dc2/109v	1512
Percival, Philip	Dublin, the city	gentry: esquire	20-Jul-24	800	Dc2/57v	1234
Percival, Philip	Dublin	gentry: esquire	17-Dec-33	400	Dc2/204r	1920
Percival, Philip	Dublin, the city	gentry: esquire	28-Feb-25	1700	Dc2/62r	1268
Percival, Philip	Dublin, the city	gentry: esquire	09-Mar-25	120	Dc2/62r	1269
Percival, Philip	Dublin	gentry: esquire	01-Dec-25	20	Dc2/71r	1326
Percival, Philip	Dublin	gentry: esquire	12-Dec-33	800	Dc2/203r	1918
Percival, Philip	Dublin, the city	gentry: esquire	17-Mar-26	1600	Dc2/75r	1351
Percival, Philip	Dublin, the city	gentry: esquire	17-Dec-25	200	Dc2/72v	1334
Percival, Philip	Dublin, the city	gentry: esquire	04-Apr-36	2000	Dc2/248r	2109

Standard	County	Occupation	Date	Amount	MS No	Ident No
Percival, Philip	Dublin, the city	gentry: esquire	11-Dec-24	400	Dc2/59v	1252
Percival, Richard	England, Leaverpole	merchant	09-Apr-59	110	B.L. 15, 635 f. 44	3340
Perkins, Richard	Meath, Athboy	gentry: esquire	08-Jun-26	200	Dc2/79r	1373
Perkins, Richard	Meath, Athboy	gentry: esquire	08-Jun-13	100	Dc1/121v	755
Perkins, Thomas	England, London	trade: ironmonger	08-Mar-05	1700	Dc1/57r	351
Perkins, William	England?, London?	trade: ironmonger?, factor and agent	03-Apr-06	1000	Dc1/66r	400
Perry, William	Limerick, Cronnon?	gentry: gent	15-Jan-41	2000	B.L. 19, 843 f. 77a	2874
Pesley, Mary	Tipperary, Roscrea	gentry: widow	08-Nov-75	1000	B.L. 19, 844 f. 86	3214
Pesley, Mary	Tipperary, Rosreain	gentry: widow	08-Nov-75	2000	Dc3/168v	2640
Pesley, William	Dublin	gentry: esquire	02-Dec-26	240	Dc2/84v	1402
Pesley, William	Dublin, the city	gentry: esquire	07-Jul-28	240	Dc2/112v	1526
Pettit, Gerald	Westmeath, Killpattoricke	gentry: esquire	19-Nov-29	87	Dc2/138v	1647
Pettit, Gerald	Westmeath, Boordstowne	gentry: gent	03-Feb-30	200	Dc2/141r	1661
Pettit, Thomas	Westmeath, Fryhton	gentry: gent	18-Nov-09	300	Dc1/92r	577
Pettit, Thomas	Westmeath, Frightowne	gentry: esquire	21-Jun-09	200	Dc1/89v	560
Petty, William	Dublin, the city	gentry: knight	05-Dec-66	1600	Dc3/46	2323
Petty, William	Dublin, the city	gentry: knight	05-Dec-66	1600	Dc3/43	2321
Petty, William	Dublin, the city	gentry: knight	05-Dec-66	1600	Dc3/44	2322
Phair, Oneciphero?	Cork, Grange	gentry: esquire	22-May-83	90	B.L. 15, 637 f. 74	3981
Pheasant, Thomas	Dublin, Baggotsrath	gentry: gent	11-Jun-25	210	Dc2/65v	1293
Phelps, Nicholas	Louth, Drogheda	gentry: gent	16-Feb-67	200	B.L. 15, 635 f. 190	3590
Phillips, Richard	Dublin, the city	trade: vintner	06-Sep-66	160	Dc3/38	2309
Phillips, Robert	Cork, the city	trade: sadler	03-Jun-67	583	B.L. 15, 635 f. 195	3600
Phillips, William	Meath, Fergunstowne		10-Feb-29	100	Dc2/124r	1578
Philpot, Michael	Dublin	merchant	30-Jun-12	120	Dc1/114v	710
Philpot, Michael	Dublin	merchant	10-Sep-13	40	Dc1/123v	766
Phipps, Benjamin	Dublin, Trinity College	gentry: gent	29-Nov-64	60	B.L. 15, 635 f. 150	3519
Pierce, Ann	Dublin, the city	other: widow	23-Mar-30	200	Dc2/143v	1672
Pierce, Ann	Dublin, the city	other: widow	10-Feb-29	600	Dc2/124r	1579
Pierce, John	Dublin, the city	trade: fishmonger	17-Dec-40	700	B.L. 19, 843 f. 117a	2954
Pierce, Martha	Westmeath, Tristernagh	gentry: widow	10-Dec-64	2000	B.L. 15, 635 f. 147	3513
Pierce, Martha	Westmeath, Tristernagh	gentry: widow	23-May-57	2000	B.L. 19, 843 f. 193	3093
Pierce, William	Westmeath, Tristernagh	gentry: knight	01-Mar-32	1500	Dc2/176v	1811
Pigot, Alexander	Cork, the city	gentry: esquire	20-Mar-53	4000	B.L. 19, 843 f. 130	2977
Pigot, Ann	Cork, the city	gentry: wife of Alexander	20-Mar-53	4000	B.L. 19, 843 f. 130	2977
Pine, Maurice	Dublin, the city	gentry: gent	04-Apr-43	100	B.L. 19, 843 f. 112a	2944
Pine, Richard	Cork, Ballinaglass	gentry: esquire	09-Mar-78	630	B.L. 19, 844 f. 150	3281
Pitchford, William	England, London, the city	trade: haberdasher	19-Jul-28	300	Dc2/113r	1529
Pitt, Walter	Dublin, the city	gentry: gent	22-Feb-67	200	Dc3/55	2340
Pitt, Walter	Dublin, the city	gentry: gent	22-Feb-67	200	B.L. 15, 636 f. 26a	3671
Plunkett, Alexander	Louth, Drogheda	merchant	30-Jan-41	200	B.L. 19, 843 f. 84	2887
Plunkett, Christopher	Dublin, Donsylye	gentry: knight	25-Nov-06	30	Dc1/72r	436
Plunkett, Christopher	Dublin, Donsaghlin	gentry: knight	27-Nov-17	2000	Dc2/11v	923

Standard	County	Occupation	Date	Amount	MS No	Ident No
Plunkett, Christopher	Meath, Donshoghlie	gentry: knight	07-Sep-05	50	Dc1/61v	375
Plunkett, Gerald	Kildare, Garvoge	gentry: gent	23-Nov-37	200	Dc2/271v	2219
Plunkett, Luke	Dublin	merchant	06-Mar-27	400	Dc2/89r	1419
Plunkett, Luke	Dublin	merchant	22-Dec-27	400	Dc2/102r	1476
Plunkett, Luke	Dublin, the city	merchant	24-Dec-28	2000	Dc2/123r	1574
Plunkett, Luke	Dublin, the city	merchant	01-Dec-27	2000	Dc2/101r	1470
Plunkett, Luke	Dublin	merchant	07-May-30	200	Dc2/146v	1685
Plunkett, Luke	Dublin, the city	merchant	11-Mar-33	1880	Dc2/192v	1873
Plunkett, Luke	Dublin	gentry: esquire	07-May-30	200	Dc2/146v	1685
Plunkett, Luke	Dublin, the city	merchant	08-Jul-31	800	Dc2/166r	1768
Plunkett, Luke	Dublin, the city	merchant	05-Aug-34	600	Dc2/216v	1970
Plunkett, Luke	Dublin	merchant	17-Feb-09	200	Dc1/87v	547
Plunkett, Maurice	Dublin, the city	prof: doctor of medicine	20-Jul-37	400	B.L. 19, 843 f. 95	2909
Plunkett, Nicholas	Dublin, Dunsoghly	gentry: esquire	04-Nov-65	1000	Dc3/14	2253
Plunkett, Nicholas	Dublin, Dunsaughly	gentry: esquire	15-Jul-72	2000	Dc3/148r	2559
Plunkett, Nicholas	Dublin, Dunsoghy	gentry: esquire	19-Dec-71	1000	Dc3/142v	2540
Plunkett, Oliver	Meath, Ballymacodd	gentry: gent	21-Nov-31	80	Dc2/171v	1790
Plunkett, Oliver	Meath, Clonybreny	gentry: esquire	02-Jun-15	200	Dc1/138r	857
Plunkett, Patrick	Roscommon, Lysloghna	gentry: esquire	25-Nov-82	400	B.L. 15, 637 f. 65a	3965
Plunkett, Richard	Meath, Rathemore	gentry: esquire	03-Feb-03	200	Dc1/44r	280
Plunkett, Richard	Louth, Dercanragh	gentry: gent	21-May-12	400	Dc1/114r	707
Plunkett, Richard	Meath, Rathmore	gentry: esquire	27-Jul-03	100	Dc1/47av	308
Plunkett, Robert	Meath, Athboy	gentry: gent	16-Feb-27	50	Dc2/88v	1417
Plunkett, Robert	Meath, Rathmore	gentry: gent	02-Apr-28	220	Dc2/106r	1495
Plunkett, Robert	Dublin	merchant	30-Nov-25	600	Dc2/71r	1327
Plunkett, Robert	Meath, Athboy	gentry: gent	18-Jul-27	100	Dc2/97r	1451
Plunkett, Thomas	Dublin, the city		17-May-26	1000	Dc2/77v	1366
Plunkett, Thomas	Dublin		23-Nov-03	600	Dc1/49v	318
Plunkett, Thomas	Dublin, the city		16-Dec-20	200	Dc2/34r	1058
Plunkett, Thomas	Dublin, the city		01-Mar-20	200	Dc2/29r	1023
Plunkett, Thomas	Dublin, the city		20-Jan-17	300	Dc2/4r	888
Plunkett, Thomas	Dublin		10-Sep-03	500	Dc1/49r	315
Plunkett, Thomas	Dublin		05-May-07	120	Dc1/76r	461
Plunkett, Thomas	Dublin, the city		10-Jan-21	600	Dc2/38r	1091
Plunkett, Thomas	Dublin		11-Sep-26	200	Dc2/82r	1390
Plunkett, Thomas	Dublin		24-Dec-03	2508	Dc1/51r	326
Plunkett, Thomas	Meath, Clowanston	gentry: gent	08-Dec-08	320	Dc1/85v	533
Plunkett, Thomas	Dublin, the city		28-Jun-15	300	Dc1/139v	864
Plunkett, Thomas	Meath, Newcastle	gentry: gent	09-Feb-32	120	Dc2/175r	1805
Plunkett, Thomas	Dublin		08-Jan-07	500	Dc1/73r	442
Plunkett, Thomas	Dublin		16-Sep-24	3000	Dc2/58r	1237
Plunkett, Thomas	Dublin		01-Apr-17	1200	Dc2/6r	898
Plunkett, Thomas	Dublin, the city		13-May-26	1000	Dc2/77r	1362
Plunkett, Thomas	Dublin		30-Oct-18	800	Dc2/16v	952
Plunkett, Thomas	Dublin		22-Nov-17	100	Dc2/11v	922

Standard	County	Occupation	Date	Amount	MS No	Ident No
Plunkett, Thomas	Dublin	merchant	06-Jun-07	100	Dc1/77v	474
Plunkett, Thomas	Dublin		18-Sep-16	1000	Dc2/—869	869
Plunkett, Thomas	Dublin, the city		26-Mar-24	6000	Dc2/54r	1208
Plunkett, Thomas	Dublin		10-Feb-19	200	Dc2/20v	973
Plunkett, Thomas	Dublin		22-May-07	50	Dc1/77r	471
Plunkett, Thomas	Dublin, the city		25-Nov-20	200	Dc2/33v	1054
Plunkett, Walter	Dublin, the Grandge	gentry: gent	14-Feb-15	1000	Dc1/135v	840
Plunkett, William	Dublin, the city	gentry: esquire	03-Mar-34	200	Dc2/208r	1937
Plunkett, William	Dublin, the city	gentry: esquire	08-Nov-34	204	Dc2/220v	1986
Plunkett, William	Dublin, the city	gentry: esquire	06-Aug-34	100	Dc2/216v	1971
Plunkett, William	Dublin, the city	gentry: esquire	07-May-32	280	Dc2/179v	1821
Plunkett, William	Dublin, the city	gentry: esquire	24-Jul-34	320	Dc2/215v	1966
Poe, Thomas	Donegal, Killerue	gentry: gent	04-Mar-39	200	B.L. 19, 843 f. 6	2730
Pollexfen, James	Dublin, the city	gentry: gent	02-Mar-35	800	Dc2/230r	2026
Pollexfen, James	Dublin, the city	gentry: esquire	20-Nov-37	600	Dc2/271v	2218
Pollidore, Elizabeth	Dublin	other: widow	24-Dec-29	220	Dc2/138v	1648
Pollidore, John	Dublin, the city	trade: factor, agent for Rob. Parkhurst, Lon, ald	24-May-26	400	Dc2/78v	1370
Pollidore, John	Dublin, the city	gentry: gent	15-Dec-28	520	Dc2/122v	1572
Pomroy, Arthur	Cork?	prof: doctor of theology, dean of Cork	10-Feb-81	400	B.L. 15, 637 f. 42a	3923
Pomroy, Arthur	Cork?	prof: doctor of theology, dean of Cork	25-Jun-83	800	B.L. 15, 637 f. 79	3991
Pomroy, Arthur	Cork?	prof: doctor of theology, dean of Cork	17-Mar-82	600	B.L. 15, 637 f. 56a	3948
Poole, Perian	Queen's Co., Ballyfin	gentry: esquire	25-Feb-73	300	Dc3/154r	2577
Pope, Thomas	Dublin, the city	gentry: esquire	01-Sep-56	200	B.L. 15, 635 f. 24	3305
Pope, Thomas	Dublin, the city	gentry: esquire	13-Dec-57	300	B.L. 15, 635 f. 28	3311
Porter, Katherine		other: widow	27-Mar-41	1000	B.L. 19, 843 f. 88a	2896
Porter, Thomas	Waterford, the city	gentry: esquire	21-Apr-40	2000	B.L. 19, 843 f. 66	2851
Portingall, Francis	Cork, Youghall	merchant	24-Oct-34	80	Dc2/220r	1984
Powell, Hassard	Limerick, Mitchelstowne Downe	gentry: gent	28-Jun-83	1790	B.L. 15, 637 f. 76	3985
Powell, Hassard	Limerick, Michaelstownydowne	gentry: gent	14-Jun-76	1000	Dc3/176av	2666
Powell, Hassard	Limerick, Michelstownenydowne	gentry: gent	14-Jun-76	1000	B.L. 19, 844 f. 97	3224
Powell, Hassard	Limerick, Mitchelstowne Down	gentry: gent	05-Sep-80	822	B.L. 15, 637 f. 39a	3917
Power, John	Cork, Cloghmore		23-Nov-97	140	Dc1/7r	50
Power, Thomas	Cork, Inshy	gentry: gent	20-Jun-15	500	Dc1/139r	861
Prendergast, Catherine	Tipperary, Carraghclony	other: widow	27-Nov-28	500	Dc2/117v	1549
Prendergast, John	Waterford, Dean of Lysmore	prof: dean of Lismore	22-Nov-06	24	Dc1/71v	435
Preston, John	Dublin		06-Jan-57	4000	B.L. 19, 843 f. 190	3087

Standard	County	Occupation	Date	Amount	MS No	Ident No
Preston, John	Dublin, the city		22-Oct-61	600	B.L. 15, 635 f. 85a	3407
Preston, John	Dublin, Royston?	gentry: gent	23-Feb-07	400	Dc1/75r	456
Preston, John	Dublin, the city		18-Jul-54	192	B.L. 19, 843 f. 150	3014
Preston, John	Dublin, the city		02-May-57	480	B.L. 19, 843 f. 193a	3094
Preston, Margaret	Meath?	peer: viscountess Gormanstowne, widow	13-May-31	500	Dc2/162v	1753
Preston, Robert	Meath, Rogerstowne	gentry: gent	16-May-31	500	Dc2/162v	1754
Preston, Robert	Meath, Gormanston	gentry: esquire	07-Feb-06	60	Dc1/65v	394
Price, Charles	Dublin	gentry: esquire	15-Jul-36	600	Dc2/255r	2144
Price, Francis	Dublin, Donore	gentry: esquire	04-Jun-68	720	Dc3/78	2401
Price, Francis	Dublin, Donore	gentry: gent	04-Jun-68	720	B.L. 15, 635 f. 220	3645
Price, Francis	Dublin, Donore	gentry: gent	07-May-66	700	Dc3/27	2284
Prine, John	Dublin, the city	gentry: gent	27-Mar-72	800	Dc3/145r	2549
Proby, William	Dublin, the city	gentry: gent	23-Jan-63	1075	B.L. 15, 635 f. 100a	3435
Procter, Robert	Dublin	merchant	23-Nov-10	40	Dc1/100v	631
Procter, Robert	Meath, Culmullen	gentry: gent	05-Jun-30	200	Dc2/148v	1693
Proctor, Robert	Meath, Culmolin	gentry: gent	10-May-28	100	Dc2/107v	1502
Proctor, Robert	Meath, Culmollen	gentry: gent	10-Apr-29	200	Dc2/127r	1597
Proctor, Robert	Meath, Culmollen	gentry: gent	09-May-29	400	Dc2/128r	1602
Proctor, Robert	Meath, Culmollen	gentry: gent	16-Jun-30	200	Dc2/152r	1707
Proctor, Thomas	Meath, Culmullen	gentry: gent	28-Sep-30	600	Dc2/155r	1720
Prowde, Nicholas	Meath, Adamstowne	prof: doctor of divinity	29-Oct-69	400	Dc3/103	2450
Prydden, Margaret	Cork, the city	other: widow	24-Apr-68	1200	B.L. 15, 635 f. 217	3639
Purbeck, Elizabeth		peer: viscountess Purbecke	09-Apr-63	600	B.L. 15, 635 f. 103	3440
Purbeck, Elizabeth		peer: viscountess Purbecke	10-Apr-63	700	B.L. 15, 635 f. 102a	3439
Purcell, Charlotte	Dublin, the city	gentry: wife of Redmond	11-Jun-63	400	B.L. 15, 635 f. 167a	3548
Purcell, Edmund	Dublin	merchant	05-Dec-97	400	Dc1/8r	58
Purcell, Edmund	Dublin	merchant	10-Mar-07	100	Dc1/57v	458
Purcell, Edmund	Dublin	merchant	19-Dec-07	60	Dc1/80v	499
Purcell, Edmund	Dublin	merchant	06-Apr-01	100	Dc1/30r	201
Purcell, Ignatius	Dublin, Cromlin	gentry: gent	22-Jun-64	312	B.L. 15, 635 f. 137	3495
Purcell, Philip	Tipperary?	peer: baron Loghmo	01-Dec-97	5000	Dc1/7v	54
Purcell, Redmond	Dublin, the city	gentry: gent	11-Jun-63	400	B.L. 15, 635 f. 167a	3548
Purcell, Richard		gentry: gent	01-Dec-97	5000	Dc1/7v	55
Purcell, Thomas	Dublin	merchant	13-Dec-14	120	Dc1/133v	831
Purcell, Thomas	Dublin	merchant	06-Dec-14	148	Dc1/133v	829
Purcell, Thomas	Dublin	merchant	09-Dec-12	120	Dc1/117r	728
Purcell, Thomas	Dublin	merchant	12-Nov-14	40	Dc1/132v	823
Purcell, Thomas	Dublin	merchant	01-Jun-13	200	Dc1/121r	753
Purcell, Thomas	Dublin	merchant	30-Nov-11	140	Dc1/110r	682
Purcell, William	Dublin, the city	merchant	27-Sep-33	200	Dc2/200r	1903
Purdon, Bartholomew	Cork, Ballicloghy	gentry: esquire	19-May-70	540	Dc3/119	2479

Standard	County	Occupation	Date	Amount	MS No	Ident No
Quatermas, Thomas	Dublin	farmer: yeoman	20-May-97	40	Dc1/4r	28
Queitrode, Nicholas	Dublin	merchant	26-Nov-99	500	Dc1/20v	138
Quin, Mark	Dublin, the city		14-Mar-66	220	B.L. 15, 635 f. 171	3551
Quin, Mark	Dublin, the city		14-May-66	220	Dc3/28	2287
Quin, Mark	Dublin, the city		14-Mar-66	400	Dc3/26	2280
Quin, Mark	Dublin, the city		03-Jun-65	100	B.L. 15, 635 f. 152	3523
Quin, Mark	Dublin, the city	trade: apothecary	17-Sep-57	200	B.L. 19, 843 f. 195a	3098
Quin, Mark	Dublin, the city		14-Mar-66	400	B.L. 15, 635 f. 166	3545
Quin, Mark	Dublin, the city	trade: apothecary	17-Sep-57	500	B.L. 19, 843 f. 196	3099
Quin, Mark	Dublin, city		03-Jun-65	100	Dc3/7	2236
Quin, Mary	Dublin, the city	trade: widow, of Mark	24-Feb-75	1000	Dc3/164v	2624
Quin, Mary	Dublin, the city	trade: widow, of Mark	24-Feb-75	1000	B.L. 19, 844 f. 56	3180
Quin, Peter	Dublin, the city	merchant	17-Nov-40	600	B.L. 19, 843 f. 89a	2898
Quin, Richard	Wicklow, Ballehoicke	gentry: gent	22-May-41	300	B.L. 19, 843 f. 90	2899
Quin, Richard	Dublin	merchant	29-Oct-17	108	Dc2/10r	914
Quin, Richard	Dublin	merchant	29-Apr-15	240	Dc1/136v	847
Quin, Thomas	Dublin, the city	gentry: gent	25-Jun-34	400	Dc2/212v	1955
Quin, Thomas	Dublin	gentry: gent	13-Feb-32	320	Dc2/175v	1807
Quin, Thomas	Dublin, the city	gentry: gent	25-Jun-34	400	B.L. 19, 843 f. 57a	2833
Radcliffe, George	Dublin, the city	gentry: knight	01-Jul-40	1000	B.L. 19, 843 f. 71	2861
Raget, Michael	Kilkenny, the city	merchant: son of Richard	08-May-39	40	B.L. 19, 843 f. 34	2786
Rainton, Nicholas	England, London		06-Nov-27	140	Dc2/99r	1461
Ram, Abel	Dublin, the city		27-Aug-77	500	B.L. 19, 844 f. 142	3272
Ram, Abel	Dublin, the city		27-Aug-77	500	Dc3/183r	2694
Ram, Andrew	Dublin, the city	gentry: gent	20-Feb-86	630	B.L. 15, 637 f. 109	4044
Rawdon, George	Antrim, Brookehill	gentry: esquire	15-Feb-56	300	B.L. 19, 843 f. 166a	3047
Rawlins, Giles	Dublin, the city	gentry: gent	01-Jul-58	110	B.L. 15, 635 f. 33	3321
Rawson, Benjamin	Dublin	gentry: son/heir of James	17-Dec-30	1000	Dc2/158r	1734
Rawson, Gilbert	Queen's Co., Grantstowne	gentry: esquire	04-Dec-67	1800	B.L. 15, 635 f. 206	3621
Rawson, Gilbert	Queen's Co., Grantstowne	gentry: esquire	04-Dec-67	400	B.L. 15, 635 f. 206a	3622
Rawson, Gilbert	Kildare, Grangemellon	gentry: gent	15-Dec-40	4000	B.L. 19, 843 f. 77	2873
Rawson, Gilbert	Kildare, Grangemellon	gentry: gent	02-Oct-40	650	B.L. 19, 843 f. 72	2863
Rawson, Gilbert	Kildare, Grangemellon	gentry: gent	27-Nov-39	1000	B.L. 19, 843 f. 36	2790
Rawson, Gilbert	Queen's Co., Grantstowne	gentry: esquire	15-Apr-63	4000	B.L. 15, 635 f. 105a	3443
Rawson, Gilbert	Queen's Co., Grantstowne	gentry: esquire	04-Dec-67	400	Dc3/70	2380
Rawson, Gilbert	Queen's Co., Grantstowne	gentry: esquire	04-Dec-67	1800	Dc3/69	2379
Rawson, James	Dublin	gentry: esquire	17-Dec-30	1000	Dc2/158r	1734
Rawson, John	Dublin	trade: victualler	29-Apr-05	240	Dc1/57v	353
Raymond, Robert	Cork, Rahinsky, Borial	farmer: yeoman	20-Aug-74	220	B.L. 19, 844 f. 40	3164
Rayner, Robert	Dublin, Rathfarnam	gentry: gent	11-May-37	400	Dc2/263v	2182
Rayner, Robert	Dublin, Rathfarnam	gentry: gent	22-Nov-31	264	Dc2/172r	1792
Rayner, Robert	Dublin, Rathfarnam?	gentry: gent	09-Aug-36	400	Dc2/255r	2146
Rayner, Robert	Dublin, Rathfarnam	gentry: gent	22-Mar-32	60	Dc2/178r	1815

Standard	County	Occupation	Date	Amount	MS No	Ident No
Rayner, Robert	Dublin, Rathfarnam	gentry: gent	14-Mar-31	60	Dc2/161r	1748
Rayner, Robert	Dublin, Rathfarnam	gentry: gent	07-Nov-36	200	Dc2/256v	2153
Reader, Enoch	Dublin, the city		17-Dec-66	320	B.L. 15, 635 f. 189a	3589
Reader, Enoch	Dublin, the city		17-Dec-66	320	Dc3/48	2326
Reader, Enoch	Dublin, the city	merchant	17-Apr-60	746	B.L. 15, 635 f. 60	3371
Reader, Enoch	Dublin, the city	merchant	21-Mar-60	500	B.L. 15, 635 f. 59a	3370
Reader, Enoch	Dublin, the city		09-Jun-73	1600	Dc3/156v	2583
Reader, Enoch	Dublin, the city		09-Jul-73	1600	B.L. 15, 636 f. 137	3850
Reader, John	Dublin	trade: baker	10-May-28	200	Dc2/107r	1501
Redmond, Patrick	Dublin, the city	merchant	28-Nov-71	300	Dc3/141v	2536
Reeves, John	Dublin, the city	gentry: gent	09-Oct-64	1000	B.L. 15, 635 f. 144	3507
Reeves, John	Dublin, the city	gentry: gent	05-Feb-64	240	B.L. 15, 635 f. 138	3497
Reeves, John	Dublin, the city	gentry: gent	14-Jul-64	113	B.L. 15, 635 f. 139a	3500
Reeves, John	Dublin, the city	gentry: gent	21-Apr-64	200	B.L. 15, 635 f. 129a	3486
Reeves, Richard	Dublin, the city	gentry: esquire	12-Nov-70	1000	B.L. 15, 636 f. 78a	3759
Reeves, Richard	Dublin, the city	gentry: esquire	14-Nov-70	800	Dc3/131r	2500
Reeves, Richard	Dublin, the city	gentry: esquire	12-Nov-70	1000	Dc3/130	2499
Reeves, Thomas	England, London	merchant	28-Jun-22	300	Dc2/41r	1114
Reeves, William	Wicklow, Rasallagh	gentry: knight	29-Nov-39	1000	B.L. 19, 843 f. 47a	2813
Reeves, William	Dublin	gentry: knight	29-Jun-35	1000	Dc2/238v	2063
Reeves, William	Dublin, the city	gentry: knight	03-Apr-34	500	Dc2/210r	1945
Reilly, Barnaby	Dublin, Rathmynes	farmer: yeoman	20-Apr-05	320	Dc1/58v	357
Reilly, Charles	Meath, Tulchanstowne	gentry: gent	23-Apr-19	240	Dc2/22v	984
Reilly, Patrick	Dublin, the city	gentry: gent	05-Sep-65	200	Dc3/14	2251
Reynell, Richard	England, London, Midletemple	gentry: esquire	20-Feb-58	300	B.L. 15, 635 f. 27	3309
Reynolds, John		soldier: comissary general of the forces, knight	16-Aug-55	216	B.L. 19, 843 f. 162a	3040
Rice, Edward	Limerick, Ballenity	gentry: gent	22-Dec-82	700	B.L. 15, 637 f. 67a	3968
Rice, Richard	Dublin	trade: perewig maker	22-Jan-01	140	Dc1/27v	185
Richard, George	Dublin, the city	gentry: esquire	24-Apr-23	450	Dc2/46r	1150
Richard, George	Dublin, the city	gentry: esquire	25-Apr-23	660	Dc2/46v	1151
Richard, Peter	England, London	merchant	11-Apr-25	3000	Dc2/63r	1278
Richardson, Thomas	Dublin, the city	gentry: esquire	15-Feb-53	1000	B.L. 19, 843 f. 141a	2997
Riche, Nathaniel	England, Essex Leez	gentry: knight	18-May-22	3000	Dc2/39v	1103
Ricke, William	England, Wapping near London	trade: mariner	02-May-07	80	Dc1/75v	460
Rickesies?, Abraham	Dublin, the city	merchant	09-Nov-40	300	B.L. 19, 843 f. 73a	2866
Ridge, John	Roscommon, Abbitowne	gentry: esquire	24-Nov-27	800	Dc2/100v	1466
Ridge, John	Roscommon, the monastery of R.	gentry: esquire	08-Jun-25	320	Dc2/65v	1291
Ridgeway, Catherine	Dublin?	other: widow, of George	12-Dec-26	200	Dc2/86r	1407
Ridgeway, Catherine	Dublin	other: widow	27-Jun-25	500	Dc2/66v	1299
Riordan, John	Cork, Cloghdae	gentry: gent	06-Aug-40	4000	B.L. 19, 843 f. 74a	2868
Riordan, John	Cork, Cloghedae?	gentry: gent	25-Oct-40	800	B.L. 19, 843 f. 74	2867

Standard	County	Occupation	Date	Amount	MS No	Ident No
Roan, John		prof: doctor of theology	12-Sep-74	200	B.L. 19, 844 f. 44	3168
Roberts, Edward	Dublin, the city	gentry: gent	01-Jul-64	580	B.L. 15, 635 f. 143a	3506
Robinson, William	Dublin, the city	gentry: esquire	10-Jan-87	1000	B.L. 15, 637 f. 111a	4051
Roche, David	Limerick, Caher Ivahillie	gentry: gent	26-Sep-39	600	B.L. 19, 843 f. 40a	2799
Roche, Dominic	Limerick		13-Feb-07	105	Dc1/74v	451
Roche, Edmund	Cork, the city	merchant	16-Nov-40	300	B.L. 19, 843 f. 81	2881
Roche, Edmund	Cork, the city	merchant	29-May-41	1000	B.L. 19, 843 f. 97	2913
Roche, John	Cork, the city	gentry: gent	14-Jul-40	400	B.L. 19, 843 f. 75	2869
Roche, Maurice	Cork, the city	gentry: gent	17-Apr-41	600	B.L. 19, 843 f. 96a	2912
Roche, Maurice	Cork, the city	gentry: gent	03-Feb-41	1000	B.L. 19, 843 f. 96	2911
Roche, Miles	Limerick, Galbally	gentry: gent	04-Nov-14	500	Dc1/132r	821
Roche, Philip	Cork, Kinsale	gentry: esquire	27-Jun-39	400	B.L. 19, 843 f. 26	2770
Roche, Theobald	Cork, Balleahowly	gentry: gent	04-Nov-14	500	Dc1/132r	820
Roche, Thomas	Limerick	gentry: gent	22-May-06	80	Dc1/68r	411
Rochford, Robert	Meath, Kylbryde	gentry: gent	30-Nov-98	300	Dc1/13v	96
Roe, Oliver	England, London	merchant	10-Jun-98	40	Dc1/11r	80
Rogers, Richard	Dublin, the city	merchant	16-Jan-40	800	B.L. 19, 843 f. 39a	2797
Rogers, Richard	Dublin ,the city	merchant	16-Dec-39	240	B.L. 19, 843 f. 38a	2795
Rogers, Richard	Dublin, the city	merchant	11-Feb-41	380	B.L. 19, 843 f. 84a	2888
Rogerson, John	Dublin, the city	merchant	01-Oct-78	800	B.L. 19, 844 f. 163	3294
Rogerson, John	England, Coventrye		13-Aug-05	440	Dc1/61r	370
Roll, Samuel	King's Co., Castletowne	gentry: esquire	15-Jul-71	420	Dc3/138v	2525
Roll, Samuel	King's Co., Castletowne	gentry: esquire	10-May-70	200	Dc3/119	2477
Roll, Samuel	King's Co., Castletown	gentry: esquire	11-Jun-78	1400	Dc3/190v	2718
Roll, Samuel	King's Co., Castletowne	gentry: esquire	06-Jun-76	400	Dc3/175v	2661
Roll, Samuel	King's Co., Castletowne	gentry: esquire	29-Nov-67	407	B.L. 15, 635 f. 204	3617
Roll, Samuel	King's Co., Castletowne	gentry: esquire	15-Nov-69	507	Dc3/107	2454
Roll, Samuel	King's Co., Castletowne	gentry: esquire	15-Nov-69	507	B.L. 15, 636 f. 50a	3710
Roll, Samuel	King's Co., Castletowne	gentry: esquire	14-Jul-71	420	B.L. 15, 636 f. 86	3772
Roll, Samuel	King's Co., Castletowne	gentry: esquire	29-Nov-67	407	Dc3/69	2377
Roll, Samuel	King's Co., Castletowne	gentry: esquire	10-May-70	200	B.L. 15, 636 f. 60a	3726
Roll, Samuel	King's Co., Castletowne	gentry: esquire	20-Feb-86	600	B.L. 15, 637 f. 109a	4045
Roll, Samuel	King's Co., Castletowne	gentry: esquire	10-Jun-65	220	Dc3/8	2239
Roll, Samuel	King's Co., Castletowne	gentry: esquire	16-Feb-66	220	Dc3/22	2273
Roll, Samuel	King's Co., Castletowne	gentry: esquire	15-Feb-70	400	B.L. 15, 636 f. 55	3717
Roll, Samuel	King's Co., Castletowne	gentry: esquire	15-Feb-70	400	Dc3/115	2469
Roll, Samuel	King's Co., Castletowne	gentry: esquire	06-Feb-66	220	B.L. 15, 635 f. 163a	3542
Rolleston, Richard	Armagh, Portdowne	gentry: esquire	17-Aug-15	1500	Dc2/0v	867
Roome, James	Dublin	trade: tailor	25-Aug-34	200	Dc2/217v	1975
Roome, James	Dublin, the city	trade: tailor	05-Sep-34	200	Dc2/218v	1978
Roome, James	Dublin, the city	trade: tailor	24-Feb-36	100	Dc2/246r	2099
Roote, Richard		soldier: captain of 'Letartmouth' a navy frigate	19-Oct-66	1200	B.L. 15, 635 f. 188	3586
Roper, Thomas	Dublin, Ropersrest	gentry: knight	27-May-26	1200	Dc2/78v	1371

Standard	County	Occupation	Date	Amount	MS No	Ident No
Roper, Thomas	Dublin, Ropersrest	gentry: knight	03-Dec-22	600	Dc2/43v	1128
Roper, Thomas	Dublin?, Ropersrest?	gentry: knight	29-Nov-21	260	Dc2/37r	1084
Roper, Thomas	Dublin, Ropersrest	gentry: knight	29-Nov-21	200	Dc2/37r	1083
Roper, Thomas	Wicklow?	peer: viscount Baltinglass	13-Aug-27	1800	Dc2/98r	1456
Roper, Thomas	Dublin	gentry: knight	22-Dec-14	600	Dc1/134v	835
Roper, Thomas	Wicklow?	peer: viscount Baltinglass	21-May-28	200	Dc2/108v	1509
Roper, Thomas	Wicklow?	peer: viscount Baltinglass	13-Nov-28	2000	Dc2/115v	1540
Roper, Thomas	Dublin, Ropersrest	gentry: knight	17-Jul-20	200	Dc2/32r	1044
Ross, James	Down, Portavo	gentry: esquire	30-Nov-75	442	B.L. 19, 844 f. 83	3211
Ross, James	Down, Portavo	gentry: esquire	20-Feb-72	1100	Dc3/144r	2546
Ross, James	Down, Portavo	gentry: esquire	12-Feb-72	1000	Dc3/143v	2544
Ross, James	Down, Portivee	gentry: gent	12-Jun-69	400	Dc3/99	2440
Ross, James	Down, Portavoe	gentry: esquire	12-Feb-72	1000	B.L. 15, 636 f. 97	3790
Ross, James	Down, Partavoe	gentry: esquire	20-Feb-72	1100	B.L. 15, 636 f.100a	3794
Rothe, David	Kilkenny	gentry: gent	30-Jun-02	400	Dc1/38v	250
Rothe, John	Kilkenny, the city	merchant	09-Jul-77	700	Dc3/183r	2692
Rothe, John	Kilkenny, the city	merchant	09-Jul-77	700	B.L. 19, 844 f. 137	3267
Rothe, Peter	Kilkenny, the city	gentry: esquire	02-Sep-39	1000	B.L. 19, 843 f. 32a	2783
Rotherham, Thomas	Dublin, the city	gentry: knight	01-Aug-33	1000	Dc2/198r	1896
Rowlandson, Joshua	Dublin, the city	merchant	06-Jun-65	80	Dc3/8	2238
Rowley, Samuel	King's Co., Castletowne	gentry: esquire	11-Jun-78	1400	B.L. 19, 844 f. 159	3290
Russell, Christopher	Down, Bangor	gentry: gent	20-Oct-04	200	Dc1/53r	335
Russell, George	Dublin, the city	merchant	10-Jun-35	100	Dc2/236v	2053
Russell, Richard	Dublin, Drenan	gentry: gent	18-Jun-00	1000	Dc1/24r	162
Russell, Richard	Dublin, Kilmachiocke	gentry: gent	21-Jul-41	400	B.L. 19, 843 f. 101	2921
Russell, Richard	Meath, Sheephowse	gentry: gent	31-Jan-12	400	Dc1/111v	691
Russell, William	Meath, Sheephouse	gentry: gent	20-Jan-40	42	B.L. 19, 843 f. 57	2832
Rutledge, Allen	Kildare, Athy	gentry: gent	02-Jul-28	400	Dc2/112r	1523
Rye, Christopher	Cork, the city		18-Jan-77	1400	B.L. 19, 844 f. 116	3245
Ryves, William		gentry: knight	22-Dec-26	400	Dc2/87r	1411
Sampson, Hugh	England, Plymothe, Devon	merchant	12-Sep-05	260	Dc1/62r	376
Sandford, Theophilus	Meath, Moyglare	gentry: gent	26-Oct-61	545	B.L. 15, 635 f. 84a	3405
Sandford, Theophilus	Dublin, the city	gentry: esquire	29-Oct-58	110	B.L. 15, 635 f. 41	3336
Sandford, Thomas	Kildare, Manooth	gentry: esquire	15-Feb-66	100	Dc3/22	2272
Sands, William	Dublin, the city	gentry: esquire	02-Oct-74	400	Dc3/162v	2616
Sands, William	Dublin	gentry: esquire	06-May-69	1500	B.L. 15, 636 f. 33a	3682
Sands, William	Dublin, the city	gentry: esquire	06-May-69	1500	Dc3/96	2433
Sankey, Henry	Longford, Toneluk?	gentry: esquire	20-Feb-58	2000	B.L. 15, 635 f. 29	3313
Sankey, John	Dublin, the city	gentry: esquire	22-Jun-65	560	B.L. 15, 636 f. 85a	3771
Sankey, John	Dublin, the city	gentry: esquire	22-Jun-65	560	Dc3/11	2246
Sankey, Ralph	Dublin	trade: apothecary	03-Mar-97	200	Dc1/2v	13
Sarsfield, John	Louth, Drogheda	merchant	02-Dec-69	400	Dc3/109	2461
Sarsfield, John	Louth, Drogheda	merchant	02-Dec-69	400	B.L. 15, 636 f. 45	3702
Sarsfield, Michael	Meath, Sarsfieldstowne	gentry: gent	14-Aug-39	600	B.L. 19, 843 f. 31a	2781

Standard	County	Occupation	Date	Amount	MS No	Ident No
Sarsfield, Peter	Meath, Moorechurche?	gentry: gent?	19-Jun-05	70	Dc1/60r	366
Saunders, Joseph	Dublin, the city	gentry: esquire	20-Feb-79	2786	B.L. 15, 637 f. 19a	3881
Savage, Arthur	Kildare, Castlereben	gentry: knight	07-Apr-30	1500	Dc2/144r	1674
Savage, Arthur	Kildare?	gentry: knight	02-Apr-23	600	Dc2/46r	1149
Savage, Patrick	Down, Ballycrannbegg	gentry: gent	19-Nov-10	120	Dc1/100v	629
Savage, Patrick	Down, Ballygalgat	gentry: gent	08-Oct-69	500	B.L. 15, 636 f. 51	3711
Savage, Robert	Down, Drumareade, Kinalagortie	gentry: gent	10-Aug-66	360	Dc3/36	2304
Savage, Rowland	Down, Baligalget	gentry: gent	19-Nov-10	400	Dc1/100r	628
Savage, William	Kildare, Reban	gentry: esquire	28-Nov-34	400	Dc2/224r	2001
Savage, William	Kildare, Castlereban	gentry: gent	15-May-26	680	Dc2/77v	1365
Savell, Robert	Dublin	gentry: esquire	09-Mar-31	44	Dc2/160v	1746
Savell, Robert	Dublin	gentry: esquire	06-Sep-33	210	Dc2/199r	1900
Savell, Robert	Dublin, the city	gentry: esquire	31-Oct-36	700	Dc2/256v	2151
Savell, Robert	Dublin, the city	gentry: esquire	18-Jul-31	80	Dc2/166v	1771
Savell, Robert	Dublin	gentry: gent	09-Apr-29	120	Dc2/127r	1596
Scanlan?, Edmund	Limerick, the city		07-May-41	1050	B.L. 19, 843 f. 91	2901
Scott, Edward	Tipperary, Kilballyherebry	gentry: esquire	17-Feb-64	4000	B.L. 15, 635 f. 128a	3484
Scott, Joseph	Louth, Drogheda		14-May-72	400	B.L. 15, 636 f. 113	3816
Scott, Joseph	Louth, Drogheda		24-May-73	200	B.L. 15, 636 f. 135a	3847
Segrave, Ann	Dublin, the city	other: widow	10-Apr-20	500	Dc2/29v	1026
Segrave, Christopher	Meath, Baltrassen	gentry: gent	12-Feb-12	200	Dc1/112r	695
Segrave, Eleanor	Dublin, the city	other: spinster	21-May-39	200	B.L. 19, 843 f. 5	2728
Segrave, Henry	Dublin, little Cabragh	gentry: gent	01-Jun-29	100	Dc2/130v	1612
Segrave, Henry	Dublin, Little Cabragh	gentry: esquire	27-Aug-34	400	Dc2/218r	1976
Segrave, Henry	Dublin, little Cabragh	gentry: gent	12-Feb-30	300	Dc2/142r	1665
Segrave, Henry	Dublin, little Cabragh	gentry: gent	09-Jun-29	100	Dc2/131r	1613
Segrave, Henry	Dublin, Little Cabragh	gentry: esquire	08-Jun-40	100	B.L. 19, 843 f. 51a	2821
Segrave, James	Dublin	merchant	09-Dec-19	1000	Dc2/27v	1014
Segrave, Jane		other: widow, wife of John	14-Mar-29	220	Dc2/126r	1591
Segrave, Nicholas	Meath, Belgerie	farmer	21-May-31	250	Dc2/164r	1759
Segrave, Nicholas	Meath, Bellgrie	farmer: yeoman	02-Mar-31	60	Dc2/160v	1745
Sergeant, William	Dublin, the city	merchant	17-Dec-79	1000	B.L. 15, 637 f. 23	3887
Sexton, George	Dublin	gentry: knight	19-Jan-19	2000	Dc2/20r	969
Sexton, George	Dublin	gentry: esquire	10-Dec-12	400	Dc1/117v	729
Sexton, George	Dublin	gentry: knight	29-Nov-17	800	Dc2/12r	926
Sexton, George	Dublin	gentry: esquire	20-Jun-15	440	Dc1/138v	859
Sexton, George	Dublin	gentry: knight	21-Nov-17	200	Dc2/11r	920
Shane, Francis	Westmeath, Byshopstowne	gentry: knight	01-Jul-12	500	Dc1/114v	712
Shane, Francis	Longford, Granarde	gentry: knight	25-Nov-08	800	Dc1/84v	528
Shane, James	Dublin, the city	gentry: knight and baronet	04-Jul-67	9000	Dc3/64	2365
Sharples, Ambrose	Dublin, the city	gentry: gent	18-May-68	300	Dc3/75	2395
Shaughnessy, Roger	Galway, Gort Insigore	gentry: esquire	21-Mar-74	1000	B.L. 15, 636 f. 131a	3840

Standard	County	Occupation	Date	Amount	MS No	Ident No
Shaughnessy, Roger	Galway, Gort Insigore	gentry: esquire	21-Mar-74	1000	B.L. 19, 844 f. 26a	3149
Shaw, John	Antrim, Glanarme	gentry: esquire	24-Sep-66	600	B.L. 15, 635 f. 175a	3560
Shaw, John	Antrim, Glenarme	gentry: esquire	24-Sep-66	600	Dc3/38	2311
Shaw, William	Dublin, the city	gentry: esquire	07-May-62	300	B.L. 15, 635 f. 113	3456
Shaw, William	Dublin, the city	gentry: esquire	07-Nov-62	627	B.L. 15, 635 f. 113a	3457
Shaw, William	Dublin, the city	gentry: esquire	29-Aug-62	900	B.L. 15, 635 f. 114	3458
Shee, John	Dublin, the city	gentry: gent	26-Jan-66	44	Dc3/20	2267
Shee, Mathew	Kilkenny, Highrath	gentry: gent	12-Dec-39	800	B.L. 19, 843 f. 54a	2827
Shee, Mathew	Kilkenny, Highrath	gentry: gent	20-Dec-39	800	B.L. 19, 843 f. 54	2826
Shee, Mathew	Kilkenny, Highrath	gentry: gent	07-Nov-39	400	B.L. 19, 843 f. 28a	2775
Shee, Mathew	Kilkenny, Highrath	gentry: gent	07-Nov-39	400	B.L. 19, 843 f. 28	2774
Shelton, Edward	Dublin, the city	merchant	07-Sep-19	90	Dc2/25r	1000
Shelton, Edward	Dublin	merchant	26-Nov-01	40	Dc1/35r	229
Shelton, John	Dublin		16-Apr-06	400	Dc1/66v	403
Shelton, John	Dublin		07-Nov-99	200	Dc1/19v	133
Shelton, Thomas	Dublin	merchant	25-Aug-24	80	Dc2/57v	1236
Shelton, William	Dublin	merchant	06-Feb-01	40	Dc1/28v	190
Shelton, William	Dublin	merchant	19-May-01	300	Dc1/31v	209
Shelton, William	Dublin	merchant	20-Apr-05	400	Dc1/58v	358
Sherlock, Christoper	Kildare, the Naace	merchant	14-Jul-23	800	Dc2/49v	1175
Sherlock, Christopher	Kildare, the Nace	merchant	24-Sep-17	400	Dc2/9v	912
Sherlock, Christopher	Kildare, Sheeginston	gentry: gent	13-May-24	300	Dc2/55r	1214
Sherlock, Christopher	Kildare, Sheeginstowne	gentry: gent	12-May-24	300	Dc2/54v	1213
Sherlock, Christopher	Kildare, Sheeginston	gentry: gent	14-May-24	300	Dc2/55r	1215
Sherlock, Christopher	Kildare, the Darr	gentry: esquire	01-Aug-34	200	Dc2/216r	1969
Sherlock, Christopher	Kildare, the Naace	merchant	10-Aug-14	200	Dc1/131v	816
Sherlock, Christopher	Kildare, the Naace	merchant	11-Aug-14	240	Dc1/131v	817
Sherlock, Christopher	Kildare, Shiggenston nr Nace	gentry: gent	30-Apr-21	120	Dc2/35r	1069
Sherlock, Patrick	Dublin, Rathcredan	gentry: esquire	22-Feb-30	400	Dc2/143r	1669
Sherlock, Thomas	Kildare, the Nace	merchant	17-Jun-05	70	Dc1/60r	365
Sherlock, Thomas	Kildare, the Nace	merchant	17-Jun-05	50	Dc1/60r	364
Sherlock, Thomas	Kildare, the Nase	gentry: gent	23-Feb-99	60	Dc1/15v	107
Sherlock, Thomas	Dublin	merchant	09-Jun-08	100	Dc1/83v	518
Sherwin, Edmund	Cavan, Creenagh	farmer: yeoman	19-May-36	120	Dc2/252r	2126
Shower, Richard	England, Devon, Topsham	merchant	21-Jul-62	200	B.L. 15, 635 f. 93	3420
Silver, Owen	Cork, Youghall	gentry: esquire	21-Sep-86	540	B.L. 15, 637 f 112	4052
Silver, Owen	Cork, Youghall	gentry: esquire	19-May-66	400	Dc3/7	2234
Silver, Owen	Cork, Youghall	gentry: esquire	24-Oct-73	338	B.L. 19, 844 f. 7	3126
Silver, Owen	Cork, Youghall	gentry: gent	06-Mar-61	600	B.L. 15, 635 f. 80	3399
Silver, Owen	Cork, Youghall	gentry: esquire	19-May-65	400	B.L. 15, 635 f. 156a	3530
Simpson, Francis	Dublin, the city	trade: inn keeper	15-Jul-72	660	B.L. 15, 636 f. 110	3810
Simpson, Francis	Dublin, the city	trade: inn holder (keeper?)	15-Jul-72	660	Dc3/148r	2558
Simpson, Jeremy	Dublin	gentry: gent	21-Jun-30	40	Dc2/152v	1710

Standard	County	Occupation	Date	Amount	MS No	Ident No
Singleton, Edward	Louth, Drogheda	merchant	20-Mar-72	600	B.L. 15, 636 f. 108	3807
Singleton, Edward	Louth, Drogheda	merchant	20-Mar-72	600	Dc3/145r	2548
Sinnott, Alexander	Wexford, Growgin	gentry: gent	24-Nov-18	120	Dc2/17v	957
Skerett, Edmund	Mayo, Cahermorish	gentry: gent	25-Jun-22	3000	Dc2/41r	1113
Skerett, James	Galway	merchant	18-Jul-70	2048	Dc3/123	2487
Skerett, James	Galway	merchant	18-Jul-70	2048	B.L. 15, 636 f. 68	3738
Skerett, Robert	Galway, the town	merchant	03-Jun-29	120	Dc2/130r	1610
Skerett, Robert	Galway, the town		04-Jun-29	120	Dc2/130v	1611
Slade, John	Dublin	gentry: gent	30-Jun-97	41	Dc1/5r	36
Slaman, Thomas	Dublin, the city	trade: shoemaker	05-Sep-34	200	Dc2/218v	1978
Slaman, Thomas	Dublin	trade: shoemaker	25-Aug-34	200	Dc2/217v	1975
Sloane, James	Down, Rowreagh	gentry: esquire	05-Jun-78	1000	B.L. 19, 844 f. 161	3292
Sloane, James	Down, Rowreagh	gentry: esquire	05-Jun-78	1000	Dc3/189v	2716
Sloane, Robert	England, London	trade: haberdasher	20-Dec-97	150	Dc1/8v	61
Smallwood, James	Louth, Milltowne	gentry: esquire	13-Nov-57	240	B.L. 19, 843 f. 200	3106
Smart, Swithin	Cork, Cworonra	gentry: gent	20-Nov-71	800	B.L. 15, 636 f. 96a	3789
Smart, William	Cork, Currowragh	gentry: gent	13-May-71	1000	B.L. 15, 636 f. 79	3761
Smart, William	Cork, Bridgetowne	gentry: gent	17-Nov-71	1000	B.L. 15, 636 f. 96	3788
Smith, Edward	King's Co., Kiltubrid	gentry: gent	05-Jul-69	240	B.L. 15, 636 f. 39a	3693
Smith, Edward	King's Co., Killtubbrid	gentry: gent	24-Nov-69	330	Dc3/107	2457
Smith, Edward	King's Co., Kiltubbar	gentry: gent	04-Aug-68	240	Dc3/82	2410
Smith, Edward	King's Co., Kiltubber	gentry: gent	21-May-69	374	Dc3/98	2438
Smith, Edward	King's Co., Kiltubrid	gentry: gent	05-Jul-69	240	Dc3/101	2443
Smith, Edward	King's Co., Kiltubber	gentry: gent	21-Mar-69	374	B.L. 15, 636 f. 38	3689
Smith, Francis	England, Netherpenn, Stafford	gentry: gent	22-May-75	400	B.L. 19, 844 f. 67	3195
Smith, Francis	England, Netherpenn Stafford	gentry: gent	22-May-75	400	Dc3/168r	2636
Smith, Grace	Dublin, the city	other: widow	07-Jun-76	300	Dc3/175v	2662
Smith, Henry	Armagh, Ballymore	gentry: esquire	10-May-26	1000	Dc2/77r	1361
Smith, Henry	Down, Loghadeggin	gentry: esquire	26-Jul-37	2000	Dc2/269v	2210
Smith, Henry	Armagh, Ballymore	gentry: esquire	01-Dec-31	400	Dc2/173r	1797
Smith, Henry	Armagh, Ballimore	gentry: esquire	11-Dec-33	880	Dc2/203v	1917
Smith, Henry			15-Dec-28	200	Dc2/123r	1573
Smith, Henry	Armagh, Ballymore	gentry: esquire	30-Dec-33	800	Dc2/206r	1927
Smith, John	Dublin, the city		21-Feb-84	350	B.L. 15, 637 f. 83a	3998
Smith, John	Dublin, the city		10-Jan-83	1700	B.L. 15, 637 f. 66	3966
Smith, John	Cork, Ballycurginay		14-Nov-74	140	B.L. 19, 844 f. 42a	3166
Smith, John	Fermanagh, Eniskillin		20-Jul-41	1200	B.L. 19, 843 f. 102	2923
Smith, John	Down, Loghsdeyne	gentry: gent	29-Nov-37	200	Dc2/272r	2221
Smith, John	Dublin, the city		11-Oct-77	8400	Dc3/183v	2695
Smith, John	Dublin, the city		12-Oct-77	8400	B.L. 19, 844 f. 140	3270
Smith, Joseph	Louth, Seatowne	gentry: gent	04-Jul-74	1000	B.L. 19, 844 f. 28	3151
Smith, Joseph	Louth, Seatowne	gentry: gent	14-May-72	400	B.L. 15, 636 f. 106	3803
Smith, Maurice	Dublin	gentry: gent	29-Apr-05	240	Dc1/57v	353

Standard	County	Occupation	Date	Amount	MS No	Ident No
Smith, Maurice	Dublin	gentry: esquire	09-Aug-33	1000	Dc2/198v	1898
Smith, Maurice	Dublin	gentry: esquire	05-Dec-33	800	Dc2/202v	1913
Smith, Maurice	Dublin, the city	gentry: esquire	12-Dec-32	500	Dc2/188v	1857
Smith, Richard	Dublin	trade: wheeler	29-Apr-05	240	Dc1/57v	353
Smith, Robert	Louth, Drogheda	gentry: gent	17-May-70	40	B.L. 15, 636 f. 70a	3743
Smith, Robert	Louth, Drogheda	gentry: gent	27-Apr-75	50	B.L. 19, 844 f. 64	3192
Smith, Robert	Louth, Drogheda	gentry: gent	28-Sep-71	115	B.L. 15, 636 f. 88	3776
Smith, Robert	Louth, Drogheda	gentry: gent	04-Mar-77	424	B.L. 19, 844 f. 118	3247
Smith, Robert	Louth, Drogheda	gentry: gent	20-Oct-71	60	B.L. 15, 636 f. 91a	3782
Smith, Robert	Limerick, the city	trade: goldsmith	15-Aug-76	140	B.L. 19, 844 f. 107	3234
Smith, Robert	Louth, Drogheda	gentry: gent	14-Feb-74	220	B.L. 19, 844 f. 21	3140
Smith, Robert	Louth, Dundalke		09-May-76	300	B.L. 19, 844 f. 94	3221
Smith, Robert	Louth, Drogheda	merchant	28-Apr-73	158	B.L. 15, 636 f. 136	3848
Smith, Robert	Louth, Drogheda	merchant	04-Aug-73	158	B.L. 15, 636 f. 138	3853
Smith, Robert	Louth, Drogheda	gentry: gent	01-Apr-73	200	B.L. 15, 636 f. 126	3833
Smith, Robert	Louth, Drogheda	merchant	04-Aug-73	40	B.L. 15, 636 f. 138	3852
Smith, Samuel	England, London	gentry: esquire	30-Apr-19	400	Dc2/23r	987
Smith, Samuel	Dublin	gentry: knight	17-Oct-29	140	Dc2/137r	1640
Smith, Samuel	Dublin	gentry: knight	08-Mar-28	400	Dc2/105v	1492
Smith, Samuel	Dublin, the city	gentry: esquire	03-Jun-20	1000	Dc2/30v	1031
Smith, William	Cork, Rathcormack	prof: doctor of theology	14-Oct-75	600	B.L. 19, 844 f. 77	3205
Smith, William	Cork, Rathcormacke	prof: doctor of theology	14-Oct-75	400	B.L. 19, 844 f. 84	3212
Smith, William	Dublin, the city		10-Mar-74	2000	Dc3/160v	2606
Smith, William	Cork, Rathcormack	prof: doctor of theology	13-Jul-70	400	B.L. 15, 636 f. 74	3750
Sober, John	Limerick, the city	gentry: esquire	23-Jan-79	420	B.L. 15, 637 f. 17	3877
Somester, Thomas	Dublin	gentry: gent	04-Mar-18	60	Dc2/113v	936
Southwell, Robert	Cork, Kingsale	gentry: esquire	22-Oct-66	2000	Dc3/40	2315
Southworth, Edward	Dublin	gentry: gent	24-Dec-14	120	Dc1/134v	836
Sparrow, Henry	Dublin, St George's Lane, near	gentry: gent	30-Sep-35	400	Dc2/239r	2066
Spence, Anthony	Dublin, the city	gentry: gent	30-May-32	210	Dc2/181v	1829
Spence, Dudley	Dublin	gentry: gent	13-May-24	300	Dc2/55r	1214
Spence, Dudley	Dublin	gentry: gent	12-May-24	300	Dc2/54v	1213
Spence, Dudley	Dublin	gentry: gent	14-May-24	300	Dc2/55r	1215
Spenser, Richard	England, Ashtowne Hall, Lanc.	gentry: esquire, son of Hon William senior	08-Dec-78	4000	B.L. 15, 637 f. 15	3874
Spottiswood, John	Scotland, Dersie, Fife	gentry: knight	23-May-28	440	Dc2/109v	1511
Spranger, Henry	Dublin, the city	gentry: gent	16-May-68	400	B.L. 19, 844 f. 21a	3141
Spranger, Henry	Dublin, the city	gentry: gent	16-May-68	400	Dc3/75	2394
Springett, Anthony	England, Sussex, Plumpton	gentry: esquire	25-Jan-62	600	B.L. 15, 635 f. 89a	3415
Springham, James	Dublin, the city	gentry: gent	30-Jul-70	700	Dc3/123	2488
Springham, Thomas	Dublin, the city	gentry: gent	06-Feb-55	172	B.L. 19, 843 f. 151a	3017
Springham, Thomas	Dublin, the city	gentry: gent	08-Jan-55	96	B.L. 19, 843 f. 148a	3011

Standard	County	Occupation	Date	Amount	MS No	Ident No
St. George, George	Leitrim, Carradrumaruske?	gentry: knight	12-Mar-55	700	B.L. 19, 843 f. 157	3028
St. George, George	Leitrim, Carrickedrumruske	gentry: knight	12-Mar-43	1100	B.L. 19, 843 f. 114	2947
St. George, George	Roscommon, Charlestowne	gentry: knight	30-Nov-28	1200	Dc2/119r	1558
St. George, George	Leitrim, Carrickdromrouske	gentry: knight	27-Apr-54	600	B.L. 19, 843 f. 138	2990
St. George, George	Leitrim, Carricke Drumrouske	gentry: knight	05-Dec-33	800	Dc2/202v	1913
St. Lawrence, Amery	Dublin, Portmernocke	gentry: esquire	04-Nov-16	80	Dc2/1v	875
St. Lawrence, Ann	Dublin, the city	other: widow	08-Jun-41	400	B.L. 19, 843 f. 117	2953
St. Lawrence, Nicholas	Dublin?	peer: baron Howth	12-May-30	800	Dc2/147r	1687
St. Lawrence, Nicholas	Dublin?	peer: baron Howth	21-Aug-37	120	Dc2/270v	2214
St. Lawrence, Richard	Dublin, Correston	gentry: gent	27-Sep-16	1000	Dc2/1r	872
St. Lawrence, Thomas	Meath, Gormanstowne	gentry: esquire	20-May-31	600	Dc2/163v	1758
St. Lawrence, Thomas	Meath, Garmanstowne	gentry: esquire	11-May-30	600	Dc2/146r	1682
St. Leger, Anthony	Dublin?, the city?	gentry: knight	23-Nov-07	600	Dc1/79av	493
St. Leger, John	Cork, Doneraile	gentry: esquire	18-Jul-74	1000	Dc3/162v	2615
St. Leger, John	Cork, Doneraile	gentry: esquire	18-Jul-74	1000	B.L. 19, 844 f. 43	3167
St. Leger, Warham	Cork, Howards Hill	gentry: esquire	18-Jun-81	1100	B.L. 15, 637 f. 46a	3929
St. Leger, William	Cork, Downeraile	gentry: esquire	20-Apr-41	800	B.L. 19, 843 f. 99	2917
Stack, Thomas	Dublin, the city	gentry: gent	02-Dec-72	200	Dc3/150r	2564
Stack, Thomas	Dublin, the city	gentry: gent	02-Dec-72	200	B.L. 15, 636 f. 133	3842
Stafford, James	Wexford	merchant	25-Nov-12	105	Dc1/116v	725
Standish, James	Dublin, the city	gentry: esquire	15-Jul-59	800	B.L. 15,635 f. 49a	3350
Standish, James	Dublin, the Inns	gentry: esquire	25-Sep-63	1000	B.L. 15, 635 f. 118	3466
Standish, James	Dublin, the city	gentry: esquire	24-Jul-63	1000	B.L. 15, 635 f. 111	3452
Stanihurst, James	Dublin, Courtduff	gentry: gent	28-Dec-11	130	Dc1/110v	687
Stanihurst, James	Dublin, Corduffe	gentry: esquire	21-May-07	200	Dc1/77r	470
Stanley, Giles	Dublin	gentry: gent	04-Oct-02	100	Dc1/40r	258
Stanley, Jane	Dublin, Grange Gorman	Gentry:	03-May-76	1200	B.L. 19, 844 f. 93	3220
Stanley, Jane	Dublin, Grangegorman	Gentry:	03-May-76	1200	Dc3/173r	2654
Stanley, John	Dublin	merchant	22-Jun-27	1000	Dc2/95r	1445
Stanley, John	Dublin, the city	merchant	13-May-40	2200	B.L. 19, 843 f. 50	2818
Stanley, John	Louth, Marlieston	gentry: esquire	05-Aug-40	120	B.L. 19, 843 f. 63	2845
Stanley, John	Louth, Marlieston	gentry: esquire	11-Aug-40	100	B.L. 19, 843 f. 64	2847
Stanley, John	Louth, Marlieston	gentry: esquire	10-Dec-40	80	B.L. 19, 843 f. 78	2875
Stanley, John	Louth, Marlieston	gentry: esquire	28-Nov-40	200	B.L. 19, 843 f. 78a	2876
Stanley, John	Louth, Marlieston	gentry: esquire	06-Aug-39	280	B.L. 19, 843 f. 63a	2846
Stanley, John	Louth, Marleystowne	gentry: esquire	24-Nov-36	40	Dc2/257r	2155
Stanley, John	Dublin	merchant	04-Dec-26	220	Dc2/85r	1403
Stanley, Walter	Dublin, the city	merchant	13-May-40	2200	B.L. 19, 843 f. 50	2818
Stapleton, James	Tipperary, Drouim?	other: son of Redmond	13-Jun-39	240	B.L. 19, 843 f. 7a	2733
Starkey, William	Dublin	gentry: gent	19-Jun-13	200	Dc1/122v	760

Standard	County	Occupation	Date	Amount	MS No	Ident No
Stearne, Dorothy	Dublin, the city	prof: widow, of John, dr of medicine, deceased	14-Nov-70	700	B.L. 15, 636 f. 79	3760
Stearne, Dorothy	Dublin, the city	prof: widow, relict of John Sterne, dr of phisick	14-Nov-70	700	Dc3/131r	2501
Stearne, John	Louth, Drogheda	gentry: gent	20-Jul-36	500	B.L. 19, 843 f. 123a	2966
Steele, Lawrence	Dublin, the city	gentry: gent	13-May-76	100	B.L. 19, 844 f. 102	3229
Steele, Lawrence	Dublin, the city	gentry: gent	13-May-76	100	Dc3/173v	2655
Stephens, John	Dublin, the city	gentry: knight	21-Feb-73	600	Dc3/154r	2576
Stephens, John	Dublin, the city	gentry: knight	21-Feb-73	600	B.L. 15, 636 f. 125	3832
Stephens, Nicholas	Dublin	merchant	23-Feb-98	140	Dc1/10r	70
Stephens, Nicholas	Dublin	merchant	15-Feb-06	300	Dc1/66r	397
Stephens, Nicholas	Dublin	merchant	19-Nov-03	1000	Dc1/49v	317
Stephens, Nicholas	Dublin	merchant	22-May-09	140	Dc1/89r	557
Stephens, Paul	Dublin, the city	gentry: gent	20-Mar-34	76	Dc2/209v	1943
Stephens, Richard	Dublin	merchant	28-Nov-03	515	Dc1/50r	320
Stephens, Stephen	Dublin	gentry: gent	21-Apr-27	60	Dc2/90r	1424
Stephens, Thomas	England, London	trade: haberdasher	06-Nov-27	140	Dc2/99r	1461
Stepney, John	Cork, Kinsale	merchant	27-Jan-64	600	B.L. 15, 635 f. 127a	3482
Stepney, John	Dublin, the city	gentry: esquire	31-Jul-69	2000	B.L. 15, 636 f. 40a	3695
Stepney, John	Dublin, the city	gentry: esquire	31-Jul-69	2000	Dc3/101	2444
Stepney, John	Cork, Kinsale	merchant	18-Aug-62	300	B.L. 15, 635 f. 112	3454
Stepney, Lancelot	Cork, the city	gentry: gent	04-Nov-70	200	B.L. 15, 636 f. 73	3748
Stewart, Andrew	Tyrone, Renhan	gentry: esquire, s/h John, baron of Castleward	19-Apr-27	1800	Dc2/90v	1425
Stewart, Hugh	Antrim, Ballyliney	gentry: gent	29-Dec-80	280	B.L. 15, 637 f. 41a	3921
Stewart, William	Tyrone, Aughenton	gentry: knight and baronet	19-Apr-27	1800	Dc2/90v	1425
Stewart, William	Donegal, Ramaltan	gentry: knight and baronet	01-Dec-28	400	Dc2/122r	1569
Stewart, William	Donegal, Ramaltan	gentry: knight and baronet	04-Dec-28	400	Dc2/122r	1570
Stokes, Nicholas	Dublin, Balhary	gentry: gent	11-May-35	120	Dc2/235r	2047
Stokes, Nicholas	Dublin, Balharie	gentry: gent	07-Apr-36	110	Dc2/249r	2112
Stokes, Nicholas	Dublin, Balharie	gentry: gent	14-May-36	60	Dc2/250v	2120
Stokes, Robert	Dublin, Balhary	gentry: gent	16-May-10	200	Dc1/96r	603
Stoughton, John	Dublin	gentry: esquire	28-Feb-28	227	Dc2/105r	1489
Stoughton, John	Dublin	gentry: esquire	03-Apr-30	130	Dc2/144r	1673
Stoughton, John	Dublin	gentry: esquire	30-Jan-28	2000	Dc2/103r	1480
Stoughton, John	Dublin	gentry: esquire	20-Jul-30	50	Dc2/154v	1717
Stoughton, John	Dublin	gentry: esquire	30-Jan-28	2000	Dc2/103r	1479
Stoughton, Nathaniel	Dublin, the city	gentry: gent	28-Apr-37	400	Dc2/261v	2174
Stout, Abigail	Cork, Youghall	gentry: wife of Jeffrey	10-Feb-57	500	B.L. 15, 635 f. 181	3572
Stout, Geoffery	Cork, Youghall	gentry: gent	10-Feb-57	500	B.L. 15, 635 f. 181	3572
Stratford, Robert	Wicklow, Baltinglass	gentry: esquire	11-Feb-82	400	B.L. 15, 637 f. 55	3945
Stritch, Lucas	Limerick, the city		02-Jul-41	840	B.L. 19, 843 f. 107	2933

Standard	County	Occupation	Date	Amount	MS No	Ident No
Stritch, Patrick	Limerick, the city	merchant	06-May-39	2000	B.L. 19, 843 f. 12a	2743
Stritch, Thomas	Limerick, the city	merchant	02-Oct-39	630	B.L. 19, 843 f. 43	2804
Stritch, Thomas	Dublin, the city	merchant: son of Patrick, merchant	10-Nov-40	1000	B.L. 19, 843 f. 85	2889
Stritch, William	Limerick, the city	other: son of William	02-Jul-41	840	B.L. 19, 843 f. 107	2933
Stritch, William	Limerick		13-Feb-07	105	Dc1/74v	451
Strobridge, Gordon	Dublin	gentry: gent	09-Jun-08	220	Dc1/83r	517
Strobridge, Gordon	Dublin	gentry: gent	27-Mar-01	160	Dc1/29v	197
Strobridge, Gordon	Dublin	gentry: gent	31-May-09	286	Dc1/89v	559
Strobridge, Gordon	Dublin	gentry: gent	16-Jun-10	300	Dc1/97v	612
Strong, Catherine	Dublin, the city	other: widow	16-Dec-36	140	Dc2/259r	2164
Strong, Catherine	Dublin, the city	other: widow	30-Jun-37	400	Dc2/266v	2195
Strong, Nicholas	Dublin, Ballycullan	farmer	06-May-35	600	Dc2/234v	2046
Strong, Nicholas	Dublin, Ballycoolan	farmer	19-Dec-35	200	Dc2/242v	2085
Strong, Patrick	Kildare, Bazardston	farmer	06-Feb-24	200	Dc2/53r	1200
Sugden, Edward	Cavan, Lyssomogan	trade: son of John the elder, tanner	24-May-26	440	Dc2/78r	1369
Sugden, Francis	Cavan, Lyssomogan	trade: son of John the elder, tanner	24-May-26	440	Dc2/78r	1369
Sugden, John	Cavan, Lyssomogan	trade: son of John the elder, tanner	24-May-26	440	Dc2/78r	1369
Sugden, Thomas	Cavan, Lysomongan?	trade: son of John the elder, tanner	24-May-26	440	Dc2/78r	1369
Sullivan, Owen	Kerry, Raithmore	gentry: gent	27-Nov-24	240	Dc2/59r	1247
Summester, Thomas	Dublin	merchant	21-Jul-17	160	Dc2/9r	910
Sweeney, Miles	Wexford, Eniscorfey		12-Jun-82	1000	B.L. 15, 637 f. 60	3955
Sweeney, Owen	Cork, Cloghda	gentry: gent	04-Dec-09	100	Dc1/93v	586
Sweet, Robert	Dublin	gentry: gent	20-May-25	200	Dc2/63v	1281
Sweet, Robert	Dublin	gentry: gent	25-Jun-29	400	Dc2/134r	1626
Sweet, Robert	Dublin	gentry: gent	23-Jun-23	100	Dc2/48v	1166
Sweet, Robert	Dublin	gentry: gent	24-Apr-29	200	Dc2/127v	1598
Sweet, Robert	Dublin	gentry: gent	23-Mar-26	400	Dc2/76r	1356
Sweetman, James	Dublin, Abbottstowne	gentry: gent	20-Mar-57	140	B.L. 19, 843 f. 192a	3092
Sweetman, John	Meath, Meymurderie	gentry: gent	25-Nov-36	400	Dc2/258r	2159
Sweetman, Lionel	Dublin, the city	gentry: gent	05-Jul-71	210	B.L. 15, 636 f. 86a	3773
Sweetman, Lionel	Dublin, the city	gentry: gent	23-Dec-68	240	Dc3/88	2420
Sweetman, Lionel	Dublin, the city	gentry: gent	17-Mar-72	210	B.L. 15, 636 f. 101	3795
Sweetman, Lionel	Dublin, the city	gentry: gent	05-Jul-71	210	Dc3/138v	2524
Sweetman, Lionel	Dublin, the city	gentry: gent	16-Mar-72	210	Dc3/144v	2547
Sweetman, Lionel	Dublin, the city	gentry: gent	23-Dec-68	240	B.L. 15, 636 f. 25a	3669
Symons, John	Armagh		20-Mar-35	2000	Dc2/231r	2030
Symons, John	Armagh, Ardmagh town		20-May-31	600	Dc2/163v	1757
Symons, John	Armagh, Ardmagh		15-May-30	1000	Dc2/148r	1690
Symons, John	Armagh, Ardmagh		13-May-30	66	Dc2/147v	1689
Symons, John	Armagh, Ardmagh		15-Feb-33	200	Dc2/191v	1870

Standard	County	Occupation	Date	Amount	MS No	Ident No
Symons, John	Armagh, Ardmagh		24-Jul-34	400	Dc2/215r	1965
Symons, John	Armagh, Ardmagh		25-Apr-35	120	Dc2/234r	2041
Symons, John	Armagh, Ardmagh		13-May-30	1000	Dc2/147v	1688
Symons, John	Armagh, the towne		04-May-32	2000	Dc2/178v	1818
Synge, Edward		prof: bishop of Cork, Cloyne and Ross	02-Nov-78	2000	B.L. 19, 844 f. 167	3298
Synge, Edward		prof: bishop of Cork, Cloyne and Ross	08-Nov-78	1000	B.L. 19, 844 f. 170	3301
Synge, Edward	Cork, Inishanon		06-Dec-66	4000	B.L. 15, 635 f. 181a	3573
Synge, Edward		prof: bishop of Cork, Cloyne and Ross	16-Dec-73	2000	B.L. 19, 844 f. 18	3136
Synge, Richard		prof: archdeacon of Cork	20-Oct-81	300	B.L. 15, 637 f. 81	3994
Synge, Richard		prof: archdeacon of Cork	11-Mar-85	1100	B.L. 13, 637 f.97	4023
Taaffe, Eilish	Louth, Cookeston	other: widow	12-Nov-02	200	Dc1/40r	259
Taaffe, John	Louth, Ballibragan	gentry: esquire	10-May-37	3000	Dc2/263r	2181
Taaffe, Richard	Louth, Cookestowne	gentry: esquire	19-Jul-34	500	Dc2/215r	1964
Taaffe, William	Louth, Smeremoore	gentry: knight	02-May-10	200	Dc1/95v	601
Taaffe, William	Dublin, Grandge of Balscaddan	gentry: gent	19-Jun-05	70	Dc1/60r	366
Tadpole, John	Dublin, the city	gentry: gent	17-Jun-56	98	B.L. 19, 843 f. 186a	3080
Talbot, Adam	Dublin, Belgard	gentry: gent	20-Dec-23	200	Dc2/52r	1192
Talbot, Adam	Dublin, the city	merchant	23-Aug-39	70	B.L. 19, 843 f. 27	2772
Talbot, Bernard	Wicklow, Radowne	gentry: gent	22-Feb-33	920	Dc2/192r	1872
Talbot, Bridget	Meath, Kibtsen?	other: spinster?, sister of John	08-Jun-27	300	Dc2/94r	1438
Talbot, Gilbert	Dublin, the city	gentry: esquire	20-Feb-67	3600	B.L. 15, 635 f. 186a	3583
Talbot, Gilbert	Dublin, the city	gentry: esquire	20-Feb-67	3600	Dc3/54	2339
Talbot, Gilbert	Dublin, the city	gentry: esquire	17-Apr-65	600	Dc3/4	2230
Talbot, Henry	Roscommon, Clondara	gentry: knight	22-Jul-61	6000	B.L. 15, 635 f. 76a	3394
Talbot, Henry	Dublin, Templeoge	gentry: knight	25-May-66	400	Dc3/29	2289
Talbot, Jane	Meath, Kibtsen?	other: spinster?, sister of John	08-Jun-27	300	Dc2/94r	1438
Talbot, John	Meath?, Corbally?	gentry: knight	24-Jun-10	100	Dc1/98v	617
Talbot, John	Meath?, Corbally?	gentry: knight	25-Jun-10	40	Dc1/98v	618
Talbot, Richard	Kildare, Cartown	gentry: esquire	06-Jun-78	1000	Dc3/189v	2717
Talbot, Richard	Dublin	merchant	30-Nov-98	200	Dc1/13v	97
Talbot, Richard	Kildare, Carrtowne	gentry: esquire	06-Jun-78	1000	B.L. 19, 844 f. 168	3299
Talbot, Richard	Dublin, Ballygriffin	gentry: esquire	30-Apr-70	2000	B.L. 15, 636 f. 67	3736
Talbot, Richard	Dublin, Balgriffin	gentry: esquire	30-Apr-70	2000	Dc3/117	2474
Talbot, Robert	Dublin, the city	prof: doctor of phisick	05-Sep-65	200	Dc3/14	2251
Talbot, Robert	Wicklow, Castletalbott	gentry: baronet	11-Jul-37	1000	Dc2/267v	2201
Talbot, Thomas	England, London	merchant	10-Jul-20	2000	Dc2/32r	1042
Talbot, Thomas	Dublin, Malahide	gentry: gent	03-Dec-05	107	Dc1/63v	384
Talbot, William	Dublin, city?	gentry: esquire	09-Jul-05	500	Dc1/60v	369

Standard	County	Occupation	Date	Amount	MS No	Ident No
Talbot, William	Kildare, Cartran	gentry: baronet	30-Jun-25	800	Dc2/67v	1305
Talbot, William	Louth, Hagarstowne	gentry: esquire	31-May-70	2000	B.L. 15, 636 f. 63	3729
Talbot, William	Louth, Hagarstowne	gentry: esquire	31-May-70	2000	Dc3/120	2480
Talbot, William	Louth, Haggerstowne	gentry: esquire	27-Sep-66	400	Dc3/39	2312
Talbot, William	Wexford		20-Nov-18	120	Dc2/17v	956
Tallant, Patrick	Dublin, the city	gentry: gent	11-Feb-57	400	B.L. 19, 843 f. 189	3085
Tallant, Patrick	Dublin, the city	gentry: gent	18-Feb-56	600	B.L. 19, 843 f. 167a	3049
Tallant, Patrick	Dublin, the city	gentry: gent	06-Apr-61	800	B.L. 15, 635 f. 66a	3381
Tallon, Ellen	Kildare, Norrogh Begg	other: widow	09-Jul-23	400	Dc2/49r	1171
Tasburgh, John	Dublin, the city	gentry: gent	23-Sep-62	500	B.L. 15, 635 f. 97	3429
Tasburgh, John	Dublin, the city	gentry: gent	07-Oct-62	4000	B.L. 15, 635 f. 96	3426
Tasburgh, John	Dublin, the city	gentry: gent	06-Oct-62	420	B.L. 15, 635 f. 97	3428
Tasburgh, John	Dublin, the city	gentry: gent	07-Oct-62	4000	B.L. 15, 635 f. 96a	3427
Taylor, Francis	Dublin		17-Jun-02	100	Dc1/38r	248
Taylor, Francis	Dublin		15-May-06	53	Dc1/67r	404
Taylor, James	Dublin	merchant	23-Nov-02	150	Dc1/40v	263
Taylor, John	Dublin, Swordes	gentry: gent	26-Feb-66	1000	B.L. 15, 635 f. 174a	3558
Taylor, John	Dublin, Swords	gentry: gent	26-Feb-66	1000	Dc3/24	2276
Taylor, Mabel	Roscommon, Roscommon	gentry: wife of Thomas	16-May-15	200	Dc1/137v	853
Taylor, Robert	Dublin, the city	merchant	28-May-24	40	Dc2/55v	1217
Taylor, Thomas	Roscommon, Cloughill	gentry: gent	14-Nov-06	300	Dc1/71r	431
Taylor, Thomas	Roscommon, Roscommon	gentry: gent	16-May-15	200	Dc1/137v	853
Taylor, Thomas	Sligo	gentry: gent	27-Apr-03	500	Dc1/46v	295
Taylor, Thomas	Roscommon, Clonaghill	gentry: gent	05-Feb-05	628	Dc1/56r	346
Taylor, Thomas	Roscommon, Clonlaughell	gentry: gent	03-Jul-07	200	Dc1/79r	482
Taylor, Thomas	Roscommon	gentry: gent	30-Sep-01	300	Dc1/33v	223
Taylor, William	Mayo, Borishoole	gentry: gent	17-Jul-63	600	B.L. 15, 635 f. 107a	3447
Teeling, Thomas	Dublin?, Mallacha	gentry: gent	28-Nov-71	300	Dc3/141v	2536
Temple, John	England, London	gentry: esquire	14-Mar-29	2000	Dc2/126v	1593
Temple, William	Dublin, the city	gentry: knight	09-Jul-24	500	Dc2/57v	1233
Tennant, Edmund	England, London	trade: clothier	14-Jul-23	400	Dc2/49v	1176
Tennant, John	England, London	trade: haberdasher	14-Jul-23	400	Dc2/49v	1176
Terry, Richard	Cork, the city	merchant	07-Apr-77	120	B.L. 19, 844 f. 121	3250
Terry, Richard	Cork, the city	trade: maltster	03-Jun-67	583	B.L. 15, 635 f. 195	3600
Thompson, Leonard	Dublin, the city		16-May-32	100	Dc2/181r	1827
Thompson, Marjory	Dublin, the city	merchant: Leonard's wife	16-May-32	100	Dc2/181r	1827
Thornhill, Robert	England, London, Middle Temple	gentry: esquire	21-Nov-79	650	B.L. 15, 637 f. 22a	3886
Thurgood, William	Dublin, the city	trade: tallow chandler	28-Apr-62	270	B.L. 15, 635 f. 94a	3423
Tichborne, William	Louth, Bewly	gentry: knight	13-Oct-70	1600	Dc3/128	2497
Tichborne, William	Louth, Bewly	gentry: knight	21-Mar-78	2000	Dc3/187v	2708
Tiffin, Rebecca	Dublin	gentry: widow	06-Nov-29	400	Dc2/137v	1642
Tiffin, Rebecca	Dublin	gentry: widow, exec of William, Dublin gent	13-May-29	240	Dc2/128v	1604
Tiffin, William	Dublin	gentry: gent	10-Feb-29	300	Dc2/124v	1582

Standard	County	Occupation	Date	Amount	MS No	Ident No
Tighe, Richard	Dublin, the city		15-Jun-65	440	B.L. 15, 635 f. 153a	3526
Tighe, Richard	Dublin, the city		25-May-63	660	B.L. 15, 635 f. 115a	3461
Tighe, Richard	Dublin		05-May-62	350	B.L. 15, 635 f. 93a	3421
Tighe, Richard	Dublin, the city		08-Dec-60	400	B.L. 15, 635 f. 61	3373
Tighe, Richard	Dublin, the city		01-Jun-63	160	B.L. 15, 635 f. 115	3460
Tighe, Richard	Dublin, the city		15-Dec-65	440	B.L. 15, 635 f. 161a	3538
Tighe, Richard	Dublin, the city		15-Jun-65	632	B.L. 15, 635 f. 154	3527
Tighe, Richard	Dublin?	gentry: esquire	11-Feb-56	216	B.L. 19, 843 f. 182a	3072
Tighe, Richard	Dublin, the city		23-Jun-64	726	B.L. 15, 635 f. 137a	3496
Tighe, Richard	Dublin, the city		08-Feb-66	1200	B.L. 15, 635 f. 169	3549
Tighe, Richard	Dublin, the city		27-Nov-63	400	B.L. 15, 635 f. 128	3483
Tighe, Richard	Dublin, the city		06-Dec-60	3000	B.L. 15, 635 f. 60a	3372
Tighe, Richard	Dublin, the city		25-May-63	660	B.L. 15, 635 f. 114a	3459
Tighe, Richard	Dublin, the city		10-Oct-70	2000	Dc3/127	2496
Tighe, Richard	Dublin, the city		10-Oct-70	2000	B.L. 15, 636 f. 71a	3745
Tighe, Richard	Dublin?	gentry: esquire	31-Mar-56	1100	B.L. 19, 843 f. 183	3073
Tighe, Richard	Dublin, the city		15-Jun-65	440	Dc3/9	2240
Tighe, Richard	Dublin, the city		08-Feb-66	1200	Dc3/21	2269
Tighe, Richard	Dublin, the city		15-Jun-65	632	Dc3/9	2241
Tighe, Richard	Dublin, the city		15-Dec-65	440	Dc3/17	2260
Tighe, Teige	Roscommon, Laragh	gentry: gent	01-Jun-33	400	Dc2/195v	1886
Tilinger, Thomas	Meath, Mullaglagh	gentry: gent	03-Feb-07	60	Dc1/73v	446
Tilson, Thomas	Dublin, the city	gentry: esquire	18-Jun-73	600	B.L. 15, 636 f. 136a	3849
Tilson, Thomas	Dublin, the city	gentry: esquire	18-Jun-73	600	Dc3/157v	2587
Tisdall, Michael	Dublin, the city	gentry: gent	03-Mar-69	2100	Dc3/92	2428
Tisdall, Michael	Dublin, the city	gentry: gent	03-Mar-69	2100	B.L. 15, 636 f. 44a	3701
Titchborne, Henry	Tyrone, Blassynborne	gentry: knight	05-Mar-30	294	Dc2/143v	1671
Tollet, George	Dublin, the city	gentry: gent	11-Jan-82	400	B.L. 15, 637 f. 54	3943
Tomlinson, John	Louth, Drogheda		13-Jul-83	1000	B.L. 15, 637 f. 77a	3988
Tomlinson, John	Louth, Drogheda	gentry: gent	08-Apr-72	105	B.L. 15, 636 f. 103a	3800
Tomlinson, John	Louth, Drogheda	merchant	03-Jun-73	500	B.L. 15, 636 f. 137a	3851
Tomlinson, John	Louth, Drogheda	gentry: gent	20-Feb-72	200	B.L. 15, 636 f. 102a	3798
Tomlinson, John	Louth, Walshstowne	gentry: gent	06-Feb-69	1340	Dc3/89	2423
Tomlinson, John	Louth, Walshestowne	gentry: gent	06-Feb-69	1340	B.L. 15, 636 f. 30a	3678
Tomlinson, John	Louth, Drogheda		31-Jan-83	160	B.L. 15, 637 f. 68a	3970
Tomlinson, John	Louth, Drogheda	merchant	16-Apr-72	300	B.L. 15, 636 f. 103	3799
Tomlinson, John	Louth, Drogheda		24-Oct-82	1100	B.L. 15, 637 f. 64	3963
Tomlinson, John	Louth, Drogheda		22-Aug-81	1200	B.L. 15, 637 f. 50	3936
Tomlinson, John	Louth, Drogheda		26-Apr-82	210	B.L. 15, 637 f. 56	3947
Tomlinson, John	Louth, Drogheda	gentry: gent	21-Feb-74	660	B.L. 19, 844 f. 22	3142
Tomlinson, John	Louth, Drogheda	gentry: gent	24-Jun-72	100	B.L. 15, 636 f. 112	3814
Tomlinson, John	Louth, Drogedagh		11-Apr-76	300	B.L. 19, 844 f. 92	3219
Tomlinson, John	Louth, Drogheda	gentry: gent	26-Aug-72	120	B.L. 15, 636 f. 124	3828
Tomlinson, John	Louth, Drogheda	gentry: gent	13-Aug-72	100	B.L. 15, 636 f. 112a	3815

Standard	County	Occupation	Date	Amount	MS No	Ident No
Tonson, Richard		soldier: major,				
		Colonel Lawrence's Reg.	24-Jun-56	200	B.L. 19, 843 f. 174a	3060
Toogood, Samson	Cork, Bandon Bridge	gentry: esquire	07-Apr-84	315	B.L. 15, 637 f.88	4005
Topham, John		prof: doctor of law	20-Nov-73	4000	Dc3/158av	2595
Topham, John		prof: doctor of law	20-Nov-73	4000	B.L. 19, 844 f. 10	3129
Towers, Anthony	Dublin, the city	gentry: esquire	05-Feb-83	200	B.L. 15, 637 f. 68	3969
Towers, Simon	Dublin, the city	gentry: gent	09-Jan-85	1400	B.L. 15, 637 f. 99	4027
Townley, Henry	Louth, Athclare	gentry: esquire	20-Jan-82	700	B.L. 15, 637 f. 54a	3944
Townsend, Cornelius	Cork, Castletowne	gentry: gent	14-Jun-72	1700	B.L. 15, 636 f. 114a	3819
Townsend, John	Cork, Tymoleage	gentry: esquire	20-Oct-74	500	B.L. 19, 844 f. 49	3172
Townsend, John	Cork, Kilbrittaine	gentry: esquire	14-Jun-72	3000	B.L. 15, 636 f. 109a	3809
Townsend, Richard	Cork, Castletowne	gentry: esquire	12-Apr-75	2400	B.L. 19, 844 f. 59	3184
Toxteth?, William	Louth, Drogheda		08-Mar-54	540	B.L. 19, 843 f. 139	2992
Travers, Joseph	Dublin, the city		07-Feb-56	250	B.L. 19, 843 f. 168a	3051
Trilbery, Tristram	Dublin, the city	gentry: gent	27-Feb-74	200	Dc3/160v	2604
Tuite, Oliver	Westmeath, Sonaghe	gentry: gent	17-Sep-12	500	Dc1/115v	717
Tuite, Oliver	Westmeath, Sonnacke	gentry: baronet	04-May-32	400	Dc2/178v	1817
Tuite, William	Westmeath, Tuitstowne	gentry: gent	04-Jul-27	600	Dc2/96v	1449
Turbin, William	Dublin	gentry: gent	18-Sep-11	110	Dc1/106v	663
Turbridge, Robert	Dublin, the city	gentry: esquire	27-Feb-58	200	B.L. 15, 635 f. 38a	3331
Turner, Paul	Dublin, the city	merchant	06-Nov-35	102	Dc2/239v	2068
Turner, Paul	Dublin	merchant	28-Jun-34	400	Dc2/213v	1958
Turner, Peter	Dublin, the city	gentry: gent	01-Dec-27	300	Dc2/101v	1471
Turner, Peter	Dublin, the city	gentry: gent	02-May-27	500	Dc2/91v	1428
Turner, Samuel	England, York, Lamhill	gentry: gent	17-Jun-61	320	B.L. 15, 635 f. 81	3401
Turner, Thomas	Dublin	merchant	23-Oct-23	200	Dc2/50v	1183
Turner, William	Dublin, the city		17-Dec-29	600	Dc2.140v	1656
Turner, William	Dublin, the city		25-Nov-28	700	Dc2/117r	1547
Turner, William	Dublin		16-Dec-23	600	Dc2/51v	1191
Tylberry, Tristram	Dublin, the city	gentry: gent	27-Feb-74	200	B.L. 19, 844 f. 20a	3139
Tyler, Francis	Dublin		17-Jul-99	110	Dc1/17v	121
Tyrrell, John	Dublin		24-Nov-97	100	Dc1/7r	51
Tyrrell, Mathew	Dublin, the city	gentry: esquire	25-Feb-24	200	Dc2/53r	1198
Tyrrell, Peter	Meath, Athboy	merchant	21-Oct-33	820	Dc2/200r	1904
Tyrrell, Philip	Westmeath, Rathcam	gentry: gent	16-May-36	600	Dc2/251r	2122
Tyrrell, Richard	Westmeath, Clownemoyle	gentry: esquire	09-Dec-18	1000	Dc2/19r	964
Tyrrell, Richard	King's Co., Coulchill	gentry: esquire	16-May-36	600	Dc2/251r	2121
Tyrrell, Richard	Dublin	trade: tailor	30-Jun-12	40	Dc1/114r	709
Tyrrell, Richard	Dublin, the city	trade: tailor	09-Aug-14	160	Dc1/131r	815
Tyrrell, Richard	Dublin	trade: tailor	27-Jan-12	40	Dc1/111r	690
Tyrrell, Richard	Westmeath, Lynn	gentry: gent	15-Feb-83	440	B.L. 15, 637 f. 75a	3984
Tyrrell, Thomas	Westmeath, Newcastle	gentry: gent, son/heir				
		of Richard	16-May-36	600	Dc2/251r	2121
Tyrrell, Thomas	Westmeath, Robbinston	gentry: esquire	21-Jul-54	120	B.L. 19, 843 f. 142a	2999
Tyrrell, Thomas	Westmeath, Newcastle	gentry: gent	06-Dec-26	400	Dc2/85r	1404

Standard	County	Occupation	Date	Amount	MS No	Ident No
Tyson, Henry	Dublin, the city	Trade: barber-surgeon	09-Mar-81	200	B.L. 15, 637 f. 43a	3925
Tyson, Thomas	Dublin, the city	gentry: esquire	09-Dec-84	1300	B.L. 15, 637 f. 96a	4022
Upton, Henry	Antrim, Carrickefergus	gentry: gent	01-May-21	800	Dc2/35v	1070
Ussher, Amy	Dublin, the city	merchant: widow	19-Jun-20	220	Dc2/31r	1036
Ussher, Amy	Dublin, the city	merchant: widow	24-Apr-19	1200	Dc2/22v	985
Ussher, Amy	Dublin, the city	merchant: widow	26-May-20	240	Dc2/30r	1030
Ussher, Amy	Dublin, the city	merchant: widow	23-Apr-19	1700	Dc2/22v	986
Ussher, Amy	Dublin, the city	merchant: widow	08-Jun-20	600	Dc2/30v	1033
Ussher, Amy	Dublin, the city	other: widow	13-May-20	200	Dc2/30r	1028
Ussher, Christopher	Dublin, the city	gentry: esquire	18-Nov-72	6000	Dc3/149r	2563
Ussher, George	Dublin	merchant	25-Oct-05	50	Dc1/62r	377
Ussher, John	Dublin, the city	merchant	07-Dec-38	660	B.L. 19, 843 f. 3	2725
Ussher, John	Dublin		30-Jun-97	700	Dc1/5v	39
Ussher, John	Dublin		30-Jun-97	600	Dc1/5v	40
Ussher, Lawrence	Dublin	merchant	24-Jan-05	140	Dc1/54v	341
Ussher, Richard	Dublin, Cromlin	gentry: gent	08-Mar-07	400	Dc1/75v	457
Ussher, Stephen	Dublin	merchant	11-Feb-19	110	Dc2/20v	974
Ussher, Stephen	Dublin, the city	merchant	20-Dec-19	150	Dc2/27v	1015
Ussher, Stephen	Dublin, the city	merchant	30-Sep-19	300	Dc2/26r	1004
Ussher, Stephen	Dublin, the city	merchant	25-Nov-20	600	Dc2/33r	1053
Ussher, Stephen	Dublin, the city	merchant	25-Jun-22	3000	Dc2/41r	1113
Ussher, Walter	Dublin		10-Jun-23	400	Dc2/48r	1164
Ussher, Walter	Dublin, the city		28-Apr-29	500	Dc2/127v	1599
Ussher, Walter	Dublin	merchant	28-Nov-10	300	Dc1/101r	634
Ussher, Walter	Dublin, the city	merchant	24-Apr-19	1200	Dc2/22v	985
Ussher, Walter	Dublin, the city	merchant	03-Jun-22	200	Dc2/40v	1111
Ussher, Walter	Dublin, the city	merchant	25-Jun-22	3000	Dc2/41r	1113
Ussher, Walter	Dublin	merchant	04-Dec-06	300	Dc1/72v	441
Ussher, Walter	Dublin, the city	merchant	22-May-22	272	Dc2/40r	1105
Ussher, Walter	Dublin, the city	merchant	23-Apr-19	1700	Dc2/22v	986
Ussher, Walter	Dublin, the city		05-May-32	100	Dc2/179r	1819
Ussher, Walter	Dublin, the city	merchant	03-Jun-22	200	Dc2/40V	1110
Ussher, William	Dublin, the city	gentry: knight	14-May-53	2000	B.L. 19, 843 f. 133	2981
Ussher, William	Dublin	gentry: knight	02-Jul-25	800	Dc2/68r	1306
Ussher, William	Dublin	gentry: esquire	09-Dec-33	400	Dc2/203r	1916
Ussher, William	Dublin	gentry: knight	16-Sep-11	800	Dc1/106v	662
Ussher, William	Dublin	gentry: esquire	17-Dec-33	400	Dc2/204r	1920
Ussher, William	Dublin	gentry: esquire	12-Dec-33	800	Dc2/203r	1918
Vanbrugh, Giles	England, Chester	merchant	29-Nov-73	880	Dc3/158av	2596
Vanbrugh, Giles	England, Chester, the city	merchant	29-Nov-73	880	B.L. 19, 844 f. 12	3131
Vanbrugh, William	England, Surrey, Waltham	gentry: gent	30-Apr-73	2000	B.L. 15, 636 f. 134a	3845

Standard	County	Occupation	Date	Amount	MS No	Ident No
Vanbrugh, William	England, London/ Waltham	gentry: gent	30-Apr-73	2000	Dc3/155r	2580
Vandeleure?, Maximilian	France, Bordeaux	merchant	13-Nov-01	200	Dc1/34r	225
Vane, William	Dublin, the city	gentry: gent	28-Apr-60	110	B.L. 15, 635 f. 58	3367
Vaughan, Owen	Mayo, Carrowmore	gentry: esquire	23-Dec-65	530	Dc3/19	2265
Veele, William	Dublin, the city	gentry: gent	21-Mar-35	500	Dc2/231v	2032
Velden, Christopher	Dublin, the city	gentry: gent	05-Sep-34	200	Dc2/218v	1979
Veldon, Christopher	Dublin, the city	gentry: gent	30-May-36	60	Dc2/252v	2129
Veldon, Christopher	Dublin, the city	gentry: gent	11-Feb-29	200	Dc2/124v	1584
Veldon, Christopher	Dublin	gentry: gent	04-May-30	400	Dc2/146r	1683
Veldon, Christopher	Dublin, the city	gentry: gent	20-Feb-36	200	Dc2/245r	2096
Veldon, Christopher	Dublin	gentry: gent	04-May-30	200	Dc2/145r	1678
Veldon, Christopher	Dublin, the city	gentry: gent	25-Feb-34	200	Dc2/207v	1934
Veldon, John	Dublin	gentry: gent	29-Oct-98	200	Dc1/13r	92
Veldon, John	Dublin	gentry: esquire	22-Feb-13	200	Dc1/119v	742
Veldon, John	Dublin?	gentry: gent	02-May-10	40	Dc1/95v	600
Veldon, John	Dublin	gentry: gent	15-Dec-01	200	Dc1/35r	231
Veldon, Peter	Dublin	merchant	27-Apr-97	100	Dc1/3r	19
Waddington, Henry	Galway, Clostokin	gentry: knight	22-Jun-65	240	Dc3/11	2245
Wadman, Judith	Antrim, Carrickfergus	other: widow, exec of John, burgess	28-Oct-72	300	B.L. 15, 636 f. 117	3822
Wafer, John	Dublin	merchant	16-Jun-99	60	Dc1/16v	113
Wafer, John	Dublin	merchant	10-Feb-98	400	Dc1/9r	64
Wafer, John	Dublin	merchant	11-Mar-01	600	Dc1/29v	195
Wafer, Roger	Meath, Granston	gentry: gent	11-Feb-18	280	Dc2/13v	934
Wafer, Roger	Meath, Gianston	gentry: gent	03-Jul-17	200	Dc2/8v	907
Wakefield, Thomas	England, London	trade: goldsmith	17-Nov-30	400	Dc2/155v	1724
Wakefield, Thomas	Dublin	merchant	01-Jun-25	100	Dc2/64v	1287
Wakley, Christopher	Meath, the Navan	gentry: gent	26-May-01	60	Dc1/32v	213
Walker, Nicholas	?, Kilmaynnam	gentry: gent	22-Sep-98	100	Dc1/12v	89
Walker, William	Dublin, the city	trade: clothier	20-Aug-59	528	B.L. 15, 635 f. 52	3355
Wall, Isobel	Dublin, the city	other: widow	12-Dec-67	280	B.L. 15, 635 f. 209	3625
Wall, Isobel	Dublin, the city	other: widow	12-Dec-67	280	Dc3/71	2383
Wall, James	Limerick, Killmallocke	merchant	14-Feb-40	1100	B.L. 19, 843 f. 43a	2805
Wall, James	Limerick, Kilmallocke		20-Jun-39	1600	B.L. 19, 843 f. 11	2740
Wall, Thomas	Dublin, the city	trade: gardener	02-Jul-55	100	B.L. 19. 843 f. 158	3030
Wallis, Thomas	Cork, Cariglasse	gentry: gent	20-Mar-79	742	B.L. 15, 637 f. 13a	3872
Wallop, Henry	Wexford, Enniscorthy	gentry: knight	28-May-06	120	Dc1/68v	415
Wallop, Henry	Wexford, Enniscorthie	gentry: knight	02-Jun-06	60	Dc1/69v	419
Wallop, Henry	illegible	gentry: knight	07-Feb-97	1000	Dc1/1r	4
Walsh, Francis	Kilkenny	other: widow	27-Feb-26	200	Dc2/74v	1348
Walsh, James	Dublin, Ballauly?	gentry: gent	05-May-32	174	Dc2/179r	1820
Walsh, James	Dublin	merchant	11-Jul-22	30	Dc2/41v	1117
Walsh, John	Dublin, Kynnowre	gentry: gent	10-Dec-02	80	Dc1/42r	270

Standard	County	Occupation	Date	Amount	MS No	Ident No
Walsh, John	Dublin, Kynnowre	gentry: gent	10-Dec-02	80	Dc1/42v	272
Walsh, John	Kildare, Castledermott		02-Jul-35	400	Dc2/238v	2064
Walsh, Mary	Antrim, Carrickfergus	other: widow, of Robert, alderman	29-Jan-72	137	B.L. 15, 636 f. 98	3792
Walsh, Oliver	Dublin, the city	gentry: gent	07-Jul-41	5000	B.L. 19, 843 f. 100	2919
Walsh, Oliver	Dublin	gentry: gent	12-Mar-25	600	Dc2/63r	1276
Walsh, Oliver	Dublin, the city	gentry: gent	06-Feb-55	2000	B.L. 19, 843 f. 156a	3027
Walsh, Peter	Limerick, Abbey Owyny	gentry: esquire	26-Jun-41	2400	B.L. 19, 843 f. 103	2925
Walsh, Randolph	Down, Hillsborrough	trade: leather worker	29-Jan-72	273	B.L. 15, 636 f. 108a	3808
Walsh, Richard	Dublin, Pimlico	gentry: gent	06-Dec-39	300	B.L. 19, 843 f. 37	2792
Walsh, Richard	Dublin, Pimlico	gentry: gent	10-May-37	220	Dc2/262v	2179
Walsh, Richard	Dublin, Pimlico	gentry: gent	08-May-37	280	Dc2/262v	2178
Walsh, Richard	Dublin, Thomascourte	gentry: gent	30-Jun-40	100	B.L. 19, 843 f. 58	2834
Walsh, Richard	Dublin, Pimlico	gentry: gent	14-Dec-39	280	B.L. 19, 843 f. 37a	2793
Walsh, Robert	Antrim, Carrickfergus		13-Mar-71	88	B.L. 15, 636 f. 82	3764
Walsh, William	Wexford	gentry: gent	27-Apr-02	300	Dc1/37v	243
Walsh, William	Dublin, Lespople	gentry: gent	30-Nov-09	500	Dc1/93r	584
Warburton, Richard	Dublin	merchant	23-Jun-30	400	Dc2/153r	1712
Ward, Richard	Dublin, the city	merchant	15-Jul-76	257	Dc3/179r	2673
Ward, Richard	Dublin, the city	merchant	15-Jul-76	357	B.L. 19, 844 f. 105	3232
Ward, Richard	Dublin, the city	gentry: gent	11-Feb-56	300	B.L. 19, 843 f. 168	3050
Ware, James	Dublin?		07-Jun-97	280	Dc1/4v	30
Ware, James	Dublin, the city	gentry: esquire	27-Jan-77	6000	Dc3/181v	2684
Ware, James	Dublin, the city	gentry: esquire	05-Feb-24	400	Dc2/53r	1201
Ware, James	Dublin, the city	gentry: esquire	27-Jan-77	6000	B.L. 19, 844 f. 128	3257
Ware, James	Dublin?	gentry: knight	12-May-65	10000	Dc3/5	2232
Ware, John	Longford, Cranelagh	gentry: esquire	22-Jun-29	200	Dc2/133v	1625
Ware, Robert	Dublin, the city	gentry: esquire	23-Mar-67	400	Dc3/57	2348
Ware, Robert	Dublin, the city	gentry: esquire	04-Nov-68	200	B.L. 15, 635 f. 229a	3664
Ware, Robert	Dublin, the city	gentry: esquire	14-Dec-68	600	B.L. 15, 635 f. 230	3665
Ware, Robert	Dublin, the city	gentry: esquire	17-Nov-69	400	Dc3/107	2455
Ware, Robert	Dublin, the city	gentry: esquire	14-Nov-68	200	Dc3/83	2412
Ware, Robert	Dublin, the city	gentry: esquire	02-Feb-67	400	Dc3/51	2335
Ware, Robert	Dublin, the city	gentry: esquire	13-Dec-66	880	Dc3/47	2324
Ware, Robert	Dublin, the city	gentry: esquire	14-Dec-68	600	Dc3/87	2418
Ware, Robert	Dublin, the city		05-Jan-84	400	B.L. 15, 637 f. 83	3997
Waring, Adam	Waterford, Kilmackoe	gentry: gent	07-Jan-41	3200	B.L. 19, 843 f. 82	2883
Warner, William	Cork, Bandonbridge	gentry: gent	14-Nov-66	1400	B.L. 15, 635 f. 182	3574
Warren, Abel	Kilkenny, Balleenlodge	gentry: esquire	15-Feb-61	360	B.L. 15, 635 f. 63	3377
Warren, Alexander	Meath, Ballibin?	gentry: gent	05-Apr-41	200	B.L. 19, 843 f. 88	2895
Warren, Edmund	Dublin, the city	merchant	16-Jan-40	800	B.L. 19, 843 f. 39a	2797
Warren, Edmund	Dublin, the city	merchant	16-Dec-39	240	B.L. 19, 843 f. 38a	2795
Warren, Edmund	Dublin, the city	merchant	29-Jul-41	1000	B.L. 19, 843 f. 104	2927
Warren, Edmund	Dublin, the city	merchant	20-Dec-24	220	Dc2/227v	2015
Warren, Edmund	Dublin, the city	merchant	27-Sep-37	189	Dc2/270v	2215

Standard	County	Occupation	Date	Amount	MS No	Ident No
Warren, Edmund	Dublin, the city	merchant	11-Feb-41	380	B.L. 19, 843 f. 84a	2888
Warren, Edward	Dublin, Swordes	gentry: gent	09-Jul-39	400	B.L. 19, 843 f. 26a	2771
Warren, Edward	Dublin, Swords	gentry: gent	21-Nov-39	66	B.L. 19, 843 f. 40	2798
Warren, Edward	Dublin, Swords	farmer	26-Sep-31	600	Dc2/168r	1777
Warren, Henry	Dublin, the city	gentry: esquire	25-Nov-70	300	Dc3/131v	2503
Warren, Henry	Dublin, the city	gentry: esquire	17-Feb-72	200	Dc3/144r	2545
Warren, Henry	Dublin, the city	gentry: esquire	17-Feb-72	200	B.L. 15, 636 f. 99	3793
Warren, Henry	Dublin	gentry: esquire	05-Feb-30	200	Dc2/141v	1662
Warren, James	Dublin, Swordes	gentry: gent	06-Nov-39	600	B.L. 19, 843 f. 39	2796
Warren, James	Dublin	merchant	08-Mar-28	300	Dc2/106r	1493
Warren, John	Kildare, Grangebeg?	gentry: esquire	18-Nov-71	200	B.L. 15, 636 f. 101a	3796
Warren, John	Dublin, Courtduffe	gentry: gent	30-May-28	200	Dc2/110v	1516
Warren, John	Kildare, Grangebegg	gentry: esquire	18-Nov-71	200	Dc3/140v	2533
Warren, Nicholas	Dublin, Sillock	gentry: gent	27-Nov-28	300	Dc2/117r	1548
Warren, Nicholas	Dublin, Sillocke	gentry: gent	20-Jun-31	300	Dc2/165v	1765
Warren, Nicholas	Dublin, Sillock	gentry: gent	03-Mar-28	200	Dc2/105v	1491
Warren, William	England, London, the city	gentry: gent	02-Jul-40	600	B.L. 19, 843 f. 65	2849
Warren, William	Dublin, Castleknocke	gentry: gent	01-Apr-41	800	B.L. 19, 843 f. 87a	2894
Warren, William	Dublin, Castleknocke	gentry: gent	26-Feb-41	1600	B.L. 19, 843 f. 87	2893
Warren, William	Dublin, the city	merchant	09-Apr-28	200	Dc2/106v	1497
Warren, William	Dublin, Collmyne	gentry: gent	19-Mar-36	220	B.L. 19, 843 f. 45	2808
Warren, William	Dublin, Colmyne	gentry: gent	19-Mar-36	220	Dc2/247r	2105
Waterhouse, Charles	Cavan, Belturbett	gentry: gent	22-Jul-20	400	Dc2/32r	1045
Waterhouse, Joseph	Dublin, the city	prof: doctor of phisick	08-Jul-57	1200	B.L. 19, 843 f. 196a	3100
Waterhouse, Thomas	Dublin, the city		17-Dec-63	360	B.L. 15, 635 f. 124a	3476
Watkins, John	Cork, Ballymee	gentry: gent	21-Jul-80	600	B.L. 15, 637 f. 38	3914
Watson, James	Dublin, the city		22-Dec-34	1000	Dc2/228r	2017
Watson, James	Dublin	merchant	09-Feb-32	110	Dc2/175v	1806
Watson, Philip	Dublin, the city	merchant: son/heir of James	22-Dec-34	1000	Dc2/228r	2017
Watson, Philip	Dublin, the city		17-Nov-40	1200	B.L. 19, 843 f. 73	2865
Wave, Richard	Dublin, the city	gentry: gent	04-Feb-24	160	Dc2/52v	1197
Wayte, Bartholomew	Dublin	gentry: gent	19-Dec-35	920	Dc2/242v	2083
Wayte, Bartholomew	Dublin	gentry: gent	24-Mar-36	200	Dc2/247v	2106
Weaver, John	Queen's Co., Ballymaddock	gentry: esquire	05-Jul-80	2000	B.L. 15, 637 f. 40	3918
Weaver, John	Dublin, the city	gentry: esquire	05-Feb-78	2600	Dc3/186v	2704
Weaver, John	Dublin, the city	gentry: esquire	05-Feb-78	2000	B.L. 19, 844 f. 147	3278
Weaver, John		other: son-in-law of Daniel	04-Dec-55	600	B.L. 19, 843 f. 206a	3119
Webb, John	Dublin	gentry: esquire	25-Sep-21	400	Dc2/36v	1078
Webb, John	Antrim, Belfast	gentry: gent	21-Feb-63	730	B.L. 15, 635 f. 101	3436
Weightman, Ann	Dublin, Spricklestowne?	other: widow	12-Nov-28	200	Dc2/115r	1539
Weldon, Robert	Kildare, Tulloghgory	gentry: esquire	10-Jun-30	240	Dc2/149v	1696
Weldon, Robert	Kildare, Tullaghgorry	gentry: esquire	20-Jul-29	1000	Dc2/133v	1624
Wenman, Thomas		gentry: knight	12-Jul-37	500	Dc2/268r	2202

Standard	County	Occupation	Date	Amount	MS No	Ident No
Wesley, Edmund	Kildare?	peer: baron of Norrosh	18-Nov-22	400	Dc2/43r	1125
West, Roger	Wicklow, Rock	gentry: esquire	15-Aug-76	500	Dc3/179v	2675
Westhenra, Henry	Limerick, Athlacka	gentry: esquire	13-Aug-85	1600	B.L. 15, 637 f. 101a	4031
Weston, Nicholas	Dublin		01-Dec-01	120	Dc1/35r	230
Weston, Nicholas	Dublin		10-Oct-98	200	Dc1/12v	90
Weston, Richard	Dublin		13-Feb-00	133	Dc1/21v	143
Weston, Richard	Dublin		06-Jul-97	84	Dc1/6r	43
Weston, Richard	Dublin		06-Jul-97	84	Dc1/6r	44
Weston, Samuel	Dublin, the city	merchant	31-Dec-59	500	B.L. 15, 635 f. 138a	3498
Weston, Warner	Dublin, the city	merchant	06-Aug-63	5000	B.L. 15, 635 f. 110a	3451
Wetherall, Elizabeth	England, London, the city	other: widow	06-Aug-55	1600	B.L. 19, 843 f. 159	3033
Wheeler, Jonas	Queen's Co., Grennan	gentry: esquire	18-Nov-72	6000	Dc3/149r	2563
Wheeler, Jonas	Dublin	prof: dean of Christchurch	16-Dec-11	110	Dc1/110r	683
Wheeler, Oliver	Queen's Co., Grennan	gentry: esquire	18-Nov-72	6000	Dc3/149r	2563
White, Arthur	Dublin, St. Katherins	gentry: esquire	27-Jan-40	3000	B.L. 19, 843 f. 44a	2807
White, Bartholomew	Louth, Carlingforde	merchant	24-Nov-29	700	Dc2/139r	1649
White, Bartholomew	Louth, Carlingford	merchant	01-Dec-26	600	Dc2/84v	1401
White, Francis	Dublin	gentry: gent	22-Aug-17	200	Dc2/9v	911
White, Francis	Dublin, the city	gentry: esquire	06-Mar-20	3000	Dc2/29r	1024
White, James	Tipperary, Clonmell	merchant	21-Nov-17	1000	Dc2/11r	921
White, James	Dublin	gentry: gent	15-Jul-36	400	Dc2/254v	2143
White, James	Tipperary, Clonmell	merchant	27-Apr-11	220	Dc1/103v	648
White, James	Dublin, the Warde	gentry: gent	08-Aug-29	400	Dc2/135v	1633
White, John	Limerick, the city		24-Oct-40	1400	B.L. 19, 843 f. 82a	2884
White, John	King's Co., Togher Crohane	gentry: gent	03-Feb-05	60	Dc1/55v	344
White, John	Antrim, Carrickfergus	gentry: gent	28-Jan-74	200	B.L. 19, 844 f. 25	3146
White, John	King's Co., Croghane	gentry: gent	12-Jan-01	160	Dc1/27v	184
White, Lawrence	Dublin, the city	gentry: gent	01-May-61	600	B.L. 15, 635 f. 72	3388
White, Lawrence	Limerick, the city	merchant	07-Jun-40	400	B.L. 19, 843 f. 68	2855
White, Lawrence	Dublin, the city	gentry: esquire	19-Sep-63	200	B.L. 15, 635 f. 118a	3467
White, Lawrence	Dublin	gentry: gent	19-Apr-61	600	B.L. 15, 635 f. 71a	3387
White, Lawrence	Limerick, the city	merchant	19-May-40	200	B.L. 19, 843 f. 58a	2835
White, Nicholas	Dublin	gentry: esquire	13-Jul-36	3000	Dc2/254v	2142
White, Nicholas	Kildare, Leixlippe	gentry: esquire	15-Feb-08	160	Dc1/81r	503
White, Nicholas	Dublin	gentry: esquire	09-May-36	1600	Dc2/250r	2117
White, Nicholas	Dublin	gentry: esquire	13-Jul-39	3000	B.L. 19, 843 f. 186	3079
White, Simon	Limerick, Cnockentry	gentry: gent	30-Nov-76	200	B.L. 19, 844 f. 133a	3242
White, Simon	Limerick, Cnockcentry	gentry: gent	28-Apr-77	110	B.L. 19, 844 f. 133	3263
White, Simon	Limerick, Cnockcentry	gentry: gent	28-Apr-77	120	B.L. 19, 844 f. 132	3262
White, Simon	Limerick, Cnockcentry	gentry: gent	28-Apr-77	240	B.L. 19, 844 f. 131	3261
White, Simon	Limerick, Knocksentry	gentry: gent	16-Jan-73	400	B.L. 15, 636 f. 127a	3835
White, Thomas	Dublin	merchant	20-Feb-05	110	Dc1/56v	349
White, Thomas	Dublin	merchant	23-Jul-23	140	Dc2/49v	1177

Standard	County	Occupation	Date	Amount	MS No	Ident No
White, Thomas	Dublin	merchant	22-Apr-00	300	Dc1/23r	155
White, Thomas	Dublin, the city	merchant	14-Apr-19	300	Dc2/21v	980
White, Thomas	Dublin	merchant	18-Jan-09	800	Dc1/85v	535
White, Thomas	Dublin	merchant	06-May-01	30	Dc1/31v	207
White, Walter	Dublin	gentry: esquire	11-Dec-32	300	Dc2/188r	1855
White, Walter	Dublin, the city	gentry: esquire	25-Apr-23	660	Dc2/46v	1151
White, William	Dublin	gentry: gent	14-Dec-34	120	Dc2/219v	1982
Wick, Oliver	Queen's Co., Brittas	gentry: gent	21-May-39	1000	B.L. 19, 843 f. 35	2788
Wigget, Richard	Dublin	trade: tailor	11-Feb-03	300	Dc1/44v	282
Wilkinson, Philip	Down, Grotto	gentry: esquire	03-Dec-78	1000	B.L. 15, 637 f. 4	3857
Wilkinson, William	Dublin, the city	merchant	17-Mar-73	100	Dc3/154v	2579
Williams, Edward	England, London	merchant	30-Jun-25	292	Dc2/67v	1304
Williams, Maurice	Dublin, the city	prof: doctor of phisick	20-Jul-37	400	Dc2/269r	2207
Williams, William	Dublin, the city	gentry: gent	28-Jun-76	1200	Dc3/179r	2672
Willis, John	Dublin	trade: smith	28-Feb-97	100	Dc1/2r	11
Willis, Richard	Dublin	gentry: gent	16-Feb-00	60	Dc1/21v	144
Willis, Thomas	Louth, Drogheda	merchant	10-Jul-76	800	B.L. 19, 844 f. 111	3239
Willis, Thomas	Louth, Drogheda	merchant	17-May-73	200	B.L. 19, 844 f. 5	3124
Willis, Thomas	Louth, Drogheda	merchant	30-Jan-73	200	B.L. 19, 844 f. 4	3123
Willoughby, Andrew	Antrim, Carrickfergus	gentry: gent	01-Sep-82	220	B.L. 15 , 637 f. 63	3961
Willoughby, Charles	Dublin, the city	prof: doctor of phisick	18-Feb-71	1600	Dc3/136r	2518
Willoughby, Nicholas	Fermanagh, Knockballymore	gentry: gent	05-May-30	140	Dc2/145v	1680
Wilmott, Arthur	Dublin, St. Mary's Abbey	gentry: esquire	04-Feb-32	2000	Dc2/174r	1801
Wilson, Ambrose	Dublin	gentry: gent	10-Nov-12	1000	Dc1/116r	721
Wilson, Ambrose	Dublin	gentry: gent	03-Mar-13	200	Dc1/120r	746
Wilson, Ambrose	Dublin	gentry: gent	03-Mar-11	200	Dc1/105r	655
Wilson, Henry	Cork, the city	merchant	02-May-72	500	B.L. 15, 636 f. 114	3818
Wilson, John	Dublin, the city	gentry: esquire	27-Aug-66	320	Dc3/37	2308
Wilson, John	Dublin, the city	gentry: esquire	27-Aug-66	320	B.L. 15, 635 f. 179a	3568
Wilson, Samuel	Dublin, the city	gentry: gent	05-Sep-55	200	B.L. 19, 843 f. 165a	3045
Wilson, Stephen		merchant	13-Jul-26	600	Dc2/81r	1385
Wilson, Thomas	Dublin, the city	gentry: esquire	24-Oct-73	2400	B.L. 19, 844 f. 14	3132
Wingfield, Thomas	Dublin, the city	gentry: gent	28-May-22	60	Dc2/40v	1109
Wingfield, Thomas	Dublin	gentry: gent	21-Jun-00	400	Dc1/24v	165
Wingfield, Thomas	Dublin	gentry: gent	29-Jun-05	600	Dc1/60v	367
Wiseman, Edward	Dublin	gentry: gent	09-Jul-40	200	B.L. 19, 843 f. 59a	2837
Wogan, Nicholas	Kildare, Rathcoffie	gentry: esquire	23-Jun-37	500	Dc2/265v	2192
Wolridge, James	Dublin, Tarby	gentry: gent	11-Dec-24	100	Dc2/59v	1251
Wolridge, James	Dublin, Tuny	gentry: gent	20-Nov-23	200	Dc2/51r	1187
Wolverston, William	Dublin, Stalorgan	gentry: esquire	19-Jun-35	300	Dc2/237r	2057
Wolverston, Christopher	Dublin	merchant	30-Jun-19	100	Dc2/24v	996
Wolverston, Christopher	Dublin, Rabock	gentry: gent	18-Nov-28	300	Dc2/116r	1542
Wolverston, George	Dublin, Balinlowre	gentry: gent	04-Mar-34	50	Dc2/209r	1940
Wolverston, James	Dublin, Stilorgan	gentry: esquire	25-Aug-65	2000	Dc3/13	2250

Standard	County	Occupation	Date	Amount	MS No	Ident No
Wolverston, James	Dublin, Stelorgan	gentry: gent	31-Oct-04	2000	Dc1/53v	337
Wolverston, James	Dublin, Stelorgan	gentry: esquire	25-Aug-65	2000	B.L. 15, 635 f. 156	3529
Wolverston, John			24-Nov-18	120	Dc2/18r	959
Wolverston, John	Wicklow, Newcastall	gentry: gent	13-May-20	1000	Dc2/30r	1029
Wolverston, William	Dublin, Raboe	gentry: gent	26-Apr-21	200	Dc2/35r	1068
Wolverston, William	Dublin, Stillorgan	gentry: gent	18-Nov-25	600	Dc2/70r	1320
Wolverston, William	Dublin, Rabo	gentry: gent	03-Dec-14	200	Dc1/133r	828
Wolverston, William	Dublin, Raboe	gentry: gent	19-Jun-18	600	Dc2/15r	944
Wolverston, William	Dublin, Roboe	gentry: gent	03-Mar-23	600	Dc2/45v	1145
Wolvey, Bridget	Cork, the city	prof: wife of James	01-Jul-67	200	B.L. 15, 635 f. 200	3609
Wolvey, James	Cork, the city	prof: doctor of medicine	01-Jul-67	200	B.L. 15, 635 f. 200	3609
Wood, Robert	Dublin, the city	prof: doctor of law	04-May-64	112	B.L. 15, 635 f. 134	3493
Wood, Robert	Dublin, the city	prof: doctor of law	23-May-64	120	B.L. 15, 635 f. 134a	3494
Wood, Simon	England, London	merchant	28-Sep-24	200	Dc2/58r	1239
Wood, Simon	England, London	merchant	18-May-25	80	Dc2/63v	1280
Woodroffe, Ffrancis	Dublin	gentry: gent	15-Jul-07	2000	Dc1/79v	487
Worrell, William	Dublin		27-Sep-00	200	Dc1/26r	174
Worrell, Francis	Dublin, the city	merchant	09-Jul-77	700	B.L. 19, 844 f. 137	3267
Worrell, Francis	Dublin, the city	merchant	09-Jul-77	700	Dc3/183r	2692
Worrell, William	Dublin		27-Sep-00	200	Dc1/26r	174
Worth, Edward		prof: bishop of Killaloe	05-Dec-66	1600	Dc3/43	2321
Worth, Edward		prof: bishop of Killaloe	03-Dec-64	3000	B.L. 15, 635 f. 146a	3512
Worth, Edward		prof: bishop of Killaloe	05-Dec-66	1600	Dc3/46	2323
Worth, Edward		prof: bishop of Killaloe	05-Dec-66	1600	Dc3/44	2322
Worth, William	Cork, the city	gentry: esquire	13-Nov-75	200	B.L. 19, 844 f. 85	3213
Worth, William	Cork, the city	gentry: esquire	13-Aug-80	1000	B.L. 15, 637 f. 38a	3915
Wotton, Thomas	Louth, Drogheda	merchant	07-May-23	200	Dc2/46v	1152
Wotton, Thomas	Louth, Drogheda	merchant	19-Nov-34	800	Dc2/222r	1992
Wotton, Walter	Dublin, Loghbragh	farmer	28-Nov-28	200	Dc2/118r	1552
Wray, Drury	Limerick, Rathcaman	gentry: esquire	25-Nov-62	800	B.L. 15, 635 f. 99a	3433
Wright, Arthur	Kilkenny, Killarie	gentry: gent	19-May-36	300	Dc2/251v	2125
Wright, Edward	Leitrim, Carrigdrumruske	prof: surgeon	11-Apr-35	400	Dc2/232r	2034
Wright, Henry	Cork, the city	merchant	22-Mar-69	480	B.L. 15, 636 f. 31a	3680
Wright, John	England, London	trade: clothworker and citizen	01-Jul-01	160	Dc1/33r	217
Wrightman, Ann	Dublin, Spricklestowne	other: widow	07-Nov-28	200	B.L. 19, 843 f. 47	2812
Wybrants, Daniel	Dublin, the city		28-Apr-57	4000	B.L. 19, 843 f. 191	3089
Wybrants, Peter	Dublin	merchant	15-Jun-27	300	Dc2/94v	1441
Wybrants, Peter	Dublin, the city	other: administrator of Theodore Schout	20-Mar-55	230	B.L. 19, 843 f. 157a	3029
Wynell, Thomas	England, London/ Middle Temple	gentry: esquire	04-Dec-67	500	Dc3/69	2378
Yard, James		merchant	30-Oct-70	2000	B.L. 15, 636 f. 77a	3757
Yarner, Abraham	Dublin, the city	gentry: esquire	09-Feb-61	1320	B.L. 15, 635 f. 65a	3380

Standard	County	Occupation	Date	Amount	MS No	Ident No
Yarner, Abraham	Dublin, the city	prof: doctor of phisick	29-Jan-53	600	B.L. 19, 843 f. 131	2978
Yeats, Richard	Cork, Youghall	merchant	03-Dec-74	380	B.L. 19, 844 f. 51a	3175
York, William	Limerick, the city	merchant	17-Jan-74	900	B.L. 19, 844 f. 25a	3147
Young, Agnes	Dublin	merchant: wife of				
		Nicholas	20-Aug-00	100	Dc1/25v	171
Young, George	Dublin		20-Apr-10	46	Dc1/95r	597
Young, Gerald	Dublin		27-Nov-07	26	Dc1/80r	494
Young, Gerald	Dublin		04-Aug-00	200	Dc1/25v	170
Young, Gerald	Dublin		03-Feb-97	400	Dc1/1r	3
Young, Gerald	Dublin		15-Apr-08	40	Dc1/81v	505
Young, Gerald	Dublin		20-Aug-00	100	Dc1/25v	171
Young, Gerald	Dublin		23-Dec-02	200	Dc1/42r	271
Young, Gerald	Dublin		05-Dec-07	130	Dc1/80v	497
Young, Gerald	Dublin		16-Nov-02	40	Dc1/40r	260
Young, Gerald	Dublin		19-Jun-07	40	Dc1/78v	479
Young, Gerald	Dublin		04-Aug-02	40	Dc1/39r	254
Young, Gerald	Dublin		07-May-97	86	Dc1/3r	20
Young, Gerald	Dublin		16-Apr-03	40	Dc1/46r	292
Young, Gerald	Dublin		01-Jul-06	40	Dc1/69v	421
Young, Gerald	Dublin		22-Apr-03	40	Dc1/46r	294
Young, Gerald	Dublin		21-Apr-08	30	Dc1/81r	507
Young, Gerald	Dublin		28-Jun-10	230	Dc1/98v	619
Young, Gerald	Dublin		12-Mar-11	40	Dc1/103r	645
Young, Gerald	Dublin		12-Aug-11	60	Dc1/106r	660
Young, Gerald	Dublin		03-Mar-98	40	Dc1/10v	74
Young, Gerald	Dublin		25-May-12	80	Dc1/114r	708
Young, Gerald	Dublin		27-Nov-06	56	Dc1/72r	437
Young, Gerald	Dublin		23-Nov-08	40	Dc1/84v	527
Young, Gerald	Dublin		06-Jun-00	40	Dc1/24r	160
Young, Gerald	Dublin		14-Jun-00	100	Dc1/24r	161
Young, Gerald	Dublin		22-Jun-99	400	Dc1/17r	116
Young, Gerald	Dublin		11-Mar-07	58	Dc1/75v	459
Young, Gerald	Dublin		18-Oct-08	40	Dc1/84r	524
Young, Gerald	Dublin		18-Oct-08	200	Dc1/84r	523
Young, Gerald	Dublin		23-Jun-00	100	Dc1/24v	166
Young, Gerald	Dublin		08-May-00	140	Dc1/23v	157
Young, Gerard	Dublin		14-Mar-00	50	Dc1/22r	147
Young, Maeve	Dublin	other: wife of Gerald	20-Aug-00	100	Dc1/25v	171
Young, Maude	Dublin	other: widow	07-Feb-14	200	Dc1/126r	782
Young, Nicholas	Dublin	merchant	05-May-03	40	Dc1/46v	297
Young, Nicholas	Dublin	merchant	30-Jan-01	30	Dc1/28r	189
Young, Nicholas	Dublin	merchant	20-Aug-00	100	Dc1/25v	171
Young, Nicholas	Dublin	merchant	23-Feb-02	60	Dc1/36v	238
Young, Richard	Dublin, the city	trade: scrivenor	21-Jun-81	140	B.L. 15, 637 f. 49	3934
Young, Richard	Dublin	trade: scrivenor	05-Jun-58	248	B.L. 15, 635 f. 55	3361

Standard	County	Occupation	Date	Amount	MS No	Ident No
Young, Richard	Dublin, the city	trade: scrivenor	22-Aug-59	120	B.L. 15, 635 f. 55a	3362
Young, Richard	Dublin	trade: scrivenor	20-Sep-59	230	B.L. 15, 635 f. 53a	3358
Young, Richard	Dublin, the city	trade: scrivenor	09-Jun-59	230	B.L. 15. 635 f. 47	3346
Young, Richard	Dublin	trade: scrivenor	01-Jun-59	100	B.L. 15, 635 f. 46a	3345
Young, Richard	Dublin	merchant	22-Apr-01	240	Dc1/30v	202
Young, Richard	Dublin, the city	trade: scrivenor	17-Jun-68	300	Dc3/78	2403
Young, Richard	Dublin	merchant	14-Nov-01	46	Dc1/34r	226
Young, Richard	Dublin, the city	trade: scrivenor	17-Jun-68	300	B.L. 15, 635 f. 219a	3644

CHAPTER 4:

ALPHABETICAL LISTING OF DEBTORS

In all over 10,000 people—5879 debtors and 4309 creditors—recorded transactions on the Irish staple towns between 1596 and 1687. Predictably the same individual appeared more than once and so the actual number of people using the staple was probably between 5000 and 6000. Here is an alphabetical listing of the standardised names of all of the debtors that appeared in the staple records, together with their address and, where given, their occupation/status (for a full discussion see Chapter 2).[1] The date on which the transaction was recorded, the amount of the bond, the reference to the original manuscript, and the identification number (which relates to the Staple CD ROM), are also listed here.[2]

---

[1] Constraints of space precluded the inclusion of any details on office held. For full details see Query 'A: Debtors - master list' on the Staple CD ROM and Jane Ohlmeyer, ed., *Using the Staple Database*, Section I.

[2] For details on the staple town or city, on the fate of the transaction, and for any accompanying text see the Staple CD ROM or the original manuscripts.

Standard	County	Occupation	Date	Amount	MS No	Ident No
?, Richard	Dublin, the city	gentry: gent	16-Jan-83	2000	B.L. 15, 637 f. 60a	3956
Abbott, Daniel	Dublin, Pimlico in the suburbs	gentry: esquire	04-Feb-76	800	Dc3/171v	2648
Abbott, Daniel	Dublin, Pimlico	gentry: esquire	04-Feb-76	800	B.L. 19, 844 f. 87	3215
Abbott, Daniel	Tipperary, Nenagh	gentry: knight	05-Apr-59	2100	B.L. 15, 635 f. 41a	3337
Abbott, Daniel	Dublin, the city	gentry: esquire	23-Jan-63	1075	B.L. 15, 635 f. 100a	3435
Acheson, Archibald	Armagh, Clancarny	gentry: knight	24-May-26	330	Dc2/78r	1368
Acheson, Archibald	Armagh, Clancarny	gentry: esquire	08-May-18	400	Dc2/14v	939
Acheson, Archibold	Armagh, Glancarry?	gentry: knight	04-Mar-26	400	Dc2/75r	1350
Acheson, George	Armagh, Cloncarny	gentry: baronet	20-Nov-59	2000	B.L. 15, 635 f. 54	3359
Adair, Andrew	Armagh, Shandrade	gentry: esquire	22-Apr-56	32	B.L. 19, 843 f. 180a	3067
Adair, Robert	Antrim, Ballemannagh	gentry: esquire	07-Dec-28	240	Dc2/120r	1561
Adair, Robert	Scotland, Kinhilt	gentry: son/heir of William	05-Dec-25	600	Dc2/71v	1329
Adair, William	Scotland, Kinhilt	gentry: esquire	05-Dec-25	600	Dc2/71v	1329
Adienke, George	Cavan, Clona	gentry: esquire	01-Jul-19	400	Dc2/24v	997
Adrian, Hubert	Dublin, the city		29-Jan-53	600	B.L. 19, 843 f. 131	2978
Adrian-Veerbeere, Catherine	Dublin, the city	other: widow	23-Jul-81	3000	B.L. 15, 637 f. 49a	3935
Adshed, Thomas	Dublin, Simonscourt	gentry: esquire	08-Jul-57	1200	B.L. 19, 843 f. 196a	3100
Adshed, Thomas	Dublin, Symonscourt	gentry: esquire	21-Jan-59	840	B.L. 15, 635 f. 40	3334
Agnew, Andrew	Scotland, Gallway, Whitehills	gentry: gent	22-Jun-85	1000	B.L. 15, 637 f. 100a	4030
Agnew, Patrick	Antrim, Killoughter	gentry: esquire	28-Jan-74	200	B.L. 19, 844 f. 25	3146
Agnew, Patrick	Antrim, Killoughter	gentry: esquire	05-Apr-79	440	B.L. 15, 637 f. 20a	3883
Aimes, Peter	Cavan, Tonnagh	gentry: esquire	15-Dec-26	300	Dc2/86v	1410
Alcock, Charles	Tipperary, Powerstowne	gentry: esquire	28-Oct-76	2000	Dc3/180r	2676
Alcock, Charles	Tipperary, Powerstowne	gentry: esquire	28-Oct-76	2000	B.L. 19, 844 f. 108	3235
Alfrey, William	Queen's Co., Ballinekill	gentry: gent	20-Jul-29	1000	Dc2/133v	1624
Allen, Charles	Cork, Kildrowinslegah?	gentry: gent	07-Apr-84	315	B.L. 15, 637 f.88	4005
Allen, Edward	Kildare, Bishopscourt	gentry: gent	25-Feb-98	300	Dc1/10r	71
Allen, George	Cork, Garigmaccowny	gentry: gent	03-Jan-72	600	B.L. 15, 636 f. 106a	3804
Allen, Henry	Kildare, Oughterard	farmer: freeholder	12-Aug-11	60	Dc1/106r	660
Allen, John	Kildare, Rewe	gentry: gent	23-May-35	100	Dc2/236r	2052
Allen, Lawrence	Kildare, Mawes	gentry: gent	20-Oct-57	600	B.L. 19, 843 f. 202	3110
Allen, Lawrence	Dublin, the city	merchant	13-Jun-53	700	B.L. 19, 843 f. 139a	2993
Allen, Lawrence	Dublin, the city	merchant	16-May-64	660	B.L. 15, 635 f. 130a	3488
Allen, Mathew	Dublin, Palmerstowne	gentry: esquire	28-Oct-31	40	Dc2/169r	1781
Allen, Mathew	Dublin, Palmerston	gentry: gent	22-Jun-26	200	Dc2/79v	1376
Allen, Mathew	Dublin, Palmerston	gentry: esquire	27-Jan-40	3000	B.L. 19, 843 f. 44a	2807
Allen, Mathew	Dublin, Palmerstowne	gentry: gent	16-Feb-36	240	Dc2/244v	2094
Allen, Mathew	Dublin, Palmerstowne	gentry: gent	09-Dec-35	240	Dc2/241v	2080
Allen, Mathew	Dublin, Palmerstowne	gentry: gent	04-May-30	400	Dc2/146r	1683
Allen, Mathew	Dublin, Palmerstowne	gentry: gent	18-Nov-31	150	Dc2/171v	1788
Allen, Mathew	Dublin, Palmerston	gentry: gent	27-Jun-27	1200	Dc2/95v	1446

Standard	County	Occupation	Date	Amount	MS No	Ident No
Allen, Mathew	Dublin, Palmerstowne	gentry: esquire	09-Jul-40	200	B.L. 19, 843 f. 59a	2837
Allen, Mathew	Dublin, Palmerston	gentry: gent	08-Jun-31	400	Dc2/164v	1762
Allen, Mathew	Dublin, Palmerston	gentry: esquire	02-Dec-26	240	Dc2/84v	1402
Allen, Mathew	Dublin, Palmerstowne	gentry: gent	05-Sep-34	200	Dc2/218v	1979
Allen, Mathew	Dublin, Palmerstowne	gentry: gent	05-Sep-34	200	Dc2/218v	1978
Allen, Mathew	Dublin, Palmerstowne	gentry: esquire	23-May-35	100	Dc2/236r	2052
Allen, Mathew	Dublin, Palmerstowne	gentry: gent	05-Sep-34	120	Dc2/219r	1980
Allen, Patrick	Kildare, Allenscourt	gentry: esquire	30-Dec-75	400	Dc3/171r	2646
Allen, Patrick	Kildare, Allenscourt/ StWoollst	gentry: esquire	30-Dec-75	400	B.L. 19, 844 f. 81	3209
Allen, Patrick	Kildare, Allenscourte	gentry: esquire	01-Jul-84	1000	B.L. 15, 637 f. 89	4007
Allen, Richard	Dublin, city	trade: tallow chandler	13-Nov-01	200	Dc1/34r	225
Allen, Richard	Kildare, Oughterard	farmer: son/heir of Henry	12-Aug-11	60	Dc1/106r	660
Allen, Thomas	Dublin		22-Feb-13	300	Dc1/119v	743
Anderson, William	Dublin	gentry: knight	09-May-36	1600	Dc2/250r	2117
Anderson, William	Dublin	gentry: knight	13-Jul-39	3000	B.L. 19, 843 f. 186	3079
Anderson, William	Dublin	gentry: knight	13-Jul-36	3000	Dc2/254v	2142
Andrews, James	Meath, the Fennor	farmer	27-Sep-37	189	Dc2/270v	2215
Andrews, Nicholas	Dublin, Castlecnocke	farmer	27-Sep-37	189	Dc2/270v	2215
Andrews, Patrick	Dublin, Terrston	farmer: husbandman	02-Jul-06	300	Dc1/69v	422
Andrews, Patrick	Dublin, the city		11-Feb-03	300	Dc1/44v	282
Andrews, Patrick	Dublin, Castlecnocke	farmer: son/heir of Nicholas	27-Sep-37	189	Dc2/270v	2215
Angon, Mable	Dublin, the city	gentry: wife of William, admin	17-Sep-56	2000	B.L. 19, 843 f. 184a	3076
Angon, William	Dublin, the city	gentry: gent, administrator	17-Sep-56	2000	B.L. 19, 843 f. 184a	3076
Annesley, Arthur		peer: earl of Anglesey	07-Oct-62	4000	B.L. 15, 635 f. 96a	3427
Annesley, Arthur		peer: earl of Anglesey	07-Oct-62	4000	B.L. 15, 635 f. 96	3426
Annesley, Francis	Kildare, Ballysonnan	gentry: esquire, s./heir of Jo	12-Nov-84	1200	B.L. 15, 637 f. 94a	4018
Annesley, John	Kildare, Ballysonnan	gentry: esquire	12-Nov-84	1200	B.L. 15, 637 f. 94a	4018
Aphugh, Richard	Louth, Carlingford	gentry: esquire	14-May-32	600	Dc2/180v	1825
Aphugh, Richard	Louth, Drogheda	gentry: esquire	16-May-33	200	Dc2/193v	1878
Aphugh, Richard	Louth, Newtowne	gentry: esquire	23-May-34	630	Dc2/211v	1951
Archbold, Andrew	Dublin	gentry: gent, s Pat of Wicklow	03-Jul-34	3000	Dc2/213v	1959
Archbold, Christopher	Kildare, Crookestowne	gentry: esquire	02-Dec-70	150	Dc3/132r	2506
Archbold, Christopher	Kildare, Crookestowne	gentry: gent	02-Jul-70	200	Dc3/122	2484
Archbold, Christopher	Dublin, Baldoyle	farmer	26-Nov-61	320	B.L. 15,635 f. 88	3412
Archbold, Christopher	Dublin, Baldoyle	farmer	26-Nov-61	220	B.L. 15, 635 f. 87a	3411
Archbold, Christopher	Cork, Crookstown	gentry: esquire	02-Dec-70	50	B.L. 15, 636 f. 80a	3762
Archbold, Christopher	Kildare, Crookestowne	gentry: gent	02-Jul-70	200	B.L. 15, 636 f. 70	3742
Archbold, Maurice	Dublin, Kilmacudd	gentry: gent	06-May-35	600	Dc2/234v	2046

Standard	County	Occupation	Date	Amount	MS No	Ident No
Archbold, Nicholas	Wicklow, Kinleiston?	gentry: gent	27-Nov-06	56	Dc1/72r	437
Archbold, Patrick	Wicklow, Kinleston	gentry: gent	11-Mar-14	80	Dc1/128r	793
Archbold, Patrick	Wicklow, Kendleston	gentry: gent	16-Jun-08	200	Dc1/83v	520
Archbold, Patrick	Dublin, the city	trade: barber-surgeon	26-Nov-61	320	B.L. 15,635 f. 88	3412
Archbold, Peter	Dublin, Baldoyle	farmer: yeoman	26-Nov-61	320	B.L. 15,635 f. 88	3412
Archbold, Richard	Dublin, the city	merchant	11-Jan-17	100	Dc2/3v	887
Archbold, Wiliam	Wicklow, Kinleston	gentry: gent	26-Apr-21	200	Dc2/35r	1068
Archbold, William	Dublin, Cloughransworde	gentry: gent	15-Jun-29	200	Dc2/132r	1618
Archbold, William	Wicklow, Kinleiston?	gentry: gent	27-Nov-06	56	Dc1/72r	437
Archbold, William	Kildare, Tymolin	gentry: gent	20-Nov-20	400	Dc2/33r	1051
Archbold, William	Kildare, Crookestowne	gentry: esquire	07-Dec-27	1000	Dc2/101v	1472
Archbold, William	Kildare, Crookstowne?	gentry: son/heir of Chris	02-Jul-70	200	Dc3/122	2484
Archbold, William	Kildare, Crookestowne	gentry: gent	02-Dec-70	150	Dc3/132r	2506
Archbold, William	Dublin, Kinleston	gentry: gent	12-May-05	120	Dc1/59r	361
Archbold, William	Cork, Crookstown	gentry: gent	02-Dec-70	50	B.L. 15, 636 f. 80a	3762
Archbold, William	Kildare, Crookestowne	gentry: gent, s./heir of Chris	02-Jul-70	200	B.L. 15, 636 f. 70	3742
Archer, Edward	Wexford, Aghclamman	gentry: gent	16-Nov-30	200	Dc2/155v	1723
Archer, John	Dublin, the city	trade: carpenter	30-Sep-35	400	Dc2/239r	2066
Archer, Patrick	Meath, Riverstowne	gentry: gent	27-May-75	300	B.L. 19, 844 f. 68	3196
Ardagh, Arthur	King's Co., Pallas	gentry: esquire	28-Jun-72	210	Dc3/147r	2555
Ardagh, Arthur	King's Co., Pallis	gentry: esquire	02-Dec-72	200	Dc3/150r	2564
Ardagh, Arthur	King's Co., Lorton More	gentry: esquire	13-Jun-73	300	Dc3/157v	2585
Ardagh, Arthur	King's Co., Loretowne	gentry: esquire	18-Jun-73	600	Dc3/157v	2587
Ardagh, Arthur	King's Co., Loretowne	gentry: esquire	18-Jun-73	600	B.L. 15, 636 f. 136a	3849
Ardagh, Arthur	King's Co., Pallice	gentry: esquire	09-Dec-84	1300	B.L. 15, 637 f. 96a	4022
Ardagh, Arthur	Queen's Co., Pallis	gentry: esquire	02-Dec-72	200	B.L. 15, 636 f. 133	3842
Ardaughstone, James	Louth	gentry: gent	08-Oct-29	200	Dc2/136v	1639
Armitage, Timothy	Louth, Atherdee	gentry: gent	12-Sep-74	200	B.L. 19, 844 f. 44	3168
Armitage, William	Dublin, Donore	gentry: esquire	07-May-66	700	Dc3/27	2284
Armitage, William	Dublin, Upper Coombe	gentry: gent	24-Dec-66	200	Dc3/50	2332
Armitage, William	Louth, Atherdee	gentry: gent	12-Sep-74	200	B.L. 19, 844 f. 44	3168
Armitage, William	Dublin, Donore	gentry: gent	04-Jun-68	720	Dc3/78	2401
Armitage, William	Dublin, Donore	gentry: gent	04-Jun-68	720	B.L. 15, 635 f. 220	3645
Armstrong, Martin	Leitrim, Launghill	gentry: esquire	21-Sep-86	540	B.L. 15, 637 f 112	4052
Arnold, Henry	Roscommon?, Athlone	merchant	17-Jun-13	140	Dc1/122r	758
Arnold, Henry	Roscommon?, Athlone	merchant	12-Jul-06	106	Dc1/70r	424
Arnop, William	Cork, Dunmanway	gentry: esquire	10-Jun-71	200	Dc3/138r	2523
Arnop, William	Cork, Dunmanway	gentry: esquire	10-Jun-71	200	B.L. 15, 636 f. 84a	3769
Arnop, William	Cork, Downmanway	gentry: esquire	10-Feb-81	400	B.L. 15, 637 f. 42a	3923
Arthur, Bennett	Dublin, Great Cabragh	gentry: gent	17-Sep-57	500	B.L. 19, 843 f. 196	3099
Arthur, Dymphna	Dublin, the city	gentry: widow	09-Jun-68	300	Dc3/78	2402
Arthur, Dymphna	Dublin, the city	gentry: widow	09-Jun-68	300	B.L. 15, 635 f. 219	3643
Arthur, Edward	Dublin	merchant	01-Jul-15	1000	Dc1/139r	866

Standard	County	Occupation	Date	Amount	MS No	Ident No
Arthur, Edward	Dublin		01-Sep-28	630	Dc2/114v	1536
Arthur, George	Dublin	merchant	01-Jul-15	1000	Dc1/139r	866
Arthur, Patrick	Dublin, Great Cabragh	gentry: gent	17-Sep-57	500	B.L. 19, 843 f. 196	3099
Arthur, Robert	Dublin, Hackettstowne	gentry: gent	17-Feb-75	200	B.L. 19, 844 f. 52	3176
Arthur, Robert	Dublin, Hacketstowne	gentry: gent	17-Feb-75	200	Dc3/164v	2623
Arthur, Robert	Dublin, Hacketstowne	gentry: esquire	12-Feb-80	3200	B.L. 15, 637 f. 27a	3896
Arthur, Robert	Dublin, the city	gentry: gent, s. of Dymphna	09-Jun-68	300	B.L. 15, 635 f. 219	3643
Arthur, Robert	Dublin, the city	gentry: gent	09-Jun-68	300	Dc3/78	2402
Arundel, George	Tyrone, Omagh	gentry: esquire	08-Jun-39	200	B.L. 19, 843 f. 20a	2759
Ash, Edward	Kildare, the Nase	gentry: gent	23-Feb-99	60	Dc1/15v	107
Ash, John	Kildare, Moyvally	gentry: gent	08-Jul-09	200	Dc1/90r	563
Ash, John	Kildare, Moyvally	gentry: gent	21-Nov-09	105	Dc1/92v	579
Ash, Richard	Cavan, Lissemayne	gentry: esquire	11-May-37	400	Dc2/263v	2182
Ash, Richard	Cavan, Lisnemeaghan	gentry: esquire	06-May-35	220	Dc2/235v	2045
Ash, Thomas	Kildare, Moyvallie	gentry: gent	12-May-35	600	Dc2/235r	2048
Ash, Thomas	Kildare, the Nase	gentry: son/heir of Edward	23-Feb-99	60	Dc1/15v	107
Ash, Thomas	Kildare, the Nace	gentry: gent	14-May-24	300	Dc2/55r	1215
Ash, Thomas	Kildare, Moyvallye	gentry: gent	12-May-35	600	B.L. 19, 843 f. 6a	2731
Ash, Thomas	Kildare, the Nace	gentry: gent	12-May-24	300	Dc2/54v	1213
Ash, Thomas	Meath, St. John's	gentry: esquire	07-Feb-56	250	B.L. 19, 843 f. 168a	3051
Ash, Thomas	Kildare, the Nace	gentry: gent	13-May-24	300	Dc2/55r	1214
Askin, John	Dublin	merchant	24-May-23	600	Dc2/47v	1160
Atkinson, James	Louth, Atherdee	gentry: gent	23-Jan-77	300	Dc3/181v	2682
Atkinson, James	Louth, Atherdee	gentry: gent	23-Jan-77	300	B.L. 19, 844 f. 115	3244
Aungier, Francis	Longford?	peer: baron Longford	11-Mar-67	2100	Dc3/56	2345
Aungier, Francis	Longford?	peer: baron Longford	11-Mar-67	1100	B.L. 15, 635 f. 203	3615
Aylmer, Andrew	Kildare, Donedea	gentry: baronet	02-Jun-76	200	Dc3/175r	2660
Aylmer, Andrew	Kildare, Donedea	gentry: baronet	02-Jun-76	200	B.L. 19, 844 f. 95	3222
Aylmer, Charles	Limerick, Mahowna	gentry: son/heir of Joshua	09-Jul-12	66	Dc1/115r	716
Aylmer, Christopher	Meath, Ballrath	gentry: knight	28-Aug-63	600	B.L. 15, 635 f. 123a	3474
Aylmer, Garret	Meath, Ballrath	gentry: baronet	21-Sep-78	800	B.L. 15, 637 f. 11a	3868
Aylmer, George	Queen's Co., Ley	gentry: esquire	17-Jun-24	100	Dc2/56v	1225
Aylmer, Gerald	Kildare, Donada	gentry: esquire	27-Jan-97	200	Dc1/1r	1
Aylmer, Gerald	Dublin, Monnckston	gentry: knight	22-Jun-15	500	Dc1/138v	858
Aylmer, Gerald	Meath, Paineston?	gentry: gent	22-Jun-15	500	Dc1/138v	858
Aylmer, Gerald	Kildare, Drunnada	gentry: knight	08-Dec-18	120	Dc2/19r	963
Aylmer, Gerald	Meath, Balrath	gentry: baronet	11-Apr-76	300	B.L. 19, 844 f. 92	3219
Aylmer, Gerald	Meath, Trym	gentry: gent, s./heir of Geo	02-Dec-97	1500	Dc1/8v	59
Aylmer, Gerald	Meath, Balrath	gentry: esquire	23-Jun-37	2060	Dc2/266r	2193
Aylmer, Gerald	Meath, Castletowne Moylagh	gentry: gent	07-Jun-97	280	Dc1/4v	30

Standard	County	Occupation	Date	Amount	MS No	Ident No
Aylmer, Gerald	Meath, Balrath	gentry: baronet	24-Oct-82	1100	B.L. 15, 637 f. 64	3963
Aylmer, Gerald	Meath, Ballrath	gentry: knight	28-Jan-73	150	B.L. 15, 636 f. 127	3834
Aylmer, Gerald	Meath, Balrath	gentry:				
		knight and baronet	03-Jun-73	500	B.L. 15, 636 f. 137a	3851
Aylmer, Gerald	Meath, Balrath	gentry: baronet	13-Jul-83	1000	B.L. 15, 637 f. 77a	3988
Aylmer, Gerald	Meath, Ballrath	gentry:				
		knight and baronet	16-Apr-72	300	B.L. 15, 636 f. 103	3799
Aylmer, Gerald	Meath, Ballrath	gentry:				
		knight and baronet	15-Jul-72	100	B.L. 15, 636 f. 115	3820
Aylmer, Gerald	Meath, Balrath	gentry: esquire	09-Oct-63	150	B.L. 15, 635 f. 122	3471
Aylmer, James	Kildare, Hartwell	gentry: son/heir of				
		James snr	20-Feb-66	500	Dc3/23	2275
Aylmer, James	Kildare, Hartwell	gentry: esquire	20-Feb-66	500	Dc3/23	2275
Aylmer, James	Kildare, Hartwell	gentry: gent, son/heir of				
		Jas	05-Sep-65	200	Dc3/14	2251
Aylmer, James	Kildare, Hartwell	gentry: esquire	05-Sep-65	200	Dc3/14	2251
Aylmer, John	Kildare, Ballykennon	gentry: esquire	22-Jun-15	500	Dc1/138v	858
Aylmer, Joshua	Limerick, Mahowna	gentry: esquire	09-Jul-12	66	Dc1/115r	716
Aylmer, Mathew	Kildare, Ballycaghan	gentry: esquire	18-Nov-35	1000	Dc2/240r	2070
Aylmer, Mathew	Kildare, Newtowne	gentry: esquire	27-May-33	400	Dc2/195r	1884
Aylmer, Thomas	Kildare, the Lyons	gentry: esquire	23-Feb-31	200	Dc2/160r	1743
Aylmer, Thomas	Kildare, Lyons	gentry: esquire	17-Jun-62	800	B.L. 15, 635 f. 92a	3419
Babe, John	Louth, Darver	gentry: gent	10-Feb-36	200	Dc2/244r	2092
Badham, Thomas	Cork, Ballyhine	gentry: gent	15-Oct-86	100	B.L. 15, 637 f. 110a	4048
Badham, Thomas	Cork, Raheene	gentry: gent	27-Sep-84	1000	B.L. 15, 637 f. 93	4015
Badham, Thomas	Cork, Ballyhoon	gentry: gent	01-Jan-39	900	B.L. 15, 637 f. 113a	4057
Bagbeere, Nicholas	Cork, Youghall	merchant	05-Jan-65	500	B.L. 15, 635 f. 202	3613
Bagnal, Dudley	Carlow, Dunleckney	gentry: esquire	25-Jan-64	1000	B.L. 15, 635 f. 127	3481
Bagnal, George	Carlow, Dunleckney	gentry: esquire	10-Jul-18	500	Dc2/15v	947
Bagnal, Nicholas	Carlow, Loghlin	gentry: gent	06-May-05	127	Dc1/58r	356
Bagnal, Walter	Carlow, Dunleckny	gentry: esquire	25-Nov-36	1000	Dc2/257v	2158
Bagot, David	Limerick, Baggottstowne	gentry: gent	02-Jul-41	840	B.L. 19, 843 f. 107	2933
Bagot, John	Limerick, Ballygormane	gentry: gent	27-Aug-40	1000	B.L. 19, 843 f. 68a	2856
Bagot, Maurice	Limerick, Boggostowne	gentry: gent	26-Sep-39	600	B.L. 19, 843 f. 40a	2799
Bagot, Maurice	Limerick, Baggottstowne	gentry: gent	02-Jul-41	840	B.L. 19, 843 f. 107	2933
Bagot, Maurice	Limerick, Baggoston	gentry: gent	07-May-41	1050	B.L. 19, 843 f. 91	2901
Bagot, Patrick	Limerick, Baggottstowne	gentry: gent	02-Jul-41	840	B.L. 19, 843 f. 107	2933
Bagot, William	Dublin, the city	merchant	25-Feb-34	200	Dc2/207v	1934
Bagshaw, Edward	Dublin, the city	gentry: knight	15-Feb-53	1000	B.L. 19, 843 f. 141a	2997
Bagshaw, Edward	Dublin, Ffinglas	gentry: knight	29-Jun-35	1000	Dc2/238v	2063
Bailey, William		prof: bishop of Clonfert	19-Apr-61	600	B.L. 15, 635 f. 71a	3387
Baker, Benjamin	Queen's Co., Milltowne	gentry: gent	16-May-68	400	Dc3/75	2394
Baker, Benjamin	King's Co., Miltowne	gentry: gent	16-May-68	400	B.L. 19, 844 f. 21a	3141
Baker, John	Cork, Carrickgrohane	gentry: esquire	16-May-68	400	B.L. 19, 844 f. 21a	3141

Standard	County	Occupation	Date	Amount	MS No	Ident No
Baker, John	Cork, Carygroghan	gentry: esquire	18-Jun-73	180	Dc3/157v	2586
Baker, John	Cork, Carrickgrohan	gentry: esquire	16-May-68	400	Dc3/75	2394
Baker, John	Cork, Carigrohane	gentry: esquire	24-Apr-68	1200	B.L. 15, 635 f. 217	3639
Baker, John	Cork, Carrygroghan	gentry: esquire	18-Jun-73	180	B.L. 15, 636 f. 135	3846
Baldwin, John	King's Co., Geeshill	gentry: esquire	15-Feb-70	400	Dc3/115	2469
Baldwin, John	King's Co., Geeshell	gentry: esquire	15-Feb-70	400	B.L. 15, 636 f. 55	3717
Balfe, Oliver	Meath, Peppardstowne	gentry: gent	21-Nov-34	200	Dc2/222v	1994
Balfe, Oliver	Meath, Gallmoulstone	gentry: gent	21-Feb-28	400	Dc2/104v	1487
Balfe, Richard	Meath, Galmoleston	gentry: gent	18-Jun-97	331	Dc1/4v	32
Balfe, Richard	Meath, Gallmerstowne	gentry: gent	30-Jan-73	200	B.L. 15, 636 f. 130	3838
Balfe, Richard	Meath, Pepperstowne	gentry: son/heir of Robert	25-Jun-63	800	B.L. 15, 635 f. 110	3450
Balfe, Robert	Meath, Pepperstowne	gentry: gent	25-Jun-63	800	B.L. 15, 635 f. 110	3450
Balfour, Charles	Fermanagh, Lisneske	gentry: esquire	13-Dec-58	400	B.L. 15, 635 f. 45	3342
Balfour, Charles	Fermanagh, Lysneskea	gentry: esquire	14-May-80	5000	B.L. 15, 637 f. 33	3906
Ball, Bartholomew	Dublin, the city	gentry: gent	24-Feb-36	100	Dc2/246r	2099
Ball, Edward	Dublin, the city		25-Nov-20	200	Dc2/33v	1054
Ball, Edward	Dublin, the city		18-May-25	80	Dc2/63v	1280
Ball, Francis	Meath, Clanee	farmer: yeoman	26-Apr-67	130	Dc3/60	2353
Ball, Robert	Dublin, the city	gentry: gent	14-Apr-71	3000	Dc3/137v	2522
Ball, Robert	Dublin, the city	gentry: gent	14-Apr-71	3000	B.L. 15, 636 f. 78	3758
Ball, Thomas	Armagh, Glasdroman	gentry: esquire	13-Feb-67	220	Dc3/53	2338
Ball, Thomas	Dublin, the city	gentry: gent, s./heir of Bart	24-Feb-36	100	Dc2/246r	2099
Bancroft, Richard	King's Co., Curroughlanty	gentry: gent	29-Nov-67	407	B.L. 15, 635 f. 204	3617
Barker, Edward	Wexford, Wexford	trade: son/heir of William	26-Sep-74	100	B.L. 19, 844 f. 39	3163
Barker, William	Wexford, Wexford	trade: tanner	26-Sep-74	100	B.L. 19, 844 f. 39	3163
Barley, John	Louth, Drogheda	trade: miller	04-Aug-73	40	B.L. 15, 636 f. 138	3852
Barnes, Toby	Dublin, the city	gentry: gent	04-Mar-70	400	Dc3/117	2473
Barnes, Toby	Dublin, the city	gentry: gent	23-Jul-67	400	Dc3/65	2369
Barnes, Toby	Dublin, the city	gentry: gent	23-Jul-67	400	B.L. 15, 635 f. 205	3619
Barnes, Toby	Dublin, the city	gentry: gent	04-Mar-70	400	B.L. 15, 636 f. 56a	3719
Barnewall, Alexander	Meath, Clowaneston	gentry: gent	27-Feb-23	50	Dc2/45v	1144
Barnewall, Christopher	Meath, Roeston	gentry: gent	20-Nov-02	300	Dc1/40v	261
Barnewall, Christopher	Louth, Rathesker	gentry: esquire	14-May-34	1600	Dc2/211r	1949
Barnewall, Christopher	Louth, Rahesker	gentry: esquire	12-Jun-29	800	Dc2/131v	1616
Barnewall, Christopher	Louth, Rahesker?	gentry: gent	17-Oct-22	200	Dc2/42v	1124
Barnewall, Christopher	Dublin, Turvy	gentry: gent	03-Aug-53	345	B.L. 19, 843 f. 133a	2982
Barnewall, Christopher	Louth, Rathesker	gentry: esquire	25-Aug-29	200	Dc2/136r	1635
Barnewall, Christopher	Meath, Crackanstowne	gentry: gent	09-Feb-28	200	Dc2/104r	1484
Barnewall, Edward	Dublin, Balbriggen	gentry: esquire	27-Sep-31	200	Dc2/168v	1778
Barnewall, Francis	Dublin, Corbally	gentry: esquire	13-Feb-67	2300	Dc3/53	2337
Barnewall, Francis	Dublin, Corbellies	gentry: esquire	29-Nov-67	264	Dc3/68	2376
Barnewall, Francis	Dublin, Corbillies	gentry: esquire	29-Nov-67	264	B.L. 15, 635 f. 213	3631

Standard	County	Occupation	Date	Amount	MS No	Ident No
Barnewall, Henry		peer: viscount Kingsland	13-Feb-67	2300	Dc3/53	2337
Barnewall, Henry	Dublin, Castleknock	gentry: esquire	15-Jan-99	800	Dc1/14r	100
Barnewall, James	Dublin, Donbroe	gentry: esquire	07-Jan-36	400	Dc2/243r	2088
Barnewall, James	Meath, Balrach Rathteboye	gentry: gent	18-Jun-07	75	Dc1/78v	478
Barnewall, James	Dublin, Donbroe?	gentry: esquire	15-Apr-36	1400	Dc2/249r	2114
Barnewall, James	Dublin, Dunbroe	gentry: gent	15-Feb-23	400	Dc2/45r	1142
Barnewall, James	Dublin, Dunbrow	gentry: esquire	17-May-64	120	B.L. 15, 635 f. 133a	3492
Barnewall, John	Meath, Angor?	gentry: son/heir of Patrick	20-Nov-30	500	Dc2/156r	1725
Barnewall, John	Meath, Rathronan	gentry: gent	04-Feb-26	200	Dc2/73v	1340
Barnewall, John	Meath, Anngor	gentry: son/heir of Patrick	21-Jun-27	400	Dc2/95r	1444
Barnewall, John	Meath, Angor	gentry: s/h Patrick of Angor	24-Feb-34	700	Dc2/207v	1933
Barnewall, Martin	Dublin, Graingediew	gentry: esquire	13-Feb-67	2300	Dc3/53	2337
Barnewall, Nicholas	Dublin, Turvey	gentry: esquire	16-May-39	2000	B.L. 19, 843 f. 15a	2749
Barnewall, Nicholas	Dublin, Turny	gentry: esquire	24-Feb-34	700	Dc2/207v	1933
Barnewall, Nicholas	Dublin, Turrie?	gentry: esquire	17-Nov-40	600	B.L. 19, 843 f. 89a	2898
Barnewall, Nicholas	Dublin, Turvy	gentry: esquire	03-Aug-53	345	B.L. 19, 843 f. 133a	2982
Barnewall, Nicholas	Dublin, Turvey	gentry: esquire	16-May-39	2000	B.L. 19, 843 f. 16	2750
Barnewall, Patrick	Meath, Angor	gentry: gent	01-Dec-26	250	Dc2/84r	1400
Barnewall, Patrick	Meath, Fflemmingston	gentry: gent	15-Oct-18	120	Dc2/16v	951
Barnewall, Patrick	Meath, Kilbrew	gentry: gent	07-May-13	140	Dc1/120v	748
Barnewall, Patrick	Meath, Kilbrewe	gentry: esquire	24-Feb-34	700	Dc2/207v	1933
Barnewall, Patrick	Meath, Angor	gentry: gent	24-Feb-34	700	Dc2/207v	1933
Barnewall, Patrick	Meath, Kilbrewe	gentry: gent	29-May-00	400	Dc1/23v	158
Barnewall, Patrick	Meath, Kilbrewe	gentry: esquire	26-Feb-41	1600	B.L. 19, 843 f. 87	2893
Barnewall, Patrick	Dublin, Grasedowe	gentry: knight	17-Feb-01	600	Dc1/29r	192
Barnewall, Patrick	Meath, Kilbrue	gentry: esquire	13-May-15	1500	Dc1/137v	852
Barnewall, Patrick	Meath, Kilbrewe	gentry: gent	12-Dec-05	108	Dc1/64r	386
Barnewall, Patrick	Meath, Kilbrew	gentry: gent	21-Jun-13	50	Dc1/122v	762
Barnewall, Patrick	Meath, Angor	gentry: gent	30-Nov-26	200	Dc2/84r	1399
Barnewall, Patrick	Meath, Kilbrewe	gentry: esquire	07-May-30	200	Dc2/146v	1685
Barnewall, Patrick	Meath, Dunboyn	gentry: gent	26-Jun-24	200	Dc2/57r	1229
Barnewall, Patrick	Dublin, Shankill	gentry: esquire	24-May-25	400	Dc2/64r	1283
Barnewall, Patrick	Meath, Angor	gentry: gent	20-Nov-30	500	Dc2/156r	1725
Barnewall, Patrick	Meath, Dunboyn	gentry: gent	20-May-01	60	Dc1/32r	210
Barnewall, Patrick	Meath, Arrardston	gentry: gent	28-May-08	40	Dc1/83r	516
Barnewall, Patrick	Meath, Kilbrew	gentry: esquire	25-Jun-29	400	Dc2/134r	1626
Barnewall, Patrick	Meath, Kilbrue	gentry: esquire	12-Jul-23	200	Dc2/49v	1174
Barnewall, Patrick	Meath, Anngor	gentry: gent	21-Jun-27	400	Dc2/95r	1444
Barnewall, Patrick	Meath, Kilbrewe	gentry: esquire	28-Apr-30	200	Dc2/144v	1675
Barnewall, Patrick	Meath, Shallan	gentry: gent, s of Dame Cecily	08-Mar-19	80	Dc2/21r	977
Barnewall, Patrick	Meath, Shallon	gentry: gent?	07-Nov-17	300	Dc2/10v	917

Standard	County	Occupation	Date	Amount	MS No	Ident No
Barnewall, Patrick	Dublin, Wespelston	gentry: esquire	28-Jun-15	300	Dc1/139v	864
Barnewall, Patrick	Dublin, Shankill	gentry: gent	15-Jun-18	200	Dc2/15r	943
Barnewall, Peter	Dublin, Tyrenure	gentry: esquire	27-Nov-10	100	Dc1/101r	633
Barnewall, Peter	Dublin, Tyrenure	gentry: esquire	15-Jul-25	400	Dc2/68v	1310
Barnewall, Peter	Dublin, Tirenure	gentry: esquire	15-Jun-18	200	Dc2/15r	943
Barnewall, Peter	Dublin, Tyrenure	gentry: esquire	10-Feb-36	1000	Dc2/244v	2093
Barnewall, Richard	Meath, Cryckeston	gentry: esquire	29-May-00	400	Dc1/23v	158
Barnewall, Richard	Dublin, Tyrenure	gentry: gent	08-Jun-41	400	B.L. 19, 843 f. 117	2953
Barnewall, Richard	Dublin, Tyrenure	gentry: esquire	17-Aug-46	100	B.L. 19, 843 f. 122	2963
Barnewall, Richard	Meath, Crickston	gentry: baronet	30-Jun-25	200	Dc2/67r	1301
Barnewall, Richard	Meath, Crickston	gentry: baronet	17-Nov-40	600	B.L. 19, 843 f. 89a	2898
Barnewall, Richard	Meath, Crickston	gentry: knight and baronet	11-Nov-25	162	Dc2/69v	1317
Barnewall, Robert	Dublin, Dunbrowe	gentry: gent	26-Jan-66	44	Dc3/20	2267
Barnewall, Robert	Meath, Rosetowne	gentry: esquire	14-Jul-66	200	Dc3/33	2296
Barnewall, Robert	Meath, Roestowne	gentry: gent	12-Dec-32	400	Dc2/188r	1856
Barnewall, Robert	Dublin, Shankill	gentry: esquire	03-Apr-34	500	Dc2/210r	1945
Barnewall, Robert	Meath, Roestowne	gentry: esquire	23-Jun-37	2060	Dc2/266r	2193
Barnewall, Robert	Dublin, Shanaghchoyle	gentry: gent	27-Sep-33	200	Dc2/200r	1903
Barnewall, Robert	Louth, Pochanstowne	gentry: gent	10-Feb-29	240	Dc2/124r	1580
Barnewall, Robert	Meath, Robertston	gentry: gent	21-Feb-06	400	Dc1/65v	396
Barnewall, Robert	Meath, Trymleston	peer: baron Trimleston	30-Nov-98	300	Dc1/13v	96
Barnewall, Robert	Meath, Trimbletston	peer: baron Trimleston	07-May-13	140	Dc1/120v	748
Barnewall, Robert	Dublin, Donbroe	gentry: esquire	27-Nov-10	100	Dc1/101r	633
Barnewall, Robert	Dublin?, Shankill?	gentry: son/heir of Patrick	24-May-25	400	Dc2/64r	1283
Barnewall, Robert	Meath, Trimbleston	peer: baron Trimletston	13-Feb-00	133	Dc1/21v	143
Barnewall, Robert	Louth, Poughanstowne	gentry: gent	14-May-34	1600	Dc2/211r	1949
Barnewall, Robert	Louth?	gentry: brother of Christopher	25-Aug-29	200	Dc2/136r	1635
Barnewall, Robert	Dublin	merchant	05-Aug-18	100	Dc2/16r	950
Barnewall, Robert	Meath, Rosetowne	gentry: esquire	14-Jul-66	200	Dc3/33	2294
Barnewall, Robert	Louth, Rathesker	gentry: son/heir of Chris	25-Aug-29	200	Dc2/136r	1635
Barnewall, Robert	Louth, Pochanstowne	gentry: gent	01-Jul-29	120	Dc2/135r	1630
Barnewall, Robert	Meath, Trimletston	peer: baron Trimleston	17-Apr-00	120	Dc1/23r	153
Barnewall, Robert	Dublin, Shankill	gentry: gent	04-May-30	200	Dc2/145r	1678
Barnewall, Robert	Meath, Rosetowne	gentry: esquire	14-Jul-66	100	Dc3/33	2295
Barnewall, Robert	Meath, Stacallane?	gentry: gent?	16-Mar-03	400	Dc1/45v	288
Barnewall, Robert	Meath, Stacalane	gentry: gent	17-Mar-03	400	Dc1/45v	289
Barnewall, Thomas	Meath, Robarston	gentry: esquire	10-Jan-27	100	Dc2/87v	1413
Barnewall, Thomas	Meath, Castlebarnewall	gentry: esquire	30-Apr-24	500	Dc2/54v	1211
Barnewall, Thomas	Meath, Castlebarnewall	gentry: esquire	05-May-26	160	Dc2/76v	1360
Barnewall, Thomas	Meath, Robertston	gentry: gent	30-Nov-09	500	Dc1/93r	584
Barnewall, Thomas	Meath, Castlebarnewall	gentry: esquire	08-Feb-23	280	Dc2/44v	1138
Barnewall, Thomas	Meath, Castlebarnewall	gentry: esquire	08-Jun-22	160	Dc2/41r	1112

Standard	County	Occupation	Date	Amount	MS No	Ident No
Barnewall, Thomas	Meath, Roberstowne	gentry: esquire	18-Aug-28	300	Dc2/114r	1533
Barnewall, Ulfran?	Dublin	merchant	07-Mar-98	40	Dc1/10r	73
Barrett, John	Cork, Castlemore	gentry: esquire	23-Aug-77	240	B.L. 19, 844 f. 141	3271
Barrett, John	Cork, Castlemore	gentry: esquire	02-May-78	140	Dc3/188r	2710
Barrett, John	Cork, Castlemore	gentry: esquire	28-Apr-77	200	B.L. 19, 844 f. 122	3251
Barrett, John	Cork, Castlemore	gentry: esquire	27-Jan-77	1000	B.L. 19, 844 f. 117	3246
Barrett, John	Cork, Castlemore	gentry: esquire	02-May-78	240	B.L. 19, 844 f. 151	3282
Barrett, John	Cork, Castlemore	gentry: esquire	26-Nov-78	600	B.L. 19, 844 f. 173	3304
Barrett, John	Cork, Castlemore	gentry: esquire	02-Jun-85	1240	B.L. 15, 637 f. 98a	4026
Barrett, John	Cork, Castlemore	gentry: esquire	27-Nov-86	2000	B.L. 15, 637 f. 111	4049
Barrett, John	Cork, Castlemore	gentry: esquire	19-Feb-87	2500	B.L. 15, 637 f. 112a	4053
Barrett, John	Cork, Castlemore	gentry: esquire	24-Feb-79	600	B.L. 15, 637 f. 12a	3870
Barrett, John	Cork, Castlemore, Barretts	gentry: esquire	23-May-83	1360	B.L. 15, 637 f. 78	3989
Barrett, John	Cork, Castlemore, Barretts	gentry: esquire	23-May-83	960	B.L. 15, 637 f. 78a	3990
Barrett, John	Cork, Castlemore	gentry: esquire	28-May-85	300	B.L. 15, 637 f. 98	4025
Barrett, Magne?	Cork, Trabolligane	gentry: gent	14-Jul-40	400	B.L. 19, 843 f. 75	2869
Barrett, William	Mayo, Rosse	gentry: gent	21-May-10	500	Dc1/96v	606
Barron, Edmund	Kildare, Kilbegge	gentry: gent, brother of James	15-Jul-11	700	Dc1/104v	654
Barron, Edward	Kildare, Courhilly?	gentry: son/heir of James	15-Jul-11	700	Dc1/104v	654
Barron, James	Kildare, Currihille	gentry: gent	15-Jul-11	700	Dc1/104v	654
Barron, James	Kildare, Cuiryhills	gentry: gent	22-May-09	140	Dc1/89r	557
Barron, James	Kildare, Kilbegges	gentry: gent	04-Aug-02	40	Dc1/39r	254
Barron, Jeffrey	Tipperary, Clonmell	gentry: esquire	10-Mar-36	100	Dc2/247r	2103
Barry, Benjamin	Tipperary, Ballicregan	gentry: gent	10-Dec-68	400	Dc3/86	2417
Barry, Benjamin	Tipperary, Ballicregan	gentry: gent	08-Jan-69	400	Dc3/88	2421
Barry, Benjamin	Dublin, Ballycregan	gentry: gent	08-Jan-69	400	B.L. 15, 636 f. 24	3666
Barry, Benjamin	Tipperary, Ballycregan	gentry: gent	10-Dec-68	400	B.L. 15, 635 f. 229	3663
Barry, David	Cork, Leambary	gentry: gent, son/heir of Garret	09-Jun-76	1100	B.L. 19, 844 f. 99	3226
Barry, David	Cork?	peer: earl of Barrymore	20-Jun-39	1600	B.L. 19, 843 f. 11	2740
Barry, David	Cork, Leannlare	gentry: son/heir of Garrett	13-Jul-70	400	B.L. 15, 636 f. 74	3750
Barry, David	Cork, Leamlare	gentry: gent	20-Mar-79	742	B.L. 15, 637 f. 13a	3872
Barry, Garret	Cork, Leambary	gentry: gent	09-Jun-76	1100	B.L. 19, 844 f. 99	3226
Barry, Garret	Cork, Carriginsky	gentry: gent	01-Oct-74	1000	B.L. 19, 844 f. 37	3161
Barry, Garret	Cork, Bishops Island	gentry: son/heir of William	01-May-65	300	B.L. 15, 635 f. 194a	3599
Barry, Garret	Cork, Barnanstowne	gentry: gent, son/heir of Wm	30-Dec-67	1772	B.L. 15, 635 f. 216a	3638
Barry, Garret	Cork, Barranstowne	gentry: son/heir of William	01-May-65	220	B.L. 15, 635 f. 157	3531
Barry, Garret	Cork, Barnanstowne	gentry: son/heir of William	30-Dec-67	3544	B.L. 15, 635 f. 216	3637
Barry, Garret	Cork, Leannlare	gentry: gent	13-Jul-70	400	B.L. 15, 636 f. 74	3750

Standard	County	Occupation	Date	Amount	MS No	Ident No
Barry, Humphrey	Dublin, Belchampe	gentry: gent	17-Sep-57	200	B.L. 19, 843 f. 195a	3098
Barry, James	Cork, Walshtonn	gentry: gent	16-Dec-14	100	Dc1/134r	834
Barry, James	Cork, Annagh	gentry: esquire	04-Apr-36	2000	Dc2/248r	2109
Barry, James	Cork, Walshtown	gentry: esquire	30-Nov-11	140	Dc1/110r	682
Barry, James	Cork, Annagh	gentry: esquire	07-Aug-33	200	Dc2/198v	1897
Barry, John	Cork, Ballycloyth	gentry: esquire	03-Dec-22	600	Dc2/43v	1128
Barry, John	Cork, Ballecloghy	gentry: gent	28-May-17	400	Dc2/7v	903
Barry, John	Cork, Monnidonnell	gentry: gent	30-Jan-79	1300	B.L. 15, 637 f. 18	3878
Barry, John	Cork, Bishops Island	gentry: gent	01-May-65	300	B.L. 15, 635 f. 194a	3599
Barry, John	Cork, Barnanstowne	gentry: gent	30-Dec-67	1772	B.L. 15, 635 f. 216a	3638
Barry, Lawrence	Cork?	peer: viscount Buttervant	14-Mar-79	2000	B.L. 15, 637 f. 19	3880
Barry, Lawrence	Cork?	peer: viscount Buttervant	29-Oct-79	1600	B.L. 15, 637 f. 36	3911
Barry, Lawrence	Cork?	peer: viscount Buttervant	20-Dec-79	300	B.L. 15, 637 f. 26	3893
Barry, Lawrence	Cork?	peer: viscount Buttervant	29-Oct-79	1600	B.L. 15, 637 f. 30a	3902
Barry, Lawrence	Cork?	peer: viscount Buttervant	29-Oct-79	800	B.L. 15, 637 f. 27	3895
Barry, Mathew	Dublin, the city	gentry: esquire	13-Dec-77	800	Dc3/184r	2698
Barry, Redmond	Cork, Rathcormick	gentry: esquire	20-Dec-65	1000	Dc3/18	2262
Barry, Redmond	Cork, Rathcormuck	gentry: esquire	02-Mar-67	800	Dc3/56	2343
Barry, Redmond	Cork, Rathcormucke	gentry: esquire	18-Nov-64	800	B.L. 15, 635 f. 145a	3510
Barry, Redmond	Cork, Rathcormack	gentry: esquire	30-Jan-79	1300	B.L. 15, 637 f. 18	3878
Barry, Redmond	Cork, Rathcormack	gentry: esquire	20-Dec-65	1000	B.L. 15, 635 f. 163	3541
Barry, Redmond	Cork, Rathcormack	gentry: esquire	17-Nov-71	1000	B.L. 15, 636 f. 96	3788
Barry, Redmond	Cork, Rathcormack	gentry: esquire	20-Nov-71	800	B.L. 15, 636 f. 96a	3789
Barry, Redmond	Cork, Rathcormack	gentry: esquire	02-Mar-67	800	B.L. 15, 635 f. 185	3580
Barry, Richard	Cork?	peer: earl of Barrymore	20-Oct-74	500	B.L. 19, 844 f. 49	3172
Barry, Richard	Cork?	peer: earl of Barrymore	21-Dec-66	500	Dc3/48	2327
Barry, Richard	Cork?	peer: earl of Barrymore	12-Nov-66	1000	Dc3/41	2317
Barry, Richard	Cork?	peer: earl of Barrymore	01-Oct-74	1000	B.L. 19, 844 f. 37	3161
Barry, Richard	Cork?	peer: earl of Barrymore	23-May-56	1000	B.L. 19, 843 f. 171	3055
Barry, Richard	Cork?	peer: earl of Barrymore	19-May-70	540	Dc3/119	2479
Barry, Richard	Cork?	peer: earl of Barrymore	12-Apr-75	2400	B.L. 19, 844 f. 59	3184
Barry, Richard	Cork?	peer: earl of Barrymore	10-Apr-75	1200	B.L. 19, 844 f. 60	3185
Barry, Richard	Cork?	peer: earl of Barrymore	10-Apr-75	2400	B.L. 19, 844 f. 65	3193
Barry, Richard	Cork?	peer: earl of Barrymore	22-Jun-75	400	B.L. 19, 844 f. 71	3199
Barry, Richard	Cork?	peer: earl of Barrymore	18-Jan-77	1400	B.L. 19, 844 f. 116	3245
Barry, Richard	Cork?	peer: earl of Barrymore	29-Aug-73	1200	B.L. 19, 844 f. 17	3135
Barry, Richard	Cork?	peer: earl of Barrymore	21-Dec-66	500	B.L. 15, 635 f. 182a	3575
Barry, Richard	Cork?	peer: earl of Barrymore	11-Jan-84	1000	B.L. 15, 637 f. 95a	4020
Barry, Richard	Dublin, the city	gentry: gent	17-Jan-83	2000	B.L. 15, 637 f. 73a	3980
Barry, Richard		peer: baron Santry	23-May-83	2000	B.L. 15, 637 f. 73	3979
Barry, Richard	Cork?	peer: earl of Barrymore	28-Mar-67	600	B.L. 15, 635 f. 189	3588
Barry, Richard	Cork?	peer: earl of Barrymore	19-Mar-69	300	B.L. 15, 636 f. 41	3696
Barry, Richard	Cork?	peer: earl of Barrymore	29-Oct-79	1600	B.L. 15, 637 f. 36	3911
Barry, Richard	Cork?	peer: earl of Barrymore	09-Apr-68	300	B.L. 15, 635 f. 215	3635
Barry, Richard	Cork?	peer: earl of Barrymore	20-Dec-79	300	B.L. 15, 637 f. 26	3893

Standard	County	Occupation	Date	Amount	MS No	Ident No
Barry, Richard	Cork?	peer: earl of Barrymore	30-Dec-67	1772	B.L. 15, 635 f. 216a	3638
Barry, Richard	Cork?	peer: earl of Barrymore	14-Jun-72	1700	B.L. 15, 636 f. 114a	3819
Barry, Richard	Cork?	peer: earl of Barrymore	02-May-72	500	B.L. 15, 636 f. 114	3818
Barry, Richard	Cork?	peer: earl of Barrymore	11-Jun-72	600	B.L. 15, 636 f. 111	3812
Barry, Richard	Cork?	peer: earl of Barrymore	14-Mar-79	2000	B.L. 15, 637 f. 19	3880
Barry, Richard	Cork?	peer: earl of Barrymore	14-Jun-72	3000	B.L. 15, 636 f. 109a	3809
Barry, Richard	Cork?	peer: earl of Barrymore	25-Aug-67	700	B.L. 15, 635 f. 215a	3636
Barry, Richard	King's Co., Ffortall	gentry: esquire	03-Nov-79	500	B.L. 15, 637 f. 22	3885
Barry, Richard	Cork?	peer: earl of Barrymore	15-Jan-70	500	B.L. 15, 636 f. 73a	3749
Barry, Richard	Cork?	peer: earl of Barrymore	05-Dec-67	1000	B.L. 15, 635 f. 204a	3618
Barry, Richard	Cork?	peer: earl of Barrymore	29-Oct-79	800	B.L. 15, 637 f. 27	3895
Barry, Richard	Cork?	peer: earl of Barrymore	04-Nov-70	200	B.L. 15, 636 f. 73	3748
Barry, Richard	Cork?	peer: earl of Barrymore	20-Jun-70	1000	B.L. 15, 636 f. 72	3746
Barry, Richard	Cork?	peer: earl of Barrymore	20-Jan-70	1000	B.L. 15, 636 f. 52a	3714
Barry, Richard	Cork?	peer: earl of Barrymore	29-Oct-79	1600	B.L. 15, 637 f. 30a	3902
Barry, Richard	Cork?	peer: earl of Barrymore	15-Jan-70	500	B.L. 15, 636 f 53	3715
Barry, Richard	Cork?	peer: earl of Barrymore	19-May-70	540	B.L. 15, 636 f. 59	3724
Barry, Richard	Cork?	peer: earl of Barrymore	19-Mar-69	800	B.L. 15, 636 f. 38a	3691
Barry, Thomas	Carlow, Rathrush	gentry: gent	10-Feb-30	400	Dc2/142r	1666
Barry, William	Cork, Courtstowne	gentry: gent	03-Feb-41	1200	B.L. 19, 843 f. 100a	2920
Barry, William	Cork, Barnanstowne	gentry: gent	30-Dec-67	3544	B.L. 15, 635 f. 216	3637
Barry, William	Cork, Barnanstowne	gentry: gent	30-Dec-67	1772	B.L. 15, 635 f. 216a	3638
Barry, William	Cork, Ringcorraine	gentry: esquire	27-Jan-64	600	B.L. 15, 635 f. 127a	3482
Barry, William	Cork, Ringcoram	gentry: esquire	18-Aug-62	300	B.L. 15, 635 f. 112	3454
Barry, William	Cork, Bishops Island	gentry: gent	01-May-65	300	B.L. 15, 635 f. 194a	3599
Barry, William	Cork, Barranstowne	gentry: gent	01-May-65	220	B.L. 15, 635 f. 157	3531
Barton, George	Kilkenny, Goslinstowne	gentry: gent	15-Feb-66	100	Dc3/22	2272
Bassett, Hanibal	Cork, the city	merchant	12-Apr-70	1000	B.L. 15, 636 f. 58a	3723
Bassett, John	Cork, the city	gentry: gent	12-Apr-70	1000	B.L. 15, 636 f. 58a	3723
Bath, Christopher	Louth, Drogheda	merchant	08-Jun-20	600	Dc2/30v	1033
Bath, Christopher	Louth, Drogheda	merchant	08-Jun-20	2000	Dc2/30v	1032
Bath, Henry	Meath, Kilkarvan?	gentry: gent	07-Nov-17	300	Dc2/10v	917
Bath, James	Dublin, Drumkonro	gentry: esquire	16-May-39	2000	B.L. 19, 843 f. 16	2750
Bath, James	Meath, Alcarne	gentry: esquire	30-May-39	1000	B.L. 19, 843 f. 18	2754
Bath, John	Galway, Lovaghan	gentry: gent	28-Nov-11	100	Dc1/109v	680
Bath, John	Meath, Athcarne	gentry: gent	12-Nov-11	50	Dc1/107v	667
Bath, John	Meath, Colpe	gentry: gent	25-Nov-40	200	B.L. 19, 843 f. 80	2879
Bath, John	Louth, Drogheda	merchant	17-May-73	200	B.L. 19, 844 f. 5	3124
Bath, John	Louth, Drogheda	merchant	09-Jul-84	700	B.L. 15, 637 f. 94	4017
Bath, John	Meath, Mountnewtowne	gentry: gent	08-Jul-86	400	B.L. 15, 637 f. 110	4047
Bath, Luke	Meath, Athcarne	gentry: baronet	23-Mar-66	200	Dc3/27	2282
Bath, Luke	Meath, Athcarne	gentry: baronet	24-Feb-70	300	Dc3/116	2472
Bath, Luke	Meath, Athcarne	gentry: baronet	20-Feb-67	3600	Dc3/54	2339
Bath, Luke	Meath, Alcaine	gentry: baronet	20-Jul-66	1000	B.L. 15, 635 f. 176	3561
Bath, Luke	Meath, Athcarne	gentry: baronet	20-Feb-67	3600	B.L. 15, 635 f. 186a	3583

Standard	County	Occupation	Date	Amount	MS No	Ident No
Bath, Luke	Meath, Acharne	gentry:				
		knight and baronet	07-Jun-64	300	B.L. 15, 635 f. 143	3505
Bath, Nicholas	Dublin, Morton psh					
	Clonmethan	gentry: gent	17-Oct-00	200	Dc1/26v	177
Bath, Nicholas	Louth, Drogheda	merchant	17-May-73	200	B.L. 19, 844 f. 5	3124
Bath, Nicholas	Louth, Paynestowne	gentry: gent	26-Aug-72	120	B.L.. 15, 636 f. 124	3828
Bath, Patrick	Dublin	trade: tailor	21-Jul-26	200	Dc2/81v	1387
Bath, Patrick	Meath, Rafeith	gentry: gent	07-Jul-41	200	B.L. 19, 843 f. 105	2929
Bath, Patrick	Dublin, the city	trade: tailor	30-Jun-25	200	Dc2/67r	1301
Bath, Patrick	Dublin	trade: tailor	28-Feb-28	200	Dc2/104v	1488
Bath, Patrick	Dublin, the city	trade: tailor	29-May-28	200	Dc2/110v	1515
Bath, Patrick	Dublin, the city	trade: tailor	08-Dec-25	200	Dc2/71v	1330
Bath, Richard	Meath, Galmorstowne	gentry: gent	30-Jan-73	200	B.L. 19, 844 f. 4	3123
Bath, Robert	Meath, Colpe	gentry: son/heir of John	25-Nov-40	200	B.L. 19, 843 f. 80	2879
Bath, Robert	Dublin, Clonturke	gentry: gent	13-Nov-33	300	Dc2/200v	1905
Bath, Robert	Meath, Beashelston	gentry: gent	20-May-14	700	Dc1/129v	804
Bath, Robert	Kilkenny	gentry: gent	06-May-01	30	Dc1/31v	207
Bath, Thomas	Dublin?, Kilbryde	gentry: gent	01-Feb-97	60	Dc1/1v	7
Bath, Thomas	Dublin, Kilbrid	gentry: gent	15-Mar-19	200	Dc2/21v	979
Bath, Thomas	Meath, Slane	other: son of Frances	03-Feb-07	60	Dc1/73v	446
Bath, Thomas	Dublin, Kilbride	gentry: gent	21-Dec-20	260	Dc2/34r	1059
Bath, Thomas	Dublin, Kilbryde	gentry: gent	05-Feb-17	60	Dc2/4v	890
Bath, Thomas	Dublin, Kilbride	gentry: gent	18-Jun-28	1000	Dc2/111r	1518
Bathurst, Henry	Cork	gentry: esquire	08-Mar-61	400	B.L. 15, 635 f. 67a	3382
Baucroft, Richard	King's Co., Curroughlanty	gentry: gent	29-Nov-67	407	Dc3/69	2377
Baxter, Garret	Sligo, Larhas	gentry: gent	19-Dec-35	300	Dc2/242r	2084
Baxter, Garret	Sligo, Karras?	gentry: esquire	01-Jul-40	1000	B.L. 19, 843 f. 71	2861
Baxter, John	Sligo, Larruske	gentry: gent	21-Jul-14	200	Dc1/131r	813
Baxter, John	Dublin, Mayestowne	gentry: esquire	31-Dec-58	500	B.L. 15, 635 f. 35a	3325
Baxter, Martin	Cavan, Carne	gentry: esquire	21-Jun-39	400	B.L. 19, 843 f. 14a	2747
Beare, John	Cork, Lyscarroll	gentry: gent	05-Jun-83	600	B.L. 15, 637 f. 74a	3982
Beavans, John	Dublin, the city	gentry: gent	19-Feb-59	400	B.L. 15, 635 f. 39	3332
Beavans, John	Dublin, the city	gentry: gent	27-Jun-57	200	B.L. 19, 843 f. 194a	3096
Beckett, William	Dublin, the city	gentry: esquire, son of				
		Randal	03-Dec-74	500	Dc3/163r	2618
Beckett, William	Dublin, the city	gentry: esquire, son of				
		Randal	03-Dec-74	500	B.L. 19, 844 f. 48	3171
Bee, John	Dublin	gentry: gent, son/heir of				
		Sam	04-Mar-34	50	Dc2/209r	1940
Bee, John	Dublin, the city	gentry: gent	22-Mar-71	100	B.L. 15, 636 f. 87a	3775
Bee, John.	Dublin, the city	merchant	05-Jun-63	100	B.L. 15, 635 f. 106	3444
Bee, Michael	Dublin	trade: tanner	22-Jan-01	140	Dc1/27v	185
Begg, Walter	Dublin, Borranstowne	gentry: gent	14-Feb-28	120	Dc2/104r	1486
Begg, Walter	Dublin, Borranstowne	gentry: gent	14-Mar-29	220	Dc2/126r	1591
Bellew, Christopher	Louth, Castletowne	gentry: knight	21-Nov-34	1000	Dc2/222v	1995

Standard	County	Occupation	Date	Amount	MS No	Ident No
Bellew, Christopher	Louth, Castletowne	gentry: knight	07-May-30	600	Dc2/146v	1684
Bellew, John	Meath, Bellewston	gentry: knight	10-Jan-21	600	Dc2/38r	1091
Bellew, John	Meath, Bellewston	gentry: esquire	01-Apr-17	1200	Dc2/6r	898
Bellew, John	Louth, Castletowne	gentry: knight	10-Jun-67	1000	Dc3/62	2358
Bellew, John	Meath, Ballymagarroie	gentry: gent	27-Jul-03	100	Dc1/47av	308
Bellew, John	Louth, Drogheda	merchant	22-Apr-00	300	Dc1/23r	155
Bellew, John	Louth, Castletowne	gentry: knight	20-Oct-66	1000	Dc3/39	2314
Bellew, John	Louth, Castletowne	gentry: knight	04-Nov-67	1000	Dc3/67	2373
Bellew, John	Louth, Castletowne	gentry: knight	10-Jun-67	1000	B.L. 15, 635 f. 193	3596
Bellew, John	Louth, Castletowne	gentry: knight	20-Oct-66	1000	B.L. 15, 635 f. 177	3563
Bellew, John	Louth, Castletown	gentry: knight	27-Nov-63	400	B.L. 15, 635 f. 128	3483
Bellew, John	Louth, Castletowne	gentry: knight	04-Nov-67	1000	B.L. 15, 635 f. 199a	3608
Bellew, John	Louth, Barmeth	gentry: esquire	16-Apr-72	300	B.L. 15, 636 f. 103	3799
Bellew, Patrick	Louth, Verdonstowne	gentry: esquire	11-Jun-30	200	Dc2/149v	1697
Bellew, Patrick	Louth, Verdonstowne	gentry: esquire	15-Feb-33	400	Dc2/191v	1869
Bellew, Patrick	Louth, Verdonstowne	gentry: esquire	20-Feb-41	621	B.L. 19, 843 f. 85a	2890
Bellew, Patrick	Louth, Verdonstowne	gentry: esquire	07-Jun-30	300	Dc2/149r	1694
Bellew, Patrick	Galway, Clanoran	gentry: esquire	22-Aug-81	1200	B.L. 15, 637 f. 50	3936
Bellew, Roger	Louth, Thomastowne	gentry: gent	07-Dec-68	400	Dc3/85	2415
Bellew, Roger	Dublin, the city	gentry: gent	01-Jul-61	108	B.L. 15, 635 f. 86	3408
Bellew, William	Louth, Slane	peer: baron Slane	23-Nov-02	150	Dc1/40v	263
Bellingham, Daniel	Dublin, the city	gentry: knight	04-Nov-65	1000	Dc3/14	2253
Bellings, Christopher	Dublin, Ballymore	gentry: gent	23-Jun-23	100	Dc2/48v	1166
Bellings, Christopher	Dublin, Ballymore	gentry: gent	17-Nov-23	250	Dc2/51r	1186
Bellings, Christopher	Kildare, Killussey	gentry: gent	03-Aug-99	540	Dc1/18v	127
Bellings, Christopher	Kildare, Kilussie	gentry: gent	23-Feb-06	300	Dc1/66r	398
Bellings, Christopher	Dublin, Ballymore	gentry: esquire	23-Dec-23	600	Dc2/52r	1193
Bellings, Henry	Kildare, Killussey	gentry: gent	03-Aug-99	540	Dc1/18v	127
Bellings, Henry	Dublin, Tyrrelston	gentry: knight	23-Dec-24	200	Dc2/60r	1255
Bellings, Henry	Dublin, Terrelston	gentry: knight	13-Feb-27	2200	Dc2/88r	1416
Bellings, Henry	Kildare, Killussy	gentry: knight	21-May-25	200	Dc2/64r	1282
Bellings, Henry	Dublin, Terrelston	gentry: gent	02-Jul-06	300	Dc1/69v	422
Bellings, Henry	Kildare, Kilussie	gentry: gent	23-Feb-06	300	Dc1/66r	398
Bellings, Henry	Kildare, Killussy	gentry: knight	23-Dec-23	600	Dc2/52r	1193
Bellings, Henry	Dublin, Tyrrelston	gentry: esquire	11-Feb-03	300	Dc1/44v	282
Bellings, Henry	Dublin, Tirrelston	gentry: gent	24-Oct-00	320	Dc1/26v	178
Bellings, Henry	Dublin, Tyrrelston	gentry: knight	23-Jun-23	100	Dc2/48v	1166
Bellings, Henry	Dublin, Tyrelston	gentry: knight	17-Nov-23	250	Dc2/51r	1186
Bellings, Henry	Dublin, Terrelston	gentry: gent	17-Feb-01	600	Dc1/29r	192
Bellings, Henry	Dublin, Tyrrelston	gentry: gent	14-Feb-03	200	Dc1/45r	286
Bellings, Henry	Dublin, Terrelston	gentry: gent	19-Sep-00	300	Dc1/25v	173
Bellings, James	Dublin, Bealingstowne	gentry: gent	31-Mar-28	400	Dc2/106r	1494
Bellings, Lawrence	Dublin, Bealingstowne	gentry: gent	12-Jul-37	300	Dc2/268r	2203
Bellings, Lawrence	Dublin, Bealingstowne	gentry: gent	07-Jul-37	200	Dc2/267v	2200
Bellings, Lawrence	Dublin, Bealingstowne	gentry: gent	01-Feb-39	160	B.L. 19, 843 f. 91a	2902

Standard	County	Occupation	Date	Amount	MS No	Ident No
Bellings, Richard	Kildare, Kyllushey?	gentry: esquire	23-Feb-98	140	Dc1/10r	70
Bellings, Richard	Dublin, Terrelston	gentry: son/heir of Sir Henry	13-Feb-27	2200	Dc2/88r	1416
Bellings, Richard	Kildare?, Killussy?	gentry: son/heir of Henry	23-Dec-23	600	Dc2/52r	1193
Bellings, Richard	Dublin, Tyrrelston?	gentry: son/heir of Sir Henry	23-Jun-23	100	Dc2/48v	1166
Bellings, Richard	Dublin, Tyrrelston?	gentry: son/heir of Sir Henry	23-Dec-24	200	Dc2/60r	1255
Bellings, Thomas	Dublin, Bellingston	gentry: gent	23-Mar-26	400	Dc2/76r	1356
Bellings, Thomas	Dublin, Bealingston	gentry: gent	20-May-25	200	Dc2/63v	1281
Bellings, Thomas	Dublin, the Combe, near Dublin	trade: baker	01-Jun-59	100	B.L. 15, 635 f. 46a	3345
Bellings, Thomas	Dublin, Bealingstowne	gentry: gent?	03-Mar-28	200	Dc2/105v	1491
Bellings, Thomas	Dublin, Bealingston	gentry: gent	31-Jan-22	240	Dc2/38v	1095
Bellings, Walter	Dublin, Ardlawe	gentry: gent	25-Jun-14	400	Dc1/130v	810
Bennett, John		soldier: captain, Col Lawrence	24-Jun-56	200	B.L. 19, 843 f. 174a	3060
Bentley, Elizabeth	King's Co., Moielie	gentry: wife of Ralph	19-Nov-03	1000	Dc1/49v	317
Bentley, Mathew	Dublin	gentry: esquire	08-Apr-37	300	Dc2/261r	2173
Bentley, Ralph	Dublin	gentry: gent	20-Dec-97	150	Dc1/8v	61
Bentley, Ralph	Meath, Clanecarnyle	gentry: gent	13-Apr-03	200	Dc1/46r	291
Bentley, Ralph	King's Co., Moielie	gentry: esquire	19-Nov-03	1000	Dc1/49v	317
Bereford, John	Meath, Kilron	gentry: esquire	18-Jun-24	200	Dc2/56v	1226
Bereford, Richard	Meath, Ballebin	gentry: gent	18-Jun-24	200	Dc2/56v	1226
Beresford, Tristram	Londonderry, Colraine	gentry: esquire	06-Oct-62	420	B.L. 15, 635 f. 97	3428
Berkeley, Maurice	Cork?	peer: viscount Ffitzharding	23-Nov-71	1680	Dc3/141r	2534
Berkeley, Maurice	Cork?	peer: viscount Ffitzharding	05-Jan-71	800	Dc3/134r	2511
Berkeley, Maurice	Cork, Berehaven	peer: viscount Ffitzharding	05-Jan-71	800	B.L. 15, 637 f. 14	3873
Berkeley, Maurice	Cork, Berehaven, Rathdowne	peer: viscount Ffitzharding	23-Nov-71	1680	B.L. 15, 636 f. 90	3779
Berkeley, Samuel	Tipperary, Castletowne	gentry: gent	28-Apr-77	120	B.L. 19, 844 f. 132	3262
Bermingham, Edmund	Kildare, Ballindrymnye	gentry: gent	25-Nov-06	30	Dc1/72r	436
Bermingham, Edmund	Kildare, Ballyndromney	gentry: gent	07-Dec-38	600	B.L. 19, 843 f. 97a	2914
Bermingham, Edward	Kildare, the Carricke	gentry: gent	22-May-09	140	Dc1/89r	557
Bermingham, Edward	Kildare, Carricke	gentry: gent	04-May-17	160	Dc2/8r	905
Bermingham, Edward	Kildare, the Carrick	gentry: esquire	15-Nov-04	160	Dc1/54r	338
Bermingham, Edward	Kildare, the Carracke	gentry: gent	07-Apr-03	210	Dc1/45v	290
Bermingham, Edward	Kildare, the Carricke	gentry: gent	15-Jun-97	80	Dc1/4v	31
Bermingham, James	Dublin, Ballough	gentry: son/heir of Robert	04-Apr-28	600	Dc2/106v	1496

Standard	County	Occupation	Date	Amount	MS No	Ident No
Bermingham, James	Dublin, Ballogh	gentry: son/heir of Robert	13-Jul-31	300	Dc2/166v	1769
Bermingham, James	Dublin, Ballogh	gentry: esquire	18-Apr-40	100	B.L. 19, 843 f. 55a	2829
Bermingham, James	Dublin, Ballagh	gentry: gent	20-Jul-36	500	B.L. 19, 843 f. 123a	2966
Bermingham, James	Dublin, Ballough	gentry: son/heir of Robert	08-Mar-28	300	Dc2/106r	1493
Bermingham, James	Dublin, Ballough	gentry: gent	14-Dec-34	120	Dc2/219v	1982
Bermingham, John	Kildare, Dunfeart	gentry: esquire	11-Feb-07	500	Dc1/74r	448
Bermingham, John	Kildare, Donfert	gentry: esquire	01-Jul-06	40	Dc1/69v	421
Bermingham, John	Kildare, Carricke	gentry: esquire	11-Jul-28	160	Dc2/112v	1527
Bermingham, John	Kildare, Donfert	gentry: esquire	29-Nov-05	500	Dc1/63r	381
Bermingham, John	Kildare, Donseirte	gentry: esquire	24-Jan-05	140	Dc1/54v	341
Bermingham, Richard	Kildare, Derelingery?	gentry: gent	07-Sep-05	50	Dc1/61v	375
Bermingham, Robert	Dublin, Ballogh	gentry: gent	31-Jan-12	400	Dc1/111v	691
Bermingham, Robert	Kildare, Carricke	gentry: esquire	24-Nov-31	150	Dc2/172r	1793
Bermingham, Robert	Dublin, Ballough	gentry: gent	04-Apr-28	600	Dc2/106v	1496
Bermingham, Robert	Dublin, Ballogh	gentry: gent	13-Jul-31	300	Dc2/166v	1769
Bermingham, Robert	Dublin, Ballough	gentry: gent	08-Mar-28	300	Dc2/106r	1493
Bermingham, Robert	Dublin, Ballgeith?	gentry: gent	21-May-18	120	Dc2/14v	940
Bermingham, Walter	Kildare, Clonkerran	gentry: gent	02-May-15	120	Dc1/136v	848
Bermingham, Walter	Kildare, the Carrick?	gentry: son of Edward	15-Nov-04	160	Dc1/54r	338
Bermingham, Walter	Kildare, Carricke	gentry: son/heir of Edward	04-May-17	160	Dc2/8r	905
Bermingham, Walter	Kildare, Donferth	gentry: esquire	10-Feb-29	600	Dc2/124r	1579
Bermingham, William	Meath, the Corballies	gentry: gent	04-Feb-13	100	Dc1/118r	733
Bermingham, William	Kildare, Parsonstowne	gentry: gent	23-Nov-37	200	Dc2/271v	2219
Bermingham, William	Kildare, Donnfort	gentry: gent	05-May-01	123	Dc1/31r	206
Bermingham, William	Meath, Corballye	gentry: gent	06-Jun-07	100	Dc1/77v	474
Beteagh, Christopher	Meath, Kells?	merchant: son/heir of Henry	06-Jul-33	200	Dc2/197r	1892
Beteagh, Edward	Meath, Moynaltie	gentry: esquire	22-May-37	800	Dc2/264r	2184
Beteagh, Edward	Meath, Moynaltie	gentry: esquire	08-Jun-33	600	Dc2/196r	1888
Beteagh, Edward	Meath, Moynaltie	gentry: esquire	24-Mar-36	200	Dc2/247v	2106
Beteagh, Henry	Meath, Kells	merchant	06-Jul-33	200	Dc2/197r	1892
Beteagh, John	Meath, Maghanstowne	gentry: gent	11-Feb-29	40	Dc2/124v	1585
Beteagh, Patrick	Meath, Moynaltie	gentry: gent, s/heir of Edward	24-Mar-36	200	Dc2/247v	2106
Beteagh, Patrick	Meath, Newtowne	gentry: gent	08-Jun-33	600	Dc2/196r	1888
Beteagh, William	Meath, Donowre	gentry: gent	10-Feb-29	100	Dc2/124r	1581
Bethell, Robert	Down?, the Ardes, Portaferry	gentry: gent	18-May-97	200	Dc1/3v	24
Bevans, Edward	Dublin	gentry: gent	10-Feb-29	100	Dc2/124r	1578
Bingham, John	Mayo, Ballynelube	gentry: son/heir of John	20-May-81	800	B.L. 15, 637 f. 48a	3933
Bingham, John	Mayo, Ffoxford	gentry: esquire	31-May-82	1400	B.L. 15, 637 f. 61	3957
Bingham, John	Mayo, Ballynelube	gentry: esquire	20-May-81	800	B.L. 15, 637 f. 48a	3933

Standard	County	Occupation	Date	Amount	MS No	Ident No
Bingham, John	Mayo, Ffoxford	gentry: esquire	12-Jun-82	1000	B.L. 15, 637 f. 60	3955
Binglie, John	Dublin	gentry: gent	25-Nov-03	4180	Dc1/49v	319
Binglie, John	Dublin	gentry: gent	24-Dec-03	2508	Dc1/50v	325
Binglie, Ralph		gentry: knight	24-Sep-16	500	Dc2/1r	871
Binglie, Richard	Down, Duffry	gentry: gent	18-Nov-06	80	Dc1/71v	432
Bird, Thomas	Dublin	merchant	03-Mar-11	200	Dc1/105r	655
Bird, Thomas	Dublin	merchant	03-Mar-13	200	Dc1/120r	746
Bishop, Thomas	Dublin	merchant	26-Nov-99	500	Dc1/20v	138
Bishop, William	Cork, Garranmony	gentry: gent	10-Apr-86	220	B.L. 15, 637 f. 105	4037
Blackiston, Thomas	Limerick, the city	gentry: gent	14-Jan-59	332	B.L. 15, 635 f. 36	3326
Blackney, John	Louth, Drogheda		29-Nov-24	200	Dc2/59r	1246
Blackney, Thomas	Louth, Drogheda		31-Oct-40	300	B.L. 19, 843 f. 80a	2880
Bladen, Thomas	Dublin, the city	prof: doctor of divinity	28-May-68	240	Dc3/76	2397
Blake, John	Galway	merchant	02-Jul-25	1000	Dc2/68r	1307
Blanchvill, Edmund	Kilkenny, Howlingstowne	gentry: esquire	04-Aug-41	700	B.L. 19, 843 f. 106	2931
Blanchvill, Edmund	Kilkenny, Howlingstone	gentry: gent, son of Edmund	08-May-39	40	B.L. 19, 843 f. 34	2786
Blaney, Edward	Monaghan?	peer: baron Monaghan	12-Oct-48	6000	B.L. 19, 843 f. 124	2967
Blaney, Henry	Monaghan?	peer: baron Monaghan	24-Jul-34	774	Dc2/215v	1967
Blaney, Henry	Monaghan?	peer: baron Monaghan	15-Jul-42	400	B.L. 19, 843 f. 108	2935
Blaney, Henry	Monaghan?	peer: baron Monaghan	07-Sep-34	112	Dc2/220r	1985
Blaney, Henry	Monaghan, Monohan	gentry: knight	07-May-28	180	Dc2/107r	1499
Blaney, Henry	Monaghan?	peer: baron Monaghan	10-Oct-43	300	B.L. 19, 843 f. 113	2945
Blaney, Henry	Monaghan?	peer: baron Monaghan	17-Nov-34	800	Dc2/221v	1990
Blaney, Henry	Monaghan?	peer: baron Monaghan	06-Aug-39	280	B.L. 19, 843 f. 63a	2846
Blaney, Henry	Monaghan?	peer: baron Blaney	30-Mar-82	900	B.L. 15, 637 f. 62	3959
Blaney, Mary	Monaghan, Carrickmacross	other: spinster	29-Nov-65	390	Dc3/16	2258
Blaney, Mary	Monaghan, Carrickmacross	other: spinster	03-Aug-69	700	Dc3/102	2445
Blaney, Mary	Monaghan, Carrickmacross	other: spinster	29-Nov-65	390	B.L. 15, 635 f. 160	3537
Blaney, Richard	Monaghan, the town	gentry: esquire	25-Jan-62	600	B.L. 15, 635 f. 89a	3415
Blennerhasset, Leonard	Fermanagh, Castlehassett	gentry: esquire	30-Oct-30	400	Dc2/155r	1721
Blennerhasset, Leonard	Fermanagh, Castlehassett	gentry: esquire	14-Jun-33	200	Dc2/196v	1889
Blennerhasset, Leonard	Fermanagh, Castlehasset	gentry: knight	01-Mar-37	500	Dc2/260r	2168
Blennerhasset, Leonard	Fermanagh, Castlehasset	gentry: esquire	10-Jun-34	200	Dc2/212r	1953
Blennerhasset, Samuel	Fermanagh, Crewenish	gentry: esquire	04-Feb-26	180	Dc2/73v	1341
Blennerhasset, Samuel	Fermanagh, Crevenyhasset	gentry: esquire	03-Jul-24	400	Dc2/57r	1231
Blennerhasset, Thomas	Fermanagh, Crevenishasset	gentry: esquire	03-Jul-24	400	Dc2/57r	1231
Blennerhasset, Ursula	Dublin, the city	gentry: widow	31-May-32	1200	Dc2/181v	1830
Blood, Neptune	Clare, Kiltonghan?, the Burren		20-Dec-58	500	B.L. 15, 635 f. 37	3328
Blood, Thomas	Meath, Sarney	gentry: esquire	18-Jun-63	400	B.L. 15, 635 f. 107	3446
Blount, James	Dublin	gentry: knight	30-Jan-28	2000	Dc2/103r	1480
Blount, Samuel	Tipperary, Lismecue	gentry: esquire	25-Feb-73	300	Dc3/154r	2577
Blount, Samuel	Tipperary, Lismacue	gentry: gent	28-Jan-81	200	B.L. 15, 637 f. 40a	3919

Standard	County	Occupation	Date	Amount	MS No	Ident No
Blount, Samuel	Tipperary, Lismakue	gentry: esquire	02-Nov-83	800	B.L. 15, 637 f. 85a	4002
Blundell, Francis	King's Co., Edenderry	gentry: baronet	27-Nov-75	1200	Dc3/170r	2643
Blundell, Francis	King's Co., Edenderry	gentry: baronet	27-Nov-75	1200	B.L. 19, 844 f. 80	3208
Blundell, Sarah	King's Co., Edenderry	gentry: widow of George, baron	27-Nov-75	1200	B.L. 19, 844 f. 80	3208
Blundell, Sarah		gentry: widow of Sir George	27-Nov-75	1200	Dc3/170r	2643
Boate, Godfrey	Dublin	gentry: gent	08-Aug-66	600	Dc3/36	2303
Boate, Godfrey	Dublin	gentry: gent	08-Aug-66	600	B.L. 15, 635 f. 183	3576
Boate, Katherine	Tipperary, Clonakenny	gentry: widow	08-Aug-66	600	Dc3/36	2303
Boate, Katherine	Tipperary, Clonakenny	gentry: widow	08-Aug-66	600	B.L. 15, 635 f. 183	3576
Bodington, Alexander	Louth, Drogheda	gentry: gent	20-Feb-72	200	B.L. 15, 636 f. 102a	3798
Bodkin, Dominic	Galway, Graigg	gentry: esquire	18-Oct-69	700	B.L. 15, 636 f. 52	3713
Bodkin, John	Galway, Carvereagh	gentry: esq, s./heir of Dominic	18-Oct-69	700	B.L. 15, 636 f. 52	3713
Boe, John	Dublin, the city	gentry: gent	22-Mar-71	100	Dc3/137r	2520
Bolton, Charles	Dublin, Swords	gentry: esquire	04-Dec-67	500	Dc3/69	2378
Bolton, Charles	Down, Mcas	gentry: esquire	28-Feb-63	1200	B.L. 15, 635 f. 101a	3437
Bolton, Edward	Dublin, Brasile	gentry: knight	14-Nov-57	200	B.L. 19, 843 f. 199a	3105
Bolton, Edward	Dublin, the city	gentry: knight	28-Apr-49	3000	B.L. 19, 843 f. 124a	2968
Bolton, Edward	Dublin, Brazile	gentry: knight	20-Mar-53	4000	B.L. 19, 843 f. 130	2977
Bolton, Edward	Dublin, Brazile	gentry: knight	13-Apr-53	400	B.L. 19, 843 f. 132	2979
Bolton, Nicholas	Dublin, Brazile	gentry: esquire, s./heir of Edward	13-Apr-53	400	B.L. 19, 843 f. 132	2979
Bolton, Nicholas	Dublin, Brazile	gentry: esquire, s./heir Walter	20-Mar-53	4000	B.L. 19, 843 f. 130	2977
Bolton, Richard	Louth, Knock	gentry: esquire	17-Mar-74	200	B.L. 19, 844 f. 22a	3143
Bolton, Richard	Louth, Knock	gentry: esquire	25-Aug-75	400	B.L. 19, 844 f. 69	3197
Boswell, John	Dublin, the city	gentry: gent	11-Sep-56	1000	B.L. 19, 843 f. 182	3071
Boswell, John	Wicklow, Ballycurry	gentry: gent	20-Feb-86	630	B.L. 15, 637 f. 109	4044
Bothell, Robert	Down, Strangford, little Ardes		01-Jul-97	200	Dc1/5r	37
Bothell, Walter	Louth, Drogheda	gentry: gent	01-Jul-97	200	Dc1/5r	37
Bothworth, Edward	Dublin, the city	gentry: esquire	10-Sep-19	80	Dc2/25v	1002
Bowen, Alice	Queen's Co., Ballintobber	other: widow	30-Nov-25	400	Dc2/71r	1325
Bowen, Alice	Queen's Co., Ballentobber	other: widow	03-Jul-24	100	Dc2/57r	1230
Bowen, Griffith	Dublin, the city	gentry: gent	02-Aug-71	100	Dc3/139v	2528
Bowen, Griffith	Dublin, the city	gentry: gent	21-Dec-66	100	Dc3/49	2329
Bowen, Griffith	Dublin, the city	gentry: gent	02-Aug-71	100	B.L. 15, 636 f. 89a	3778
Bowen, Oliver	Mayo, Castlecarre	gentry: gent	30-Nov-25	400	Dc2/71r	1325
Bowen, Oliver	Queen's Co., Ballentober	gentry: gent	03-Jul-24	100	Dc2/57r	1230
Bowen, Oliver	Mayo, Castlecarre	gentry: gent	20-Dec-25	300	Dc2/72v	1336
Bowen, Robert	Queen's Co., Ballyadams	gentry: esquire	11-May-05	2000	Dc1/59r	359
Bowen, Thomas	Mayo, Liskillen	gentry: gent	20-Dec-25	300	Dc2/72v	1336

Standard	County	Occupation	Date	Amount	MS No	Ident No
Bowen, William	Queen's Co., Ballyadams	gentry: esquire	18-Aug-70	5000	Dc3/124	2489
Bowles, Thomas	Dublin, the city	gentry: esquire	06-Feb-55	1000	B.L. 19, 843 f. 149a	3013
Boyd, John	Antrim, Ballyclare	gentry: gent	29-Dec-80	280	B.L. 15, 637 f. 41a	3921
Boyle, Barry	Cork, Castle Lyons	gentry: gent	09-Jul-78	500	B.L . 19, 844 f.171	3302
Boyle, Francis	Cork?	peer: viscount Shannon	22-Jan-69	1000	B.L. 15, 636 f. 28a	3675
Boyle, Richard	Limerick, Hosbytall	gentry: gent	03-Mar-97	200	Dc1/2v	13
Boyle, Richard	Dublin	gentry: gent	29-Mar-97	150	Dc1/3r	17
Boyle, Roger	Cork?	peer: baron Broghill	03-Feb-73	1000	Dc3/153r	2572
Boyle, Roger	Cork?	peer: baron Broghill	03-Feb-73	1000	B.L. 15, 636 f. 131	3839
Brabazon, Chambre	Dublin, the city	gentry: esquire	22-Dec-76	4000	Dc3/181r	2681
Brabazon, Chambre	Dublin, the city	gentry: esquire	22-Dec-76	1000	B.L. 19, 844 f. 119	3248
Brabazon, Edward	Roscommon, Killemollcana	gentry: esquire	12-Dec-26	500	Dc2/86r	1408
Brabazon, Malby	Roscommon, Ballenesloe	gentry: esquire	10-Nov-12	110	Dc1/116r	722
Brabazon, Malby	Roscommon	gentry: esquire	03-Jul-26	200	Dc2/80v	1383
Brabazon, Malby	Roscommon, Ballenesloe	gentry: esquire	11-Feb-19	110	Dc2/20v	974
Brabazon, Malby	Roscommon, Ballesloe?	gentry: esquire	12-Dec-26	500	Dc2/86r	1408
Brabazon, Malby	Roscommon, Ballinesloe	gentry: esquire	22-Feb-33	920	Dc2/192r	1872
Brabazon, Malby	Roscommon, Ballenesloe	gentry: esquire	09-Dec-30	200	Dc2/157v	1733
Brabazon, Malby	Roscommon, Ballenesloe	gentry: esquire	10-Dec-16	400	Dc2/3v	885
Brabazon, William	Louth?	peer: earl of Meath	07-Dec-33	3000	Dc2/202v	1914
Brabazon, William	Louth?	peer: earl of Meath	17-Feb-30	4000	Dc2/142v	1667
Brady, Charles	Donegal, Rahine	gentry: gent	18-Nov-05	107	Dc1/61v	373
Brady, Luke	Clare, Tomgreany	gentry: esquire	03-Mar-34	3000	Dc2/208v	1938
Brady, Patrick	Cavan, Cavan	merchant	15-May-26	300	Dc2/77v	1364
Brady, Philip	Cavan, Cornagile	gentry: gent	04-Dec-28	600	Dc2/120r	1562
Brady, Robert	Dublin, the city	merchant	28-Sep-75	200	Dc3/168v	2639
Brady, Robert	Dublin, the city	merchant	29-Sep-75	200	B.L. 19, 844 f. 72	3200
Brady, Robert	Cavan, Cavan	gentry: gent	17-May-31	300	Dc2/163r	1755
Brady, Robert	Dublin, St. Patrick's Close	trade: tailor	19-Jun-68	200	Dc3/79	2404
Brady, Robert	Dublin, St. Patrick's Close	trade: tailor	19-Jun-68	200	B.L. 15, 635 f. 222	3649
Brady, Terrence	Cavan, the Cavan	gentry: gent	29-Nov-20	300	Dc2/33v	1055
Brady, Walter	Louth, Drogheda	merchant	15-Jan-04	400	Dc1/51v	328
Brady?, Flann	Clare, Moynes	gentry: gent	03-Jul-37	80	Dc2/266v	2196
Bramhall, Thomas	Dublin, the city	gentry: baronet	05-Mar-67	8000	Dc3/56	2344
Brandon, Edward	Louth, Dundalk	gentry: gent	21-Jun-32	300	Dc2/183v	1838
Brandon, James	Louth, Dundalke	gentry: gent	11-Aug-40	100	B.L. 19, 843 f. 64	2847
Brandon, Richard	Dublin	gentry: gent	19-Jun-98	220	Dc1/11r	81
Brazier, Kilnor	Donegal, Ray	gentry: esquire	16-Feb-80	418	B.L. 15, 637 f. 28	3897
Brereton, Edward	Queen's Co., Loughteoge	gentry: gent	12-Jul-56.	200	B.L. 19, 843 f. 181	3068
Brereton, Henry	Dublin, Little Clonshagh		10-Nov-56	110	B.L. 19, 843 f. 185a	3078
Brett, Bartholomew	Louth, Drogheda	merchant	08-Jun-20	2000	Dc2/30v	1032
Brett, Bartholomew	Louth, Drogheda	merchant	08-Jun-20	600	Dc2/30v	1033
Brett, Christopher	Meath, Coraghton	gentry: gent	16-Jun-99	60	Dc1/16v	113
Brett, George	Meath, Tullocke	gentry: gent	15-Jun-32	1200	Dc2/183r	1835
Brett, George	Meath, Tullock	gentry: gent	14-Jun-30	200	Dc2/151r	1703

Standard	County	Occupation	Date	Amount	MS No	Ident No
Brett, Henry	Louth, Drogheda	merchant	28-Jun-22	300	Dc2/41r	1114
Brett, James	Tipperary, Heathstowne	gentry: gent	13-Jun-39	240	B.L. 19, 843 f. 7a	2733
Brett, Richard	Meath, Tullocke	gentry: gent	20-Jul-33	2000	Dc2/198r	1895
Brett, Richard	Meath, Tullok	gentry: gent	27-Mar-01	160	Dc1/29v	197
Brett, Richard	Meath?, Tullogg	gentry: gent	21-Jun-39	160	B.L. 19, 843 f. 13	2744
Brett, Richard	Meath, Tullocke	gentry: esquire	28-Feb-31	100	Dc2/160r	1744
Brett, Richard	Meath, Tullocke	gentry: gent	26-Oct-31	200	Dc2/169r	1780
Brett, Richard	Meath, Tullocke	gentry: gent	15-Jun-32	1200	Dc2/183r	1835
Brett, Richard	Meath, Tullock	gentry: gent	14-Jun-30	200	Dc2/151r	1703
Brett, Richard	Meath?, Tolloke	gentry: gent?	12-May-97	200	Dc1/3v	25
Brett, Robert	Clare, Kells	gentry: gent	25-Nov-14	600	Dc1/133r	826
Brett, Walter	Meath, Tulloke	gentry: gent	07-Feb-05	102	Dc1/55v	345
Brett, Walter	Meath, Tulloke	gentry: gent	12-Feb-11	400	Dc1/102v	642
Brett, Walter	Meath, Tullocke	gentry: gent	09-Jul-05	500	Dc1/60v	369
Brewster, Francis	Dublin, the city	gentry: knight	04-Mar-78	2600	Dc3/186v	2706
Brewster, Francis	Dublin, the city	gentry: knight	09-Mar-78	2600	B.L. 19, 844 f. 148	3279
Brewster, Francis	Dublin, the city	gentry: knight	20-Feb-79	2786	B.L. 15, 637 f. 19a	3881
Brice, Randolph	Down, Bangor	gentry: esquire	29-Oct-78	1200	B.L. 15, 637 f. 5	3858
Brice, Robert	Down, Bally Trinston	gentry: gent	08-Apr-63	600	B.L. 15, 636 f. 82a	3765
Brice, Walter	Dublin, the city	merchant	19-Sep-63	200	B.L. 15, 635 f. 118a	3467
Brice, Walter	Dublin, the city	merchant	11-May-63	200	B.L. 15, 635 f. 106a	3445
Brice, Walter	Dublin, the city	merchant	20-Oct-64	200	B.L. 15, 635 f. 145	3509
Bringhurst, Thomas	Dublin, the city	gentry: gent	02-Jan-55	80	B.L. 19, 843 f. 148	3010
Bringhurst, Thomas	Dublin, the city	gentry: gent	27-Aug-34	400	Dc2/218r	1976
Bringhurst, Thomas	Dublin, the city	gentry: gent	02-Jul-55	100	B.L. 19. 843 f. 158	3030
Broderick, John	Cork, Ballyanan	gentry: knight	09-Dec-68	2000	Dc3/86	2416
Broderick, John	Cork, Ballyannin	gentry: knight	09-Nov-66	1000	Dc3/40	2316
Broderick, John	Cork, Ballyannin	gentry: knight	09-Nov-66	1000	B.L. 15, 635 f. 177a	3564
Brombey, Nicholas	Limerick, Newcastle	gentry: gent	16-Dec-73	2000	B.L. 19, 844 f. 18	3136
Bromwell, Robert	Dublin, the city	gentry: esquire	28-Sep-65	70	Dc3/14	2252
Brookes, Eusebi?	Kerry, Carnefilly	gentry: esquire	27-Sep-13	200	Dc1/123v	767
Brookes, George	Dublin, the city	gentry: esquire	21-Feb-84	350	B.L. 15, 637 f. 83a	3998
Brookes, George	Dublin, the city	gentry: esquire	01-Jun-85	90	B.L. 15, 637 f. 100	4029
Brookes, George	Dublin, the city	gentry: esquire	10-Jan-83	1700	B.L. 15, 637 f. 66	3966
Brookes, William	Dublin, the city	trade: brewer	25-May-63	660	B.L. 15, 635 f. 114a	3459
Broomfield, William	Carlow, Catherlagh	gentry: gent	18-Sep-32	1200	Dc2/185v	1846
Browne, George	Mayo, the Neale	gentry: esquire	03-Apr-77	1561	Dc3/182v	2687
Browne, George	Mayo, Neale	gentry: esquire	03-Apr-77	1561	B.L. 19, 844 f. 125	3254
Browne, Henry	Kildare, Newton More	gentry: son/heir of Nicholas	08-Jun-40	100	B.L. 19, 843 f. 51a	2821
Browne, Ignatius	Mayo, Blackrath	gentry: gent	06-Jun-79	120	B.L. 15, 637 f. 20	3882
Browne, James	Dublin	merchant	26-May-01	60	Dc1/32v	213
Browne, James	Dublin, the city	merchant	12-Dec-32	500	Dc2/188v	1857
Browne, John	Dublin, the city	gentry: esquire	27-Feb-75	400	B.L. 19, 844 f. 54	3178
Browne, John	Dublin, the city	gentry: esquire	03-Apr-77	1561	B.L. 19, 844 f. 125	3254

Standard	County	Occupation	Date	Amount	MS No	Ident No
Browne, John	Mayo, the Neale	gentry: esquire	18-Jul-31	80	Dc2/166v	1771
Browne, John	Dublin, the city	gentry: esquire	25-Nov-70	300	Dc3/131v	2503
Browne, John	Dublin	merchant	09-Dec-07	300	Dc1/80v	498
Browne, John	Dublin, the city	gentry: esquire	03-Apr-77	1561	Dc3/182v	2687
Browne, John	Dublin, Neilstowne	gentry: gent	12-Mar-62	200	B.L. 15, 635 f. 92	3418
Browne, John	Dublin, the city	gentry: esquire	27-Feb-75	400	Dc3/165v	2626
Browne, John	Mayo, Kinturke	gentry: esquire	31-May-82	1400	B.L. 15, 637 f. 61	3957
Browne, John	Mayo, Kentwike	gentry: esquire	12-Jun-82	1000	B.L. 15, 637 f. 60	3955
Browne, Joseph	Dublin, Fynston	gentry: gent	23-Jun-20	90	Dc2/31r	1037
Browne, Josias	Mayo, Neale	gentry: esquire	20-May-23	500	Dc2/47r	1158
Browne, Josias	Mayo, the Neale	gentry: esquire	06-Dec-12	500	Dc1/117r	727
Browne, Nicholas	Kildare, Newtowne of Moone	gentry: gent	10-Feb-29	400	Dc2/124v	1583
Browne, Nicholas	Kildare, Newtone a More	farmer: freeholder	18-Oct-08	200	Dc1/84r	523
Browne, Nicholas	Kildare, Newton More	gentry: gent	08-Jun-40	100	B.L. 19, 843 f. 51a	2821
Browne, Nicholas	Kildare, Newtoneamore	farmer: freeholder	18-Oct-08	40	Dc1/84r	524
Browne, Nicholas	Kildare, Kardiston	gentry: gent	23-Feb-02	60	Dc1/36v	238
Browne, Patrick	Dublin, Neilstowne	gentry: gent	24-Apr-40	2000	B.L. 19, 843 f. 53	2824
Browne, Patrick	Dublin, Nealestowne	gentry: gent	30-Mar-36	240	Dc2/248r	2108
Browne, Patrick	Dublin, Nealestowne	gentry: gent	21-Nov-39	66	B.L. 19, 843 f. 40	2798
Browne, Richard		gentry: baronet	23-Jul-27	1300	Dc2/97v	1453
Browne, Richard	Kildare, Newtonamore	farmer: freeholder	23-Dec-02	200	Dc1/42r	271
Browne, Simon			10-Feb-97		Dc1/1v	6
Browne, Thomas	Limerick, Camno	gentry: gent	06-May-39	2000	B.L. 19, 843 f. 12a	2743
Browne, Thomas	Cork, the city	gentry: gent	25-Mar-72	240	B.L. 15, 636 f. 105	3801
Browne, Valentine	Kerry, Mollahive	gentry: esquire	04-Dec-13	400	Dc1/125v	778
Browne, William	Wexford, Malrankan	gentry: esquire	08-Jun-41	400	B.L. 19, 843 f. 117	2953
Browne, William	Dublin, Rowelagh	gentry: gent	23-Jun-20	90	Dc2/31r	1037
Brownlow, John	Armagh, Brownlowesderry	gentry: gent	19-Dec-35	920	Dc2/242v	2083
Brownlow, John	Armagh, Brownlowesderry	gentry: gent	12-Dec-33	800	Dc2/203r	1918
Brownlow, William	Armagh, Brownlowesderry	gentry: knight	09-Aug-34	4000	Dc2/217r	1973
Brownlow, William	Armagh, Brownlowesderry	gentry: knight	12-Dec-33	800	Dc2/203r	1918
Brownlow, William	Armagh, Brownlowederry	gentry: knight	14-Dec-42	80	B.L. 19, 843 f. 118a	2956
Brownlow, William	Armagh, Brownelowesderry	gentry: knight	27-Nov-33	350	Dc2/201v	1909
Brownlow, William	Armagh, Brownelowesderry	gentry: knight	27-Nov-33	418	Dc2/201r	1908
Brownlow, William	Armagh, Brownlowesderry	gentry: knight	27-Jun-34	3000	Dc2/213r	1957
Brownlow, William	Armagh, Brownlowesderry	gentry: knight	19-Dec-35	920	Dc2/242v	2083
Brownlow, William	Armagh, Brownloderry	gentry: knight	19-Feb-24	400	Dc2/53v	1205
Brownlow, William	Armagh, Brownlowesderry	gentry: knight	09-Aug-33	1000	Dc2/198v	1898
Bryan, James	England, Kent/the Nash	gentry: esquire	23-Feb-70	700	Dc3/116	2470
Bryan, James	England, Kent/the Nash	gentry: esquire	23-Feb-70	1400	Dc3/116	2471
Bryan, James	Kilkenny, Bawnmore	gentry: esquire	27-Mar-72	800	Dc3/145r	2549
Bryan, James	Dublin, the city	gentry: esquire	19-Feb-68	200	Dc3/74	2391
Bryan, James	England, Kent, Nash	gentry: esquire	23-Feb-70	700	B.L. 15, 636 f. 46	3704
Bryan, James	Dublin, the city	gentry: esquire	29-Feb-68	200	B.L. 15, 635 f. 218	3641

Standard	County	Occupation	Date	Amount	MS No	Ident No
Bryan, Walter	Wexford, the Skarr	gentry: gent	31-Jan-09	160	Dc1/86v	541
Bulkley, Arthur	Louth, Dundalk	trade: draper	07-Aug-58	550	B.L. 15, 635 f. 32	3319
Bulkley, Arthur	Louth, Dundalk	trade: draper	07-Aug-58	450	B.L. 15, 635 f. 31a	3318
Bunbury, John	Dublin, the city	gentry: gent	13-Jun-56	200	B.L. 19, 843 f. 181a	3070
Burdett, Jane	Kilkenny, Thomastowne	gentry: wife of Robert	05-Apr-76	220	B.L. 19, 844 f. 89	3216
Burdett, Jane	Kilkenny, Thomastowne	gentry: wife of Robert	05-Apr-76	220	Dc3/173r	2653
Burdett, Robert	Kilkenny, Thomastowne	gentry: esquire	05-Apr-76	220	Dc3/173r	2653
Burdett, Robert	Kilkenny, Thomastowne	gentry: esquire	05-Apr-76	220	B.L. 19, 844 f. 89	3216
Burgate, John	Limerick, Lisseenarrue	gentry: son of Thomas	06-May-40	800	B.L. 19, 843 f. 93a	2906
Burgate, John	Limerick, Clohir	gentry: esquire	06-May-40	800	B.L. 19, 843 f. 93a	2906
Burgate, Thomas	Limerick, Lisseenarrue	gentry: gent, son/heir of John	06-May-40	800	B.L. 19, 843 f. 93a	2906
Burke, David	Mayo, Moynulla	gentry: esquire	21-Jan-37	600	Dc2/259v	2166
Burke, Edmund	Mayo, Corran	gentry: esquire	07-Jun-25	606	Dc2/65r	1290
Burke, Edmund	Mayo, Roppagh	gentry: esquire	12-Dec-26	500	Dc2/86v	1409
Burke, Feagh	Galway, Glinske	gentry: esquire	18-May-07	440	Dc1/76v	467
Burke, Feagh	Galway, Glynske	gentry: esquire	17-May-14	2000	Dc1/129r	802
Burke, Henry	Limerick, Kishiquirke	gentry: gent	03-Dec-29	120	Dc2/139r	1651
Burke, John	Galway, Derremclaghny	gentry: knight	23-Jun-18	220	Dc2/15v	945
Burke, John	Galway, Dermaclaghlen	gentry: esquire	18-Nov-05	140	Dc1/62r	378
Burke, John	Galway, Derrymaklaghny	gentry: esquire	24-Feb-14	200	Dc1/127r	788
Burke, John	Mayo, Touskirte	gentry: gent	02-Dec-33	1000	Dc2/202r	1912
Burke, John	Galway, Dirremelagh	gentry: knight	18-Nov-16	100	Dc2/2r	877
Burke, Miles	Mayo, Gallaghe	gentry: gent	24-Feb-20	320	Dc2/28v	1021
Burke, Miles	Mayo?	peer: viscount Mayo	21-Mar-35	500	Dc2/231v	2032
Burke, Miles	Mayo, Carrigcowly	gentry: esq s/heir of Sir Theobald	24-Feb-20	320	Dc2/28v	1021
Burke, Miles	Mayo?	peer: viscount Mayo	23-Feb-31	200	Dc2/160r	1743
Burke, Miles	Mayo?	peer: viscount Mayo	23-Nov-33	1000	Dc2/201r	1907
Burke, Miles	Mayo?	peer: viscount Mayo	03-Mar-34	200	Dc2/208r	1937
Burke, Miles	Mayo, Kinturke	gentry: esquire	09-Dec-25	100	Dc2/72r	1331
Burke, Miles	Mayo?	peer: viscount Mayo	21-Feb-35	600	Dc2/229v	2024
Burke, Miles	Mayo, Kentowk	gentry: esquire	13-Dec-18	110	Dc2/19v	966
Burke, Miles	Mayo, Kintarke	gentry: esquire	11-May-27	4000	Dc2/92v	1432
Burke, Miles	Mayo, Carrigachowly	gentry: esquire	09-Jul-18	105	Dc2/15v	946
Burke, Miles	Mayo?	peer: viscount Mayo	21-Jan-37	600	Dc2/259v	2166
Burke, Miles	Mayo?	peer: viscount Mayo	13-Mar-34	205	Dc2/209r	1941
Burke, Miles	Mayo?	peer: viscount Mayo	17-Jun-35	960	Dc2/237r	2056
Burke, Miles	Mayo, Carrickoly	gentry: esquire	18-Nov-16	100	Dc2/2r	877
Burke, Oliver	Mayo, Ropagh	gentry: esquire	07-Jun-25	606	Dc2/65r	1290
Burke, Richard	Galway, Derrymaclaghna	gentry: esquire	07-Jul-37	2000	Dc2/267v	2199
Burke, Richard	Mayo, Lisgoule	gentry: esquire	21-Jan-37	600	Dc2/259v	2166
Burke, Richard	Galway?	peer: earl of Clanricard	12-Aug-05	2752	Dc1/61r	371
Burke, Richard	Mayo, Ballintobber in Tyrawlie	gentry: esquire	14-Mar-36	400	Dc2/247r	2104

Standard	County	Occupation	Date	Amount	MS No	Ident No
Burke, Richard	Galway, Deremchalga[n]or[agh]?	gentry: gent	08-Nov-97	41	Dc1/6v	47
Burke, Theobald	Limerick?	peer: baron Castleconnell	13-Feb-07	105	Dc1/74v	451
Burke, Theobald	Limerick, Ballynegarde	gentry: gent	26-Sep-39	600	B.L. 19, 843 f. 40a	2799
Burke, Theobald	Mayo, Kintork	gentry: knight	19-Feb-13	40	Dc1/119v	741
Burke, Theobald		peer: baron Brittas	13-Sep-61	4000	B.L. 15, 635 f. 88a	3413
Burke, Theobald		peer: baron Brittas	23-Dec-62	150	B.L. 15, 635 f. 100	3434
Burke, Thomas	Mayo, Ardnary	gentry: knight	11-May-27	4000	Dc2/92v	1432
Burke, Thomas	Roscommon, Balleneslo	gentry: knight	04-Dec-05	320	Dc1/63r	383
Burke, Thomas	Mayo, Loughmaske	gentry: knight	28-Nov-06	200	Dc1/72v	439
Burke, Thomas	Dublin, the city	gentry: gent	16-Jan-79	500	B.L. 15, 637 f. 12	3869
Burke, Tibbot	Tipperary, Burres o Leigh	gentry: gent	19-May-06	150	Dc1/67v	409
Burke, Tibbot	Mayo, Kentoirke	gentry: knight	19-Jul-09	440	Dc1/90r	565
Burke, Ulick	Galway, Downeoman	gentry: gent	17-May-14	2000	Dc1/129r	803
Burke, Ulick	Galway, Lynske	gentry: gent	13-Dec-18	110	Dc2/19v	966
Burke, Ursula	Roscommon, Ballenesloe	gentry: widow	11-Feb-19	110	Dc2/20v	974
Burke, Walter	Tipperary, Borres o Leigh	gentry: gent	19-May-06	150	Dc1/67v	409
Burnell, Christopher	Dublin, Castleknock	gentry: esquire	09-Jul-24	300	Dc2/57r	1232
Burnell, Christopher	Dublin, Castleknock	gentry: esquire	29-Jan-25	300	Dc2/60v	1258
Burnell, Christopher	Kildare, Kelliston	gentry: gent	09-Jun-20	200	Dc2/31r	1034
Burnell, Henry	Meath, Castlerickard	gentry: gent	11-Feb-34	200	Dc2/206v	1929
Burnell, Henry	Dublin, Castleknock	gentry: son/heir of Chris	29-Jan-25	300	Dc2/60v	1258
Burnell, Michael	Louth, Callaghstowne	gentry: gent	27-Jun-39	300	B.L. 19, 843 f. 27a	2773
Burnell, Michael	Louth, Drogheda	merchant	23-Jun-30	400	Dc2/153r	1712
Burnell, Michael	Louth, Drogheda	gentry: gent	27-Feb-36	3000	Dc2/246v	2101
Burnell, Richard	Dublin, the city	trade: barber-surgeon	09-Dec-28	100	Dc2/121v	1568
Burnell, Richard	Dublin	trade: barber-surgeon	25-Jun-19	300	Dc2/24r	994
Burnett, Thomas	Monaghan, Ballelecke	gentry: gent	11-Jul-39	2000	B.L. 19, 843 f. 17	2752
Burrowes, Walter	Dublin, the city	gentry: esquire	20-Nov-52	400	B.L. 19, 843 f. 128	2974
Burt, Richard	Waterford, Tallow	merchant	06-Feb-77	500	B.L. 19, 844 f. 120	3249
Burt, Richard	Waterford, Tallogh	gentry: esquire	01-May-84	1000	B.L. 15, 637 f. 91a	4012
Bury, John	Carlow, Hacketstowne	gentry: esquire	15-Jun-65	440	Dc3/9	2240
Bury, John	Carlow, Haoketstowne	gentry: esquire	15-Jun-65	440	B.L. 15, 635 f. 153a	3526
Butler, Edmund	Tipperary, Fitzmoone	gentry: esquire	21-Nov-17	1000	Dc2/11r	921
Butler, Edmund	Meath?	peer: baron Dunboyne	27-Nov-28	500	Dc2/117v	1549
Butler, Edmund	Tipperary, Clogheully	gentry: esquire	21-Nov-17	1000	Dc2/11r	921
Butler, Edmund	Carlow, Lisnewae	gentry: gent	20-Apr-35	400	Dc2/233r	2038
Butler, Edmund	Kilkenny?	peer: viscount Mountgarrett	18-Feb-97	200	Dc1/2r	9
Butler, Edmund	Meath?	peer: baron Dunboyne	16-May-29	1000	Dc2/129r	1606
Butler, Edmund	Kilkenny, Kilmocker?	gentry: esquire	09-Dec-33	400	Dc2/203r	1916
Butler, Edmund	Meath?	peer: baron of Dunboyne	17-Jun-26	400	Dc2/78r	1374
Butler, Edmund	Kilkenny?	peer: viscount Mountgarrett	14-Dec-70	5000	Dc3/133r	2509

Standard	County	Occupation	Date	Amount	MS No	Ident No
Butler, Edmund	Meath?	peer: baron Dunboyne	23-May-28	600	Dc2/109v	1512
Butler, Edward	Wexford, Monehore	gentry: esquire	10-Nov-12	140	Dc1/116r	720
Butler, Edward	Dublin, the city	gentry: esquire	14-Dec-70	5000	Dc3/133r	2509
Butler, Elizabeth	Kilkenny?	peer: countess of Ormond	24-Feb-58	800	B.L. 19, 843 f. 206	3118
Butler, Elizabeth	Kilkenny?	peer: wife of Edmund	14-Dec-70	5000	Dc3/133r	2509
Butler, Elizabeth	Kilkenny?	peer: countess of Ormonde	19-Oct-59	1000	B.L. 15, 635 f. 53	3357
Butler, Emily	Kilkenny, the city	gentry: wife of Richard	14-Dec-70	5000	Dc3/133v	2510
Butler, James	Carlow, Tennehinch	gentry: esquire	28-Jun-26	300	Dc2/80r	1380
Butler, James	Tipperary, Knockloughty	gentry: esquire	18-Jun-24	200	Dc2/56v	1227
Butler, James	Kilkenny?	peer: earl of Ormond	27-Jun-35	1600	Dc2/238r	2061
Butler, James	Tipperary, Knockloghtie	gentry: esquire	16-May-29	1000	Dc2/129v	1607
Butler, James	Tipperary, Ballinekill	gentry: esquire	14-Mar-66	140	Dc3/26	2279
Butler, James	Kilkenny?	peer: earl of Ormond	06-Jun-40	4000	B.L. 19, 843 f. 56a	2831
Butler, James	Kilkenny, Kilkenny castle	peer: earl of Ormond	30-Apr-39	4000	B.L. 19, 843 f. 5a	2729
Butler, James	Carlow, Tennehinch	gentry: esquire	28-Jun-26	300	Dc2/80r	1380
Butler, John	Tipperary, Cloghbridie	gentry: gent	16-Jun-37	160	Dc2/264v	2187
Butler, John	Tipperary, Cloghbridie	gentry: esquire	16-Jun-37	160	Dc2/264v	2187
Butler, Peter	Tipperary, Banshaghe	gentry: esquire	10-Mar-36	100	Dc2/247r	2103
Butler, Pierce	Tipperary, Kilvoylagher	gentry: esquire	30-Apr-72	400	Dc3/145v	2551
Butler, Pierce	Meath?	peer: baron Dunboyne	09-Dec-72	80	Dc3/151r	2566
Butler, Pierce	Meath?	peer: baron Dunboyne	14-Mar-66	140	Dc3/26	2279
Butler, Pierce	Wicklow, Caheire	gentry: esquire	21-Nov-34	1400	Dc2/223r	1996
Butler, Pierce	Tipperary, Nodeston	gentry: gent	15-May-06	53	Dc1/67r	404
Butler, Pierce	Tipperary, Kilvoylegher	gentry: esquire	03-May-76	1000	B.L. 19, 844 f. 104	3231
Butler, Pierce	Kilkenny, Grange?	peer: viscount Galmoy	22-Feb-82	1800	B.L. 15, 637 f. 59	3953
Butler, Pierce	Kilkenny, Grange?	peer: viscount Galmoy	07-Apr-82	4000	B.L. 15, 637 f. 59a	3954
Butler, Pierce	Tipperary, Kilvoylagher	gentry: esquire	30-Apr-72	400	B.L. 15, 636 f. 105a	3802
Butler, Richard	Tipperary, Ballykeanasy	gentry: gent	07-Jul-41	240	B.L. 19, 843 f. 99a	2918
Butler, Richard	Kilkenny, the city	gentry: esquire	14-Dec-70	5000	Dc3/133v	2510
Butler, Richard		peer: earl of Burrimore	05-Dec-67	1000	Dc3/70	2382
Butler, Richard	Kilkenny, Knocktopher	gentry: knight	09-Jul-40	200	B.L. 19, 843 f. 59a	2837
Butler, Richard		peer: earl of Arran	16-Mar-67	7800	Dc3/57	2347
Butler, Richard		peer: son/heir of Edmund	18-Feb-97	200	Dc1/2r	9
Butler, Richard	Kilkenny, Knockosser	gentry: knight	30-Apr-39	4000	B.L. 19, 843 f. 5a	2729
Butler, Stephen	Cavan, Belterbett	gentry: knight	22-Mar-32	60	Dc2/178r	1815
Butler, Stephen	Fermanagh, Castlecowle	gentry: knight	22-Jul-20	400	Dc2/32r	1045
Butler, Stephen	Cavan, Belturbet	gentry: knight	29-May-23	500	Dc2/48r	1163
Butler, Stephen	Cavan, Belturbett	gentry: knight	14-Mar-31	60	Dc2/161r	1748
Butler, Stephen	Cavan, Belturbet	gentry: knight	05-Mar-23	4000	Dc2/45v	1146
Butler, Stephen	Cavan, Belturbett	gentry: knight	19-May-36	120	Dc2/252r	2126
Butler, Theobald	Tipperary, Ballyhemekin	gentry: esquire	05-Mar-39	400	B.L. 19, 843 f. 20	2758
Butler, Thomas	Tipperary, Brittas	gentry: gent	15-Feb-08	160	Dc1/81r	503

Standard	County	Occupation	Date	Amount	MS No	Ident No
Butler, Thomas	Carlow, Cloghgrenan	gentry: knight and baronet	07-May-32	280	Dc2/179v	1821
Butler, Thomas	Carlow, Cloghgrenan	gentry: baronet	15-Dec-28	520	Dc2/122v	1572
Butler, Thomas	Carlow, Sroughboe	gentry: gent	21-Nov-34	1400	Dc2/223r	1996
Butler, Thomas	Carlow, Shrughboe	gentry: gent	20-Apr-35	400	Dc2/233r	2038
Butler, Thomas	Carlow, Newstone	gentry: esquire	29-Nov-12	200	Dc1/117r	726
Butler, Thomas	Tipperary?	peer: baron Cahir	27-Apr-11	220	Dc1/103v	648
Butler, Thomas	Tipperary?	peer: baron Cahir	21-Nov-17	1000	Dc2/11r	921
Butler, Walter	Carlow, Shrughboe?	gentry: son/heir of Thomas	20-Apr-35	400	Dc2/233r	2038
Butler, Walter	Tipperary, Cloghbridie	gentry: gent	16-Jun-37	160	Dc2/264v	2187
Butler, Walter	Kilkenny, Paulestowne	gentry: gent	20-Feb-40	700	B.L. 19, 843 f. 52a	2823
Butler, Walter	Tipperary, Nodstowne	gentry: esquire	13-Jun-39	240	B.L. 19, 843 f. 7a	2733
Butterfield, Henry	Dublin, the city	trade: tailor	21-May-36	200	Dc2/252r	2127
Buttle, John	Dublin, the city	gentry: gent	07-Jan-79	560	B.L. 15, 637 f. 8	3862
Byran, James	Westmeath, Killouckin		02-Jul-12	500	Dc1/115r	714
Byrne, Barnaby	Wicklow, Ballenecor	gentry: son of Phelim	03-Mar-23	600	Dc2/45v	1145
Byrne, Barnaby	Meath, Balentre		17-Feb-02	20	Dc1/36r	237
Byrne, Barnaby	Carlow?, Ouldtowne?	gentry: son/heir of William	15-May-27	100	Dc2/92v	1433
Byrne, Brian	Roscommon, Mologhneshee	gentry: gent	21-Nov-11	60	Dc1/108v	676
Byrne, Brian	Wicklow, Ballynecor	gentry: esquire	21-Nov-34	1400	Dc2/223r	1996
Byrne, Brian	Wicklow, Kildea	gentry: gent	30-Jun-19	500	Dc2/24v	995
Byrne, Cahir	Wicklow, Knocklowe	gentry: gent	18-Nov-28	300	Dc2/116r	1542
Byrne, Callagh	Wicklow, Courtfoyle	gentry: gent	13-May-20	1000	Dc2/30r	1029
Byrne, Callagh	Wicklow, Kilteemyn	gentry: gent	30-Jun-19	500	Dc2/24v	995
Byrne, Connor	Roscommon, Clonfadda	gentry: gent	28-May-13	60	Dc1/121r	752
Byrne, Daniel	Dublin, the city	trade: tailor	17-Feb-76	400	B.L. 19, 844 f. 123	3252
Byrne, Daniel	Wicklow, Ballinderry	gentry: gent?	15-May-26	400	Dc2/77r	1363
Byrne, Daniel	Dublin, the city	trade: tailor	10-Jul-74	480	B.L. 19, 844 f. 30	3153
Byrne, Daniel	Dublin, the city	trade: tailor	19-Apr-69	1200	Dc3/95	2432
Byrne, Daniel	Roscommon, Drombodan	gentry: gent	14-Nov-11	60	Dc1/107v	670
Byrne, Daniel	Dublin, the city	trade: tailor	11-Mar-76	500	Dc3/172v	2652
Byrne, Daniel	Dublin, the city	trade: tailor	10-Jul-74	480	Dc3/162r	2613
Byrne, Daniel	Dublin, the city	trade: tailor	09-Jun-73	1600	Dc3/156v	2583
Byrne, Daniel	Dublin, the city	trade: tailor	17-Feb-76	400	Dc3/172v	2651
Byrne, Daniel	Dublin, the city	trade: tailor	19-Apr-69	1200	B.L. 15, 636 f. 37	3687
Byrne, Daniel	Dublin, the city	trade: tailor	09-Jul-73	1600	B.L. 15, 636 f. 137	3850
Byrne, Denis	Carlow, Tenrylan	gentry: gent	12-Nov-14	40	Dc1/132v	823
Byrne, Donogh	Roscommon, Downyn	gentry: esquire	20-Nov-11	60	Dc1/108v	675
Byrne, Donogh	Roscommon, Drowyn	gentry: gent	15-Nov-11	100	Dc1/108r	671
Byrne, Donogh	Roscommon, Downyn	gentry: gent	15-Nov-11	50	Dc1/108r	672
Byrne, Donogh	Roscommon, Downyn	gentry: gent	13-Nov-11	60	Dc1/107v	669
Byrne, Donogh	Roscommon, Downyn	gentry: gent	14-Nov-11	50	Dc1/107v	668

Standard	County	Occupation	Date	Amount	MS No	Ident No
Byrne, Donogh	Roscommon, Downyn	gentry: esquire	20-Nov-11	60	Dc1/108v	674
Byrne, Donogh	Roscommon, Downine	gentry: gent	14-Nov-10	50	Dc1/100r	626
Byrne, Donogh	Roscommon, Downyn	gentry: esquire	21-Nov-11	60	Dc1/109r	677
Byrne, Donogh	Roscommon, Downine	gentry: gent	14-Nov-10	50	Dc1/99v	625
Byrne, Dudley	Wicklow, Ballemcshennan	gentry: gent	28-May-22	60	Dc2/40v	1109
Byrne, Edmund	Carlow, Ravillye	gentry: esquire	31-May-17	220	Dc2/7v	904
Byrne, Edmund	Carlow, Rathvilly	gentry: esquire	20-Nov-18	120	Dc2/17v	956
Byrne, Edmund	Wicklow, Tinneparke	gentry: gent	25-Apr-35	1600	Dc2/233v	2040
Byrne, Edmund	Wicklow, Downecallibeere	gentry: gent	06-May-37	800	Dc2/262r	2177
Byrne, Edmund	Wicklow, Ballyhursy	gentry: gent	09-Aug-31	120	Dc2/167r	1773
Byrne, Edmund	Wicklow, Tyneparke	gentry: gent	05-May-32	174	Dc2/179r	1820
Byrne, Edmund	Wicklow, Culmore	gentry: gent	02-May-27	500	Dc2/91v	1428
Byrne, Edmund	Wicklow, Tinneparke	gentry: gent	24-Nov-34	1200	Dc2/223r	1997
Byrne, George	Wicklow, Toonhleyn	gentry: gent	25-May-22	600	Dc2/40r	1107
Byrne, George	Wicklow, Ardmary	gentry: gent	28-Jun-34	400	Dc2/213v	1958
Byrne, George	Wicklow, Templeleyne	gentry: gent	05-May-32	174	Dc2/179r	1820
Byrne, Gerald	Carlow, Bushardstowne	gentry: gent	12-Nov-34	400	Dc2/221r	1989
Byrne, Gerald	Wicklow, the Downe	gentry: gent	09-Aug-31	120	Dc2/167r	1773
Byrne, Gerald	Wicklow, Ballenvallee	gentry: gent	15-Jun-24	240	Dc2/56r	1223
Byrne, Gregory	Queen's Co., Killoen	gentry: baronet	17-Feb-76	400	B.L. 19, 844 f. 123	3252
Byrne, Gregory	Dublin, the city	gentry: gent, son of Daniel	19-Apr-69	1200	Dc3/95	2432
Byrne, Gregory	Queen's Co., Killowen	gentry: baronet	10-Jul-74	480	Dc3/162r	2613
Byrne, Gregory	Queen's Co., Killowen	gentry: baronet	10-Jul-74	480	B.L. 19, 844 f. 30	3153
Byrne, Gregory	Queen's Co., Killone	gentry: baronet	09-Jun-73	1600	Dc3/156v	2583
Byrne, Gregory	Queen's Co., Killoen	gentry: knight and baronet	17-Feb-76	400	Dc3/172v	2651
Byrne, Gregory	Queen's Co., Killone	gentry: baronet	09-Jul-73	1600	B.L. 15, 636 f. 137	3850
Byrne, Gregory	Queen's Co., Tymoge	gentry: baronet	05-Jan-84	400	B.L. 15, 637 f. 83	3997
Byrne, Gregory	Dublin, the city	trade: son of Daniel	19-Apr-69	1200	B.L. 15, 636 f. 37	3687
Byrne, Hugh	Wicklow, Ballenecor	gentry: son of Phelim	03-Mar-23	600	Dc2/45v	1145
Byrne, James	Carlow, Rahell	gentry: gent	18-Nov-24	400	Dc2/59r	1245
Byrne, James	Carlow, Seaskeanrean	gentry: gent	27-Mar-32	200	Dc2/178r	1816
Byrne, James	Carlow, Rathuill	gentry: gent	21-Nov-34	1400	Dc2/223r	1996
Byrne, James	Roscommon, late of Abby Boyle	merchant	14-Feb-57	520	B.L. 19, 843 f. 187a	3082
Byrne, John	Wicklow, Kilmartin	gentry: gent	01-May-22	350	Dc2/39v	1102
Byrne, John	Wicklow?	gentry: son of Murrough	17-Apr-19	100	Dc2/22r	981
Byrne, John	Wicklow, Courtfoyle	gentry: gent	28-May-22	60	Dc2/40v	1109
Byrne, John	Kilkenny, Banemore	gentry: gent	11-Nov-34	200	Dc2/221r	1988
Byrne, John	Wicklow, Courtfoyle	gentry: gent	13-May-20	1000	Dc2/30r	1029
Byrne, John	Wicklow, Courtfoyle	gentry: gent	14-Feb-23	240	Dc2/45r	1141
Byrne, John	Wicklow, Courtfoyle	gentry: gent	15-Jun-24	240	Dc2/56r	1223
Byrne, Laughlin	Wicklow, Knockomree	gentry: gent	30-Jun-19	500	Dc2/24v	995
Byrne, Luke	Wicklow, Killouana	gentry: gent	14-Jul-37	1200	Dc2/268v	2204

Standard	County	Occupation	Date	Amount	MS No	Ident No
Byrne, Luke	Wicklow, Killenane?	gentry: son/heir of Redmond	27-Aug-32	600	Dc2/185r	1844
Byrne, Luke	Wicklow, Kilmachnoe	gentry: gent	11-Jul-22	30	Dc2/41v	1117
Byrne, Melaghlen	Roscommon, Clonfadda	gentry: gent	15-Nov-10	50	Dc1/100r	627
Byrne, Murrough	Wicklow, Cowlemony	gentry: gent	17-Apr-19	100	Dc2/22r	981
Byrne, Phelim	Wicklow, Ballenecor	gentry: esquire	03-Mar-23	600	Dc2/45v	1145
Byrne, Redmond	Wicklow, Killevane	gentry: esquire	18-Nov-28	300	Dc2/116r	1542
Byrne, Redmond	Wicklow, Killenane	gentry: gent	27-Aug-32	600	Dc2/185r	1844
Byrne, Redmond	Wicklow, Kilmaghe	gentry: esquire	13-Dec-20	600	Dc2/33v	1056
Byrne, Redmond	Wicklow, Kilmacow	gentry: gent	23-Jul-23	140	Dc2/49v	1177
Byrne, Redmond	Wicklow, Kilmacow	gentry: gent	16-Dec-23	600	Dc2/51v	1191
Byrne, Richard	Wicklow, Tenne-Parke	gentry: gent	01-May-22	350	Dc2/39v	1102
Byrne, Richard	Wicklow, Tyneparke	gentry: gent	14-Feb-23	240	Dc2/45r	1141
Byrne, Richard	Wicklow, Tenneparke	gentry: gent	13-May-20	1000	Dc2/30r	1029
Byrne, Richard	Wicklow, Tyneparke	gentry: gent	12-May-23	350	Dc2/46v	1154
Byrne, Richard	Wicklow, Tynneparke	gentry: gent	28-May-22	60	Dc2/40v	1109
Byrne, Richard	Wicklow, Tynneparke	gentry: gent	25-May-22	600	Dc2/40r	1107
Byrne, Richard	Wicklow, Teneparke	gentry: gent	15-Jun-24	240	Dc2/56r	1223
Byrne, Teige	Wicklow, Ballenevallee	gentry: gent	30-Jun-19	500	Dc2/24v	995
Byrne, Turlough	Westmeath, Kilmore, Athlone	gentry: gent	16-Aug-55	600	B.L. 19, 843 f. 163a	3041
Byrne, Turlough	Wicklow, Cnocknearaid	gentry: gent	12-May-23	350	Dc2/46v	1154
Byrne, William	Carlow, Ouldtowne	gentry: gent	15-May-27	100	Dc2/92v	1433
Bysse, John	Dublin, the city	gentry: esquire	13-Feb-34	240	Dc2/206v	1930
Bysse, Robert	Dublin	gentry: esquire	02-Sep-22	1240	Dc2/42v	1121
Caddell, Andrew	Dublin, the city	merchant	09-Sep-25	360	Dc2/69r	1314
Caddell, John	Dublin, the Naull	gentry: gent	29-Oct-58	110	B.L. 15, 635 f. 41	3336
Caddell, Patrick	Dublin, Surgostown	gentry: gent	22-Nov-20	200	Dc2/33r	1052
Caddell, Patrick	Dublin, Surgotstone	gentry: gent	23-Mar-26	80	Dc2/76r	1355
Caddell, Patrick	Dublin, Surgoldston	gentry: gent	14-Feb-15	60	Dc1/135r	839
Caddell, Patrick	Dublin, Glassenhall	gentry: gent	22-Jun-37	300	Dc2/265r	2190
Caddell, Patrick	Dublin, Surgotston	gentry: gent	21-Sep-24	100	Dc2/58r	1238
Caddell, Patrick	Dublin, Surgoston	gentry: gent	05-Mar-27	160	Dc2/88v	1418
Caddell, Patrick	Dublin, Surgolston	gentry: gent	02-Dec-17	200	Dc2/12r	927
Caddell, Richard	Meath, Doveston	gentry: gent	25-Jun-10	40	Dc1/98v	618
Caddell, Richard	Meath, Dowstone	gentry: gent	07-May-18	320	Dc2/14r	938
Caddell, Richard	Meath, Daneston	gentry: gent	18-Nov-06	120	Dc1/71v	433
Caddell, Robert	Dublin, the Moreton	gentry: gent	03-Dec-06	750	Dc1/72v	440
Caddell, Robert	Dublin, Mooreton	gentry: gent	19-Jun-11	105	Dc1/104v	652
Caddell, Robert	Meath, Harbardstowne	gentry: gent	05-Dec-97	400	Dc1/8r	58
Cairnes, John	Tyrone, Aghronan	gentry: gent	20-Jun-78	200	B.L. 15, 637 f. 2a	3855
Caldwell, James	Fermanagh, Wollsborrough	gentry: esquire	13-Nov-78	5000	B.L. 15, 637 f. 9	3863
Callaghan, Callaghan	Cork, Clonmyne	gentry: esquire	09-Dec-12	120	Dc1/117r	728
Callaghan, Callaghan	Cork, Clonmyne	gentry: gent	09-Jun-13	60	Dc1/122r	757

Standard	County	Occupation	Date	Amount	MS No	Ident No
Callaghan, Callaghan	Cork, Clounmyne	gentry: esquire	23-May-28	600	Dc2/109v	1512
Callaghan, Callaghan	Cork, Clonmyne	gentry: gent	06-Dec-14	148	Dc1/133v	829
Callaghan, Callaghan	Cork, Clonmyne	gentry: esquire	08-Jun-13	60	Dc1/121v	756
Callaghan, Callaghan	Cork, Clonmyn	gentry: esquire	10-Dec-12	400	Dc1/117v	729
Callaghan, Callaghan	Cork, Clonmyne	gentry: gent	01-Jun-13	200	Dc1/121r	753
Callaghan, Con	Cork, Cooleroe	gentry: esquire	29-Aug-73	1200	B.L. 19, 844 f. 17	3135
Callaghan, Donogh	Cork, Cluonmyne	gentry: gent	07-Apr-39	400	B.L. 19, 843 f. 30a	2779
Callaghan, Donogh	Cork, Cluonemyne	gentry: gent	24-Mar-38	440	B.L. 19, 843 f. 19	2756
Callaghan, Donogh	Cork, Castlenaninshy	gentry: esquire	16-Feb-82	800	B.L. 15, 637 f. 58	3951
Callaghan, Donogh	Cork, Clonmeone	gentry: esquire	25-Aug-68	300	B.L. 15, 635 f. 227a	3660
Callaghan, Donogh	Cork, Clonmeone	gentry: gent, son/heir of Donagh	25-Aug-68	300	B.L. 15, 635 f. 227a	3660
Callan, David	Westmeath, Athlone	farmer: yeoman	16-Dec-99	100	Dc1/20r	137
Callan, Mathew	Louth, Monesterboyse?	farmer: yeoman	12-Jul-98	300	Dc1/11v	84
Calthorpe, Charles		gentry: knight	12-Sep-05	260	Dc1/62r	376
Campbell, Hugh	Down, Donoghadee	gentry: gent	12-Jun-69	400	Dc3/99	2440
Candler, William	Queen's Co., Ballybrittas	farmer: yeoman	14-Mar-68	60	Dc3/74	2392
Canning, George	Londonderry, Aghevey	gentry: esquire	31-Jul-69	2000	Dc3/101	2444
Canning, George	Londonderry, Aghevey	gentry: esquire	31-Jul-69	2000	B.L. 15, 636 f. 40a	3695
Cantwell, John	Kilkenny, Cantwell Courte	gentry: gent	13-Feb-07	105	Dc1/74r	449
Cantwell, Thomas	Tipperary, Kiltelloge	gentry: esquire	13-Mar-35	400	Dc2/230v	2028
Cantwell, William	Tipperary, Muckarke	gentry: esquire	20-Mar-34	76	Dc2/209v	1943
Cardiff, John	Dublin, Dunsinke	gentry: gent	23-Mar-00	200	Dc1/22r	148
Cardiff, Robert	Dublin, Scribleston	gentry: gent	23-Mar-00	200	Dc1/22r	148
Cardiff, Robert	Dublin, Ffinglas	gentry: gent	02-Dec-02	160	Dc1/41v	266
Carew, Robert	Wexford, Belaborow	gentry: gent	24-Jun-76	600	B.L. 19, 844 f. 112	3240
Carew, Robert	Wexford, Belaborough	gentry: gent	17-May-74	300	B.L. 19, 844 f. 26	3148
Carew, Robert	Wexford, Belaborow	gentry: gent	24-Jun-76	600	Dc3/178v	2671
Carew, Robert	Cork, Carrivd	gentry: knight	26-Jun-37	400	Dc2/266r	2194
Carew, Robert	Wexford, Bellaboree	gentry: esquire	22-Feb-86	2000	B.L. 15, 637 f. 105a	4038
Carey, John	Dublin	merchant	09-Dec-16	120	Dc2/3r	883
Carleton, George	Dublin, Oxmantowne, suburbs	gentry: esquire	07-Feb-59	866	B.L. 15, 635 f. 43a	3339
Carleton, Lancelot	Fermanagh, Little Carleton	gentry: gent	02-May-59	300	B.L. 15, 635 f. 44a	3341
Carr, William	Dublin, Ffinglas	gentry: gent	20-Jul-99	40	Dc1/18r	124
Carr, William	Dublin, Ffinglas	gentry: gent	27-Nov-99	60	Dc1/20r	136
Carrick, Simon	Dublin, the city	merchant	11-Jun-73	240	Dc3/157r	2584
Carrick, Simon	Dublin, the city	merchant	11-Jun-73	240	B.L. 15, 636 f. 134	3844
Carrick, William	Kerry, Glandine	gentry: esquire	06-Sep-78	460	B.L. 15, 637 f.10	3865
Carroll, Charles	King's Co., Beaghernagh	gentry: esquire	09-Apr-29	120	Dc2/127r	1596
Carroll, James	Dublin, the city	gentry: knight	13-Feb-24	120	Dc2/53v	1203
Carroll, James	Dublin, the city	gentry: knight	24-Sep-32	200	Dc2/186r	1847
Carroll, James	Dublin	gentry: knight	27-May-26	1200	Dc2/78v	1371
Carroll, James	Dublin?	gentry: knight	23-Feb-15	666	Dc1/136r	843
Carroll, John	King's Co., Clonluske	gentry: esquire	05-Jul-34	600	Dc2/214r	1961

Standard	County	Occupation	Date	Amount	MS No	Ident No
Carroll, John	King's Co., Clonliske	gentry: esquire	28-Jun-25	400	Dc2/67r	1300
Carroll, John	King's Co., Clonliske	gentry: esquire	07-Jul-37	3000	Dc2/267r	2198
Carroll, John	King's Co., Clunliske	gentry: esquire	31-Jul-40	10000	B.L. 19, 843 f. 69a	2858
Carroll, John	King's Co., Clonliske	gentry: esquire	07-Aug-33	200	Dc2/198v	1897
Carroll, John	King's Co., Clonliske	gentry: esquire	10-Feb-34	700	Dc2/206r	1928
Carroll, John	King's Co., Leape	gentry: esquire	14-Jan-25	160	Dc2/60r	1256
Carroll, John	King's Co., Clonliske	gentry: esquire	17-Dec-30	1000	Dc2/158r	1734
Carroll, John	King's Co., Clonliske	gentry: esquire	18-Jul-28	200	Dc2/113v	1531
Carroll, John	King's Co., Clonlaske	gentry: esquire	30-Jun-28	180	Dc2/112r	1524
Carroll, John	King's Co., Clonluske	gentry: esquire	25-Nov-28	200	Dc2/117r	1546
Carroll, Mulronee	King's Co., Clonlyske	gentry: knight	23-May-06	400	Dc1/68r	412
Carroll, Teige	King's Co., Ballyneclohe		23-May-06	400	Dc1/68r	412
Carter, Nicholas	Dublin, Jamestowne	gentry: esquire	05-Jun-58	248	B.L. 15, 635 f. 55	3361
Casey, William	Westmeath, Molingare	gentry: gent	18-Nov-09	300	Dc1/92r	577
Casey, William	Westmeath, Mollingarre	merchant	13-Nov-06	30	Dc1/71r	430
Casey, William	Westmeath, Mollingarr	merchant	21-Jun-09	200	Dc1/89v	560
Cashell, Oliver	Louth, Dundalk	gentry: gent	04-Dec-26	220	Dc2/85r	1403
Cashell, Oliver	Louth, Dondalke	gentry: gent	01-Dec-26	600	Dc2/84v	1401
Cashell, Patrick	Louth, Doundalke	gentry: esquire	24-Nov-29	700	Dc2/139r	1649
Cashell, Patrick	Louth, Dondalke	gentry: esquire	01-Dec-26	600	Dc2/84v	1401
Cashell, Patrick	Louth, Dundalk	gentry: esquire	04-Dec-26	220	Dc2/85r	1403
Cashell, Patrick	Louth, Dundalk	gentry: esquire	05-Jul-36	2000	Dc2/254v	2141
Cashin, Owney	Queen's Co., Crosse	gentry: gent	20-Aug-39	1000	B.L. 19, 843 f. 35a	2789
Cashin, Patrick	Queen's Co., Crosse	gentry: gent	28-Mar-40	1000	B.L. 19, 843 f. 49	2816
Cassell, Patrick	Dublin, Surgotston		20-Nov-23	200	Dc2/51r	1187
Cassidy, Rory	Monaghan, Rathcowelle	gentry: gent	25-Nov-20	600	Dc2/33r	1053
Caulfield, Robert	Armagh?	peer: baron Charlemont	02-Dec-42	1000	B.L. 19, 843 f. 110	2939
Caulfield, Robert	Armagh?	peer: baron Charlemont	12-Sep-42	600	B.L. 19, 843 f. 109a	2938
Caulfield, Thomas	Roscommon, Donamon	gentry: esquire	07-Feb-77	660	Dc3/181v	2685
Caulfield, Thomas	Roscommon, Donamon	gentry: esquire	07-Feb-77	660	B.L. 19, 844 f. 113	3241
Caulfield, William	Armagh?	peer: baron Charlemont	03-Jan-56	210	B.L. 19, 843 f. 169	3052
Caulfield, William	Armagh?	peer: baron Charlemont	05-Dec-33	800	Dc2/202v	1913
Caulfield, William	Armagh?	peer: baron Charlemont	07-Apr-30	1500	Dc2/144r	1674
Caulfield, William	Armagh?	peer: baron Charlemont	02-Mar-29	400	Dc2/125v	1589
Caulfield, William	Armagh?	peer: baron Charlemont	02-Mar-29	2000	Dc2/125v	1588
Caulfield, William	Armagh?	peer: baron Charlemont	07-Apr-55	500	B.L. 19, 843 f. 159a	3034
Caulfield, William	Armagh?	peer: baron Charlemont	30-May-36	2000	Dc2/252v	2130
Caulfield, William	Armagh?	peer: baron Charlemont	20-Jun-54	500	B.L. 19, 843 f. 141	2996
Caulfield, William	Armagh?	peer: baron Charlemont	13-Feb-61	620	B.L. 15, 635 f. 64a	3378
Caulfield, William	Armagh?	peer: baron Charlemont	20-Sep-61	700	B.L. 15, 635 f. 84	3404
Cayne, Stephen	Londonderry, the city	gentry: esquire	20-Feb-58	300	B.L. 15, 635 f. 27	3309
Chaff, Robert	King's Co., Rathmoore	gentry: esquire	16-Feb-66	220	Dc3/22	2273
Challenor, James	Louth, Drogheda	trade: clothier	27-Apr-75	50	B.L. 19, 844 f. 64	3192
Challoner, James	Louth, Drogheda	gentry: gent	07-May-64	280	B.L. 15, 635 f. 148	3515
Chamberlain, Marcus	Dublin, Kilreske	gentry: gent	16-Oct-00	400	Dc1/26r	176

Standard	County	Occupation	Date	Amount	MS No	Ident No
Chamberlain, Michael	Dublin		12-Jul-06	200	Dc1/70r	423
Chamberlain, Michael	Dublin	merchant	08-Mar-07	400	Dc1/75v	457
Chamberlain, Michael	Dublin	merchant	02-May-07	80	Dc1/75v	460
Chamberlain, Michael	Dublin		18-Sep-11	200	Dc1/664	664
Chamberlain, Michael	Dublin		24-Dec-03	2508	Dc1/50v	324
Chamberlain, Michael	Dublin		23-Sep-09	400	Dc1/91v	573
Chamberlain, Richard	Dublin, Kilreske	gentry: son/heir of Marcus	16-Oct-00	400	Dc1/26r	176
Chamberlain, Rowland	Dublin, the city	merchant	11-Jan-17	100	Dc2/3v	887
Chamberlain, Rowland	Dublin	merchant: son/heir of Micheal	18-Sep-11	200	Dc1/664	664
Chamberlain, William	Dublin, Ffinglas	gentry: gent	13-Jul-01	80	Dc1/33r	219
Chamberlain, William	Dublin, Ffinglas	gentry: gent	20-Jul-00	100	Dc1/25r	169
Chamberlain, William	Dublin, Ffinglas	farmer: freeholder	23-Apr-99	40	Dc1/17r	117
Chambers, Francis	Armagh, Drumully	gentry: gent, son/heir of Franas	17-Jan-72	340	B.L. 15, 636 f. 102	3797
Chambers, Francis	Armagh, Drumully	gentry: esquire	17-Jan-72	340	B.L. 15, 636 f. 102	3797
Chambre, Calcott	Wicklow, Carnowe	gentry: esquire	12-Jan-30	1000	Dc2/140v	1658
Chambre, Calcott	Wicklow, Carnow	gentry: esquire	07-Dec-33	1500	Dc2/203r	1915
Champant, Thomas	Cork, Cashell McAwlye	gentry: gent	23-May-14	340	Dc1/129v	805
Chase, Robert	King's Co., Rathmoore	gentry: esquire	06-Feb-66	220	B.L. 15, 635 f. 163a	3542
Cheeke, Thomas	Kildare, Blackrath	gentry: gent	09-Oct-57	200	B.L. 19, 843 f. 197	3101
Cheeke, Thomas	Kildare, Blackerath	gentry: gent	02-May-59	1200	B.L. 15, 635 f. 43	3338
Cheeke, Thomas	Dublin, the city	trade: brewer	11-Feb-56	300	B.L. 19, 843 f. 168	3050
Cheevers, Christopher	Meath, Maston	gentry: esquire	02-Mar-01	2000	Dc1/29r	194
Cheevers, Christopher	Meath, Muston	gentry: esquire	21-Jun-39	4000	B.L. 19, 843 f. 21a	2761
Cheevers, Christopher	Meath, Maceton	gentry: esquire	01-Jul-09	40	Dc1/89v	561
Cheevers, Henry	Dublin, Hounton	gentry: gent	27-Sep-33	200	Dc2/200r	1903
Cheevers, Henry	Dublin, Mounckton	gentry: esquire	28-Apr-37	1000	Dc2/261v	2175
Cheevers, Henry	Dublin, Maunton	gentry: gent	04-May-30	200	Dc2/145r	1678
Cheevers, Henry	Dublin, Monnckton	gentry: esquire	24-May-25	400	Dc2/64r	1283
Cheevers, Jeremy	Louth, Drogheda	merchant	20-Mar-72	600	Dc3/145r	2548
Cheevers, Jeremy	Louth, Drogheda	merchant	20-Mar-72	600	B.L. 15, 636 f. 108	3807
Cheevers, John	Meath, Ballyhoe	gentry: gent	20-Jan-40	42	B.L. 19, 843 f. 57	2832
Cheevers, John	Carlow, Grangfortt	gentry: son/heir of Chris	21-Jun-39	4000	B.L. 19, 843 f. 21a	2761
Cheevers, John	Carlow, Grangeforth	gentry: esquire	16-Nov-39	600	B.L. 19, 843 f. 32	2782
Cheevers, John	Dublin, Glasniven	gentry: gent	01-Jun-29	100	Dc2/130v	1612
Cheevers, John	Meath, Masetowne	gentry: esquire	27-Jan-65	2000	Dc3/1	2223
Cheevers, John	Meath, Maston	gentry: esquire	12-Jan-99	200	Dc1/14r	99
Cheevers, John	Meath, Maston	gentry: esquire	06-Nov-98	200	Dc1/12v	91
Cheevers, John	Carlow, Grangforth	gentry: esquire	11-Nov-34	200	Dc2/220v	1987
Cheevers, John	Meath, Maston	gentry: esquire	10-Oct-98	200	Dc1/12v	90
Cheevers, John	Meath, Masetowne	gentry: esquire	27-Jan-65	2000	B.L. 15, 635 f. 214	3633
Cheevers, Mark	Wexford, the grange of Roslare	gentry: gent?	15-Nov-16	240	Dc2/2r	876

Standard	County	Occupation	Date	Amount	MS No	Ident No
Cheevers, Nicholas	Meath, Gerraldston	gentry: gent	06-Nov-98	200	Dc1/12v	91
Cheevers, Philip	Dublin, Beverston	gentry: gent	17-Jun-02	100	Dc1/38r	248
Cheevers, Richard	Wexford, Attramman	gentry: gent	29-May-68	700	Dc3/77	2398
Cheevers, Richard	Wexford, Antramnan?	gentry: gent	29-May-68	700	B.L. 15, 635 f. 218a	3642
Cheevers, Robert	Louth, Drogheda [Carnaghton]	gentry: gent	18-Aug-40	400	B.L. 19, 843 f. 66a	2852
Cheevers, Walter	Dublin, Monktowne	gentry: esquire	06-Nov-73	459	Dc3/158ar	2593
Cheevers, Walter	Dublin, Mountaine?	gentry: esquire	08-Apr-65	220	Dc3/3	2229
Cheevers, Walter	Dublin, Monckstowne	gentry: esquire	03-Mar-69	1200	Dc3/92	2427
Cheevers, Walter	Dublin, Monkstowne	gentry: esquire	17-Feb-71	420	Dc3/136r	2517
Cheevers, Walter	Dublin, Mounckton?	gentry: son/heir of Henry	28-Apr-37	1000	Dc2/261v	2175
Cheevers, Walter	Dublin, Monktowne	gentry: esquire	06-Nov-73	450	B.L. 19, 844 f. 15	3133
Cheevers, Walter	Dublin, Monckestowne	gentry: esquire	03-Mar-69	1200	B.L. 15, 636 f. 38	3690
Chichester, Arthur	Antrim?	peer: viscount Chichester	01-May-57	200	B.L. 19, 843 f. 197a	3102
Chichester, Arthur	Tyrone, Dungannon	gentry: knight	13-Feb-68	300	Dc3/73	2390
Chichester, Arthur	Antrim?	peer: viscount Chichester	29-Apr-55	1000	B.L. 19, 843 f. 160	3035
Chichester, Arthur	Antrim?	peer: earl of Donegal	09-Jun-76	1400	Dc3/176v	2664
Chichester, Arthur	Tyrone, Dungannon	gentry: knight	25-Nov-65	1500	Dc3/16	2257
Chichester, Arthur	Tyrone, Dongannon	gentry: knight	28-Mar-65	30	B.L. 15, 635 f. 150a	3520
Chichester, Arthur	Antrim?	peer: earl of Donegal	25-Mar-66	3240	B.L. 15, 635 f. 172a	3554
Chichester, Arthur	Tyrone, Dungannon	gentry: knight	13-Feb-68	300	B.L. 15, 635 f. 220a	3646
Chichester, Arthur	Tyrone, Dungannon	gentry: knight	25-Nov-65	1500	B.L. 15, 635 f. 159a	3536
Chichester, Arthur	Tyrone, Dungannon	gentry: knight	09-Jul-61	300	B.L. 15, 635 f. 83a	3403
Chichester, Edward	Wexford, Prospecte	gentry: esquire	26-Jul-37	2000	Dc2/269v	2210
Chichester, Edward	Antrim, Stranmillis	soldier: lieutenant colonel	05-Feb-58	100	B.L. 15, 635 f. 28a	3312
Chichester, Edward	Wexford, Prospect	gentry: esquire	03-Dec-69	1460	Dc3/110	2463
Chichester, Edward	Antrim, Stranmillis	soldier: s/heir of Lt Col Edward	05-Feb-58	100	B.L. 15, 635 f. 28a	3312
Chichester, Edward	Antrim?	peer: viscount Chichester	21-Dec-32	2000	Dc2/189r	1859
Chichester, Edward	Wexford, Prospect	gentry: esquire	09-Jul-61	300	B.L. 15, 635 f. 83a	3403
Chichester, John	Dublin, the city	gentry: gent	01-Dec-73	700	Dc3/159r	2597
Child, Joshua	Westmeath, Kilbeggan	gentry: gent	12-Feb-24	1000	Dc2/53v	1202
Chillam, Christopher	Louth, Drogheda		18-Sep-23	800	Dc2/50r	1181
Chillam, Christopher	Louth, Drogheda		13-Feb-26	300	Dc2/73v	1342
Chillam, Christopher	Louth, Drogheda	merchant	23-Dec-35	96	Dc2/243r	2086
Chillam, Christopher	Louth, Drogheda		23-Mar-23	900	Dc2/54r	1207
Chillam, Christopher	Louth, Drogheda	merchant: son/heir of Robert	01-Mar-32	1500	Dc2/176v	1811
Chillam, Christopher	Meath, Gaffine	gentry: gent	30-Aug-39	200	B.L. 19, 843 f. 36a	2791
Chillam, Christopher	Louth, Drogheda	merchant	17-Dec-29	600	Dc2.140v	1656
Chillam, Christopher	Louth, Drogheda	merchant	04-Feb-29	400	Dc2/123v	1577
Chillam, Christopher	Louth, Drogheda	other: son/heir of Robert	27-Jan-29	100	Dc2/123v	1576

Standard	County	Occupation	Date	Amount	MS No	Ident No
Chillam, Christopher	Louth, Drogheda	merchant	01-Dec-35	80	Dc2/23	2087
Chillam, Christopher	Meath, Gaffine	gentry: gent	26-Jun-40	400	B.L. 19, 843 f. 59	2836
Chillam, Christopher	Louth, Drogheda	merchant	04-Dec-22	400	Dc2/43v	1130
Chillam, Christopher	Meath, Gaffnie	gentry: son/heir of Robert	05-May-28	200	Dc2/106v	1498
Chillam, Christopher	Louth, Drogheda	gentry: son of Robert	29-Apr-26	100	Dc2/76v	1359
Chillam, James	Meath, Gaffny	gentry: gent	19-May-69	480	Dc3/98	2437
Chillam, James	Meath, Gafny	gentry: gent	02-Dec-69	400	Dc3/109	2461
Chillam, James	Meath, Gaffny	gentry: gent	06-Apr-72	400	Dc3/145v	2550
Chillam, James	Meath, Gaffny	gentry: gent	02-Dec-69	400	B.L. 15, 636 f. 45	3702
Chillam, James	Meath, Gaffny	gentry: gent	06-Apr-72	400	B.L. 15, 636 f. 113a	3817
Chillam, James	Meath, Gaffney	gentry: gent	19-May-69	480	B.L. 15, 636 f. 43a	3700
Chillam, Patrick	Meath, Gaffine	gentry: son/heir of Chris	30-Aug-39	200	B.L. 19, 843 f. 36a	2791
Chillam, Richard	Dublin, Palmerstowne	trade: miller	28-Oct-31	40	Dc2/169r	1781
Chillam, Robert	Louth, Drogheda		18-Sep-23	800	Dc2/50r	1181
Chillam, Robert	Louth, Drogheda		15-Jan-04	400	Dc1/51v	328
Chillam, Robert	Louth, Drogheda		29-Apr-26	100	Dc2/76v	1359
Chillam, Robert	Meath, Gafnie	gentry: gent	01-Mar-32	1500	Dc2/176v	1811
Chillam, Robert	Meath, Gaffnie	gentry: gent	05-May-28	200	Dc2/106v	1498
Chillam, Robert	Louth, Drogheda		13-Feb-26	300	Dc2/73v	1342
Chillam, Robert	Louth, Drogheda		27-Jan-29	100	Dc2/123v	1576
Church, John	Dublin, Newcastle, near Lyons	farmer: son of Ric freeholder	22-Jun-99	400	Dc1/17r	116
Churchman, Samuel	Dublin	trade: upholster	04-Jul-33	240	Dc2/197r	1891
Clancy, Cornelius	Clare, Vrely	gentry: gent	28-May-41	1200	B.L. 19, 843 f. 95a	2910
Clancy, Donogh	Clare, Warlyn	gentry: gent	13-Feb-07	87	Dc1/74v	450
Clancy, Murrough	Clare, Vrely	gentry: gent, s./heir of Cornelius	28-May-41	1200	B.L. 19, 843 f. 95a	2910
Clarke, John	Dublin, the city	gentry: gent	19-Jun-68	200	Dc3/79	2405
Clarke, John	Cork, Twomolty	gentry: gent	27-Mar-82	720	B.L. 15, 637 f. 57	3949
Clarke, Lawrence	Dublin, Dyswelston	farmer	04-Apr-00	40	Dc1/22v	150
Clarke, Richard	Dublin, Dyswelston	farmer	04-Apr-00	40	Dc1/22v	150
Clarke, Simon	Dublin, Tirrelston	farmer: yeoman	19-Apr-05	400	Dc1/57v	352
Clarke, Thomas	Dublin, Hollewood Rath	farmer	04-Apr-00	40	Dc1/22v	150
Clarke, Thomas	Dublin	merchant	28-Nov-10	300	Dc1/101r	634
Clarke, William	Cork, Ballywolaghanein?	gentry: gent	27-Mar-82	720	B.L. 15, 637 f. 57	3949
Cleyborne, William	Wexford	gentry: esquire	05-Nov-58	800	B.L. 15, 635 f. 37a	3329
Cleyborne, William	Wexford, the town	gentry: esquire	28-Sep-59	600	B.L. 15, 635 f. 51a	3354
Clifford, Knight	Dublin, the city	gentry: gent	21-Jan-74	2000	Dc3/159v	2600
Clifford, Mary	Meath, Castle Jordan	gentry: widow of Rich esq	09-Feb-99	203	Dc1/15v	106
Clinch, Patrick	Dublin, the city	trade: baker	23-Mar-30	200	Dc2/143v	1672
Clinch, Peter	Dublin, Newcastle neer Lyon	gentry: gent	24-Jan-18	200	Dc2/13r	932
Clinch, Robert	Dublin, Dunsincke	farmer	20-Nov-28	220	Dc2/116r	1543

Standard	County	Occupation	Date	Amount	MS No	Ident No
Clinton, Peter	Louth, Dowdestowne	gentry: esquire	25-Nov-36	200	Dc2/257r	2156
Clinton, Sebastian	Louth, Port	gentry: gent	20-Feb-72	200	B.L. 15, 636 f. 102a	3798
Clotworthy, Hugh	Antrim, Antrim	gentry: esquire	18-Apr-10	400	Dc1/95r	596
Clotworthy, John	Antrim?	peer:				
		viscount Massereene	05-Jul-70	1000	Dc3/123	2486
Clotworthy, John	Antrim, Antrim	gentry: knight	20-Feb-55	2400	B.L. 19, 843 f. 161	3037
Clotworthy, Mary	Kildare, Grangemillon	other: widow	02-Dec-70	2000	Dc3/132r	2505
Clotworthy, Mary	Kildare, Grangemillon	other: widow	02-Dec-70	2000	B.L. 15, 636 f. 75	3752
Codd, Balthazar	Wexford, Garrylogh	gentry: gent	16-May-09	160	Dc1/88r	551
Codd, Edward	Wexford, Enneeskorthy	gentry: gent	10-Nov-12	140	Dc1/116r	720
Codd, Martin	Wexford, Castilton	gentry: gent	30-Jun-12	120	Dc1/114v	710
Coffey, Hugh	Cork, Killmore	gentry: gent	23-Nov-97	140	Dc1/7r	50
Colclough, Anthony	Wexford, Old Ross	gentry: gent	11-Jul-22	120	Dc2/41v	1116
Colclough, Dudley	Wexford, Moynart	gentry: esquire	14-Sep-63	1000	B.L. 15, 635 f. 125	3477
Colclough, Patrick	Wexford, Moynart	gentry: son/heir of				
		Dudley	14-Sep-63	1000	B.L. 15, 635 f. 125	3477
Cole, John	Monaghan, Ballinveaghan	gentry: gent	28-Feb-63	240	B.L. 15, 635 f. 105	3442
Coleman, James	Tipperary, Nenagh	gentry: gent	16-Feb-67	200	B.L. 15, 635 f. 190	3590
Coleman, Samuel	Dublin, Wailshton	gentry: gent	28-Jul-26	100	Dc2/81v	1388
Coleman, Samuel	Dublin, Walshton	gentry: gent	27-Feb-23	50	Dc2/45v	1144
Coleman, William	Limerick, Ardagh	gentry: esquire	30-Nov-11	140	Dc1/110r	682
Colley, Gerard	Louth, Ardee	gentry: esquire	24-Nov-30	100	Dc2/156v	1728
Colvill, Margaret	Dublin, the city	other: widow	23-Feb-65	1300	Dc3/3	2227
Colvill, Robert	Antrim, Goltgorme	gentry: esquire	09-Jun-76	2400	Dc3/176r	2663
Coman, James	Clare, Downebegg	gentry: gent	24-Nov-27	100	Dc2/100r	1465
Coman, Patrick	Clare, Ardnekelly	gentry: gent	24-Nov-27	100	Dc2/100r	1465
Coman, Thomas	Dublin, Wyanston	gentry: gent	17-Feb-26	600	Dc2/74r	1345
Comerford, Edward	Kilkenny, Callan	gentry: esquire	06-Jun-40	4000	B.L. 19, 843 f. 56a	2831
Comerford, George	Carlow, Wells	gentry: esquire	10-Feb-30	400	Dc2/142r	1666
Comerford, George	Carlow, Wells	gentry: esquire	25-Oct-40	800	B.L. 19, 843 f. 74	2867
Comerford, George	Carlow, Wells	gentry: esquire	25-Nov-36	1000	Dc2/257v	2158
Comerford, George	Carlow, Wells	gentry: esquire	13-Feb-32	320	Dc2/175v	1807
Comerford, George	Carlow, Wells	gentry: esquire	28-Nov-28	240	Dc2/118r	1553
Comingan, William	Dublin	gentry: gent	26-Aug-29	320	Dc2/136r	1636
Condon, Maurice	Cork, Kilbarrie	gentry: gent	07-Jan-41	3200	B.L. 19, 843 f. 82	2883
Conner, Cary	Kildare, Lexlippe	gentry: gent	13-Jun-28	800	Dc2/111r	1517
Connolly, Patrick	Dublin, the city	merchant	09-Jul-07	704	Dc1/79v	486
Conran, John	Westmeath, Athlone	merchant	02-Dec-25	120	Dc2/71v	1328
Conran, John	Westmeath, Athlone	merchant	17-Dec-25	200	Dc2/72v	1334
Conran, John	Westmeath, Athlone	merchant	07-Jun-25	606	Dc2/65r	1290
Conran, John	Westmeath, Athlone	merchant	18-Feb-15	200	Dc1/135v	842
Conran, John	Westmeath, Athlone	merchant	17-Dec-25	40	Dc2/72r	1333
Conran, John	Westmeath, Athlone	merchant	09-Mar-25	120	Dc2/62r	1269
Conran, John	Westmeath, Athlone	merchant	11-Jun-25	606	Dc2/65v	1292
Conran, Mary	Dublin, the city	merchant: wife of Walter	17-Jun-31	200	Dc2/165r	1763

Standard	County	Occupation	Date	Amount	MS No	Ident No
Conran, Walter	Dublin, the city	merchant	17-Jun-31	200	Dc2/165r	1763
Conran, William	Dublin	merchant	01-Dec-19	120	Dc2/26v	1007
Conroy, Maurice	Wicklow, Holliwood		30-Apr-30	80	Dc2/144v	1676
Conroy, Maurice	Wicklow, Holliwood		30-Apr-30	63	Dc2/144v	1677
Conway, Foulke	Antrim?	gentry: knight	29-Nov-17	800	Dc2/12r	926
Conway, Foulke	Antrim, Carrickfergus	gentry: knight	16-Mar-09	500	Dc1/88r	549
Conway, Foulke	Antrim, Carrickfergus	gentry: knight	23-May-15	400	Dc1/138r	855
Conway, Foulke	Antrim, Lysnegarvee	gentry: knight	01-May-21	800	Dc2/35v	1070
Conway, Jenkin	Kerry, Killorgan	gentry: esquire	19-Nov-13	20	Dc1/124r	770
Cooche, Thomas	Queen's Co., Stradballie	gentry: knight	16-Apr-06	400	Dc1/66v	403
Cooke, Walshingham	Meath, Donnshaghlyin	gentry: esquire	25-Jul-18	620	Dc2/16r	949
Cooke, Walshingham	Meath, Dunshaglin	gentry: esquire	06-Apr-20	300	Dc2/29v	1025
Cooke, Walshingham	Meath, Donsaghlin	gentry: esquire	01-Apr-17	280	Dc2/6r	899
Cooke, Walshingham	Meath, Dunshaghlin	gentry: esquire	13-May-29	240	Dc2/128v	1604
Cooke, Walshingham	Meath, Donshaghlen	gentry: esquire	25-Jul-18	310	Dc2/16r	948
Cooke, Walshingham	Meath, Dunsaghlen	gentry: esquire	22-Aug-17	200	Dc2/9v	911
Cooke, Walshingham	Meath, Donsaghlin	gentry: esquire	10-Dec-17	200	Dc2/12v	930
Cooke, Walsingham	Meath, Donsaghlen	gentry: esquire	30-Mar-17	300	Dc2/6r	897
Cooke, Walsingham	Meath, Dunshaghlin	gentry: esquire	19-Feb-17	300	Dc2/4v	892
Cooke, Walsingham	Meath, Donsaghlin	gentry: esquire	30-Mar-17	200	Dc2/5v	896
Cooke, William	Dublin, the city	gentry: esquire	20-Nov-37	600	Dc2/271v	2218
Cooley, Dudley	Kildare, Castlekerberry	gentry: esquire	16-Dec-57	200	B.L. 19, 843 f. 202a	3111
Cooley, Dudley	Kildare, Castlcarbary	gentry: esquire	06-Feb-55	2000	B.L. 19, 843 f. 156a	3027
Cooley, Dudley	Kildare, Castlecarbry	gentry: esquire	06-Feb-55	1000	B.L. 19, 843 f. 156	3026
Cooley, Henry	Kildare, CastleCarbery	gentry: esquire	05-Dec-97	400	Dc1/8r	58
Cooley, Henry	Kildare, Castel Carbry	gentry: knight	19-Dec-18	500	Dc2/19v	967
Cooley, John	Dublin, Cantrelston	farmer: yeoman	01-Apr-41	800	B.L. 19, 843 f. 87a	2894
Cooley, Randolph	Dublin, Stonebatter	farmer: yeoman	01-Apr-41	800	B.L. 19, 843 f. 87a	2894
Cooney, Nicholas	Louth, Drogheda		04-Aug-73	158	B.L. 15, 636 f. 138	3853
Cooney, Nicholas	Louth, Drogheda		28-Apr-73	158	B.L. 15, 636 f. 136	3848
Cooper, John	Clare, Meelick	gentry: esquire	30-Aug-60	1200	B.L. 15, 635 f. 75a	3393
Cooper, John	Limerick	gentry: gent	20-Jan-59	4000	B.L. 15, 635 f. 75	3392
Cooper, John	Clare, Meleek	gentry: esquire	25-Oct-61	500	B.L. 15, 635 f. 86a	3409
Coote, Charles	Roscommon, Castlecoote	gentry: knight and baronet	01-May-57	1200	B.L. 19, 843 f. 192	3091
Coote, Charles	Roscommon, Castlecoote	gentry: knight and baronet	27-Jul-55	2000	B.L. 19, 843 f. 158	3031
Coote, Charles	Roscommon, Castlecourte	gentry: knight and baronet	18-May-22	3000	Dc2/39v	1103
Coote, Charles	Roscommon, Castlecoote	gentry: knight and baronet	11-Feb-57	400	B.L. 19, 843 f. 189	3085
Coote, Charles	Roscommon, Castlecoote	gentry: esquire, s./heir of Ch	27-Jul-55	2000	B.L. 19, 843 f. 158	3031
Coote, Charles	Roscommon, Castlecoote	gentry: esquire, s./heir of Ch	08-Feb-53	2600	B.L. 19, 843 f. 129a	2976

Standard	County	Occupation	Date	Amount	MS No	Ident No
Coote, Charles	Roscommon, Castlecoote	gentry: knight and baronet	08-Feb-53	2600	B.L. 19, 843 f. 129a	2976
Coote, Charles	Roscommon, Castlecoote	gentry: esquire, s./heir Ch	08-Feb-53	1400	B.L. 19, 843 f. 129	2975
Coote, Charles	Roscommon, Castlecoote	gentry: knight and baronet	08-Feb-53	1400	B.L. 19, 843 f. 129	2975
Coote, Charles	Dublin, the city	gentry: esquire, s./heir	01-May-57	1200	B.L. 19, 843 f. 192	3091
Coote, Charles	Queen's Co., Castlecuffe	gentry: knight and baronet	09-May-36	1600	Dc2/250r	2117
Coote, Charles	Roscommon, Castlecoote	gentry: knight and baronet	16-Oct-54	650	B.L. 19, 843 f. 146a	3007
Coote, Charles	Roscommon?	peer: lord Castlecoote	13-Jul-61	1400	B.L. 15, 635 f. 77	3395
Coote, Charles	Roscommon?	peer: earl of Mountrath	26-Jul-61	750	B.L. 15, 635 f. 78	3397
Coote, Chidley	Limerick, Kilmallock	gentry: esquire	06-Sep-78	800	B.L. 15, 637 f. 10a	3866
Coote, Philip	Dublin, Killester	gentry: knight	14-Jan-86	1200	B.L. 15, 637 f. 103	4034
Coote, Richard	Meath?	peer: baron Colooney, 3rd s Ch	10-Jul-76	800	B.L. 19, 844 f. 111	3239
Coote, Richard	Meath?	peer: baron Colooney	12-Jun-67	400	Dc3/63	2360
Coote, Richard	Meath?	peer: baron Colooney	28-Jun-76	1200	Dc3/179r	2672
Coote, Richard	Kilkenny, Balleraggett	gentry: esquire	03-Sep-74	500	B.L. 19, 844 f. 41	3165
Coote, Richard	Kilkenny, Tullagh Maine	gentry: esquire	20-Jun-73	200	Dc3/158r	2588
Coote, Richard	Meath?	peer: baron Colooney 3rd s Charles	12-Jul-67	400	B.L. 15, 635 f. 197a	3605
Coote, Thomas	Cavan, Cootehill	gentry: esquire	22-Dec-66	520	Dc3/49	2330
Coote, Thomas	Antrim, Portmore	gentry: esquire	26-Oct-54	660	B.L. 19, 843 f. 145	3004
Coote, Thomas	Cavan, Cootehill	gentry: esquire	22-Dec-66	520	B.L. 15, 635 f. 180	3569
Coote, Thomas	Cavan, Cootehill	gentry: esquire	17-Aug-61	1000	B.L. 15, 635 f. 83	3402
Cope, Anthony	Armagh, Ballerath	gentry: esquire	13-May-33	2000	Dc2/193r	1876
Cope, Anthony	Armagh, Drommoolly	gentry: esquire	15-Jun-18	600	Dc2/15r	942
Cope, Anthony	Armagh, Ballyrah	gentry: esquire	05-Feb-31	200	Dc2/159r	1739
Cope, Anthony	Armagh, Ballyrath	gentry: esquire	09-Jun-30	1000	Dc2/149r	1695
Cope, Richard	Wexford, Banbery	gentry: esquire	17-Aug-15	1500	Dc2/0v	867
Coppinger, Dominic	Cork, Dominick St.?	merchant	07-Nov-72	160	B.L. 15, 636 f. 128	3836
Coppinger, John	Cork, the city		16-Feb-14	120	Dc1/126v	786
Coppinger, John	Cork, the city		03-Dec-13	276	Dc1/125r	777
Coppinger, Robert	Cork, the city	gentry: gent	29-May-41	1000	B.L. 19, 843 f. 97	2913
Coppinger, Stephen	Cork, Crogh	gentry: gent, son/heir of Thomas	26-Nov-72	800	B.L. 19, 844 f. 9	3128
Coppinger, Stephen	Cork, Croghin	gentry: gent, son/heir of Thomas	13-May-71	1000	B.L. 15, 636 f. 79	3761
Coppinger, Thomas	Cork, Crogh	gentry: gent	26-Nov-72	800	B.L. 19, 844 f. 9	3128
Coppinger, Thomas	Cork, Crogh	gentry: gent	19-May-66	400	Dc3/7	2234
Coppinger, Thomas	Cork, Croghin	gentry: gent	13-May-71	1000	B.L. 15, 636 f. 79	3761

Standard	County	Occupation	Date	Amount	MS No	Ident No
Coppinger, Thomas	Cork, Crogh	gentry: gent	19-May-65	400	B.L. 15, 635 f. 156a	3530
Coppinger, Walter	Cork, the city	gentry: esquire	03-Dec-13	276	Dc1/125r	777
Coppinger, Walter	Cork, the city	gentry: esquire	16-Feb-14	120	Dc1/126v	786
Corker, Edward	Dublin, the city	gentry: gent	27-Mar-72	800	Dc3/145r	2549
Cormack, Ellen	Mayo, Enver	gentry: widow of				
		Michael, esq	01-Jun-36	400	B.L. 19, 843 f. 38	2794
Cormack, Michael	Mayo, Ineiver	gentry: gent	06-Jun-14	300	Dc1/130r	808
Cormack, Richard	Mayo, Barranagh	gentry: gent	01-Jun-36	400	B.L. 19, 843 f. 38	2794
Cormick, Michael	Mayo, Inver	gentry: esquire	20-Jul-30	50	Dc2/154r	1717
Corry, John	Tipperary, Tuborhany	gentry: gent	05-Mar-39	400	B.L. 19, 843 f. 20	2758
Cosby, Alexander	Queen's Co., Stradbally	gentry: esquire	05-Feb-78	2000	B.L. 19, 844 f. 147	3278
Cosby, Alexander	Queen's Co., Stradbally	gentry: esquire	05-Feb-78	2600	Dc3/186v	2704
Cosby, Alexander	Queen's Co., Stradbally	gentry: esquire	08-Nov-75	2000	Dc3/168v	2640
Cosby, Alexander	Westmeath, Stradbally	gentry: esquire	08-Nov-75	1000	B.L. 19, 844 f. 86	3214
Cosby, Francis	Queen's Co., Stradbally	gentry: esquire	13-Aug-54	502	B.L. 19, 843 f. 144	3002
Cosby, Francis	Queen's Co., Stradbally	gentry: esquire	10-Oct-51	200	B.L. 19, 843 f. 127	2972
Cosby, Richard	Queen's Co., Stradbally	gentry: esquire	15-Jul-07	2000	Dc1/79v	487
Costigan, Augustus	Queen's Co., Ballemoy	gentry: gent	04-Nov-40	200	B.L. 19, 843 f. 83	2885
Costigan, Augustus	Queen's Co., Ballevoy	gentry: gent	07-Nov-39	400	B.L. 19, 843 f. 28	2774
Costigan, Augustus	Queen's Co., Ballevoy	gentry: gent	07-Nov-39	400	B.L. 19, 843 f. 28a	2775
Cotterell, John	Wexford, Wexford	gentry: gent	16-Feb-71	100	Dc3/135r	2515
Cotterell, John	Wexford, Wexford	gentry: gent	16-Feb-71	100	B.L. 15, 636 f. 77	3756
Cottle, Walter	Wexford, Newross	gentry: gent	01-Jun-25	100	Dc2/64v	1287
Couche, Thomas	Queen's Co., Stradbally	gentry: knight	15-Jul-07	2000	Dc1/79v	487
Coughlan, Joseph	Limerick, the city	gentry: esquire	20-Feb-86	600	B.L. 15, 637 f. 109a	4045
Coughlan, Terence	King's Co., Kincorra	gentry: gent	04-Dec-30	2564	Dc2/157v	1732
Coughlan, Terence	King's Co., Kilcolgan	gentry: gent	18-Dec-33	70	Dc2/204v	1922
Coughlan, Terrence	King's Co., Kilcolgan	gentry: esquire	24-Dec-39	560	B.L. 19, 843 f. 48	2814
Coursey, Thomas	Louth, Drogheda	gentry: gent	22-Mar-98	60	Dc1/10v	76
Courthop, Peter	Dublin, the city	gentry: knight	20-Dec-65	1000	Dc3/18	2262
Courthop, Peter	Dublin, the city	gentry: knight	20-Dec-65	1000	B.L. 15, 635 f. 163	3541
Courtney, George	Limerick, Newcastle	gentry: esquire	14-Dec-22	1000	Dc2/44r	1133
Courtney, George	Limerick, Newcastel	gentry: esquire	28-May-17	600	Dc2/7r	902
Covert, Christiana	Cork, the city	gentry: widow, exec				
		Richard, esq.	11-Mar-85	1100	B.L. 13, 637 f.97	4023
Covert, Richard	Cork, the city	gentry: gent, son/heir of				
		Richard	11-Mar-85	1100	B.L. 13, 637 f.97	4023
Cowley, Gerald	Louth, Ardee	gentry: esquire	06-Jul-33	200	Dc2/197v	1893
Cowley, Gerald	Louth, Atherdie	gentry: esquire	16-Jun-38	200	B.L. 19, 843 f. 25	2768
Cowley, Gerald	Louth, Atherdy	gentry: esquire	08-Feb-23	150	Dc2/44v	1137
Cowley, Gerald	Louth, Atherdee	gentry: esquire	15-Jul-34	200	Dc2/214v	1963
Cowley, Gerard	Louth, Atherdee	gentry: esquire	28-Nov-32	400	Dc2/187r	1851
Cowley, Henry	Kildare, Castlecarbry	gentry: knight	02-Dec-18	200	Dc2/18v	961
Cowley, Henry	Kildare, Castlecarbery	gentry: knight	23-Oct-29	300	Dc2/137r	1641
Cowley, James	Queen's Co., Killennye	gentry: esquire	02-Sep-39	1000	B.L. 19, 843 f. 32a	2783

Standard	County	Occupation	Date	Amount	MS No	Ident No
Cowley, Thomas	Kildare, Castlecarbry	gentry: knight	17-Jul-22	280	Dc2/42r	1119
Cowse, Richard	Dublin, the city	gentry: esquire	29-Sep-63	150	B.L. 15, 635 f. 117a	3465
Cox, Read	Dublin	gentry: gent	22-Feb-12	160	Dc1/112v	699
Cox, William	Limerick, Ballynoe	gentry: esquire	04-Apr-83	4000	B.L. 15, 637 f. 72a	3978
Coyle, Nicholas	Mayo, Gerrardstowne	farmer: yeoman	10-Feb-66	200	Dc3/21	2270
Coyne, Thady	Queen's Co., Tignahincy	gentry: esquire	20-Nov-16	300	Dc2/2r	878
Craig, James	Cavan, Crohan	gentry: knight	05-Mar-30	294	Dc2/143v	1671
Craig, James	Cavan, Croghan	gentry: knight	25-Sep-22	400	Dc2/42v	1123
Craig, James	Dublin, the city	gentry: knight	25-Apr-23	660	Dc2/46v	1151
Craig, James	Dublin, the city	gentry: knight	24-Apr-23	450	Dc2/46r	1150
Crante, Thomas	Cavan, Cavan	gentry: gent	11-May-37	400	Dc2/263v	2182
Crante, Thomas	Cavan, Cavan	gentry: gent	07-Nov-36	200	Dc2/256v	2153
Crawford, William	Down, Ballykillard	gentry: gent	13-May-71	200	B.L. 15, 636 f. 87	3774
Creighton, Abraham	Fermanagh, Crum	gentry: esquire	06-Dec-73	1300	Dc3/159r	2598
Creighton, Abraham	Fermanagh, Crum	gentry: esquire	22-Jun-78	2400	B.L. 19, 844 f. 165	3296
Creighton, Abraham	Fermanagh, Crum	gentry: esquire	22-Jun-78	2000	B.L. 19, 844 f. 164	3295
Creighton, George	Fermanagh, Aghlane		23-May-64	120	B.L. 15, 635 f. 134a	3494
Crelly, Denis	Down, Newry	merchant	23-Nov-40	200	B.L. 19, 843 f. 110a	2940
Crelly, Patrick	Down, Newry	merchant	13-Dec-34	600	Dc2/226r	2009
Crelly, Robert	Down, Newry	merchant	23-Nov-40	200	B.L. 19, 843 f. 110a	2940
Crimble, Charles	Down, Donoghodee	merchant: s/heir of Waterhouse	09-Aug-36	600	Dc2/256r	2149
Crimble, Roger	Down, Donnoghadee	gentry: gent	04-Jun-68	400	Dc3/77	2400
Crimble, Roger	Monaghan, Emy	gentry: esquire	12-Feb-72	1000	Dc3/143v	2544
Crimble, Roger	Down, Donaghadee	gentry: esquire	26-Aug-71	540	B.L. 15, 636 f. 92a	3784
Crimble, Roger	Monaghan, Emy	gentry: esquire	12-Feb-72	1000	B.L. 15, 636 f. 97	3790
Crimble, Waterhouse	Down, Donghdie	gentry: gent	28-Nov-28	200	Dc2/117v	1551
Crimble, Waterhouse	Down, Donnoghodee	gentry: esquire	09-Aug-36	600	Dc2/256r	2149
Crimble, William	Antrim, Carrickfergus	gentry: gent	28-Oct-72	300	B.L. 15, 636 f. 117	3822
Crimble, William	Antrim, Carrickfergus	gentry: gent	30-Oct-72	1200	B.L. 15, 636 f. 118	3823
Crocker, Thomas	Waterford, Ballyanker?	gentry: gent	13-Apr-81	850	B.L. 15, 637 f. 47	3930
Croft, Silvester	Dublin	merchant	11-Apr-25	3000	Dc2/63r	1278
Crofton, George	Roscommon, the Mott	gentry: esquire	23-Nov-37	830	Dc2/272r	2220
Crofts, Benjamin	Cork, the city	gentry: esquire	06-Mar-61	600	B.L. 15, 635 f. 80	3399
Crolly, Thomas	Louth, Drogheda	merchant	28-Apr-30	200	Dc2/144v	1675
Crosby, Ann	Kerry, Ballynoe	gentry: widow	23-Jul-55	240	B.L. 19, 843 f. 158a	3032
Crosby, Brian	Kerry, Gottneskey	gentry: gent	29-Nov-21	200	Dc2/37r	1083
Crosby, David	Kerry, Ardfert	gentry: esquire	13-Apr-35	320	Dc2/232v	2036
Crosby, John	Kildare, Walterstowne	gentry: knight and baronet	23-Jul-55	240	B.L. 19, 843 f. 158a	3032
Crosby, Patrick	Kerry, Ballinprior	gentry: gent	10-Nov-68	600	Dc3/83	2411
Crosby, Pierce	Queen's Co., Maryburrow	gentry: knight	13-Nov-28	2000	Dc2/115v	1540
Crosby, Pierce	Kerry, Tarbart	gentry: knight	10-Jul-18	500	Dc2/15v	947
Crosby, Walter	Kerry, Newton	gentry: knight and baronet	13-Apr-35	320	Dc2/232v	2036

Standard	County	Occupation	Date	Amount	MS No	Ident No
Crosby, Walter	Kerry, Gortneskehie	gentry: gent	19-Jul-40	100	B.L. 19, 843 f. 62a	2844
Cross, Epentus?	Cork, Ringroane	gentry: esquire	03-Dec-64	3000	B.L. 15, 635 f. 146a	3512
Crossed out	Dublin, the city	gentry: esquire	16-Jan-83	2000	B.L. 15, 637 f. 60a	3956
Crossed out	Dublin, the city	gentry: gent	16-Jan-83	2000	B.L. 15, 637 f. 60a	3956
Crossed out	Dublin, the city	gentry: esquire	16-Jan-83	2000	B.L. 15, 637 f. 60a	3956
Crowe, John	England, Northampton	gentry: esquire	30-Jun-25	120	Dc2/67r	1302
Crowe, John	Dublin, the city	gentry: esquire	04-Dec-67	700	Dc3/70	2381
Crowe, John	Dublin, the city	gentry: esquire	05-Dec-67	700	B.L. 15, 635 f. 208a	3624
Crowe, Stephan	Dublin	gentry: esquire	13-Jul-39	3000	B.L. 19, 843 f. 186	3079
Crowe, Stephen	Dublin	gentry: esquire	13-Jul-36	3000	Dc2/254v	2142
Crowley, Patrick	Dublin, the city	trade: shoemaker	23-Apr-19	1700	Dc2/22v	986
Cruise, Christopher	Louth, Drumkath	gentry: gent	21-Jun-67	160	Dc3/64	2363
Cruise, Christopher	Louth, Dunnrath	gentry: gent	21-Jun-67	160	B.L. 15, 635 f. 195a	3601
Cruise, Gerald	Meath, Brittace	gentry: gent	07-Jun-14	300	Dc1/130r	809
Cruise, James	Dublin, the city	gentry: gent	21-Jun-67	160	Dc3/64	2363
Cruise, James	Dublin, the city	gentry: gent	21-Jun-67	160	B.L. 15, 635 f. 195a	3601
Cruise, Valentine	Meath, Crueseton	gentry: gent	25-Nov-14	600	Dc1/133r	826
Cuffe, James	Mayo, Ballinrobe	gentry: knight	09-Mar-75	3300	Dc3/166v	2631
Cuffe, Robert	Cork, Killeagh	gentry: gent	21-Jun-70	800	B.L. 15, 636 f. 71	3744
Cullen, Daniel	Wicklow, Ballenouine	gentry: gent	03-Jun-65	100	Dc3/7	2236
Cullen, Daniel	Cork, Ballincurry	gentry: gent	20-Aug-40	120	B.L. 19, 843 f. 121a	2962
Cullen, Daniel	Wicklow, Ballegomme	gentry: gent	03-Jun-65	100	B.L. 15, 635 f. 152	3523
Cullen, Edmund	Dublin	trade: barber-surgeon	20-Aug-00	100	Dc1/25v	171
Cullen, Farrell	Wicklow, Balligarny	gentry: gent	29-Jun-22	600	Dc2/41v	1115
Cullen, Farrell	Wicklow, Ballegarme	gentry: gent	20-Jun-21	200	Dc2/36r	1075
Cullen, Farrell	Wicklow, Ballegarnee	gentry: gent?	15-May-26	400	Dc2/77r	1363
Cullen, Farrell	Wicklow, Couledyle?	gentry: gent	25-Jun-19	300	Dc2/24r	994
Cullen, Farrell	Wicklow, Balle o Kerny	gentry: gent	25-May-22	600	Dc2/40r	1107
Cullen, Morgan	Wicklow, Balledonnoghreagh	gentry: gent	25-May-22	600	Dc2/40r	1107
Cullen, Morgan	Wicklow, Ballydonnaghreagh	gentry: gent	16-Jun-32	200	Dc2/183v	1837
Cullen, Robert	Limerick, Lysmote	gentry: esquire	24-Jul-13	200	Dc1/123r	764
Cullen, Robert	Limerick, Lismote	gentry: esquire	31-Aug-13	200	Dc1/123r	765
Cullen, Thomas	Wexford, Cullen	gentry: gent	15-Nov-16	240	Dc2/2r	876
Culme, Hugh	Cavan, Cloghoughter	gentry: knight	06-May-30	600	Dc2/145v	1681
Culme, Hugh	Cavan, Cloghulter	gentry: esquire	04-Dec-21	600	Dc2/37v	1088
Cunningham, George	Longford, Killeffara?	gentry: esquire	14-Jun-81	5000	B.L. 15, 637 f. 45a	3928
Cunningham, Henry	Donegal, Castle Coningham	gentry: esquire	30-Apr-86	800	B.L. 15, 637 f. 109	4043
Cunningham, John	Dublin, the city	trade: tailor	11-Apr-35	400	Dc2/232r	2034
Curragh, William	Dublin?, the Curraghe	gentry: gent	26-Apr-08	105	Dc1/82r	510
Curtin, Daniel	Dublin	trade: tailor	10-Feb-97	50	Dc1/1v	5
Cusack, Adam	Meath?, Lesmollen?	gentry: son/heir of Richard	29-Mar-25	4000	Dc2/63r	1277

Standard	County	Occupation	Date	Amount	MS No	Ident No
Cusack, Adam	Meath, Trevett	gentry: gent	12-Feb-30	300	Dc2/142r	1665
Cusack, Adam	Meath, Trevett	gentry: esquire	05-Jul-34	600	Dc2/214r	1961
Cusack, Andrew	Meath, Triblestowne	gentry: gent	19-Jun-18	600	Dc2/15r	944
Cusack, Bartholomew	Meath, Trubly	gentry: gent	27-Nov-27	204	Dc2/101r	1468
Cusack, Bartholomew	Meath, Troublie	gentry: gent	19-Jul-25	80	Dc2/68v	1311
Cusack, Bartholomew	Meath, Trobly	gentry: gent	22-Nov-16	300	Dc2/2v	879
Cusack, Bartholomew	Meath, Trubly	gentry: gent	09-Feb-32	120	Dc2/175r	1805
Cusack, Bartholomew	Meath, Trubly	gentry: gent	14-Nov-27	120	Dc2/99v	1462
Cusack, Bartholomew	Meath, Harishtowne	gentry: gent	19-Jun-18	600	Dc2/15r	944
Cusack, Bartholomew	Meath, Trubly	gentry: gent	01-Dec-27	180	Dc2/101r	1469
Cusack, Bartholomew	Meath, Troublie	gentry: gent	14-May-28	100	Dc2/108r	1506
Cusack, Bartholomew	Meath, Troublie	gentry: gent	16-May-28	200	Dc2/108v	1507
Cusack, Bartholomew	Meath, Trooblie	gentry: gent	30-May-25	84	Dc2/64r	1284
Cusack, Cecily	Dublin, Howthe	peer: widow, of Howth	30-Jan-11	70	Dc1/102v	640
Cusack, Cecily	Dublin, Howth	peer: widow, lady dowager	08-Mar-19	80	Dc2/21r	977
Cusack, Christopher	Meath, Trymme?	gentry: gent	16-Nov-31	80	Dc2/170r	1784
Cusack, Edward	Meath, Rathkenny	gentry: esquire	14-Jul-66	100	Dc3/33	2295
Cusack, Edward	Meath, Rathkenny	gentry: esquire	14-Jul-66	200	Dc3/33	2296
Cusack, Edward	Meath, Rathkenny	gentry: esquire	14-Jul-66	200	Dc3/33	2294
Cusack, James	Meath, Gerrardston	gentry: gent	21-May-10	500	Dc1/96v	607
Cusack, James	Meath, Cloneenardran	gentry: gent?	04-Feb-13	100	Dc1/118r	733
Cusack, James	Meath, Gerardston	gentry: gent	21-May-10	500	Dc1/96v	605
Cusack, James	Meath, Gerrardston	gentry: gent	28-Nov-13	2000	Dc1/124r	773
Cusack, John	Meath, Cussenston	gentry: gent	10-Feb-19	200	Dc2/20v	973
Cusack, John	Meath, Cussenston	gentry: gent	28-Sep-09	300	Dc1/91v	574
Cusack, John	Meath, Cussinston	gentry: gent	24-Nov-13	160	Dc1/124v	772
Cusack, Lawrence	Meath, Knockston	gentry: gent	30-May-25	84	Dc2/64r	1284
Cusack, Lawrence	Kildare, Bushops Courte	gentry: gent	19-Jun-18	600	Dc2/15r	944
Cusack, Michael	Meath, Balreske	gentry: gent, son/heir of Patrick	19-Jun-20	220	Dc2/31r	1036
Cusack, Michael	Meath, Balreask	gentry: gent	10-Jul-29	2000	Dc2/135r	1631
Cusack, Patrick	Meath, Cussingstowne	gentry: gent	12-Nov-11	50	Dc1/107v	667
Cusack, Patrick	Meath, Rathalron	gentry: esquire	24-Nov-09	150	Dc1/92v	581
Cusack, Patrick	Meath, Rahalron	gentry: gent	18-Apr-03	300	Dc1/46r	293
Cusack, Patrick	Meath, Cussentown	gentry: son/heir of John	28-Sep-09	300	Dc1/91v	574
Cusack, Patrick	Meath, Rahalron	gentry: esquire	11-Feb-13	240	Dc1/118v	735
Cusack, Patrick	Meath, Cousenstowne	gentry: gent	04-May-37	2000	Dc2/262r	2176
Cusack, Patrick	Meath, Gerrardstowne	gentry: esquire	28-May-31	3000	Dc2/164v	1761
Cusack, Patrick	Meath, Rathlalron	gentry: esquire	19-Jun-20	220	Dc2/31r	1036
Cusack, Patrick	Meath, Cussingstowne	gentry: gent	13-May-31	160	Dc2/162r	1752
Cusack, Patrick	Meath, Cussenston	gentry: son/heir of John	10-Feb-19	200	Dc2/20v	973
Cusack, Patrick	Meath, Rathalron	gentry: esquire	10-Jul-29	2000	Dc2/135r	1631
Cusack, Patrick	Meath, Gerrardstowne	gentry: esquire	17-Feb-35	1400	Dc2/229v	2023
Cusack, Patrick	Meath, Cussinston	gentry: son/heir of John	24-Nov-13	160	Dc1/124v	772

Standard	County	Occupation	Date	Amount	MS No	Ident No
Cusack, Patrick	Meath, Cussinston	gentry: gent	10-Feb-12	60	Dc1/112r	696
Cusack, Patrick	Mayo, Cusackstowne	gentry: esquire	10-Jul-29	2000	Dc2/135r	1631
Cusack, Patrick	Meath, Cowssingstowne	gentry: gent	16-Nov-31	80	Dc2/170r	1784
Cusack, Patrick	Meath, Cossingstowne	gentry: gent	05-Jul-30	200	Dc2/154r	1715
Cusack, Patrick	Meath, Gerrardstowne	gentry: esquire	22-Jun-37	500	Dc2/265r	2189
Cusack, Patrick	Meath, Rathalron	gentry: gent	29-Aug-05	160	Dc1/61r	372
Cusack, Patrick	Meath, Cussingstowne	gentry: gent	07-May-30	200	Dc2/146v	1685
Cusack, Philip	Meath, Ballemolchan	gentry: gent	19-Jun-20	220	Dc2/31r	1036
Cusack, Richard	Dublin, the city	gentry: gent	14-Jul-66	200	Dc3/33	2296
Cusack, Richard	Meath, Lesmullin	gentry: esquire	25-Nov-10	200	Dc1/100v	630
Cusack, Richard	Dublin, the city	gentry: gent	14-Jul-66	200	Dc3/33	2294
Cusack, Richard	Dublin, the city	gentry: gent	14-Jul-66	100	Dc3/33	2295
Cusack, Richard	Meath, Lesmollin	gentry: gent	02-Dec-97	1500	Dc1/8v	59
Cusack, Richard	Meath, Lesmollen	gentry: esquire	29-Jan-11	250	Dc1/102r	639
Cusack, Richard	Meath, Lesmollen	gentry: esquire	28-May-08	40	Dc1/83r	516
Cusack, Richard	Meath, Lesmullen	gentry: esquire	29-Mar-25	4000	Dc2/63r	1277
Cusack, Richard	Meath, Lesmullen	gentry: gent	11-May-07	200	Dc1/76r	464
Cusack, Richard	Meath, Lesmollen	gentry: esquire	22-Nov-11	400	Dc1/109r	678
Cusack, Richard	Meath, Lesmollen	gentry: esquire	24-Apr-10	200	Dc1/95v	598
Cusack, Richard	Meath, Lysmullen	gentry: esquire	17-Apr-22	200	Dc2/29r	1100
Cusack, Robert	Meath, Cousenstowne	gentry: son/heir of Patrick	04-May-37	2000	Dc2/262r	2176
Cusack, Robert	Meath, Cussingstowne?	gentry: son/heir of Patrick	13-May-31	160	Dc2/162r	1752
Cuthbert, William	Armagh, Castledawson		01-Jul-58	110	B.L. 15, 635 f. 33	3321
Daley, Hugh	Galway, Killeveny	gentry: gent	01-Dec-57	120	B.L. 19, 843 f. 201	3108
Daley, Owen	Cork, Duglashe	gentry: gent	03-Dec-25	120	B.L. 19, 843 f. 93	2905
Dallway, Alexander	Antrim, Ballyhill	gentry: esquire	18-Sep-66	600	B.L. 15, 635 f. 178a	3566
Dalton, Edmund	Westmeath, Mylton	gentry: son/heir of Thomas	12-May-06	130	Dc1/67r	405
Dalton, Gerald	Westmeath, Ballisallaughe	gentry: gent?	06-Jul-97	300	Dc1/5v	42
Dalton, Henry	King's Co., Ralihin	gentry: gent	20-May-97	40	Dc1/4r	28
Dalton, John	Westmeath, Daleston	gentry: gent	26-May-20	240	Dc2/30r	1030
Dalton, Nicholas	Westmeath, Ballynecarrow	gentry: gent	26-May-28	300	Dc2/110r	1514
Dalton, Richard	Westmeath, Laleston	gentry: esquire	26-May-20	240	Dc2/30r	1030
Dalton, Richard	Westmeath, Ballybullen	gentry: gent	16-May-15	200	Dc1/137v	853
Dalton, Thomas	Westmeath, Mylton	gentry: gent	12-May-06	130	Dc1/67r	405
Dalton, William	Donegal, Greenefort	gentry: esquire	15-Dec-69	210	Dc3/111	2464
Daniel, John	Dublin	merchant: son of Thady, merchant	03-Aug-10	60	Dc1/99r	621
Darcy, Edmund	Westmeath, Redmondstowne	gentry: gent	22-Nov-28	200	Dc2/116v	1545
Darcy, George	Meath, Platton	gentry: esquire	07-May-97	86	Dc1/3r	20
Darcy, George	Meath?, Platten	gentry: esquire	22-Apr-01	240	Dc1/30v	202

Standard	County	Occupation	Date	Amount	MS No	Ident No
Darcy, John	Meath, Donmore	gentry: esquire	27-Jan-12	40	Dc1/111r	690
Darcy, Nicholas	Meath, Plattin	gentry: esquire	16-May-39	2000	B.L. 19, 843 f. 16	2750
Darcy, Nicholas	Meath, Platten	gentry: esquire	16-May-39	2000	B.L. 19, 843 f. 15a	2749
Darcy, Nicholas	Meath, Plattin	gentry: esquire	03-Mar-69	2100	Dc3/92	2428
Darcy, Nicholas	Meath, Platten	gentry: esquire	17-Feb-35	1400	Dc2/229v	2023
Darcy, Nicholas	Meath, Platten	gentry: esquire	10-Mar-37	2600	Dc2/263r	2180
Darcy, Nicholas	Meath, Plattin	gentry: esquire	17-Nov-68	1600	Dc3/84	2413
Darcy, Nicholas	Meath, Paltten	gentry: esquire	01-Feb-83	230	B.L. 15, 637 f. 69	3971
Darcy, Nicholas	Meath, Platten	gentry: esquire	17-Nov-68	1600	B.L. 15, 636 f. 27	3672
Darcy, Nicholas	Meath, Platting	gentry: gent	11-Jun-63	400	B.L. 15, 635 f. 167a	3548
Darcy, Nicholas	Meath, Plattin	gentry: gent	29-May-41	600	B.L. 19, 843 f. 92	2903
Darcy, Nicholas	Meath, Plattin	gentry: esquire	03-Mar-69	2100	B.L. 15, 636 f. 44a	3701
Darcy, Patrick	Galway, the town	gentry: esquire	26-Jun-54	300	B.L. 19, 843 f. 143a	3001
Dardis, John	Westmeath, Gartlanstowne	gentry: gent	16-May-28	100	Dc2/108r	1505
Dardis, Thomas	Westmeath, Johnston	gentry: gent	15-Jun-24	200	Dc2/56r	1222
Darling, Richard	Dublin, the city	gentry: gent	17-Jan-83	2000	B.L. 15, 637 f. 73a	3980
Daton, Edmund	Kilkenny, Kildaton	gentry: gent	05-Dec-17	300	Dc2/12v	929
Davells, Henry	Carlow, Clonw?lske	gentry: esquire	30-Jun-02	400	Dc1/38v	250
Davells, Henry	Carlow, Clonnuilske	gentry: esquire	23-May-09	400	Dc1/89v	558
Davells, Thomas	Queen's Co., Ballehide	gentry: esquire	09-Dec-33	400	Dc2/203r	1916
Davells, Thomas	Queen's Co., Ballyhide	gentry: esquire	01-Aug-39	400	B.L. 19, 843 f. 46a	2811
Davells, Thomas	Queen's Co., Killeshin	gentry: esquire	26-Oct-30	300	B.L. 19, 843 f. 11a	2741
Davells, Thomas	Queen's Co., Ballyhide	gentry: esquire	25-Nov-36	1000	Dc2/257v	2158
Davells, Thomas	Queen's Co., Killeshin	gentry: esquire	10-Mar-36	300	B.L. 19, 843 f.12	2742
Davenport, Roland,	Waterford, Assane	gentry: esquire	21-Nov-28	200	Dc2/116v	1544
Davis, John	Kildare, Kill	gentry: gent	12-Mar-11	40	Dc1/103r	645
Davis, Paul	Dublin, the city	gentry: gent	30-Aug-25	200	Dc2/69r	1313
Davis, Richard	Roscommon, Ballindeary	gentry: gent	11-Dec-24	100	Dc2/59v	1251
Dawson, Thomas	Londonderry, Meola	gentry: esquire	25-Aug-74	2000	B.L. 19, 844 f. 34	3158
Dawson, Thomas	Dublin, Bridg St. the suburbs	gentry: esquire	06-Feb-56	500	B.L. 19, 843 f. 170a	3054
Dawson, Thomas	Londonderry, Moolow	gentry: esquire	02-Oct-73	2000	Dc3/158v	2592
Dawson, Thomas	Londonderry, Meola	gentry: esquire	12-Dec-74	880	B.L. 19, 844 f. 45	3169
Dawson, Thomas	Dublin, the city	gentry: esquire	15-Jul-59	800	B.L. 15,635 f. 49a	3350
Dawson, Thomas	Londonderry, Castle Dawson	gentry: esquire	16-Jun-80	2000	B.L. 15, 637 f. 35a	3910
De la Sale, William	Meath, Saleston	gentry: gent	24-Sep-17	400	Dc2/9v	912
Deane, Abraham	Wexford, Hilltowne	gentry: gent	13-Nov-69	210	Dc3/106	2453
Deane, Abraham	Wexford, Hilltowne	gentry: gent	13-Nov-69	210	B.L. 15, 636 f. 55a	3718
Deane, Joesph	Dublin, Crumlin	gentry: esquire	15-Jul-72	660	Dc3/148r	2558
Deane, Joseph	Dublin, Crumlin	gentry: esquire	15-Jul-72	660	B.L. 15, 636 f. 110	3810
Deane, Mathew	Cork, the city	gentry: knight	22-May-83	90	B.L. 15, 637 f. 74	3981
Dee, Thomas	Dublin	trade: girdler	06-Jun-06	250	Dc1/69v	420
Delacourt, John	Cork, Ballinrea	gentry: gent	01-May-67	240	B.L. 15, 635 f. 210a	3626
Delacourt, John	Cork, Ballyknockane	gentry: gent	22-Jan-69	1000	B.L. 15, 636 f. 28a	3675

Standard	County	Occupation	Date	Amount	MS No	Ident No
Delahyde, Francis	Clare, Keyllnacarhungary	gentry: gent	09-Nov-41	1124	B.L. 15, 635 f. 140	3501
Delahyde, Gerald	Dublin	gentry: gent	03-Aug-99	540	Dc1/18v	127
Delahyde, Gerald	Kildare, Kyllussey?	gentry: gent	23-Feb-98	140	Dc1/10r	70
Delahyde, Gerald	Louth, Drogheda	gentry: gent	24-Oct-00	320	Dc1/26v	178
Delahyde, Joan	Meath, Moyglare	gentry: widow	15-Jan-99	800	Dc1/14r	100
Delahyde, John	Meath, Bellantrye	gentry: gent	17-Feb-07	200	Dc1/74v	453
Delahyde, John	Meath, Donshaghlen	gentry: gent, s/heir of Walter	12-May-99	1000	Dc1/16v	112
Delahyde, John	Meath, Ballentry	gentry: gent	19-Jun-98	220	Dc1/11r	81
Delahyde, John	Meath, Bellantry	gentry: gent	20-Aug-99	500	Dc1/18v	129
Delahyde, John	Meath, Belantrye	gentry: esquire	06-Feb-08	100	Dc1/81r	502
Delahyde, John	Meath, Roeston?	gentry: gent, s./heir of Walter	18-May-97	666	Dc1/3v	23
Delahyde, John	Kildare, Puncheston	gentry: gent	24-Jun-10	100	Dc1/98v	617
Delahyde, John	Meath?, Reston?	gentry: son/heir of Walter	15-Nov-99	1000	Dc1/19v	134
Delahyde, John	Kerry, Kyllaha	gentry: gent	28-Nov-98	800	Dc1/13v	95
Delahyde, John	Meath, Bellantrie	gentry: gent	27-Sep-00	200	Dc1/26r	174
Delahyde, John	Meath, Bellantne	gentry: gent	13-Jun-01	200	Dc1/32v	215
Delahyde, Lawrence	Meath, Maglare	gentry: esquire	29-May-28	200	Dc2/110v	1515
Delahyde, Lawrence	Meath, Bryneston	gentry: gent	23-Nov-35	600	Dc2/240v	2073
Delahyde, Luke	Meath, Moyglare	gentry: esquire	10-Aug-14	200	Dc1/131v	816
Delahyde, Luke	Meath, Moyglare	gentry: esquire	23-Nov-35	600	Dc2/240v	2073
Delahyde, Luke	Meath, Moyglare	gentry: gent	21-Jul-26	200	Dc2/81v	1387
Delahyde, Luke	Meath, Moyglare	gentry: esquire	30-Jun-25	200	Dc2/67r	1301
Delahyde, Luke	Meath, Moyglare	gentry: esquire	15-Feb-33	450	Dc2/192r	1871
Delahyde, Luke	Dublin, Moyglare	gentry: esquire	12-Feb-25	120	Dc2/61v	1266
Delahyde, Luke	Westmeath, Moyglare	gentry: esquire	09-Aug-14	160	Dc1/131r	815
Delahyde, Luke	Meath, Moyclare	gentry: esquire	05-Jun-24	500	Dc2/55v	1218
Delahyde, Luke	King's Co., Castletowne	gentry: esquire	22-Mar-56	120	B.L. 19, 843 f. 185	3077
Delahyde, Luke	Meath, Moyglare	gentry: esquire	05-Feb-35	1400	Dc2/229r	2021
Delahyde, Luke	King's Co., Castletowne	gentry: esquire	20-Feb-41	621	B.L. 19, 843 f. 85a	2890
Delahyde, Michael	Kildare, Palmerston	gentry: gent	22-Jun-26	1000	Dc2/79v	1377
Delahyde, Oliver	Clare, Tullagh	gentry: esquire	09-Nov-41	1124	B.L. 15, 635 f. 140	3501
Delahyde, Peter	Kildare, Puncheston	gentry: esquire	05-Jun-24	500	Dc2/55v	1218
Delahyde, Peter	Dublin, Pheiposton	gentry: esquire	21-Mar-22	200	Dc2/39r	1098
Delahyde, Peter	Kildare, Puncheston	gentry: gent	24-Jun-10	100	Dc1/98v	617
Delahyde, Peter	Dublin, Corbally	gentry: gent	13-Nov-14	120	Dc1/132r	822
Delahyde, Peter	Dublin, Corballies	gentry: gent	10-Aug-14	200	Dc1/131v	816
Delahyde, Peter	Meath, Bellantrye	gentry: gent	17-Feb-07	200	Dc1/74v	453
Delahyde, Richard	Meath, Moiclare	gentry: gent	19-Jun-98	220	Dc1/11r	81
Delahyde, Richard	Meath, Moyglare	gentry: son/heir of Luke	15-Feb-33	450	Dc2/192r	1871
Delahyde, Thomas	Dublin, Loghshenney	gentry: gent	05-Jun-32	300	Dc2/182v	1833
Delahyde, Thomas	Dublin, Loggsheny	gentry: gent	28-Nov-28	200	Dc2/118r	1552
Delahyde, Thomas	Dublin, Loggshinny	gentry: gent	19-Apr-41	100	B.L. 19, 843 f. 101a	2922
Delarock, Richard	Meath, Ballicurry	gentry: gent	08-Nov-65	240	Dc3/15	2254

Standard	County	Occupation	Date	Amount	MS No	Ident No
Dempsey, Owen	King's Co., Clownegawne	gentry: esquire	02-Jul-28	400	Dc2/112r	1523
Dempsey, Owen	King's Co., Clownygaunagh?	gentry: esquire	17-Nov-30	400	Dc2/155v	1724
Dempsey, Owen	King's Co., Clowneyawney	gentry: esquire	12-Dec-29	400	Dc2/140r	1654
Dennell, John	Dublin, Palmerstowne	farmer: yeoman	28-Oct-31	40	Dc2/169r	1781
Denny, Arthur	Kerry, Trali	gentry: esquire	18-Nov-09	600	Dc1/92r	576
Denny, Arthur	Kerry, Traly	gentry: esquire	17-Jun-13	240	Dc1/122r	759
Denny, Arthur	Kerry, Traly	gentry: esquire	27-Sep-13	200	Dc1/123v	767
Dering, Edmund	Kildare, Roban	gentry: gent	02-Jun-06	120	Dc1/69r	418
Devenish, George	Westmeath, Athloane	gentry: esquire	17-Jun-29	800	Dc2/132v	1620
Devenish, Katherine	Westmeath, Athlone	gentry: wife of William	08-Aug-63	200	B.L. 15, 635 f. 116a	3463
Devenish, Peter	Westmeath, Athlone	gentry: gent	08-Aug-63	200	B.L. 15, 635 f. 116a	3463
Devenish, William	Westmeath, Athlone	gentry: gent	08-Aug-63	200	B.L. 15, 635 f. 116a	3463
Devereux, Philip	Wexford, The Dipps	gentry: gent	24-Nov-18	120	Dc2/17v	957
Devlin, John	Louth, Mayne	gentry: gent	20-Jun-77	500	B.L. 19, 844 f. 129	3259
Devlin, John	Louth, Mayne	gentry: gent	20-Jun-77	500	Dc3/183r	2691
Devlin, John	Louth, Magne	gentry: gent	26-Nov-75	300	B.L. 19, 844 f. 79	3207
Devlin, John	Louth, Mayne	gentry: gent	26-Nov-75	300	Dc3/170r	2642
Devlin, John	Louth, Mayn	gentry: gent	25-May-72	500	Dc3/146r	2552
Devlin, John	Louth, Mayne	gentry: gent	14-Jul-80	200	B.L. 15, 637 f. 35	3909
Devlin, John	Louth, Maine	gentry: gent	10-May-81	600	B.L. 15, 637 f. 43	3924
Dexter, Walter	Mayo, Carrymacullen	gentry: gent	21-Jun-30	100	Dc2/152v	1709
Dexter, Walter	Mayo, Carrymacullen	gentry: gent	21-Jun-30	40	Dc2/152v	1710
Dickson, Patrick	Dublin	merchant	28-Feb-97	100	Dc1/2r	11
Dillon, Andrew	Meath, Riverstowne	gentry: esquire	25-Nov-36	400	Dc2/258r	2159
Dillon, Andrew	Meath, Riverstowne	gentry: esquire	10-May-37	220	Dc2/262v	2179
Dillon, Andrew	Meath, Riverstowne	gentry: esquire	10-Feb-35	200	Dc2/229r	2022
Dillon, Andrew	Meath, Riverstowne	gentry: esquire	07-Dec-35	800	Dc2/241v	2079
Dillon, Andrew	Meath, Riverstowne	gentry: esquire	19-Jun-35	400	Dc2/237v	2059
Dillon, Arthur	Meath, Ladyhill	gentry: esquire	26-Nov-68	1000	Dc3/83	2414
Dillon, Arthur	Meath, Ladyhill	gentry: esquire	10-Jul-76	800	B.L. 19, 844 f. 111	3239
Dillon, Arthur	Meath, Ladyhill	gentry: esquire	26-Nov-68	1000	B.L. 15, 636 f. 29a	3677
Dillon, Arthur	Meath, Lismullin, Skreene	gentry: esquire	13-May-62	1800	B.L. 15, 635 f. 95a	3425
Dillon, Bartholomew	Meath, Riverston	gentry: esquire	14-May-12	240	Dc1/113v	703
Dillon, Bartholomew	Meath, Riverston	gentry: esquire	27-Jan-03	800	Dc1/43v	277
Dillon, Bartholomew	Meath, Riverston	gentry: esquire	16-May-10	200	Dc1/96r	603
Dillon, Bartholomew	Meath, Riverston	gentry: esquire	10-Feb-12	60	Dc1/112r	696
Dillon, Bartholomew	Meath, Riverston	gentry: esquire	10-Feb-10	300	Dc1/94r	590
Dillon, Bartholomew	Meath, Riverston	gentry: esquire	13-Dec-97	240	Dc1/8v	60
Dillon, Bartholomew	Meath, Ryverston	gentry: gent	19-May-09	400	Dc1/89r	556
Dillon, Bartholomew	Meath, Ryverston	gentry: esquire	30-Sep-99	900	Dc1/19v	132
Dillon, Bartholomew	Meath, Riverston	gentry: esquire	16-Sep-11	800	Dc1/106v	662
Dillon, Bartholomew	Meath, Riverston	gentry: esquire	23-Apr-19	240	Dc2/22v	984
Dillon, Christopher	Mayo, Ballelahen	gentry: knight	18-May-22	3000	Dc2/39v	1103
Dillon, Christopher	Dublin, Cappocke	gentry: gent, son of Bart	01-Dec-35	400	Dc2/240v	2075

Standard	County	Occupation	Date	Amount	MS No	Ident No
Dillon, Edmund	Westmeath, Portlock	gentry: gent	04-Aug-66	300	Dc3/35	2302
Dillon, Eleanor	Meath, Kilbride	other: widow	22-May-06	400	Dc1/68v	413
Dillon, Elizabeth	Meath, Kenteston	other: widow	19-May-10	160	Dc1/96r	604
Dillon, Ellis	Dublin, Newgrange	other: widow	17-Jun-10	200	Dc1/98r	615
Dillon, Ellis	Dublin, Newgrange	other: widow	17-Jun-10	400	Dc1/98r	616
Dillon, Farrell	Wicklow, Ballegarnee	gentry: gent	26-Feb-21	200	Dc2/34v	1065
Dillon, Francis	Meath, Mooretowne	gentry: gent	18-Jun-36	100	Dc2/253v	2135
Dillon, Francis	Meath, Moorestowne	gentry: gent	08-May-37	280	Dc2/262v	2178
Dillon, Garret	Westmeath, Portlock	gentry: son/heir of Edmund	04-Aug-66	300	Dc3/35	2302
Dillon, George	Dublin, Killeghe	gentry: gent	05-May-07	120	Dc1/76r	461
Dillon, George	Dublin, Killiegh	gentry: gent	22-Jan-14	80	Dc1/125v	780
Dillon, George	Dublin, Killeghe	gentry: gent	30-Jun-12	60	Dc1/115	711
Dillon, Gerald	Dublin, Lessonhall	gentry: esquire	13-Dec-97	240	Dc1/8v	60
Dillon, Gerald	Meath, Balgoth		31-Jan-99	300	Dc1/15r	104
Dillon, Gerald	Meath, Balgothe	gentry: esquire	27-Jan-03	800	Dc1/43v	277
Dillon, Gerald	Meath, Balgethe	gentry: esquire	21-Nov-09	105	Dc1/92v	579
Dillon, Gerald	Meath, Balgieth	gentry: gent	08-Jul-09	200	Dc1/90r	563
Dillon, Gerald	Meath, Balgeth	gentry: gent	14-May-12	240	Dc1/113v	703
Dillon, Gerald	Dublin, Haroldsgrandge	gentry: gent	04-Dec-06	300	Dc1/72v	441
Dillon, Gerald	Meath, Balgothe	gentry: gent	19-May-09	400	Dc1/89r	556
Dillon, Gerald	Meath, Balgeth	gentry: gent	10-Feb-10	300	Dc1/94r	590
Dillon, Gilbert	Westmeath, Killenyny	gentry: gent	24-Nov-18	60	Dc2/18r	958
Dillon, Henry	Meath, Kenston		08-Jan-07	500	Dc1/73r	442
Dillon, Henry	Meath, Moymot	gentry: gent	30-Jun-97	700	Dc1/5v	39
Dillon, Henry	Meath, Moymet	gentry: gent	30-Jun-97	600	Dc1/5v	40
Dillon, Henry	Roscommon, Clunrebrecan	gentry: esquire	10-Feb-35	200	Dc2/229r	2022
Dillon, Henry	Meath, Lescarnan	gentry: gent	13-May-26	1000	Dc2/77r	1362
Dillon, Henry	Meath, Kentstowne	gentry: esquire	29-Jun-05	600	Dc1/60v	367
Dillon, Hubert	Westmeath, Killenynen?	gentry: gent	18-May-22	3000	Dc2/39v	1103
Dillon, Hubert	Longford, Laragh	gentry: gent	24-Sep-33	800	Dc2/199v	1902
Dillon, James	Mayo, Ballavill?	gentry: knight	04-Dec-30	2564	Dc2/157v	1732
Dillon, James	Meath, Moymet	gentry: knight	30-Oct-18	800	Dc2/16v	952
Dillon, James	Mayo, Costello and Gallen	gentry: esquire	02-Mar-75	2500	B.L. 19, 844 f. 55	3179
Dillon, James	Meath, Moymot	gentry: knight	24-Dec-03	2508	Dc1/51r	326
Dillon, James	Mayo, Bellavill	gentry: knight	04-Dec-28	400	Dc2/120v	1564
Dillon, James	Dublin, Hunteston		31-Jan-99	300	Dc1/15r	104
Dillon, James	Meath?, Moymot	gentry: knight	24-Dec-03	2508	Dc1/50v	324
Dillon, James	Mayo?	gentry: esquire	02-Mar-75	2500	Dc3/165v	2627
Dillon, James		peer: earl of Roscommon	06-Sep-42	2000	B.L. 19, 843 f. 108a	2936
Dillon, James	Mayo, Costolo and Gallin	gentry: esquire	02-Mar-75	3000	Dc3/166r	2628
Dillon, James		peer: earl of Roscommon	20-Jun-43	400	B.L. 19, 843 f. 112	2943
Dillon, James	Mayo, Ballevile	gentry: knight	07-Nov-28	500	Dc2/115v	1541
Dillon, James	Westmeath, Killnifagh	gentry: knight	20-Dec-33	800	Dc2/205r	1924
Dillon, James	Westmeath, Killfaghny	gentry: knight	29-May-28	200	Dc2/110v	1515

Standard	County	Occupation	Date	Amount	MS No	Ident No
Dillon, James	Mayo, Bellauill	gentry: knight	08-Dec-26	800	Dc2/85v	1405
Dillon, James	Westmeath, Killnifaghny	gentry: knight	20-Dec-33	1000	Dc2/205r	1923
Dillon, James	Westmeath, Clouchullan	gentry: knight	20-Feb-41	621	B.L. 19, 843 f. 85a	2890
Dillon, James	Mayo, Costello and Gallen	gentry: esquire	02-Mar-75	3000	B.L. 19, 844 f. 60a	3186
Dillon, James		peer: earl of Roscommon	12-Dec-57	800	B.L. 19, 843 f. 204a	3115
Dillon, John	Armagh, Castledillon	gentry: esquire	13-May-30	66	Dc2/147v	1689
Dillon, John	Armagh, Castledillon	gentry: esquire	13-May-30	1000	Dc2/147v	1688
Dillon, John	Armagh, Castledillon	gentry: esquire	30-May-36	3000	Dc2/252v	2131
Dillon, John	Armagh, Castledillon	gentry: esquire	04-Dec-35	700	Dc2/241r	2077
Dillon, John	Armagh, Mullabane	gentry: esquire	18-Nov-20	600	Dc2/33r	1050
Dillon, Luke	Roscommon, Loghglin	gentry: esquire	18-May-22	3000	Dc2/39v	1103
Dillon, Luke	Roscommon, Loghglynn	gentry: knight	04-Aug-53	4000	B.L. 19, 843 f. 135	2984
Dillon, Luke	Roscommon, Loughglyn	gentry: knight	04-Aug-53	448	B.L. 19, 843 f. 134	2983
Dillon, Luke	Mayo, Costello and Gallen	peer: viscount Costello-Gallen	02-Mar-75	2500	B.L. 19, 844 f. 55	3179
Dillon, Luke	Mayo, Costello and Gallen	peer: viscount Dillon, Gallen	02-Mar-75	3000	B.L. 19, 844 f. 60a	3186
Dillon, Luke	Mayo?	peer: viscount Costello-Gallen	02-Mar-75	2500	Dc3/165v	2627
Dillon, Luke	Roscommon, Loghlin	gentry: knight	05-Aug-34	600	Dc2/216v	1970
Dillon, Luke	Westmeath, Kilnefaghny	gentry: knight	07-Nov-28	500	Dc2/115v	1541
Dillon, Luke	Cavan, Trynnett Island	gentry: esquire	11-Feb-34	200	Dc2/206v	1929
Dillon, Luke	Mayo, Costolo and Gallin	peer: viscount Costello-Gallen	02-Mar-75	3000	Dc3/166r	2628
Dillon, Luke	Meath, Moymett	gentry: esquire	03-Jun-22	200	Dc2/40V	1110
Dillon, Luke	Westmeath, Kilnelaghnee	gentry: knight	04-Jun-25	800	Dc2/65r	1289
Dillon, Luke	Cavan, Trinitie Island	gentry: esquire	28-Feb-28	200	Dc2/104v	1488
Dillon, Luke	Mayo, Benfadda	gentry: gent	17-May-14	2000	Dc1/129r	802
Dillon, Luke	Westmeath, Killenefaghner	gentry: knight	08-Dec-26	800	Dc2/85v	1405
Dillon, Luke	Roscommon, Loghglin	gentry: knight	08-Dec-25	200	Dc2/71v	1330
Dillon, Luke	Westmeath, Killinfaghny	gentry: knight	04-Dec-30	2564	Dc2/157v	1732
Dillon, Luke	Roscommon, Loghlin	gentry: knight	28-Nov-25	240	Dc2/70v	1322
Dillon, Pierce	Westmeath, Baskonnogh	gentry: gent	16-May-15	200	Dc1/137v	853
Dillon, Richard	Meath, Prudston	gentry: gent	20-May-98	320	Dc1/11r	79
Dillon, Robert	Meath, Moymet	gentry: knight, s./heir Sr James	30-Oct-18	800	Dc2/16v	952
Dillon, Robert	Meath, Carnarston	gentry: esquire	01-Dec-19	500	Dc2/26r	1006
Dillon, Robert	Meath, Newton	gentry: knight	03-Jun-22	200	Dc2/40V	1110
Dillon, Robert	Meath?, Moymot	gentry: son/heir of Sir James	24-Dec-03	2508	Dc1/51r	326
Dillon, Robert	Galway, Clonebroke	gentry: esquire	17-Jun-10	200	Dc1/98r	615
Dillon, Robert	Galway, Clonbrocke	gentry: esquire	05-Jul-23	120	Dc2/48v	1169
Dillon, Robert	Kilkenny?	peer: baron Kilkenny West	28-Feb-28	200	Dc2/104v	1488
Dillon, Robert	Dublin, Blanchardstone	gentry: gent	30-May-28	200	Dc2/110v	1516

Standard	County	Occupation	Date	Amount	MS No	Ident No
Dillon, Robert	Meath, Ladyrath	gentry: gent	27-Nov-27	204	Dc2/101r	1468
Dillon, Robert	Meath, Laderath	gentry: gent	09-Dec-26	400	Dc2/85v	1406
Dillon, Robert	Dublin, Blanchardstowne	gentry: gent	16-Sep-30	300	Dc2/155r	1719
Dillon, Robert	Dublin, Blancherston	gentry: gent	21-Apr-40	100	B.L. 19, 843 f. 46	2810
Dillon, Robert	King's Co., Klummore	gentry: gent	08-Dec-60	400	B.L. 15, 635 f. 61	3373
Dillon, Thomas	Kildare, Barbistowne	gentry: esquire	11-Feb-34	200	Dc2/206v	1929
Dillon, Thomas	Westmeath, Ardnecrary	other: s./heir Talbot Dillon	01-Dec-19	500	Dc2/26r	1005
Dillon, Thomas	Westmeath?, Ardnecrany?	other: son of Talbot	25-Jul-14	400	Dc1/131r	814
Dillon, Thomas	Mayo, Costello and Gallen	peer: viscount Dillon, Gallen	29-Nov-67	1000	Dc3/68	2375
Dillon, Thomas	Westmeath, Ardnecrany	gentry: gent	21-Nov-25	400	Dc2/70r	1321
Dillon, Thomas	Mayo, Costello-Gallen?	peer: viscount Costello-Gallen	29-Nov-67	1000	B.L. 15, 635 f. 217a	3640
Dillon, Tibbot	Westmeath, Killnifaghny	gentry: knight	17-May-14	2000	Dc1/129r	803
Dillon, Walter	Dublin, Coulmine	gentry: gent	02-Dec-02	160	Dc1/41v	266
Dillon, Wentworth	Roscommon?	peer: earl of Roscommon	12-Oct-66	4000	Dc3/39	2313
Dillon, Wentworth	Roscommon?	peer: earl of Roscommon	14-May-70	4000	Dc3/119	2478
Dillon, Wentworth	Roscommon?	peer: earl of Roscommon	10-Nov-71	3200	Dc3/140r	2531
Dillon, Wentworth	Roscommon?	peer: earl of Roscommon	03-Jan-73	900	Dc3/152v	2569
Dillon, Wentworth	Roscommon?	peer: earl of Roscommon	13-Jul-66	1000	Dc3/31	2291
Dillon, Wentworth	Roscommon?	peer: earl of Roscommon	15-Jan-72	6000	Dc3/143v	2542
Dillon, Wentworth	Roscommon?	peer: earl of Roscommon	15-Jan-72	6000	B.L. 15, 636 f. 95	3787
Dillon, Wentworth	Roscommon?	peer: earl of Roscommon	14-May-70	4000	B.L. 15, 636 f. 66a	3735
Dillon, Wentworth	Roscommon?	peer: earl of Roscommon	19-Apr-82	3000	B.L. 15, 637 f. 55a	3946
Dillon, Wentworth	Roscommon?	peer: earl of Roscommon	23-Sep-62	500	B.L. 15, 635 f. 97	3429
Dillon, Wentworth	Roscommon?	peer: earl of Roscommon	03-Jan-73	90	B.L. 15, 636 f. 123	3830
Dillon, Wentworth	Roscommon?	peer: earl of Roscommon	10-Nov-71	3200	B.L. 15, 636 f. 92	3783
Dillon, William	Meath, Flynston	gentry: gent	18-May-04	120	Dc1/52v	333
Dillon, William	Meath, Fflynston	gentry: gent	19-May-09	400	Dc1/89r	556
Dillon, William	Meath, Fflinstowne	gentry: gent	26-Jun-28	200	Dc2/111v	1520
Disbrowe, John	Kilkenny, the city	gentry: gent	31-Dec-79	2000	B.L. 15, 637 f. 24	3889
Disney, George	Louth, Strabanon	gentry: gent	16-Apr-78	43	B.L. 19, 844 f. 154	3285
Disney, William	Louth, Stabanan	gentry: esquire	24-Jun-72	100	B.L. 15, 636 f. 112	3814
Dobbs, Richard	Antrim, Castledobb	gentry: esquire	26-May-79	280	B.L. 15, 637 f. 21	3884
Dobbs, Richard	Antrim, Castledobb	gentry: esquire	21-Mar-65	315	B.L. 15, 635 f. 151	3521
Dobbs, Richard	Antrim, Castledobb	gentry: esquire	11-Oct-66	85	B.L. 15, 635 f. 178	3565
Dobson, Isaac	Dublin, Clookers Lane	soldier: lieutenant colonel	16-Apr-56	216	B.L. 19, 843 f. 183a	3074
Dobson, Isaac	Dublin, the city	gentry: esquire	31-Mar-56	1100	B.L. 19, 843 f. 183	3073
Dobson, Katherine	Dublin, Clookers Lane	soldier: wife of Isaac	16-Apr-56	216	B.L. 19, 843 f. 183a	3074
Dodwell, Henry	Galway, Killion		03-Dec-40	230	B.L. 19, 843 f. 89	2897
Dodwell, William	Roscommon, grange of Thallan?		15-Dec-34	100	Dc2/226r	2010
Dodwell, William	Galway, Killion	other: son/heir of Henry	03-Dec-40	230	B.L. 19, 843 f. 89	2897

Standard	County	Occupation	Date	Amount	MS No	Ident No
Doe, Paul	Galway		02-Aug-65	680	B.L. 15, 635 f. 157a	3532
Doherty, Patrick	Monaghan, Monohan		07-May-28	180	Dc2/107r	1499
Donaldson, Hugh	Antrim, Ballymoney,					
	Isl. Magee	gentry: gent	01-Sep-82	220	B.L. 15 , 637 f. 63	3961
Done, Richard	Antrim, Carrickfergus	soldier: captain	02-Jan-56	800	B.L. 19, 843 f. 164a	3043
Dongan, Edward	Kildare, Kilteghan	gentry: esquire	16-Feb-30	600	Dc2/142v	1668
Dongan, Edward	Kildare, Killteghan	gentry: esquire	12-Dec-29	600	Dc2/140r	1655
Dongan, John	Kildare,					
	Castletownekildrought	gentry: baronet	16-Feb-30	600	Dc2/142v	1668
Dongan, John	Kildare, Castletowne	gentry:				
		knight and baronet	22-Jan-35	800	Dc2/228v	2019
Dongan, Mary	Dublin?, Castletowne	gentry:				
		widow of John, baronet	24-Sep-61	640	B.L. 15, 635 f. 85	3406
Dongan, Robert	Kildare, Castletowne	gentry: esquire	24-Sep-61	640	B.L. 15, 635 f. 85	3406
Dongan, Walter	Kildare, Possockston	gentry: gent	09-May-10	100	Dc1/96r	602
Dongan, Walter	Kildare, Passickston	gentry: gent	11-Jun-07	200	Dc1/78r	475
Dongan, Wiliam	Kildare?	peer:				
		viscount Dungan, Clane	18-Nov-71	200	Dc3/140v	2533
Dongan, William	Kildare?	peer:				
		viscount Dungan, Clane	08-Feb-70	400	Dc3/113	2467
Dongan, William	Kildare?	peer:				
		viscount Dungan, Clane	10-Nov-71	3200	Dc3/140r	2531
Dongan, William	Kildare?	peer:				
		viscount Dungan, Clane	21-May-69	400	Dc3/99	2439
Dongan, William	Dublin	gentry: gent	22-Nov-99	100	Dc1/20r	135
Dongan, William	Dublin	gentry: gent	01-Dec-98	133	Dc1/14r	98
Dongan, William	Kildare?	peer:				
		viscount Dungan, Clane	17-Feb-72	200	Dc3/144r	2545
Dongan, William	Kildare?	peer:				
		viscount Dungan, Clane	18-Nov-71	200	B.L. 15, 636 f. 101a	3796
Dongan, William	Kildare?	peer:				
		viscount Dungan, Clane	08-Feb-70	400	B.L. 15, 636 f. 53a	3716
Dongan, William	Kildare?	peer:				
		viscount Dungan, Clane	08-Aug-63	1000	B.L. 15, 635 f. 116	3462
Dongan, William	Kildare?	peer:				
		viscount Dungan, Clane	17-Feb-72	200	B.L. 15, 636 f. 99	3793
Dongan, William	Kildare?	peer:				
		viscount Dungan, Clane	10-Nov-71	3200	B.L. 15, 636 f. 92	3783
Donie?, William	Carlow, Katherlagh	merchant	11-May-05	2000	Dc1/59r	359
Donnellan, Edmund	Roscommon, Cloghan	gentry: esquire	17-Apr-60	746	B.L. 15, 635 f. 60	3371
Donovan, Richard	Waterford?		22-Nov-06	24	Dc1/71v	435
Dowd, Charles	Sligo, Cottletowne,					
	Tyreragh?	gentry: esquire	09-Dec-29	200	Dc2/139v	1653
Dowd, David	Sligo, Killeglaishin	gentry: gent	30-Nov-13	60	Dc1/124v	774
Dowd, David	Sligo, Castleconnor	gentry: esquire	15-Feb-13	50	Dc1/119r	740

Standard	County	Occupation	Date	Amount	MS No	Ident No
Dowd, David	Sligo, Gilleglash	gentry: gent	03-Dec-13	60	Dc1/125r	776
Dowd, David	Sligo, Castletowne	gentry: esquire	30-Nov-28	1000	Dc2/119v	1559
Dowd, Donal	Sligo, Rosloy	gentry: gent	09-Jul-18	105	Dc2/15v	946
Dowd, Donogh	Sligo, Enescrone	gentry: esquire	12-Feb-13	62	Dc1/118v	736
Dowd, Donogh	Sligo, Ennescrone	gentry: esquire	12-Feb-13	16	Dc1/118v	737
Dowd, John	Dublin		22-Feb-13	200	Dc1/119v	742
Dowdall, Alexander	Meath, Athboy	merchant	11-Nov-13	400	Dc1/123v	768
Dowdall, Alexander	Westmeath, Cloran	merchant	03-Jun-22	200	Dc2/40v	1111
Dowdall, Allexander	Westmeath, Cloghrane	merchant	13-May-20	200	Dc2/30r	1028
Dowdall, Charles	Louth, Castledowdall	gentry: gent	05-Apr-41	200	B.L. 19, 843 f. 88	2895
Dowdall, Christopher	Louth, Donleer	gentry: son/heir of William	22-Apr-08	200	Dc1/82r	508
Dowdall, Christopher	Louth, Killally	gentry: esquire	25-Jun-29	400	Dc2/134r	1626
Dowdall, Edward	Meath, Athlumny	gentry: esquire	13-May-20	200	Dc2/30r	1028
Dowdall, Edward	Meath, Athlumny	gentry: esquire	26-May-20	240	Dc2/30r	1030
Dowdall, Edward	Meath, Athlumny	gentry: esquire	03-Jun-22	200	Dc2/40v	1111
Dowdall, Edward	Meath, Rathmore	gentry: esquire	11-Nov-13	400	Dc1/123v	768
Dowdall, Edward	Meath, Athlumny	gentry: esquire	03-Jun-22	200	Dc2/40V	1110
Dowdall, Edward	Meath, Munckston	gentry: esquire	01-Mar-32	600	Dc2/177r	1812
Dowdall, Edward	Meath, Rathmore	gentry: gent	21-May-12	400	Dc1/114r	707
Dowdall, Francis	Meath, parish of Timoule	gentry: gent	12-May-69	800	Dc3/96	2434
Dowdall, Francis	Meath, Tomoole	gentry: gent	12-May-69	800	B.L. 15, 636 f. 37a	3688
Dowdall, George	Louth, Drogheda	gentry: gent, s./heir of Walter	01-Sep-40	200	B.L. 19, 843 f. 64a	2848
Dowdall, George	Louth, Drogheda	gentry: gent, s. of Walter	24-Sep-41	240	B.L. 19, 843 f. 115a	2950
Dowdall, James	Louth, Dundalk		28-Dec-11	130	Dc1/110v	687
Dowdall, James	Louth, Baggotston	gentry: gent	12-Feb-03	200	Dc1/45r	285
Dowdall, John	Louth, Ardee?	gentry: son/heir of Luke	01-Dec-34	200	Dc2/224v	2002
Dowdall, John	Louth, Drogheda	gentry: gent	27-Jul-07	300	Dc1/79ar	488
Dowdall, John	Meath, Clonlion	gentry: gent	14-Feb-29	200	Dc2/125r	1587
Dowdall, John	Meath, Prymetston	gentry: gent	20-Nov-01	140	Dc1/34v	228
Dowdall, John	Louth, Drogheda	gentry: gent	09-May-98	105	Dc1/11r	78
Dowdall, John	Louth, Glaspistell	gentry: gent	22-Jan-41	100	B.L. 19, 843 f. 79a	2878
Dowdall, John	Meath, Prymetston	gentry: gent	26-Nov-01	40	Dc1/35r	229
Dowdall, John	Meath, Prymetston	gentry: gent	11-Dec-00	200	Dc1/27r	182
Dowdall, John	Meath, Clonlion	gentry: gent	11-Mar-37	400	Dc2/260v	2170
Dowdall, Lancelot	Meath, Monketowne	gentry: gent	23-Aug-66	600	Dc3/37	2307
Dowdall, Lancelot	Meath, Monckstowne	gentry: gent	23-Aug-66	600	B.L. 15, 635 f. 180a	3570
Dowdall, Lawrence	Meath, Athlumny	gentry: esquire	11-Mar-37	400	Dc2/260v	2170
Dowdall, Lawrence	Meath, Athlumny	gentry: gent	09-Dec-35	240	Dc2/241v	2080
Dowdall, Lawrence	Meath, Athlumny	gentry: esquire	16-Feb-36	240	Dc2/244v	2094
Dowdall, Lawrence	Meath, Athlomney	gentry: esquire	20-Mar-55	80	B.L. 19, 843 f. 154a	3023
Dowdall, Lawrence	Meath, Athlummie	gentry: gent	07-Dec-38	660	B.L. 19, 843 f. 3	2725
Dowdall, Luke	Louth, Ardee	gentry: gent	01-Dec-34	200	Dc2/224v	2002
Dowdall, Luke	Louth, Atherdee	gentry: gent	28-Nov-35	120	Dc2/240v	2074

Standard	County	Occupation	Date	Amount	MS No	Ident No
Dowdall, Luke	Louth, Atherdee	gentry: gent	17-May-36	80	Dc2/251v	2123
Dowdall, Mathew	Westmeath, Cloran	gentry: gent	26-Aug-67	200	Dc3/66	2371
Dowdall, Michael	Louth, Atherdee	merchant	28-Nov-35	120	Dc2/240v	2074
Dowdall, Michael	Louth, Atherdee	gentry: gent, son of Luke	17-May-36	80	Dc2/251v	2123
Dowdall, Nicholas	Meath, Brownston	gentry: gent	01-Mar-32	600	Dc2/177r	1812
Dowdall, Nicholas	Meath, Brownston	gentry: gent	15-Oct-18	120	Dc2/16v	951
Dowdall, Patrick	Meath, Kenoge	gentry: gent	12-May-69	800	Dc3/96	2434
Dowdall, Patrick	Meath, Kenoge	gentry: gent	12-May-69	800	B.L. 15, 636 f. 37a	3688
Dowdall, Patrick	Limerick, the city	gentry: esquire	09-Aug-60	1000	B.L. 15, 635 f. 68	3383
Dowdall, Richard	Cavan, Latt	gentry: gent	28-Dec-11	130	Dc1/110v	687
Dowdall, Robert	Wicklow, Talbotston	gentry: gent	03-Dec-14	200	Dc1/133r	828
Dowdall, Stephen	Louth, Killally	gentry: gent	25-Jun-29	400	Dc2/134r	1626
Dowdall, Stephen	Louth, Killaley	gentry: esquire	05-Apr-41	200	B.L. 19, 843 f. 88	2895
Dowdall, Walter	Louth, Atherdie	merchant	06-Feb-06	100	Dc1/65r	393
Dowdall, Walter	Louth, Drogheda	gentry: gent	30-Nov-98	200	Dc1/13v	97
Dowdall, William	Louth, Donleere	gentry: gent	22-Apr-08	200	Dc1/82r	508
Dowding, James	Louth, Drogheda	merchant	01-May-41	120	B.L. 19, 843 f. 90a	2900
Downey, Edward	Queen's Co., Tignahincy	gentry: gent	20-Nov-16	300	Dc2/2r	878
Downing, Robert	Mayo, Castlelaygy	gentry: gent	13-Dec-80	4000	B.L. 15, 637 f. 44a	3927
Doyle, Daniel	Wicklow, Kilbride	trade: butcher	24-Oct-34	80	Dc2/220r	1984
Doyle, Donal	Wexford, Garrysinod	gentry: gent	14-Feb-32	120	Dc2/176r	1808
Doyle, John	Cavan, Balliheyes	gentry: esquire	11-Dec-18	200	Dc2/19r	965
Doyle, Thomas	Meath, Kilmoore	gentry: gent	12-Nov-11	50	Dc1/107v	667
Doyle, William	Wexford, Fortechichester	gentry: gent?	23-Nov-30	100	Dc2/157r	1729
Doyle, William	Wexford, Ffortchichester	gentry: gent	14-Feb-32	120	Dc2/176r	1808
Doyne, Barnaby	Queen's Co., Brittas	gentry: esquire	17-Dec-30	1000	Dc2/158r	1734
Doyne, George	Dublin, the city	gentry: gent	26-Jun-67	400	Dc3/64	2364
Doyne, Henry	Dublin, the city	merchant	06-Nov-35	102	Dc2/239v	2068
Doyne, Patrick	Dublin, the city	merchant	26-May-28	120	Dc2/110r	1513
Doyne, Terrence	Cork, Castletowne	gentry: gent	11-May-30	400	Dc2/147r	1686
Drake, John	Meath, Drakerath	gentry: gent	22-Apr-11	120	Dc1/103v	646
Drake, Roger	Wexford, Stokestowne	gentry: gent	17-Jul-66	50	Dc3/34	2297
Draycott, Christopher	Meath, Mornanstowne	gentry: gent	16-Jan-40	800	B.L. 19, 843 f. 39a	2797
Draycott, Henry	Meath, Morningtowne	gentry: esquire	07-Jun-64	300	B.L. 15, 635 f. 143	3505
Draycott, Henry	Meath, Morlingtowne	gentry: esquire	06-Aug-63	600	B.L. 15, 635 f. 122a	3472
Draycott, John	Meath, Mornantowne	gentry: esquire	29-May-41	600	B.L. 19, 843 f. 92	2903
Draycott, John	Meath, Mornington	gentry: esquire	18-Feb-41	600	B.L. 19, 843 f. 102a	2924
Draycott, John	Meath, Mornanstowne	gentry: esquire	16-Jan-40	800	B.L. 19, 843 f. 39a	2797
Draycott, Marcus	Meath, Athcarne	gentry: gent	07-May-23	200	Dc2/46v	1152
Draycott, Marcus	Meath, Odder	gentry: gent	03-May-00	200	Dc1/23v	156
Drew, John	Clare, Dromaneene	gentry: gent	04-Jul-85	240	B.L. 15, 637 f. 113	4055
Duff, ?	Dublin?	merchant	28-Feb-97	100	Dc1/2r	11
Duff, Edward	Dublin, the city	merchant: son of Richard	26-Jan-32	200	Dc2/174r	1800
Duff, George	Louth, Termonfeighen	gentry: gent	16-Nov-11	200	Dc1/108r	673

Standard	County	Occupation	Date	Amount	MS No	Ident No
Duff, Lawrence	Dublin, the city	trade: butcher	13-Aug-23	150	Dc2/50v	1178
Duff, Peter	Louth, Drogheda	merchant	16-Nov-12	250	Dc1/116v	724
Duff, Peter	Louth, Drogheda	merchant	14-Nov-12	200	Dc1/116v	723
Duff, Peter	Louth, Drogheda	merchant: brother of				
		George	16-Nov-11	200	Dc1/108r	673
Duff, Richard	Dublin, the city	gentry: esquire	04-Feb-73	800	Dc3/153r	2573
Duff, Richard	Dublin, the city	merchant	26-Jan-32	200	Dc2/174r	1800
Duff, Richard	Dublin, the city	gentry: esquire	04-Feb-73	800	B.L. 15, 636 f. 122	3829
Duff, Robert	Dublin	merchant	23-Mar-14	60	Dc1/128v	799
Duff, Robert	Dublin, the city	merchant	19-Dec-34	150	Dc2/227r	2013
Duff, Robert	Dublin	merchant	21-Sep-24	100	Dc2/58r	1238
Duff, Stephen	Dublin, the city	merchant	10-Mar-27	200	Dc2/89v	1421
Duff, Stephen	Louth, Drogheda	gentry: gent	14-Nov-12	200	Dc1/116v	723
Duignan, John	King's Co., Ballyduffe	gentry: gent	27-Nov-39	1000	B.L. 19, 843 f. 36	2790
Duignan, Rory	King's Co., Corre	gentry: gent	17-Nov-30	400	Dc2/155v	1724
Duls, Andrew	Dublin, the city	gentry: gent	05-Dec-23	240	Dc2/51v	1190
Dunbar, James	Fermanagh, Garrison	gentry: esquire	02-Jun-36	2000	Dc2/253r	2134
Dunbar, James	Fermanagh, Kiltowe	gentry: esquire	20-Jul-41	1200	B.L. 19, 843 f. 102	2923
Dunbar, John	Fermanagh, Dumbarr	gentry: esquire	22-Feb-17	450	Dc2/5v	895
Dunbar, John	Fermanagh, Dunbare	gentry: knight	13-May-28	200	Dc2/107v	1503
Dunbar, John	Fermanagh, Dunbarr	gentry: knight	02-Jun-36	2000	Dc2/253r	2134
Dunne, Barnaby	Queen's Co., Brittas	gentry: esquire	07-Jul-37	3000	Dc2/267r	2198
Dunne, Donugh	Queen's Co., Ballybrittas	farmer: yeoman	14-Mar-68	60	Dc3/74	2392
Dunne, Terrence	Queen's Co., Ballynekill	gentry: esquire	15-Feb-83	440	B.L. 15, 637 f. 75a	3984
Dutton, Charles	Longford, Rathcleene	gentry: esquire	03-Dec-36	1000	Dc2/258v	2162
Dwyer, John	Tipperary, Downedroma	gentry: esquire	17-May-09	1000	Dc1/88v	552
Dwyer, Derby	Tipperary, Clonyhirma	gentry: esquire	17-May-09	1000	Dc1/88v	553
Dwyer, Philip	Tipperary, Dundromy	gentry: esquire	30-Apr-39	4000	B.L. 19, 843 f. 5a	2729
East, Samuel	Wicklow, Rathduffe	gentry: esquire	12-Nov-40	240	B.L. 19, 843 f. 71a	2862
East, Samuel	Wicklow, Rathduffe	gentry: esquire	13-Feb-39	240	B.L. 19, 843 f. 51	2820
East, William	Kildare, Ballysonnan		12-Nov-40	240	B.L. 19, 843 f. 71a	2862
East, William	Kildare, Ballysonan		13-Feb-39	240	B.L. 19, 843 f. 51	2820
Eastwood, Stephen	Limerick, the city	gentry: gent	15-Jan-62	200	B.L. 15, 635 f. 90	3416
Echlin, Robert	Down, Castleboy, Ardes,	gentry: esquire	20-Mar-55	230	B.L. 19, 843 f. 157a	3029
Edgeworth, John	Longford, Carnelagh	gentry: esquire	09-Aug-67	800	Dc3/66	2370
Edgeworth, John	Longford, Lizard	gentry: knight	30-Apr-73	2000	Dc3/155r	2580
Edgeworth, John	Longford, Carnelagh	gentry: esquire	09-Aug-67	800	B.L. 15, 635 f. 205a	3620
Edgeworth, John	Longford, Lizard	gentry: knight	30-Apr-73	2000	B.L. 15, 636 f. 134a	3845
Edmonston, Archibald	Antrim, Brad Island	gentry: esquire	08-Apr-63	600	B.L. 15, 636 f. 82a	3765
Edmonston, Archibald	Antrim, Brade Island	gentry: esquire	22-Jan-66	600	B.L. 15, 635 f. 167	3547
Edmonston, Archibald	Antrim, Broad Island		13-Jun-68	320	B.L. 15, 635 f. 223a	3652
Edmonston, James	Antrim, Ballybantro	gentry: gent	01-Sep-82	220	B.L. 15 , 637 f. 63	3961
Edmonston, John	Antrim, Ballybartra	gentry: gent	02-Nov-65	200	B.L. 15, 636 f. 83a	3767
Edmonston, John	Antrim, Ballybantro	gentry: gent	01-Sep-82	220	B.L. 15 , 637 f. 63	3961

Standard	County	Occupation	Date	Amount	MS No	Ident No
Edwards, Edward	Tyrone, Castlederg	gentry: esquire	23-May-76	3000	B.L. 19, 844 f. 110	3238
Edwards, Edward	Tyrone, Castledarge	gentry: esquire	23-May-76	3000	Dc3/174r	2657
Edwards, Edward	Tyrone, Castlederige	gentry: esquire	23-May-76	1600	Dc3/174r	2658
Edwards, Edward	Tyrone, Castledergg	gentry: esquire	06-Dec-73	1300	Dc3/159r	2598
Edwards, Edward	Tyrone, Castlederg	gentry: esquire	20-Jun-86	2300	B.L. 15, 637 f. 110	4046
Edwards, Richard	Dublin, the city	trade: tailor	11-Apr-35	400	Dc2/232r	2034
Edwards, Thomas	Dublin, Castleknocke	gentry: gent	11-Apr-35	400	Dc2/232r	2034
Edwards, William	Louth, Phillippstowne	gentry: gent	08-Apr-72	105	B.L. 15, 636 f. 103a	3800
Elliott, Christopher	Meath, Donshaghlen	gentry: esquire	28-Sep-30	600	Dc2/155r	1720
Elliott, Henry	Cavan, Aghinmaddie	gentry: esquire	01-Dec-40	1500	B.L. 19, 843 f. 76	2871
Elliott, Henry	Meath, Balreaske	gentry: son of Sir John	26-Nov-16	1000	Dc2/2v	881
Elliott, Henry	Meath, Ballryeske	gentry: gent	04-May-12	200	Dc1/133r	702
Elliott, John	Meath, Balreaske	gentry: knight	01-Jul-15	1000	Dc1/139v	865
Elliott, John	Meath, Balreske	gentry: esquire	27-Jan-03	800	Dc1/43v	278
Elliott, Oliver	Meath, Bridgend	gentry: gent	14-Feb-29	200	Dc2/125r	1587
Elliott, Oliver	Meath, Bridgend	gentry: gent	13-May-29	400	Dc2/128v	1603
Elliott, Oliver	Meath, Bridgend	gentry: gent	28-Sep-30	600	Dc2/155r	1720
Elliott, Thomas	Meath, Balreaske	gentry: esquire	15-Dec-28	200	Dc2/123r	1573
Elliott, Thomas	Meath, Balreske	gentry: esquire	14-Feb-29	200	Dc2/125r	1587
Elliott, Thomas	Meath, Balreske	gentry: esquire	16-May-28	200	Dc2/108v	1507
Elliott, Thomas	Meath, Balreske	gentry: esquire	14-May-28	100	Dc2/108r	1506
Elliott, Thomas	Meath, Balriske	gentry: esquire	27-Nov-27	204	Dc2/101r	1468
Elliott, Thomas	Meath, Balreske	gentry: esquire	02-Sep-28	200	Dc2/114v	1537
Elliott, Thomas	Meath, Balreske	gentry: esquire	13-May-29	400	Dc2/128v	1603
Elliott, Thomas	Meath, Balreske	gentry: esquire	30-Sep-19	300	Dc2/26r	1004
Elliott, Thomas	Meath, Balreaske	gentry: son/heir of Sir John	01-Jul-15	1000	Dc1/139v	865
Elliott, Thomas	Meath, Balreske	gentry: esquire	28-Nov-22	700	Dc2/43r	1127
Elliott, Thomas	Meath, Balreske	gentry: esquire	25-Nov-20	200	Dc2/33v	1054
Elliott, Thomas	Meath, Balryeske	gentry: gent?	04-May-12	200	Dc1/133r	702
Elliott, Thomas	Meath, Balriske	gentry: esquire	14-Nov-27	120	Dc2/99v	1462
English, Nicholas	Dublin, Shallon	farmer: yeoman	04-May-03	300	Dc1/46v	296
English, Richard	Dublin	illegible	10-Mar-27	40	Dc2/89r	1420
Ennis, John	Kildare, the Naace	gentry: gent	07-May-14	100	Dc1/129r	801
Erskine, James		gentry: knight	19-Apr-27	1800	Dc2/90v	1425
Esmond, Lawrence	Wexford, Limerick	gentry: esquire	30-Apr-70	2000	Dc3/117	2474
Esmond, Lawrence	Carlow, Huntington	gentry: baronet	21-Nov-79	650	B.L. 15, 637 f. 22a	3886
Esmond, Lawrence	Wexford, Limick	gentry: esquire	30-Apr-70	2000	B.L. 15, 636 f. 67	3736
Etchingham, John	Wexford, Dunbrody	gentry: esquire	20-Mar-46	140	B.L. 19, 843 f. 121	2961
Etchingham, Sarah	Wexford, Dunbrody	gentry: wife of John	20-Mar-46	140	B.L. 19, 843 f. 121	2961
Eustace, Christopher	Meath, Lescartan	gentry: esquire	23-Oct-12	250	Dc1/115v	719
Eustace, Christopher	Meath, Lescartan	gentry: gent	03-Dec-05	107	Dc1/63v	384
Eustace, Christopher	Meath, Lescartan	gentry: gent	03-Jul-07	40	Dc1/79	484
Eustace, Christopher	Meath, Lescartan	gentry: gent	03-Jul-07	400	Dc1/79r	483
Eustace, Christopher	Meath, Lescartan	gentry: gent	03-May-05	80	Dc1/58r	354

Standard	County	Occupation	Date	Amount	MS No	Ident No
Eustace, Christopher	Meath, Lescarten	gentry: gent	13-May-08	200	Dc1/82v	513
Eustace, Christopher	Kildare, Giginstowne	gentry: gent	28-May-33	280	Dc2/195v	1885
Eustace, Christopher	Meath, Lescarten	gentry: gent	07-May-11	1000	Dc1/104r	649
Eustace, James	Kildare, Newland	gentry: gent	15-Mar-19	240	Dc2/21v	978
Eustace, James	Kildare, Newland	gentry: gent	27-Jan-20	160	Dc2/28v	1019
Eustace, James	Kildare?	gentry: gent	25-Aug-24	80	Dc2/57v	1236
Eustace, James	Kildare, Clongoweswodd	gentry: gent	28-Jun-26	200	Dc2/81r	1386
Eustace, James	Kildare, Confy	gentry: esquire	15-Nov-52	494	B.L. 19, 843 f. 127a	2973
Eustace, James	Kildare, Newland	gentry: esquire	13-May-24	300	Dc2/55r	1214
Eustace, James	Kildare, Newland	gentry: esquire	14-May-24	300	Dc2/55r	1215
Eustace, James	Kildare, Newland	gentry: esquire	28-May-33	280	Dc2/195v	1885
Eustace, James	Kildare, Newland	gentry: esquire	19-Aug-34	200	Dc2/217v	1974
Eustace, James	Kildare, Confy	gentry: esquire	26-Jun-54	655	B.L. 19, 843 f. 142	2998
Eustace, James	Kildare, Newlan	gentry: esquire	12-May-24	300	Dc2/54v	1213
Eustace, James	Kildare, Confie	gentry: esquire	01-Jul-61	600	B.L. 15, 635 f. 74a	3391
Eustace, James	Kildare, Newlan	gentry: gent	26-May-23	300	Dc2/47v	1161
Eustace, John	Kildare, Brenockstowne	gentry: knight	09-Mar-75	680	Dc3/166r	2630
Eustace, John	Kildare, Harristowne	gentry: gent	31-Jan-22	270	Dc2/38v	1093
Eustace, John	Dublin, the city	gentry: knight	18-May-67	500	Dc3/61	2355
Eustace, John	Kildare, Brecknockstowne	gentry: knight	09-Mar-75	680	B.L. 19, 844 f. 57	3181
Eustace, John	Dublin, the city	gentry: knight	18-May-67	500	B.L. 15, 635 f. 191a	3593
Eustace, Maurice	Kildare, Clongoweswood		10-Sep-03	500	Dc1/49r	315
Eustace, Maurice	Kildare, Clongoweswood	gentry: gent	18-Jun-02	200	Dc1/38v	249
Eustace, Maurice	Kildare, Harristowne	gentry: knight	19-Dec-83	2400	B.L. 15, 637 f. 82	3996
Eustace, Maurice	Kildare, Harristowne	gentry: knight	04-Jul-85	2000	B.L. 15, 637 f. 113	4056
Eustace, Maurice	Kildare?	gentry: knight	09-Apr-63	600	B.L. 15, 635 f. 103	3440
Eustace, Nicholas	Dublin, Clareston	gentry: gent	14-Jul-25	123	Dc2/68v	1309
Eustace, Nicholas	Dublin, Elverston	gentry: gent	11-Nov-25	200	Dc2/69v	1318
Eustace, Nicholas	Wicklow, Burgadge Moyle?	gentry: gent	16-Mar-35	200	Dc2/231r	2029
Eustace, Nicholas	Kildare, Crookestowne	gentry: gent	10-Sep-70	220	Dc3/124	2490
Eustace, Nicholas	Kildare, Crookestowne	gentry: gent	10-Sep-70	220	B.L. 15, 636 f. 69a	3741
Eustace, Oliver	Carlow, Kilknocke	gentry: gent	13-Feb-07	105	Dc1/74r	449
Eustace, Oliver	Carlow, Ballynunri	gentry: esquire	09-Feb-41	1200	B.L. 19, 843 f. 83a	2886
Eustace, Richard	Kildare, Moylaghcash	gentry: gent	08-Apr-01	40	Dc1/30r	199
Eustace, Roland	Kildare, Moone	gentry: gent	16-Nov-37	400	Dc2/271r	2217
Eustace, Thomas	Kildare, Couby	gentry: gent	04-Feb-68	300	Dc3/72	2387
Eustace, Thomas	Kildare, Confy	gentry: gent	04-Feb-68	300	B.L. 15, 635 f. 224a	3654
Eustace, Walter	Dublin, Elverestowne	gentry: gent, son/heir of Nicholas	16-Mar-35	200	Dc2/231r	2029
Eustace, Walter	Dublin, Eluerstowne	gentry: gent	15-Jun-29	200	Dc2/132r	1618
Eustace, Walter	Dublin?, Elverston?	gentry: son/heir of Nicholas	11-Nov-25	200	Dc2/69v	1318
Eustace, William	Kildare, Castelmarten	gentry: esquire	17-Jul-20	200	Dc2/32r	1044
Eustace, William	Kildare, CastleMarten	gentry: esquire	05-Dec-97	400	Dc1/8r	58
Eustace, William	Kildare, Galmorstowne	gentry: gent	02-May-35	460	Dc2/234v	2044

Standard	County	Occupation	Date	Amount	MS No	Ident No
Eustace, William	Kildare, Castlemartin	gentry: esquire	03-May-05	80	Dc1/58r	354
Eustace, William	Kildare, Castelmartin	gentry: esquire	10-Sep-03	500	Dc1/49r	315
Eustace, William	Kildare, Castlemarten	gentry: esquire	26-Feb-14	500	Dc1/127r	789
Eustace, William	Kildare, Castlemarten	gentry: esquire	08-Feb-10	400	Dc1/94r	589
Eustace, William	Kildare, Clongoweswood	gentry: son/heir of				
		Maurice	18-Jun-02	200	Dc1/38v	249
Eustace, William	Kildare, Castlemarten	gentry: esquire	17-Apr-06	1000	Dc1/66v	402
Eustace, William	Kildare, Castlemarten	gentry: gent	28-Jan-05	105	Dc1/55r	343
Eustace, William	Kildare, Castlemarten	gentry: esquire	27-Jan-97	200	Dc1/1r	1
Evans, George	Mayo, Ballinrobe	gentry: knight	09-Mar-75	3300	B.L. 19, 844 f. 51	3174
Evans, George	Cork, Phylipstown	gentry: esquire	30-Jul-75	6000	B.L. 19, 844 f. 74	3202
Everard, Charles	Waterford, Glanbally					
	Cullynam	gentry: gent	25-May-39	2200	B.L. 19, 843 f. 14	2746
Everard, Thomas	Meath, the Newton	gentry: gent	28-Aug-02	120	Dc1/39v	255
Everard, Walter	Meath, the Navan	merchant	28-Aug-02	120	Dc1/39v	255
Evers, Christopher	Meath, Ballardon	gentry: gent	01-Dec-69	200	Dc3/109	2460
Ewer, John	Wicklow, Tombore	gentry: gent	15-May-26	400	Dc2/77r	1363
Fagan, Thomas	Dublin	gentry: gent	12-May-99	400	Dc1/16v	111
Fair, Miles	Westmeath, Comberston	gentry: gent	21-May-23	800	Dc2/47v	1159
Fanning, Dominic	Limerick, the city	gentry: esquire	24-Oct-40	1400	B.L. 19, 843 f. 82a	2884
Fanning, Henry	Westmeath, Killare	gentry: esquire	09-Dec-30	200	Dc2/157v	1733
Fanning, John	Carlow, Cloghnea	gentry: esquire	21-Jun-83	2000	B.L. 15, 637 f. 75	3983
Fare, Robert	Cork, Grange	gentry: esquire	21-Mar-78	2000	Dc3/187v	2708
Farrell, Connel	Longford, Killenlyke	gentry: esquire	31-Oct-07	300	Dc1/79ar	490
Farrell, Connel	Longford, Tyneleke	gentry: esquire	19-May-10	160	Dc1/96r	604
Farrell, Fachtna	Longford, Mote	gentry: esquire	13-May-34	2000	Dc2/210v	1947
Farrell, Fachtna	Longford, Moate	gentry: esquire	22-Jun-29	200	Dc2/133v	1625
Farrell, Francis	Longford, Clankerin	gentry: esquire	09-Jul-77	700	B.L. 19, 844 f. 137	3267
Farrell, Francis	Longford, Clanker	gentry: esquire	09-Jul-77	700	Dc3/183r	2692
Farrell, Gerald	Longford, Newcastel	gentry: gent	27-Jul-03	1000	Dc1/47av	310
Farrell, Honora	Sligo, Ardneglass	gentry: widow of				
		Moylemorrye	11-Aug-38	100	B.L. 19, 843 f.10	2738
Farrell, James	Longford, Tinnelicke	gentry: esquire	08-May-32	200	Dc2/179v	1822
Farrell, James	Longford, Castelruighe	gentry: gent?	27-Jul-03	1000	Dc1/47av	309
Farrell, James	Longford, Killenlyke	gentry: son/heir of Conel	31-Oct-07	300	Dc1/79ar	490
Farrell, John	Longford, Ardenragh	gentry: esquire	17-May-14	2000	Dc1/129r	803
Farrell, John	Longford, Ardenraghe	gentry: gent	27-Jul-03	1000	Dc1/47av	309
Farrell, Murrough	Longford, Reyne	gentry: gent	09-May-34	400	Dc2/210v	1946
Farrell, Roger	Longford, Mamin	gentry: son/heir of				
		Francis	09-Jul-77	700	B.L. 19, 844 f. 137	3267
Farrell, Roger	Longford, Marnin	gentry: gent	09-Jul-77	700	Dc3/183r	2692
Farrell, Ross	Longford, the Moate	gentry: esquire	25-Nov-08	800	Dc1/84v	528
Farrell, Shane	Dublin, Ballinecorny	Farmer: husbandman	08-Feb-03	200	Dc1/44r	281

Standard	County	Occupation	Date	Amount	MS No	Ident No
Farrell, William	Longford, Ballintobber	gentry: esquire	08-May-32	200	Dc2/179v	1822
Farrell, William	Longford, Ballintobber	gentry: esquire	01-Dec-28	200	Dc2/119v	1560
Farrell, William	?, Ffurlough, Cloonarte	gentry: gent	16-May-29	80	Dc2/129r	1605
Fay, Edward	Westmeath, Connorston	gentry: son/heir of Meyler	04-Jul-26	250	Dc2/80v	1384
Fay, Geoffrey	Kildare?, Harbartston?	gentry: son/heir of Meyler	17-Jun-24	100	Dc2/56v	1225
Fay, Geoffrey	Kildare?, Harbarston?	gentry: son/heir of Meyler	06-Dec-22	200	Dc2/43v	1131
Fay, Gerald	Westmeath, Derinygarragh	gentry: esquire	30-Nov-71	240	Dc3/142r	2537
Fay, Gerald	Westmeath, Dernegarah	gentry: esquire	15-Jul-76	357	B.L. 19, 844 f. 105	3232
Fay, Gerald	Westmeath, Dernegarah	gentry: esquire	15-Jul-76	257	Dc3/179r	2673
Fay, Meyler	Kildare, Harbartston	gentry: gent	17-Jun-24	100	Dc2/56v	1225
Fay, Meyler	Kildare, Harbarston	gentry: gent	06-Dec-22	200	Dc2/43v	1131
Fay, Meyler	Westmeath, Connorston	gentry: gent	04-Jul-26	250	Dc2/80v	1384
Feltham, Henry	Tipperary, Liskelly	gentry: gent	04-Aug-68	240	Dc3/82	2410
Feltham, Henry	Tipperary, Liskilley, Owney	gentry: gent	24-Nov-69	330	Dc3/107	2457
Fennell, Gerald	Tipperary, Ballygriffin	gentry: esquire	30-Apr-39	4000	B.L. 19, 843 f. 5a	2729
Fennell, Gerald	Tipperary, Ballygriffin	gentry: esquire	06-Jun-40	4000	B.L. 19, 843 f. 56a	2831
Fernley, Philip	Dublin, the city	gentry: esquire	11-Jun-56	600	B.L. 19, 843 f. 175	3061
Fernley, Philip	Dublin	gentry: esquire	20-Apr-55	600	B.L. 19, 843 f. 155a	3025
Fernley, Philip	Dublin, the city	gentry: esquire	20-Nov-37	600	Dc2/271v	2218
Fernley, Philip	Dublin, the city	gentry: esquire	13-Apr-53	400	B.L. 19, 843 f. 132a	2980
Ferris, John	Antrim, Dunmurry	trade: leather worker	29-Jan-72	137	B.L. 15, 636 f. 98	3792
Ferris, John	Antrim, Dunmurry	trade: leather worker	29-Jan-72	273	B.L. 15, 636 f. 108a	3808
Field, James	Monaghan, Coulry	gentry: esquire	15-Jun-30	2000	Dc2/151v	1705
Field, James	Monaghan, Ballireagh	gentry: esquire	25-Jun-28	220	Dc2/111v	1519
Field, John	Dublin, the city	gentry: son/heir of Simon	19-Dec-34	220	Dc2/226v	2012
Field, John	Dublin, the city?	gentry: son/heir of Simon	18-Mar-34	200	Dc2/209v	1942
Field, John	Dublin, the city	gentry: son/heir of Simon	27-Aug-34	400	Dc2/218r	1976
Field, John	Dublin, the city	gentry: son/heir of Simon	19-Dec-34	220	B.L. 19, 843 f. 98	2915
Field, Simon	Dublin, the city	gentry: gent	18-Mar-34	200	Dc2/209v	1942
Field, Simon	Dublin	gentry: gent	10-May-28	200	Dc2/107r	1501
Field, Simon	Dublin, the city	gentry: gent	27-Aug-34	400	Dc2/218r	1976
Field, Simon	Dublin, the city	gentry: gent	19-Dec-34	220	Dc2/226v	2012
Field, Simon	Dublin, the city	gentry: gent	19-Dec-34	220	B.L. 19, 843 f. 98	2915
Finan, Daniel	Kerry, Ardtully	gentry: esquire	09-Jun-13	60	Dc1/122r	757
Finan, Daniel	Kerry, Ardtullyhy	gentry: esquire	28-May-13	40	Dc1/121r	751
Finan, Daniel	Kerry, Ardthuly	gentry: gent	19-Feb-14	240	Dc1/127r	787
Finan, Daniel	Kerry, Ardtullyhy	gentry: esquire	01-Jun-13	200	Dc1/121r	753
Finan, Donogh	Queen's Co., Mannen	gentry: gent	04-Nov-40	200	B.L. 19, 843 f. 83	2885

Standard	County	Occupation	Date	Amount	MS No	Ident No
Finan, Donogh	Queen's Co., Mannen	gentry: gent	07-Nov-39	400	B.L. 19, 843 f. 28a	2775
Finan, Donogh	Queen's Co., Mannen	gentry: gent	07-Nov-39	400	B.L. 19, 843 f. 28	2774
Finglas, Andrew	Dublin, Tobbertowne	gentry: gent	19-Apr-71	600	B.L. 15, 636 f. 84	3768
Finglas, Christopher	Dublin, Wespelston	gentry: gent	27-Nov-97	200	Dc1/7v	53
Finglas, Christopher	Dublin, Morroghe	gentry: gent	07-Nov-17	120	Dc2/10v	916
Finglas, Christopher	Dublin, Morroghe	gentry: gent	06-Mar-00	200	Dc1/22r	146
Finglas, Christopher	Dublin, Westpelston	gentry: brother of Richard	09-Dec-19	1000	Dc2/27v	1014
Finglas, Christopher	Dublin, Murragh	gentry: gent	09-Dec-19	1000	Dc2/27v	1014
Finglas, Christopher	Dublin, Stephenston	gentry: gent	29-Jul-09	120	Dc1/90v	568
Finglas, Elizabeth	Dublin, Luttrelston	other: widow	27-Jun-01	40	Dc1/33r	216
Finglas, John	Dublin, Tobbertowne	gentry: gent	28-Nov-28	200	Dc2/118r	1552
Finglas, John	Dublin, Tobbertowne	gentry: gent	15-Jun-35	200	Dc2/236v	2054
Finglas, John	Dublin, Tobberton	gentry: gent	02-Aug-32	200	Dc2/185r	1843
Finglas, John	Dublin, Tobbertowne	gentry: gent	14-May-34	1600	Dc2/211r	1949
Finglas, John	Dublin, Tobbertonn	gentry: gent	16-Dec-20	200	Dc2/34r	1058
Finglas, John	Dublin, Wespelston	gentry: esquire	06-Mar-00	200	Dc1/22r	146
Finglas, John	Dublin, Tobbertowne	gentry: gent	05-Dec-28	200	Dc2/121r	1566
Finglas, John	Dublin, Tobberton	gentry: gent	13-Dec-28	400	Dc2/122v	1571
Finglas, John	Dublin, Wespelton	gentry: gent	03-Jun-03	500	Dc1/47r	299
Finglas, John	Dublin, Toberton	gentry: gent	12-Jun-29	400	Dc2/131v	1615
Finglas, John	Dublin, Toberton	gentry: gent	17-Oct-22	200	Dc2/42v	1124
Finglas, John	Dublin, Porterane	gentry: gent	02-Apr-29	1000	Dc2/127r	1595
Finglas, John	Dublin, Toberton	gentry: gent	12-Jun-29	800	Dc2/131v	1616
Finglas, John	Dublin, Tubberstowne	gentry: gent	01-Feb-28	400	Dc2/103v	1482
Finglas, John	Dublin, Porterane	gentry: gent	07-May-23	200	Dc2/46v	1152
Finglas, John	Dublin, Tobberton	gentry: gent	04-Apr-26	400	Dc2/76v	1358
Finglas, John	Dublin, Wespelston	gentry: esquire	27-Nov-97	200	Dc1/7v	53
Finglas, John	Dublin, Tobbertown	gentry: esquire	21-Dec-24	400	Dc2/60r	1254
Finglas, Richard	Dublin, Stephenstowne	gentry: esquire	01-Aug-31	300	Dc2/167r	1772
Finglas, Richard	Dublin, Westpelston	gentry: esquire	09-Dec-19	1000	Dc2/27v	1014
Finglas, Richard	Dublin, Wespelston	gentry: esquire	01-Feb-28	400	Dc2/103v	1482
Finglas, Richard	Dublin, Stephinstowne	gentry: esquire	27-Nov-28	300	Dc2/117r	1548
Finglas, Richard	Dublin, Wespelston	gentry: esquire	05-Mar-27	160	Dc2/88v	1418
Finglas, Richard	Dublin, Waspelston	gentry: esquire	21-Dec-24	400	Dc2/60r	1254
Finglas, Richard	Dublin, Wespelstone	gentry: esquire	13-Dec-28	400	Dc2/122v	1571
Finglas, Richard	Dublin, Wespeltowne	gentry: esquire	05-Dec-28	200	Dc2/121r	1566
Finglas, Richard	Dublin, Wespailston?	gentry: gent	28-Jul-26	100	Dc2/81v	1388
Finn, William	Kildare, Leixlipp	gentry: gent	12-Sep-25	48	Dc2/69r	1315
Finn, als Barnewall, Mary	Kildare, Leixlipp	other: widow	12-Sep-25	48	Dc2/69r	1315
Finn, Daniel	Queen's Co., Rathniculinan?	gentry: gent	02-Dec-33	100	Dc2/201v	1910
Finn, Edmund	Queen's Co., Rathniculinan?	gentry: son/heir of Daniel	02-Dec-33	100	Dc2/201v	1910
Finn, William	Dublin	merchant	05-Apr-10	150	Dc1/95r	595

Standard	County	Occupation	Date	Amount	MS No	Ident No
Fish, Edmund	Dublin	gentry: baronet	24-May-26	440	Dc2/78r	1369
Fish, Edward		gentry: baronet, s of				
		Sir John	13-Jun-25	1000	Dc2/66r	1294
Fish, John	Cavan, Lesmeen	gentry: esquire	19-Jan-19	2000	Dc2/20r	969
Fish, Joseph	Dublin	merchant	05-Dec-56	1000	B.L. 19, 843 f. 188	3083
Fish, Mary		gentry: daughter of				
		Sir John	13-Jun-25	1000	Dc2/66r	1295
Fitton, Alexander	England, London,					
	Inner Temple	gentry: esquire	22-May-75	2909	Dc3/167v	2635
Fitton, Alexander	England, London,					
	Inner Temple	gentry: esquire	22-May-75	2909	B.L. 19, 844 f. 62	3189
Fitton, Alexander	Limerick, Awney	gentry: esquire	08-Oct-66	500	B.L. 15, 635 f. 179	3567
Fitton, Edward	Limerick, Amy	gentry: gent	10-Apr-39	1000	B.L. 19, 843 f. 4	2726
Fitton, William	Limerick, Amy	gentry: esquire	10-Apr-39	1000	B.L. 19, 843 f. 4	2726
Fitton, William	Limerick, Any	gentry: esquire	15-Jan-41	2000	B.L. 19, 843 f. 77a	2874
Fitzgerald, Clement	Dublin, Kilcoghlan	gentry: gent	01-Feb-39	160	B.L. 19, 843 f. 91a	2902
Fitzgerald, Clement	Dublin, Kilcoskan	gentry: gent	12-Jul-37	300	Dc2/268r	2203
Fitzgerald, Clement	Dublin, Kilkosker	gentry: gent	31-Jan-22	240	Dc2/38v	1095
Fitzgerald, Clement	Dublin, Kilcoskan	gentry: gent	23-Mar-26	400	Dc2/76r	1356
Fitzgerald, Clement	Dublin, Kilcaskan	gentry: gent	07-Jul-37	200	Dc2/267v	2200
Fitzgerald, Clement	Dublin, Kilcoskan	gentry: gent	04-Dec-17	200	Dc2/12v	928
Fitzgerald, David	Kerry, Balledaniell	gentry: gent	24-May-23	600	Dc2/47v	1160
Fitzgerald, David	Limerick, Ballynacourtie	gentry: son/heir of				
		Gerald	07-Jun-40	400	B.L. 19, 843 f. 68	2855
Fitzgerald, Edmund	Cork, Ballymollowe	gentry: esquire	29-May-41	1000	B.L. 19, 843 f. 97	2913
Fitzgerald, Edmund	Cork, Ballymoloe	gentry: esquire	06-May-41	1500	B.L. 19, 843 f. 98a	2916
Fitzgerald, Edmund	Cork, Imokilly,					
	Glannagueare	gentry: gent	16-Dec-67	560	B.L. 15, 635 f. 214a	3634
Fitzgerald, Edward	Kildare?, Blackhall	gentry: gent	10-Nov-18	200	Dc2/17r	953
Fitzgerald, Edward	Kildare, Blackhall	gentry: esquire	22-Nov-32	140	Dc2/187r	1852
Fitzgerald, Edward	Dublin	merchant	20-Jul-30	50	Dc2/154v	1717
Fitzgerald, Edward	Kildare, Blackehall	gentry: gent	05-Jul-17	200	Dc2/8v	908
Fitzgerald, Edward	Kildare, Blackhill	gentry: esquire	15-Nov-31	100	Dc2/169v	1783
Fitzgerald, Edward	Kildare, Blackhall	gentry: gent	27-Jan-20	160	Dc2/28v	1019
Fitzgerald, Edward	Kildare, Blackhall	gentry: esquire	07-Feb-24	200	Dc2/53r	1199
Fitzgerald, Edward	Meath, Tecroghan	gentry: knight	12-May-99	400	Dc1/16v	111
Fitzgerald, Edward	Kildare, Rasillagh	gentry: gent	24-Jun-00	140	Dc1/25r	167
Fitzgerald, Edward	Kildare, Blackhall	gentry: gent	22-Feb-30	100	Dc2/143r	1670
Fitzgerald, Edward	Kildare, Blackhall	gentry: gent	21-Nov-21	500	Dc2/36v	1079
Fitzgerald, Edward	Kildare, Blackhall	gentry: gent	15-Jun-24	200	Dc2/56r	1224
Fitzgerald, Edward	Kildare, Blackehall	gentry: gent	01-Aug-34	200	Dc2/216r	1969
Fitzgerald, Florence	Queen's Co.,					
	Castletonaffarlan	gentry: son/heir of John	26-May-23	300	Dc2/47v	1161
Fitzgerald, Garret	Kildare, Donore	gentry: gent	10-May-27	1000	Dc2/92r	1431
Fitzgerald, Garret	Kildare, Dunover	gentry: gent	27-Jun-20	120	Dc2/31v	1039

Standard	County	Occupation	Date	Amount	MS No	Ident No
Fitzgerald, Garret	Kildare, Dunower	gentry: gent	03-Dec-21	200	Dc2/37v	1086
Fitzgerald, Garret	Kildare, Dunower	gentry: gent	30-Jun-25	800	Dc2/67v	1305
Fitzgerald, Garret	Kildare, Dunover	gentry: gent	27-Jun-20	120	Dc2/31v	1038
Fitzgerald, Garret	Kildare, Dunower	gentry: gent	03-Dec-21	200	Dc2/37v	1087
Fitzgerald, Garret	Kildare, Doonaure	gentry: gent	23-Nov-22	600	Dc2/43r	1126
Fitzgerald, Garret	Cork, Lisquinlan	gentry: esquire	07-Feb-79	2000	B.L. 15, 637 f. 16	3875
Fitzgerald, George	Kildare?,	peer: earl of Kildare	19-Dec-49	2000	B.L. 19, 843 f. 125	2969
Fitzgerald, George	Meath, Tecrahan	gentry: esquire	09-May-63	190	B.L. 15, 635 f. 120a	3469
Fitzgerald, George	Meath, Tecrahan	gentry: esquire	25-May-63	1500	B.L. 15, 635 f. 119	3468
Fitzgerald, George	Meath, Terrahan	gentry: esquire	09-May-63	200	B.L. 15, 635 f. 111a	3453
Fitzgerald, Gerald	Limerick, Ballynacourtie	gentry: gent	07-Jun-40	400	B.L. 19, 843 f. 68	2855
Fitzgerald, Gerald	Kildare, Ballysonan	gentry: son/heir	28-Jun-17	160	Dc2/8r	906
Fitzgerald, Gerald	King's Co., Corbetston	gentry: gent	17-Jul-99	110	Dc1/17v	121
Fitzgerald, Gerald	Kildare, Ballysonnan?	gentry: son/heir of James	31-May-10	500	Dc1/97r	609
Fitzgerald, Gerald	Cork?, Ballyhonocke		29-May-41	1000	B.L. 19, 843 f. 97	2913
Fitzgerald, Gerald	Kildare, Osbertstowne	gentry: gent	06-Feb-32	200	Dc2/175r	1804
Fitzgerald, Gerald	Kildare, Glashelie	gentry: esquire	23-Nov-35	200	Dc2/240r	2072
Fitzgerald, Gerald	Kildare, Pounchiston	gentry: gent	22-Apr-03	40	Dc1/46r	294
Fitzgerald, Helen	Cork, Ballymoloe	peer: widow, lady	06-May-41	1500	B.L. 19, 843 f. 98a	2916
Fitzgerald, James	Kildare, Osberston	gentry: gent	14-Jun-00	100	Dc1/24r	161
Fitzgerald, James	Kildare, Carrick	gentry: gent	13-May-69	300	Dc3/97	2435
Fitzgerald, James	Kildare, Ballysonan	gentry: knight	18-Nov-22	400	Dc2/43r	1125
Fitzgerald, James	Kildare, Osberston	gentry: gent	03-Dec-21	200	Dc2/37v	1086
Fitzgerald, James	Kildare, Killrush	gentry: son/heir of Maurice	10-Jul-39	5000	B.L. 19, 843 f. 17a	2753
Fitzgerald, James	Kildare, Ballysonnan?	gentry: knight	31-May-10	500	Dc1/97r	609
Fitzgerald, James	Kildare, Osberston	gentry: gent	15-Jun-24	200	Dc2/56r	1224
Fitzgerald, James	Kildare, Kilrush	gentry: gent	22-Sep-98	100	Dc1/12v	89
Fitzgerald, James	Kildare, Osberton	gentry: esquire	13-May-24	300	Dc2/55r	1214
Fitzgerald, James	Kildare, Ballesuran?	gentry: esquire	16-Aug-98	200	Dc1/12r	87
Fitzgerald, James	Kildare, Osbersten	gentry: gent	01-Oct-00	200	Dc1/26r	175
Fitzgerald, James	Kildare, Osberston	gentry: esquire	12-May-24	300	Dc2/54v	1213
Fitzgerald, James	Kildare, Ballesuran	gentry: esquire	12-Aug-98	1000	Dc1/12r	86
Fitzgerald, James	Kildare, Osberton	gentry: esquire	14-May-24	300	Dc2/55r	1215
Fitzgerald, James	Kildare, Bealan	gentry: gent?	31-Jan-25	100	Dc2/61r	1259
Fitzgerald, James	Kildare, Ballysonan	gentry: knight	28-Jun-17	160	Dc2/8r	906
Fitzgerald, James	Kildare, Osberston	gentry: gent	30-Apr-21	120	Dc2/35r	1069
Fitzgerald, James	Kildare, Osberston	gentry: gent	07-Apr-15	300	Dc1/136r	845
Fitzgerald, James	Cork?, Glennanie		29-May-41	1000	B.L. 19, 843 f. 97	2913
Fitzgerald, James	Cork, Ballyfine		29-May-41	1000	B.L. 19, 843 f. 97	2913
Fitzgerald, James	Westmeath, Laraghe	gentry: esquire	28-Nov-05	189	Dc1/63r	382
Fitzgerald, James	Kildare, Osberston	gentry: gent	27-Jun-20	120	Dc2/31v	1038
Fitzgerald, James	Kildare, Osbartston	gentry: gent	11-Feb-05	144	Dc1/56v	348
Fitzgerald, James	Kildare, Taghdowein	gentry: gent	26-Nov-05	44	Dc1/62v	380
Fitzgerald, James	Cork, Glinane	gentry: esquire	25-Nov-82	600	B.L. 15, 637 f. 69a	3972

Standard	County	Occupation	Date	Amount	MS No	Ident No
Fitzgerald, John	Cork, the city	gentry: gent	13-Aug-66	600	Dc3/36	2305
Fitzgerald, John	Kerry, Innismore	gentry: esquire	08-Jul-31	2200	Dc2/166r	1767
Fitzgerald, John	Waterford, Ballyheny	gentry: esquire	11-May-19	200	Dc2/23v	990
Fitzgerald, Lucas	Meath, Taroghan	gentry: knight	16-May-39	2000	B.L. 19, 843 f. 15a	2749
Fitzgerald, Maurice	Kildare, Kilrush	gentry: gent	09-May-28	200	Dc2/107r	1500
Fitzgerald, Maurice	Westmeath, Belagh	gentry: gent	17-Jul-99	110	Dc1/17v	121
Fitzgerald, Maurice	Longford, Newcashell	gentry: esquire	24-Nov-18	60	Dc2/18r	958
Fitzgerald, Maurice	Kildare, Allon	gentry: esquire	22-Nov-32	140	Dc2/187r	1852
Fitzgerald, Maurice	Kildare, Allon	gentry: esquire	23-Nov-35	600	Dc2/240v	2073
Fitzgerald, Maurice	Kildare, Stablerston	gentry: gent	27-Jan-20	160	Dc2/28v	1019
Fitzgerald, Maurice	Kildare, Lackagh	gentry: esquire	05-Mar-34	200	Dc2/208v	1939
Fitzgerald, Maurice	Kildare, Burton	gentry: esquire	12-Aug-98	1000	Dc1/12r	86
Fitzgerald, Maurice	Kildare, Allonn	gentry: gent	02-Dec-26	240	Dc2/84v	1402
Fitzgerald, Maurice	Meath, Balfeaghan	gentry: esquire	11-Dec-32	300	Dc2/188r	1855
Fitzgerald, Maurice	Kildare, Killrush	gentry: gent	10-Jul-39	5000	B.L. 19, 843 f. 17a	2753
Fitzgerald, Maurice	Kildare, Burton	gentry: gent	16-Aug-98	200	Dc1/12r	87
Fitzgerald, Maurice	Kildare, Scullockstowne	gentry: gent	06-Feb-32	200	Dc2/175r	1804
Fitzgerald, Maurice	Cork, Imokilly Inchincerennagh	gentry: gent	16-Dec-67	560	B.L. 15, 635 f. 214a	3634
Fitzgerald, Oliver	Longford, Portnoure	gentry: esquire	16-Feb-36	320	Dc2/245r	2095
Fitzgerald, Oliver	Dublin, Chaple Isode	gentry: gent	04-Dec-02	240	Dc1/42r	269
Fitzgerald, Oliver	Longford, Ffortenuyre	gentry: esquire	16-May-32	100	Dc2/181r	1827
Fitzgerald, Oliver	Longford, Ffortinure	gentry: esquire	04-Feb-32	200	Dc2/174v	1802
Fitzgerald, Oliver	Longford, Ffortenuyre	gentry: esquire	20-Feb-40	100	B.L. 19, 843 f. 44	2806
Fitzgerald, Oliver	Longford, Portenuyre	gentry: esquire	08-May-32	200	Dc2/179v	1822
Fitzgerald, Oliver	Dublin, Chapel Isod	gentry: gent	16-Mar-03	400	Dc1/45v	288
Fitzgerald, Oliver	Longford, Myleckan	gentry: gent	03-Dec-19	200	Dc2/26v	1009
Fitzgerald, Patrick	Kildare, Kilmorry?	gentry: son/heir of Thomas	16-Dec-36	140	Dc2/259r	2164
Fitzgerald, Pierce	Kildare, Bellane	gentry: gent	23-Nov-08	40	Dc1/84v	527
Fitzgerald, Richard	Dublin	merchant	13-Nov-01	200	Dc1/34r	225
Fitzgerald, Richard	Meath, Rathtrone	gentry: esquire	17-Apr-65	600	Dc3/4	2230
Fitzgerald, Richard	Cork, Imokilly, Glannagueare	gentry: esquire	16-Dec-67	560	B.L. 15, 635 f. 214a	3634
Fitzgerald, Robert	Kildare, Grangemellon	gentry: esquire	02-Dec-69	600	Dc3/109	2462
Fitzgerald, Robert	Kildare, Grangemellon	gentry: esquire	07-May-75	2200	B.L. 19, 844 f. 61a	3188
Fitzgerald, Robert	Kildare, Grangemillon	gentry: esquire	02-Dec-70	2000	Dc3/132r	2505
Fitzgerald, Robert	Westmeath, Laraghe	gentry: s./heir of James	28-Nov-05	189	Dc1/63r	382
Fitzgerald, Robert	Kildare, Grangemellon	gentry: esquire	28-Feb-66	300	Dc3/24	2277
Fitzgerald, Robert	Kildare, Grangemellon	gentry: esqire	21-May-78	2000	Dc3/188av	2713
Fitzgerald, Robert	Kildare, Grangemullin	gentry: esquire	05-Dec-66	1288	Dc2/42	2320
Fitzgerald, Robert	Kildare, Grangemellon	gentry: esquire	21-May-78	2000	B.L. 19, 844 f. 153	3284
Fitzgerald, Robert	Kildare, Grangmellon	gentry: esquire	07-May-75	2200	Dc3/167r	2633
Fitzgerald, Robert	Meath, Newton	gentry: gent	16-Dec-36	140	Dc2/259r	2164
Fitzgerald, Robert	Kildare, Grangemellon	gentry: esquire	17-Sep-67	1000	B.L. 15, 635 f. 202a	3614

Standard	County	Occupation	Date	Amount	MS No	Ident No
Fitzgerald, Robert	Kildare, Grange Mollon	gentry: esquire	02-Dec-69	600	B.L. 15, 636 f. 49	3708
Fitzgerald, Robert	Kildare, Grangemillon	gentry: esquire	02-Dec-70	2000	B.L. 15, 636 f. 75	3752
Fitzgerald, Robert	Kildare, Grangemellon	gentry: esquire	28-Feb-66	300	B.L. 15, 635 f. 174	3557
Fitzgerald, Robert	Kildare, Grangemullin	gentry: esquire	05-Dec-66	1288	B.L. 15, 636 f. 24a	3667
Fitzgerald, Thomas	Waterford, Woodhouse	gentry: gent	28-Jun-28	200	Dc2/111v	1521
Fitzgerald, Thomas	Limerick, Gortnetubberd	gentry: esquire	04-Dec-32	2000	Dc2/187v	1853
Fitzgerald, Thomas	Kildare, Elliston	gentry: gent?	25-Aug-24	80	Dc2/57v	1236
Fitzgerald, Thomas	Kildare, Rodstone	gentry: gent	02-Dec-17	200	Dc2/12r	927
Fitzgerald, Thomas	Kildare, Kilmorry	gentry: gent	16-Dec-36	140	Dc2/259r	2164
Fitzgerald, Thomas	Limerick, Gurtnytubberitt	gentry: gent	13-Dec-14	120	Dc1/133v	831
Fitzgerald, Thomas	Kildare, Trodston	gentry: gent	03-Feb-19	160	Dc2/20r	971
Fitzgerald, Thomas	Kildare, Lackaghe	gentry: esquire	18-May-07	60	Dc1/77r	468
Fitzgerald, William	Kildare, Blackhall	gentry: son/heir of Edward	22-Feb-30	100	Dc2/143r	1670
Fitzgerald, William	Kildare, Laundestowne	gentry: gent	01-Aug-34	200	Dc2/216r	1969
Fitzgerald, William	Kildare?, Blackhall?	gentry: son/heir of Edward	15-Jun-24	200	Dc2/56r	1224
Fitzgerald, William	Kildare?, Blackhall?	gentry: son/heir of Edward	21-Nov-21	500	Dc2/36v	1079
Fitzgibbon, Maurice	Limerick, Ballynehinshye	gentry: gent	06-May-40	800	B.L. 19, 843 f. 93a	2906
Fitzgibbon, William	Cork, Milltowne	gentry: gent	14-Feb-40	1100	B.L. 19, 843 f. 43a	2805
Fitzjames, Patrick	Kilkenny, the city	merchant	16-Nov-18	105	Dc2/17r	955
Fitzjohn, James	Cork, Ballyfyne	gentry: gent	06-May-41	1500	B.L. 19, 843 f. 98a	2916
Fitzkeery, Robert	Dublin, Collotrath	gentry: gent	09-Dec-16	80	Dc2/3r	882
FitzMaurice, Giles	Kerry?	peer: widow, of Kerry Lixnaw	08-Jul-31	2200	Dc2/166r	1767
Fitzmaurice, Thomas	Limerick, Gortnetobberhood	gentry: esquire	28-Jun-23	37	Dc2/48v	1167
Fitzmorris, Edmund	Kerry, Listowell	gentry: esquire	08-Jul-31	2200	Dc2/166r	1767
Fitzmorris, Eugene	Cork?, Carrignyshinne		29-May-41	1000	B.L. 19, 843 f. 97	2913
Fitzmorris, Gerald	Kerry, Listowell	gentry: esquire	08-Jul-31	2200	Dc2/166r	1767
Fitzmorris, Thomas	Kerry, Lickswan	peer: baron Lixnaw	28-May-06	300	Dc1/69r	416
Fitzpatrick, Barnaby	Kilkenny, Upper Ossory	peer: baron Upper Ossory	02-Sep-39	1000	B.L. 19, 843 f. 32a	2783
Fitzpatrick, Barnaby	Tipperary?, Upper Osserye	merchant: son of Fflorence	04-Dec-06	300	Dc1/72v	441
Fitzpatrick, Barnaby	Queen's Co., Canniclone	gentry: gent	12-Dec-39	800	B.L. 19, 843 f. 54a	2827
Fitzpatrick, Barnaby	Queen's Co., Garran McCunly	gentry: esquire	17-Jun-26	400	Dc2/78r	1374
Fitzpatrick, Dermot	Queen's Co., Clonibe	gentry: esquire	02-Sep-39	1000	B.L. 19, 843 f. 32a	2783
Fitzpatrick, Edmund	Queen's Co., Sraghenarrowe	gentry: esquire	20-Dec-39	800	B.L. 19, 843 f. 54	2826
Fitzpatrick, Florence	King's Co., Castletowne	gentry: esquire	18-May-33	400	Dc2/194r	1879
Fitzpatrick, Florence	Queen's Co., Castletowne	gentry: esquire	20-Dec-39	800	B.L. 19, 843 f. 54	2826
Fitzpatrick, Florence	Queen's Co., Castletowne	gentry: esquire	17-Nov-30	400	Dc2/155v	1724

Standard	County	Occupation	Date	Amount	MS No	Ident No
Fitzpatrick, Florence	Queen's Co., Castletowne	gentry: esquire	17-Dec-30	1000	Dc2/158r	1734
Fitzpatrick, Florence	Queen's Co., Castletowne	gentry: esquire	02-Oct-40	650	B.L. 19, 843 f. 72	2863
Fitzpatrick, Florence	Queen's Co., Castletowne	gentry: esquire	15-Dec-40	4000	B.L. 19, 843 f. 77	2873
Fitzpatrick, Florence	Tipperary, Upper Ossoryie	peer:				
		baron of Upper Ossory	04-Dec-06	300	Dc1/72v	441
Fitzpatrick, Florence	Queen's Co., Castletown	gentry: esquire	19-Dec-34	600	Dc2/227r	2014
Fitzpatrick, Florence	Kilkenny, Upper Ossory	peer:				
		baron Upper Ossory	22-May-02	1000	Dc1/38r	246
Fitzpatrick, Florence	Queen's Co., Castletowne	gentry: esquire	12-Dec-29	400	Dc2/140r	1654
Fitzpatrick, Geoffrey	Queen's Co.,					
	Beallagherahin	gentry: esquire	22-May-02	1000	Dc1/38r	246
Fitzpatrick, Geoffrey	Queen's Co., Ballaghrahin	gentry: esquire	19-Aug-34	200	Dc2/217v	1974
Fitzpatrick, Joan		gentry: widow	01-Dec-97	5000	Dc1/7v	54
Fitzpatrick, John	Queen's Co., Ballygeeghin	gentry: gent	27-Nov-39	1000	B.L. 19, 843 f. 36	2790
Fitzpatrick, John	Tipperary?, Upper Osseryie	gentry: s./heir of Florens	04-Dec-06	300	Dc1/72v	441
Fitzpatrick, John	Queen's Co., Castletowne	gentry: esquire	04-Dec-67	1800	Dc3/69	2379
Fitzpatrick, John	Queen's Co.,					
	Castletonaffarlan	gentry: esquire	26-May-23	300	Dc2/47v	1161
Fitzpatrick, John	Queen's Co., Castletowne	gentry: esquire	04-Dec-67	400	Dc3/70	2380
Fitzpatrick, John	Queen's Co., Castletowne	gentry: esquire	04-Dec-67	400	B.L. 15, 635 f. 206a	3622
Fitzpatrick, John	Queen's Co., Castletowne	gentry: esquire	15-Apr-63	4000	B.L. 15, 635 f. 105a	3443
Fitzpatrick, John	Queen's Co., Castletowne	gentry: esquire	04-Dec-67	1800	B.L. 15, 635 f. 206	3621
Fitzpierce, James	Kildare, Ballesonan	gentry: knight	02-Apr-04	600	Dc1/52r	331
Fitzrobert, John	Cork, Ballylinnugge	gentry: gent	09-Nov-40	160	B.L. 19, 843 f. 81a	2882
Fitzrory, Robert	Dublin, Colotray	gentry: gent	03-May-00	200	Dc1/23v	156
Fitzrory, Robert	Dublin, Collatrath	gentry: gent	22-Nov-69	100	B.L. 15, 636 f. 48	3706
Fitzrory, Robert	Dublin, Colerath	gentry: esquire	14-Jul-64	200	B.L. 15, 635 f. 144a	3508
Fitzrory, Robert	Dublin, Colerath	gentry: esquire	14-Jul-64	113	B.L. 15, 635 f. 139a	3500
Fitzrory, Robert	Dublin, Collatrath	gentry: gent	22-Nov-69	100	Dc3/107	2456
Fitzrory, Robert	Dublin, Gollatrath	gentry: gent	23-Dec-65	92	Dc3/18	2263
Fitzsimons, Christopher	Dublin, Grandge of					
	Baldoile	gentry: gent	14-Nov-01	46	Dc1/34r	226
Fitzsimons, Christopher	Dublin, Grange of					
	Baldoyle	gentry: gent	01-Aug-99	50	Dc1/18v	126
Fitzsimons, James	Louth, Drogheda	merchant: s of late				
		Richard, ald	18-Feb-25	200	Dc2/62r	1267
Fitzsimons, John	Dublin, Balmadrought	gentry: gent	04-Apr-12	200	Dc1/113r	700
Fitzsimons, John	Dublin, Balmadrought	gentry: gent	15-Jan-09	120	Dc1/85v	536
Fitzsimons, John	Dublin, Balmadroughte	gentry: gent	25-Oct-09	200	Dc1/92r	575
Fitzsimons, John	Dublin, Balmadroght	gentry: gent	27-Jun-11	120	Dc1/104v	653
Fitzsimons, Mark	Dublin, Ballmadraught	gentry: gent	14-Nov-68	200	Dc3/83	2412
Fitzsimons, Mark	Dublin, Balmadrought	gentry: gent	18-Dec-68	267	Dc3/88	2419
Fitzsimons, Mark	Dublin, Ballymadroght	gentry: gent	22-Nov-67	400	Dc3/68	2374
Fitzsimons, Mark	Dublin, Ballimadroght	gentry: gent	17-Nov-69	400	Dc3/107	2455
Fitzsimons, Mark	Dublin, Balmadraught	gentry: gent	04-Nov-68	200	B.L. 15, 635 f. 229a	3664

Standard	County	Occupation	Date	Amount	MS No	Ident No
Fitzsimons, Nicholas	Kildare, Grandgemore	gentry: gent	12-Nov-20	600	Dc2/32v	1048
Fitzsimons, Nicholas	Down, Kilclese	gentry: gent	20-Oct-04	200	Dc1/53r	335
Fitzsimons, Nicholas	Down, Kilcleeffe	gentry: esquire	27-Mar-56	383	B.L. 19, 843 f. 181	3069
Fitzsimons, Nicholas	Down, Killclisse	gentry: gent	28-Jun-38	600	B.L. 19, 843 f. 7	2732
Fitzsimons, Richard	Dublin?, Balmadroughte?	gentry: son/heir of John	25-Oct-09	200	Dc1/92r	575
Fitzsimons, Richard	Dublin, Balmadroght	gentry: son/heir of John	27-Jun-11	120	Dc1/104v	653
Fitzsimons, Richard	Dublin, Balmadrought	gentry: son of John	15-Jan-09	120	Dc1/85v	536
Fitzsimons, Richard	Dublin, Balmadrought	gentry: son/heir of John	04-Apr-12	200	Dc1/113r	700
Fitzsimons, Walter	Down, ?	gentry: gent	20-Oct-04	200	Dc1/53r	335
Fitzthomas, Maurice	Cork, Rochestowne	gentry: gent	29-May-41	1000	B.L. 19, 843 f. 97	2913
Fitzwilliam, John	Dublin	merchant	03-Mar-11	200	Dc1/105r	655
Fitzwilliam, John	Dublin	merchant	03-Mar-13	200	Dc1/120r	746
Fitzwilliam, John	Dublin	merchant	03-Mar-11	400	Dc1/105r	656
Fitzwilliam, John	Dublin	merchant	03-Mar-13	400	Dc1/120r	747
Fitzwilliam, John	Dublin, Merrion	gentry: knight	13-Dec-22	1000	Dc2/44r	1132
Fitzwilliam, John	Dublin	merchant	05-Mar-14	240	Dc1/127v	792
Fitzwilliam, Michael	Meath, Dunamoore	gentry: gent	13-Jul-20	300	Dc2/32r	1043
Fitzwilliam, Michael	Dublin, the city	gentry: gent	03-Apr-26	1000	Dc2/76r	1357
Fitzwilliam, Oliver	Dublin, Merrion	gentry: gent, 2nd s of Thomas	17-Mar-26	1600	Dc2/75r	1351
Fitzwilliam, Richard	Dublin, Merrion	gentry: son/heir of Thomas	21-Jun-32	800	Dc2/184r	1839
Fitzwilliam, Richard	Dublin, Merrion	gentry: s/heir of Thomas, vis	11-May-36	2000	Dc2/250r	2118
Fitzwilliam, Richard	Dublin, Merrion?	gentry: son/heir of Thomas	31-May-32	2000	Dc2/182r	1831
Fitzwilliam, Richard	Dublin, the Meryon	gentry: son/heir of Sir Thomas	13-Sep-26	800	Dc2/82v	1391
Fitzwilliam, Richard	Dublin, Merrion	gentry: son/heir of Sir Thomas	22-Dec-26	400	Dc2/87r	1411
Fitzwilliam, Richard	Dublin, Merrion	gentry: esquire	08-May-40	600	B.L. 19, 843 f. 61	2841
Fitzwilliam, Richard	Dublin, Merrion	gentry: esquire, s/h Sir Thomas	17-Mar-26	1600	Dc2/75r	1351
Fitzwilliam, Richard	Dublin, Merrion?	gentry: esquire, s/h of Thomas	13-Oct-31	2000	Dc2/168v	1779
Fitzwilliam, Richard	Dublin, Merrion	gentry: son/heir of Thomas	20-Dec-34	1200	Dc2/227v	2016
Fitzwilliam, Richard	Dublin, Merrion?	gentry: son/heir of Thomas	27-Dec-32	700	Dc2/189v	1862
Fitzwilliam, Richard	Dublin, Merrion?	gentry: son/heir of Thomas	09-Jan-33	1000	Dc2/190r	1864
Fitzwilliam, Richard	Dublin, Merrion	gentry: son/heir of Thomas	30-Nov-25	600	Dc2/71r	1327
Fitzwilliam, Richard	Dublin?, Merrion?	gentry: son/heir of Thomas	13-Dec-22	1000	Dc2/44r	1132

Standard	County	Occupation	Date	Amount	MS No	Ident No
Fitzwilliam, Richard	Dublin, Merryon	gentry: son/heir of Thomas	20-May-33	2000	Dc2/194r	1880
Fitzwilliam, Richard	Dublin, Merryon	gentry: son/heir of Thomas	23-Oct-34	1200	Dc2/219v	1983
Fitzwilliam, Stephen	Dublin, Jobstowne	gentry: gent	27-Jan-30	300	Dc2/141r	1660
Fitzwilliam, Stephen	Dublin, Jobstowne	gentry: gent	18-Apr-31	500	Dc2/161v	1750
Fitzwilliam, Stephen	Dublin, Jobstowne	gentry: gent	28-Nov-34	800	Dc2/223v	1999
Fitzwilliam, Thomas	Dublin?	peer: viscount Fitzwilliams	08-Jul-31	800	Dc2/166r	1768
Fitzwilliam, Thomas	Dublin, Jobeston	gentry: gent	05-Mar-14	240	Dc1/127v	792
Fitzwilliam, Thomas	Dublin, Merrion	peer: viscount Fitzwilliams	21-Jun-32	800	Dc2/184r	1839
Fitzwilliam, Thomas	Meath, Castelton Moylagh	gentry: gent	14-Jun-10	40	Dc1/97r	611
Fitzwilliam, Thomas	Dublin, Merrion	peer: viscount Fitzwilliams	31-May-32	2000	Dc2/182r	1831
Fitzwilliam, Thomas	Meath, Castleton Moilaghe	gentry: gent	02-May-10	40	Dc1/95v	600
Fitzwilliam, Thomas	Dublin, Meryon	gentry: knight	16-Jun-10	300	Dc1/97v	612
Fitzwilliam, Thomas	Dublin, Merryon	peer: viscount Fitzwilliams	20-May-33	2000	Dc2/194r	1880
Fitzwilliam, Thomas	Dublin, Jobeston	gentry: gent	03-Mar-11	200	Dc1/105r	655
Fitzwilliam, Thomas	Dublin, Merrion	peer: viscount Fitzwilliams	27-Dec-32	700	Dc2/189v	1862
Fitzwilliam, Thomas	Dublin, Merrion	gentry: knight	17-Mar-26	1600	Dc2/75r	1351
Fitzwilliam, Thomas	Dublin, the city	gentry: esquire	10-Mar-74	2000	Dc3/160v	2606
Fitzwilliam, Thomas	Dublin, Meryon	gentry: knight	31-May-09	286	Dc1/89v	559
Fitzwilliam, Thomas	Dublin, Merrion	gentry: knight	30-Nov-25	600	Dc2/71r	1327
Fitzwilliam, Thomas	Dublin, Merrion	gentry: esquire, s vis Merrion	10-Nov-71	1000	Dc3/140v	2532
Fitzwilliam, Thomas	Meath, Castleton Moylagh	gentry: gent	15-Jun-11	320	Dc1/104r	651
Fitzwilliam, Thomas	Dublin, Merrion	peer: viscount Fitzwilliams	13-Oct-31	2000	Dc2/168v	1779
Fitzwilliam, Thomas	Dublin, Merryon	peer: viscount Fitzwilliams	24-May-33	500	Dc2/194v	1882
Fitzwilliam, Thomas	Dublin, Merrion	peer: viscount Fitzwilliams	09-Jan-33	1000	Dc2/190r	1864
Fitzwilliam, Thomas	Dublin, Myrryon	peer: viscount Fitzwilliams	11-Mar-33	1880	Dc2/192v	1873
Fitzwilliam, Thomas	Meath, Castleton Moylagh	gentry: gent	28-Jun-10	230	Dc1/98v	619
Fitzwilliam, Thomas	Meath, Castellton Moylaghe	gentry: gent	22-Dec-09	80	Dc1/93v	587
Fitzwilliam, Thomas	Dublin, Merrion	gentry: knight	22-Dec-27	400	Dc2/102r	1476
Fitzwilliam, Thomas	Dublin, Merrion	peer: viscount Fitzwilliams	20-Dec-34	1200	Dc2/227v	2016
Fitzwilliam, Thomas	Dublin, Merrion	peer: viscount Fitzwilliams	11-May-36	2000	Dc2/250r	2118

Standard	County	Occupation	Date	Amount	MS No	Ident No
Fitzwilliam, Thomas	Dublin, Merrion	peer:				
		viscount Fitzwilliams	04-Jul-34	400	Dc2/214r	1960
Fitzwilliam, Thomas	Dublin, Merrion	gentry: knight	01-Dec-27	2000	Dc2/101r	1470
Fitzwilliam, Thomas	Dublin, Jobeston	gentry: gent	03-Mar-13	400	Dc1/120r	747
Fitzwilliam, Thomas	Dublin, Merrion	gentry: knight	28-Jun-27	400	Dc2/96v	1450
Fitzwilliam, Thomas	Dublin, Merrion	gentry: knight	23-Mar-27	2000	Dc2/90r	1423
Fitzwilliam, Thomas	Dublin, Merrion	gentry: knight	03-Aug-27	200	Dc2/98r	1455
Fitzwilliam, Thomas	Dublin, the Meryon	gentry: knight	13-Sep-26	800	Dc2/82v	1391
Fitzwilliam, Thomas	Dublin, Merrion	peer:				
		viscount Fitzwilliams	23-May-34	200	Dc2/212r	1952
Fitzwilliam, Thomas	Dublin, Merrion	gentry: knight	09-Jun-08	220	Dc1/83r	517
Fitzwilliam, Thomas	Dublin, Meryon	gentry: knight	03-Jul-26	200	Dc2/80v	1382
Fitzwilliam, Thomas	Dublin, Jobeston	gentry: gent	03-Mar-13	200	Dc1/120r	746
Fitzwilliam, Thomas	Dublin, Jobston	gentry: esquire	13-Dec-21	160	Dc2/37v	1089
Fitzwilliam, Thomas	Dublin, Merrion	gentry: knight	22-Dec-26	400	Dc2/87r	1411
Fitzwilliam, Thomas	Dublin, Jobeston	gentry: gent	03-Mar-11	400	Dc1/105r	656
Fitzwilliam, Thomas	Dublin, Merryon	peer:				
		viscount Fitzwilliams	23-Oct-34	1200	Dc2/219v	1983
Fitzwilliam, Thomas	Dublin, Merrion	gentry: knight	04-Nov-20	2000	Dc2/32v	1047
Fitzwilliam, Thomas	Meath, Castleton Moylaghe	gentry: gent	15-Feb-06	300	Dc1/66r	397
Fitzwilliam, Thomas	Dublin, Merrion	gentry: knight	27-Sep-20	120	Dc2/32v	1046
Fitzwilliam, Thomas	Dublin, Meryon	gentry: knight	24-Dec-28	2000	Dc2/123r	1574
Fitzwilliam, Thomas	Dublin, Merion	gentry: knight	21-Sep-11	200	Dc1/107r	666
Fitzwilliam, Thomas	Dublin, Merrion	gentry: esquire, s./heir				
		William	10-Nov-71	1000	B.L. 15, 636 f. 91	3781
Fitzwilliam, Thomas	Dublin, city, Merion	gentry: knight	04-Jul-25	600	Dc2/68r	1308
Fitzwilliam, William	Dublin, Merrion?	gentry: son of Thomas	23-May-34	200	Dc2/212r	1952
Fitzwilliam, William	Dublin, Merrion	peer: viscount Merrion	10-Nov-71	1000	Dc3/140v	2532
Fitzwilliam, William	Dublin, Merryon	gentry: son, 3rd son of				
		Thomas	23-Oct-34	1200	Dc2/219v	1983
Fitzwilliam, William	Dublin, Merrion?	gentry: esquire, 3rd s of				
		Thomas	13-Oct-31	2000	Dc2/168v	1779
Fitzwilliam, William	Kildare, Dollarstowne	gentry: esquire	10-Nov-71	1000	Dc3/140v	2532
Fitzwilliam, William	Dublin, Merrion	peer:				
		viscount Fitzwilliams	10-Nov-71	1000	B.L. 15, 636 f. 91	3781
Fitzwilliam, William	Kildare, Dollarstowne	gentry: esquire	10-Nov-71	1000	B.L. 15, 636 f. 91	3781
Flaherty, Murrough	Galway, Bunowen	gentry: esquire	08-May-32	300	Dc2/180r	1823
Flannagan, Gillebride	Roscommon	gentry: gent	17-May-14	2000	Dc1/129r	803
Flatisbury, James	Kildare, Palmerstowne	gentry: gent	12-Jun-19	1000	Dc2/23v	992
Flatisbury, James	Kildare, Palmerstonn	gentry: gent	17-Jun-23	100	Dc2/48r	1165
Flatisbury, James	Kildare, Palmerstowne	gentry: gent	18-Sep-11	110	Dc1/106v	663
Flatisbury?, James	Dublin, Palmerston		19-May-17	600	Dc2/6v	900
Flatsbury, James	Kildare, Palmerston	gentry: gent	26-Apr-21	80	Dc2/35r	1067
Fleming, Bestian?	Louth, Drogheda	merchant	30-Jun-99	220	Dc1/17v	118

Standard	County	Occupation	Date	Amount	MS No	Ident No
Fleming, Catherine	Dublin	other: widow	03-Feb-98	7	Dc1/9v	67
Fleming, Christopher	Meath?, Deerpatricke?	gentry: son/heir of James	16-Sep-24	3000	Dc2/58r	1237
Fleming, Francis	Louth, Drogheda	merchant: son of Martin, merchant	07-May-64	280	B.L. 15, 635 f. 148	3515
Fleming, George	Meath, Killarue	gentry: gent	08-Jul-41	120	B.L. 19, 843 f. 104a	2928
Fleming, James	Meath, Derpatricke	gentry: gent	08-Dec-08	320	Dc1/85v	533
Fleming, James	Meath, Derpatricke	gentry: gent	16-Sep-24	3000	Dc2/58r	1237
Fleming, James	Meath, Stephenstowne	gentry: esquire	15-Jun-30	1000	Dc2/151v	1704
Fleming, James	Meath, Baytston	gentry: gent	29-Nov-37	200	Dc2/272r	2221
Fleming, John	Meath, Ardagh	gentry: gent	08-Jul-41	120	B.L. 19, 843 f. 104a	2928
Fleming, John	Monaghan, Ballmeforagh	gentry: gent	02-Jul-27	310	Dc2/96r	1448
Fleming, John	Meath, Stephenstowne	gentry: esquire	28-Aug-63	600	B.L. 15, 635 f. 123a	3474
Fleming, Patrick	Dublin, the city	trade: baker	19-Jun-35	20	Dc2/237v	2058
Fleming, Robert	Tipperary, Loghkent	gentry: gent	27-Nov-28	500	Dc2/117v	1549
Flower, Benjamin	Meath, Knockmarke	farmer	20-Nov-29	100	Dc2/137v	1643
Flower, George	Waterford, Knockmore	gentry: knight	08-Feb-06	400	Dc1/65v	395
Folliott, Thomas	Donegal?	peer: baron Bealshanny	17-May-34	3000	Dc2/211v	1950
Foran, Thady	Dublin, Castle Cnocke	farmer	01-Apr-41	800	B.L. 19, 843 f. 87a	2894
Ford, Andrew	Meath, Moygaddy	gentry: gent	07-Sep-22	60	Dc2/42v	1122
Ford, Stephen	Meath, Chamb[er]linston	gentry: gent	17-May-26	1000	Dc2/77v	1366
Ford, Stephen	Meath, Chamberlinstowne	gentry: gent	02-Apr-28	220	Dc2/106r	1495
Fortescue, Thomas	Louth, Druminiskin	gentry: knight	01-Jun-74	1200	Dc3/161v	2611
Fortescue, Thomas	Louth, Dromeskin	gentry: esquire	10-Apr-63	700	B.L. 15, 635 f. 102a	3439
Forth, Edward	Dublin, the city	gentry: esquire	15-Feb-75	400	B.L. 19, 844 f. 53	3177
Forth, Edward	Dublin, the city	gentry: esquire	15-Feb-75	400	Dc3/164v	2622
Forth, John	King's Co., Redwood	gentry: esquire	15-Feb-75	400	B.L. 19, 844 f. 53	3177
Forth, John	King's Co., Redwood	gentry: esquire	15-Feb-75	400	Dc3/164v	2622
Foster, Charles	Dublin, the city		05-Sep-55	200	B.L. 19, 843 f. 165a	3045
Foster, Charles	Dublin, the city	gentry: gent, son/heir of Richard	20-Aug-28	400	Dc2/114r	1534
Foster, Charles	Dublin, Clonshagh	gentry: esquire	09-Sep-36	400	Dc2/255v	2148
Foster, Charles	Dublin, the city		19-Nov-35	100	Dc2/240r	2071
Foster, Charles	Dublin, Clunsagh	gentry: gent	27-Apr-33	160	Dc2/193r	1875
Foster, Charles	Dublin, the city		08-Jul-58	400	B.L. 15, 635 f. 31	3317
Foster, Christopher	Dublin, the city		20-Dec-23	200	Dc2/52r	1192
Foster, Christopher	Dublin	gentry: knight	21-Nov-32	300	Dc2/186v	1850
Foster, Christopher	Dublin, the city		30-Jun-25	292	Dc2/67v	1304
Foster, Christopher	Dublin, the city		02-Sep-28	200	Dc2/114v	1537
Foster, Christopher	Dublin, the city		18-May-25	80	Dc2/63v	1280
Foster, Gerald	Meath, Kilgrege	gentry: gent	19-Nov-01	500	Dc1/34v	227
Foster, John	Dublin	merchant	03-Mar-15	600	Dc1/136r	844
Foster, John	Monaghan, Tullaghan	gentry: esquire	13-Feb-61	620	B.L. 15, 635 f. 64a	3378
Foster, Richard	Dublin, the city		10-Jan-21	500	Dc2/34r	1060
Foster, Richard	Dublin, the city		30-Sep-19	300	Dc2/26r	1004

Standard	County	Occupation	Date	Amount	MS No	Ident No
Foster, Richard	Dublin, the city		10-Jul-19	700	Dc2/25r	998
Foster, Richard	Meath, Kilgrege	gentry: son/heir of Gerald	19-Nov-01	500	Dc1/34v	227
Foster, Richard	Dublin, Clonsagh	gentry: gent	08-Jul-58	400	B.L. 15, 635 f. 31	3317
Foster, Richard	Dublin		27-Nov-18	120	Dc2/18v	960
Foster, Richard	Dublin, Clonshagh	gentry: gent	01-May-61	600	B.L. 15, 635 f. 72	3388
Foster, William	Dublin, Kyllagh	gentry: gent	24-Feb-97	100	Dc1/2r	12
Foster, William	Dublin, Killeghe	other: son/heir of Robt, dec'd	18-Jun-97	1000	Dc1/5r	35
Foster, William	Kildare, Nass	gentry: gent	06-Sep-66	160	Dc3/38	2309
Foster, William	Dublin, Kyllegh	gentry: gent, s./heir Robert	23-Mar-97	200	Dc1/2v	16
Fottrell, Thomas	Dublin, Ballybaghall	farmer	24-May-26	400	Dc2/78v	1370
Foulke, Christopher	Meath, Athlumny	gentry: esquire	05-Dec-18	200	Dc2/18v	962
Foulke, Francis	Waterford, Camphire	gentry: knight	03-Nov-74	800	B.L. 19, 844 f. 38	3162
Foulke, Francis	Waterford, Camplure	gentry: knight	14-Jun-61	300	B.L. 15, 635 f. 73	3390
Fountain, John	Dublin, the city	gentry: esquire	08-Jan-55	96	B.L. 19, 843 f. 148a	3011
Fountain, John	Wexford, Middletowne	gentry: gent	17-Jul-84	300	B.L. 15, 637 f. 92	4013
Fountain, John	Wexford, Middletowne	gentry: gent	20-Feb-86	630	B.L. 15, 637 f. 109	4044
Fox, Charles	Longford, Rathreagh	gentry: esquire	02-May-65	333	Dc3/4	2231
Fox, Charles	Longford, Rathreagh	gentry: esquire	20-Apr-67	800	Dc3/60	2352
Fox, Charles	Longford, Rathreagh	gentry: esquire	02-May-65	333	B.L. 15, 635 f. 166a	3546
Fox, Charles	Longford, Rathreagh	gentry: esquire	20-Apr-67	800	B.L. 15, 635 f. 187a	3585
Fox, Edmund	Limerick, Balligidine	gentry: gent	27-Aug-40	1000	B.L. 19, 843 f. 68a	2856
Fox, John	Limerick, Ballyrenoge	gentry: esquire	02-May-40	600	B.L. 19, 843 f. 49a	2817
Fox, Mathew	Longford, Rathreagh	gentry: esquire	21-Nov-25	400	Dc2/70r	1321
Foy, Meyler	Kildare, Harbartston	gentry: gent	09-Jul-23	400	Dc2/49r	1171
Frane, Henry	King's Co., Barnan	gentry: gent	05-May-29	400	Dc2/128r	1601
Frane, Henry	King's Co., the Barnon	gentry: gent	09-Mar-31	44	Dc2/160v	1746
Frane, Henry	King's Co., Barnon	gentry: gent	05-Dec-28	200	Dc2/121v	1567
Frane, Henry	King's Co., Barnon?	gentry: son and heir to Henry	05-Dec-28	200	Dc2/121v	1567
Frane, James	King's Co., Barnan	gentry: son/heir of Henry	05-May-29	400	Dc2/128r	1601
Frane, James	King's Co., the Barnon?	gentry: son/heir of Henry	09-Mar-31	44	Dc2/160v	1746
Frane, William	Dublin, Balmakellye	farmer: freeholder	15-Jul-06	100	Dc1/70r	425
Frank, John	Meath, Tecrohan	gentry: esquire	24-May-58	400	B.L. 15, 635 f. 30	3315
Franklin, James	Louth, Drogheda	merchant	23-Aug-39	70	B.L. 19, 843 f. 27	2772
Freeney, Patrick	Dublin, Balgriffen	farmer	31-Jul-01	400	Dc1/33v	221
Freeney, Richard	Dublin, Galroeston	farmer	31-Jul-01	400	Dc1/33v	221
French, Bate	Cork, the city	merchant	14-Oct-75	600	B.L. 19, 844 f. 77	3205
French, Dominic	Mayo, Robin	gentry: esquire	03-Apr-30	130	Dc2/144r	1673
French, Richard	Galway	gentry: gent	16-Aug-55	600	B.L. 19, 843 f. 163a	3041
Friend, John	Dublin, Scribleston	farmer	16-May-07	20	Dc1/76v	465

Standard	County	Occupation	Date	Amount	MS No	Ident No
Furey, Henry	Meath, Johns[towne]	gentry: gent	26-May-20	240	Dc2/30r	1030
Furey, Terence	Meath, Fforsterstowne	gentry: gent	05-Dec-29	200	Dc2/139v	1652
Furey, Terence	Meath, Trime	gentry: gent	21-May-28	200	Dc2/108v	1509
Furey, Terence	Meath, St. John's	gentry: gent	03-Jun-22	200	Dc2/40v	1110
Furley, Nathaniel	Dublin, the city	trade: tailor	15-Jun-65	70	Dc3/10	2243
Furley, Nathaniel	Dublin, the city	trade: tailor	15-Jun-65	70	B.L. 15, 635 f. 159	3535
Furlong, William	Wexford, Haresmeade	gentry: gent	25-Jun-34	400	B.L. 19, 843 f. 57a	2833
Furlong, William	Wexford, Haresmeade	gentry: gent	25-Jun-34	400	Dc2/212v	1955
Furlong, William	Wexford, Harsmeade	gentry: esquire	09-Dec-33	400	Dc2/203r	1916
Furlong, William	Wexford, Hortton	gentry: gent	05-Feb-24	400	Dc2/53r	1201
Furlong, William	Wexford, Horetowne	gentry: gent	11-Jul-22	120	Dc2/41v	1116
Furlong, William	Wexford, Haresmerde	gentry: gent	13-Feb-32	320	Dc2/175v	1807
Fyan, George	Louth, Drogheda	merchant	27-May-37	80	Dc2/264v	2186
Fyan, James	Dublin	merchant	24-Dec-27	280	Dc2/102v	1477
Fyan, Jasper	Louth, Drogheda	merchant	15-Jan-08	150	Dc1/80v	500
Fyan, John	Meath, Proudsfootstowne	gentry: gent	04-Mar-77	424	B.L. 19, 844 f. 118	3247
Fyan, William	Kildare, Leixlipp	gentry: gent	28-May-24	40	Dc2/55v	1217
Galbraith, Humphery	Dublin, the city		18-Feb-56	600	B.L. 19, 843 f. 167a	3049
Gallan, Patrick	Cork, Cahiren	gentry: gent	14-Nov-74	140	B.L. 19, 844 f. 42a	3166
Gallan, Patrick	Cork, Cahirew	gentry: gent	03-Dec-74	380	B.L. 19, 844 f. 51a	3175
Galland, John	Antrim, Vow	gentry: esquire	19-Aug-74	880	B.L. 19, 844 f. 31	3154
Galland, John	Antrim, Vow	gentry: esquire	12-Apr-80	350	B.L. 15, 637 f. 32	3905
Galtron, Simon	Dublin	merchant	20-Jun-03	400	Dc1/47v	301
Galway, Andrew	Cork	gentry: gent	14-Nov-09	40	Dc1/92v	580
Galway, Arthur	Cork, Ballypheaghane	gentry: gent	02-Apr-74	1000	B. L. 19, 844 f. 24	3145
Galway, Arthur	Cork, Ballypheaghane	gentry: gent, son/heir of John	04-May-70	120	B.L. 15, 636 f. 62	3728
Galway, Arthur	Cork, Ballyfeaghan	gentry: gent	21-Dec-71	1000	B.L. 15, 636 f. 107	3805
Galway, Arthur	Cork, Ballypheaghane	gentry: gent, son/heir of John	04-May-70	240	B.L. 15, 636 f. 61	3727
Galway, Arthur	Cork, Ballyfeaghan	gentry: son/heir of John	19-Oct-66	1200	B.L. 15, 635 f. 188	3586
Galway, Arthur	Cork, Ballyfeaghane	gentry: gent	21-Dec-71	1000	B.L. 15, 636 f. 107a	3806
Galway, Arthur	Cork, Ballypheaghane	gentry: son/heir of John	12-May-69	200	B.L. 15, 636 f. 39	3692
Galway, John	Cork, Ballypheaghane	gentry: gent	04-May-70	120	B.L. 15, 636 f. 62	3728
Galway, John	Cork, Ballypheaghane	gentry: gent	04-May-70	240	B.L. 15, 636 f. 61	3727
Galway, John	Cork, Ballyfeaghan	gentry: gent	19-Oct-66	1200	B.L. 15, 635 f. 188	3586
Galway, John	Cork, Ballypheaghane	gentry: gent	12-May-69	200	B.L. 15, 636 f. 39	3692
Galway, Walter	Cork, the city	gentry: gent	15-Dec-20	200	Dc2/33v	1057
Garaway, Ann	Longford, Rathcleene	gentry: widow	03-Dec-36	1000	Dc2/258v	2162
Garland, Anthony	Meath, Agherpalles	gentry: gent	22-Dec-00	120	Dc1/27v	183
Garland, Nicholas	Louth, Mylton	gentry: gent	17-Jun-05	50	Dc1/60r	364
Garland, Proncias	Meath, Agherpalles?	gentry: son/heir of Anthony	22-Dec-00	120	Dc1/27v	183
Garnet, Bartholomew	Louth, Drogheda	trade: clothier	24-Sep-41	240	B.L. 19, 843 f. 115a	2950

Standard	County	Occupation	Date	Amount	MS No	Ident No
Garnet, Nicholas	Louth, Drogheda	merchant	15-May-26	300	Dc2/77v	1364
Garret, Oliver	Dublin, Chapel Isod	gentry: gent	23-Nov-03	600	Dc1/49v	318
Garth, Nicholas	Dublin, the city	gentry: gent	16-Jun-29	120	Dc2/133r	1621
Garvey, Philip	Dublin, late of Odder,					
	Meath	gentry: esquire	30-Oct-01	40	Dc1/34r	224
Gash, John	Cork, Castle Lyons	gentry: gent	09-Jul-78	500	B.L. 19, 844 f. 166	3297
Gaydon, John	Kildare, late of Irishtowne	gentry: esquire	23-Aug-66	500	Dc3/37	2306
Gaydon, John	Kildare, Irishtowne	gentry: gent	27-Nov-69	350	Dc3/108	2459
Gaydon, John	Kildare, Irishtowne	gentry: esquire	26-Jun-54	655	B.L. 19, 843 f. 142	2998
Gaydon, John	Kildare, Irishtown	gentry: esquire	14-May-35	500	Dc2/235v	2049
Gaydon, John	Kildare, Irishtowne	gentry: esquire	12-May-55	156	B.L. 19, 843 f. 184	3075
Gaydon, John	Kildare, Irishtowne	gentry: gent	27-Nov-69	350	B.L. 15, 636 f. 48a	3707
Gaydon, John	Kildare, Irishtowne	gentry: esquire	23-Aug-66	560	B.L. 15, 635 f. 176a	3562
Gaydon, John	Kildare, Irishtowne	gentry: esquire	23-Jun-64	726	B.L. 15, 635 f. 137a	3496
Gaydon, Patrick	Kildare, Strafan	gentry: gent	27-Nov-69	350	Dc3/108	2459
Gaydon, Patrick	Kildare, Irishtowne	gentry: son/heir of John	12-May-55	156	B.L. 19, 843 f. 184	3075
Gaydon, Patrick	Kildare, Straffan	gentry: gent, son/heir of				
		John	23-Aug-66	500	Dc3/37	2306
Gaydon, Patrick	Kildare, Irishtowne	gentry: son/heir of John	23-Jun-64	726	B.L. 15, 635 f. 137a	3496
Gaydon, Patrick	Kildare, Straffan	gentry: gent, son/heir of				
		John	23-Aug-66	560	B.L. 15, 635 f. 176a	3562
Gaydon, Patrick	Kildare, Strafan	gentry: gent	27-Nov-69	350	B.L. 15, 636 f. 48a	3707
Geane, Hugh	Antrim, Broghshane	gentry: gent	20-Nov-66	600	B.L. 15, 635 f. 183a	3577
Geashell, Edmund	Dublin, Pastostone	gentry: gent	21-Nov-17	200	Dc2/11r	920
Geashell, Edmund	Dublin, Posteston	gentry: gent	31-Jan-22	240	Dc2/38v	1095
Geashell, Edmund	Dublin, Pastostone	gentry: gent	02-Dec-17	200	Dc2/12r	927
Geashell, Edmund	Dublin, Pastoston	gentry: gent	04-Dec-17	200	Dc2/12v	928
Geashell, Edmund	Dublin, Parslockstowne	gentry: gent	06-May-35	600	Dc2/234v	2046
Geashell, Edmund	Dublin	gentry: gent	14-Feb-15	60	Dc1/135r	839
Geashell, Edmund	Dublin, Pastoston	gentry: gent	20-Nov-23	200	Dc2/51r	1187
Geashell, Edmund	Dublin, Pastockestowne	gentry: gent	19-Dec-35	200	Dc2/242v	2085
Geashell, Edmund	Dublin, Pastoston	gentry: gent	23-Mar-26	80	Dc2/76r	1355
Geashell, Edmund	Dublin, the city	gentry: gent	15-Jul-14	200	Dc1/131r	812
Geoghegan, Arthur	Meath, Castletowne	gentry: gent	25-Aug-28	1000	Dc2/114v	1535
Geoghegan, Callagh	Westmeath, Syonan	gentry: esquire	19-Nov-29	87	Dc2/138v	1647
Geoghegan, Charles	Westmeath, Syonan	gentry: gent	25-May-66	1000	Dc3/29	2288
Geoghegan, Edward	Longford, Robinstowne	gentry: gent	25-May-66	1000	Dc3/29	2288
Geoghegan, Hugh	Westmeath, Castletowne	gentry: esquire	16-May-15	200	Dc1/137v	853
Geoghegan, Hugh	Westmeath, Lara,					
	b. Moycashell	gentry: gent	01-Jul-12	500	Dc1/114v	712
Geoghegan, James	Westmeath, Billera	gentry: gent	23-Dec-03	100	Dc1/50r	322
Geoghegan, Owen	Westmeath, Curreawogh	gentry: gent	15-Apr-22	36	Dc2/39r	1099
Geoghegan, Ross	Westmeath, Moycashell	gentry: gent	03-Jul-07	200	Dc1/79r	482
Geoghegan, Thomas	Longford, Robinstowne	gentry: gent	25-May-66	1000	Dc3/29	2288
George, Robert	Queen's Co., Tawne	gentry: esquire	02-Apr-23	600	Dc2/46r	1149

Standard	County	Occupation	Date	Amount	MS No	Ident No
George, Robert	Meath, Kilbrew	prof: doctor of law	13-Feb-83	1000	B.L. 15, 637 f. 70	3973
Gerald, Edmund	Kerry, Glaudyn	gentry: gent	19-Nov-13	20	Dc1/124r	770
Gerald, Gerald	Limerick, Ballegloghan	gentry: gent	28-Jun-23	37	Dc2/48v	1167
Gerald, Gerald	Limerick, Ballynacourty	gentry: gent	19-May-40	200	B.L. 19, 843 f. 58a	2835
Gernon, Anthony	Meath, Agherpalles	gentry: esquire	07-Feb-07	180	Dc1/74r	447
Gernon, Anthony	Meath, Agherparis	gentry: esquire	07-Sep-19	90	Dc2/25r	1000
Gernon, Edward	Louth, Garnonston	gentry: gent	11-Apr-21	272	Dc2/35r	1066
Gernon, Edward	Louth, Gernonston	gentry: esquire	19-May-06	500	Dc1/67v	407
Gernon, George	Louth, Milton	gentry: esquire	30-Nov-26	200	Dc2/84r	1399
Gernon, George	Louth, Donmoghan	gentry: gent	24-Nov-30	100	Dc2/156v	1728
Gernon, Henry	Louth, Milton	gentry: gent	27-Sep-31	200	Dc2/168v	1778
Gernon, Hugh	Louth, Killincoole	gentry: gent	13-Aug-72	100	B.L. 15, 636 f. 112a	3815
Gernon, Nicholas	Dublin, the city	merchant	15-Jun-65	632	Dc3/9	2241
Gernon, Nicholas	Louth, Newton	gentry: gent	21-Nov-17	200	Dc2/11r	920
Gernon, Nicholas	Dublin, the city	merchant	16-May-65	740	Dc3/6	2233
Gernon, Nicholas	Dublin, the city	merchant	16-May-65	740	B.L. 15, 635 f. 175	3559
Gernon, Nicholas	Dublin, the city	merchant	05-Aug-64	400	B.L. 15, 635 f. 142a	3504
Gernon, Nicholas	Dublin, the city	trade: barber-surgeon	27-Jun-64	600	B.L. 15, 635 f. 139	3499
Gernon, Nicholas	Dublin, the city	merchant	27-Jun-64	600	B.L. 15, 635 f. 139	3499
Gernon, Nicholas	Dublin, the city	merchant	15-Jun-65	632	B.L. 15, 635 f. 154	3527
Gernon, Patrick	Dublin, Edmonston	gentry: son/heir of Edward	11-Apr-21	272	Dc2/35r	1066
Gernon, Patrick	Louth, Gernonstowne	gentry: esquire	07-Dec-27	280	Dc2/98v	1458
Gernon, Patrick	Louth, Mainbradon	gentry: gent	21-Nov-17	200	Dc2/11r	920
Gernon, Patrick	Louth, Gernanston	gentry: gent	27-Jan-27	200	Dc2/87v	1415
Gernon, Patrick	Louth, Gernonston	gentry: gent	22-May-22	272	Dc2/40r	1105
Gernon, Pierce	Meath?, Agherpalllles	gentry: son/heir of Anthony	07-Feb-07	180	Dc1/74r	447
Gernon, Richard	Louth, Mylton	gentry: gent	24-Nov-00	100	Dc1/26v	179
Gernon, Roger	Dublin	merchant	07-Dec-27	280	Dc2/98v	1458
Gernon, Roger	Dublin, the city	merchant	15-May-35	200	Dc2/235v	2050
Gernon, Roger	Dublin, the city	merchant	29-Nov-21	160	Dc2/37r	1082
Gernon, Roger	Dublin, the city	merchant	22-May-22	272	Dc2/40r	1105
Gernon, Roger	Louth, Stabanan	gentry: gent	16-Jun-37	150	Dc2/264v	2188
Gernon, Roger	Dublin	gentry: merchant	11-Apr-21	272	Dc2/35r	1066
Gernon, Thomas	Louth, Mullaghyloe	gentry: gent	15-Jul-14	200	Dc1/131r	812
Gernon, Thomas	Louth, Mullinstowne	gentry: esquire	25-Jun-28	220	Dc2/111v	1519
Gernon, Thomas	Louth, Mollenstone	gentry: gent	21-Nov-17	200	Dc2/11r	920
Gernon, Thomas	Louth, Mollenton	gentry: gent	02-Dec-17	200	Dc2/12r	927
Gernon, Thomas	Louth, Mollinstowne	gentry: esquire	13-Feb-26	230	Dc2/74r	1343
Gernon, Thomas	Louth, Mollenston	gentry: gent	04-Dec-17	200	Dc2/12v	928
Gettins, John	Wexford	trade: tanner	01-May-18	60	Dc2/14v	941
Gettins, Richard	Cork, Ballyfeniter	gentry: baronet	14-Jun-76	1000	Dc3/177v	2667
Gettins, Richard	Cork, Ballyfeniter	gentry: esquire	14-Jun-76	1000	Dc3/177v	2667
Gettins, Richard	Cork, Ballinfeniter	gentry: esquire	14-Jun-76	1000	B.L. 19, 844 f. 96	3223

Standard	County	Occupation	Date	Amount	MS No	Ident No
Gettins, Richard	Dublin, the city	gentry: baronet	22-Oct-66	2000	Dc3/40	2315
Gettins, Richard	Cork, Gethingsgrott	gentry: baronet	02-Apr-74	1000	B. L. 19, 844 f. 24	3145
Gettins, Richard	Cork, Ballinfeniter	gentry: baronet?	14-Jun-76	1000	B.L. 19, 844 f. 96	3223
Gettins, Richard	Cork, Gethinsgrott	gentry: knight and baronet	27-Aug-79	400	B.L. 15, 637 f. 23a	3888
Gettins, Richard	Cork, Gething's growth	gentry: baronet	21-Dec-71	1000	B.L. 15, 636 f. 107a	3806
Gettins, Richard	Cork, Gethin's grouth	gentry: baronet	21-Dec-71	1000	B.L. 15, 636 f. 107	3805
Gettins, Teige	Dublin, Ballinecorny	farmer: husbandman	08-Feb-03	200	Dc1/44r	281
Gibbon, John	Cork, Garranes	gentry: gent	27-Jan-83	400	B.L. 15, 637 f. 70a	3974
Gibbon, John	Cork, Garranes	gentry: gent	04-Jun-84	1000	B.L. 15, 637 f. 92a	4014
Gibbon, Simon	Limerick, Shannagolin	gentry: gent	18-Apr-77	300	B.L. 19, 844 f. 139	3269
Gibbon, Thomas	Dublin, the city	trade: maltster	12-Dec-67	280	Dc3/71	2383
Gibbon, Thomas	Dublin, the city	trade: maltster	12-Dec-67	280	B.L. 15, 635 f. 209	3625
Gibbon, William	Mayo, Ballygolman	gentry: gent	01-Jun-36	400	B.L. 19, 843 f. 38	2794
Gibbon, William	Dublin, the county	farmer: freeholder	06-Oct-12	120	Dc1/115v	718
Gibbon, William	Down, Ballekenlor	gentry: gent	28-Jun-38	600	B.L. 19, 843 f. 7	2732
Gibbon, William	Mayo, Ballygolman	gentry: gent	30-Jun-36	400	Dc2/254r	2138
Gibbon, William	Dublin, Clondalkan	farmer: yeoman, s./heir of John	19-Dec-07	60	Dc1/80v	499
Gibbon, William	Dublin, Tyrenure	farmer: yeoman	18-May-07	200	Dc1/76v	466
Gibbon, William	Mayo, Ballygolman	gentry: gent	30-Jun-36	400	Dc2/253v	2137
Gibson, John	Dublin, the city		21-Mar-37	350	Dc2/261r	2171
Gifford, John	Meath, Castlegordon	gentry: esquire	02-May-73	2600	Dc3/155v	2581
Gifford, John	Meath, Castlejordan	gentry: esquire	02-May-73	2600	B.L. 15, 636 f. 129	3837
Gifford, Thomas	Meath, Castlejordan	gentry: knight	27-Jul-61	210	B.L. 15, 635 f. 79a	3398
Gilbert, Christopher	Westmeath, Ballybrack	gentry: esquire	06-Jun-76	400	Dc3/175v	2661
Gilbert, George	Dublin, the city		29-Jul-59	200	B.L. 15, 635 f. 50a	3352
Gilbert, George	Dublin, the city		16-Jul-59	200	B.L. 15, 635 f. 50	3351
Gilbert, George	Dublin, the city		13-Feb-60	200	B.L. 15, 635 f. 57	3365
Gilbert, George	Dublin, the city		13-Feb-60	200	B.L. 15, 635 f. 57a	3366
Gilbert, Henry	Queen's Co., Knockmay	gentry: esquire	26-Jun-68	3000	Dc3/80	2407
Gilbert, Henry	Queen's Co., ?	gentry: esquire	19-Nov-55	1500	B.L. 19, 843 f. 162	3039
Gilbert, Henry	Queen's Co., Kilmynsye	gentry: esquire	06-Feb-55	1400	B.L. 19, 843 f. 152	3018
Gilbert, Henry	Queen's Co., Knockmay	gentry: esquire	26-Jun-68	3000	B.L. 15, 635 f. 226	3657
Gilbert, John	Queen's Co., Kilminchy	gentry: esquire	05-Jul-80	2000	B.L. 15, 637 f. 40	3918
Gilbert, William	Meath, Dowanstowne	gentry: gent	04-May-70	800	Dc3/118	2476
Gilbert, William	Meath, Dowanstowne	gentry: gent	04-May-70	800	B.L. 15, 636 f. 57	3720
Gilliott, Job	Dublin, Sturmynston	gentry: esquire	16-May-23	200	Dc2/47r	1157
Gilliott, Job	Dublin, Sturmynston	gentry: esquire	16-May-23	200	Dc2/47r	1155
Gilliott, Job	Dublin, Sturmynston	gentry: esquire	15-Feb-23	400	Dc2/45r	1142
Gilliott, Job	Dublin, Sturmynston	gentry: esquire	16-May-23	200	Dc2/47r	1156
Gillott, Job	Dublin, Ballcurris	gentry: esquire	31-May-27	1500	Dc2/93r	1434
Goegh, Edward	Waterford, Killmanihine	gentry: son of Patrick, esq	17-Feb-64	4000	B.L. 15, 635 f. 128a	3484

Standard	County	Occupation	Date	Amount	MS No	Ident No
Gogan, James	Cork, Knockane Guarodigge?	gentry: gent	03-May-39	240	B.L. 19, 843 f. 31	2780
Golburne, Richard	Dublin, the city	merchant	17-Dec-22	200	Dc2/44r	1134
Golburne, William	Kildare?	prof: archdeacon of Kildare	17-Dec-22	200	Dc2/44r	1134
Golding, Christopher	Meath, Donakerny	gentry: gent	01-Jul-39	160	B.L. 19, 843 f. 34a	2787
Goodman, James	Dublin, Laghnanstowne	gentry: gent	03-Mar-28	200	Dc2/105v	1491
Goodman, James	Dublin, Loghnanston	gentry: gent	23-Mar-26	400	Dc2/76r	1356
Goodman, James	Dublin, Laughnanstowne	gentry: gent	06-May-35	600	Dc2/234v	2046
Goodman, James	Dublin, Laughnanstowne	gentry: gent	01-Sep-32	200	Dc2/185v	1845
Goodman, James	Dublin, Laughnanston	gentry: gent	07-Jul-32	1000	Dc2/184v	1842
Goodman, James	Dublin, Laughnanstowne	gentry: gent	20-Jul-35	440	Dc2/239r	2065
Goodman, James	Dublin, Laughnanstowne?	gentry: son/heir of James	20-Jul-35	440	Dc2/239r	2065
Goodman, James	Dublin, Loghnanston	gentry: gent	20-May-25	200	Dc2/63v	1281
Goodman, James	Meath, Beaton	gentry: gent	31-Jan-22	240	Dc2/38v	1095
Goodman, James	Meath, Bewtun	gentry: gent	09-Dec-19	1000	Dc2/27v	1014
Goodman, Robert	Dublin, Rocheston	gentry: gent	24-Nov-18	120	Dc2/18r	959
Goodman, Robert	Dublin, Rocheston	gentry: gent	11-Feb-05	200	Dc1/56r	347
Goodman, William	Dublin, Loghnanston	gentry: gent	11-Feb-05	200	Dc1/56r	347
Goodman, William	Dublin, Loughnanston	gentry: gent	16-Jun-10	300	Dc1/97v	612
Goodman, William	Dublin, Loghnanston	gentry: gent	31-May-09	286	Dc1/89v	559
Goodman, William	Dublin, Laghnanston	gentry: gent	09-Jun-08	220	Dc1/83r	517
Goodwin, John	Dublin, the city		19-Jan-21	200	Dc2/34r	1061
Goodwin, Matthew	Dublin, the city	merchant	19-Jan-21	200	Dc2/34r	1061
Gookin, Robert	Cork, Kilcolman	gentry: gent	27-Apr-82	1600	B.L. 15, 637 f. 57a	3950
Gooley, Stephen	Cork, the city	gentry: gent	13-Apr-69	400	B.L. 15, 636 f. 34a	3683
Gore, Paul	Kilkenny, the city	gentry: esquire	19-Aug-81	200	B.L. 15, 637 f. 48	3932
Gorey, John	Mayo, Rahince	gentry: esquire	18-Jul-31	300	Dc2/166v	1770
Gorman, Patrick	Louth, Gornonston	gentry: gent	29-Nov-21	160	Dc2/37r	1082
Gorman, Teige	Carlow, Newton	gentry: gent?	31-May-17	220	Dc2/7v	904
Gough, James	Waterford, Kilmanhyn	gentry: knight	18-Nov-07	600	Dc1/79av	491
Gough, Patrick	Dublin	gentry: gent	29-Apr-05	240	Dc1/57v	353
Gould, Christopher	Cork, the city	merchant	21-Feb-39	600	B.L. 19, 843 f. 53a	2825
Gould, Francis	Cork, the city	merchant	05-Nov-40	1000	B.L. 19, 843 f. 92a	2904
Gould, Gerald	Cork, Inislinnsi	gentry: gent	14-Jul-40	400	B.L. 19, 843 f. 75	2869
Gould, James	Cork, the city	gentry: gent, son/heir of Henry	05-Nov-40	1000	B.L. 19, 843 f. 92a	2904
Gould, James	Cork, the city	other: s./heir Thom, alderman	20-Mar-63	800	B.L. 15, 635 f. 146	3511
Gould, James	Cork	gentry: gent	24-Oct-60	240	B.L. 15, 635 f. 126a	3480
Gould, James	Cork, the city	gentry: gent	26-May-70	320	B.L. 15, 636 f. 60	3725
Gould, James	Cork, the city	gentry: gent	04-Jan-66	308	B.L. 15, 635 f. 162a	3540
Gould, James	Cork, the city	gentry: gent	23-Jan-65	600	B.L. 15, 635 f. 149a	3518
Gould, John	Cork, the city	gentry: gent	16-Nov-40	300	B.L. 19, 843 f. 81	2881
Gould, John	Cork, the city	merchant	05-Nov-40	1000	B.L. 19, 843 f. 92a	2904

Standard	County	Occupation	Date	Amount	MS No	Ident No
Goulding, Richard	Dublin, Rathowlke	gentry: gent	15-Jun-29	200	Dc2/132r	1618
Grace, Gerald	Kilkenny, Legan	gentry: gent	24-Nov-10	200	Dc1/101r	632
Grace, Gerald	Kilkenny, Legan	gentry: esquire	15-Feb-08	160	Dc1/81r	503
Grace, Gerald	Tipperary, Kilboy	gentry: gent	21-May-39	1000	B.L. 19, 843 f. 35	2788
Grace, John	Kilkenny, Courtstowne	gentry: esquire	23-Feb-70	700	Dc3/116	2470
Grace, John	Galway, Ballimussen	gentry: gent	03-Jul-56	268	B.L. 19, 843 f. 176a	3063
Grace, John	Tipperary, Thurles	gentry: gent	08-Feb-10	400	Dc1/94r	589
Grace, John	Kilkenny, Aghviller	gentry: gent	15-Feb-08	160	Dc1/81r	503
Grace, John	Kilkenny, Courtstowne	gentry: esquire	23-Feb-70	700	B.L. 15, 636 f. 46	3704
Grace, Richard	King's Co., Moyelly, Kilcoursy	gentry: esquire	12-May-81	800	B.L. 15, 637 f. 51	3939
Grace, Richard	King's Co., Moyely	gentry: esquire	03-Jun-63	660	B.L. 15, 635 f. 108	3448
Grace, Robert	Kilkenny, Killagh	gentry: esquire	12-May-81	800	B.L. 15, 637 f. 51	3939
Grady, Dermot	Limerick, Ballniskullie	gentry: gent	06-May-39	2000	B.L. 19, 843 f. 12a	2743
Grady, Dermot	Limerick, Kilballeowin	gentry: esquire	28-Sep-72	720	B.L. 15, 636 f. 116	3821
Grady, Standish	Limerick, Elton	gentry: gent	20-Mar-79	742	B.L. 15, 637 f. 13a	3872
Grady, Thady	Limerick, Kilkillane	gentry: esquire	26-Sep-39	600	B.L. 19, 843 f. 40a	2799
Grady, Thady	Limerick, Kilkillane		02-Jul-41	840	B.L. 19, 843 f. 107	2933
Grady, Thomas	Limerick, Kilballeowin	gentry: gent	28-Sep-72	720	B.L. 15, 636 f. 116	3821
Graham, George	Wicklow, Ballynure	gentry: gent	31-Dec-19	200	Dc2/28r	1016
Graham, George	Queen's Co., Kilfecle	gentry: gent	26-Jun-34	440	Dc2/213r	1956
Graham, George	Kildare, Castlewarnyne	gentry: esquire	23-Jul-03	500	Dc1/47av	307
Graham, Mark	Kildare, Castlewarning	gentry: esquire	31-Dec-19	200	Dc2/28r	1016
Graham, Mark	Kildare, Castlewarning	gentry: esquire	31-Dec-19	200	Dc2/28r	1017
Graham, Richard	Queen's Co., Lynanston	gentry: knight	19-Jun-13	200	Dc1/122v	760
Graham, Richard	Queen's Co., Lynanston	gentry: knight	22-Feb-17	450	Dc2/5v	895
Graham, Richard	Queen's Co., Killfeatly	gentry: esquire	17-Mar-73	100	Dc3/154v	2579
Graham, Thomas	Kildare, Kilberry	gentry: esquire	04-Dec-34	400	Dc2/224v	2003
Graham, Thomas	Cork, Killathy	gentry: esquire	09-Mar-76	300	B.L. 19, 844 f. 103	3230
Graham, William	Wexford, Ould Rosse	gentry: esquire	10-Apr-41	120	B.L. 19, 843 f. 103a	2926
Graham, William	Wicklow, Kilballiowen	gentry: esquire	17-Aug-29	300	Dc2/135v	1634
Graham, William	Wicklow, Kilballiowen	gentry: gent	26-Jun-34	440	Dc2/213r	1956
Greatrakes, Allen	Carlow, Garrenno	gentry: esquire	11-Apr-35	1000	Dc2/232v	2035
Greatrakes, Richard	Waterford, Aghafane	gentry: gent	11-Apr-35	1000	Dc2/232v	2035
Greatrakes, Valentine	Waterford, Afaune	gentry: esquire	20-May-78	800	B.L. 19, 844 f. 156	3287
Greatrakes, Valentine	Waterford, Afane	gentry: esquire	21-Mar-78	2000	Dc3/187v	2708
Greatrakes, Valentine	Waterford, Afanne	gentry: esquire	09-Mar-78	630	B.L. 19, 844 f. 150	3281
Greatrakes, William	Waterford, Aghafane	gentry: esquire	11-Apr-35	1000	Dc2/232v	2035
Greatrakes, William	Carlow, Catherlagh	gentry: esquire	28-Nov-28	240	Dc2/118r	1553
Greatrakes, William	Carlow, Catherlagh	gentry: esquire	28-Nov-28	300	Dc2/118r	1554
Greatrakes, William	Waterford, Affane	gentry: esquire	18-Sep-32	1200	Dc2/185v	1846
Green, Andrew	Sligo, Annagh	gentry: esquire	11-May-27	4000	Dc2/92v	1432
Green, Godfrey	Tipperary, Moorestowne	gentry: gent	04-Apr-83	4000	B.L. 15, 637 f. 72a	3978
Green, John	Waterford, Killmanaheene	gentry: gent	04-Apr-83	4000	B.L. 15, 637 f. 72a	3978
Grimes, George	Wicklow, Ballinure	gentry: gent	20-Mar-26	300	Dc2/75v	1352

Standard	County	Occupation	Date	Amount	MS No	Ident No
Grimes, George	Wicklow, Ballynewe	gentry: gent	23-Jul-23	140	Dc2/49v	1177
Grimes, Mark	Carlow, Tobinston	gentry: esquire	20-Mar-26	300	Dc2/75v	1352
Grimes, Mark	Kildare, Castlewarden	gentry: gent	23-Jul-23	140	Dc2/49v	1177
Grimes, Mark	Carlow, Tobinston	gentry: esquire	20-Mar-26	600	Dc2/75v	1353
Grimley, Andrew	Meath, Ratowth	farmer: yeoman	27-Jun-36	100	Dc2/253v	2136
Gwynn, Evan	Cork, Garranagranoge	gentry: gent	24-Jul-73	754	B.L. 19, 844 f. 11	3130
Hackett, Barnaby	Dublin, Blancherstowne	gentry: gent	20-Mar-57	140	B.L. 19, 843 f. 192a	3092
Hackett, Patrick	Dublin, Ballibought	gentry: gent	08-Jun-27	1000	Dc2/93v	1437
Hackett, Patrick	Dublin, Sutton	gentry: gent	14-Sep-14	80	Dc1/131v	818
Hackett, Patrick	Dublin, Sutton	gentry: gent	14-Nov-25	400	Dc2/70r	1319
Hackett, Thomas	Wicklow, Wicklow, the town	gentry: gent	16-Jan-61	600	B.L. 15, 635 f. 61a	3374
Hagan, Brian	Armagh, Losdeyne	gentry: gent	29-Nov-37	200	Dc2/272r	2221
Halgan, Patrick	Meath, Prymetston	farmer: freeholder	12-Jul-98	300	Dc1/11v	84
Hall, Francis	Down, Laggan	gentry: gent	15-Aug-76	500	Dc3/179v	2675
Hall, Francis	Armagh, Glassdromin	gentry: gent	21-Nov-70	2000	Dc3/131r	2502
Hall, Francis	Armagh, Glasdromin	gentry: gent	21-Nov-70	2000	B.L. 15, 636 f. 74a	3751
Hall, Richard	Meath, Rath mc Crechan	gentry: gent	14-Feb-74	220	B.L. 19, 844 f. 21	3140
Hall, Richard	Meath, Rathin Crochan	gentry: gent	28-Sep-71	115	B.L. 15, 636 f. 88	3776
Hall, Richard	Meath, Rathin Crucan	gentry: gent	17-May-70	40	B.L. 15, 636 f. 70a	3743
Hall, William	Cork, the city	gentry: esquire	05-Aug-75	660	B.L. 19, 844 f. 70	3198
Hally, Carbery	Sligo, Carowkile?	gentry: gent	10-Sep-13	40	Dc1/123v	766
Hally, Robert	Cork, the city	gentry: gent	18-Jan-68	700	B.L. 15, 635 f. 213a	3632
Hamill, Hugh	Tyrone, Strabane	gentry: gent	06-Dec-73	1300	Dc3/159r	2598
Hamill, Hugh	Tyrone, Strabane	gentry: esquire	22-Jun-78	2400	B.L. 19, 844 f. 165	3296
Hamill, Hugh	Dublin, the city	gentry: gent	21-Feb-73	600	Dc3/154r	2576
Hamill, Hugh	Tyrone, Strabane	gentry: esquire	23-May-76	3000	Dc3/173v	2656
Hamill, Hugh	Tyrone, Strabane	gentry: esquire	22-Jun-78	2000	B.L. 19, 844 f. 164	3295
Hamill, Hugh	Dublin, the city	gentry: gent	21-Feb-73	600	B.L. 15, 636 f. 125	3832
Hamilton, Archibald	Tyrone, Tallycosher	gentry: esquire	19-Jul-36	1200	Dc2/255r	2145
Hamilton, Archibald	Tyrone, Tallycosher	gentry: esquire	15-Jul-36	600	Dc2/255r	2144
Hamilton, Archibald	Tyrone, Ballegallie	gentry: esquire	02-Jul-40	600	B.L. 19, 843 f. 65	2849
Hamilton, Charles	Donegal, Letterkenny	gentry: esquire	08-Feb-56	1080	B.L. 19, 843 f. 173a	3059
Hamilton, Francis	Cavan, Castlekeylagh	gentry: knight and baronet	15-Jul-36	600	Dc2/255r	2144
Hamilton, Francis	Cavan, Castlekeylagh	gentry: knight	04-Jul-36	200	Dc2/254r	2140
Hamilton, Francis	Cavan, Keilagh	gentry: knight and baronet	22-Nov-33	400	Dc2/200v	1906
Hamilton, Francis	Cavan, Castlekilagh	gentry: knight and baronet	08-Feb-56	1080	B.L. 19, 843 f. 173a	3059
Hamilton, Frederick	Leitrim, Mannorhamilton	gentry: knight	04-Dec-35	800	Dc2/241r	2076
Hamilton, George	Tyrone, Donelonge?	gentry: knight and baronet	11-Jun-47	2000	B.L. 19, 843 f. 123	2965
Hamilton, George	Tipperary, Nenagh	gentry: knight and baronet	08-Nov-69	3000	Dc3/104	2451

Standard	County	Occupation	Date	Amount	MS No	Ident No
Hamilton, Hans	Armagh, Hamilton Bawn	gentry: knight	19-Jun-78	10000	Dc3/190v	2719
Hamilton, Hans	Armagh, Hamilton Bawn	gentry: knight	05-Jun-78	1000	Dc3/189v	2716
Hamilton, Hans	Armagh, Hamilton Bawn	gentry: knight and baronet	05-Jun-78	4000	Dc3/189r	2715
Hamilton, Hans	Armagh, Hamilstowne	gentry: knight and baronet	05-Jun-78	1000	B.L. 19, 844 f. 161	3292
Hamilton, Hans	Armagh, Hamilton's Barne?	gentry: knight and baronet	02-Dec-71	400	Dc3/142r	2538
Hamilton, Hans	Armagh, Hamilstowne Bawne	gentry: knight and baronet	19-Jun-78	10000	B.L. 19, 844 f. 162	3293
Hamilton, Hans	Armagh, Hamiltons Bawne	gentry: knight and baronet	05-Jun-78	4000	B.L. 19, 844 f. 157	3288
Hamilton, Hans	Armagh, Hamilton's Bawne	gentry: knight and baronet	03-Dec-78	1000	B.L. 15, 637 f. 3	3856
Hamilton, Hans	Armagh, Hamilton's Bawne	gentry: knight and baronet	03-Dec-78	600	B.L. 15, 637 f. 7	3860
Hamilton, Hans	Armagh, Hamilton's Bawne	gentry: knight and baronet	03-Dec-78	1000	B.L. 15, 637 f. 4	3857
Hamilton, Hans	Armagh, Hamilton's Bawn	gentry: knight	03-Dec-78	400	B.L. 15, 637 f. 7a	3861
Hamilton, Hans	Armagh, Hamilton's Bawne	gentry: knight and baronet	08-Dec-78	4000	B.L. 15, 637 f. 15	3874
Hamilton, Henry	Down?	peer: earl of Clanbrassill	20-Feb-72	1100	Dc3/144r	2546
Hamilton, Henry	Kildare, Tully	gentry: esquire	19-Jun-78	10000	Dc3/191r	2720
Hamilton, Henry	Kildare, Tully	gentry: esquire	19-Jun-78	10000	B.L. 15, 637 f. 2	3854
Hamilton, Henry	Down?	peer: earl of Clanbrassill	20-Feb-72	1100	B.L. 15, 636 f.100a	3794
Hamilton, Hugh	Tyrone, Tullidowy	gentry: gent	23-Dec-65	530	Dc3/19	2265
Hamilton, James	Down, Newcastle	gentry: esquire	19-Jun-78	10000	B.L. 19, 844 f. 162	3293
Hamilton, James	Down, Newcastle	gentry: esquire	05-Jun-78	4000	Dc3/189r	2715
Hamilton, James	Down, Newcastle	gentry: esquire	05-Jun-78	1000	B.L. 19, 844 f. 161	3292
Hamilton, James	Down, Newcastle	gentry: esquire	05-Jun-78	1000	Dc3/189v	2716
Hamilton, James	Antrim, Neilsbrooke	gentry: esquire	07-Aug-71	780	Dc3/139v	2529
Hamilton, James	Down, Newcastle	gentry: esquire	05-Jun-78	4000	B.L. 19, 844 f. 157	3288
Hamilton, James	Down, Newcastle	gentry: esquire	19-Jun-78	10000	Dc3/190v	2719
Hamilton, James	Down, Bangoer	gentry: knight		2000	Dc2/25r	999
Hamilton, James	Down, Bangore	gentry: knight	17-Mar-14	1000	Dc1/128v	797
Hamilton, James	Down, Bangoer	gentry: knight	21-Apr-19	2000	Dc2/22r	983
Hamilton, James	Cavan, Carenary	gentry: esquire	07-Oct-26	233	Dc2/82v	1392
Hamilton, James	Down?	peer: viscount Clandeboy	27-Jan-55	1200	B.L. 19, 843 f. 149	3012
Hamilton, James	Down, Newcastle	gentry: esquire	08-Dec-78	4000	B.L. 15, 637 f. 15	3874
Hamilton, James	Down, Newcastle	gentry: esquire	03-Dec-78	400	B.L. 15, 637 f. 7a	3861
Hamilton, James	Antrim, Nelsbrooke	gentry: esquire	10-Aug-63	1280	B.L. 15, 635 f. 171	3552
Hamilton, James	Galway, Clonefert	gentry: esquire	29-Mar-64	200	B.L. 15, 635 f. 132a	3490
Hamilton, James	Down, Newcastle	gentry: esquire	03-Dec-78	600	B.L. 15, 637 f. 7	3860
Hamilton, James	Down, Newcastle	gentry: esquire	03-Dec-78	1000	B.L. 15, 637 f. 4	3857
Hamilton, James	Down, Newcastle	gentry: esquire	03-Dec-78	1000	B.L. 15, 637 f. 3	3856

Standard	County	Occupation	Date	Amount	MS No	Ident No
Hamilton, James	Antrim, Neilsbrooke	gentry: esquire	22-Mar-69	480	B.L. 15, 636 f. 31a	3680
Hamilton, James	Cavan, Derrinekesh	gentry: esquire	19-Apr-61	600	B.L. 15, 635 f. 71a	3387
Hamilton, James	Antrim, Neilsbrooke	gentry: esquire	07-Aug-70	700	B.L. 15, 636 f. 90a	3780
Hamilton, James	Down, Newcastle	gentry: esquire	03-Dec-78	400	B.L. 15, 637 f. 6	3859
Hamilton, John	Cavan, Correnery	gentry: esquire	04-Jul-36	200	Dc2/254r	2140
Hamilton, Malcolm	Down, Ballyhenry	gentry: esquire	09-May-15	1000	Dc1/137r	850
Hamilton, William	Scotland, Eliston	gentry: knight	18-Mar-25	553	Dc2/63r	1275
Hamilton, William	Tyrone, Bollefatten	gentry: gent	20-Feb-55	600	B.L. 19, 843 f. 154	3022
Hamilton, William	Tyrone, Callidon	gentry: esquire	14-Feb-71	400	Dc3/135r	2514
Hamilton, William	Scotland, Eliston	gentry: knight	18-Mar-25	1100	Dc2/62r	1270
Hamilton, William	King's Co., Liscloony	gentry: esquire	22-Jun-69	200	Dc3/99	2441
Hamilton, William	Tyrone, Calidon	gentry: esquire	10-Nov-69	2000	Dc3/106	2452
Hamilton, William	King's Co., Liscloony	gentry: esquire	19-Jul-71	200	Dc3/139r	2526
Hamilton, William	Dublin, the city	gentry: esquire	22-May-67	200	Dc3/61	2357
Hamilton, William	Scotland, Eliston	gentry: knight	18-Mar-25	555	Dc2/62v	1273
Hamilton, William	Dublin, the city	gentry: esquire	30-May-66	500	Dc3/30	2290
Hamilton, William	Scotland, Eliston	gentry: knight	18-Mar-25	680	Dc2/62v	1271
Hamilton, William	Scotland, Eliston	gentry: knight	18-Mar-25	660	Dc2/62v	1272
Hamilton, William	Tyrone, Kinard	gentry: esquire	13-Dec-66	880	Dc3/47	2324
Hamilton, William	Scotland, Eliston	gentry: knight	18-Mar-25	554	Dc2/62v	1274
Hamilton, William	Tyrone, Loughcurrine	gentry: esquire	23-Dec-65	530	Dc3/19	2265
Hamilton, William	Tyrone, Callidon	gentry: esquire	10-Nov-69	2400	B.L. 15, 636 f. 57a	3721
Hamilton, William	Dublin, the city	gentry: esquire	22-May-67	200	B.L. 15, 635 f. 196	3602
Hamilton, William	King's Co., Liscloony	gentry: esquire	22-Jun-69	200	B.L. 15, 636 f. 50	3709
Hamilton, William	King's Co., Liscloony	gentry: esquire	19-Jul-71	200	B.L. 15, 636 f. 89	3777
Hamlin, Andrew	Louth, Drogheda		08-Jun-20	2000	Dc2/30v	1032
Hamlin, Andrew	Louth, Drogheda		08-Jun-20	600	Dc2/30v	1033
Hamlin, Bartholomew	Louth, Drogheda	merchant	27-Apr-81	400	B.L. 15, 637 f. 42	3922
Hamlin, Edmund	Dublin, the city	merchant	29-Aug-29	350	Dc2/136v	1637
Hamlin, Edmund	Dublin	merchant	11-Feb-29	200	Dc2/124v	1584
Hamlin, Edmund	Dublin, the city	merchant	29-Aug-31	100	Dc2/168r	1776
Hamlin, Patrick	Dublin, the city	trade: miller	10-Nov-73	480	B.L. 19, 844 f. 16	3134
Hamlin, Patrick	Dublin, the city	trade: baker	10-Nov-73	480	Dc3/158ar	2594
Hamlin, Thomas	Meath, Smytheston	gentry: gent	27-Nov-06	500	Dc1/72r	438
Hamlin, Thomas	Dublin, the city	merchant	29-Aug-29	350	Dc2/136v	1637
Hamlin, Thomas	Meath, Smithston	gentry: gent	08-Jun-20	2000	Dc2/30v	1032
Hamlin, Thomas	Dublin	merchant	11-Feb-29	200	Dc2/124v	1584
Hamlin, William	Louth, Drogheda		15-Aug-41	100	B.L. 19, 843 f. 111	2941
Hamlin, William	Louth, Drogheda		27-Mar-44	120	B.L. 19, 843 f. 113a	2946
Hammond, William	Wexford, Prishuggard	gentry: gent	13-Feb-65	400	Dc3/2	2226
Hammond, William	Wexford, Prishagared	gentry: gent	13-Feb-65	400	B.L. 15, 635 f. 148a	3516
Hand, James	Antrim, Glinarme	gentry: gent	18-Jun-70	160	Dc3/120	2481
Hand, James	Antrim, Glinarme	gentry: gent	18-Jun-70	160	B.L. 15, 636 f. 69	3740
Handcock, Christopher	Dublin, the city	merchant	20-May-29	200	Dc2/129v	1608
Handcock, Christopher	Dublin, the city	merchant	30-Apr-19	400	Dc2/23r	987

Standard	County	Occupation	Date	Amount	MS No	Ident No
Handcock, Christopher	Dublin	merchant	27-Feb-26	200	Dc2/74v	1348
Handcock, Mathew	Dublin		16-Sep-11	105	Dc1/106r	661
Hanlon, Patrick		gentry: gent	17-Dec-11	500	Dc1/110v	685
Hanlon, Redmond	Louth, Dondalke	gentry: gent	23-Apr-19	1700	Dc2/22v	986
Hannon, Edward	Meath, Trym	gentry: gent	01-Dec-08	60	Dc1/85r	532
Hannon, Robert	Meath, Trym	gentry: gent	06-Feb-01	40	Dc1/28v	190
Hansard, Elizabeth	Donegal, Ballindrate	other: widow	19-Oct-64	252	B.L. 15, 635 f. 147a	3514
Harding, Richard	Kerry, Balleneskellick	gentry: esquire	20-May-12	200	Dc1/113v	705
Harman, Ann	Carlow, Castlerow	gentry: widow	22-Jun-76	1000	B.L. 19, 844 f. 101	3228
Harman, Ann	Carlow, Castlerow	gentry: widow	22-Jun-76	1000	Dc3/178r	2669
Harman, Ann	Carlow, Castlerow	gentry: widow	22-Jun-76	1000	Dc3/178r	2670
Harman, Ann	Carlow, Castlerow	gentry: widow	22-Jun-76	1000	B.L . 19, 844 f.106	3233
Harman, Edward	Carlow, Kelstowne	gentry: gent	18-Sep-32	1200	Dc2/185v	1846
Harman, Wentworth	Dublin, the city	gentry: esquire	10-Jan-87	1000	B.L. 15, 637 f. 111a	4051
Harman, Wentworth	Dublin, the city	gentry: esquire	29-Nov-84	1000	B.L. 15, 637 f. 96	4021
Harmer, John	Cork, Downmaghon	gentry: gent	27-Sep-84	500	B.L. 15, 637 f. 93a	4016
Harold, Edmund	Dublin, Kilmachioke	gentry: gent	19-May-06	300	Dc1/67v	408
Harold, James	Waterford	merchant	18-Jun-10	120	Dc1/97v	614
Harold, Thomas	Limerick, the city	merchant	24-Apr-79	600	B.L. 15, 637 f. 16a	3876
Harrington, Henry	Dublin, Grandgegorman	gentry: knight	30-Oct-04	1000	Dc1/53v	336
Harrington, Henry	Dublin, Grandgegorman	gentry: knight	31-Oct-04	2000	Dc1/53v	337
Harrington, William	Dublin, the city	gentry: esquire	11-Mar-14	1600	Dc1/128r	795
Harrington, William	Wicklow, Newcastell	gentry: esquire	11-Mar-14	2500	Dc1/128r	794
Harris, Gladdis	Antrim, Carrickfergus	merchant: widow	10-Oct-68	99	B.L. 15, 636 f. 25	3668
Harris, John	Antrim, Carrickfergus	merchant	10-Oct-68	99	B.L. 15, 636 f. 25	3668
Harrison, William	Queen's Co., Killaban	gentry: gent	16-Oct-39	500	B.L. 19, 843 f. 41	2800
Harrison, William	Dublin, the city	gentry: gent	21-Jul-59	200	B.L. 15, 635 f. 54a	3360
Hart, Henry	Clare, Carriggourane	gentry: esquire	27-May-40	800	B.L. 19, 843 f. 70a	2860
Hart, William	Dublin, Blommelston	farmer	04-Aug-00	200	Dc1/25v	170
Hartpole, George	Queen's Co., Shrowell	gentry: esquire	11-May-05	2000	Dc1/59r	359
Hartpole, George	Queen's Co., Rathnemannagho	gentry: gent	16-Apr-01	120	Dc1/30r	200
Hartpole, George	Carlow, Catherlaghe	gentry: esquire	29-Aug-03	200	Dc1/48v	314
Hartpole, Pierce	Queen's Co., Shrowle	gentry: gent	15-Dec-14	1000	Dc1/134r	833
Hartpole, Robert	Queen's Co., Shrule	gentry: esquire	11-Nov-34	200	Dc2/221r	1988
Hartpole, Robert	Queen's Co., Shrule	gentry: esquire	11-Nov-34	200	Dc2/220v	1987
Hartpole, Robert	Queen's Co., Shrewle	gentry: esquire	01-Feb-33	600	Dc2/190v	1866
Hartpole, Robert	Queen's Co., Shrule	gentry: esquire	04-Jul-39	2000	B.L. 19, 843 f. 16a	2751
Hartpole, Robert	King's Co., Shrowle	gentry: esquire	07-Jul-41	5000	B.L. 19, 843 f. 100	2919
Hartpole, Robert	Queen's Co., Shrewle	gentry: esquire	24-Nov-36	420	Dc2/257v	2157
Hartpole, Robert	Queen's Co., Shrowle	gentry: esquire	09-Dec-33	400	Dc2/203r	1916
Hartpole, Robert	Queen's Co., Ballikillkeavan	gentry: gent	21-Nov-27	200	Dc2/100r	1464
Hartpole, William	Carlow, Katherloghe	gentry: knight	13-May-05	2000	Dc1/59r	360
Hartpole, William	Carlow, Catherlaghe	gentry: esquire	29-Aug-03	200	Dc1/48v	314

Standard	County	Occupation	Date	Amount	MS No	Ident No
Hartpole, William	Carlow, Katherloghe	gentry: knight	21-May-05	4000	Dc1/59v	363
Hartpole, William	Carlow, Catherlagh	gentry: esquire	02-Jun-00	1000	Dc1/24r	159
Harvey, William	Dublin, the city	trade: hatband-maker	25-May-63	660	B.L. 15, 635 f. 115a	3461
Hasking, Patrick	Kildare, the little Rathe	farmer: freeholder	24-May-22	160	Dc2/40r	1106
Hatch, John	Meath, Duleeke	gentry: son/heir of John	20-Jul-70	200	B.L. 15, 636 f. 72a	3747
Hatch, John	Meath, Duleeke	gentry: esquire	20-Jul-70	200	B.L. 15, 636 f. 72a	3747
Hatton, Edward	Monaghan, Ardagh	prof: archdeacon of Ardagh	06-Nov-29	400	Dc2/137v	1642
Hawkes, Edward	Roscommon, Cloonemoore		25-Nov-71	500	Dc3/141v	2535
Hay, William	Kildare, Cotlandstowne	gentry: esquire	20-Nov-73	4000	Dc3/158av	2595
Hayden, Edmund	Tipperary, Ballymurren	gentry: gent	23-Nov-30	46	Dc2/156r	1726
Heatley, Elizabeth	Dublin, the city	trade: spinster, wife Thomas	16-Jun-84	800	B.L. 15, 637 f. 87	4004
Heatley, Thomas	Dublin, the city	trade: hogler/hegler	16-Jun-84	800	B.L. 15, 637 f. 87	4004
Henzey, Annanias	King's Co., Somertowne	gentry: esquire	05-Jul-69	240	Dc3/101	2443
Henzey, Annanias	King's Co., Somertowne	gentry: esquire	05-Jul-69	240	B.L. 15, 636 f. 39a	3693
Herbert, Gerald	Limerick, Inglanston	gentry: gent	31-Jan-07	200	Dc1/73v	445
Herbert, Jasper	King's Co., Monestrorigh	gentry: knight	24-Dec-29	220	Dc2/138v	1648
Herbert, John	Kildare, Cottlanstown	gentry: esquire	21-May-02	500	Dc1/38r	245
Herbert, John	Kildare, Coclanstone	gentry: gent	22-May-06	600	Dc1/68r	410
Herbert, John	Kildare, Cottlanston	gentry: esquire	06-Sep-02	200	Dc1/39v	256
Herbert, John	Kildare, Cottlanston	gentry: esquire	03-Mar-03	200	Dc1/45r	287
Herbert, Maurice	Limerick?, Inglanston?	gentry: gent	31-Jan-07	200	Dc1/73v	445
Herlighy, Donald	Cork, Ballyworgny	gentry: gent	16-Mar-28	180	B.L. 19, 843 f. 19a	2757
Herlighy, Thady	Cork, Ballyvourny	gentry: gent	16-Mar-28	180	B.L. 19, 843 f. 19a	2757
Herlighy, William	Cork, Ballyworgny	gentry: son/heir of Donnogh?	16-Mar-28	180	B.L. 19, 843 f. 19a	2757
Heskett, Thomas	England, Lancaster, Rufforde	gentry: esquire	12-Jul-01	300	Dc1/33v	220
Hetherington, Richard	Dublin, Donakerny	gentry: son/heir of Robert	16-Jun-10	250	Dc1/97v	613
Hetherington, Robert	Dublin, Donakerny	gentry: gent	16-Jun-10	250	Dc1/97v	613
Hetherington, Robert	Dublin, Donakry	gentry: gent	10-Feb-97	200	Dc1/1v	8
Hetherington, Robert	Dublin, Dunakerny	gentry: gent	06-Aug-08	120	Dc1/83v	521
Hetherington, William	Queen's Co., Tully	gentry: gent	26-Jun-34	440	Dc2/213r	1956
Hewson, Christopher	Kilkenny, Thomastowne	gentry: gent	25-Sep-58	170	B.L. 15, 635 f. 45a	3343
Hewson, Richard	Kildare, Castlecarbery	gentry: gent	23-Oct-29	300	Dc2/137r	1641
Hewson, Robert	Carlow, Cloghna	gentry: gent?	31-May-17	220	Dc2/7v	904
Hewston, Thomas	Kildare, Gray Abbie	gentry: esquire	11-Jan-82	400	B.L. 15, 637 f. 54	3943
Hickman, Thomas	Clare, Ballehenane	gentry: esquire	13-Sep-73	3012	B.L. 19, 844 f. 20	3138
Hicks, Walter	Galway	merchant	30-Oct-70	2000	B.L. 15, 636 f. 77a	3757
Higgins, William	Dublin, the city	merchant	07-May-38	200	B.L. 19, 843 f. 114a	2948
Higgins, William	Dublin, the city	merchant	20-Feb-40	100	B.L. 19, 843 f. 44	2806
Hill, John	Cork, Newmarkett	merchant	18-Apr-85	305	B.L. 15, 367 f. 97a	4024

Standard	County	Occupation	Date	Amount	MS No	Ident No
Hill, John	Dublin, Kilmainham	trade: brewer	19-Dec-83	2400	B.L. 15, 637 f. 82	3996
Hill, Peter	Down, Downpatricke	gentry: gent	21-Feb-35	300	Dc2/230r	2025
Hill, Thomas	Dublin, the city	gentry: gent	20-Nov-37	600	Dc2/271v	2218
Hill, Thomas	Cork, Newmarkett	gentry: gent	18-Apr-85	305	B.L. 15, 367 f. 97a	4024
Hill, William	Dublin, Howth	gentry: gent	23-Feb-39	30	B.L. 19, 843 f. 45a	2809
Hill, William	Dublin, the city	prof: surgeon	06-Jun-56	242	B.L. 19, 843 f. 171a	3056
Hoare, Philip	Dublin, Kilsalghan	gentry: gent	22-Jun-37	300	Dc2/265r	2190
Hoey, John	Kildare, Collanstowne	gentry: knight	29-Jan-55	1200	B.L. 19, 843 f. 153	3020
Hoey, John	Kildare, Collanstowne	gentry: knight	01-Feb-55	400	B.L. 19, 843 f. 153a	3021
Hoey, John	Kildare, Cotlanstowne	gentry: knight	20-Nov-57	400	B.L. 19, 843 f. 200a	3107
Hoey, John	Wicklow, Donganstowne	gentry: esquire	26-Jul-37	2000	Dc2/269v	2210
Hoey, John	Kildare, Cottlanstowne	gentry: knight	09-Feb-61	1320	B.L. 15, 635 f. 65a	3380
Hoey, William	Kildare, Cottlandstowne	gentry: esquire	14-Jun-76	5200	Dc3/176ar	2665
Hoey, William	Kildare, Cotlanstowne	gentry: son/heir of Sir John	20-Nov-57	400	B.L. 19, 843 f. 200a	3107
Hoey, William	Kildare, Cotlanestowne	gentry: esquire	20-Nov-73	4000	B.L. 19, 844 f. 10	3129
Hoey, William	Kildare, Cottlingstowne	gentry: esquire	29-Jul-65	500	Dc3/12	2248
Hoey, William	Kildare, Cottlandstowne	gentry: esquire	14-Jun-76	5200	B.L. 19, 844 f. 98	3225
Hoey, William	Kildare, Cottlanstowne	gentry: esquire	29-Jul-65	400	B.L. 15, 635 f. 158a	3534
Holbert, John	Wicklow, Wickloe	trade: soap-boiler	14-Mar-65	260	Dc3/3	2228
Holder, Richard	Kildare, the Nace	merchant	20-May-13	160	Dc1/120v	750
Hollywood, Christopher	Dublin, Tartam	gentry: gent	08-Jun-41	400	B.L. 19, 843 f. 117	2953
Hollywood, Edward	Louth, Hamonstowne	gentry: gent	25-Apr-35	640	Dc2/333v	2039
Hollywood, Edward	Louth, Hamanstowne	gentry: gent	02-Jul-28	600	Dc2/112r	1522
Hollywood, Edward	Louth, Hamonstowne	gentry: gent	22-Nov-36	600	Dc2/257r	2154
Hollywood, Lucas	Meath, Perisetowne	gentry: gent	03-Aug-61	220	B.L. 15, 635 f. 80a	3400
Hollywood, Luke	Meath, Pierstowne	gentry: gent	05-May-62	350	B.L. 15, 635 f. 93a	3421
Hollywood, Patrick	Louth, Hamonstowne?	gentry: son/heir of Edward	25-Apr-35	640	Dc2/333v	2039
Holman, John	Dublin	gentry: gent	20-Dec-02	60	Dc1/43r	275
Holman, John	Dublin, Kilmainhame	farmer: yeoman	20-Dec-03	300	Dc1/51r	327
Holman, John	Dublin, the city	gentry: gent	26-May-28	120	Dc2/110r	1513
Holman, John	Dublin?	gentry: gent?	20-Dec-02	60	Dc1/43r	274
Holmon, John	Dublin	farmer: yeoman	20-Jun-98	80	Dc1/11v	83
Holt, John	Louth, Drumcar	gentry: gent	25-May-76	700	Dc3/175r	2659
Hooper, Nicholas	Wexford, Wexford	gentry: esquire	27-Feb-74	200	Dc3/160v	2604
Hooper, Nicholas	Wexford, Wexford	gentry: esquire	27-Feb-74	200	B.L. 19, 844 f. 20a	3139
Hope, Alexander	Westmeath, Mullengare	gentry: gent	28-May-23	500	Dc2/48r	1162
Hope, Alexander	Westmeath, Molingare	gentry: gent	22-Nov-28	200	Dc2/116v	1545
Hope, Alexander	Westmeath, Molnegar	gentry: gent	05-Dec-29	200	Dc2/139v	1652
Hope, Alexander	Westmeath, Mollyngare	gentry: gent	15-Jun-19	150	Dc2/24r	993
Hope, Walter	Westmeath, Mollingarr	gentry: gent	13-Feb-13	100	Dc1/119r	738
Hope, Walter	Westmeath, Mollingare	gentry: gent	16-May-12	100	Dc1/113v	704
Hope, Walter	Westmeath, Mollingare	gentry: gent	03-Mar-14	1000	Dc1/127v	791
Hopton, James	Louth, Warrenstowne	gentry: esquire	13-May-62	1800	B.L. 15, 635 f. 95a	3425

Standard	County	Occupation	Date	Amount	MS No	Ident No
Hore, George	Wexford, Ballychoge	gentry: gent	24-Jun-72	3000	Dc3/146v	2554
Hore, George	Wexford, Ballychoge	gentry: gent	24-Jun-72	3000	B.L. 15, 636 f.110a	3811
Hore, Martin	Waterford, Ardigenagh	gentry: gent	21-Jul-74	240	B.L. 19, 844 f. 33	3157
Hore, Phelim	Wexford, Ballychoge	gentry: esquire	24-Jun-72	3000	B.L. 15, 636 f.110a	3811
Hore, Phelim	Wexford, Ballicheogh	gentry: gent	11-Jun-73	240	B.L. 15, 636 f. 134	3844
Hore, Philip	Wexford, Ballicheogh	gentry: gent	11-Jun-73	240	Dc3/157r	2584
Hore, Philip	Wexford, Drinagh	gentry: esquire	20-Jul-66	1000	Dc3/34	2299
Hore, Philip	Dublin, Kilsalghan	gentry: gent	23-Aug-09	160	Dc1/91r	571
Hore, Philip	Wexford, Ballychoge	gentry: esquire	24-Jun-72	3000	Dc3/146v	2554
Hore, Philip	Dublin, Kilsalghan	gentry: esquire	07-Jun-64	300	B.L. 15, 635 f. 143	3505
Hore, Philip	Wexford, Ballechioge	gentry: esquire	27-Aug-80	1000	B.L. 15, 637 f. 37	3912
Hore, Philip	Dublin, Kilsauchan	gentry: esquire	28-Aug-63	600	B.L. 15, 635 f. 123a	3474
Hore, Philip	Dublin, Kilsalchan	gentry: esquire	24-Jul-63	300	B.L. 15, 635 f. 123	3473
Hore, Philip	Dublin, Kilsalgan	gentry: esquire	20-Jul-66	1000	B.L. 15, 635 f. 176	3561
Hore, William	Wexford, Harperstowne	gentry: esquire	13-Feb-32	320	Dc2/175v	1807
Hore, William	Wexford, Harperstowne	gentry: esquire	25-Jun-34	400	B.L. 19, 843 f. 57a	2833
Hore, William	Wexford, Harperstowne	gentry: esquire	25-Jun-34	400	Dc2/212v	1955
Horish, John	Dublin, the city	merchant	24-May-26	400	Dc2/78v	1370
Horish, Richard	Dublin, the city	merchant	24-May-26	400	Dc2/78v	1370
Houston, William	Antrim, Craigs	gentry: gent	30-Nov-75	442	B.L. 19, 844 f. 83	3211
Houston, William	Antrim, Craigs	gentry: esquire	30-Nov-75	442	B.L. 19, 844 f. 83	3211
Hovendon, James	Queen's Co., Ballyfoyle	gentry: gent	01-Feb-25	200	Dc2/61r	1260
Hovendon, James	Queen's Co., Killeene	gentry: gent	21-Nov-27	200	Dc2/100r	1464
Hovendon, James	Queen's Co., Killeene	gentry: esquire	25-Jun-30	250	Dc2/153v	1713
Hovendon, James	Queen's Co., Killine	gentry: gent	04-May-30	200	Dc2/145r	1679
Hovendon, Robert	Armagh, Ballinemeatagh	gentry: esquire	24-May-37	300	Dc2/264r	2185
Hovendon, Robert	Armagh, Ballnnemetagh	gentry: esquire	07-Jul-37	2000	Dc2/267r	2197
Hovendon, Robert	Armagh, Ballynemetagh	gentry: esquire	17-Jun-35	1200	Dc2/236v	2055
Hovendon, Robert	Armagh, Ballynemeatagh	gentry: esquire	27-Jun-35	2000	Dc2/238r	2062
Hovendon, Robert	Armagh, Ballinemetagh	gentry: esquire	04-May-32	2000	Dc2/178v	1818
Hovendon, Robert	Armagh, Ballynemeetagh	gentry: esquire	01-Dec-31	400	Dc2/173r	1797
Hovendon, Robert	Armagh, Ballinemetagh	gentry: esquire	24-Jul-34	400	Dc2/215r	1965
Hovendon, Thomas	Queen's Co., Tankardstowne	gentry: esquire	15-Nov-31	100	Dc2/169v	1783
Howard, William	Meath, Galtrim	gentry: gent	16-Jul-68	200	Dc3/81	2408
Hubbart, Derek	Dublin, Holmpatricke	gentry: esquire	03-Jul-30	120	Dc2/153v	1714
Hubbart, Derek	Dublin, Holpatricke	merchant	20-Jun-29	600	Dc2/133r	1622
Hubbart, Derek	Dublin, Holmepatrick	gentry: gent	12-Oct-32	500	Dc2/186v	1849
Hubbart, Redmond	Galway, Gortenemakenne	gentry: gent	10-May-15	100	Dc1/137r	851
Hull, George	Down, Lignegappocke	gentry: gent	27-Mar-56	383	B.L. 19, 843 f. 181	3069
Hull, Richard	Cork, Inchinabacky	gentry: esquire	19-Jun-76	280	B.L. 19, 844 f. 109	3236
Humphrey, Edward	Carlow, Oldtowne	gentry: gent	01-Feb-78	600	B.L. 19, 844 f. 145	3276
Humphrey, Edward	Carlow, Oldtowne	gentry: gent	01-Feb-78	600	Dc3/185r	2702
Humphrey, Edward	Dublin, the city	gentry: gent	16-Feb-71	200	Dc3/135v	2516
Humphrey, Henry	Wicklow, Knockandaragh	gentry: gent	01-Feb-78	600	B.L. 19, 844 f. 145	3276

Standard	County	Occupation	Date	Amount	MS No	Ident No
Humphrey, Henry	Wicklow, Knockandaragh	gentry: gent	01-Feb-78	600	Dc3/185r	2702
Humphrey, John	Dublin, the city	gentry: gent	01-Feb-78	600	B.L. 19, 844 f. 145	3276
Humphrey, John	Wicklow, Dunnard	gentry: esquire	16-Feb-71	200	Dc3/135v	2516
Humphrey, John	Dublin, the city	gentry: gent	01-Feb-78	600	Dc3/185r	2702
Humphrey, John	Dublin, the city	gentry: gent	01-Feb-78	1200	Dc3/185v	2703
Humphrey, William	Dublin, the city	gentry: gent	16-Feb-71	200	Dc3/135v	2516
Hunt, Richard	Dublin, the city	gentry: gent	09-Dec-72	500	Dc3/151v	2567
Hunt, Richard	Dublin, the city	gentry: gent	09-Dec-72	500	B.L. 15, 636 f. 119	3825
Hunt, Thomas	Wexford, Homestowne	gentry: gent	03-Jul-56	268	B.L. 19, 843 f. 176a	3063
Hussey, Bartholomew	Dublin, the city	gentry: esquire	05-Nov-58	800	B.L. 15, 635 f. 37a	3329
Hussey, Edward	Meath, Mollassey	gentry: esquire	16-Jun-30	200	Dc2/152r	1707
Hussey, Hilkiah	Cork?, Brownestowne	prof: doctor of theology	17-Mar-82	600	B.L. 15, 637 f. 56a	3948
Hussey, James	Meath, Galtrie	gentry: gent	07-Jun-97	280	Dc1/4v	30
Hussey, Joan	Meath, Moyclare	gentry: widow	18-Jun-97	150	Dc1/4v	33
Hussey, Joan	Meath, Moyclare	gentry: widow	18-Jun-97	200	Dc1/5r	34
Hussey, Joan	Meath, Moyglare	gentry: widow	28-Nov-98	800	Dc1/13v	95
Hussey, John	Meath, Rodanston	gentry: gent	11-Nov-37	300	Dc2/271r	2216
Hussey, John	Cork?, Ardeteige	gentry: gent, son of doctor	17-Mar-82	600	B.L. 15, 637 f. 56a	3948
Hussey, Martin	Dublin	merchant	18-Jun-97	150	Dc1/4v	33
Hussey, Martin	Meath, Culmullen	gentry: gent	15-Jan-99	800	Dc1/14r	100
Hussey, Patrick	Meath, Galtrym	gentry: esquire	10-Apr-29	200	Dc2/127r	1597
Hussey, Patrick	Meath?	peer: baron Galtrim	05-Jun-30	200	Dc2/148v	1693
Hussey, Patrick	Meath, Galtrim	gentry: esquire	30-Nov-28	200	Dc2/121r	1565
Hussey, Patrick	Meath?	peer: baron Galtrim	04-Feb-26	200	Dc2/73r	1339
Hussey, Patrick	Meath, Galtrim	gentry: esquire	27-Apr-24	200	Dc2/54v	1210
Hussey, Peter	Meath, Galtrim	gentry: esquire	30-Nov-28	200	Dc2/121r	1565
Hussey, Peter	Dublin, Weston	gentry: esquire	10-Apr-29	200	Dc2/127r	1597
Hussey, Peter	Meath, Galtrim	gentry: gent	04-Feb-26	200	Dc2/73v	1340
Hussey, Peter	Meath, Galtrim	gentry: gent	27-Apr-24	200	Dc2/54v	1210
Hussey, Robert	Meath, Rodanston	gentry: gent	10-May-09	120	Dc1/88r	550
Hussey, Robert	Meath, Roddanston	gentry: gent	14-Jan-07	66	Dc1/73r	443
Hussey, Thomas	Meath, Galloe	gentry: gent	30-Jun-12	40	Dc1/114r	709
Hussey, Thomas	Meath, Oldstowne	gentry: gent	28-Nov-71	300	Dc3/141v	2536
Hussey, Thomas	Meath, Nyllussy?	gentry: s./heir of Walter	11-Feb-98	200	Dc1/9v	66
Hussey, Thomas	Meath, Milhusy	gentry: esq	12-Jul-22	200	Dc2/42r	1118
Hussey, Walter	Dublin, Maylush?	gentry: gent	08-May-00	140	Dc1/23v	157
Hussey, Walter	Meath, Nyllussy?	gentry: gent	11-Feb-98	200	Dc1/9v	66
Hutchinson, Daniel	Dublin, the city		28-Apr-57	4000	B.L. 19, 843 f. 191	3089
Hutchinson, Daniel	Dublin, the city		04-Jun-59	2100	B.L. 15, 635 f. 48	3348
Hutchinson, Daniel	Dublin, the city		06-Jan-57	4000	B.L. 19, 843 f. 190	3087
Hutchinson, Daniel	Dublin, the city		06-Oct-70	500	Dc3/125	2491
Hutchinson, Daniel	Dublin, the city		06-Dec-60	3000	B.L. 15, 635 f. 60a	3372
Huxton, Barnard	Dublin	gentry: gent	06-Aug-07	200	Dc1/79ar	489
Hyde, Arthur	Cork, Castlehyde	gentry: esquire	02-Apr-74	1000	B. L. 19, 844 f. 24	3145

Standard	County	Occupation	Date	Amount	MS No	Ident No
Hyde, Arthur	Cork, Castlehide	gentry: esquire	21-Dec-71	1000	B.L. 15, 636 f. 107a	3806
Hyde, Arthur	Cork, Castlehyde	gentry: esquire	21-Dec-71	1000	B.L. 15, 636 f. 107	3805
Hyde, Arthur	Cork, Castlehyde	gentry: esquire	29-Nov-79	600	B.L. 15, 637 f. 25a	3892
Irwin, Gerard	Tyrone, Ardstrae	gentry: gent	02-May-59	300	B.L. 15, 635 f. 44a	3341
Irwin, William	Leitrim, Newton	gentry: knight	06-Nov-23	200	Dc2/50v	1184
Isaac, Robert	Kilkenny, Killmadully	gentry: esquire	16-Aug-55	216	B.L. 19, 843 f. 162a	3040
Jackson, Oliver	Mayo, Eniscoe?	gentry: esquire	07-Jun-84	1600	B.L. 15, 637 f. 90a	4010
Jackson, Thomas	Limerick, the city	gentry: esquire	24-Oct-73	2400	B.L. 19, 844 f. 14	3132
Jacob, Edward	Kildare, Dullardstowne	gentry: gent	17-Nov-31	200	Dc2/170r	1785
Jacob, Lawrence	Dublin, the city	merchant	01-Jun-27	200	Dc2/94v	1442
Jacob, Lawrence	Dublin, the city	merchant	20-Jun-27	200	Dc2/94v	1443
Jacob, Nicholas	Dublin, Laghton	gentry: knight	01-Jun-27	200	Dc2/94v	1442
Jacob, Nicholas	Dublin, Laghton		01-Jun-27	200	Dc2/94v	1442
Jacob, Nicholas	Kildare, Ernehill	gentry: gent	17-Nov-31	200	Dc2/170r	1785
Jans, Edward	Dublin, the city		31-May-26	2000	Dc2/78v	1372
Jarvis, Humphrey	Dublin, the city		27-Jan-77	6000	Dc3/181v	2684
Jarvis, Humphrey	Dublin, the city		27-Jan-77	6000	B.L. 19, 844 f. 128	3257
Jarvis, John	King's Co., Roscorah	gentry: gent	21-May-69	374	Dc3/98	2438
Jarvis, John	King's Co., Roscorath	gentry: gent	21-Mar-69	374	B.L. 15, 636 f. 38	3689
Jeffreys, John	Dublin, the city	gentry: esquire	29-Aug-63	600	B.L. 15, 635 f. 112a	3455
Jellose, Laughlin	Meath, Jelloston	gentry: gent	21-Feb-12	60	Dc1/112v	698
Jellose, Stephen	Meath, Jelonston	gentry: gent	16-Feb-00	60	Dc1/21v	144
Jellose, Stephen	Meath, Jellonston	gentry: gent	24-Jun-13	120	Dc1/123r	763
Jephson, John	Cork, Moyallow	gentry: esquire	27-Apr-77	1160	B.L. 19, 844 f. 126	3255
Jephson, John	Cork, Malloe	gentry: knight	03-Dec-09	600	Dc1/93v	585
Jephson, John	Cork, Malloe	gentry: knight	02-Jun-15	2000	Dc1/138r	856
Jephson, John	Cork, Moyallow	gentry: esquire	22-Oct-67	1200	B.L. 15, 635 f. 212a	3630
Jephson, John	Cork, Moyallow	gentry: esquire	20-Jan-69	220	B.L. 15, 636 f. 31	3679
Johns, George	Dublin	trade: apothecary	30-Mar-17	200	Dc2/5v	896
Johns, John	Carlow, Catherlogh	gentry: gent	10-Jul-18	500	Dc2/15v	947
Johnston, Elias	Dublin	merchant	04-Jul-33	240	Dc2/197r	1891
Johnston, John	Tyrone, Clare	gentry: gent	22-Jun-78	2000	B.L. 19, 844 f. 164	3295
Johnston, John	Tyrone, Clare	gentry: gent	22-Jun-78	2400	B.L. 19, 844 f. 165	3296
Jones, Ambrose		gentry: esquire, s/heir Oliver	14-Jun-76	1000	B.L. 19, 844 f. 97	3224
Jones, Ambrose		gentry: esquire, s/heir Oliver	14-Jun-76	1000	Dc3/176av	2666
Jones, Ambrose	Limerick, the city	gentry: esquire	28-Jun-83	1790	B.L. 15, 637 f. 76	3985
Jones, Ambrose	Tipperary, Cashell, the city	gentry: gent	05-Sep-80	822	B.L. 15, 637 f. 39a	3917
Jones, Arthur	Kildare, Osbaldstow	gentry: knight, s./heir Theophilus	22-Jun-76	1000	B.L . 19, 844 f.106	3233

Standard	County	Occupation	Date	Amount	MS No	Ident No
Jones, Arthur	Meath?	peer: viscount Ranelagh	15-Dec-53	2000	B.L. 19, 843 f. 135a	2985
Jones, Arthur	Kildare, Asbalstowne	gentry: knight, s/h Sir Theophilus	22-Jun-76	1000	Dc3/178r	2669
Jones, Arthur	Dublin, the city	gentry: knight, s./heir Theophilus	13-Dec-77	900	B.L. 19, 844 f. 143	3274
Jones, Arthur	Dublin, the city	gentry: knight, s./heir Theophilus	13-Dec-77	900	Dc3/184r	2699
Jones, Arthur	Kildare, Osbaldstowne	gentry: knight, s./heir Theophilus	22-Jun-76	1000	B.L. 19, 844 f. 101	3228
Jones, Arthur	Kildare, Asbalstowne	gentry: son/heir of Sir Theophilus	22-Jun-76	1000	Dc3/178r	2670
Jones, Arthur	Meath?	peer: viscount Ranelagh	13-Jul-61	1400	B.L. 15, 635 f. 77	3395
Jones, George	Dublin	trade: apothecary	25-Jul-18	310	Dc2/16r	948
Jones, Henry		prof: dean of Ardagh	31-Oct-36	700	Dc2/256v	2151
Jones, Henry	Dublin, the city	prof: doctor in divinity	06-Aug-55	1600	B.L. 19, 843 f. 159	3033
Jones, Henry		prof: bishop of Meath	18-Jul-66	130	Dc3/34	2298
Jones, Jane	Tipperary, Cashell, the city	gentry: wife of Ambrose	05-Sep-80	822	B.L. 15, 637 f. 39a	3917
Jones, Oliver	Carlow, Laughlinsbridge	gentry: esquire	06-Feb-55	172	B.L. 19, 843 f. 151a	3017
Jones, Owen	Dublin, the city	merchant	17-Jun-68	300	Dc3/78	2403
Jones, Owen	Dublin, the city	merchant	17-Jun-68	300	B.L. 15, 635 f. 219a	3644
Jones, Richard	Dublin, the city	gentry: esquire	22-Oct-69	400	Dc3/103	2449
Jones, Richard	Meath?	peer: viscount Ranelagh	07-Oct-70	3000	Dc3/check	2494
Jones, Richard	Meath?	peer: viscount Ranelagh	06-Oct-70	2200	Dc3/125	2492
Jones, Richard	Meath?	peer: viscount Ranelagh	06-Oct-70	2200	Dc3/126	2493
Jones, Richard	Meath, Durhamston?	gentry: s/h of vis Ranelagh	13-Jul-61	1400	B.L. 15, 635 f. 77	3395
Jones, Roger	Dublin, the city	gentry: gent	18-May-68	300	Dc3/75	2395
Jones, Theophilus	Kildare, Osbaldstowne	gentry: knight	22-Jun-76	1000	B.L. 19, 844 f. 101	3228
Jones, Theophilus	Kildare, Asbalstowne	gentry: knight	22-Jun-76	1000	Dc3/178r	2670
Jones, Theophilus	Kildare, Osbaldstowne	gentry: knight	28-Apr-75	2800	B.L. 19, 844 f. 58	3182
Jones, Theophilus	Dublin, the city	gentry: knight	13-Dec-77	900	Dc3/184r	2699
Jones, Theophilus	Dublin, the city	gentry: knight	05-Dec-66	1600	Dc3/43	2321
Jones, Theophilus	Kildare, Osbaldstowne	gentry: knight	22-Jun-76	1000	B.L . 19, 844 f.106	3233
Jones, Theophilus	Kildare, Osbaldstowne	gentry: knight	28-Apr-75	2800	Dc3/167r	2632
Jones, Theophilus	Dublin, the city	gentry: knight	13-Dec-77	900	B.L. 19, 844 f. 143	3274
Jones, Theophilus	Kildare, Asbalstowne	gentry: knight	22-Jun-76	1000	Dc3/178r	2669
Jones, Walter	Dublin, the city	gentry: esquire	18-Aug-69	1000	Dc3/102	2446
Jones, Walter	Dublin, the city	gentry: esquire	18-Aug-69	1000	B.L. 15, 636 f. 42	3697
Jones, William	Louth, Stabbannan	gentry: esquire	13-Nov-57	240	B.L. 19, 843 f. 200	3106
Jordan, Nicholas	Dublin, Ballymagwier	gentry: gent	04-Jul-14	40	Dc1/130v	811
Jordan, Richard	Dublin, Swordes	gentry: son/heir of Walter	09-Jul-39	400	B.L. 19, 843 f. 26a	2771
Jordan, Richard	Dublin, Swords	gentry: gent	06-Feb-99	300	Dc1/15r	105
Jordan, Walter	Dublin, Swordes	gentry: gent	09-Jul-39	400	B.L. 19, 843 f. 26a	2771

Standard	County	Occupation	Date	Amount	MS No	Ident No
Karle?, Rory	Donegal, Tirechonylle	peer: earl of Tyrconnell	23-Apr-04	2006	Dc1/52v	332
Kavanagh, Arthur	Wexford, Newton	gentry: gent	11-Mar-07	58	Dc1/75v	459
Kavanagh, Arthur	Carlow, Ballyenlaghlin	gentry: gent	29-Nov-39	1000	B.L. 19, 843 f. 47a	2813
Kavanagh, Arthur	Queen's Co., Ballytaggart	gentry: gent	02-Sep-39	1000	B.L. 19, 843 f. 32a	2783
Kavanagh, Brian	Carlow, Ballycormucke	gentry: gent	12-Nov-14	40	Dc1/132v	823
Kavanagh, Darby	Wexford, Tinkarry	gentry: gent	25-Nov-28	700	Dc2/117r	1547
Kavanagh, Darby	Wexford, Tinekurrie	gentry: gent	01-Dec-27	300	Dc2/101v	1471
Kavanagh, Dermot	Wexford, Tennorry	gentry: gent	02-May-27	50	Dc2/91v	1429
Kavanagh, Donnel	Carlow, Clonmullen	gentry: gent	02-May-01	74	Dc1/31r	204
Kavanagh, Donogh	Wexford, Ballingarry	gentry: gent	14-Jun-30	120	Dc2/150v	1701
Kavanagh, Donogh	Wexford, Ballingarry	gentry: gent	13-Jun-30	300	Dc2/150v	1700
Kavanagh, Edward	Wexford, Kilmehill	gentry: gent	23-Nov-30	100	Dc2/157r	1729
Kavanagh, Edward	Wexford, Kilmeehell	gentry: gent	14-Feb-32	120	Dc2/176r	1808
Kavanagh, Griffin	Carlow, Dromgeene	gentry: gent	13-Jun-30	300	Dc2/150v	1700
Kavanagh, Griffin	Carlow, Dromgeene	gentry: gent	14-Jun-30	120	Dc2/150v	1701
Kavanagh, Humphry	Wexford, Garreduffe	gentry: gent	02-May-27	50	Dc2/91v	1429
Kavanagh, Maurice	Carlow, Knockullard	gentry: gent	18-Nov-25	600	Dc2/70r	1320
Kavanagh, Morgan	Carlow, Clonemullen	gentry: knight	14-Jul-37	1200	Dc2/268v	2204
Kavanagh, Morgan	Carlow, Clanmullin	gentry: knight	20-Dec-24	220	Dc2/227v	2015
Kavanagh, Morgan	Carlow, Pulmontye	gentry: gent	10-Dec-04	100	Dc1/54r	339
Kavanagh, Morgan	Carlow, Clonmullin	gentry: knight	07-Feb-31	600	Dc2/159v	1740
Kavanagh, Mulmorry	Wexford, Couleroe	gentry: brother of Walter	06-Aug-34	100	Dc2/216v	1971
Kavanagh, Murrough	Carlow, Castletowne	gentry: gent	20-Feb-40	700	B.L. 19, 843 f. 52a	2823
Kavanagh, Murrough	Wexford, Cloghney	gentry: gent	11-Jul-22	120	Dc2/41v	1116
Kavanagh, Murrough	Carlow, Burreis	gentry: esquire	18-Nov-25	600	Dc2/70r	1320
Kavanagh, Murrough	Carlow, Polmontye	gentry: esquire	06-May-07	300	Dc1/76r	462
Kavanagh, Walter	Wexford, Couleroe	gentry: gent	06-Aug-34	100	Dc2/216v	1971
Kearney, Christopher	Louth, Drogheda	merchant	30-Jul-99	200	Dc1/18r	125
Kearney, Edmund	Limerick, Kilmallocke		23-Nov-14	300	Dc1/132v	825
Kearney, Patrick	Limerick, Kilmallocke		23-Nov-14	300	Dc1/132v	825
Kearns, John	Tyrone, Aghronan	gentry: gent	20-Jun-78	200	Dc3/191v	2722
Keating, Arthur	Wexford, Kilcowan	gentry: gent	13-Feb-32	320	Dc2/175v	1807
Keating, Arthur	Wexford, Kilcowan	gentry: esquire	05-Mar-34	200	Dc2/208v	1939
Keating, Gerald	Kildare, Castlewarning	gentry: gent	16-Feb-30	600	Dc2/142v	1668
Keating, Gerald	Kildare, Castlewaring	gentry: gent	12-Dec-29	600	Dc2/140r	1655
Keating, Maurice	Dublin, the city	gentry: esquire	27-Jul-63	430	B.L. 15, 635 f. 109a	3449
Keating, Maurice	Dublin, the city	gentry: gent	22-Aug-59	120	B.L. 15, 635 f. 55a	3362
Keating, Redmond	Queen's Co., Clonoghe	gentry: gent	03-Feb-15	300	Dc1/135r	838
Keating, Richard	Tipperary, Mourstowne	gentry: gent?	05-Mar-39	400	B.L. 19, 843 f. 20	2758
Keating, Thomas	Queen's Co., Crottentegill	gentry: gent	24-Nov-36	420	Dc2/257v	2157
Keating, William	Meath, Possockstowne	farmer: freeholder	11-May-11	60	Dc1/104r	650
Keeffe, Arthur	Cork, Dromagh	gentry: gent	28-May-13	40	Dc1/121r	751
Keeffe, Arthur	Cork, Dromagh	gentry: gent	06-Dec-14	148	Dc1/133v	829
Keeffe, Arthur	Cork, Dromagh?	gentry: gent	08-Jun-13	60	Dc1/121v	756
Keeffe, Arthur	Cork, Dromaghe	gentry: gent	01-Jun-13	200	Dc1/121r	753

Standard	County	Occupation	Date	Amount	MS No	Ident No
Keegan, Carbery	?, Ffurlough, Corbegge	gentry: gent	16-May-29	80	Dc2/129r	1605
Kelly, Coll	Galway, Moylagh	gentry: esquire	18-May-07	440	Dc1/76v	467
Kelly, David	Mayo, Donnamonoe	gentry: gent	30-Jun-36	400	Dc2/254r	2138
Kelly, David	Mayo, Donnamoune	gentry: gent	01-Jun-36	400	B.L. 19, 843 f. 38	2794
Kelly, David	Mayo, Donnamonoe	gentry: gent	30-Jun-36	400	Dc2/253v	2137
Kelly, Edmund	Roscommon, Glannetobber	gentry: gent	14-May-32	40	Dc2/180v	1826
Kelly, Feardorcha	Galway, Agherin o Maurye	gentry: esquire	18-May-07	440	Dc1/76v	467
Kelly, Nicholas	Dublin, the city	merchant	28-Sep-24	200	Dc2/58r	1239
Kelly, Nicholas	Dublin		06-Nov-27	140	Dc2/99r	1461
Kelly, Owen	Dublin, the city	trade: smith	20-Jun-65	800	Dc3/10	2244
Kelly, Robert	Dublin, the city	merchant	20-Jun-65	800	Dc3/10	2244
Kelly, William	Galway, Killawogy	gentry: gent	25-Aug-27	120	Dc2/98v	1457
Kelly, William	Galway, Killinoggy	gentry: gent	26-Aug-29	320	Dc2/136r	1636
Kennagh, Robert	Kildare, the Naace	merchant	03-Mar-05	110	Dc1/57r	350
Kennan, Towle	Monaghan, Dawagh/ Mullaghdawagh	gentry: gent	08-Feb-20	120	Dc2/28v	1020
Kennedy, Dermot	Tipperary, Donnally	gentry: gent?	19-Sep-16	200	Dc2/1r	870
Kennedy, George	Dublin, the city	merchant	31-May-82	1400	B.L. 15, 637 f. 61	3957
Kennedy, George	Dublin, the city	merchant	12-Jun-82	1000	B.L. 15, 637 f. 60	3955
Kennedy, John	Dublin	gentry: gent	12-Mar-31	500	Dc2/161r	1747
Kennedy, John	Dublin, the city	gentry: gent	17-Dec-32	100	Dc2/188v	1858
Kennedy, John	Dublin, the city	gentry: gent	04-Apr-43	100	B.L. 19, 843 f. 112a	2944
Kennedy, John	Dublin, the city	gentry: gent	04-Nov-36	2000	Dc2/256v	2152
Kennedy, John	Dublin	gentry: esquire	30-Jun-25	200	Dc2/67v	1303
Kennedy, John	Dublin, the city	gentry: gent	10-Jun-35	100	Dc2/236v	2053
Kennedy, John	Dublin, the city	gentry: gent	30-May-36	60	Dc2/252v	2129
Kennedy, John	Dublin, the city	gentry: gent	01-Mar-36	1000	Dc2/246v	2102
Kennedy, John	Dublin, the city	gentry: gent	18-Dec-30	100	Dc2/158r	1735
Kennedy, Keadagh	Tipperary, Killykarren	gentry: gent	19-Sep-16	200	Dc2/1r	870
Kennedy, Robert	Dublin, the city		04-Dec-22	200	Dc2/43v	1129
Kennedy, Thomas	Dublin, the city	gentry: esquire	05-Apr-76	220	B.L. 19, 844 f. 89	3216
Kennedy, Thomas	Dublin, the city	gentry: esquire	05-Apr-76	220	Dc3/173r	2653
Kennedy, Walter	Dublin, the city	merchant	04-Dec-22	200	Dc2/43v	1129
Kennedy, William	Longford, Mollogh	gentry: esquire	04-May-64	112	B.L. 15, 635 f. 134	3493
Kennedy, William	Longford, Mullogh	gentry: esquire	09-Jun-62	232	B.L. 15, 635 f. 98	3430
Kennington, Thomas	Louth, Drogheda	merchant	18-Jul-54	192	B.L. 19, 843 f. 150	3014
Kenny, James	Dublin, the city	merchant	01-Aug-37	200	Dc2/270r	2212
Kenny, Nicholas	Dublin, Newcastle near Lyons?	gentry: gent	26-May-01	300	Dc1/32v	214
Kenny, Nicholas	Dublin	gentry: gent	27-Apr-97	100	Dc1/3r	19
Kenny, Richard	Dublin, county of city Dublin	gentry: esquire	26-Feb-99	60	Dc1/15v	108
Kent, Alexander	Meath, Ffreffans	gentry: gent	05-Feb-33	200	Dc2/191r	1867
Kent, Alexander	Meath, the Navan	gentry: gent	28-Apr-29	500	Dc2/127v	1599
Kent, Hugh	Meath, the Navan	merchant	28-Apr-29	500	Dc2/127v	1599

Standard	County	Occupation	Date	Amount	MS No	Ident No
Kent, Nicholas	Meath, Rathowne	gentry: gent	19-Jun-29	100	Dc2/133v	1623
Kent, Thomas	Meath, Dainston	gentry: gent	04-Dec-02	400	Dc1/41v	267
Kent, Thomas	Meath, Danistowne	gentry: gent	07-Jul-41	200	B.L. 19, 843 f. 105	2929
Kent, Thomas	Meath, Dainston	gentry: gent	31-Aug-05	600	Dc1/61v	374
Kent, Thomas	Meath, Dainstowne	gentry: gent	10-Aug-97	240	Dc1/6r	46
Kent, Thomas	Meath, Daneston	gentry: gent	25-Apr-08	300	Dc1/82r	509
Kent, Thomas	Meath, Daneston	gentry: gent	21-Jun-00	400	Dc1/24v	165
Kent, Thomas	Meath, Danestowne	gentry: gent	19-Jun-29	100	Dc2/133v	1623
Kent, Thomas	Meath, Daniston	gentry: gent	05-Feb-33	200	Dc2/191r	1867
Kent, Thomas	Meath, Danestowne	gentry: gent	28-Apr-29	500	Dc2/127v	1599
Kent, Thomas	Meath, Daniston	gentry: esquire	07-Jul-09	100	Dc1/90r	562
Kent, Thomas	Meath, Downeston?	gentry: gent	21-Apr-08	30	Dc1/81r	507
Keogh, Elizabeth	Dublin, Ballenmraher?	gentry: widow	08-Feb-03	200	Dc1/44r	281
Keppock, Stephen	Louth, Atherdie	gentry: gent	02-Jun-97	200	Dc1/4r	29
Keppock, Thomas	Louth, Atherdee	gentry: gent	19-Jul-34	500	Dc2/215r	1964
Keppock, Thomas	Louth, Atherdy	gentry: gent	30-Apr-35	200	Dc2/234r	2043
Keppock, Thomas	Louth, Atherdee	gentry: gent	01-Apr-34	400	Dc2/210r	1944
Keppock, Thomas	Louth, Atherdy	gentry: gent	28-Apr-35	600	Dc2/234r	2042
Keppock, Thomas	Louth, Atherdee	gentry: gent	24-Oct-35	200	Dc2/239v	2067
Kerdiff, James	Kildare, Keardiffestowne	gentry: gent	07-Dec-27	1000	Dc2/101v	1473
Kerdiff, John	Meath, Ratowth	gentry: gent	05-Mar-23	60	Dc2/46r	1147
Kerdiff, John	Meath, Rataoth	gentry: gent	14-Feb-12	100	Dc1/112v	697
Kiernan, Phelim	Cavan, Cloan	gentry: gent	04-Dec-28	600	Dc2/120r	1562
Kiernan, Thomas	Dublin, Newrow	gentry: gent	21-Feb-83	1800	B.L. 15, 637 f. 77	3987
Kilpatrick, Dermot	Wicklow, Kilmacurra	gentry: gent	22-May-41	300	B.L. 19, 843 f. 90	2899
Kindelon, Edward	Meath, Ballenekill	gentry: gent	23-Nov-10	40	Dc1/100v	631
King, Bascocke	Dublin, the city	gentry: son/heir of Henry	05-Feb-05	628	Dc1/56r	346
King, Bascocke	Dublin	gentry: son/heir of Henry	14-Nov-06	300	Dc1/71r	431
King, Bascocke	Dublin?	gentry: son of Henry	27-Apr-03	500	Dc1/46v	295
King, George	Dublin, Clontarffe	gentry: gent	14-Feb-15	1000	Dc1/135v	840
King, George	Dublin, Clontarfe	gentry: gent	11-Feb-25	300	Dc2/61v	1264
King, George	Dublin, Clontarffe	gentry: gent	07-Nov-99	200	Dc1/19v	133
King, George	Dublin, Clontarffe	gentry: esquire	12-Jun-29	400	Dc2/131v	1615
King, George	Dublin, Clontarfe	gentry: esquire	15-Mar-27	700	Dc2/89v	1422
King, George	Dublin, Clontarf	gentry: esquire	04-Apr-26	400	Dc2/76v	1358
King, George	Dublin, Clontarfe	gentry: esquire	02-Apr-29	1000	Dc2/127r	1595
King, George	Dublin, Clontarfe	gentry: esquire	01-Jul-29	120	Dc2/135r	1630
King, George	Dublin, Clontarf	gentry: gent	30-Sep-01	300	Dc1/33v	223
King, Henry	Dublin, the city	gentry: gent	05-Feb-05	628	Dc1/56r	346
King, Henry	Meath, Ardnemolon	gentry: gent	07-Nov-99	200	Dc1/19v	133
King, Henry	Dublin, St. Mary's Abbey		30-Sep-01	300	Dc1/33v	223
King, Henry	Dublin	gentry: gent	14-Nov-06	300	Dc1/71r	431
King, Henry	Dublin	gentry: gent	27-Apr-03	500	Dc1/46v	295

Standard	County	Occupation	Date	Amount	MS No	Ident No
King, John	Dublin, Dunnakerny	gentry: gent	04-Apr-26	400	Dc2/76v	1358
King, John	Dublin	gentry: gent?	24-Dec-03	2508	Dc1/50v	325
King, John	Dublin, Clontarfe	gentry: son/heir of George	11-Feb-25	300	Dc2/61v	1264
King, John	Dublin, Clontarfe	gentry: gent	14-May-34	1600	Dc2/211r	1949
King, John	Dublin, Dunakerny	gentry: gent	17-Oct-22	200	Dc2/42v	1124
King, John	Roscommon?	peer: baron Kingston	12-Jun-67	2000	Dc3/62	2359
King, John	Dublin, Clontarffe	gentry: son/heir of George	14-Feb-15	1000	Dc1/135v	840
King, John	Dublin	gentry: gent?	25-Nov-03	4180	Dc1/49v	319
King, John	Roscommon?	peer: baron Kingston	14-Mar-66	1800	Dc3/25	2278
King, John	Dublin, Clontarfe	gentry: son/heir of George	15-Mar-27	700	Dc2/89v	1422
King, John	Dublin, Clontarffe	gentry: son/heir of George	12-Jun-29	400	Dc2/131v	1615
King, John	Roscommon, Abbyboyle	gentry: esquire	08-Jul-57	400	B.L. 19, 843 f. 195	3097
King, John	Roscommon?	peer: baron Kingston	10-Jun-61	2000	B.L. 15, 635 f. 70a	3385
King, John	Roscommon?	peer: baron Kingston	14-Mar-66	1800	B.L. 15, 635 f. 169a	3550
King, John	Roscommon?	peer: baron Kingston	12-Jun-67	2000	B.L. 15, 635 f. 192a	3595
King, John	Roscommon?	peer: baron Kingston	30-Aug-62	2500	B.L. 15, 635 f. 94	3422
King, Murrough	King's Co., Keppoghdonnill	gentry: gent	02-Nov-03	80	Dc1/50r	321
King, Robert	Roscommon, Boyle	gentry: knight	20-Nov-28	800	Dc2/118v	1556
King, Robert	Roscommon, Abbayboyle	gentry: knight	07-Apr-30	1500	Dc2/144r	1674
Kinsella, Donogh	Wexford, Ballyteige	gentry: gent	06-Dec-39	300	B.L. 19, 843 f. 37	2792
Kitchinman, John	Dublin, the city	gentry: gent	16-Feb-58	500	B.L. 15, 635 f. 27a	3310
Kitchinman, John	Dublin, the city	gentry: gent	22-Oct-61	600	B.L. 15, 635 f. 85a	3407
Knight, Nicholas	Dublin, the city	gentry: esquire	05-Aug-65	100	Dc3/13	2249
Knight, Nicholas	Dublin, the city	gentry: esquire	30-Jul-70	700	Dc3/123	2488
Knowde, James	Kerry, the Abbey of Dorney?	gentry: gent	19-Feb-14	240	Dc1/127r	787
Knowles, James	Carlow, Caterlagh	merchant	29-Nov-12	200	Dc1/117r	726
Knox, Thomas	Wexford, Taguman	gentry: esquire	11-Dec-80	800	B.L. 15, 637 f. 41	3920
Kyan, Denis	Westmeath, Mollingarr	merchant	13-Nov-06	40	Dc1/71r	429
Kyan, James	Meath, Cossanstowne		09-Mar-81	200	B.L. 15, 637 f. 43a	3925
Kyrle, Richard	Cork, Dromynyne	soldier: captain	16-May-57	1200	B.L. 19, 843 f. 198	3103
Kyrle, Richard	Cork, Clonmeene	gentry: knight	02-Aug-78	400	B.L. 19, 844 f.172	3303
Kyrle, Richard	Cork, Dromynyne	gentry: esquire	29-Mar-60	1400	B.L. 15, 635 f. 65	3379
Kyrle, Richard	Cork, Dromginne	gentry: esquire	03-May-59	800	B.L. 15, 636 f. 76	3754
Labitte?, Robert	Kildare, Goodwingston	gentry: gent	05-Jul-20	200	Dc2/31v	1041
Lambert, Charles	Westmeath?	peer: baron Cavan	08-Mar-28	400	Dc2/105v	1492
Lambert, Charles	Westmeath, Kilbeggan	peer: lord Lambert, s of earl of Cavan	04-Mar-74	2000	B.L. 19, 844 f. 27	3150
Lambert, Charles	Westmeath?	peer: baron Cavan, ld Lambert	03-Mar-28	860	Dc2/105r	1490

Standard	County	Occupation	Date	Amount	MS No	Ident No
Lambert, Charles	Westmeath, Kilbeggan	peer:				
		son/heir of earl Cavan	18-Jul-74	1000	B.L. 19, 844 f. 43	3167
Lambert, Charles	Westmeath, Kilbegan	peer: lord Lambert	04-Mar-74	2000	Dc3/160v	2605
Lambert, Charles	Westmeath?	peer:				
		son/heir of earl Cavan	18-Jul-74	1000	Dc3/162v	2615
Lambert, Charles	Westmeath?	peer: earl of Cavan	20-Sep-59	230	B.L. 15, 635 f. 53a	3358
Lambert, Oliver	Westmeath, Kibeggon	gentry: knight	22-Nov-16	500	Dc2/2v	880
Lambert, Richard	Westmeath?	peer: earl of Cavan	12-May-65	10000	Dc3/5	2232
Lambert, Thomas	Dublin, Balrothery	gentry: gent	05-Mar-00	200	Dc1/21v	145
Lane, Richard	Roscommon, Ballyoughter	gentry: esquire	20-Nov-28	800	Dc2/118v	1556
Lane, Richard	Roscommon, Ballyougther	gentry: esquire	30-Nov-28	1000	Dc2/119r	1557
Lane, Richard	Roscommon, Tulske	gentry: esquire	12-Mar-55	700	B.L. 19, 843 f. 157	3028
Lane, Richard	Roscommon, Ballyoughter	gentry: esquire	30-Nov-28	1200	Dc2/119r	1558
Lang, Richard	Roscommon, Ballyoughter	gentry: esquire	05-Feb-30	200	Dc2/141v	1662
Langley, Henry	Waterford, Grenan	gentry: gent	06-Jun-56	242	B.L. 19, 843 f. 172a	3057
Langton, Nicholas	Kilkenny	merchant	18-Feb-07	750	Dc1/75r	455
Largan, William	Kildare, the Nase	trade: tanner	06-Jun-00	40	Dc1/24r	160
Large, James	Cavan, Tullocullen	gentry: gent	08-Mar-28	400	Dc2/105v	1492
Large, James	Cavan, Tullecullen	gentry: gent	03-Mar-28	860	Dc2/105r	1490
Large, James	Cavan, Tullocullin	gentry: gent	12-Feb-24	1000	Dc2/53v	1202
Lattin, William	Kildare, Morristowne	gentry: gent	28-Jun-72	160	Dc3/147r	2557
Lattin, William	Kildare, Morristowne	gentry: gent	28-Jun-72	160	B.L. 15, 636 f. 111a	3813
Lawless, John	Queen's Co., Ley	gentry: gent	06-Dec-22	200	Dc2/43v	1131
Leach, Edmund	Dublin, the city	gentry: esquire	03-Jul-57	500	B.L. 19, 843 f. 194	3095
Leary, Donald	Cork, Carriggny Gillagh	gentry: gent	16-Mar-28	180	B.L. 19, 843 f. 19a	2757
Ledwich, Hubbert	Westmeath, Kappagh	gentry: gent	01-Feb-28	100	Dc2/103v	1481
Ledwich, John	Meath, Cookstowne	gentry: son/heir of				
		Richard	10-Feb-30	400	Dc2/141v	1663
Ledwich, John	Meath, Cookestowne	gentry: son/heir of				
		Richard	22-Jun-26	360	Dc2/79r	1375
Ledwich, Richard	Meath, Cookestowne	gentry: gent	22-Jun-26	360	Dc2/79r	1375
Ledwich, Richard	Meath, Cookestowne	gentry: gent	22-Jun-26	360	Dc2/79v	1378
Ledwich, Richard	Meath, Cookstowne	gentry: gent	10-Feb-30	400	Dc2/141v	1663
Lee, Arthur	Tyrone, Ffentenagh	gentry:				
		knight and baronet	25-Apr-35	120	Dc2/234r	2041
Lee, Arthur	Tyrone, Ffentenagh	gentry: baronet	24-Jul-34	400	Dc2/215r	1965
Lee, Emanuel	Tyrone, Lysmore	gentry: esquire	27-Jun-25	500	Dc2/66v	1299
Lee, James	Meath, Clonross	gentry: gent	18-Jun-99	200	Dc1/17v	119
Lee, James	Meath, Clonross	gentry: gent	02-Jul-99	200	Dc1/18r	123
Lee, James	Meath, Clonross	gentry: gent	17-Jul-99	200	Dc1/18r	122
Lee, John	Tyrone, Ffentonagh	gentry: esquire	07-Jul-28	240	Dc2/112v	1526
Lee, Thomas	Louth, Drogheda		30-Aug-71	200	Dc3/140r	2530
Leech, Edmund	Dublin, the city	merchant	01-Jul-64	580	B.L. 15, 635 f. 143a	3506
Leicester, John	King's Co., Kilcarmicke	gentry: gent	10-Nov-65	240	Dc3/15	2255
Leicester, John	King's Co., Kilcarmick	gentry: gent	10-Nov-65	240	B.L. 15, 635 f. 158	3533

Standard	County	Occupation	Date	Amount	MS No	Ident No
Leicester, Robert	King's Co., Clonfrill?	gentry: esquire	19-Nov-31	200	Dc2/171v	1789
Leinagh, Edmund	Mayo, the Neale	gentry: gent	18-Jul-31	80	Dc2/166v	1771
Lennon, Patrick	Dublin	trade: shoemaker	10-Jun-03	400	Dc1/47r	300
Leonard, John	Kilkenny, Tybraghnie	gentry: esquire	28-Jun-28	200	Dc2/111v	1521
Leslie, Charles	Monaghan, Castle Leslie		15-May-83	1200	B.L. 15, 637 f. 72	3977
Leslie, John	Monaghan?	prof: bishop of Clogher	31-Jan-65	1000	Dc3/2	2224
Leslie, John	Monaghan, Castle Lesley	prof: bishop of Clogher?	15-Feb-73	600	Dc3/153v	2575
Leslie, John	Monaghan, Castleleslie	prof: bishop of Clogher	17-Dec-64	1000	B.L. 15, 635 f. 151a	3522
Leslie, John	Monaghan, Castlelesley		15-Feb-73	600	B.L. 15, 636 f. 124	3831
Leslie, John	Monaghan, Castle Leslie	prof: deacon of Dromore	15-May-83	1200	B.L. 15, 637 f. 72	3977
Leslie, William	Antrim, Dunluce	gentry: esquire	20-Aug-74	600	B.L. 19, 844 f. 32	3156
Lester, Robert	Dublin	gentry: gent	27-Jan-97	200	Dc1/1r	1
Lester, Thomas	Galway, Millick	gentry: esquire	26-Nov-27	160	Dc2/100v	1467
Lestrange, Thomas	Roscommon, Castlestrandge	gentry: esquire	24-Nov-26	1000	Dc2/83r	1396
Lestrange, William	Queen's Co., Castelcuffe	gentry: esquire	08-Nov-75	2000	Dc3/168v	2640
Lestrange, William	Queen's Co., Castlecuffe	gentry: esquire	13-Jun-73	300	Dc3/157v	2585
Lestrange, William	Queen's Co., Castlecuffe	gentry: esquire	28-Jun-72	220	Dc3/147r	2556
Lestrange, William	Queen's Co., Castle Cuffe	gentry: esquire	08-Nov-75	1000	B.L. 19, 844 f. 86	3214
Levion, Thomas	Dublin	gentry: gent	22-Nov-31	264	Dc2/172r	1792
Lewis, Nicholas	Dublin, the city	merchant	25-Aug-34	200	Dc2/217v	1975
Leyne, Gerald	Meath, Donower	gentry: gent	17-Apr-35	1500	Dc2/233r	2037
Leyne, Peter	Dublin, the city	merchant	21-Jan-74	800	Dc3/159v	2599
Leyne, Turlough	Carlow, Carrickneslane	gentry: gent	12-Nov-34	400	Dc2/221r	1989
Lilly, Nicholas	Dublin, the city	trade: tailor	17-Dec-40	700	B.L. 19, 843 f. 117a	2954
Lincoll, Robert	Waterford	merchant	05-Aug-18	100	Dc2/16r	950
Lindsay, Andrew	Monaghan, Castleleslie	gentry: esquire	10-Feb-70	800	Dc3/114	2468
Lindsay, Andrew	Monaghan, Castleleslie	gentry: esquire	10-Feb-70	800	B.L. 15, 636 f. 63a	3730
Lloyd, Andrew	Dublin, the city	gentry: esquire, s. And Ashton	27-Jul-54	600	B.L. 19, 843 f. 151	3016
Lloyd, Trevor	King's Co., Tomagh	gentry: esquire	18-May-69	200	Dc3/97	2436
Locke, John	Dublin, the city	trade: tanner	30-Aug-25	200	Dc2/69r	1313
Locke, John	Dublin, Colmanstowne	gentry: gent	09-May-63	240	B.L. 15, 635 f. 104a	3441
Locke, Patrick	Dublin, the city	trade: tanner	11-Feb-56	216	B.L. 19, 843 f. 182a	3072
Locke, Thomas	Dublin, Aderge	farmer	31-Jul-01	400	Dc1/33v	221
Loftus, Adam	Dublin, Rathfarnam	gentry: esquire	04-Jul-67	9000	Dc3/64	2365
Loftus, Adam	Dublin?	gentry: knight	31-Jul-28	1600	Dc2/113v	1532
Loftus, Adam	Dublin, Rathfarnam	gentry: knight	05-May-45	800	B.L. 19, 843 f.119	2957
Loftus, Adam	Dublin, Rathfarnam	gentry: knight	02-May-31	2000	Dc2/162r	1751
Loftus, Adam	King's Co., Ely	gentry: knight	17-Jul-39	4000	B.L. 19, 843 f. 22a	2763
Loftus, Adam	Dublin, Dromnegh	gentry: knight	02-Mar-08	2000	Dc1/81v	504
Loftus, Adam	Dublin, Rathfarnam	gentry: knight	02-Mar-35	800	Dc2/230r	2026
Loftus, Adam	Dublin, Rathfarnan	gentry: knight, s./heir Dudley	08-Feb-11	3000	Dc1/103r	643
Loftus, Adam	Dublin, Rathfarnam	gentry: knight	23-Jun-29	2000	Dc2/134v	1628

Standard	County	Occupation	Date	Amount	MS No	Ident No
Loftus, Adam	Dublin, Rathfarnam	gentry: knight	22-May-30	220	Dc2/148r	1691
Loftus, Adam	Dublin, Rathfarnam	gentry: knight	22-Jun-35	1600	Dc2/237v	2060
Loftus, Arthur	Wexford, Kilclogan	gentry: knight	02-Mar-35	800	Dc2/230r	2026
Loftus, Arthur	Wexford, Kilclogan	gentry: knight	22-Jun-35	1600	Dc2/237v	2060
Loftus, Dudley	Meath, Killian	gentry: knight	22-Nov-31	400	Dc2/171v	1791
Loftus, Dudley	Dublin, the city	prof: doctor of law	30-Sep-69	600	Dc3/103	2448
Loftus, Dudley	Dublin, the city	gentry: knight	29-May-45	100	B.L. 19, 843 f. 120a	2960
Loftus, Dudley	Dublin, Rafarnam	gentry: knight	02-Mar-08	2000	Dc1/81v	504
Loftus, Dudley	Dublin, Rathfarnan	gentry: knight	08-Feb-11	3000	Dc1/103r	643
Loftus, Dudley	Dublin, the city	prof: doctor of law	30-Sep-69	600	B.L. 15, 636 f. 45a	3703
Loftus, Godfrey	Meath, Kilmone		20-Apr-14	120	Dc1/128v	800
Loftus, Godfrey	Meath, Kilmore	prof: parson of Kilmore	30-Nov-10	120	Dc1/101v	635
Loftus, Nicholas	Wexford, Kilcloggan	gentry: esquire	02-May-31	2000	Dc2/162r	1751
Loftus, Nicholas	Dublin, the city	gentry: esquire	01-Feb-33	600	Dc2/190v	1866
Loftus, Nicholas	Wexford, Kilclogan	gentry: esquire	22-May-30	220	Dc2/148r	1691
Loftus, Nicholas	Wexford, Kilclogan	gentry: esquire	23-Jun-29	2000	Dc2/134v	1628
Loftus, Nicholas	Dublin, the city	gentry: esquire	30-May-32	210	Dc2/181v	1829
Loftus, Nicholas	Dublin, the city	gentry: esquire	31-Jul-28	1600	Dc2/113v	1532
Loftus, Nicholas	Wexford, Ffetherd	gentry: esquire	20-Apr-54	1000	B.L. 19, 843 f. 137	2988
Loftus, Nicholas	Dublin, the city	gentry: esquire	22-Jun-35	1600	Dc2/237v	2060
Loftus, Nicholas	Dublin, Rathfarnan	gentry: son of Dudley	08-Feb-11	3000	Dc1/103r	643
Loftus, Nicholas	Dublin, the city	gentry: esquire	02-Mar-35	800	Dc2/230r	2026
Loftus, Nicholas	Dublin	gentry: esquire	03-Mar-34	800	Dc2/208r	1936
Loftus, Robert	Dublin	gentry: knight	11-Dec-33	880	Dc2/203v	1917
Loftus, Robert	Dublin, St Mary's Abbey	gentry: knight	24-Feb-36	2000	Dc2/245v	2098
Loftus, Robert	Monaghan, Clownes	gentry: knight	13-May-40	2200	B.L. 19, 843 f. 50	2818
Loftus, Samuel	Dublin, the city	gentry: gent	30-May-32	210	Dc2/181v	1829
Loftus, Thomas	Queen's Co., Temoghoe	gentry: knight	16-Apr-01	120	Dc1/30r	200
Loftus, Thomas	Queen's Co., Tymogho/e	gentry: knight	15-Dec-14	1000	Dc1/134r	833
Loftus, Thomas	Meath, Killain?	gentry: knight	20-Oct-06	220	Dc1/70v	427
Lombard, William	Cork, Gortinelire?	gentry: gent	29-May-67	300	B.L. 15, 635 f. 211	3627
Long, Bartholomew	Kildare, the Derr	gentry: gent	06-Feb-11	200	Dc1/102v	641
Long, Felix	Wexford, Ballineclash	gentry: esquire	27-Aug-66	320	Dc3/37	2308
Long, Felix	Wexford, Ballineclash	gentry: esquire	27-Aug-66	320	B.L. 15, 635 f. 179a	3568
Long, John	Dublin	merchant	12-Feb-03	600	Dc1/44v	284
Long, John	Dublin	merchant	18-Jun-99	100	Dc1/117r	115
Long, John	Dublin	merchant	19-Sep-01	200	Dc1/33v	222
Long, Martin	Kildare, Bowdenston	gentry: gent	24-Sep-17	400	Dc2/9v	912
Long, Patrick	Roscommon, Corskeagh	gentry: gent	22-Apr-57	80	B.L. 19, 843 f. 190a	3088
Long, Patrick	Dublin, Donsaghlee	farmer: yeoman	27-Nov-07	26	Dc1/80r	494
Losse, Ambrose	Dublin	gentry: esquire	02-Jul-35	400	Dc2/238v	2064
Loughlin, Turlough	Kilkenny, Dunmore	gentry: gent	05-Jul-20	200	Dc2/31v	1041
Lound, Lebbens	Louth, Drogheda		01-Apr-73	200	B.L. 15, 636 f. 126	3833
Lovett, Christopher	Dublin, the city		12-Nov-74	1000	B.L. 19, 844 f. 36	3160
Lovett, Christopher	Dublin, the city		12-Nov-74	1000	Dc3/163r	2617

Standard	County	Occupation	Date	Amount	MS No	Ident No
Lowe, Ebenezer	Westmeath, Newtown	gentry: gent	11-Jun-78	1400	Dc3/190v	2718
Lowe, Ebenezer	Westmeath, Newtowne	gentry: gent	11-Jun-78	1400	B.L. 19, 844 f. 159	3290
Lowe, Edward	Dublin	gentry: gent	20-Nov-29	100	Dc2/137v	1643
Lowe, George	Dublin	gentry: gent	08-Feb-12	86	Dc1/112r	694
Lowman, James	Kilkenny, Glannagowe?	gentry: gent	15-Apr-36	1600	Dc2/249v	2115
Lowman, James	Kilkenny, Glannagowe	gentry: gent	29-Aug-36	100	Dc2/255v	2147
Lowther, George	Meath, Skrine	gentry: gent	18-Aug-56	500	B.L. 19, 843 f. 180	3066
Lucy, John	Limerick, Cowlruse	gentry: gent	16-Dec-14	100	Dc1/134r	834
Lundy, Edward	Cork, Youghall	merchant	06-Feb-77	500	B.L. 19, 844 f. 120	3249
Luttrell, Henry	Kildare, Caraghbryne		23-Apr-97	90	Dc1/3r	18
Luttrell, John	Dublin	merchant	04-Apr-00	40	Dc1/2v	151
Luttrell, John	Dublin, Bussardeston	gentry: gent	16-May-07	20	Dc1/76v	465
Luttrell, John	Dublin	merchant	12-Jul-02	40	Dc1/38v	251
Luttrell, John	Dublin, Killeghe	gentry: gent	22-May-07	50	Dc1/77r	471
Luttrell, Oliver	Meath, Tanckardstowne	gentry: gent	19-Nov-31	500	Dc2/170v	1787
Luttrell, Richard	Kildare, the Naace	gentry: gent	07-May-14	100	Dc1/129r	801
Luttrell, Richard	Dublin	gentry: son of John	12-Jul-02	40	Dc1/38v	251
Luttrell, Richard	Meath, Tankardston	gentry: gent	13-Apr-00	60	Dc1/23r	152
Luttrell, Richard		gentry: gent	09-Dec-16	80	Dc2/3r	882
Luttrell, Robert	Dublin, the city	gentry: gent	07-Nov-28	200	B.L. 19, 843 f. 47	2812
Luttrell, Robert	Dublin	gentry: gent	28-Jul-27	100	Dc2/97v	1454
Luttrell, Robert	Dublin, the city	merchant	21-Nov-27	200	Dc2/100r	1464
Luttrell, Robert	Dublin, the city	gentry: gent	12-Nov-28	200	Dc2/115r	1539
Luttrell, Robert	Dublin	gentry: gent	22-Jun-26	200	Dc2/79v	1376
Luttrell, Robert	Meath, Porterston	gentry: gent	13-Apr-00	60	Dc1/23r	152
Luttrell, Thomas	Westmeath, Ronaghan	gentry: esquire	26-Feb-73	400	B.L. 15, 636 f. 132	3841
Luttrell, Thomas	Dublin, the city	gentry: esquire	28-Jun-73	200	B.L. 19, 844 f. 3	3122
Luttrell, Thomas	Westmeath, Ranaghan	gentry: esquire	31-Jan-73	200	Dc3/153r	2571
Luttrell, Thomas	Dublin	trade: tanner	16-May-07	20	Dc1/76v	465
Luttrell, Thomas	Westmeath, Ronaghan	gentry: esquire	26-Feb-73	400	Dc3/154v	2578
Luttrell, Thomas	Dublin, Killeghe	gentry: son/heir of John	22-May-07	50	Dc1/77r	471
Luttrell, Thomas	Dublin, the city		28-Jun-73	200	Dc3/158v	2590
Luttrell, Thomas	Westmeath, Ronnaghan	gentry: gent	06-May-64	200	B.L. 15, 635 f. 130	3487
Luttrell, Thomas	Dublin, the city	gentry: esquire	14-Jul-64	113	B.L. 15, 635 f. 139a	3500
Lynan, Patrick	Dublin	merchant	03-Feb-97	400	Dc1/1r	3
Lynch, Garret	Meath, the Knock	gentry: esquire	29-Nov-25	600	Dc2/70v	1324
Lynch, Garret	Meath, Kilmeer	gentry: gent	29-Nov-25	700	Dc2/70v	1323
Lynch, Marcus	Galway, Galway		21-Nov-09	500	Dc1/83r	582
Lynch, Nathaniel	Waterford	prof: archdeacon of Waterford	20-Jan-34	400	Dc2/205v	1925
Lynch, Richard	Dublin, the city	gentry: gent?	15-Jul-14	200	Dc1/131r	812
Lynington, George	Wexford, Wexford	gentry: gent	25-Mar-84	300	B.L. 15, 637 f. 84a	4000
Lyons, William	King's Co., Duffield	gentry: esquire	12-Feb-24	1000	Dc2/53v	1202
Lyons, William	King's Co., Mucklough	gentry: esquire	08-Mar-28	400	Dc2/105v	1492

The Irish Statute Staple Books: Debtors, 1596-1687

Standard	County	Occupation	Date	Amount	MS No	Ident No
Lyons, William	King's Co., Mullouck	gentry: esquire	03-Mar-28	860	Dc2/105r	1490
Lysaght, John	Cork, Ardywhoige	gentry: esquire	03-Feb-73	1000	Dc3/153r	2572
Lysaght, John	Cork, Ardnihioge	gentry: esquire	03-Feb-73	1000	B.L. 15, 636 f. 131	3839
MacAuley, James	Westmeath, Carne?	gentry: gent	28-Jul-64	1000	B.L. 15, 635 f. 201a	3612
MacAuley, John	Westmeath, Downigan	gentry: gent	28-Jul-64	1000	B.L. 15, 635 f. 201a	3612
MacAuley, Malachy	Cork, Carrigcashell	gentry: gent	13-Dec-14	120	Dc1/133v	831
MacAuley, Malachy	Cork, Carrigecashell	gentry: gent	30-Nov-11	140	Dc1/110r	682
MacBrien, Hugh	Fermanagh, Dereney	gentry: gent	30-Jun-27	800	Dc2/96r	1447
MacBrien, Hugh	Fermanagh, Derrinenny	gentry: gent	18-Jul-28	1100	Dc2/113v	1530
MacCann, Brian	Dublin	trade: haberdasher	14-Jul-00	40	Dc1/25r	168
MacCart, Donell	Cork, Glannsphreghan	gentry: gent	30-Nov-09	20	Dc1/93r	583
MacCartan, Patrick	Down, Loghenelan	gentry: esquire	27-Nov-33	350	Dc2/201v	1909
MacCartan, Patrick	Down, Loghenelan	gentry: esquire	27-Nov-33	418	Dc2/201r	1908
MacCartan, Patrick	Down, Loghanelan	gentry: esquire	12-Dec-33	800	Dc2/203r	1918
MacCarthy, Callaghan		peer: earl of Clancarty	03-May-76	1200	Dc3/173r	2654
MacCarthy, Callaghan		peer: earl of Clancarty	03-May-76	1200	B.L. 19, 844 f. 93	3220
MacCarthy, Callaghan	Cork, Kilenykahirrowie	gentry: gent	23-Jul-36	270	B.L. 19, 843 f. 41a	2801
MacCarthy, Callaghan	Cork, Culefnarny?	gentry: gent	23-Oct-18	120	B.L. 19, 843 f. 4a	2727
MacCarthy, Callaghan	Cork, Kilenycahirrowne	gentry: gent	23-Jul-36	800	B.L. 19, 843 f. 42	2802
MacCarthy, Callaghan	Cork, Bealabahallagh		28-Feb-25	1700	Dc2/62r	1268
MacCarthy, Charles	Cork, Kilcrea	gentry: esquire	20-Feb-17	60	Dc2/5r	893
MacCarthy, Charles	Cork, Kilivydy	gentry: gent	10-Dec-36	800	B.L. 19, 843 f. 18a	2755
MacCarthy, Charles	Cork, Montyrie?	gentry: gent	27-Apr-30	800	B.L. 19, 843 f. 29a	2777
MacCarthy, Charles	Cork, Carrignimucke	gentry: gent	10-Dec-36	800	B.L. 19, 843 f. 18a	2755
MacCarthy, Charles	Cork, Cloghroe	gentry: esquire	26-Jul-86	1200	B.L. 15, 637 f. 111	4050
MacCarthy, Cormac	Cork?, Byrne Cleaghy?	gentry: son/heir of Owen	11-Dec-24	400	Dc2/59v	1252
MacCarthy, Cormac	Cork, Corra	gentry: gent	13-Dec-14	120	Dc1/133v	831
MacCarthy, Cormac	Cork, Cloghroe	gentry: gent	28-May-17	400	Dc2/7v	903
MacCarthy, Daniel	Kerry, Casterlogh	gentry: esquire	17-May-21	400	Dc2/35v	1071
MacCarthy, Daniel	Kerry, Pallice	gentry: esquire	05-Dec-34	1000	Dc2/225r	2005
MacCarthy, Daniel	Cork, Dishert	gentry: gent	24-Mar-38	440	B.L. 19, 843 f. 19	2756
MacCarthy, Dermot	Cork, Downyue	gentry: gent, son/heir of Donnogh	23-Jul-36	270	B.L. 19, 843 f. 41a	2801
MacCarthy, Dermot	Cork, Lohurt	gentry: esquire	29-Nov-23	600	Dc2/51v	1189
MacCarthy, Dermot	Cork, Loghert	gentry: esquire	05-Jun-13	40	Dc1/121v	754
MacCarthy, Dermot	Cork, Inshirahillie	gentry: gent	01-Apr-39	800	B.L. 19, 843 f. 30	2778
MacCarthy, Dermot	Kerry, Killane	gentry: gent	09-Dec-12	120	Dc1/117r	728
MacCarthy, Dermot	Cork, the Loughurt?	gentry: esquire	22-Dec-14	600	Dc1/134v	835
MacCarthy, Dermot	Cork, Downyne	gentry: gent, s. of Donnogh	23-Jul-36	800	B.L. 19, 843 f. 42	2802
MacCarthy, Dermot	Cork, Drowmsirkane	gentry: son/heir of Dermot	29-Nov-23	600	Dc2/51v	1189
MacCarthy, Donnel	Cork, Kilbertin	gentry: esquire	11-May-30	400	Dc2/147r	1686
MacCarthy, Donnel	Kerry, Cashelloghe	gentry: gent	24-Feb-06	200	Dc1/66r	399

Standard	County	Occupation	Date	Amount	MS No	Ident No
MacCarthy, Donnel	Kerry, Castelloughre	gentry: gent	03-May-05	1000	Dc1/58r	355
MacCarthy, Donnel	Kerry, Dunagyle	gentry: gent	21-Nov-23	300	Dc2/51v	1188
MacCarthy, Donnel	Kerry, Castlelough	gentry: gent s/h Donell				
		MacCarthy	07-Nov-23	1000	Dc2/50v	4058
MacCarthy, Donogh	Cork, Canturk	gentry: gent	23-Feb-98	60	Dc1/9v	69
MacCarthy, Donogh	Cork, Blarny	gentry: knight	06-Sep-33	210	Dc2/199r	1900
MacCarthy, Donogh	Cork, Blarnie	gentry: knight	06-Jun-40	4000	B.L. 19, 843 f. 56a	2831
MacCarthy, Donogh	Cork, Downen	gentry: gent	04-Dec-09	100	Dc1/93v	586
MacCarthy, Donogh	Cork, ?	gentry: knight	30-Apr-39	4000	B.L. 19, 843 f. 5a	2729
MacCarthy, Elizabeth		peer: widow, of				
		Clancarthy	06-Mar-80	1800	B.L. 15, 637 f. 31	3903
MacCarthy, Florence	Cork, Banduffe	gentry: gent	05-Jun-13	40	Dc1/121v	754
MacCarthy, Florence	Cork, Montine Castle	gentry: gent	01-Apr-39	800	B.L. 19, 843 f. 30	2778
MacCarthy, Florence	Kerry, Bannduffe	gentry: gent	01-Jun-13	200	Dc1/121r	753
MacCarthy, Owen	Cork, Byrne Cleaghy	gentry: gent	11-Dec-24	400	Dc2/59v	1252
MacCarthy, Thady	Cork, Carrignymuck?	gentry: gent	23-Oct-18	120	B.L. 19, 843 f. 4a	2727
MacCarthy, Thady	Cork, Blarny	gentry: gent	20-Feb-17	60	Dc2/5r	893
MacCarthy, Thady	Cork, Ouldcashell	gentry: gent	24-Mar-38	440	B.L. 19, 843 f. 19	2756
MacCarthy, Thady	Cork, Kylcrone	gentry: gent	23-Feb-98	60	Dc1/9v	69
MacCarthy, Thady	Cork, Carrignimucke	gentry: gent, s./heir of				
		Charles	10-Dec-36	800	B.L. 19, 843 f. 18a	2755
MacConnell, Coll	Louth, Wingson	gentry: gent	29-Apr-01	40	Dc1/30v	203
MacCooey, Edmund	Galway, Ballygasta	gentry: gent	15-Feb-10	300	Dc1/94v	591
MacCooey, Francis	Meath, Rahinston	gentry: gent	10-May-28	100	Dc2/107v	1502
MacCooey, John	Galway, Killemedyma	gentry: gent	15-Feb-10	300	Dc1/94v	591
MacCooey, William	Meath, Balleneskeagh	gentry: esquire	10-May-28	100	Dc2/107v	1502
MacCormack, Ellen	Mayo?	gentry: widow of				
		Michael, esq	30-Jun-36	400	Dc2/254r	2138
MacCormack, Ellen	Mayo?	gentry: widow of				
		Michael, esq	30-Jun-36	400	Dc2/253v	2137
MacCormack, Michael	Mayo, Inver?	gentry: gent	28-Feb-28	227	Dc2/105r	1489
MacCormack, Richard	Mayo, Barranagh	gentry: gent	30-Jun-36	400	Dc2/253v	2137
MacCormack, Richard	Mayo, Barrenagh	gentry: gent	28-Feb-28	227	Dc2/105r	1489
MacCormack, Richard	Mayo, Barranagh	gentry: gent	30-Jun-36	400	Dc2/254r	2138
MacCormack, Thomas	Donegal, Lifford	gentry: gent	19-Oct-64	252	B.L. 15, 635 f. 147a	3514
MacDermot, Brien	Roscommon,					
	Carrigmacdermott	gentry: esquire	09-Dec-25	100	Dc2/72r	1331
MacDermot, Charles	Roscommon, Meery	gentry: gent	05-Jun-39	1000	B.L. 19, 843 f.8a	2735
MacDermot, Terence	Roscommon, Carricke	gentry: esquire	14-Aug-39	600	B.L. 19, 843 f. 31a	2781
MacDermot, Terence	Roscommon, Caricke	gentry: esquire	05-Jun-39	1000	B.L. 19, 843 f.8a	2735
MacDermot, Terrence	Roscommon, Carricke					
	McDermot	gentry: esquire	03-Dec-40	6000	B.L. 19, 843 f. 75a	2870
MacDermot, Terrence	Roscommon, Carricke	gentry: esquire	26-Aug-40	3000	B.L. 19, 843 f. 67	2853
MacDonagh, Brian	Sligo, Cowleowny	gentry: esquire	09-Jul-18	105	Dc2/15v	946
MacDonagh, Callaghan	Cork, Bealebahallagh	gentry: gent	28-Feb-25	1700	Dc2/62r	1268

Standard	County	Occupation	Date	Amount	MS No	Ident No
MacDonagh, Henry	Sligo, Cloncashell	gentry: gent	12-Dec-26	500	Dc2/86v	1409
MacDonagh, Henry	Sligo, Clouingashell, Curren	gentry: gent	09-Dec-29	200	Dc2/139v	1653
MacDonagh, Laughlin	Sligo, Balinagan	gentry: gent	13-May-39	200	B.L. 19, 843 f. 23a	2765
MacDonagh, Owen	Cork, Ballymackmorregh	gentry: gent	09-Jun-13	60	Dc1/122r	757
MacDonagh, Robert	Sligo, Clowncunny	gentry: gent	08-Jul-34	400	Dc2/214v	1962
MacDonnell, Alexander	Dublin, the city	gentry: gent	21-Mar-35	500	Dc2/231v	2032
MacDonnell, Alexander	Mayo, Mayo	gentry: gent	13-Mar-34	205	Dc2/209r	1941
MacDonnell, Alexander	Antrim, Glenarme	gentry: esquire	24-Sep-66	600	Dc3/38	2311
MacDonnell, Alexander	Antrim, Glenarme	gentry: esquire	20-Nov-78	660	B.L. 15, 637 f. 9a	3864
MacDonnell, Alexander	Antrim, Glenarme	gentry: esquire	24-Sep-66	600	B.L. 15, 635 f. 175a	3560
MacDonnell, Fergus	Queen's Co., Tenikellie	gentry: esquire	08-Feb-28	800	Dc2/103v	1483
MacDonnell, Randal	Antrim?	peer: earl of Antrim	04-Jun-41	1600	B.L. 19, 843 f. 94	2907
MacDonnell, Thady	Queen's Co., Killpurcell	gentry: gent	20-Aug-39	1000	B.L. 19, 843 f. 35a	2789
MacEdward, Cuconnacht	Down, Derrineale	gentry: gent	30-Dec-33	800	Dc2/206r	1927
MacGill, John	Down, Dromore	gentry: esquire	10-Apr-63	700	B.L. 15, 635 f. 102a	3439
MacGillecuddy, Connor	Kerry, Castlecurrig	gentry: gent	27-Nov-24	240	Dc2/59r	1247
MacGlancy, Melaghlyn	Leitrim, Clointiprohillis	gentry: gent	03-Dec-36	600	Dc2/258v	2161
MacGrane, Philip	Meath, Birtinston Galwaye	farmer	25-Oct-05	50	Dc1/62r	377
Machet, James	Armagh, Kerhanagh?		22-Feb-13	60	Dc1/120r	744
MacHugh, Owen		soldier: provost-marshall	29-Apr-01	40	Dc1/30v	203
MacHugh, Tomoltagh?	Roscommon, Ballyclannhugh	gentry: gent	05-Jun-39	1000	B.L. 19, 843 f.8a	2735
Mackay, William	Meath, Ballyneskeaghe	gentry: gent	01-Dec-07	200	Dc1/80r	496
Mackay, William	Meath, Balleneskagh	gentry: gent	16-May-01	200	Dc1/31v	208
Mackay, William	Meath, Balleneskagh	gentry: gent	19-May-01	300	Dc1/31v	209
MacKenna, Neill	Monaghan, Lower Trough	gentry: esquire	14-Nov-27	160	Dc2/99v	1463
MacKenna, Toole	Monaghan, Tonnynvmcry?	gentry: gent	21-Nov-21	240	Dc2/36v	1080
MacLellan, Robert	Scotland, Bombey	gentry: knight	19-Feb-19	400	Dc2/21r	976
MacMahon, Arthur	Monaghan, Rowskie	gentry: esquire	04-Dec-28	400	Dc2/120v	1563
MacMahon, Arthur	Monaghan, Calmore	gentry: gent	25-Nov-20	600	Dc2/33r	1053
MacMahon, Arthur	Monaghan, Dartry, Rowske	gentry: esquire	09-Jul-24	500	Dc2/57v	1233
MacMahon, Arthur	Monaghan, Monnoghan Duffe	gentry: gent	01-Dec-30	300	Dc2/157r	1730
MacMahon, Arthur	Monaghan, Ruskie	gentry: esquire	16-Jun-30	100	Dc2/151v	1706
MacMahon, Arthur	Monaghan, Rowskie	gentry: esquire	18-Jun-30	2000	Dc2/152r	1708
MacMahon, Arthur	Monaghan, Ballinterr	gentry: esquire	29-Nov-31	400	Dc2/173r	1796
MacMahon, Brian	Monaghan, Ruske	gentry: knight	22-Nov-13	200	Dc1/124r	771
MacMahon, Brian	Monaghan, Kilshanlisse	gentry: gent	18-Jun-30	2000	Dc2/152r	1708
MacMahon, Brian	Monaghan, Rowske	gentry: knight	19-Nov-13	600	Dc1/123r	769
MacMahon, Brian	Monaghan, Rowskie/ Darbrie	gentry: knight	25-Nov-20	600	Dc2/33r	1053
MacMahon, Brian	Monaghan, Kilshanlisse	gentry: gent	05-May-30	140	Dc2/145v	1680
MacMahon, Brian	Monaghan, Crymowrne	gentry: gent	22-Nov-13	200	Dc1/124r	771
MacMahon, Brian	Monaghan, Lysnecryne	gentry: gent	25-Nov-20	600	Dc2/33r	1053

Standard	County	Occupation	Date	Amount	MS No	Ident No
MacMahon, Coll	Monaghan, Monaghan Duffe	gentry: gent	30-Jan-41	200	B.L. 19, 843 f. 84	2887
MacMahon, Coll	Monaghan, Tulloglasse	gentry: esquire	13-Feb-34	1000	Dc2/207r	1931
MacMahon, Coll	Fermanagh, Farny	gentry: esquire	18-Jul-28	1100	Dc2/113v	1530
MacMahon, Dermot	Limerick, Ballyrodane	gentry: son/heir of Murrough	10-Jun-40	200	B.L. 19, 843 f. 67a	2854
MacMahon, Hugh	Monaghan, Tullaghgallghan	gentry: gent	16-Jun-30	100	Dc2/151v	1706
MacMahon, Hugh	Monaghan, Tullaghgallegan	gentry: gent	18-Jun-30	2000	Dc2/152r	1708
MacMahon, Hugh	Fermanagh, Derinennie	gentry: gent	18-Jul-28	1100	Dc2/113v	1530
MacMahon, James	Monaghan, Ballymechan	gentry: gent	13-Feb-34	1000	Dc2/207r	1931
MacMahon, John	Clare, Killygartin	gentry: gent	01-Dec-25	20	Dc2/71r	1326
MacMahon, Mathew	Clare, Killtumper	gentry: gent	17-Jan-74	900	B.L. 19, 844 f. 25a	3147
MacMahon, Murrough	Limerick, Ballyrodane	gentry: gent	10-Jun-40	200	B.L. 19, 843 f. 67a	2854
MacMahon, Nicholas	Roscommon, Ballinamilly	gentry: esquire	22-Jun-69	400	Dc3/100	2442
MacMahon, Nicholas	Roscommon, Ballynemony	gentry: esquire	15-Feb-77	300	B.L. 19, 844 f. 135	3265
MacMahon, Nicholas	Roscommon, Ballynemony	gentry: esquire	15-Feb-77	300	Dc3/182r	2686
MacMahon, Nicholas	Roscommon, Ballinamilly	gentry: esquire	22-Jun-69	200	Dc3/99	2441
MacMahon, Nicholas	Roscommon, Strokestowne	gentry: esquire	28-Jun-80	800	B.L. 15, 637 f. 34	3908
MacMahon, Nicholas	Roscommon, Ballynamilley	gentry: esquire	22-Jun-69	200	B.L. 15, 636 f. 50	3709
MacMahon, Nicholas	Roscommon, Strokestowne	gentry: esquire	25-Jun-80	500	B.L. 15, 637 f. 33a	3907
MacMahon, Owen	Monaghan, Kenocke	gentry: gent	16-Jun-30	100	Dc2/151v	1706
MacMahon, Patrick	Monaghan, Roaskie	gentry: son/heir of Arthur	04-Dec-28	400	Dc2/120v	1563
MacMahon, Patrick	Monaghan, Rowskie	gentry: gent, s/h of Arthur	18-Jun-30	2000	Dc2/152r	1708
MacMahon, Rory	Monaghan, Ballymagarahan	gentry: gent	05-May-30	140	Dc2/145v	1680
MacMahon, Ross	Monaghan, Monaghandowne	gentry: gent	01-Jun-27	60	Dc2/93v	1436
MacMahon, Teige	Clare, Cleunagh	gentry: esquire	13-Jul-66	200	Dc3/32	2293
MacMahon, Teige	Clare, Clunahg	gentry: esquire	13-Jul-66	200	Dc3/32	2292
MacMahon, Teige	Clare, Clenagh	gentry: esquire	13-Jul-66	200	B.L. 15, 636 f. 35	3684
MacMahon, Teige	Clare, Clenagh	gentry: esquire	13-Jul-66	200	B.L. 15, 636 f. 35a	3685
MacMahon, Thady	Clare, Killtumper	gentry: gent	17-Jan-74	900	B.L. 19, 844 f. 25a	3147
MacMahon, Turlough	Clare, Clonederelagh	gentry: esquire	13-Feb-13	100	Dc1/119r	739
MacMahon, Turlough	Clare, Clonderela	gentry: esquire	27-Apr-08	500	Dc1/82r	511
MacNamara, Daniel	Clare, Dungenviggen	gentry: gent	01-Dec-25	20	Dc2/71r	1326
MacNamara, John	Clare, Monccallen	gentry: knight	06-Dec-26	400	Dc2/85r	1404
MacQuillan, Ever	Antrim, Carnvinky	gentry: gent	20-Jun-15	440	Dc1/138v	859
MacQuillan, Rory	Antrim, Galgorme?	gentry: gent	20-Jun-15	440	Dc1/138v	859
MacWilliam, Owen	Waterford, Ballencourt	gentry: gent	11-May-19	200	Dc2/23v	990
Madison, John	Fermanagh, Cloncailliga	gentry: gent	03-Jun-74	200	Dc3/162r	2612

Standard	County	Occupation	Date	Amount	MS No	Ident No
Magennis, Arthur	Down, Quillin	gentry: gent	10-Dec-34	200	Dc2/225v	2007
Magennis, Brian	Down, Shancoll	gentry: gent	30-Dec-33	800	Dc2/206r	1927
Magennis, Connor	Down, Newcastle	gentry: knight	25-Nov-34	2000	Dc2/223v	1998
Magennis, Connor	Down, Newcastle	gentry: knight	21-Nov-34	1000	Dc2/222v	1995
Magennis, Daniel	Down, Narrowwater	gentry: esquire	21-Nov-34	1000	Dc2/222v	1995
Magennis, Donald	Down, Narrowwater	gentry: esquire	25-Nov-34	2000	Dc2/223v	1998
Magennis, Edmund	Down, Corrocks	gentry: gent	30-Dec-33	800	Dc2/206r	1927
Magennis, Ever	Down, Ballycrin	gentry: gent	24-Mar-35	500	Dc2/232r	2033
Magennis, Ever	Down, Ballycryn	gentry: gent	21-Mar-35	2000	Dc2/231v	2031
Magennis, Hugh	Down?	peer: viscount Iveagh	25-Nov-34	2000	Dc2/223v	1998
Magennis, Rory	Down, Ballycryn	gentry: son/heir of Ever	21-Mar-35	2000	Dc2/231v	2031
Magennis, Rory	Down, Ballycrin	gentry: son/heir of Ever	24-Mar-35	500	Dc2/232r	2033
Mageoghegan, Owen	Westmeath, Bushopston	gentry: gent	10-Jun-23	400	Dc2/48r	1164
Magner, Richard	Cork, Ahaddi	gentry: gent	14-Jul-40	400	B.L. 19, 843 f. 75	2869
Magrath, James	Donegal, Culenuer	gentry: esquire	21-Jan-37	600	Dc2/259v	2166
Magrath, James	Donegal, Tyrmondmagrath	gentry: esquire	04-Dec-34	400	Dc2/224v	2004
Magrath, James	Donegal, Culenver	gentry: esquire	22-Dec-36	600	Dc2/259v	2165
Magrath, James	Down, Tarmanmagrath	gentry: gent	13-Mar-34	205	Dc2/209r	1941
Magrath, Terence	Tipperary, Gourtin	gentry: gent	16-May-79	440	B.L. 15, 637 f. 18a	3879
Magrath, Turlough	Donegal, Tyrmondmagrath?	gentry: son/heir of James	04-Dec-34	400	Dc2/224v	2004
Magrath, Turlough	Donegal, Culenver?	gentry: son/heir of James	22-Dec-36	600	Dc2/259v	2165
Maguire, Brian	Fermanagh, Tympodessell	gentry: esquire	18-Jun-30	2000	Dc2/152r	1708
Maguire, Brian	Fermanagh, Derineny	gentry: knight	22-Jun-27	1000	Dc2/95r	1445
Maguire, Brian	Fermanagh, Dereneny	gentry: knight	30-Jun-27	800	Dc2/96r	1447
Maguire, Brian	Fermanagh?	peer: baron Enniskillen	18-Jul-28	1100	Dc2/113v	1530
Maguire, Connor	Fermanagh?	peer: baron Enniskillen	12-Dec-34	2000	Dc2/225v	2008
Maguire, Connor	Fermanagh?	peer: baron Enniskillen	06-Dec-34	2000	Dc2/225r	2006
Maguire, Cormac	Fermanagh, Abboe	gentry: gent	22-Jun-39	441	B.L. 19, 843 f. 23	2764
Maguire, Cowcho?	Fermanagh, Irrish	gentry: gent	22-Jun-39	441	B.L. 19, 843 f. 23	2764
Maguire, Cuconnacht	Fermanagh, Aghowkrewill	gentry: esquire	22-Jun-27	1000	Dc2/95r	1445
Maguire, Cuconnacht	Fermanagh, Aghowdrefuill	gentry: esquire	30-Jun-27	800	Dc2/96r	1447
Maguire, Richard	Limerick, Mahonagh	gentry: esquire	26-Mar-68	200	B.L. 15, 635 f. 221a	3648
Maguire, Rory	Fermanagh, Castlehassett	gentry: esquire	10-Jun-41	200	B.L. 19, 843 f. 118	2955
Mahony, Donogh	Limerick, the city	merchant	13-Apr-40	600	B.L. 19, 843 f. 56	2830
Mahony, Mahony	Clare, Canovrighane	gentry: gent	13-Apr-40	600	B.L. 19, 843 f. 56	2830
Mahony, Mortagh	Clare, Carrig Errie	gentry: gent	28-May-41	1200	B.L. 19, 843 f. 95a	2910
Malady, Hugh	Westmeath, Rathwire	gentry: gent	09-Dec-76	1000	Dc3/180v	2677
Malady, Redmond	Westmeath, Rathwire	gentry: gent	09-Dec-76	1000	Dc3/180v	2677
Malby, George	Roscommon, Roscommon	gentry: esquire	29-Mar-23	1200	Dc2/46r	1148
Malby, George	Roscommon, Roscommon	gentry: esquire	12-Jun-24	200	Dc2/56r	1221
Malby, George	Roscommon, Roscommon	gentry: esquire	23-Dec-23	400	Dc2/52r	1194
Malby, George	Roscommon, Roscommon	gentry: knight	24-Nov-27	800	Dc2/100v	1466
Malby, George	Roscommon, Roscommon	gentry: esquire	21-Jun-24	300	Dc2/56v	1228

Standard	County	Occupation	Date	Amount	MS No	Ident No
Malby, George	Roscommon, Roscommon	gentry: esquire	25-Feb-24	200	Dc2/53r	1198
Malby, George	Roscommon, Roscommon	gentry: knight	27-Oct-28	3000	Dc2/115r	1538
Malby, George	Roscommon, Roscommon	gentry: esquire	04-Feb-24	160	Dc2/52v	1197
Malby, George	Roscommon, Roscommon	gentry: esquire	08-Jun-25	320	Dc2/65v	1291
Malby, George	Roscommon, Roscommon	gentry: knight	11-Jun-25	210	Dc2/65v	1293
Malby, Henry	Roscommon	gentry: esquire	22-Jul-98	100	Dc1/11v	85
Malby, Henry	Roscommon, Roscommon	gentry: esquire	07-Apr-02	500	Dc1/37r	240
Malby, Henry	Roscommon, Roscommon	gentry: esquire	28-Nov-97	1000	Dc1/8r	57
Mall, Thomas	Dublin	gentry: esquire	30-Jan-28	2000	Dc2/103r	1480
Mall, Thomas	Dublin	gentry: esquire	30-Jan-28	2000	Dc2/103r	1479
Malone, Edmund	Westmeath, Ballynehowne	gentry: esquire	08-Nov-75	2000	Dc3/168v	2640
Malone, Edmund	Westmeath, Clontonnan	gentry: gent	28-Jul-64	1000	B.L. 15, 635 f. 201a	3612
Malone, Edward	Westmeath, Ballynehowne	gentry: esquire	08-Nov-75	1000	B.L. 19, 844 f. 86	3214
Malone, John	Dublin	gentry: gent	20-Apr-05	400	Dc1/58v	358
Malone, John	Dublin		30-Apr-01	240	Dc1/31r	205
Malone, John	Dublin	gentry: gent	02-Aug-99	140	Dc1/19r	130
Malone, John	Dublin	gentry: gent	08-Jan-01	200	Dc1/28r	186
Malone, John	Dublin	gentry: gent	13-Feb-09	40	Dc1/87r	545
Malone, John	Dublin		26-Jan-00	200	Dc1/20v	140
Malone, Thomas	Dublin	merchant: son of John	13-Feb-09	40	Dc1/87r	545
Malone, William	Meath, Lismullen	gentry: esquire	15-Aug-44	500	B.L. 19, 843 f. 116	2951
Mann, Bartholomew	Louth, Ardee	gentry: gent	16-Jun-32	30	Dc2/183r	1836
Mann, James	Louth, Ardee	gentry: son/heir of Bart	16-Jun-32	30	Dc2/183r	1836
Mannering, Richard	Dublin, Rathcredan	gentry: gent	23-Feb-09	60	Dc1/87v	548
Manning, Charles	Fermanagh, Mannorhigate	gentry: gent	20-Jul-41	1200	B.L. 19, 843 f. 102	2923
Manning, Henry	Fermanagh, Mannorhigate	gentry: esquire	20-Jul-41	1200	B.L. 19, 843 f. 102	2923
Mansfield, Walter	Waterford, BallyMcMoltenagh	gentry: gent	04-Jun-25	200	Dc2/65r	1288
Manwaring, Richard	Dublin, Rathcredan	gentry: gent	27-Sep-00	200	Dc1/26r	174
Mapas, Christopher	Dublin, the city	merchant	31-Oct-36	700	Dc2/256v	2151
Mapas, Christopher	Dublin	merchant	01-Sep-28	630	Dc2/114v	1536
Mapas, Christopher	Dublin	merchant	13-Mar-35	400	Dc2/230v	2028
Mapas, Christopher	Dublin, the city	merchant	14-Mar-29	200	Dc2/126r	1592
Mapas, Patrick	Dublin		01-Sep-28	630	Dc2/114v	1536
Mapas, Patrick	Dublin, the city	gentry: gent	02-Oct-58	164	B.L. 15, 635 f. 36a	3327
Mapas, Patrick	Dublin, the city	gentry: gent	16-Jun-57	600	B.L. 19, 843 f. 199	3104
Mapas, Patrick	Dublin, the city	merchant	24-Apr-19	1200	Dc2/22v	985
Mapas, Patrick	Dublin, the city	gentry: gent	28-Apr-62	270	B.L. 15, 635 f. 94a	3423
Mape, Gerald	Meath, Maperath	gentry: gent	17-Nov-38	150	B.L. 19, 943 f.2a	2724
Mape, Gerald	Meath, Maperath	gentry: gent	26-Aug-31	100	Dc2/167v	1775
Mape, Henry	Meath, Maperath	gentry: son/heir of Gerald	17-Nov-38	150	B.L. 19, 943 f.2a	2724
Mapother, Thomas	Roscommon, Kiltinan	gentry: esquire	27-Apr-54	600	B.L. 19, 843 f. 138	2990
Marron, James	Tyrone, Castletuch	gentry: esquire	03-Apr-37	540	Dc2/261r	2172
Martin, Giles	Dublin, Dromconra	gentry: esquire	08-Jul-85	400	B.L. 15, 637 f. 99a	4028

Standard	County	Occupation	Date	Amount	MS No	Ident No
Martin, Henry	Mayo, Barishoule	gentry: esquire	23-May-57	2000	B.L. 19, 843 f. 193	3093
Martin, Henry	Kilkenny	gentry: esquire	31-Jan-67	400	Dc3/51	2334
Martin, Henry	Dublin, the city	gentry: esquire	13-Jan-59	250	B.L. 15, 635 f. 46	3344
Martin, Henry	Kilkenny, the city	gentry: esquire	31-Jan-66	300	Dc3/20	2268
Martin, Henry	Dublin, the city	gentry: esquire	19-Dec-65	600	Dc3/17	2261
Martin, Henry	Dublin, the city	gentry: esq, s./heir of Anthony	01-Mar-54	600	B.L. 19, 843 f. 140	2994
Martin, Henry	Kilkenny, the city	gentry: esquire	17-Jul-63	600	B.L. 15, 635 f. 107a	3447
Martin, Henry	Kilkenny, the city	gentry: esquire	10-Dec-64	2000	B.L. 15, 635 f. 147	3513
Martin, Henry	Kilkenny, the city	gentry: esquire	31-Jan-66	300	B.L. 15, 635 f. 164	3543
Martin, Henry	Kilkenny	gentry: esquire	31-Jan-67	400	B.L. 15, 635 f. 185a	3581
Martin, John	Louth, Drogheda	gentry: esquire	04-Feb-36	3000	Dc2/244r	2091
Martin, Robert	Galway, Ross, Muccullin	gentry: gent	29-Jan-68	600	B.L. 15, 635 f. 223	3651
Marward, Janet	Meath?	gentry: d/h, Walter bar Skryne	20-Jul-09	80	Dc1/90v	566
Marward, Janet	Meath, Skryne	gentry: d/h, Walter bar Skryne	13-May-08	320	Dc1/82v	514
Mason, Richard	Dublin, Shalcockeswood	farmer: yeoman	01-Apr-41	800	B.L. 19, 843 f. 87a	2894
Mason, William	Dublin	gentry: gent	13-Feb-29	212	Dc2/125r	1586
Masterson, Edward	Wexford, Boris	gentry: gent	25-Jun-34	400	B.L. 19, 843 f. 57a	2833
Masterson, Edward	Wexford, Boris	gentry: gent	25-Jun-34	400	Dc2/212v	1955
Masterson, Henry	Wexford, Castletowne	gentry: gent	23-Nov-30	100	Dc2/157r	1729
Masterson, Henry	Wexford, Monnyseade	gentry: esquire	26-Jul-37	2000	Dc2/269v	2210
Masterson, Henry	Wexford, Clonee	gentry: esquire	22-Nov-61	200	B.L. 15, 635 f. 87	3410
Masterson, John	Wicklow, Owre	gentry: gent	21-Jul-17	160	Dc2/9r	910
Masterson, John	Wexford, Clahamon	gentry: esquire	15-Apr-02	500	Dc1/37r	241
Masterson, Nicholas	Wexford, Ardcroman	gentry: gent	24-Nov-02	300	Dc1/41r	265
Masterson, Nicholas	Wexford, Ardcroman	gentry: esquire	28-May-06	120	Dc1/68v	415
Masterson, Nicholas	Wexford, Ardcroman	gentry: esquire	15-Apr-02	500	Dc1/37r	241
Masterson, Richard	Wexford, Fferns	gentry: knight	24-Nov-02	300	Dc1/41r	265
Masterson, Roger	Wicklow, Ballenestow	gentry: gent	14-Feb-23	240	Dc2/45r	1141
Masterson, Roger	Queen's Co., Donnoghmore	gentry: gent	04-May-30	200	Dc2/145r	1679
Masterson, Roger	Wicklow, Ballenestoe	gentry: gent	25-Jun-19	300	Dc2/24r	994
Masterson, Roger	Wicklow, Ballenestow	gentry: gent	30-Jun-19	100	Dc2/24v	996
Masterson, Roger	Wexford, Clonee	gentry: son/heir of Henry	22-Nov-61	200	B.L. 15, 635 f. 87	3410
Masterson, Thomas	Wexford, Townequoile	gentry: gent	06-Dec-39	300	B.L. 19, 843 f. 37	2792
Masterson, Thomas	Wexford, Crouekrinnaght	gentry: esquire	30-Jun-40	100	B.L. 19, 843 f. 58	2834
Mather, Griffith	Dublin, the city	gentry: gent	27-Jun-40	600	B.L. 19, 843 f. 61a	2842
Mathews, George	Tipperary, Reighill	gentry: esquire	19-Aug-63	200	B.L. 15, 635 f. 125a	3478
Maxwell, Robert	Down, Killyleagh	gentry: knight	03-Dec-79	400	B.L. 15, 637 f. 31a	3904
Mayne, Thomas	Waterford	merchant	05-Aug-18	100	Dc2/16r	950
Maypother, Thomas	Roscommon, Killinbay	gentry: esquire	13-Sep-55	150	B.L. 19, 843 f. 166	3046
McGranill, Daniel	Leitrim, Dromard	gentry: gent	02-Sep-34	160	Dc2/218r	1977

Standard	County	Occupation	Date	Amount	MS No	Ident No
McKee, Frances	Meath, Rayhinston	gentry: gent	22-Feb-26	100	Dc2/74v	1346
McKee, Francis	Meath, Rachinstowne	gentry: son/heir of William	25-May-31	120	Dc2/164r	1760
McKee, Francis	Meath?, Ballencheagh?	gentry: s/h of Wm	12-Jul-22	200	Dc2/42r	1118
McKee, William	Meath, Balleneskeagh	gentry: esquire	25-May-31	120	Dc2/164r	1760
McKee, William	Meath, Ballencheagh	gentry: esquire	12-Jul-22	200	Dc2/42r	1118
McKee, William	Meath, Balleneskeogh	gentry: gent	22-Feb-26	100	Dc2/74v	1346
McKeon, Arthur	Monaghan, Rowskie	gentry: esquire	04-Dec-28	600	Dc2/120r	1562
McKeon, Brian	Monaghan, Kilshanligh	gentry: gent	04-Dec-28	600	Dc2/120r	1562
McKeon, Hugh	Monaghan, Killencroe	gentry: gent	04-Dec-28	600	Dc2/120r	1562
McKeon, Patrick	Monaghan, Rowske	gentry: son/heir of Art Oge	04-Dec-28	600	Dc2/120r	1562
McNawa, Thady	Leitrim, Tullycorcke	gentry: gent	03-Dec-36	600	Dc2/258v	2161
Meade, David	Cork	gentry: gent?	14-Nov-09	40	Dc1/92v	580
Meade, John	Cork	gentry: esquire	20-Jun-15	500	Dc1/139r	861
Meade, William	Cork, Ballintober	gentry: esquire	13-Sep-78	660	B.L. 19, 844 f. 169	3300
Meagher, David	Cork, Kinsale	gentry: gent	25-Nov-12	105	Dc1/116v	725
Meagher, Richard	Kilkenny, Clonmore	gentry: gent	15-May-06	53	Dc1/67r	404
Meagher, Robert	Limerick, Kilmallocke		13-Jul-30	200	Dc2/154r	1716
Meagher, Thomas	Tipperary, Boilybane	gentry: gent	17-May-09	300	Dc1/88v	554
Mercer, Hubert	Dublin, Ballyforman	gentry: knight	26-Oct-61	545	B.L. 15, 635 f. 84a	3405
Meredith, Charles	Dublin, the city	gentry: knight	04-May-70	800	Dc3/117	2475
Meredith, Charles	Dublin, the city	gentry: knight	04-May-70	800	B.L. 15, 636 f. 68a	3739
Meredith, Robert	Dublin, the city	gentry: knight	06-Oct-54	660	B.L. 19, 843 f. 145a	3005
Merrifield, Thomas	Dublin, the city	trade: brick maker	13-Sep-82	200	B.L. 15, 637 f. 62a	3960
Merriman, Richard	Dublin, Cowlocke	farmer	04-Nov-16	80	Dc2/1v	875
Mervyn, Audley	Dublin	gentry: knight	15-Oct-70	2000	Dc3/129	2498
Mervyn, Audley	Dublin, the city	gentry: knight	14-Dec-70	480	Dc3/132v	2508
Mervyn, Audley	Tyrone, Castle Tutchet	gentry: esquire	29-Jul-41	1000	B.L. 19, 843 f. 104	2927
Mervyn, Audley		gentry: knight	29-Jun-70	3300	Dc3/122	2483
Mervyn, Audley	Dublin, the city		14-Dec-70	480	B.L. 15, 636 f. 81	3763
Mervyn, Audley	Dublin?		29-Jun-70	3300	B.L. 15, 636 f. 64	3731
Mervyn, Henry	Tyrone, Trelick	gentry: esquire	29-Jun-70	3300	Dc3/122	2483
Mervyn, Henry	Tyrone, Trelick	gentry: esquire	29-Jun-70	3300	B.L. 15, 636 f. 64	3731
Mervyn, James	Tyrone, Castletuchett	gentry: esquire	21-Aug-37	120	Dc2/270v	2214
Mervyn, James	Tyrone, Castle Tutchett	gentry: esquire	16-Dec-39	240	B.L. 19, 843 f. 38a	2795
Mervyn, James	Tyrone, Castetuchett	gentry: esquire	04-Mar-37	400	Dc2/260v	2169
Mervyn, James	Tyrone, Castletuchett	gentry: esquire	04-Mar-39	200	B.L. 19, 843 f. 6	2730
Mervyn, James	Tyrone, Castle Tutchett	gentry: esquire	11-Feb-41	380	B.L. 19, 843 f. 84a	2888
Mervyn, James	Tyrone, Castle Tutchett	gentry: esquire	10-Jun-40	800	B.L. 19, 843 f. 70	2859
Michael, John	Dublin, the city	gentry: esquire	22-Jul-65	120	Dc3/12	2247
Miles, Ralph	Dublin	gentry: gent	15-May-28	200	Dc2/107v	1504
Miles, Ralph	Dublin, the city	gentry: gent	09-Apr-28	200	Dc2/106v	1497
Miles, Ralph	Dublin	merchant	01-Jul-01	160	Dc1/33r	217
Miles, Ralph	Dublin, the city	gentry: gent	08-Feb-25	200	Dc2/61v	1263

Standard	County	Occupation	Date	Amount	MS No	Ident No
Miller, Robert	Mayo, Cushinstowne	gentry: esquire	28-Jul-82	600	B.L. 15, 637 f. 63a	3962
Mills, Daniel	Dublin, the city	merchant	08-Jun-84	90	B.L. 15, 637 f. 88a	4006
Mills, Ralph	Dublin	merchant	06-Feb-02	200	Dc1/36r	234
Mills, Robert	Dublin, the city		09-Apr-59	110	B.L. 15, 635 f. 44	3340
Mills, William	Dublin, the city	gentry: esquire	21-Mar-78	200	B.L. 19, 844 f. 152	3283
Mills, William	Dublin, the city	gentry: esquire	21-Mar-78	200	Dc3/187v	2709
Mills, William	Dublin, the city	gentry: esq, fath of Daniel	08-Jun-84	90	B.L. 15, 637 f. 88a	4006
Mills, William	Dublin, the city	trade: cloth seller?	21-Jun-81	140	B.L. 15, 637 f. 49	3934
Misset, Adam	Kildare, Dowdington	gentry: gent	21-Nov-21	500	Dc2/36v	1079
Misset, Adam	Kildare, Stickin	gentry: gent	15-Nov-31	100	Dc2/169v	1783
Molloy, Callogh	King's Co., Ralye/Ralehin	gentry: gent	05-Dec-07	130	Dc1/80v	497
Molloy, Charles	King's Co., Rathhan	gentry: esquire	24-Nov-69	80	Dc3/108	2458
Molloy, Connell	King's Co., Rathlion	gentry: esquire	17-May-97	200	Dc1/4r	26
Molloy, Connell	King's Co., Ralihin	gentry: esquire	20-May-97	40	Dc1/4r	28
Molloy, Philip	King's Co., Diridalny	gentry: gent	02-Dec-72	200	Dc3/150r	2564
Molloy, Philip	Queen's Co., Dirricalny	gentry: gent	02-Dec-72	200	B.L. 15, 636 f. 133	3842
Molyneux, Daniel			21-May-07	200	Dc1/77r	470
Molyneux, Daniel	Dublin, Newland	gentry: esquire	07-Jun-24	220	Dc2/55v	1220
Molyneux, Samuel	Wexford, St. John's	gentry: esquire	07-Jun-24	220	Dc2/55v	1220
Monroe, Andrew	Down, Cherry Valley	gentry: gent	20-Apr-77	240	B.L. 19, 844 f. 127	3256
Monroe, Andrew	Down, Cherry vally	gentry: gent	03-Apr-78	200	B.L. 19, 844 f. 160	3291
Montgomery, George	Meath?	prof: bp of Meath & Clogher	22-Feb-17	1600	Dc2/5r	894
Montgomery, Henry	Dublin, the city	gentry: esquire	27-Nov-75	3000	Dc3/170v	2644
Montgomery, Henry	Dublin, the city	gentry: esquire	27-Nov-75	3000	B.L. 19, 844 f. 82	3210
Montgomery, Hugh	Down, the Ards	peer: earl of Mount Alexander	27-Nov-75	3000	B.L. 19, 844 f. 82	3210
Montgomery, Hugh	Dublin, the city	gentry: esquire	12-Jun-69	400	Dc3/99	2440
Montgomery, Hugh	Down, the Ards	peer: earl of Mount Alexander	22-Nov-75	10640	B.L. 19, 844 f. 75	3203
Montgomery, Hugh	Down?	peer: earl of Mount Alexander	30-Nov-75	1870	Dc3/170v	2645
Montgomery, Hugh	Down?	peer: earl of Mount Alexander	27-Nov-75	3000	Dc3/170v	2644
Montgomery, Hugh	Down, the Ards	peer: earl of Mount Alexander	30-Nov-75	1870	B.L. 19, 844 f. 78	3206
Montgomery, Hugh	Down?	peer: earl of Mount Alexander	22-Nov-75	10640	Dc3/169r	2641
Montgomery, Hugh	Down, the great Ardes	peer: viscount Montgomery	24-Nov-26	200	Dc2/83r	1395
Montgomery, Hugh	Down, Newton	gentry: knight	22-Feb-17	1600	Dc2/5r	894
Montgomery, Hugh	Down, the Ards	peer: earl of Mount Alexander	27-Nov-79	10000	B.L. 15, 637 f. 24a	3890

Standard	County	Occupation	Date	Amount	MS No	Ident No
Montgomery, Hugh	Down, the Ards	peer: viscount Montgomery	06-Apr-61	800	B.L. 15, 635 f. 66a	3381
Montgomery, Hugh	Down, the Ards	peer: viscount Montgomery	25-Jun-58	900	B.L. 15, 635 f. 56a	3364
Montgomery, Robert	Fermanagh, Ruskee	gentry: esquire	12-Mar-25	600	Dc2/63r	1276
Montgomery, William	Down, the Fflorida	gentry: esquire	25-Jun-58	900	B.L. 15, 635 f. 56a	3364
Montgomery, William	Down, Rostoman	gentry: esquire	02-May-62	280	B.L. 15, 635 f. 207	3623
Mooney, James	Dublin, the city	merchant	23-Mar-30	200	Dc2/143v	1672
Moore, Abigail	Louth, Ardaghstown	other: widow	02-Sep-75	400	B.L. 19, 844 f. 76	3204
Moore, Arthur	Armagh, Drumbannaghar	gentry: esquire	11-Dec-33	880	Dc2/203v	1917
Moore, Arthur	Armagh, Drombaunaghar	gentry: esquire	04-May-32	2000	Dc2/178v	1818
Moore, Bartholomew	Meath, Dowanstowne	gentry: gent	26-Feb-66	1000	Dc3/24	2276
Moore, Bartholomew	Meath, Dowanst[owne]	gentry: gent	20-May-17	50	Dc2/7r	901
Moore, Bartholomew	Meath, Downestowne	gentry: gent	26-Feb-66	1000	B.L. 15, 635 f. 174a	3558
Moore, Brent	Louth, Turlagh Donnell	gentry: esquire	10-Apr-63	700	B.L. 15, 635 f. 102a	3439
Moore, Callagh	Kildare, Ballina	gentry: esquire	18-May-07	60	Dc1/77r	468
Moore, Charles	Louth?	peer: viscount Moore, Drogheda	16-May-39	2000	B.L. 19, 843 f. 16	2750
Moore, Charles	Louth?	peer: viscount Moore, Drogheda	20-Mar-35	2000	Dc2/231r	2030
Moore, Charles	Louth?	peer: viscount Moore, Drogheda	31-May-36	1000	Dc2/253r	2132
Moore, Charles	Louth?	peer: viscount Moore, Drogheda	24-Jul-34	774	Dc2/215v	1967
Moore, Charles	Louth?	peer: viscount Moore, Drogheda	17-Nov-34	800	Dc2/221v	1990
Moore, Charles	Louth?	peer: viscount Moore, Drogheda	16-May-39	2000	B.L. 19, 843 f. 15a	2749
Moore, Emanuel	Cork, Ross Carbery	gentry: esquire	25-Aug-68	200	B.L. 15, 635 f. 228	3661
Moore, Henry	Louth?	peer: viscount Moore, Drogheda	26-Sep-44	800	B.L. 19, 843 f. 122a	2964
Moore, Henry	Louth?	peer: viscount Moore, Drogheda	16-Feb-55	300	B.L. 19, 843 f. 150a	3015
Moore, Henry	Louth?	peer: viscount Moore, Drogheda	08-Mar-54	540	B.L. 19, 843 f. 139	2992
Moore, Henry	Louth?	peer: viscount Moore, Drogheda	05-Dec-55	600	B.L. 19, 843 f. 169a	3053
Moore, Henry	Louth?	peer: earl of Drogheda	20-May-69	2008	B.L. 15, 636 f. 36a	3686
Moore, John	Galway, Cloghan	gentry: esquire	04-Dec-19	300	Dc2/27r	1011
Moore, John	Louth, Dunmaghan	gentry: esquire	05-Dec-73	460	Dc3/150v	2565
Moore, John	King's Co., Crouchan	gentry: esquire	03-Feb-65	100	Dc3/2	2225
Moore, John	Mayo, Bryse	gentry: esquire	09-Feb-14	200	Dc1/126r	783
Moore, John	Louth, Dunmaghan	gentry: esquire	05-Dec-72	460	B.L. 15, 636 f. 133a	3843
Moore, Melchior	Westmeath, Cromston	gentry: gent	21-May-12	400	Dc1/114r	707

Standard	County	Occupation	Date	Amount	MS No	Ident No
Moore, Nicholas	Cork, Creg, barony of					
	Ffermoy	gentry: esquire	10-May-75	500	B.L. 19, 844 f. 66	3194
Moore, Nicholas	Limerick, Bulgadin	gentry: gent	04-Apr-83	4000	B.L. 15, 637 f. 72a	3978
Moore, Nicholas	Cork, Fermoy, Carrygonedy		29-Nov-64	60	B.L. 15, 635 f. 150	3519
Moore, Patrick	Meath, Dowanstowne	gentry: gent, son/heir of				
		Bartholomew	26-Feb-66	1000	Dc3/24	2276
Moore, Patrick	Dublin, Balloghe	farmer	31-Jul-01	400	Dc1/33v	221
Moore, Patrick	Meath, Downestown	gentry: son/heir of Bart	26-Feb-66	1000	B.L. 15, 635 f. 174a	3558
Moore, Robert	Louth, Drogheda	merchant	27-Jun-39	300	B.L. 19, 843 f. 27a	2773
Moore, Robert	Louth, Drogheda	merchant	28-Jan-36	600	Dc2/243v	2090
Moore, Roger	Dublin, the city	merchant	01-Oct-78	800	B.L. 19, 844 f. 163	3294
Moore, Roger	Louth, Dundalke	gentry: esquire	12-May-35	600	Dc2/235r	2048
Moore, Roger	Louth, Dundalke	gentry: esquire	12-May-35	600	B.L. 19, 843 f. 6a	2731
Moore, Roger	Dublin, the city	merchant	30-Apr-73	2000	Dc3/155r	2580
Moore, Roger	Dublin	gentry: gent	26-Feb-41	1600	B.L. 19, 843 f. 87	2893
Moore, Roger	Kildare, Ballena	gentry: esquire	04-Dec-28	400	Dc2/120v	1563
Moore, Roger	Dublin, the city	merchant	30-Apr-73	2000	B.L. 15, 636 f. 134a	3845
Moore, Roger	Dublin, the city	gentry: esquire	13-Dec-80	4000	B.L. 15, 637 f. 44a	3927
Moore, Thomas	King's Co., Crochan	gentry: esquire	05-Jul-34	600	Dc2/214r	1961
Moore, Thomas	King's Co., Kadromann	gentry: esquire	11-Feb-28	300	Dc2/104r	1485
Moore, William	Louth, Moorestowne	gentry: gent	15-Jul-34	200	Dc2/214v	1963
Moore, William	Louth, Mosetowne	gentry: gent	06-Jul-33	200	Dc2/197v	1893
Moore, William	Louth, Deanrath	gentry: gent	05-Aug-40	120	B.L. 19, 843 f. 63	2845
Moore, William	Louth, Barneath	gentry: gent	05-Aug-40	120	B.L. 19, 843 f. 63	2845
Moore, William	Louth, Drogheda	gentry: brother? Henry,				
		earl of Drogheda	15-Jun-87	4000	B.L. 15, 637 f. 108	4042
Moran, John	Carlow, Katherlagh	farmer	11-May-05	2000	Dc1/59r	359
Morgan, Charles	Galway, Kilcolgan	gentry: esquire	09-Dec-76	300	Dc3/181r	2678
Morgan, Charles	Galway, Kilcolgan	gentry: esquire	09-Dec-76	300	Dc3/181r	2679
Morgan, George	Dublin, the city	merchant	24-Apr-19	1200	Dc2/22v	985
Morgan, George	Dublin, the city	merchant	23-Apr-19	1700	Dc2/22v	986
Morgan, Patrick	Meath, Ballybine	farmer	09-Jun-29	100	Dc2/131r	1613
Morgan, Robert	Sligo, Cottlestown	gentry: esquire	30-Jul-75	6000	B.L. 19, 844 f. 73	3201
Morley, James	Dublin, the city	gentry: esquire	18-May-58	600	B.L. 15, 635 f. 25	3307
Morris, John	Tipperary, Beakestowne	gentry: knight	19-Aug-63	200	B.L. 15, 635 f. 125a	3478
Morris, Richard	Dublin, the city	gentry: esquire	23-Jul-81	3000	B.L. 15, 637 f. 49a	3935
Morris, Samuel	Dublin, the city	gentry: gent	19-Jul-40	100	B.L. 19, 843 f. 62a	2844
Mortimer, Richard	Louth, Drogheda	gentry: gent	01-Jul-74	500	B.L. 19, 844 f. 35	3159
Mortimer, Richard	Louth, Drogheda	merchant	17-Sep-73	220	B.L. 19, 844 f. 6	3125
Mortimer, Richard	Louth, Drogheda	merchant	07-Mar-76	700	B.L. 19, 844 f. 91	3218
Moss, Suzanna	Dublin, the city	other: widow	07-Jun-76	300	Dc3/175v	2662
Moston, Hugh	Galway, Cloyan	gentry: gent	25-Nov-97	400	Dc1/7r	52
Motley, Walter	Dublin, the city	merchant	19-Jun-77	700	B.L. 19, 844 f. 134	3264
Motley, Walter	Dublin, the city	merchant	19-Jun-77	700	Dc3/182v	2690

Standard	County	Occupation	Date	Amount	MS No	Ident No
Mulholland, John	Monaghan, Counogtty	gentry: gent	07-Feb-68	308	Dc3/72	2388
Mulholland, John	Monaghan, Clonnoghy	gentry: gent	07-Feb-68	308	B.L. 15, 635 f. 222a	3650
Mullis, Joseph	Dublin	gentry: gent	19-Dec-18	240	Dc2/19v	968
Mulshinoch, Anthony	Cork, Ballynahilskie	prof: physician [phistie]	07-Apr-39	400	B.L. 19, 843 f. 30a	2779
Mulshinoch, Anthony	Cork, Ballydahine	prof: doctor of phisick	17-Apr-41	600	B.L. 19, 843 f. 96a	2912
Mulshinoch, Meollmurry?	Cork, Garrane Itoale	gentry: gent	17-Apr-41	600	B.L. 19, 843 f. 96a	2912
Murphy, Thomas	Dublin, Clondalkon	farmer	20-Apr-24	80	Dc2/54r	1209
Murray, Roger	Sligo, Ardneglass	gentry: gent	09-May-39	154	B.L. 19, 843 f. 8	2734
Murtagh, Henry	Wexford, Mottibegg	gentry: gent	09-Dec-16	120	Dc2/3r	883
Muschamp, Denis	Dublin, the city	gentry: esquire	05-Feb-86	3400	B.L. 15, 637 f. 104	4035
Myagh, James	Cork, the city	gentry: gent	26-May-65	300	B.L. 15, 635 f. 152a	3524
Myagh, Thomas	Cork, Kinsale	gentry: gent	14-Aug-69	800	B.L. 15, 636 f. 47a	3705
N.S.	Wicklow, Killevana	gentry: gent	11-Jul-22	30	Dc2/41v	1117
Nagle, Edmund	Longford, Ballimakigging	gentry: gent	06-Jun-65	80	Dc3/8	2238
Nagle, John	Cork, Moaneanymye	gentry: son/heir of Richard	06-Aug-40	4000	B.L. 19, 843 f. 74a	2868
Nagle, John	Cork, Moaneanymny	gentry: gent, son/heir of Richard	20-Apr-41	800	B.L. 19, 843 f. 99	2917
Nagle, Richard	Cork, Moaneanymye	gentry: gent	06-Aug-40	4000	B.L. 19, 843 f. 74a	2868
Nagle, Richard	Cork, Moaneanymny	gentry: gent	20-Apr-41	800	B.L. 19, 843 f. 99	2917
Nagle, Richard	Cork, Moneanymny	gentry: gent	17-Apr-41	600	B.L. 19, 843 f. 96a	2912
Nangle, George	Meath, Ardsallagh	gentry: gent	17-Feb-35	1400	Dc2/229v	2023
Nangle, Gerald	Meath, Kildarke	gentry: gent	11-Jun-07	700	Dc1/78r	476
Nangle, John	Dublin	gentry: gent	22-May-01	120	Dc1/32r	212
Nangle, John	Kerry, Dungleicouch	merchant	23-Oct-23	200	Dc2/50v	1183
Nangle, Mathew	Kildare, Ballysan	gentry: gent	30-Apr-21	120	Dc2/35r	1069
Nangle, Patrick	Meath, Ardsallagh	peer: son/heir of Thomas	13-May-20	400	Dc2/29v	1027
Nangle, Thomas	Meath, Arsalloghe	peer: baron Navan	19-Jun-07	500	Dc1/78v	480
Nangle, Thomas	Meath, Ardsallagh	gentry: esquire	11-May-08	70	Dc1/82v	512
Nangle, Thomas	Meath, Ardsallagh	peer: baron Navan	08-Feb-12	86	Dc1/112r	694
Nangle, Thomas	Meath, Ardsallagh	peer: baron Navan	13-Feb-19	100	Dc2/21r	975
Nangle, Thomas	Meath, Ardsallagh	gentry: esq b. Navan	03-Jul-17	200	Dc2/8v	907
Nangle, Thomas	Meath, Ardshallagh	peer: baron Navan	28-Nov-22	700	Dc2/43r	1127
Nangle, Thomas	Meath, Ardsallagh	peer: baron Navan	11-Feb-18	280	Dc2/13v	934
Nangle, Thomas	Meath, Ardsallagh	peer: baron Navan	14-Nov-10	400	Dc1/99v	624
Nangle, Thomas	Meath, Ardsallagh	peer: baron Navan	13-May-20	400	Dc2/29v	1027
Nangle, Thomas	Meath?	peer: baron Navan	12-May-06	200	Dc1/67r	406
Nangle, Thomas	Meath, Ardsallagh	gentry: esquire	20-Dec-04	105	Dc1/54r	340
Nangle, Thomas	Meath, Ardsallagh	peer: baron Navan	22-Jun-15	200	Dc1/139r	863
Nangle, Thomas	Meath, Ardsallagh	gentry: esquire	28-Apr-10	160	Dc1/95v	599
Nangle, Thomas	Meath?	peer: baron Navan	28-Apr-10	160	Dc1/95v	599
Nangle, Thomas	Meath?	peer: baron Navan	19-May-36	140	Dc2/251v	2124
Nangle, Thomas	Meath, Ardsallagh	gentry: esquire	04-Dec-17	200	Dc2/12v	928

Standard	County	Occupation	Date	Amount	MS No	Ident No
Nangle, Thomas	Meath, Ardsallagh	gentry: esquire	22-May-01	120	Dc1/32r	212
Nangle, Thomas	Meath, Ardsallagh	peer: baron Navan	11-May-13	60	Dc1/120v	749
Nangle, Thomas	Meath?	peer: baron Navan	19-May-36	300	Dc2/251v	2125
Nangle, Thomas	Meath, Ardsallagh	peer: baron Navan	08-Jun-13	100	Dc1/121v	755
Nangle, Thomas	Meath, Ardsallagh	peer: baron Navan	14-Feb-22	600	Dc2/38v	1096
Nangle, Thomas	Meath, Ardsallagh	gentry: esquire	28-Nov-08	120	Dc1/85r	530
Nangle, Thomas	Meath?	peer: baron Navan	28-Nov-08	120	Dc1/85r	530
Nangle, Thomas	Meath, Ardsallgh	peer: baron Navan	18-Sep-10	400	Dc1/99r	622
Nangle,Thomas	Meath, Ardsallagh	gentry: esquire	09-Sep-02	105	Dc1/39v	257
Naughton, Rory	Roscommon, Clanegawnye	gentry: gent	06-Nov-06	100	Dc1/70v	428
Nealon, William	Clare, Deesert	gentry: esquire	30-Aug-60	1200	B.L. 15, 635 f. 75a	3393
Nelson, John	King's Co., Clonegaune	gentry: esquire	14-Nov-62	1080	B.L. 15, 635 f. 99	3432
Nesbitt, James	Leitrim, Drumad	gentry: esquire, s./heir of John	12-Feb-86	1000	B.L. 15, 637 f. 107	4041
Nesbitt, James	Leitrim, Drumad	gentry: esquire, s./heir of John	13-Feb-86	1000	B.L. 15, 637 f. 106a	4040
Nesbitt, John	Donegal, Tully Donnell	gentry: esquire	13-Feb-86	1000	B.L. 15, 637 f. 106a	4040
Nesbitt, John	Donegal, Tully Donnell	gentry: esquire	12-Feb-86	1000	B.L. 15, 637 f. 107	4041
Netterville, James	Dublin, Tobber	gentry: gent	27-Feb-32	500	Dc2/176v	1810
Netterville, James	Wicklow, Tobber	gentry: gent	04-Jun-32	240	Dc2/182r	1832
Netterville, James	Kildare, Tober	gentry: gent	20-Mar-26	60	Dc2/75v	1354
Netterville, James	Kildare, Tober	gentry: gent	09-Nov-26	100	Dc2/83r	1394
Netterville, James	Wicklow, Tobber	gentry: gent	22-Feb-30	400	Dc2/143r	1669
Netterville, Nicholas	Meath, Ballegarte	gentry: esquire	19-Feb-21	1000	Dc2/34v	1064
Netterville, Richard	Dublin, Corballes	gentry: gent	18-Jun-00	200	Dc1/24v	164
Netterville, Richard	Dublin, Corballies	gentry: esquire	18-Jun-99	400	Dc1/17r	114
Neville, Richard	Dublin, Cromlyne	gentry: gent	28-Jun-54	200	B.L. 19, 843 f. 143	3000
Newbold, Francis	Queen's Co., Ballyfenane	gentry: gent	26-Jul-77	400	B.L. 19, 844 f. 138	3268
Newbold, Francis	Queen's Co., Ballyfenane	gentry: gent	26-Jul-77	400	Dc3/183r	2693
Newburgh, Thomas	Cavan, Ballyhaies	gentry: esquire	02-Feb-74	2000	Dc3/160r	2602
Newburgh, Thomas	Galway, Portumny	gentry: esquire	02-Jun-56	800	B.L. 19, 843 f. 173a	3058
Newce, William	Cork	gentry: esquire	16-Aug-20	500	B.L. 19, 843 f. 29	2776
Newcomen, Beverly	Dublin, the city	gentry: knight, heir of Robert	06-Mar-20	3000	Dc2/29r	1024
Newcomen, Robert	Longford, Ballyloge	gentry: esquire	03-Dec-36	1000	Dc2/258v	2162
Newcomen, Robert	Dublin, the city	gentry: knight	06-Mar-20	3000	Dc2/29r	1024
Newcomen, Robert	Dublin, the same	gentry: knight and baronet	16-Feb-24	867	Dc2/53v	1204
Newcomen, Thomas	Dublin, the city	gentry: son of Robert	06-Mar-20	3000	Dc2/29r	1024
Newcomen, Thomas	Dublin, the city	gentry: esquire, s./heir Robert	13-Feb-66	600	Dc3/21	2271
Newcomen, Thomas	Longford, Kenogh	gentry: baronet	03-Jun-68	200	Dc3/77	2399
Newcomen, Thomas	Longford, Isenogh	gentry: baronet	03-Jun-68	200	B.L. 15, 635 f. 226a	3658
Newcomen, Thomas	Longford, Barranamore	gentry: esquire	15-Feb-61	360	B.L. 15, 635 f. 63	3377

Standard	County	Occupation	Date	Amount	MS No	Ident No
Newcomen, Thomas	Kildare, Caretowne	gentry: esquire	24-Sep-61	640	B.L. 15, 635 f. 85	3406
Newcomen, Thomas	Dublin, the city	gentry: esquire, s./heir Robert	12-Sep-63	600	B.L. 15, 635 f. 131	3489
Newcomen, Thomas	Dublin, the city	gentry: baronet, s./heir Robert	13-Feb-66	600	B.L. 15, 635 f. 164a	3544
Newell, Thomas	Kilkenny, Callin	gentry: gent	20-Mar-71	500	Dc3/136v	2519
Neylan, Redmond	Clare, Ballyvickahill	gentry: gent	05-Feb-39	600	B.L. 19, 843 f.2	2723
Nicholl, Henry	Waterford, Kilmedin	gentry: esquire	02-Apr-67	600	Dc3/58	2350
Nicholl, Henry	Waterford, Kilmeden	gentry: esquire	29-Jul-71	446	Dc3/139r	2527
Nicholl, Henry	England, London	gentry: esquire	06-Jun-72	800	Dc3/146v	2553
Noble, Richard	Dublin, Grandgegorman	gentry: gent	30-Oct-04	1000	Dc1/53v	336
Noel, Thomas	Kilkenny, Callen	gentry: gent	20-Mar-71	500	B.L. 15, 636 f. 85	3770
Nolan, Gregory	Mayo, Ballinrobe	gentry: esquire	04-Dec-28	400	Dc2/122r	1570
Nolan, Gregory	Mayo, Ballinrobe	gentry: esquire	01-Dec-28	400	Dc2/122r	1569
Nolan, James	Mayo, Ballinrobe	gentry: gent	17-Dec-25	40	Dc2/72r	1333
Nolan, James	Mayo, Ballinrobe	gentry: gent	02-Dec-25	120	Dc2/71v	1328
Nolan, James	Mayo, Ballinrobe	gentry: gent	17-Dec-25	200	Dc2/72v	1334
Nolan, James	Mayo, Ballinrobe	gentry: gent	09-Mar-25	120	Dc2/62r	1269
Nolan, John	Dublin, Gallanston	gentry: esquire	17-Dec-25	40	Dc2/72r	1333
Nolan, John	Dublin, Gallanston	gentry: esquire	17-Dec-25	200	Dc2/72v	1334
Nolan, John	Sligo, Eskerowne	gentry: esquire	02-Dec-33	1000	Dc2/202r	1911
Nolan, John	Dublin	gentry: esquire	21-Jun-30	100	Dc2/152v	1709
Nolan, John	Dublin, Gallantston	gentry: esquire	09-Mar-25	120	Dc2/62r	1269
Nolan, John	Dublin	gentry: esquire	21-Jun-30	40	Dc2/152v	1710
Nolan, John	Dublin, the city	gentry: esquire	04-Dec-28	400	Dc2/122r	1570
Nolan, John	Dublin, the city	gentry: esquire	01-Dec-28	400	Dc2/122r	1569
Nolan, John	Dublin, Gallanston	gentry: esquire	02-Dec-25	120	Dc2/71v	1328
Nolan, John	Mayo, Ballenrobe	gentry: gent	25-Jun-22	3000	Dc2/41r	1113
Nolan, John	Sligo, Eskerowen	gentry: esquire	01-Aug-33	1000	Dc2/198r	1896
Nolan, John	Dublin, Gallanston	gentry: esquire	07-Jun-25	606	Dc2/65r	1290
Nolan, Richard	Dublin	gentry: gent	26-Oct-26	200	Dc2/82v	1393
Nolan, Thomas	Mayo, Ballenrobe	gentry: esquire	25-Jun-22	3000	Dc2/41r	1113
Nolan, Thomas	Mayo, Ballinrobe	gentry: gent	24-May-10	300	Dc1/97r	608
Norris, Thomas	illegible	gentry: knight	07-Feb-97	1000	Dc1/1r	4
Northeast, Jonathan	Dublin, the city	merchant	10-Feb-68	1500	Dc3/73	2389
Norton, John	Dublin, Cornells Court	farmer	08-Apr-65	220	Dc3/3	2229
Note, Thomas	Cork, Aghdowne	gentry: gent	11-May-30	400	Dc2/147r	1686
Noton, Humphrey	Antrim, Templepatricke	gentry: esquire	13-Feb-18	1000	Dc2/13v	935
Nottingham, Lamencke?	Dublin, Deanerath	gentry: gent	23-Feb-09	60	Dc1/87v	548
Nottingham, Lamoracke	Dublin, Ballyowen	gentry: esquire	24-Dec-32	200	Dc2/189r	1860
Nottingham, Roger	Dublin, Luske	gentry: gent	17-Apr-06	1000	Dc1/66v	402
Nottingham, William	Dublin, Ballyowen?	gentry: s/heir of Lamoracke	24-Dec-32	200	Dc2/189r	1860
Nugent, Andrew	Westmeath, Donowre	gentry: gent	11-May-19	100	Dc2/23v	991
Nugent, Christoper	Westmeath, Robinston	gentry: esquire	15-Feb-23	400	Dc2/45r	1142

Standard	County	Occupation	Date	Amount	MS No	Ident No
Nugent, Christopher	Meath, Moyrath	gentry: gent	15-Jul-02	200	Dc1/39r	252
Nugent, Christopher	Dublin, Cloghran Sworde	gentry: gent	19-Sep-11	120	Dc1/107r	665
Nugent, Christopher	Westmeath, Robinson	gentry: gent	13-Jun-25	600	Dc2/66r	1296
Nugent, Christopher	Meath, Moyrath	gentry: esquire	03-Mar-98	170	Dc1/10r	72
Nugent, Christopher	Meath, Moyrath	gentry: esquire	24-Jan-01	80	Dc1/28r	187
Nugent, Christopher	Meath, Moyrath	gentry: esquire	25-Aug-00	200	Dc1/25v	172
Nugent, Christopher	Dublin, Kilmore	gentry: gent	29-Apr-24	300	Dc2/54v	1212
Nugent, Christopher	Westmeath, Wardinstowne?	gentry: gent	04-Mar-78	410	Dc3/187r	2707
Nugent, Christopher	Westmeath, Robinstowne	gentry: esquire	21-Jun-31	1500	Dc2/165r	1764
Nugent, Christopher	Westmeath, Robinston	gentry: esquire	15-Apr-36	1400	Dc2/249r	2114
Nugent, Christopher	Westmeath, Robintowne	gentry: esquire	08-Nov-34	204	Dc2/220v	1986
Nugent, Christopher	Dublin, Kilmoore	gentry: gent	21-Dec-16	100	Dc2/3v	886
Nugent, Christopher	Westmeath, Robinston	gentry: gent	20-May-24	400	Dc2/55r	1216
Nugent, Christopher	Westmeath, Robinstowne	gentry: esquire	10-Jun-34	400	Dc2/212v	1954
Nugent, Edmund	Dublin, the city	merchant	15-Jul-02	200	Dc1/39r	252
Nugent, Edmund	Westmeath, Taffarnan	gentry: gent	07-Mar-98	40	Dc1/10r	73
Nugent, Edmund	Westmeath, Carlonstowne	gentry: esquire	14-Nov-85	600	B.L. 15, 637 f. 102a	4033
Nugent, Edward	Westmeath, Morton	gentry: gent	20-Feb-98	120	Dc1/9v	68
Nugent, Edward	Westmeath, Bracklyn	gentry: gent	03-Mar-98	40	Dc1/10v	74
Nugent, Edward	Westmeath, Bracklyn	gentry: esquire	07-Mar-98	40	Dc1/10r	73
Nugent, Ignatius	Cavan, Sullegollen?	gentry: esquire	01-Jul-45	400	B.L. 19, 843 f. 120	2959
Nugent, James	Westmeath, Portloman	gentry: esquire, s./heir Walter	20-May-37	4000	Dc2/263v	2183
Nugent, James	Dublin, the city	merchant	07-Jan-36	400	Dc2/243r	2088
Nugent, James	Dublin	merchant: brother, Christopher	21-Dec-16	100	Dc2/3v	886
Nugent, James	Dublin, the city	merchant	15-Apr-36	1400	Dc2/249r	2114
Nugent, James	Dublin, the city	merchant	25-Aug-34	200	Dc2/217v	1975
Nugent, James	Dublin, the city	merchant	08-Nov-34	204	Dc2/220v	1986
Nugent, James	Westmeath, Collamber	gentry: esquire	21-Jul-54	120	B.L. 19, 843 f. 142a	2999
Nugent, James	Dublin	merchant	10-Jun-34	400	Dc2/212v	1954
Nugent, James	Westmeath, Portlamon		25-Apr-43	320	B.L. 19, 843 f. 111a	2942
Nugent, James	Westmeath, Teffernan	gentry: gent	23-May-07	80	Dc1/77v	472
Nugent, James	Meath, Kilcarne	gentry: son of William	01-Dec-19	1000	Dc2/26v	1008
Nugent, James	Meath, Rosse	gentry: esquire	22-Jun-30	3000	Dc2/153r	1711
Nugent, James	Meath, Kilcarne	gentry: son/heir of William	23-Apr-18	260	Dc2/14r	937
Nugent, Janet	Meath, Kilcarne	gentry: wife of William	17-Dec-05	40	Dc1/64r	388
Nugent, Janet	Meath, Kilkarne	gentry: wife of William	27-May-07	300	Dc1/77v	473
Nugent, Janet	Meath, Kilkarne	gentry: gent[lewoman]	21-Aug-09	400	Dc1/91r	570
Nugent, Janet	Meath, Kilcarne	gentry: wife of William	01-Dec-19	1000	Dc2/26v	1008
Nugent, Janet	Meath, Kilcarne	gentry: wife of William	23-Apr-18	260	Dc2/14r	937
Nugent, Janet	Meath, Kilcarne		17-Feb-07	300	Dc1/75r	454
Nugent, John	Westmeath, Culuin	gentry: gent	26-Nov-31	500	Dc2/172v	1794
Nugent, John	Westmeath, Killagh	gentry: gent	16-Feb-66	120	Dc3/23	2274

Standard	County	Occupation	Date	Amount	MS No	Ident No
Nugent, John	Westmeath, Cinluni	gentry: gent	12-Jun-27	250	Dc2/94r	1440
Nugent, John	Westmeath , Cinluni	gentry: gent	12-Jun-27	250	Dc2/94r	1439
Nugent, John	Longford, Ballinlagh	gentry: esquire	20-Jun-45	600	B.L. 19, 843 f. 119a	2958
Nugent, John	Westmeath, Culuin	gentry: gent	24-Jul-34	320	Dc2/215v	1966
Nugent, Mary	Meath?	peer: widow, of Delvin	13-Jul-03	260	Dc1/47ar	305
Nugent, Oliver	Westmeath, Mapstowne	gentry: gent	04-Feb-32	50	Dc2/174v	1803
Nugent, Oliver	Westmeath, Mabstowne	gentry: gent	28-Nov-34	220	Dc2/224r	2000
Nugent, Oliver	Westmeath, Mapestowne	gentry: gent	04-Jul-32	50	Dc2/184v	1841
Nugent, Richard	Meath?	peer: baron Delvin	13-Jul-03	260	Dc1/47ar	305
Nugent, Richard	Westmeath, the Rossa?	gentry: son/heir of William	12-May-99	200	Dc1/16r	110
Nugent, Richard	Westmeath, Rosse	gentry: son/heir of William	16-Nov-98	120	Dc1/13r	94
Nugent, Richard	Dublin	merchant	19-Sep-11	120	Dc1/107r	665
Nugent, Robert	Longford, Aghnagarim	gentry: gent	25-May-66	1000	Dc3/29	2288
Nugent, Robert	Meath, Kilkarne	gentry: son/heir of Wm Nugent	13-May-08	320	Dc1/82v	514
Nugent, Robert	Westmeath, Cavolanston	gentry: esquire	11-Nov-17	200	Dc2/11r	919
Nugent, Robert	Westmeath, Taghman	gentry: baronet	28-Jun-73	400	Dc3/158v	2591
Nugent, Robert	Westmeath, Taghmon	gentry: baronet	20-Sep-69	600	Dc3/102	2447
Nugent, Robert	Westmeath, Ballinsillod	gentry: gent	04-May-32	400	Dc2/178v	1817
Nugent, Robert	Westmeath, Rosse, Lough Sillan	gentry: son/heir of William	17-Feb-09	200	Dc1/87v	547
Nugent, Robert	Westmeath, Taghman	gentry: baronet	28-Jun-73	400	B.L. 19, 844 f. 2	3121
Nugent, Robert	Westmeath, Taghman	gentry: baronet	28-Jun-73	200	B.L. 19, 844 f. 3	3122
Nugent, Robert	Westmeath, Taghman	gentry: baronet	28-Jun-73	200	Dc3/158v	2590
Nugent, Robert	Meath, Kilkarne	gentry: gent	27-May-07	300	Dc1/77v	473
Nugent, Robert	Wicklow, Dunmore	gentry: esquire	08-Feb-66	1200	B.L. 15, 635 f. 169	3549
Nugent, Robert	Roscommon, Corkreagh	gentry: son/heir of Sir Thomas	22-Jul-61	6000	B.L. 15, 635 f. 76a	3394
Nugent, Robert	Westmeath, Taghman	gentry: baronet	01-Oct-64	800	B.L. 15, 635 f. 149	3517
Nugent, Robert	Meath, Kilkarne	gentry: gent	21-Aug-09	400	Dc1/91r	570
Nugent, Robert	Westmeath, Taghmon	gentry: baronet	20-Sep-69	600	B.L. 15, 636 f. 51a	3712
Nugent, Thomas	Westmeath, Cavolanston	gentry: gent, brother of Robert	11-Nov-17	200	Dc2/11r	919
Nugent, Thomas	Westmeath, Balreagh	gentry: gent	10-Sep-27	200	Dc2/98v	1459
Nugent, Thomas	Meath, Daylistowne	gentry: gent	16-Nov-31	80	Dc2/170r	1784
Nugent, Thomas	Galway, Pallace	gentry: esquire	08-Feb-84	1000	B.L. 15, 637 f. 84	3999
Nugent, Thomas	Louth, Drogheda		09-Aug-62	160	B.L. 15, 635 f. 95	3424
Nugent, Thomas	Roscommon, Corkreagh	gentry: knight and baronet	22-Jul-61	6000	B.L. 15, 635 f. 76a	3394
Nugent, William	Meath, the Rosse	gentry: esquire	28-Jun-98	120	Dc1/11v	82
Nugent, William	Westmeath, Rosse, LoughSilian	gentry: esquire	27-Jan-00	130	Dc1/21r	141
Nugent, William	Meath, Kilkarne	gentry: esquire	13-May-08	320	Dc1/82v	514

Standard	County	Occupation	Date	Amount	MS No	Ident No
Nugent, William	Meath, Kilcarne	gentry: esquire	01-Mar-14	200	Dc1/127v	790
Nugent, William	Meath, Kilcarne	gentry: esquire	27-May-07	300	Dc1/77v	473
Nugent, William	Westmeath, the Rosse	gentry: esquire	12-May-99	200	Dc1/16r	110
Nugent, William	Meath, Kilcarne		17-Feb-07	300	Dc1/75r	454
Nugent, William	Meath, Kilcarne	gentry: esquire	17-Dec-05	40	Dc1/64r	388
Nugent, William	Meath, Kilcarne	gentry: esquire	23-Aug-03	240	Dc1/48r	312
Nugent, William	Meath, Kilcarne	gentry: esquire	16-Sep-11	105	Dc1/106r	661
Nugent, William	Westmeath, Rosse, Loghsylan	gentry: esquire	16-Nov-98	120	Dc1/13r	94
Nugent, William	Meath, Kilcarne	gentry: esquire	23-Apr-18	260	Dc2/14r	937
Nugent, William	Meath, Kilcarne?	gentry: gent	20-Jul-09	80	Dc1/90v	566
Nugent, William	Meath, Kilcarne	gentry: esquire	01-Dec-19	1000	Dc2/26v	1008
Nugent, William	Meath, Kilcarne	gentry: esquire	05-Mar-10	120	Dc1/94v	592
Nugent, William	Westmeath, Rosse, Lough Sillan	gentry: esquire	17-Feb-09	200	Dc1/87v	547
Nugent, William	Meath, Kilcarne	gentry: esquire	21-Aug-09	400	Dc1/91r	570
O'Brien, Brian	Clare, Agherin	gentry: gent	25-Nov-14	600	Dc1/133r	826
O'Brien, Connor	Clare, Derryowen	gentry: gent	01-Dec-25	20	Dc2/71r	1326
O'Brien, Connor	Clare, Ballymulcashell	gentry: gent	01-Dec-25	20	Dc2/71r	1326
O'Brien, Connor	Tipperary, Belanaha?	gentry: son/heir of Donogh	16-Dec-33	3000	Dc2/204r	1919
O'Brien, Daniel	Tipperary, Annagh	gentry: esquire	10-Dec-35	200	Dc2/242r	2081
O'Brien, Daniel	Clare?	peer: viscount Clare	19-Jun-76	2800	Dc3/178r	2668
O'Brien, Daniel	Clare?	peer: viscount Clare	21-Mar-74	1000	B.L. 19, 844 f. 26a	3149
O'Brien, Daniel	Clare, Carrigholt	gentry: esquire	05-Dec-66	500	Dc3/42	2319
O'Brien, Daniel	Clare?	peer: viscount Clare	19-Jun-76	2000	B.L. 19, 844 f. 100	3227
O'Brien, Daniel	Tipperary, Annagh	gentry: esquire	02-Jul-26	140	Dc2/80r	1381
O'Brien, Daniel	Clare?	peer: viscount Clare	21-Mar-74	1000	B.L. 15, 636 f. 131a	3840
O'Brien, Daniel	Clare, Carrighall	gentry: esquire	05-Dec-66	500	B.L. 15, 635 f. 184	3578
O'Brien, Dermot	Clare?,	peer: baron Inchiquin	25-Nov-14	600	Dc1/133r	826
O'Brien, Donald	Cork, Dungullane	gentry: gent	07-Jan-41	3200	B.L. 19, 843 f. 82	2883
O'Brien, Donogh	Clare, Newtowne	gentry: esquire	26-Jun-32	60	Dc2/184r	1840
O'Brien, Donogh	Tipperary, Belanaha	gentry: esquire	16-Dec-33	3000	Dc2/204r	1919
O'Brien, Donogh	Clare, Newton	gentry: esquire	17-Jun-35	960	Dc2/237r	2056
O'Brien, Donogh	Tipperary, Bellanahy	gentry: esquire	06-Dec-26	400	Dc2/85r	1404
O'Brien, Donogh	Clare, Luneneagh	gentry: esquire	26-Jul-69	300	B.L. 15, 636 f. 42a	3698
O'Brien, Kennedy	Tipperary, Ballyurgan	gentry: gent	10-Dec-35	200	Dc2/242r	2081
O'Brien, Murrough	Tipperary?, Annagh?	gentry: gent, son/heir of Daniel	02-Jul-26	140	Dc2/80r	1381
O'Brien, Murrough	Tipperary, Derry	gentry: son/heir of Daniel	10-Dec-35	200	Dc2/242r	2081
O'Brien, Murrough	Clare?	peer: earl of Inchiquin	02-Aug-66	600	Dc3/35	2300
O'Brien, Murrough	Tipperary, Annagh, Ormond	gentry: esquire	09-Mar-39	1200	B.L. 19, 843 f. 21	2760

Standard	County	Occupation	Date	Amount	MS No	Ident No
O'Brien, Murrough	Clare?	peer: earl of Inchiquin	22-Oct-66	2000	Dc3/40	2315
O'Brien, Murrough	Clare?	peer: earl of Inchiquin	22-Jun-68	2000	B.L. 15, 635 f. 225a	3656
O'Brien, Murrough	Clare?	peer: earl of Inchiquin	13-Jun-70	2000	B.L. 15, 636 f. 65	3733
O'Brien, Murrough	Clare?	peer: earl of Inchiquin	13-Jun-70	960	B.L. 15, 636 f. 64a	3732
O'Brien, Teige	Cork, Kilnesur	gentry: gent	29-Aug-73	1200	B.L. 19, 844 f. 17	3135
O'Brien, Terence	Tipperary, Castletowne Arra	gentry: esquire	27-Jan-24	300	Dc2/52v	1196
O'Brien, Thady	Clare, Luneneagh	gentry: gent	26-Jul-69	300	B.L. 15, 636 f. 42a	3698
O'Brien, Turlough	Clare, Tullaghmore	gentry: esquire	14-Mar-36	400	Dc2/247r	2104
O'Brien, Turlough	Clare, Tullamore	gentry: gent	24-Nov-27	100	Dc2/100r	1465
O'Brien, William		peer: lord O'Brien, son of Murrough	22-Jun-68	2000	B.L. 15, 635 f. 225a	3656
O'Brien, William		peer: lord O'Brien, son of Murrough	13-Jun-70	2000	B.L. 15, 636 f. 65	3733
O'Brien, William		peer: lord O'Brien, son of Murrough	13-Jun-70	960	B.L. 15, 636 f. 64a	3732
O'Connor, Charles	Roscommon, Ballintobber	gentry: esquire	01-Jun-33	400	Dc2/195v	1886
O'Connor, Charles	King's Co., Kilclanturke	gentry: gent	15-Jun-27	300	Dc2/94v	1441
O'Connor, Charles	Roscommon, Ballintobber	gentry: esquire	27-Jun-33	300	Dc2/196v	1890
O'Connor, Charles	Roscommon, Ballintobber	gentry: esquire	07-Jun-33	800	Dc2/196r	1887
O'Connor, Charles	Clare, Loughcloven	gentry: gent	24-Nov-27	100	Dc2/100r	1465
O'Connor, Charles	Sligo, Sligo	gentry: knight and baronet	03-Aug-22	1200	Dc2/42r	1120
O'Connor, Charles	King's Co., Kilcloncorkery	gentry: gent	04-Sep-30	400	Dc2/154v	1718
O'Connor, Donogh	Sligo, Sligo	gentry: esquire	27-May-29	2000	Dc2/130r	1609
O'Connor, Donogh	Sligo, Sligo	gentry: esquire	30-Nov-28	1000	Dc2/119v	1559
O'Connor, Donogh	Sligo, Sligo	gentry: esquire	09-Dec-25	100	Dc2/72r	1331
O'Connor, Donogh	Sligo, Sligo	gentry: esquire	12-Dec-26	500	Dc2/86v	1409
O'Connor, Donogh	Sligo, Sligo	gentry: esquire	11-May-27	4000	Dc2/92v	1432
O'Connor, John	Kerry, Carrigfoille	gentry: gent	03-Dec-97	30	Dc1/9r	62
O'Connor, John	Kerry, Carrickfoile	gentry: esquire	19-Nov-13	20	Dc1/124r	770
O'Connor, Mathew	Dublin, the city	gentry: gent	27-Aug-77	500	B.L. 19, 844 f. 142	3272
O'Connor, Mathew	Dublin, the city	gentry: gent	27-Aug-77	500	Dc3/183r	2694
O'Connor, Roger	Sligo, Scardane	gentry: gent	01-Jul-38	100	B.L. 19, 843 f. 9a	2737
O'Dempsey, Owny	King's Co., Clonegowny	gentry: esquire	08-Dec-18	120	Dc2/19r	963
O'Donnell, Neill		gentry: knight	21-May-04	300	Dc1/53r	334
O'Donnell, Nigel	Donegal, Castellfinne	gentry: knight	26-Apr-05	1200	Dc1/60v	368
O'Donnell, Rory	Donegal?	peer: earl of Tyrconnell	09-Jul-07	500	Dc1/79v	485
O'Doron, Patrick	Down, Killcowe	gentry: gent	10-Dec-34	200	Dc2/225v	2007
O'Gara, Farrell	Sligo, Moighgane	gentry: gent	20-Jun-25	200	Dc2/66v	1297
O'Gara, Farrell	Sligo, Copnagh	gentry: gent	07-Jun-24	280	Dc2/55v	1219
O'Gara, Farrell	Sligo, Moighgane	gentry: gent	25-Jun-25	300	Dc2/66v	1298
O'Gormogan?, Thady	Carlow, Newton	gentry: gent	20-Nov-18	120	Dc2/17v	956
O'Hara, Cahill	Antrim, Slatte	gentry: gent	10-Aug-39	5000	B.L. 19, 843 f. 33	2784
O'Hara, Cormac	Sligo, Mollon	gentry: esquire	14-May-34	400	Dc2/211r	1948

Standard	County	Occupation	Date	Amount	MS No	Ident No
O'Hara, Cormac	Sligo, Molane	gentry: esquire	19-Dec-29	300	Dc2/140v	1657
O'Hara, Cyril	Antrim, Townaghbracke	gentry: gent	10-Aug-39	5000	B.L. 19, 843 f. 33	2784
O'Hara, Henry	Antrim, Cregbilly	gentry: son of Teige	17-May-55	2240	B.L. 19, 843 f. 160a	3036
O'Hara, Kane	Dublin	gentry: esquire	09-May-36	1600	Dc2/250r	2117
O'Hara, Oliver	Sligo, Mollon?	gentry: son/heir of				
		Cormack	14-May-34	400	Dc2/211r	1948
O'Hara, Teige	Antrim, Cregbilly	gentry: esquire	17-May-55	2240	B.L. 19, 843 f. 160a	3036
O'Keefe, Arthur	Cork, Dromophe	gentry: gent	09-Jun-13	60	Dc1/122r	757
O'Mara, William	Tipperary, Lyssenuske	gentry: esquire	19-Sep-16	200	Dc2/1r	870
O'More, Rory	Meath, Kilmaynamwood	gentry: gent	02-Jun-15	200	Dc1/138r	857
O'Neill, Barnaby	Armagh, Tullaghlish	gentry: esquire	05-Jul-23	114	Dc2/49r	1170
O'Neill, Brian	Down, Ballyhornan	gentry: knight	22-Dec-54	160	B.L. 19, 843 f. 147	3008
O'Neill, Brian	Armagh, Tulloglasse	gentry: esquire	24-May-37	300	Dc2/264r	2185
O'Neill, Brian	Dublin	gentry: gent	21-Jun-30	40	Dc2/152v	1710
O'Neill, Brian	Dublin	gentry: gent	21-Jun-30	100	Dc2/152v	1709
O'Neill, Conn	Kildare, Castlewarnyne	gentry: esquire	23-Jul-03	500	Dc1/47av	307
O'Neill, Cormac	Antrim, Tullymore	gentry: esquire	29-Mar-78	220	B.L. 19, 844 f. 158	3289
O'Neill, Cormac	Antrim, Tullymore	gentry: esquire	27-Mar-82	800	B.L. 15, 637 f. 58a	3952
O'Neill, Henry	Antrim, Edendufcarricke	gentry: knight	25-Feb-24	100	Dc2/54r	1206
O'Neill, John	Dublin	gentry: esquire	14-Mar-29	2000	Dc2/126v	1593
O'Neill, John	Antrim, Magherleane	gentry: esquire	29-Mar-78	220	B.L. 19, 844 f. 158	3289
O'Neill, John	Tipperary, Carrick	gentry: esquire	12-Nov-66	1000	Dc3/41	2318
O'Neill, Neill	Antrim, Killelagh	gentry: esquire	10-May-27	2000	Dc2/92r	1430
O'Neill, Phelim	Tyrone, Keynard	gentry: esquire	27-Jun-35	2000	Dc2/238r	2062
O'Neill, Phelim	Tyrone, Kinard	gentry: esquire	01-Dec-31	400	Dc2/173r	1797
O'Neill, Phelim	Tyrone, Kynard	gentry: esquire	04-May-32	2000	Dc2/178v	1818
O'Neill, Phelim	Tyrone, Kinard					
	[Monnterberry]	gentry: esquire	19-Feb-39	1000	B.L. 19,843 f. 50a	2819
O'Neill, Phelim	Tyrone, Kennard	gentry: esquire	07-Jul-37	2000	Dc2/267r	2197
O'Neill, Phelim	Tyrone, Kynnard	gentry: esquire	17-Jun-35	1200	Dc2/236v	2055
O'Neill, Phelim	Dublin, the city	gentry: gent	19-Dec-83	2400	B.L. 15, 637 f. 82	3996
O'Neill, Stephen	Louth, Carlingford	gentry: gent	30-Aug-39	200	B.L. 19, 843 f. 24a	2767
O'Neill, Terence	Armagh, Ardgonnell	gentry: gent	04-May-32	2000	Dc2/178v	1818
O'Neill, Turlough	Armagh, Ardgonnell	gentry: esquire	27-Jun-35	2000	Dc2/238r	2062
O'Neill, Turlough	Armagh, Argonell	gentry: esquire	07-Jul-37	2000	Dc2/267r	2197
O'Rourke, Con	Leitrim,					
	Aghloghdonnoghery	gentry: gent	03-Dec-36	600	Dc2/258v	2161
O'Rourke, John	Leitrim, Cloncoricke	gentry: esquire	21-Nov-31	80	Dc2/171v	1790
O'Rourke, Mary	Leitrim, Newton	gentry: widow of Sir Teige	29-Oct-17	108	Dc2/10r	914
O'Rourke, Mary	Leitrim, Newton	gentry: widow of Sir Teige	30-Oct-17	120	Dc2/10r	915
O'Rourke, Teige	Leitrim, Lethram	gentry: esquire	03-Feb-04	666	Dc1/52r	330
O'Shaughnessy, Roger	Galway, Gortinchyuorin	gentry: knight	11-May-27	4000	Dc2/92v	1432
Oakely, Rowland	Dublin, the city	gentry: esquire	01-Sep-56	200	B.L. 15, 635 f. 24	3305
Odel, Charles	Limerick, Castletowne					
	Macinery	gentry: gent	05-Nov-83	1500	B.L. 15, 637 f. 80	3993

Standard	County	Occupation	Date	Amount	MS No	Ident No
Ormsby, Edward	Mayo, Shruel	gentry: knight	22-Feb-75	4200	B.L. 19, 844 f. 50	3173
Ormsby, Edward	Mayo, Shruell	gentry: knight	25-Feb-75	4200	Dc3/165r	2625
Ormsby, Robert	Mayo, Shrule	gentry: esquire	21-Mar-60	500	B.L. 15, 635 f. 59a	3370
Orr, Thomas	Dublin	merchant	13-Jun-59	200	B.L. 15, 635 f. 47a	3347
Osbaldston, John	Westmeath, St.Bridget's Well	gentry: gent	16-Aug-55	600	B.L. 19, 843 f. 163a	3041
Osbourne, James	Dublin, the city	trade: barber-surgeon	09-Dec-28	100	Dc2/121v	1568
Osbourne, John	Dublin, Butterlane	gentry: gent	04-Dec-71	400	Dc3/142v	2539
Owen, Henry	Dublin, the city	gentry: esquire	05-Dec-66	1600	Dc3/46	2323
Owen, Nicholas	Kildare, Blackhall	gentry: esquire	13-May-24	300	Dc2/55r	1214
Owen, Nicholas	Kildare, Blackhall	gentry: esquire	14-May-24	300	Dc2/55r	1215
Owen, Richard	Kildare, Blackhall	gentry: gent	12-May-24	300	Dc2/54v	1213
Oxburgh, Henry	King's Co., Bovne?	gentry: esquire	13-Aug-85	1600	B.L. 15, 637 f. 101a	4031
Oxburgh, Howard	Galway, Lisenacade	gentry: gent	01-Dec-57	120	B.L. 19, 843 f. 201	3108
Packenham, Henry	Westmeath, Tullenalley	gentry: esquire	03-May-73	200	Dc3/156v	2582
Packington, William	Waterford, the city	gentry: gent	22-Apr-68	200	B.L. 15, 635 f. 228a	3662
Page, John	Kildare, Newhall	gentry: gent	28-Apr-37	400	Dc2/261v	2174
Page, Thomas	Limerick, Glynn	gentry: gent	28-May-77	800	B.L. 19, 844 f. 128a	3258
Page, Thomas	Limerick, Glynn	gentry: gent	28-May-77	800	Dc3/182v	2689
Page, Thomas	Limerick, Glynn	gentry: gent	31-Jul-76	2000	Dc3/179v	2674
Page, Thomas	Limerick, Corkamore	gentry: gent	14-Aug-80	1800	B.L. 15, 637 f. 39	3916
Paisley, William	Dublin	gentry: esquire	21-Nov-29	200	Dc2/138r	1645
Paisley, William	Dublin	gentry: esquire	17-Oct-29	140	Dc2/137r	1640
Pallas, Andrew	Dublin, the city	gentry: gent	03-Dec-36	1200	Dc2/259r	2163
Pallas, James	Meath, Longwood	gentry: gent	23-Dec-65	92	Dc3/18	2263
Pallas, James	Meath, Longwood	gentry: gent	21-Apr-64	200	B.L. 15, 635 f. 129a	3486
Pallas, William	Dublin, the city	gentry: gent	20-Feb-41	621	B.L. 19, 843 f. 85a	2890
Paris, John	Tipperary, Ardmale	gentry: esquire	08-Nov-78	1000	B.L. 19, 844 f. 170	3301
Parker, Giles	Dublin, Sk?blestoy?	gentry: gent	10-Sep-19	80	Dc2/25v	1002
Parker, Giles	Kildare, Athie	gentry: esquire	30-Jun-10	120	Dc1/99r	620
Parker, John		prof: bishop of Elphin	23-Feb-67	4000	Dc3/55	2341
Parker, John		prof: bishop of Elphin	23-Feb-67	4000	B.L. 15, 635 f. 187	3584
Parker, Roger	Carlow, Ballyduffe	gentry: gent	09-Nov-40	300	B.L. 19, 843 f. 73a	2866
Parker, William	Wexford, Crondanill	gentry: gent	15-Feb-73	300	Dc3/153v	2574
Parkinson, Edward	Louth, Atherdee		24-Dec-66	200	Dc3/50	2332
Parkinson, Edward	Louth, Atherdee		02-Jan-78	700	B.L. 19, 844 f. 144	3275
Parkinson, Edward	Louth, Atherdee		09-May-76	300	B.L. 19, 844 f. 94	3221
Parkinson, Edward	Louth, Atherdee		12-Sep-74	200	B.L. 19, 844 f. 44	3168
Parry, John		prof: bishop of Ossory	29-Nov-73	880	B.L. 19, 844 f. 12	3131
Parry, John		prof: bishop of Ossory	29-Nov-73	880	Dc3/158av	2596
Parsons, Lawrence	King's Co., Birre	gentry: esquire	21-Feb-63	730	B.L. 15, 635 f. 101	3436
Parsons, Lawrence	King's Co., Birr	gentry: baronet	19-Apr-81	3000	B.L. 15, 637 f. 47a	3931
Parsons, Lawrence	King's Co., Birre/ Parsonstowne	gentry: esquire	05-Jun-67	3000	B.L. 15, 635 f. 200a	3610

Standard	County	Occupation	Date	Amount	MS No	Ident No
Parsons, Richard	Dublin, Ballymount	gentry: baronet	18-May-81	20000	B.L. 15, 637 f. 44	3926
Parsons, William	Dublin, the city	gentry: baronet	16-Aug-55	1200	B.L. 19, 843 f. 161a	3038
Pasmer, Patrick	Dublin, Baldoyle, the grange	farmer	26-Nov-61	320	B.L. 15,635 f. 88	3412
Pasmer, Patrick	Dublin, Grange of Baldoyle	farmer	26-Nov-61	220	B.L. 15, 635 f. 87a	3411
Pasmer, Robert	Dublin, Balscaddan	farmer	10-Dec-02	80	Dc1/42r	270
Pawlett, John	Roscommon, Derritoman	gentry: esquire	02-Dec-56	300	B.L. 19, 843 f. 189a	3086
Peake, Phillip	Dublin, the city	gentry: esquire	06-Feb-55	172	B.L. 19, 843 f. 151a	3017
Peard, Richard	Cork, Coole	soldier: ensign	10-Apr-75	1200	B.L. 19, 844 f. 60	3185
Peard, Richard	Cork, Coole	soldier: ensign	12-Apr-75	2400	B.L. 19, 844 f. 59	3184
Peard, Richard	Cork, Coole	gentry: gent	18-Jan-77	880	B.L. 19, 844 f. 130	3260
Peard, Richard	Cork, Coole	gentry: gent, son/heir of Richard	12-Apr-75	2400	B.L. 19, 844 f. 59	3184
Peard, Richard	Cork, Coole	gentry: gent, son/heir of Richard	10-Apr-75	1200	B.L. 19, 844 f. 60	3185
Peard, Richard	Cork, Coole	gentry: gent	29-Oct-79	800	B.L. 15, 637 f. 27	3895
Peckham, James	Down, Downdrowe	gentry: esquire	23-May-34	630	Dc2/211v	1951
Pemberton, Thomas	Dublin, the city	gentry: gent	18-May-68	300	Dc3/76	2396
Pench, John	Carlow, Orchard	gentry: esquire	23-Nov-77	1600	Dc3/183v	2697
Penery, Nathan	Dublin, the city	trade: coach-maker	29-Jun-82	1200	B.L. 15, 637 f. 61a	3958
Pentony, Edward	Meath, Cabragh	gentry: gent	27-Jul-24	200	Dc2/57v	1235
Pentony, Edward	Meath, Cabragh	gentry: gent	01-Jun-25	340	Dc2/64v	1286
Pentony, Edward	Meath, the Cabragh	gentry: gent	12-Jun-30	600	Dc1/150r	1699
Pentony, Edward	Meath, Cabragh	gentry: gent	27-Sep-23	40	Dc2/50v	1182
Pentony, Gilbert	Meath, the Cabragh	gentry: gent, 2nd s of Edward	12-Jun-30	600	Dc1/150r	1699
Pentony, Mathew	Meath, the Cabragh	gentry: gent, s/h of Edward	12-Jun-30	600	Dc1/150r	1699
Peppard, Christopher	Louth, Drogheda	merchant	29-Jan-79	600	B.L. 15, 637 f. 11	3867
Peppard, George	Meath, Sarsfieldstowme	gentry: gent	30-Jan-73	200	B.L. 19, 844 f. 4	3123
Peppard, George	Louth, Drogheda		07-Dec-65	217	Dc3/17	2259
Peppard, George	Louth, Drogheda		02-Dec-65	261	B.L. 15, 635 f. 173a	3556
Peppard, Ignatius	Louth, Drogheda	merchant	29-Jan-79	600	B.L. 15, 637 f. 11	3867
Peppard, Patrick	Wexford, Glascarricke	gentry: gent	21-Jul-17	160	Dc2/9r	910
Peppard, Patrick	Wexford, Glascarricke	gentry: esquire	12-Nov-24	300	Dc2/58r	1240
Peppard, Patrick	Wexford, Glascarricke	gentry: gent	14-Jul-37	1200	Dc2/268v	2204
Peppard, Patrick	Wexford, Mannor of Peppard	gentry: esquire	01-Dec-21	200	Dc2/37r	1085
Peppard, Thomas	Wexford, Glascarrige	gentry: gent	18-Nov-28	300	Dc2/116r	1542
Peppard, Thomas	Wexford, Glascarricke	gentry: gent, s/h of Patrick	14-Jul-37	1200	Dc2/268v	2204
Pepper, John	Louth, Peppardstowne	gentry: gent	16-Apr-78	300	B.L. 19, 844 f. 155	3286
Percival, John	Dublin, the city	gentry: esquire	18-May-54	2000	B.L. 19, 843 f. 138a	2991
Percival, John	Dublin, the city	gentry: esquire	19-Jul-58	500	B.L. 15, 635 f. 32a	3320
Percival, John	Dublin, the city	gentry: baronet	13-Nov-62	420	B.L. 15, 635 f. 98a	3431

Standard	County	Occupation	Date	Amount	MS No	Ident No
Percival, Philip	Dublin, the city	gentry: esquire	04-Apr-36	2000	Dc2/248v	2110
Percy, Henry	Westmeath, Trysternagh	gentry: esquire	27-Jan-99	200	Dc1/15r	103
Perry, William	Limerick	gentry: gent	12-Feb-21	400	Dc2/34v	1063
Pesly, William	King's Co., Knocknemease	gentry: esquire	09-Feb-32	110	Dc2/175v	1806
Pettit, Adam	Westmeath, Ballindiry	gentry: esquire	05-Dec-29	200	Dc2/139v	1652
Pettit, Garret	Westmeath, Kilpatricke	gentry: esquire	10-Jul-23	200	Dc2/49r	1173
Pettit, Gerald	Meath, Bourdstowne	gentry: gent	25-Aug-28	1000	Dc2/114v	1535
Pettit, Gerald	Westmeath, Irishstowne	gentry: esquire	05-Dec-29	200	Dc2/139v	1652
Pettit, Gerald	Westmeath, Boordstowne	gentry: esquire	26-Nov-31	200	Dc2/172v	1795
Pettit, Gerald	Westmeath, Lynne	gentry: gent	27-Apr-15	120	Dc1/136v	846
Pettit, Gerrot	Westmeath, Frashton	gentry: esquire	10-Feb-23	100	Dc2/45r	1139
Pettit, Thomas	Westmeath, Kilpatricke	gentry: esquire	25-Nov-36	1200	Dc2/258r	2160
Phair, Robert	Cork, Grange	gentry: esquire	09-Mar-78	630	B.L. 19, 844 f. 150	3281
Phillips, George	Londonderry, Lemevaddy	gentry: gent, son/heir of Dudley	14-May-53	2000	B.L. 19, 843 f. 133	2981
Phillips, George	Londonderry, NewtownKinnevaddy	gentry: esquire	18-Jun-81	1100	B.L. 15, 637 f. 46a	3929
Phillips, George	Londonderry, Lymavady	gentry: esquire	18-Jun-54	1060	B.L. 15, 635 f. 62	3375
Phillips, Richard	Dublin, the city	gentry: esquire	08-Jul-57	400	B.L. 19, 843 f. 195	3097
Philpot, Edward	Louth, Drogheda	gentry: esquire	27-Feb-58	200	B.L. 15, 635 f. 38a	3331
Philpot, Edward	Louth, Drogheda	gentry: esquire	26-Mar-39	400	B.L. 19, 843 f. 25a	2769
Phipps, Michael	Meath, the Rowan	gentry: son/heir of Richard	13-Sep-09	126	Dc1/91v	572
Phipps, Richard	Meath, the Rowane	gentry: gent, son/heir of Patrick	01-Dec-00	500	Dc1/27r	180
Phipps, Richard	Meath, the Rowan	gentry: gent	13-Sep-09	126	Dc1/91v	572
Phipps, Richard	Meath, Rowan	gentry: gent	20-Mar-01	100	Dc1/29v	198
Pierce, Eleanor	Dublin, Merrion	gentry: wife of Richard	08-May-40	600	B.L. 19, 843 f. 61	2841
Pierce, Henry	Westmeath, Tristernagh	gentry: baronet	02-Feb-67	400	Dc3/51	2335
Pierce, Henry	Westmeath, Trysternagh	gentry: esquire	07-Jul-03	700	Dc1/47v	302
Pierce, Henry	Cavan, Pierscourte	gentry: knight and baronet	10-Feb-31	500	Dc2/160v	1742
Pierce, Henry	Cavan, Pierscourte	gentry: knight and baronet	04-Feb-32	2000	Dc2/174r	1801
Pierce, John	Louth, Clintonstowne	gentry: esquire	15-Jul-59	320	B.L. 15, 635 f. 52a	3356
Pierce, Mary	Louth, Clintonstown	gentry: wife of John	15-Jul-59	320	B.L. 15, 635 f. 52a	3356
Pierce, Nicholas	Dublin, the city	merchant	11-Oct-77	8400	Dc3/183v	2695
Pierce, Nicholas	Dublin, the city	merchant	12-Oct-77	8400	B.L. 19, 844 f. 140	3270
Pierce, William	Westmeath, Tristernaugh	gentry: esquire	03-Feb-25	200	Dc2/61r	1261
Pierce, William	Westmeath, Tristernaugh	gentry: esquire	04-Feb-25	200	Dc2/61r	1262
Pigot, Alexander	Cork, Enishonane	gentry: esquire	17-Apr-75	1100	B.L. 19, 844 f. 61	3187
Pigot, Griffith	Dublin, Kilmaynam	gentry: gent	31-May-10	500	Dc1/97r	610
Pigot, Thomas	Queen's Co., Dysart	gentry: esquire	09-May-74	690	B.L. 19, 844 f. 31a	3155
Pigot, Thomas	Queen's Co., Dysart	gentry: esquire	09-May-74	690	Dc3/161r	2608
Pilkington, Thomas	Wexford, Wexford	gentry: gent	14-Sep-66	400	Dc3/38	2310

Standard	County	Occupation	Date	Amount	MS No	Ident No
Pine, Richard	Dublin, the city	gentry: esquire	09-Nov-79	500	B.L. 15, 637 f. 29	3899
Pipher, Kenborowe?	Dublin, the city	other: widow	02-Nov-57	400	B.L. 19, 843 f. 203a	3113
Piphoe, Michael	Meath, the Rowan	gentry: son/heir of				
		Richard	12-Aug-09	600	Dc1/91r	569
Piphoe, Michael	Meath, the Rowan	gentry: son/heir of				
		Richard	08-Apr-10	80	Dc1/95r	594
Piphoe, Richard	Meath, the Rowan	gentry: gent	11-Aug-03	400	Dc1/48v	313
Piphoe, Richard	Meath, the Rowan	gentry: gent	12-Aug-09	600	Dc1/91r	569
Piphoe, Richard	Meath, Rowan	other: son/heir of				
		Patrick	01-May-97	120	Dc1/3v	22
Piphoe, Richard	Meath, Rowan		01-May-97	120	Dc1/3v	22
Piphoe, Richard	Meath, the Rowan	gentry: gent	08-Apr-10	80	Dc1/95r	594
Pitchford, Thomas	Tyrone, Derricke Creene	gentry: gent	19-Jul-28	300	Dc2/113r	1529
Plowden, Richard	Dublin, the city	gentry: esquire	15-Jul-72	2000	Dc3/148r	2559
Plowden, Richard	Galway, Treswell	gentry: esquire	19-Dec-71	1000	Dc3/142v	2540
Plunkett, Alexander	Meath, Geerly	gentry: esquire	26-Mar-24	6000	Dc2/54r	1208
Plunkett, Alexander	Meath, Rathmore	gentry: son/heir of				
		Richard	01-Apr-00	200	Dc1/22v	149
Plunkett, Alexander	Meath, Rathmore?	gentry: son/heir of				
		Richard	23-Apr-02	1000	Dc1/37v	242
Plunkett, Alexander	Meath, Armaghebrege	gentry: gent	03-Feb-03	200	Dc1/44r	280
Plunkett, Alexander	Meath, Gyrley	gentry: esquire	08-Feb-23	280	Dc2/44v	1138
Plunkett, Alexander	Meath, Dullene	gentry: gent	19-Nov-14	80	Dc1/132v	824
Plunkett, Alexander	Meath, Greley	gentry: esquire	14-Feb-22	600	Dc2/38v	1096
Plunkett, Allexander	Meath, Rathmore	gentry: son/heir of				
		Richard	30-Jun-97	41	Dc1/5r	36
Plunkett, Allexander	Meath, Rathmore	gentry: son/heir of				
		Richard	29-Oct-98	200	Dc1/13r	92
Plunkett, Ambrose	Carlow, Urny	gentry: esquire	11-Jul-37	1000	Dc2/267v	2201
Plunkett, Ambrose	Dublin, the city	gentry: esquire	21-Apr-64	200	B.L. 15, 635 f. 129a	3486
Plunkett, Christopher	Meath, Tathrath	gentry: gent	19-Mar-36	220	Dc2/247r	2105
Plunkett, Christopher	Meath, Tathrath	gentry: gent	19-Mar-36	220	B.L. 19, 843 f. 45	2808
Plunkett, Christopher	Meath, Dunsary	gentry: esquire, s/h of				
		Edward	25-Aug-65	2000	Dc3/13	2250
Plunkett, Christopher	Meath, Dunsaney	gentry: esquire	29-Oct-69	400	Dc3.103	2450
Plunkett, Christopher	Meath, Dunsany?	gentry: son/heir of				
		Edward	17-Jun-67	600	Dc3/63	2361
Plunkett, Christopher	Meath, Clonbreny	gentry: esquire	27-Apr-02	300	Dc1/37v	243
Plunkett, Christopher	Meath, Kells	merchant: son of George	08-Dec-32	50	Dc2/187v	1854
Plunkett, Christopher	Meath, Ardmaghe Breege	gentry: gent	10-Feb-97	50	Dc1/1v	5
Plunkett, Christopher	Meath, Dunsany	gentry: son/heir of				
		Edward	25-Aug-65	2000	B.L. 15, 635 f. 156	3529
Plunkett, Christopher	Meath, Dunsany	gentry: son/heir of				
		Edward	07-Jun-67	600	B.L. 15, 635 f. 193a	3597
Plunkett, Edward	Meath, Dunsany	gentry: esquire	17-Jun-67	600	Dc3/63	2361

Standard	County	Occupation	Date	Amount	MS No	Ident No
Plunkett, Edward	Meath, Berrelston	gentry: gent	11-Sep-26	200	Dc2/82r	1390
Plunkett, Edward	Meath, Dunsary	gentry: esquire	25-Aug-65	2000	Dc3/13	2250
Plunkett, Edward	Meath, Barrelston	gentry: gent	18-Dec-16	60	Dc2/3r	884
Plunkett, Edward	Meath, Carlanston	other: s/heir of Gerald	21-Jun-13	100	Dc1/122v	761
Plunkett, Edward	Meath, Drombarach?	gentry: son/heir of Gerald	21-Oct-33	820	Dc2/200r	1904
Plunkett, Edward	Meath, Carlanston	gentry: gent	21-Jun-13	100	Dc1/122v	761
Plunkett, Edward	Monaghan, Donserkyn	gentry: gent	25-Nov-20	600	Dc2/33r	1053
Plunkett, Edward	Meath?	gentry: son/heir of Patrick	07-May-62	300	B.L. 15, 635 f. 113	3456
Plunkett, Edward	Meath, Dunsany	gentry: esquire	07-Jun-67	600	B.L. 15, 635 f. 193a	3597
Plunkett, Edward	Meath, Dunsany	gentry: esquire	25-Aug-65	2000	B.L. 15, 635 f. 156	3529
Plunkett, Ellen	Meath, Kilcarne	other: widow	23-Aug-03	240	Dc1/48r	312
Plunkett, George	Louth, Dunleere	gentry: gent	10-Dec-40	80	B.L. 19, 843 f. 78	2875
Plunkett, George	Louth, Dunleere	gentry: gent	22-Dec-40	200	B.L. 19, 843 f. 79	2877
Plunkett, George	Meath, Kells	gentry: gent	08-Dec-32	50	Dc2/187v	1854
Plunkett, Gerald	Dublin, the Grange	gentry: gent	16-Nov-98	100	Dc1/13r	93
Plunkett, Gerald	Meath, Robbinstowne	gentry: gent	18-Jul-27	100	Dc2/97r	1451
Plunkett, Gerald	Meath, Robinson	gentry: gent	16-Feb-27	50	Dc2/88v	1417
Plunkett, Gerald	Meath, Drombarach	gentry: gent	21-Oct-33	820	Dc2/200r	1904
Plunkett, Gerald	Cavan, Knockneny	gentry: esquire	18-Sep-16	1000	Dc2/—869	869
Plunkett, Henry	Meath, Blackrath	gentry: gent	10-Dec-02	80	Dc1/42v	272
Plunkett, Henry	Meath, Eiskerowne?	gentry: gent	24-Nov-36	40	Dc2/257r	2155
Plunkett, Henry	Meath, Blackrath	gentry: gent	10-Dec-02	80	Dc1/42r	270
Plunkett, James	Meath, Longewood	gentry: esquire	25-Jun-14	400	Dc1/130v	810
Plunkett, James	Meath, Longwoode	gentry: esquire	19-Nov-34	800	Dc2/222r	1992
Plunkett, James	Dublin, Dunsaghley	gentry: esquire	14-Dec-39	280	B.L. 19, 843 f. 37a	2793
Plunkett, James	Meath, Longwood	gentry: esquire	04-Nov-25	332	Dc2/69v	1316
Plunkett, James	Meath, Longwoode	gentry: esquire	26-Dec-32	400	Dc2/189v	1861
Plunkett, James	Dublin, Dunshaughly	gentry: esquire	08-Oct-36	1600	Dc2/256r	2150
Plunkett, James	Dublin, Dunshaghly	gentry: esquire	03-Dec-36	1200	Dc2/259r	2163
Plunkett, James	Meath, Belpear	gentry: gent	21-Jun-13	50	Dc1/122v	762
Plunkett, John	Louth, Banoon	gentry: gent	28-Nov-40	200	B.L. 19, 843 f. 78a	2876
Plunkett, John	Meath, Longwood	gentry: son/heir of James	04-Nov-25	332	Dc2/69v	1316
Plunkett, John	Meath, Clonardan	gentry: gent	08-Feb-98	30	Dc1/9r	65
Plunkett, John	Meath, the Stan Rath	gentry: gent	10-Dec-03	201	Dc1/50v	323
Plunkett, John	Meath, Marshalston?	gentry: gent	06-Jun-14	80	Dc1/130r	807
Plunkett, John	Dublin, the city	gentry: gent	21-Apr-19	40	Dc2/22r	982
Plunkett, Martin	Dublin, the city	merchant	18-Dec-16	60	Dc2/3r	884
Plunkett, Mathew	Louth?	peer: baron Louth	24-Nov-81	1200	B.L. 15, 637 f. 53a	3942
Plunkett, Nicholas	Louth, Castlelomnaght	gentry: gent, s/h of Oliver	12-Jun-30	200	Dc2/150r	1698
Plunkett, Nicholas	Dublin, Dunsaghly	gentry: esquire	16-Mar-72	210	Dc3/144v	2547

Standard	County	Occupation	Date	Amount	MS No	Ident No
Plunkett, Nicholas	Louth, Castlelomnaght	gentry: son/heir of Oliver	11-Jun-30	200	Dc2/149v	1697
Plunkett, Nicholas	Dublin, Dunsaghly	gentry: esquire	22-Sep-63	200	B.L. 15, 635 f. 126	3479
Plunkett, Nicholas	Dublin, Dunsaughly	gentry: esquire	21-Apr-64	200	B.L. 15, 635 f. 129a	3486
Plunkett, Nicholas	Dublin, Dunsaghly	gentry: esquire	17-Mar-72	210	B.L. 15, 636 f. 101	3795
Plunkett, Oliver	Meath, Croskyle	gentry: gent	10-Dec-02	80	Dc1/42v	272
Plunkett, Oliver	Meath, Clonebtrny	gentry: gent	19-Nov-14	80	Dc1/132v	824
Plunkett, Oliver	Meath, Balrath	gentry: gent	10-Feb-98	400	Dc1/9r	64
Plunkett, Oliver	Meath, Balrath	gentry: gent	11-Mar-01	600	Dc1/29v	195
Plunkett, Oliver	Louth?	peer: baron Louth	10-May-37	3000	Dc2/263r	2181
Plunkett, Oliver	Louth, Castlelomnaght	gentry: gent	11-Jun-30	200	Dc2/149v	1697
Plunkett, Oliver	Louth?	peer: baron Louth	10-Mar-37	2600	Dc2/263r	2180
Plunkett, Oliver	Meath, the grandge	gentry: gent	11-Sep-26	200	Dc2/82r	1390
Plunkett, Oliver	Louth, Castlelomnaght	gentry: gent	12-Jun-30	200	Dc2/150r	1698
Plunkett, Oliver	Louth?	peer: baron Louth	19-Mar-39	800	B.L. 19, 843 f. 13a	2745
Plunkett, Oliver	Meath, grandge of Derpatricke	gentry: gent	18-Dec-16	60	Dc2/3r	884
Plunkett, Oliver	Meath, Clonebreny	gentry: gent	06-Jun-14	80	Dc1/130r	807
Plunkett, Patrick	Meath?	peer: baron Dunsany	18-Sep-16	1000	Dc2/—869	869
Plunkett, Patrick	Sligo, Rathcrany	gentry: esquire	08-Oct-36	1600	Dc2/256r	2150
Plunkett, Patrick	Meath, Longwoode?	gentry: son/heir of James	26-Dec-32	400	Dc2/189v	1861
Plunkett, Patrick	Meath, Longwoode	gentry: gent	19-Nov-34	800	Dc2/222r	1992
Plunkett, Patrick	Meath, Longwood	gentry: gent, son of James	03-Dec-36	1200	Dc2/259r	2163
Plunkett, Patrick	Meath?	peer: baron of Dunsany	28-Jun-15	300	Dc1/139v	864
Plunkett, Patrick	Meath?	peer: baron Dunsany	07-May-62	300	B.L. 15, 635 f. 113	3456
Plunkett, Richard	Meath, Rathmore	gentry: esquire	29-Oct-98	200	Dc1/13r	92
Plunkett, Richard	Meath, Rathmore	gentry: esquire	14-Jul-09	2000	Dc1/90r	564
Plunkett, Richard	Meath, Rathmore	gentry: esquire	26-Mar-24	6000	Dc2/54r	1208
Plunkett, Richard	Meath, Muchebooles	gentry: gent	16-Jul-03	1000	Dc1/47ar	306
Plunkett, Richard	Meath, the Bolees	gentry: gent	10-May-03	520	Dc1/47r	298
Plunkett, Richard	Meath, Rathmore	gentry: esquire	01-Apr-00	200	Dc1/22v	149
Plunkett, Richard	Meath, Muchebooles	gentry: gent	10-Dec-03	201	Dc1/50v	323
Plunkett, Richard	Meath, Rathmore	gentry: esquire	04-Feb-06	1200	Dc1/65r	392
Plunkett, Richard	Meath, Rathmore	gentry: esquire	16-Jul-03	1000	Dc1/47ar	306
Plunkett, Richard	Meath, the Boolyes	gentry: gent	31-Jul-02	120	Dc1/39r	253
Plunkett, Richard	Meath, Rathmore	gentry: gent	18-Nov-97	120	Dc1/6v	49
Plunkett, Richard	Meath, the Bollies	gentry: gent	04-Feb-06	1200	Dc1/65r	392
Plunkett, Richard	Meath, Rathmore	gentry: esquire	23-Mar-97	300	Dc1/2v	14
Plunkett, Richard	Meath, Rathmore?	gentry: esquire	23-Apr-02	1000	Dc1/37v	242
Plunkett, Richard	Meath, Rathmore	gentry: esquire	23-Mar-97	40	Dc1/2v	15
Plunkett, Richard	Meath, Rothmore	gentry: esquire	27-Feb-97		Dc1/2r	10
Plunkett, Richard	Meath, Bolyes	gentry: gent	23-Mar-97	300	Dc1/2v	14
Plunkett, Richard	Meath, Bolyes	gentry: gent	30-Jan-01	30	Dc1/28r	189

Standard	County	Occupation	Date	Amount	MS No	Ident No
Plunkett, Richard	Meath, Rathmore	gentry: esquire	30-Jun-97	41	Dc1/5r	36
Plunkett, Richard	Meath, Crosskelle	gentry: gent	24-Nov-97	100	Dc1/7r	51
Plunkett, Richard	Meath, Rathmore	gentry: gent	10-Nov-97	200	Dc1/6v	48
Plunkett, Richard	Meath, the Boolies		18-Nov-97	120	Dc1/6v	49
Plunkett, Richard	Meath, Boles	gentry: gent	27-Mar-01	160	Dc1/29v	197
Plunkett, Richard	Meath, Rathmore	gentry: esquire	10-May-03	520	Dc1/47r	298
Plunkett, Richard	Meath, Muchbolies, Doleecke	gentry: gent	10-Aug-97	240	Dc1/6r	46
Plunkett, Robert	Meath, Gibstown	gentry: gent	13-May-20	400	Dc2/29v	1027
Plunkett, Robert	Meath, Gibston	gentry: esquire	14-Feb-22	600	Dc2/38v	1096
Plunkett, Robert	Meath, Gibston	gentry: esquire	14-Feb-22	600	Dc2/39r	1097
Plunkett, Robert	Meath, Polextowne	gentry: gent	17-Feb-32	800	Dc2/176r	1809
Plunkett, Robert	Meath, Gibston	gentry: gent	22-May-37	800	Dc2/264r	2184
Plunkett, Rowland	Meath, Dowston	gentry: gent	14-Feb-22	600	Dc2/38v	1096
Plunkett, Rowland	Meath, Dowestown	gentry: gent	13-May-20	400	Dc2/29v	1027
Plunkett, Thomas	Meath, Athboye	gentry: gent	21-Apr-08	300	Dc1/81v	506
Plunkett, Thomas	Dublin		24-Dec-03	2508	Dc1/50v	324
Plunkett, Thomas	Meath, Loghcrue	gentry: esquire	28-Nov-22	700	Dc2/43r	1127
Plunkett, Thomas	Meath, Castelkeran	gentry: gent	27-Apr-02	300	Dc1/37v	243
Plunkett, Thomas	Meath, Clowanston	gentry: gent	08-Dec-08	120	Dc1/85v	534
Plunkett, Walter	Dublin, the city	gentry: esquire	13-Jun-56	200	B.L. 19, 843 f. 181a	3070
Plunkett, Walter	Dublin, Portmarnocke	gentry: gent	07-Apr-36	1000	Dc2/249r	2113
Plunkett, Walter	Dublin, Grandge of Portmernock	gentry: gent	20-Feb-02	200	Dc1/36r	236
Plunkett, Walter	Dublin, Portmarnocke	gentry: gent	31-Jan-31	160	Dc2/159r	1738
Plunkett, Walter	Dublin, Grandge of Portmarnock	gentry: gent	29-Apr-24	300	Dc2/54v	1212
Plunkett, Walter	Dublin, Grange of Portmarnock	gentry: gent	19-Apr-41	100	B.L. 19, 843 f. 101a	2922
Plunkett, Walter	Dublin, the city	gentry: esquire	27-Jun-57	200	B.L. 19, 843 f. 194a	3096
Plunkett, Walter	Dublin, Portmarnocke	gentry: gent	22-Nov-17	100	Dc2/11v	922
Plunkett, Walter	Dublin, Portmarnocke	gentry: gent	27-Jun-21	200	Dc2/36r	1077
Plunkett, Walter	Dublin, the city	gentry: esquire	07-Mar-59	600	B.L. 15, 635 f. 39a	3333
Plunkett, Walter	Dublin, Rabeele	gentry: esquire	23-Jul-58	200	B.L. 15, 635 f. 34	3323
Plunkett, Walter	Dublin, Rathleale	gentry: esquire	19-Feb-59	400	B.L. 15, 635 f. 39	3332
Plunkett, Walter	Dublin, Portmarnocke	gentry: gent	22-May-15	240	Dc1/137v	854
Plunkett, Walter	Dublin, the Grandge	gentry: gent	17-Feb-15	400	Dc1/135v	841
Plunkett, Walter	Dublin, Rathdale	gentry: esquire	19-Oct-59	1000	B.L. 15, 635 f. 53	3357
Plunkett, Walter	Dublin, Rathbeale	gentry: knight	09-Feb-61	1320	B.L. 15, 635 f. 65a	3380
Plunkett, William	Louth, Beawly	gentry: esquire	06-Mar-41	200	B.L. 19, 843 f. 94a	2908
Plunkett, William	Louth, Bewly	gentry: esquire	10-Oct-39	600	B.L. 19, 843 f. 115	2949
Ponsonby, John	Wicklow, Powerscourte	gentry: esquire	08-Dec-54	400	B.L. 19, 843 f. 147a	3009
Ponsonby, John	Wicklow, Powerscourte	gentry: esquire	04-Oct-54	400	B.L. 19, 843 f. 144a	3003
Ponsonby, John	Kilkenny, Kildalton	gentry: knight	21-Dec-66	200	Dc3/49	2328
Ponsonby, John	Kilkenny, Kildalton	gentry: knight	01-Dec-66	200	B.L. 15, 635 f. 188a	3587

Standard	County	Occupation	Date	Amount	MS No	Ident No
Poole, Nathaniel	Meath, Gerrardstowne	gentry: esquire	15-Jul-71	420	Dc3/138v	2525
Poole, Nathaniel	Meath, Gerraldstowne	gentry: esquire	10-May-70	200	Dc3/119	2477
Poole, Nathaniel	Meath, Gerrardstowne	gentry: esquire	09-Jan-85	1400	B.L. 15, 637 f. 99	4027
Poole, Nathaniel	Meath, Gerrardstowne	gentry: esquire	05-Feb-83	200	B.L. 15, 637 f. 68	3969
Poole, Nathaniel	Meath, Gerrardstowne	gentry: esquire	10-May-70	200	B.L. 15, 636 f. 60a	3726
Poole, Nathaniel	Meath, Gerrardstowne	gentry: esquire	14-Jul-71	420	B.L. 15, 636 f. 86	3772
Poole, Nicholas	Dublin	merchant	28-Apr-37	400	Dc2/261v	2174
Poole, Perry	Queen's Co., Ballyfirin	gentry: esquire	17-Dec-86	1000	B.L. 15, 637 f. 113	4054
Poole, Thomas	Carlow, Croneskagh	farmer: yeoman	28-Apr-37	400	Dc2/261v	2174
Poole, Thomas	Dublin, the city	gentry: esquire	05-Nov-58	800	B.L. 15, 635 f. 37a	3329
Porter, Richard	Meath, Ouldbridge	gentry: gent	27-Mar-41	1000	B.L. 19, 843 f. 88a	2896
Poulter, Anthony	Dublin, the city	prof: surgeon	03-Dec-70	800	Dc3/132v	2507
Powell, Giles	Cork, Corneveagh	soldier: coronet	10-Feb-57	500	B.L. 15, 635 f. 181	3572
Power, Katherine	Dublin, the city	other: spinster?	02-Nov-57	400	B.L. 19, 843 f. 203a	3113
Power, Pierce	Waterford, Curraghmoore	gentry: esquire	22-Dec-66	220	Dc3/50	2331
Power, Pierce	Cork, Conbinny	gentry: gent	07-Apr-64	1350	B.L. 15, 635 f. 129	3485
Power, Pierce	Waterford, Curraghmore	gentry: esquire	22-Dec-66	220	B.L. 15, 635 f. 184a	3579
Power, Richard	Dublin, the city	gentry: s. of bar				
		Curraghmore	02-Nov-57	400	B.L. 19, 843 f. 203a	3113
Power, Richard	Waterford?	peer:				
		baron Curraghmore	12-Nov-70	1000	Dc3/130	2499
Power, Richard	Waterford?	peer:				
		baron Curraghmore	14-Nov-70	800	Dc3/131r	2500
Power, Richard	Waterford?	peer:				
		baron Curraghmore	14-Nov-70	700	Dc3/131r	2501
Power, Richard	Waterford?	peer:				
		baron Curraghmore	12-Nov-70	1000	B.L. 15, 636 f. 78a	3759
Power, Richard	Waterford?	peer:				
		baron Curraghmore	14-Nov-70	700	B.L. 15, 636 f. 79	3760
Power, Richard	Cork, Carrigline	gentry: gent	22-Jan-69	1000	B.L. 15, 636 f. 28a	3675
Power, Thomas	Cork, Inshye	gentry: gent	20-Jun-15	500	Dc1/139r	862
Power, Thomas	Cork, Inshye	gentry: gent	03-Dec-25	120	B.L. 19, 843 f. 93	2905
Power, Walter	Waterford, Castletowne	gentry: gent	23-Nov-30	220	Dc2/156v	1727
Prendergast, Edmund	Tipperary, Killnecarrigie	gentry: gent	14-Mar-40	800	B.L. 19, 843 f. 60	2838
Prendergast, Edmund	Tipperary, Newcastle	gentry: esquire	14-Mar-40	800	B.L. 19, 843 f. 60	2838
Prendergast, Robert	Tipperary, Poultarrie	gentry: gent	14-Mar-40	800	B.L. 19, 843 f. 60	2838
Prendergast, Walter	Tipperary, Ballybegg	gentry: gent	14-Mar-40	800	B.L. 19, 843 f. 60	2838
Prestly, Robert	Waterford, Ballycanan	merchant	20-Apr-54	200	B.L. 19, 843 f. 137a	2989
Preston, Jenico	Meath?	peer:				
		viscount Gormanstown	27-Sep-66	400	Dc3/39	2312
Preston, Jenico	Meath?	peer:				
		viscount Gormanstown	05-Jul-71	210	Dc3/138v	2524
Preston, Jenico	Meath?	peer:				
		viscount Gormanstown	14-Dec-68	600	Dc3/87	2418

Standard	County	Occupation	Date	Amount	MS No	Ident No
Preston, Jenico	Meath?	peer: viscount Gormanstown	03-Aug-66	1000	Dc3/35	2301
Preston, Jenico	Meath?	peer: viscount Gormanstown	23-Dec-68	240	Dc3/88	2420
Preston, Jenico	Meath?	peer: viscount Gormanstown	14-Dec-68	600	B.L. 15, 635 f. 230	3665
Preston, Jenico	Meath?	peer: viscount Gormanstown	23-Dec-68	240	B.L. 15, 636 f. 25a	3669
Preston, Jenico	Meath?	peer: viscount Gormanstown	05-Jul-71	210	B.L. 15, 636 f. 86a	3773
Preston, Nicholas	Dublin, the city	gentry: esquire	03-Aug-66	1000	Dc3/35	2301
Preston, Robert	Dublin, Ballmadoin	gentry: esquire	20-Dec-26	400	Dc2/87r	1412
Preston, Robert	Dublin, Balmadame	gentry: esquire	04-Oct-06	60	Dc1/70v	426
Preston, Robert	Dublin, Balmadane	gentry: esquire	23-Feb-07	400	Dc1/75r	456
Preston, Robert	Meath, Rogerstowne	gentry: gent	13-May-31	500	Dc2/162v	1753
Preston, William	Dublin	merchant	20-May-98	320	Dc1/11r	79
Pretty, Henry	Tipperary, Garranes	gentry: esquire	08-Jan-69	400	Dc3/88	2421
Pretty, Henry	Tipperary, Garrawes	gentry: esquire	10-Dec-68	400	Dc3/86	2417
Pretty, Henry	Tipperary, Garranes	gentry: esquire	10-Dec-68	400	B.L. 15, 635 f. 229	3663
Pretty, Henry	Tipperary, Garranes	gentry: esquire	08-Jan-69	400	B.L. 15, 636 f. 24	3666
Pricker?, Richard	Dublin	merchant	08-Mar-01	120	Dc1/29v	196
Proudfoot, John	Meath, Prudsfotestowne	gentry: gent	08-Jul-03	200	Dc1/47ar	304
Proudfoot, John	Meath, Prudsfotestowne	gentry: gent	08-Jul-03	200	Dc1/47ar	304
Pue, Robert	Dublin, the city	gentry: gent	13-Dec-57	300	B.L. 15, 635 f. 28	3311
Puntney, William	King's Co., Phillippstowne	gentry: gent	06-Jun-56	242	B.L. 19, 843 f. 172a	3057
Purcell, Edmund	Tipperary, Aghall	farmer: yeoman	20-May-22	200	Dc2/39v	1104
Purcell, Edmund	Dublin, the city	merchant: son of William	09-Jun-62	500	B.L. 15, 635 f. 102	3438
Purcell, Edmund	Dublin, the city	merchant	22-Jun-64	312	B.L. 15, 635 f. 137	3495
Purcell, Ignatius	Dublin, the city	merchant: son of William	09-Jun-62	500	B.L. 15, 635 f. 102	3438
Purcell, John	Limerick, Cloenanna	gentry: gent	17-Jun-40	400	B.L. 19, 843 f. 69	2857
Purcell, Patrick	Limerick, Ballynacarrigie	other: son of Richard	10-Jun-40	200	B.L. 19, 843 f. 67a	2854
Purcell, Patrick	Limerick, Ballynacarrgie	gentry: gent, son of Richard	17-Jun-40	400	B.L. 19, 843 f. 69	2857
Purcell, Philip	Tipperary, Loughmo	peer: baron Loughmo	01-Dec-97	5000	Dc1/7v	55
Purcell, Richard	Waterford, Ballycashin	gentry: gent	23-Nov-30	220	Dc2/156v	1727
Purcell, Richard	Dublin	trade: baker	13-Nov-01	200	Dc1/34r	225
Purcell, Richard		gentry: gent	01-Dec-97	5000	Dc1/7v	54
Purcell, Thomas	Dublin	merchant	05-Jul-17	200	Dc2/8v	908
Purcell, William	Dublin, the city	merchant	09-Jun-62	500	B.L. 15, 635 f. 102	3438
Purdon, Bartholomew	Cork, Ballyclough	gentry: esquire, s./heir Nicholas	03-Jan-72	600	B.L. 15, 636 f. 106a	3804
Purdon, George	Clare, Ogannah?	gentry: esquire	05-Jun-65	300	Dc3/8	2237
Purdon, Nicholas	Cork, Ballyclough	gentry: knight	03-Jan-72	600	B.L. 15, 636 f. 106a	3804
Purdon, Richard	Dublin, Mylton	gentry: gent	01-Mar-02	200	Dc1/36v	239
Purdon, Simon	Clare, Ogonello	gentry: gent	28-Apr-77	240	B.L. 19, 844 f. 131	3261

Standard	County	Occupation	Date	Amount	MS No	Ident No
Purdon, Simon	Clare, Ogenello	gentry: gent	28-Apr-77	120	B.L. 19, 844 f. 132	3262
Purdue, Richard	Meath, Kilskerry		22-Nov-31	400	Dc2/171v	1791
Purefoy, Arthur	Meath, Skreeine	gentry: esquire	10-Jun-65	220	Dc3/8	2239
Purefoy, Basil	King's Co., Derringboy	gentry: esquire	10-Jun-65	220	Dc3/8	2239
Purefoy, Patrick	King's Co., Ballylackin	gentry: esquire	15-Nov-69	507	B.L. 15, 636 f. 50a	3710
Purefoy, Peter	King's Co., Ballylackin	gentry: esquire	15-Nov-69	507	Dc3/107	2454
Queitrode, Janet	Dublin	merchant: widow of James, mer	26-Jan-00	200	Dc1/20v	140
Queitrode, Nicholas	Dublin, the city	merchant	15-Jan-04	400	Dc1/51v	328
Queitrode, Nicholas	Dublin	merchant	24-Sep-14	150	Dc1/131v	819
Queitrode, Nicholas	Dublin	merchant	28-Mar-10	80	Dc1/94v	593
Queitrode, Richard	Dublin	merchant	26-Jan-00	200	Dc1/20v	140
Queitrode, Richard	Dublin	merchant	08-Jan-01	200	Dc1/28r	186
Queitrode, Richard	Dublin	merchant: son/heir of Nicholas	28-Mar-10	80	Dc1/94v	593
Queitrode, Richard	Dublin	merchant: son/heir of Nicholas	24-Sep-14	150	Dc1/131v	819
Quigley, Laughlin	Monaghan, Drumhaven	gentry: gent	25-Feb-78	600	B.L. 19, 844 f. 146	3277
Quigley, Laughlin	Monaghan, Drumhawan	gentry: gent	25-Feb-78	600	Dc3/186v	2705
Quigley?, Derby	Dublin	farmer: yeoman	15-Dec-01	200	Dc1/35r	231
Quin, Thomas	Dublin, the city	prof: doctor, apothecary	24-Feb-75	1000	B.L. 19, 844 f. 56	3180
Quin, Thomas	Dublin, the city	trade: apothecary,son of Mark	24-Feb-75	1000	Dc3/164v	2624
Quin, William	Meath, Donshaghlen	farmer: yeoman	31-Oct-08	120	Dc1/84r	525
Quincey, Francis	Dublin, Smithfield, Oxmantowne	gentry: gent	28-Jul-68	100	Dc3/82	2409
Quincey, Francis	Dublin, Smythfield/ Oxmantowne	gentry: gent	28-Jul-68	100	B.L. 15, 635 f. 225	3655
Rawdon, George	Antrim, Lisburne	gentry: baronet of Moira	11-Dec-76	1000	B.L. 19, 844 f. 114	3243
Rawdon, George	Antrim, Lisburne	gentry: baronet	03-Apr-74	612	B.L. 19, 844 f. 23	3144
Rawdon, George	Antrim, Lisburne	gentry: baronet	11-Dec-76	1000	Dc3/181r	2680
Rawdon, George	Antrim, Lysborn	gentry: baronet	27-Mar-79	2000	B.L. 15, 637 f. 13	3871
Rawley, James	Limerick, Killmore	gentry: gent	07-May-41	1050	B.L. 19, 843 f. 91	2901
Rawley, Maurice	Limerick, Rawlieghstowne	gentry: gent	07-May-41	1050	B.L. 19, 843 f. 91	2901
Rawley, Maurice	Limerick, Rawlestowne	gentry: gent	02-Jul-41	840	B.L. 19, 843 f. 107	2933
Rawlins, Henry	Queen's Co., Ballynekill	merchant	10-Jun-30	240	Dc2/149v	1696
Rawlins, John	Queen's Co., Tymoge	gentry: esquire	21-Jul-59	200	B.L. 15, 635 f. 54a	3360
Rawson, Gilbert	Queen's Co., Granstowne	gentry: esquire	20-Nov-52	400	B.L. 19, 843 f. 128	2974
Reade, Thomas	Dublin	gentry: gent	23-Aug-03	120	Dc1/48r	311
Reader, Enoch	Dublin, the city		09-Dec-79	800	B.L. 15, 637 f. 28a	3898
Reader, Robert	Cavan, Ballyhaies	gentry: gent	30-Jun-20	40	Dc2/31v	1040
Reader, Robert	Cavan, Ballahais	gentry: gent	24-May-22	70	Dc2/40r	1108
Redich, Richard	England, London, the city	gentry: gent	13-May-28	200	Dc2/108v	1508

Standard	County	Occupation	Date	Amount	MS No	Ident No
Redman, Daniel	Kilkenny, Ballylynch	gentry: esquire	14-Jul-74	4000	Dc3/162v	2614
Reeves, Richard	Dublin, the city	gentry: esquire	12-May-74	500	B.L. 19, 844 f. 29	3152
Reeves, Richard	Dublin, the city	gentry: esquire	12-May-74	500	Dc3/161r	2609
Reeves, William	Limerick, Lyckelly	gentry: gent	24-Oct-73	338	B.L. 19, 844 f. 7	3126
Reid, Patrick	Meath, the Navan	other: son/heir of Richard	07-Feb-14	200	Dc1/126r	782
Reid, Richard	Meath, the Navan		07-Feb-14	200	Dc1/126r	782
Reilly, Edmund	Dublin, Castleknocke	gentry: gent	19-Mar-36	220	B.L. 19, 843 f. 45	2808
Reilly, Edmund	Dublin, Castleknocke	farmer: yeoman, s./heir of Terence	16-May-35	200	Dc2/236r	2051
Reilly, Edmund	Dublin, Castleknocke	gentry: gent	19-Mar-36	220	Dc2/247r	2105
Reilly, Edward	Dublin, the city	gentry: gent	10-Apr-86	3000	B.L. 15, 637 f. 104a	4036
Reilly, Garret	Dublin, Castleknock	farmer	29-Jan-25	300	Dc2/60v	1258
Reilly, Garret	Dublin, Castleknock	farmer	09-Jul-24	300	Dc2/57r	1232
Reilly, Hugh	Cavan, Bille	gentry: gent	27-Nov-28	200	Dc2/117v	1550
Reilly, Hugh	Cavan, Liskennan	gentry: esquire	04-Dec-28	600	Dc2/120r	1562
Reilly, Hugh	Cavan, Killevahen	gentry: gent	22-May-37	800	Dc2/264r	2184
Reilly, John	Cavan, Killmore	gentry: gent	27-Nov-28	200	Dc2/117v	1550
Reilly, Mulmore	Cavan, Bellanecargie	gentry: esquire	29-Nov-11	200	Dc1/109v	681
Reilly, Owen	Cavan, Killmore	gentry: gent	27-Nov-28	200	Dc2/117v	1550
Reilly, Phelim	Cavan, Crossbane	gentry: gent	21-Sep-33	140	Dc2/199v	1901
Reilly, Philip	Cavan, Ballentrosse	gentry: esquire	03-Mar-28	860	Dc2/105r	1490
Reilly, Philip	Cavan, Bellahost	gentry: esquire	08-Mar-28	400	Dc2/105v	1492
Reilly, Philip	Cavan, Crosbane	gentry: gent	21-Jul-37	200	Dc2/269r	2208
Reilly, Richard	Dublin, Kinowre	gentry: gent	20-May-01	400	Dc1/32r	211
Reilly, Terence	Dublin, Castleknocke	gentry: gent	19-Mar-36	220	Dc2/247r	2105
Reilly, Terence	Dublin, Castleknocke	farmer: yeoman	16-May-35	200	Dc2/236r	2051
Reilly, Terence	Dublin, Castleknocke	gentry: gent	19-Mar-36	220	B.L. 19, 843 f. 45	2808
Reilly, Thomas	Dublin, Stonebatter	farmer: yeoman	01-Apr-41	800	B.L. 19, 843 f. 87a	2894
Reilly, William	Queen's Co., Tyrnanne	farmer: yeoman	28-Apr-37	400	Dc2/261v	2174
Rellick, James	Dublin, the city	trade: maltster	23-Mar-67	400	Dc3/57	2348
Reynolds, Edward	Carlow, Catherlagh	gentry: gent	18-Sep-32	1200	Dc2/185v	1846
Reynolds, Henry	Leitrim, Lisneggan	gentry: esquire	19-Feb-34	1254	Dc2/207r	1932
Reynolds, John	Leitrim, Loughskire?	gentry: gent	07-Feb-06	60	Dc1/65v	394
Reynolds, Richard	Dublin, city	merchant	20-Apr-10	46	Dc1/95r	597
Reynolds, Thomas	Leitrim, Rosclogher	gentry: esquire	22-Jun-29	200	Dc2/133v	1625
Rice, Edward	Limerick, Ballinity	gentry: son of James, gent	15-Nov-82	4000	B.L. 15, 637 f. 67	3967
Rice, William	Clare, Killestree	gentry: gent	28-Apr-77	120	B.L. 19, 844 f. 132	3262
Richards, George	Dublin, the city	gentry: esquire	16-Feb-24	867	Dc2/53v	1204
Richardson, Thomas	Dublin, the city	gentry: esquire	09-Jul-58	420	B.L. 15, 635 f. 30a	3316
Ridge, John	Roscommon, Abbytowne	gentry: esquire	12-Mar-43	1100	B.L. 19, 843 f. 114	2947
Ridgeway, John		gentry: esquire	12-Nov-10	200	Dc1/99v	623
Ridgeway, Thomas	Londonderry?	peer: earl of Londonderry	12-Dec-26	200	Dc2/86r	1407

Standard	County	Occupation	Date	Amount	MS No	Ident No
Ridgeway, Thomas	Londonderry?	peer:				
		earl of Londonderry	29-Nov-26	1000	Dc2/83v	1398
Rind, David	Fermanagh, Inniskillin	merchant	02-May-59	300	B.L. 15, 635 f. 44a	3341
Robbins, Connor	Kildare, Newton a Moore	farmer	16-Apr-03	40	Dc1/46r	292
Robbins, James	Kildare, the Naas	farmer: yeoman	16-Apr-03	40	Dc1/46r	292
Robbins, Patrick	Kildare, Newton a Moore	farmer	16-Apr-03	40	Dc1/46r	292
Robbins, Robert	Kilkenny, the city	trade: clothier	14-Jun-61	600	B.L. 15, 635 f. 71	3386
Roberts, Edward	Dublin, the city	gentry: gent	06-May-69	1500	Dc3/96	2433
Roberts, Edward	Dublin	gentry: gent	06-May-69	1500	B.L. 15, 636 f. 33a	3682
Roberts, Francis	Cork, Britsfieldstowne	gentry: esquire	14-Nov-66	1400	B.L. 15, 635 f. 182	3574
Roberts, Thomas	Cork, the city		06-Dec-66	4000	B.L. 15, 635 f. 181a	3573
Robley, Thomas	Dublin	gentry: gent	01-Dec-98	133	Dc1/14r	98
Roche, David	Limerick, the city	other: son of Thomas	27-May-40	800	B.L. 19, 843 f. 70a	2860
Roche, Dominic	Cork, Kinsale		03-Feb-41	1000	B.L. 19, 843 f. 96	2911
Roche, Dominic	Limerick, the city		24-Feb-36	600	Dc2/246r	2100
Roche, Dominic	Limerick		22-May-06	80	Dc1/68r	411
Roche, John	Wexford, Mulmintir	gentry: gent	30-Jun-12	120	Dc1/114v	710
Roche, John	Cork, Ballynymuanye	gentry: gent	06-Aug-40	4000	B.L. 19, 843 f. 74a	2868
Roche, John	Cork, the city	gentry: gent	12-Jan-69	200	B.L. 15, 636 f. 26	3670
Roche, Maurice	Cork, Creige	gentry: esquire	07-Aug-33	200	Dc2/198v	1897
Roche, Maurice	Cork, Cregge	gentry: esquire, s./heir				
		Fermo	23-May-28	600	Dc2/109v	1512
Roche, Maurice	Cork, Fermoy	peer:				
		viscount Ffitzharding	17-Jun-56	98	B.L. 19, 843 f. 186a	3080
Roche, Maurice	Cork, Creige	gentry: esquire	06-Sep-33	210	Dc2/199r	1900
Roche, Maurice	Cork, Fermoy	peer:				
		viscount Ffitzharding	26-Oct-36	2440	B.L. 19, 843 f. 42a	2803
Roche, Miles	Limerick, Galbally	gentry: gent	04-Nov-14	500	Dc1/132r	820
Roche, Patrick	Cork, the city	gentry: gent	16-Nov-40	300	B.L. 19, 843 f. 81	2881
Roche, Patrick	Cork, the city	gentry: gent	12-Feb-69	600	Dc3/89	2424
Roche, Patrick	Cork, the city	gentry: gent	10-Feb-69	600	B.L. 15, 636 f. 27a	3673
Roche, Patrick	Cork, Downdamonim	gentry: esquire	21-Mar-83	2800	B.L. 15, 637 f. 71a	3976
Roche, Redmond	Cork, Ballyheindin	gentry: esquire	06-Aug-40	4000	B.L. 19, 843 f. 74a	2868
Roche, Redmond	Cork, Ballyheiden	gentry: esquire	07-Apr-39	400	B.L. 19, 843 f. 30a	2779
Roche, Richard	Cork, Ffartie	gentry: gent	27-Jun-39	400	B.L. 19, 843 f. 26	2770
Roche, Richard	Cork, Kinsale		03-Feb-41	1000	B.L. 19, 843 f. 96	2911
Roche, Robert	Wexford, Mallimonte	gentry: gent	31-Jan-09	160	Dc1/86r	538
Roche, Theobald	Cork, Balleahowly	gentry: gent	04-Nov-14	500	Dc1/132r	821
Roche, Thomas	Wexford, Harreistowne	gentry: esquire	11-Aug-31	400	Dc2/167v	1774
Roche, Ulick	Cork, Ballymognollie	gentry: esquire	06-Aug-40	4000	B.L. 19, 843 f. 74a	2868
Roche, Ulick	Cork, Ballymognolly	gentry: esquire	07-Apr-39	400	B.L. 19, 843 f. 30a	2779
Rochford, Henry	Meath, Kilbride	gentry: esquire	05-May-62	350	B.L. 15, 635 f. 93a	3421
Rochford, Henry	Meath, Kilbride	gentry: esquire	03-Aug-61	220	B.L. 15, 635 f. 80a	3400
Rochford, John	Meath, Killbride	gentry: esquire	25-Nov-20	200	Dc2/33v	1054
Rochford, Robert	Meath, Kilbride	gentry: esquire	27-Jan-03	800	Dc1/43v	278

Standard	County	Occupation	Date	Amount	MS No	Ident No
Rochford, Thomazin?	Meath, Streamestowne	soldier: lieut. col.	06-Jul-56	242	B.L. 19, 843 f. 178	3064
Rochford, Walter	Dublin	gentry: gent	08-Apr-01	40	Dc1/30r	199
Rochford, Walter	Meath, Newton of					
	Mygaddye?	gentry: gent	05-May-03	40	Dc1/46v	297
Roe, Richard	Dublin, the city	trade: shoemaker	24-Jul-37	200	Dc2/269v	2209
Roe, William	Kildare, Branganstowne	gentry: gent	23-Jun-37	500	Dc2/265v	2192
Roe, William	Kildare, Branganstowne	gentry: gent	15-Jul-36	400	Dc2/254v	2143
Rolleston, Richard	Armagh, Magherlecowlee	gentry: gent	25-Nov-14	60	Dc1/133r	827
Rolleston, Richard	Armagh, Portadownan	gentry: esquire	04-Mar-18	60	Dc2/113v	936
Rolleston, Richard	Armagh, Magherlecho	gentry: gent	15-Dec-14	200	Dc1/134r	832
Rolleston, Richard	Armagh, Portdowne	gentry: gent	17-Aug-16	400	Dc2/0v	868
Ronan, Patrick	Cork, the city	merchant	13-Nov-75	200	B.L. 19, 844 f. 85	3213
Ronan, Patrick	Cork, the city	merchant	13-Jul-76	260	B.L. 19, 844 f. 109a	3237
Ronowe, James	Westmeath, Mollingarr	gentry: gent	04-Oct-02	100	Dc1/40r	258
Ronowe, James	Dublin, Ballenmraher?	gentry: gent	08-Feb-03	200	Dc1/44r	281
Ronowe, Morgan	Dublin	gentry: gent?	08-Feb-03	200	Dc1/44r	281
Ronowe, Owen	Dublin, Ballinecorny	gentry: gent	08-Feb-03	200	Dc1/44r	281
Roper, Thomas		gentry: knight	12-Mar-11	1200	Dc1/105r	657
Roper, Thomas	Kerry, Kerry	gentry: knight	23-May-14	340	Dc1/129v	805
Roper, Thomas	Dublin, Ropersrest, near	gentry: knight	03-Jun-20	1000	Dc2/30v	1031
Roper, Thomas	Dublin, Ropersrest	gentry: knight	24-May-23	600	Dc2/47v	1160
Roper, Thomas	Dublin, Ropersrest	gentry: knight	02-Jul-25	800	Dc2/68r	1306
Roper, Thomas	Wicklow?	peer: viscount Baltinglass	17-Jun-35	960	Dc2/237r	2056
Roper, Thomas	Dublin, Ropersrest	gentry: knight	11-Apr-25	3000	Dc2/63r	1278
Roper, Thomas	Dublin, Ropersrest	gentry: knight	17-Dec-25	2000	Dc2/72v	1335
Roper, Thomas	Wicklow?	peer: viscount Baltinglass	03-Mar-34	200	Dc2/208r	1937
Roper, Thomas	Dublin, Ropersrest	gentry: knight	10-Jul-20	2000	Dc2/32r	1042
Roper, Thomas	Wicklow?	gentry: s./heir vis				
		Baltinglass	15-Apr-36	1600	Dc2/249v	2115
Roper, Thomas	Wicklow?	peer: viscount Baltinglass	15-Apr-36	1600	Dc2/249v	2115
Roper, Thomas	Dublin, Ropersrest	gentry: knight	26-Dec-21	1500	Dc2/38r	1090
Roper, Thomas	Dublin, Ropersrest	gentry: knight	28-Feb-26	2000	Dc2/75r	1349
Roper, Thomas	Dublin, Ropersrest	gentry: knight	23-Oct-23	200	Dc2/50v	1183
Rossiter, Robert	Wexford, the bridge of					
	Bargcie	gentry: gent	31-Jan-09	160	Dc1/86r	539
Rossiter, William	Wexford, Tomhaggar	gentry: gent	31-Jan-09	160	Dc1/86v	540
Rothery, John	Kilkenny	merchant	18-Feb-07	750	Dc1/75r	455
Routledge, Allen	Dublin, the city	gentry: gent	24-Sep-32	200	Dc2/186r	1847
Routledge, Nicholas	Roscommon,					
	Clonegormegan	gentry: gent	04-Feb-24	160	Dc2/52v	1197
Rowles, Henry	Dublin, the city	gentry: esquire	20-Mar-57	140	B.L. 19, 843 f. 192a	3092
Rowles, Henry	Dublin, Milltowne	gentry: esquire	28-Oct-67	720	Dc3/67	2372
Rowles, Henry	Dublin, Milltowne	gentry: esquire	01-Mar-67	400	Dc3/55	2342
Rowles, Henry	Dublin, Milltowne	gentry: esquire	28-Oct-67	720	B.L. 15, 635 f. 199	3607
Rowles, Henry	Dublin, Milltowne	gentry: esquire	01-Mar-67	400	B.L. 15, 635 f. 190a	3591

Standard	County	Occupation	Date	Amount	MS No	Ident No
Rowley, Edward	Armagh, Ardgonnell?	gentry: esquire	07-Nov-62	627	B.L. 15, 635 f. 113a	3457
Rowley, Hugh	Londonderry, Kalmore	gentry: esquire	07-Nov-62	627	B.L. 15, 635 f. 113a	3457
Rowley, Hugh	Londonderry, Aghedowey	gentry: gent	21-Jun-64	840	B.L. 15, 636 f. 83	3766
Rowley, John	Londonderry, Castleroe	gentry: knight	21-Jun-64	840	B.L. 15, 636 f. 83	3766
Ruddock, Andrew	Cork, Walletowne	gentry: esquire	14-Nov-62	800	B.L. 15, 635 f. 198a	3606
Ruddock, Andrew	Cork, Wallstowne	gentry: esquire	21-Jul-80	600	B.L. 15, 637 f. 38	3914
Russell, Alison	Dublin, Mabeston	other: widow of George	03-Aug-99	300	Dc1/19r	131
Russell, Alison	Dublin, Mabeston	other: widow of George	02-Aug-99	140	Dc1/19r	130
Russell, Bartholomew	Dublin, Seaton	gentry: gent	06-Nov-39	600	B.L. 19, 843 f. 39	2796
Russell, Christopher	Down, Ballevalton	gentry: gent	28-Jun-38	600	B.L. 19, 843 f. 7	2732
Russell, David	Meath, Cookestone	gentry: gent	02-Mar-31	60	Dc2/160v	1745
Russell, David	Meath, Cookeston	gentry: gent	23-Sep-08	120	Dc1/84r	522
Russell, Edward	Donegal, Lyfford	gentry: gent	16-Dec-11	60	Dc1/110r	684
Russell, Edward	Donegal, Lyfford	gentry: gent	16-Dec-11	110	Dc1/110r	683
Russell, George	Down, Rathmolline	gentry: esquire	12-Dec-33	800	Dc2/203r	1918
Russell, George	Down, Rathmollyn	gentry: gent	30-Jun-36	200	Dc2/254r	2139
Russell, George	Down, Rathmollynn	gentry: gent	15-Dec-34	600	Dc2/226v	2011
Russell, George	Down, Rathmollen	gentry: esquire	07-Dec-39	40	B.L. 19,843 f. 3a	4062
Russell, Gerald	Dublin, Newton near Swordes	gentry: gent	21-Nov-09	105	Dc1/92v	579
Russell, John	Down, Killawgh	gentry: gent	08-May-23	200	Dc2/46v	1153
Russell, Mathew	Dublin, Rushe	gentry: gent	08-Feb-10	400	Dc1/94r	589
Russell, Mathew	Dublin, Rush	gentry: gent	24-Nov-10	200	Dc1/101r	632
Russell, Nicholas	Dublin, Collinston	gentry: gent	04-Jul-14	40	Dc1/130v	811
Russell, Richard	Dublin, Mabeston	other: son/heir of George	03-Aug-99 ˋ	300	Dc1/19r	131
Russell, Richard	Dublin, Mabeston	other: son/heir of George	02-Aug-99	140	Dc1/19r	130
Russell, Richard	Down, Ballinaston	gentry: gent	24-May-33	700	Dc2/195r	1883
Russell, Richard	Meath, Cookestone?	gentry: son/heir of Thomas	02-Mar-31	60	Dc2/160v	1745
Russell, Richard	Meath, Sheephouse	gentry: gent	31-Jan-12	400	Dc1/111v	692
Russell, Robert	Louth, Droghodah	merchant	04-Jul-14	40	Dc1/130v	811
Russell, Thomas	Meath, Cookestone?	gentry: son/heir of David	02-Mar-31	60	Dc2/160v	1745
Ruxton, John	Louth, Atherdee	gentry: son/heir of John	21-Feb-74	660	B.L. 19, 844 f. 22	3142
Ruxton, John	Louth, Atherdee	gentry: esquire	21-Feb-74	660	B.L. 19, 844 f. 22	3142
Ryan, Anthony	Clare, Cappagh	gentry: gent	17-Jan-74	900	B.L. 19, 844 f. 25a	3147
Ryan, Dermot	Tipperary, Sallaghoe	gentry: esquire	10-Nov-40	1000	B.L. 19, 843 f. 85	2889
Ryburne, Christopher	Dublin, Oxmantowne, the suburbs	gentry: gent	04-Nov-59	96	B.L. 15, 635 f. 56	3363
Ryder, John	Dublin	prof: dean of St. Patrick's	01-Dec-98	133	Dc1/14r	98
Ryder, John		prof: bp of Dromore? Laonensio	09-Sep-19	1332	Dc2/25v	1001
Ryte, Roger	Limerick, Askeatin	gentry: gent	28-May-17	600	Dc2/7r	902

Standard	County	Occupation	Date	Amount	MS No	Ident No
Sacheverell, Francis	Armagh, Mollodroy	gentry: esquire	15-May-30	1000	Dc2/148r	1690
Sacheverell, Francis	Armagh, Mollodroy	gentry: gent, s/h of Francis	15-May-30	1000	Dc2/148r	1690
Sacheverell, Francis	Antrim?, Leggacory	gentry: esquire	25-Sep-21	400	Dc2/36v	1078
Sacheverell, Francis	Antrim?, Leggacory?	gentry: son/heir of Francis	25-Sep-21	400	Dc2/36v	1078
Sacheverell, Francis	Armagh, Mulladroy	gentry: gent	20-May-31	600	Dc2/163v	1757
Sacheverell, Francis	Armagh, Mullaydroy	gentry: gent	15-Feb-33	200	Dc2/191v	1870
Sacheverell, William	Wexford, Ffithard	gentry: gent	20-Jul-37	400	B.L. 19, 843 f. 95	2909
Sacheverell, William	Wexford, Ffithard	gentry: gent	20-Jul-37	400	Dc2/269r	2207
Sadler, Thomas	Galway	gentry: esquire	20-Feb-59	1000	B.L. 15, 635 f. 40a	3335
Sale, Richard	Meath, Saleston	gentry: gent	20-May-01	60	Dc1/32r	210
Salt, John	Kildare, Coubaustowne	gentry: esquire	09-Jun-59	230	B.L. 15. 635 f. 47	3346
Salt, John	Kildare, Corkanstowne	gentry: esquire	07-Feb-59	200	B.L. 15, 645 f. 38	3330
Salt, John	Kildare, Covcanstown	gentry: esquire	05-Feb-64	240	B.L. 15, 635 f. 138	3497
Salt, John	Kildare, Corkanstowne	gentry: esquire	25-Nov-62	800	B.L. 15, 635 f. 99a	3433
Salt, John	Kildare, Corkenstowne	gentry: esquire	17-Jun-62	800	B.L. 15, 635 f. 92a	3419
Sandford, Francis	Wicklow, Carnwne	gentry: esquire	12-Jan-30	1000	Dc2/140v	1658
Sands, John	Wexford, Pallard, Gory	gentry: esquire	21-Jul-62	200	B.L. 15, 635 f. 93	3420
Sands, Lancelot	Kerry, Carrickfoyle	gentry: esquire	29-Aug-62	900	B.L. 15, 635 f. 114	3458
Sands, William	Dublin, the city	gentry: esquire	21-Jul-62	200	B.L. 15, 635 f. 93	3420
Sankey, Henry	Dublin, the city	gentry: esquire	03-Mar-75	200	Dc3/166r	2629
Sankey, Henry	Dublin, the city	gentry: esquire	03-Mar-75	200	B.L. 19, 844 f. 62a	3190
Sankey, Henry	Longford, Tenclicke	gentry: esquire	21-Feb-63	730	B.L. 15, 635 f. 101	3436
Sankey, John	Dublin, the city	gentry: esquire	22-Jun-65	240	Dc3/11	2245
Sarsfield, Michael	Meath, Sarsffieldstowne?	gentry: son/heir of Thomas	13-May-31	500	Dc2/162v	1753
Sarsfield, Michael	Meath, Sarsfieldstowne	gentry: son/heir of Thomas	16-May-31	500	Dc2/162v	1754
Sarsfield, Patrick	Kildare, Tully	gentry: esquire	27-Nov-17	400	Dc2/11v	924
Sarsfield, Patrick	Kildare, Tully	gentry: esquire	05-Jun-24	500	Dc2/55v	1218
Sarsfield, Patrick	Cork, Ballyshangaule	gentry: gent	29-Oct-72	320	B.L. 19, 844 f. 8	3127
Sarsfield, Patrick	Kildare, Rosberry	gentry: esquire	14-May-66	220	Dc3/28	2287
Sarsfield, Patrick	Dublin, the city	gentry: esquire	09-Jul-67	282	Dc3/65	2368
Sarsfield, Patrick	Kildare, Tully	gentry: esquire	20-Jan-17	300	Dc2/4r	888
Sarsfield, Patrick	Kildare, Rosberry	gentry: esquire	14-May-66	220	Dc3/28	2286
Sarsfield, Patrick	Kildare, Tully	gentry: esquire	25-Jun-21	200	Dc2/36r	1076
Sarsfield, Patrick	Kildare, Tully	gentry: esquire	31-Jan-22	400	Dc2/38v	1094
Sarsfield, Patrick	Kildare, Tully	gentry: esquire	05-Feb-13	1000	Dc1/118r	734
Sarsfield, Patrick	Kildare, Rosberry	gentry: esquire	14-Mar-66	220	B.L. 15, 635 f. 171	3551
Sarsfield, Patrick	Dublin, the city	gentry: esquire	09-Jul-67	282	B.L. 15, 635 f. 197	3604
Sarsfield, Patrick	Kildare, Rossberry	gentry: esquire	14-May-66	220	B.L. 15, 636 f. 58	3722
Sarsfield, Peter	Kildare, Tullie	gentry: gent	12-Dec-27	200	Dc2/102r	1474
Sarsfield, Peter	Kildare, Rosberry	gentry: son/heir of Patrick	25-Jun-21	200	Dc2/36r	1076

Standard	County	Occupation	Date	Amount	MS No	Ident No
Sarsfield, Peter	Kildare?, Tully?	gentry: son/heir of Patrick	31-Jan-22	400	Dc2/38v	1094
Sarsfield, Peter	Kildare, Tully	gentry: gent	02-Jul-28	400	Dc2/112r	1523
Sarsfield, Peter	Meath, Morechurche	gentry: gent	17-Jun-05	70	Dc1/60r	365
Sarsfield, Peter	Kildare, Tully	gentry: gent	05-Feb-13	1000	Dc1/118r	734
Sarsfield, Peter	Kildare, Rosberry	gentry: son/heir of Patrick	27-Nov-17	400	Dc2/11v	924
Sarsfield, Robert	Dublin, Tobertowne	gentry: gent	28-Jun-80	800	B.L. 15, 637 f. 34	3908
Sarsfield, Thomas	Meath, Sarsffieldstowne	merchant	13-May-31	500	Dc2/162v	1753
Sarsfield, Thomas	Meath, Sarsffieldstowne	gentry: gent	16-May-31	500	Dc2/162v	1754
Sarsfield, William	Cork, the Grange	gentry: knight	02-Dec-30	200	Dc2/157r	1731
Sarsfield, William	Dublin, Lucan	gentry: esquire	16-Dec-17	700	Dc2/13r	931
Sarsfield, William	Dublin, Lukane	gentry: knight	05-Feb-13	1000	Dc1/118r	734
Sarsfield, William	Dublin, Lukan	gentry: esquire	20-Jan-17	300	Dc2/4r	888
Sarsfield, William	Limerick?	peer: viscount Kilmallock	07-Jan-41	3200	B.L. 19, 843 f. 82	2883
Sarsfield,Thomas	Meath?, Sarsfeldston		20-May-98	320	Dc1/11r	79
Saunders, John	Dublin, the city	trade: plummer	29-Aug-31	100	Dc2/168r	1776
Saunders, Joseph	Dublin, the city	gentry: esquire	01-May-78	1350	Dc3/188ar	2712
Saunders, Joseph	Dublin, the city	gentry: esquire	01-May-78	1350	B.L. 15, 637 f. 29a	3900
Saunders, Joseph	Dublin, the city	gentry: gent	12-Aug-64	200	B.L. 15, 635 f. 142	3503
Saunders, Robert	Cork, Youghall	gentry: esquire	22-Feb-58	100	B.L. 19, 843 f. 205	3117
Saunders, Robert	Dublin, the city	gentry: esquire	17-Jan-83	2000	B.L. 15, 637 f. 73a	3980
Saunders, Robert	Wexford, Deepes	gentry: esquire	12-Aug-64	200	B.L. 15, 635 f. 142	3503
Saunderson, Robert	Cavan, Parta	gentry: esquire	29-Jan-70	200	Dc3/113	2466
Savage, Henry	Down, Arghin, the little Ardes	gentry: gent, son/heir of Jenk	19-Nov-10	120	Dc1/100v	629
Savage, Henry	Down, Arghin, the little Ardes	gentry: gent, son/heir of Jenk	19-Nov-10	400	Dc1/100r	628
Savage, Henry	Down, Arckyn	gentry: esquire	24-Nov-26	200	Dc2/83r	1395
Savage, Hugh	Down, Porteffore	gentry: esquire	10-Aug-66	360	Dc3/36	2304
Savage, Hugh	Down, Carneshure	gentry: gent	03-Nov-71	160	B.L. 15, 636 f. 93	3785
Savage, James	Down, Kirkistowne	gentry: gent	08-Oct-69	500	B.L. 15, 636 f. 51	3711
Savage, Patrick	Down, Portferry	gentry: esquire	24-Nov-26	200	Dc2/83r	1395
Savage, Phelim	Dublin, the city	gentry: esquire	12-May-74	500	B.L. 19, 844 f. 29	3152
Savage, Philip	Dublin, the city	gentry: esquire	12-May-74	500	Dc3/161r	2609
Savage, Thomas	England, Cardingto, Bedford	gentry: knight	28-Nov-34	400	Dc2/224r	2001
Savage, William	Kildare, Castleroban	gentry: esquire	20-Feb-58	2000	B.L. 15, 635 f. 29	3313
Scalrie?, John	Dublin, the Warde	farmer	06-Jul-03	120	Dc1/47v	303
Scott, Thomas	Wexford, Newboy	gentry: esquire	16-Sep-84	200	B.L. 15, 637 f. 90	4009
Scott, Thomas	Wexford, Newboy	gentry: gent	16-Sep-84	200	B.L. 15, 637 f. 90	4009
Scott, William	Queen's Co., Shannaghan	gentry: esquire	26-Jun-73	200	Dc3/158r	2589
Seaton, Christopher	Tyrone, Kilskerry	prof: parson of Kilskerry	06-Nov-29	400	Dc2/137v	1642
Segrave, James	Dublin	merchant	28-Jun-23	200	Dc2/48v	1168
Segrave, John	Dublin, Little Cabragh	gentry: esquire	13-Jan-71	600	Dc3/134r	2512

Standard	County	Occupation	Date	Amount	MS No	Ident No
Segrave, John	Dublin, Little Cabragh	gentry: esquire	24-Jul-63	1000	B.L. 15, 635 f. 111	3452
Segrave, Lawrence	Dublin	merchant	19-Aug-99	200	Dc1/18v	128
Segrave, Lawrence	Westmeath, Logangore	gentry: gent	08-Dec-60	400	B.L. 15, 635 f. 61	3373
Segrave, Nicholas	Meath, Ballyhacke	gentry: esquire	02-Apr-29	500	Dc2/126v	1594
Segrave, Nicholas	Meath, Ballehack	gentry: gent	01-Dec-01	120	Dc1/35r	230
Segrave, Nicholas	Dublin	merchant	19-Aug-99	200	Dc1/18v	128
Segrave, Patrick	Meath, Killeglan	gentry: esquire	21-May-39	200	B.L. 19, 843 f. 5	2728
Segrave, Patrick	Meath, Killeglane	gentry: esquire	23-Sep-29	200	Dc2/136v	1638
Segrave, Patrick	Meath, Killeglan?	gentry: son/heir of Richard	03-Mar-98	300	Dc1/10v	75
Segrave, Patrick	Meath, Killeglen	gentry: esquire	12-Feb-12	200	Dc1/112r	695
Segrave, Patrick	Meath, Killeglan	gentry: esquire	11-Feb-03	2000	Dc1/44v	283
Segrave, Patrick	Meath, Killeglan	gentry: esquire	13-May-15	1500	Dc1/137v	852
Segrave, Patrick	Meath, Killeglan	gentry: gent	31-Jul-34	210	Dc2/216r	1968
Segrave, Patrick	Meath, Killeglan	gentry: esquire	24-Mar-36	600	Dc2/247v	2107
Segrave, Patrick	Dublin, Little Johnstowne	gentry: gent	31-Mar-69	400	Dc3/94	2431
Segrave, Richard	Meath	gentry: esquire, s/h of Patrick	04-Jul-27	600	Dc2/96v	1449
Segrave, Richard	Meath, Killeglan	gentry: esquire	04-Jul-28	170	Dc2/112v	1525
Segrave, Richard	Meath, Rathkenny	gentry: gent	18-May-05	1000	Dc1/59v	362
Segrave, Richard	Meath, Killeglan?	gentry: esquire	03-Mar-98	300	Dc1/10v	75
Segrave, Richard	Meath, Killoglane	gentry: son/heir of Patrick	23-Sep-29	200	Dc2/136v	1638
Segrave, Richard	Meath, Ballyhacke	other: son/heir of Richard	02-Apr-29	500	Dc2/126v	1594
Segrave, Richard	Meath, Rathbeggan	gentry: gent	23-Jun-37	1200	Dc2/265v	2191
Segrave, Walter	Dublin		13-May-15	1500	Dc1/137v	852
Segrave, William	Dublin, Curranston	gentry: gent	03-Feb-03	100	Dc1/44r	279
Selling, John	Dublin, the city	merchant	13-Dec-54	1000	B.L. 19, 843 f. 152a	3019
Sexton, George	Dublin, the city	gentry: knight	28-Feb-20	500	Dc2/29r	1022
Shane, Eilish		other: widow	28-Nov-11	100	Dc1/109v	680
Shane, Francis	Westmeath, Killare	gentry: esquire	02-Dec-97	1600	Dc1/8r	56
Shane, Francis	Meath, Byshopstowne	gentry: knight	01-Jul-12	200	Dc1/114v	713
Shane, Francis	Westmeath, Ballemore	gentry: esquire	25-Nov-97	400	Dc1/7r	52
Shane, James	Dublin, the city	gentry: knight and baronet	04-Jul-67	4000	Dc3/65	2366
Shane, James	Dublin, the city	gentry: knight and baronet	04-Jul-67	5000	Dc3/65	2367
Shane, James	Westmeath, Bishopstowne	gentry: esquire	02-May-57	480	B.L. 19, 843 f. 193a	3094
Shane, James	Westmeath, Killare	gentry: esquire	03-Jul-56	400	B.L. 19, 843 f. 175a	3062
Sharples, Ambrose	Dublin, the city	gentry: gent	18-May-68	300	Dc3/76	2396
Shaw, Francis	Westmeath, Ballymore	gentry: knight	23-Feb-15	666	Dc1/136r	843
Shaw, John	Antrim, Ballygelly	gentry: esquire	10-Apr-73	1300	B.L. 19, 844 f. 1	3120
Shee, Robert	Kilkenny, Bonninstowne	gentry: esquire	27-Nov-39	1000	B.L. 19, 843 f. 36	2790
Sheehy, Edmund	Limerick, Ballyallinane	gentry: gent	09-Nov-39	3600	B.L. 19, 843 f. 33a	2785

Standard	County	Occupation	Date	Amount	MS No	Ident No
Shelley, Toby	Dublin, the city	merchant	28-Jan-36	600	Dc2/243v	2090
Shelton, William	Dublin	merchant	20-Apr-05	320	Dc1/58v	357
Shelton, William	Dublin	merchant	25-Nov-08	400	Dc1/84v	529
Shelton, William	Dublin	merchant	14-Dec-05	500	Dc1/64r	387
Shelton, William	Tipperary, Cnockananeena	gentry: gent	30-Nov-76	200	B.L. 19, 844 f. 133a	3242
Shelton, William	Dublin	merchant	23-Aug-03	120	Dc1/48r	311
Shelton, William	Dublin	merchant	16-May-01	200	Dc1/31v	208
Shelton, William	Tipperary, Cnockananeene	gentry: gent	28-Apr-77	240	B.L. 19, 844 f. 131	3261
Shelton, William	Dublin	merchant	26-Jan-00	200	Dc1/20v	140
Shelton, William	Dublin	merchant	13-Aug-05	440	Dc1/61r	370
Shelton, William	Tipperary, Cnockananeene	gentry: gent	28-Apr-77	110	B.L. 19, 844 f. 133	3263
Shelton, William	Tipperary, Carockaninyn	gentry: gent	16-Jan-73	400	B.L. 15, 636 f. 127a	3835
Sherlock, Andrew	Kildare, the Nace	gentry: gent	17-Dec-13	200	Dc1/125v	779
Sherlock, Barnaby	Meath, Scurlockstowne	gentry: gent	13-Nov-35	600	Dc2/239v	2069
Sherlock, Barnaby	Meath, Scurlockestowne	gentry: gent	05-Apr-31	930	Dc2/161v	1749
Sherlock, Barnaby	Meath, the Ffrayne?	gentry: gent	01-Mar-20	200	Dc2/29r	1023
Sherlock, Christopher	Kildare, Sheginston	gentry: esquire	07-Feb-24	200	Dc2/53r	1199
Sherlock, Christopher	Kildare, the Darre	gentry: esquire	23-Apr-29	200	Dc2/128r	1600
Sherlock, George	Dublin	merchant	23-Nov-03	600	Dc1/49v	318
Sherlock, James	Kildare, Forenaught	gentry: gent	09-Nov-30	220	Dc2/155v	1722
Sherlock, James	Kildare, Ffornaughte	gentry: gent	12-Feb-30	110	Dc2/141v	1664
Sherlock, John	Kildare, little Rath	gentry: knight	23-Jun-40	264	B.L. 19, 843 f. 62	2843
Sherlock, Martin	Dublin, Newcastle	gentry: gent	03-Mar-54	200	B.L. 19, 843 f. 136a	2987
Sherlock, Oliver	Meath, Scurlockston	gentry: gent	23-Dec-02	200	Dc1/42v	273
Sherlock, Oliver	Meath, Cloncarnyle	gentry: gent	20-Feb-05	110	Dc1/56v	349
Sherlock, Oliver	Meath, Scorlockeston	gentry: gent	08-Dec-02	40	Dc1/41v	268
Sherlock, Patrick	Dublin, Rathcredan	gentry: gent	16-Aug-23	60	Dc2/50r	1179
Sherlock, Patrick	Dublin, Rathcredan	gentry: gent	10-Aug-14	200	Dc1/131v	816
Sherlock, Patrick	Waterford, St Katerins near	gentry: gent	15-May-06	53	Dc1/67r	404
Sherlock, Philip	Kildare, the Nace		07-Feb-24	200	Dc2/53r	1199
Sherlock, Philip	Kildare, Littlerath	gentry: esquire	09-Mar-75	680	B.L. 19, 844 f. 57	3181
Sherlock, Philip	Kildare, Littlerath	gentry: esquire	09-Mar-75	680	Dc3/166r	2630
Sherlock, Philip	Kildare, Littlerath	gentry: gent	07-Jul-83	600	B.L. 15, 637 f. 76a	3986
Sherlock, Richard	Mayo, Newcastle	gentry: gent	13-Jun-08	120	Dc1/83v	519
Sherlock, Roland	Wexford, Codston	gentry: gent	24-Nov-18	120	Dc2/17v	957
Sherlock, Thomas	Dublin	merchant	02-Jun-15	200	Dc1/138r	857
Shield, Robert	Meath, Wyanstowne	gentry: gent	04-Jul-70	220	Dc3/122	2485
Shield, Robert	Meath, Wyanstowne	gentry: gent	04-Jul-70	220	B.L. 15, 636 f. 67a	3737
Short, Edward	Dublin, the city	gentry: gent	09-Jul-61	600	B.L. 15, 634 f. 89	3414
Shortall, Oliver	Kilkenny, Upperclaragh	gentry: esquire	30-Nov-29	400	Dc2/139r	1650
Shortall, Oliver	Kilkenny, Claragh	gentry: gent	05-Jul-20	200	Dc2/31v	1041
Sibthorpe, Robert	Kildare, Maynouth		12-Dec-35	1000	Dc2/242r	2082
Sinnott, Edmund	Wexford, Monevollen	gentry: gent	31-Jan-09	160	Dc1/86v	542
Sinnott, Edmund	Wexford, Garryvadden	gentry: gent?	16-May-09	160	Dc1/88r	551
Sinnott, Edmund	Wexford, Lingeston	gentry: gent?	31-Jan-09	160	Dc1/86v	541

Standard	County	Occupation	Date	Amount	MS No	Ident No
Sinnott, Edmund	Wexford, Tobbercullen	gentry: son/heir of				
		Gerott	31-Jan-09	160	Dc1/87r	543
Sinnott, Gerald	Wexford, Ballinihaske	gentry: gent?	31-Jan-09	160	Dc1/87r	543
Sinnott, John	Wexford, Cowledyne	gentry: gent?	31-Jan-09	160	Dc1/86v	542
Sinnott, John	Wexford, Rathdownie?	gentry: gent	31-Jan-09	160	Dc1/86v	540
Sinnott, John	Wexford, Ballyoran	gentry: gent	21-May-36	600	Dc2/252r	2128
Sinnott, Nicholas	Wexford	merchant	28-May-06	120	Dc1/68v	415
Sinnott, Richard	Wexford, Ffarrolston	gentry: gent?	31-Jan-09	160	Dc1/86r	538
Sinnott, Robert	Wexford, Balliorran	gentry: gent?	31-Jan-09	160	Dc1/86r	539
Sinnott, Thomas	Wexford, Clone	gentry: gent	21-May-36	600	Dc2/252r	2128
Sinnott, Walter	Wexford, Bolenevoroke	gentry: esquire	12-Nov-24	300	Dc2/58r	1240
Sinnott, Walter	Wexford, Ballinerincke	gentry: esquire	18-Dec-24	80	Dc2/59v	1253
Sinnott, Walter	Wexford, Enniscorthie	gentry: son/heir of of				
		Sir William	13-Feb-07	800	Dc1/74v	452
Sinnott, William	Wexford, Enniscorthie	gentry: knight	13-Feb-07	800	Dc1/74v	452
Skelton, Anthony	Limerick, Ballyniwranny	gentry: gent	26-Sep-39	600	B.L. 19, 843 f. 40a	2799
Skiddy, Nicholas	Cork, the city	gentry: gent	20-Aug-74	220	B.L. 19, 844 f. 40	3164
Skiddy, Nicholas	Cork, the city	gentry: gent	21-Feb-39	600	B.L. 19, 843 f. 53a	2825
Skiddy, Nicholas	Cork, the city	gentry: gent	27-Sep-72	500	B.L. 15, 636 f. 118a	3824
Skiddy, Nicholas	Cork, the city	gentry: gent	25-Aug-66	170	B.L. 15, 635 f. 180a	3571
Skiddy, Roger	Dublin	gentry: gent	05-Aug-18	100	Dc2/16r	950
Skiddy, Thomas	Cork, the city	gentry: gent	15-Dec-20	200	Dc2/33v	1057
Skiddy, William	Cork, the city	gentry: son/heir of				
		Nicholas	20-Aug-74	220	B.L. 19, 844 f. 40	3164
Skiddy, William	Cork, the city	gentry: gent, son/heir of				
		Nicholas	27-Sep-72	500	B.L. 15, 636 f. 118a	3824
Smallwood, James	Louth, Whiterath	gentry: esquire	04-Jul-74	1000	B.L. 19, 844 f. 28	3151
Smallwood, James	Louth, Miltowne	gentry: esquire	21-Feb-57	200	B.L. 19, 843 f. 187	3081
Smallwood, James	Louth, Whiterath	gentry: esquire	24-May-73	200	B.L. 15, 636 f. 135a	3847
Smallwood, James	Louth, Whiterath	gentry: esquire	14-May-72	400	B.L. 15, 636 f. 106	3803
Smallwood, James	Louth, Whiterath	gentry: esquire	14-May-72	400	B.L. 15, 636 f. 113	3816
Smith, Anthony	Armagh, Moyerie	gentry: esquire	10-May-26	1000	Dc2/77r	1361
Smith, James	Londonderry, Monymore	gentry: gent	20-Jul-41	1200	B.L. 19, 843 f. 102	2923
Smith, James	Kildare, Athie	gentry: gent	13-Nov-24	100	Dc2/58v	1242
Smith, Joseph	Louth, Seatowne	gentry: gent	24-May-73	200	B.L. 15, 636 f. 135a	3847
Smith, Richard	Cork, Bridgefeild	gentry: esquire	09-Feb-69	332	B.L. 15, 636 f. 33	3681
Smith, Richard	Kilkenny, the city	gentry: gent	11-Feb-61	1000	B.L. 15, 635 f. 70	3384
Smith, Thomas	Galway, the town	gentry: esquire	26-Jul-09	200	Dc1/90v	567
Smith, Thomas	Galway, the town	gentry: esquire	10-Nov-12	1000	Dc1/116r	721
Smith, William	Dublin, the city		27-Aug-77	500	B.L. 19, 844 f. 142	3272
Smith, William.	Dublin, the city		24-Mar-57	200	B.L. 15, 635 f. 24a	3306
Smith, William	Kildare, Athy	gentry: gent	22-Sep-98	100	Dc1/12v	89
Smith, William	Dublin, the city		10-Mar-74	800	Dc3/161r	2607
Smith, William	Kildare, Athye	gentry: gent	12-Aug-98	1000	Dc1/12r	86
Smith, William	Dublin, the city		27-Aug-77	500	Dc3/183r	2694

Standard	County	Occupation	Date	Amount	MS No	Ident No
Smithsby, Thomas	Dublin, the city	gentry: gent	02-May-68	220	Dc3/74	2393
Soar, William	King's Co., Barnebuy	gentry: gent	15-Jul-29	100	Dc2/135v	1632
Sowthlie, Henry	Dublin, the city		11-Nov-20	200	Dc2/32v	1049
Sparke, Peter	Meath, Ratouth	gentry: gent	21-May-31	250	Dc2/164r	1759
Spenser, William	Roscommon, Ballneslow	gentry: esquire	03-Jul-84	2000	B.L. 15, 637 f. 89a	4008
Spenser, William	Cork, Andicanes	gentry: esquire	21-May-68	400	B.L. 15, 635 f. 224	3653
Spenser, William	Cork, Ardeenes	gentry: esquire	21-May-68	100	B.L. 15, 635 f. 227	3659
Spensfield, John	Galway, Castlegarryaghcart	gentry: gent	17-Jun-10	400	Dc1/98r	616
Spensfield, John	Galway, Castlegareaghcart	gentry: gent	28-Nov-11	100	Dc1/109v	680
Spottiswood, Henry	Tyrone, Clogher	gentry: knight	06-Nov-29	400	Dc2/137v	1642
Spottiswood, Henry	Monaghan, Drumbrate	gentry: knight	22-Dec-49	400	B.L. 19, 843 f. 126	2971
Spottiswood, Henry	Fermanagh, Portora	gentry: knight	12-Jun-29	160	Dc2/132r	1617
Spottiswood, Henry	Dublin, the city	gentry: knight	18-Apr-50	130	B.L. 19, 843 f. 125a	2970
Spottiswood, Henry	Fermanagh, Portora	gentry: knight	23-May-28	440	Dc2/109v	1511
Spottiswood, Henry	Fermanagh, Portora	gentry: knight	23-May-28	300	Dc2/109r	1510
Spottiswood, James		prof: bishop of Clogher	06-Nov-29	400	Dc2/137v	1642
Spottiswood, John	Scotland, Dersie, Ffife	gentry: knight	23-May-28	300	Dc2/109r	1510
Spring, Walter	Kerry, Killaghy	gentry: esquire	13-Feb-13	100	Dc1/119r	739
Springham, Thomas	Dublin, the city	merchant	05-Sep-55	1800	B.L. 19, 843 f. 165	3044
St. George, George	Roscommon, Charlestowne	gentry: knight	20-Nov-28	800	Dc2/118v	1556
St. George, George	Roscommon, Karleston?	gentry: knight	30-Nov-28	1000	Dc2/119r	1557
St. George, George	Galway, Drumore	gentry: knight	13-May-62	1800	B.L. 15, 635 f. 95a	3425
St. George, Oliver	Galway, Hedford	gentry: baronet	28-Jun-76	1200	Dc3/179r	2672
St. George, Oliver	Leitrim, Carrickdromrude	gentry: knight	27-Apr-65	650	B.L. 15, 635 f. 153	3525
St. George, Oliver	Galway, Akin	gentry: knight	27-Jul-61	210	B.L. 15, 635 f. 79a	3398
St. Lawrence, Ambrose	Dublin	gentry: gent	27-Sep-16	1000	Dc2/1r	872
St. Lawrence, Christopher	Dublin?	peer: baron Howth	18-Jan-09	800	Dc1/85v	535
St. Lawrence, Christopher	Louth, Crueston	gentry: esquire	22-Jan-41	100	B.L. 19, 843 f. 79a	2878
St. Lawrence, Christopher	Louth, Cruestowne	gentry: gent	28-Apr-30	200	Dc2/144v	1675
St. Lawrence, Christopher	Dublin?	peer: baron Howth	19-Dec-12	1000	Dc1/117v	730
St. Lawrence, Christopher	Dublin?	peer: baron Howth	23-Dec-10	400	Dc1/101v	636
St. Lawrence, Nicholas	Dublin?	peer: baron Howth	11-May-30	600	Dc2/146r	1682
St. Lawrence, Nicholas	Dublin?	peer: baron Howth	20-May-31	600	Dc2/163v	1758
St. Lawrence, William	Dublin?	peer: baron Howth	25-Sep-56	300	B.L. 19, 843 f. 188a	3084
St. Lawrence, William	Dublin?	peer: baron Howth	06-May-61	600	B.L. 15, 635 f. 72a	3389
St. Leger, Anthony	Carlow, Clonmolske	gentry: esquire	10-Nov-18	200	Dc2/17r	953
St. Leger, Hayward	Cork, Heywardshill	gentry: esquire	09-Dec-68	2000	Dc3/86	2416
St. Leger, Howard	Cork, Castlemoore	gentry: esquire	22-Oct-66	2000	Dc3/40	2315
St. Leger, John	Cork, Downerayle	gentry: esquire	02-Jan-56	6000	B.L. 19, 843 f. 164	3042
Stack, Edmund	Kerry, Dromnoren	gentry: gent	28-May-06	300	Dc1/69r	416
Stack, Thomas	Kerry, Garyna	gentry: gent	28-May-06	300	Dc1/69r	416
Stafford, John	Wexford, Balmaghharne	gentry: gent	24-Nov-18	120	Dc2/17v	957
Stafford, John	Wexford, Balmahearne	gentry: gent	15-Nov-16	240	Dc2/2r	876
Stafford, Nicholas	Wexford, Balmakehem	gentry: esquire	08-Jun-41	400	B.L. 19, 843 f. 117	2953
Stanihurst, James	Dublin, Curduffe	gentry: esquire	21-May-07	300	Dc1/77r	469

Standard	County	Occupation	Date	Amount	MS No	Ident No
Stanihurst, James	Dublin, Curduffe	gentry: gent	06-Feb-02	60	Dc1/36r	235
Stanihurst, James	Dublin, Curduff in psh Luske	gentry: gent	19-Nov-06	150	Dc1/71v	434
Stanihurst, James	Dublin, Curduff	gentry: gent	21-Dec-11	300	Dc1/110v	686
Stanihurst, James	Dublin, late of Corduffe	gentry: gent	31-Jan-12	3000	Dc1/111v	693
Stanihurst, James	Dublin, Curduffe	gentry: esquire	16-Feb-11	200	Dc1/103r	644
Stanley, Giles	Westmeath, Kilkennye?		07-May-07	600	Dc1/76r	463
Stanley, Giles	Westmeath, Kilkennye	gentry: gent	13-Jun-07	600	Dc1/78r	477
Stanley, John	Louth, Drogheda		28-Jan-36	600	Dc2/243v	2090
Stanley, John	Dublin, the city	merchant	09-Feb-30	1200	Dc2/159v	1741
Stanley, John	Louth, Drogheda		10-Nov-31	800	Dc2/169v	1782
Stanley, John	Dublin	merchant	10-Nov-31	800	Dc2/169v	1782
Stanley, John	Dublin, the city	gentry: esquire	30-May-32	210	Dc2/181v	1829
Stanley, John	Dublin, the city	merchant	12-Dec-32	500	Dc2/188v	1857
Stanley, John	Louth, Drogheda		09-Feb-30	1200	Dc2/159v	1741
Stanley, John	Dublin, the city	merchant	27-Feb-23	2000	Dc2/45v	1143
Stanley, John	Louth, Drogheda	merchant	19-Jun-21	200	Dc2/35v	1073
Stanley, John	Dublin, the city	merchant	06-Oct-32	300	Dc2/186r	1848
Stanley, John	Louth, Drogheda		06-Oct-32	300	Dc2/186r	1848
Stanley, John	Dublin	merchant	09-Sep-36	400	Dc2/255v	2148
Stanley, Patrick	Dublin	merchant	21-Jun-00	400	Dc1/24v	165
Stanley, Thomas	Dublin	trade: tanner	13-Jun-07	600	Dc1/78r	477
Stanley, Thomas	Dublin	trade: tanner	07-May-07	600	Dc1/76r	463
Stanley, Walter	Meath, Ffennor	gentry: gent	12-Dec-32	500	Dc2/188v	1857
Stanley, Walter	Dublin, the city	merchant	09-Jul-40	200	B.L. 19, 843 f. 59a	2837
Staples, Alexander	Londonderry, Ffaghanule, city	gentry: esquire	11-Sep-60	400	B.L. 15, 635 f. 59	3369
Staples, Bartholomew	Louth, Drogheda	merchant	04-Apr-28	600	Dc2/106v	1496
Staples, Bartholomew	Louth, Drogheda	merchant	23-Apr-19	1700	Dc2/22v	986
Staples, Bartholomew	Louth, Drogheda	merchant	09-Jun-20	200	Dc2/31r	1035
Staples, Bartholomew	Louth, Drogheda	merchant	08-Mar-28	300	Dc2/106r	1493
Staples, Bartholomew	Louth, Drogheda	merchant	08-Jun-20	600	Dc2/30v	1033
Stapleton, Pierce	Tipperary, Drommwarren	gentry: gent	19-May-06	150	Dc1/67v	409
Staughton, William	Westmeath, Kilbeggan	gentry: gent	12-Feb-24	1000	Dc2/53v	1202
Stawell, Anthony	Cork, Kinsale	gentry: esquire	02-Nov-78	2000	B.L. 19, 844 f. 167	3298
Steanek, Henry	Kilkenny, Tybraughny	gentry: esquire	19-Jun-21	1000	Dc2/36r	1074
Stearne, Robert	Westmeath, Tullevally	gentry: esquire	06-Nov-58	900	B.L. 15, 635 f. 33a	3322
Stenes, Henry	Kilkenny, Tyboroughny	gentry: esquire	20-Dec-19	150	Dc2/27v	1015
Stephens, John	Dublin, the city	gentry: knight	01-Apr-71	200	Dc3/137v	2521
Stephens, John	Dublin, the city	gentry: knight	13-Sep-72	450	Dc3/149r	2562
Stephens, Richard	Dublin, the city	gentry: esquire	28-Jun-70	540	Dc3/121	2482
Stephens, Richard	Wexford, New Rosse	gentry: esquire	01-Jun-63	160	B.L. 15, 635 f. 115	3460
Stephens, Richard	Dublin, the city	gentry: esquire	28-Jul-70	540	B.L. 15, 636 f. 66	3734
Stephens, Robert	Dublin	merchant	12-Mar-31	500	Dc2/161r	1747
Stephenson, John	Down, Bangor	gentry: gent	13-May-71	200	B.L. 15, 636 f. 87	3774

Standard	County	Occupation	Date	Amount	MS No	Ident No
Stephenson, Rachel	Down, Bangor	gentry: wife of John	13-May-71	200	B.L. 15, 636 f. 87	3774
Stephenson, Richard	Limerick, Ballyvoughan	gentry: esquire	22-Dec-82	700	B.L. 15, 637 f. 67a	3968
Stepney, Lancelot	Cork, the city	gentry: esquire	14-Oct-75	400	B.L. 19, 844 f. 84	3212
Sterling, Jane	Louth, Atherdee	gentry: widow	22-Feb-67	200	Dc3/55	2340
Sterling, Jane	Louth, Atherdee	gentry: widow of Sir Robert	22-May-67	431	Dc3/61	2356
Sterling, Jane	Louth, Ardee	gentry: widow of Sir Robert	22-May-67	431	B.L. 15, 635 f. 194	3598
Sterling, Jane	Louth, Atherdee	gentry: widow	22-Feb-67	200	B.L. 15, 636 f. 26a	3671
Sterling, Robert	Dublin, the city	gentry: esquire, s.of Sir Robert	22-May-67	431	Dc3/61	2356
Sterling, Robert	Louth, Atherdee	gentry: esquire	22-Feb-67	200	Dc3/55	2340
Sterling, Robert	Louth, Atherdee	gentry: esquire	22-Feb-67	200	B.L. 15, 636 f. 26a	3671
Sterling, Robert	Dublin, the city	gentry: son/heir of Sir Robert	22-May-67	431	B.L. 15, 635 f. 194	3598
Stewart, Andrew		peer: baron Castlestewart	07-Aug-44	140	B.L. 19, 843 f. 116a	2952
Stewart, Henry	Tyrone, Carragon	gentry: esquire	24-Dec-34	160	Dc2/228r	2018
Stokes, Henry	Kildare, Calueston	gentry: gent	15-May-26	680	Dc2/77v	1365
Stokes, Henry	Kildare, Calveston	gentry: gent	13-Nov-24	400	Dc2/58v	1241
Stopford, James	Dublin, King's Inns	gentry: esquire	19-Dec-72	560	Dc3/152r	2568
Stopford, James	Dublin, the city	gentry: esquire	10-Dec-68	400	Dc3/86	2417
Stopford, James	Dublin, the city	gentry: esquire	08-Jan-69	400	Dc3/88	2421
Stopford, James	Dublin, King's Inns	gentry: esquire	18-Feb-71	1600	Dc3/136r	2518
Stopford, James	Dublin, the city	gentry: esquire	08-Jan-69	400	B.L. 15, 636 f. 24	3666
Stopford, James	Dublin, King's Inns	gentry: esquire	19-Dec-72	560	B.L. 15, 636 f. 120	3827
Stopford, James	Dublin, the city	gentry: esquire	10-Dec-68	400	B.L. 15, 635 f. 229	3663
Stopford, James	Dublin, the Inns	gentry: esquire	25-Sep-63	1000	B.L. 15, 635 f. 118	3466
Stopford, James	Dublin, the city	gentry: esquire	09-Oct-64	1000	B.L. 15, 635 f. 144	3507
Stopford, William	Dublin, the city	gentry: gent, son/heir of James	19-Dec-72	560	Dc3/152r	2568
Stopford, William	Dublin, the city	gentry: gent, son/heir of James	19-Dec-72	560	B.L. 15, 636 f. 120	3827
Stoughton, Anthony	Dublin, the city	gentry: esquire	17-Dec-33	200	Dc2/204v	1921
Stoughton, Anthony	Dublin, the city	gentry: esquire	17-Dec-33	400	Dc2/204r	1920
Stoughton, Anthony	Dublin, the city	gentry: esquire	31-Oct-36	700	Dc2/256v	2151
Stoughton, Arthur	Dublin, the city	gentry: gent	17-Dec-33	200	Dc2/204v	1921
Stoughton, Arthur	Dublin, the city	gentry: gent	17-Dec-33	400	Dc2/204r	1920
Strange, Lawrence	Kilkenny, Dromdowny	gentry: gent	27-Nov-39	1000	B.L. 19, 843 f. 36	2790
Strange, Richard	Kilkenny, Dunkitt	gentry: esquire	27-Nov-39	1000	B.L. 19, 843 f. 36	2790
Strassie, Thomas	Wexford, Cloghaman	gentry: gent	06-Dec-39	300	B.L. 19, 843 f. 37	2792
Stritch, Bartholomew	Limerick, the city	merchant: son of Nicholas	02-Oct-39	630	B.L. 19, 843 f. 43	2804
Stritch, Nicholas	Limerick, the city	merchant	02-Oct-39	630	B.L. 19, 843 f. 43	2804

Standard	County	Occupation	Date	Amount	MS No	Ident No
Stritch, William	Limerick, the city	merchant: son of Nicholas	02-Oct-39	630	B.L. 19, 843 f. 43	2804
Strong, Patrick	Waterford	merchant	18-Nov-02	200	Dc1/40v	262
Sullivan, Daniel	Kerry, Dunlohe	gentry: esquire	28-May-13	40	Dc1/121r	751
Sullivan, Daniel	Kerry, Donloe	gentry: gent	01-Dec-13	300	Dc1/125r	775
Sullivan, Daniel	Kerry, Ardey	gentry: gent	04-Jun-29	120	Dc2/130v	1611
Sullivan, Daniel	Kerry, Donlogh	gentry: esquire	19-Nov-13	20	Dc1/124r	770
Sullivan, Daniel	Kerry, Donloe	gentry: son/heir of Owen	25-Nov-11	130	Dc1/109r	679
Sullivan, Daniel	Kerry, Dookernan	gentry: esquire	29-Nov-21	260	Dc2/37r	1084
Sullivan, Daniel	Kerry, Ardey	gentry: gent	03-Jun-29	120	Dc2/130r	1610
Sullivan, Owen	Kerry, Donkarron	gentry: esquire	25-Nov-11	130	Dc1/109r	679
Sullivan, Owen	Kerry, Ballymacgullnyullan	gentry: gent	01-Jun-13	200	Dc1/121r	753
Sullivan, Owen	Kerry, Dunkerran	gentry: gent	09-Dec-12	120	Dc1/117r	728
Supple, William	Cork, Aghaddagh	gentry: esquire	07-Feb-79	2000	B.L. 15, 637 f. 16	3875
Sutton, Edward	Kildare, Scolloge	gentry: knight and baronet	05-Feb-64	240	B.L. 15, 635 f. 138	3497
Sutton, John	Kildare, Ikeathy/Richardstowne	gentry: gent, son/heir of Gar	03-Apr-67	161	Dc3/59	2351
Sutton, John	Kildare, Richardstown	gentry: gent, son/heir of Garet	03-Apr-67	160	B.L. 15, 635 f. 186	3582
Sutton, Katherine	Kildare, Ikeathy/Richardstowne	gentry: widow of Gerrot	03-Apr-67	161	Dc3/59	2351
Sutton, Katherine	Kildare, Richardstown	gentry: widow of Garet	03-Apr-67	160	B.L. 15, 635 f. 186	3582
Sutton, William	Kildare, Barbistowne	gentry: gent	12-Feb-30	110	Dc2/141v	1664
Sutton, William	Wexford, Ballekerran	gentry: gent?	30-Jun-12	120	Dc1/114v	710
Sutton, William	Kildare, Barbistowne	gentry: gent	09-Nov-30	220	Dc2/155v	1722
Swan, John	Dublin, the city	gentry: gent	09-Nov-55	270	B.L. 19, 843 f. 167	3048
Sweeney, Brian	Cork, Cloghda?	gentry: gent	24-Dec-14	120	Dc1/134v	836
Sweeney, Brian	Cork, Clogheda	gentry: gent	13-Mar-14	30	Dc1/128r	796
Sweeney, Brian	Cork, Clonday	gentry: esquire	19-Feb-14	240	Dc1/127r	787
Sweeney, Donogh	Donegal, Rahine	gentry: gent	18-Nov-05	107	Dc1/61v	373
Sweeney, Edmund	Sligo, Ardneglass	other: son of Alexander	26-Jan-33	160	B.L. 19, 843 f. 9	2736
Sweeney, Edmund	Cork, Clogheda	gentry: gent	13-Mar-14	30	Dc1/128r	796
Sweeney, Everard	Sligo, Ardneglass	gentry: gent	26-Jan-33	160	B.L. 19, 843 f. 9	2736
Sweeney, Mulmorry	Donegal, Castletonagh	gentry: knight	20-Aug-33	1000	Dc2/199r	1899
Sweeney, Mulmurry	Sligo, Ardneglasse, Tyreragh	gentry: gent	09-Dec-29	200	Dc2/139v	1653
Sweeney, Murrough	Cork, Ballintober	gentry: gent	23-Feb-13	300	Dc1/120r	745
Sweeney, Owen	Cork, Masshaneglasse?	gentry: gent	13-Mar-14	30	Dc1/128r	796
Sweeney, Owen	Cork, Masshanglane	gentry: gent	19-Feb-14	240	Dc1/127r	787
Sweeney, Roger	Sligo, Ardneglass	gentry: gent	10-Jan-38	80	B.L. 19, 843 f. 24	2766
Sweeney, Roger	Sligo, Ardneglass	gentry: gent	09-May-39	154	B.L. 19, 843 f. 8	2734
Sweeney, Roger	Sligo, Ardneglass	gentry: gent	01-Jul-38	100	B.L. 19, 843 f. 9a	2737
Sweeney, Roger	Sligo, Ardneglass	gentry: gent	11-Aug-38	100	B.L. 19, 843 f.10	2738

Standard	County	Occupation	Date	Amount	MS No	Ident No
Sweeney, Roger	Sligo, Ardneglass	gentry: gent	06-Jun-39	170	B.L. 19, 843 f. 10a	2739
Sweeney, Rory	Sligo, Ardneglass	gentry: gent	11-Aug-38	100	B.L. 19, 843 f.10	2738
Sweet, Henry		gentry: esquire	30-Jun-97	140	Dc1/5v	38
Sweet, Stephan	Cork, the city	gentry: gent	17-Apr-86	330	B.L. 15, 637 f. 106	4039
Sweetman, Andrew	Dublin, Magilston	farmer	14-May-36	60	Dc2/250v	2120
Sweetman, John	Dublin, Daneston	farmer	14-May-36	60	Dc2/250v	2120
Swift, Godwin	Dublin, the city	gentry: esquire	17-Jan-83	2000	B.L. 15, 637 f. 73a	3980
Swinfield, Raphael	Armagh, Maherlecowe	trade: chapman	22-Mar-14	186	Dc1/128v	798
Swords, Robert	Down, Ballindonell	gentry: gent	07-May-19	400	Dc2/23r	988
Taaffe, Christopher	Louth, Ballebragan	gentry: esquire	29-Nov-21	300	Dc2/36v	1081
Taaffe, Christopher	Louth, Branganstowne	gentry: son/heir of John	21-Jul-41	400	B.L. 19, 843 f. 101	2921
Taaffe, Christopher	Louth, Braganston	gentry: esquire	13-Feb-26	200	Dc2/74r	1344
Taaffe, Christopher	Kildare, Jagostowne (Jiggins)	gentry: gent	17-May-97	60	Dc1/4r	27
Taaffe, Christopher	Louth, Braganstowne	gentry: esquire	14-Jun-30	200	Dc2/151r	1702
Taaffe, Christopher	Louth, Stephenstowne	gentry: gent	15-Jun-65	280	Dc3/9	2242
Taaffe, Christopher	Louth, Stephenstowne	gentry: gent	15-Jun-65	280	B.L. 15, 635 f. 154a	3528
Taaffe, Edward	Louth, Cookeston	gentry: esquire	12-Nov-02	200	Dc1/40r	259
Taaffe, Edward	Louth, Cookston	gentry: gent	02-May-10	200	Dc1/95v	601
Taaffe, George	Louth, Rathbaddie	gentry: gent	19-Mar-39	800	B.L. 19, 843 f. 13a	2745
Taaffe, George	Louth, Rathboddie	gentry: gent	07-Dec-39	40	B.L. 19,843 f. 3a	4062
Taaffe, John	Louth, Braganstowne	gentry: esquire	15-Dec-34	600	Dc2/226v	2011
Taaffe, John	Louth, Braganstowne	gentry: esquire	27-Feb-40	1200	B.L. 19, 843 f. 52	2822
Taaffe, John	Louth, Braganstowne	gentry: esquire	30-Jun-36	200	Dc2/254r	2139
Taaffe, John	Louth, Stephenstowne	gentry: gent	21-Nov-34	200	Dc2/222r	1993
Taaffe, John	Sligo?	peer: viscount Taaffe, Corren	09-Dec-29	200	Dc2/139v	1653
Taaffe, John	Sligo?	peer: viscount Taaffe, Corren	04-Dec-28	400	Dc2/120v	1564
Taaffe, John	Sligo?	peer: viscount Taaffe, Corren	07-Nov-28	500	Dc2/115v	1541
Taaffe, John	Louth, Ballibragan	gentry: esquire	21-Nov-34	200	Dc2/222r	1993
Taaffe, John	Sligo, Ballymote	gentry: knight	08-Dec-26	800	Dc2/85v	1405
Taaffe, John	Sligo?	peer: viscount Taaffe, Corren	11-May-36	400	Dc2/250v	2119
Taaffe, John	Sligo, Ballymote	gentry: knight	25-Jun-25	300	Dc2/66v	1298
Taaffe, John	Sligo, Ballymote	gentry: knight	20-Jun-25	200	Dc2/66v	1297
Taaffe, John	Sligo, Ballymote	gentry: knight	04-Jun-25	800	Dc2/65r	1289
Taaffe, John	Sligo, Ballymote	gentry: esquire	07-Jun-24	280	Dc2/55v	1219
Taaffe, John	Louth, Ballibragan	gentry: esquire	10-Mar-37	2600	Dc2/263r	2180
Taaffe, John	Sligo?	peer: viscount Taaffe, Corren	15-Jul-37	3150	Dc2/268v	2205
Taaffe, John	Sligo?	peer: viscount Taaffe, Corren	15-Jul-37	800	Dc2/269r	2206

Standard	County	Occupation	Date	Amount	MS No	Ident No
Taaffe, John	Louth, Branganstowne	gentry: esquire	21-Jul-41	400	B.L. 19, 843 f. 101	2921
Taaffe, John	Sligo?	peer:				
		viscount Taaffe, Corren	05-Aug-34	600	Dc2/216v	1970
Taaffe, John	Louth, Braganstowne	gentry: esquire	08-Sep-34	200	Dc2/219r	1981
Taaffe, John	Louth, Ballybragan	gentry: esquire	21-Nov-34	200	B.L. 19, 843 f. 15	2748
Taaffe, John	Sligo?	peer:				
		viscount Taaffe, Corren	20-Dec-33	800	Dc2/205r	1924
Taaffe, John	Sligo?	peer:				
		viscount Taaffe, Corren	19-Dec-31	2000	Dc2/173v	1798
Taaffe, John	Sligo?	peer:				
		viscount Taaffe, Corren	20-Dec-33	1000	Dc2/205r	1923
Taaffe, John	Louth, Stephenstowne	gentry: gent	21-Nov-34	200	B.L. 19, 843 f. 15	2748
Taaffe, John	Louth, Braganston	gentry: esquire	19-Mar-39	800	B.L. 19, 843 f. 13a	2745
Taaffe, John	Sligo?	peer:				
		viscount Taaffe, Corren	06-Aug-34	1200	Dc2/217r	1972
Taaffe, John	Louth, Braganston	gentry: esquire	07-Dec-39	40	B.L. 19,843 f. 3a	4062
Taaffe, Lawrence	Louth, Rosmacha	gentry: gent	30-Apr-12	300	Dc1/113r	701
Taaffe, Nicholas	Louth, Stephenstowne	gentry: son/heir of John	21-Nov-34	200	Dc2/222r	1993
Taaffe, Nicholas	Louth, Stephenstowne	gentry: son/heir of John	21-Nov-34	200	B.L. 19, 843 f. 15	2748
Taaffe, Richard	Louth, Cookestowne	gentry: esquire	15-Feb-33	400	Dc2/191v	1869
Taaffe, Richard	Louth, Cookstowne	gentry: esquire	07-Jun-30	300	Dc2/149r	1694
Taaffe, Richard	Louth, Cookstowne	gentry: esquire	14-Jun-30	200	Dc2/151r	1702
Taaffe, Richard	Louth, Cookstowne	gentry: esquire	01-Apr-34	400	Dc2/210r	1944
Taaffe, Robert	Louth, Cookestowne	gentry: son/heir of				
		Richard	21-Jul-41	400	B.L. 19, 843 f. 101	2921
Taaffe, Stephen	Louth, Aclare	gentry: gent	02-Jul-28	600	Dc2/112r	1522
Taaffe, Theobald	Louth?	peer: earl of Carlingford	30-Nov-70	2800	Dc3/132r	2504
Taaffe, Theobald	Sligo, Corren	gentry: son/heir of John	15-Jul-37	800	Dc2/269r	2206
Taaffe, Theobald	Louth?	peer: earl of Carlingford	11-Mar-69	1600	Dc3/94	2430
Taaffe, Theobald	Sligo, Corren	gentry: son/heir of John	11-May-36	400	Dc2/250v	2119
Taaffe, Theobald	Louth?	peer: earl of Carlingford	11-Mar-69	1600	Dc3/93	2429
Taaffe, Theobald	Louth?	peer: earl of Carlingford	06-Feb-69	1340	Dc3/89	2423
Taaffe, Theobald	Sligo, Ballymoate	gentry: esquire	12-Jul-37	500	Dc2/268r	2202
Taaffe, Theobald	Sligo?	gentry: esquire, s/h of				
		John	06-Aug-34	1200	Dc2/217r	1972
Taaffe, Theobald	Sligo?	gentry: son/heir of John	15-Jul-37	3150	Dc2/268v	2205
Taaffe, Theobald	Sligo, Ballymote	gentry: esquire, s/h of				
		John	20-Dec-33	1000	Dc2/205r	1923
Taaffe, Theobald	Louth?	peer: earl of Carlingford	17-May-75	1000	Dc3/167v	2634
Taaffe, Theobald	Sligo, Ballymote	gentry: esquire, s./heir				
		of John	20-Dec-33	800	Dc2/205r	1924
Taaffe, Theobald	Louth?	peer: earl of Carlingford	30-Nov-70	2800	B.L. 15, 636 f. 76a	3755
Taaffe, Theobald	Louth?	peer: earl of Carlingford	11-Mar-69	1600	B.L. 15, 636 f. 29	3676
Taaffe, Theobald	Louth?	peer: earl of Carlingford	06-Feb-69	1340	B.L. 15, 636 f. 30a	3678
Taaffe, Theobald	Louth?	peer: earl of Carlingford	18-Oct-63	1600	B.L. 15, 635 f. 124	3475

Standard	County	Occupation	Date	Amount	MS No	Ident No
Taaffe, Theobald	Louth?	peer: earl of Carlingford	10-Mar-69	1600	B.L. 15, 636 f. 40	3694
Taaffe, William	Louth, Sintramon	gentry: knight	04-Jun-25	800	Dc2/65r	1289
Taaffe, William	Sligo?	peer:				
		viscount Taaffe, Corren	11-Mar-69	1600	Dc3/93	2429
Taaffe, William	Sligo?	gentry: s, vis Taaffe,				
		Corren	06-Feb-69	1340	Dc3/89	2423
Taaffe, William	Sligo, Ballymot	gentry: knight	15-Nov-18	110	Dc2/17r	954
Taaffe, William	Sligo, Ballimote	gentry: knight	05-May-19	1000	Dc2/23r	989
Taaffe, William	Sligo, Ballymott	gentry: knight	29-Nov-21	300	Dc2/36v	1081
Taaffe, William	Louth, Smermore	gentry: knight	04-Dec-22	200	Dc2/43v	1129
Taaffe, William	Louth, Smermot	gentry: knight	13-Feb-26	200	Dc2/74r	1344
Taaffe, William	Sligo, Ballymoate	gentry: knight	08-Jul-23	140	Dc2/49r	1172
Taaffe, William	Sligo?	gentry: s, vis Taaffe,				
		Corren	11-Mar-69	1600	Dc3/94	2430
Taaffe, William	Louth, Smarman	gentry: knight	28-Nov-25	240	Dc2/70v	1322
Taaffe, William	Sligo?	gentry: s, vis Taaffe,				
		Corren	30-Nov-70	2800	Dc3/132r	2504
Taaffe, William	Dublin, Grandge of					
	Balscaddan	gentry: gent	17-Jun-05	70	Dc1/60r	365
Taaffe, William	Louth, Smarmore	gentry: knight	06-Dec-24	200	Dc2/59v	1250
Taaffe, William	Sligo?	gentry: s, vis Taaffe,				
		Corren	06-Feb-69	1340	B.L. 15, 636 f. 30a	3678
Taaffe, William	Sligo?	peer:				
		viscount Taaffe, Corren	11-Mar-69	1600	B.L. 15, 636 f. 29	3676
Taaffe, William	Sligo?	gentry: s, vis Taaffe,				
		Corren	10-Mar-69	1600	B.L. 15, 636 f. 40	3694
Taaffe, William	Sligo?	gentry: s, vis Taaffe,				
		Corren	30-Nov-70	2800	B.L. 15, 636 f. 76a	3755
Talbot, ?	Dublin, Balmadyn	gentry: gent	01-Feb-97	60	Dc1/1v	7
Talbot, Bernard	Wicklow, Rathdowne	gentry: esquire	08-Feb-66	1200	Dc3/21	2269
Talbot, Bernard	Wicklow, Rathdowne	gentry: esquire	08-Feb-66	1200	B.L. 15, 635 f. 169	3549
Talbot, George	Roscommon, Castleruvy?	gentry: esquire	25-Nov-82	400	B.L. 15, 637 f. 65a	3965
Talbot, Henry	Dublin, Templeoge	gentry: knight	31-May-65	200	Dc3/7	2235
Talbot, Henry	Dublin, Templeoge	gentry: gent	21-May-36	200	Dc2/252r	2127
Talbot, Henry	Dublin, Templeoge	gentry: knight	15-Dec-65	440	Dc3/17	2260
Talbot, Henry	Dublin, Templeoge	gentry: knight	24-Sep-61	640	B.L. 15, 635 f. 85	3406
Talbot, Henry	Dublin, Templeoge	gentry: knight	15-Dec-65	440	B.L. 15, 635 f. 161a	3538
Talbot, Henry	Dublin, Temple Oge	gentry: knight	18-Oct-63	1600	B.L. 15, 635 f. 124	3475
Talbot, Henry	Dublin, Templeoge	gentry: knight	17-Dec-63	360	B.L. 15, 635 f. 124a	3476
Talbot, James	Dublin, Templeoge	gentry: esquire	18-Nov-71	200	Dc3/140v	2533
Talbot, James	Meath, Robtston	gentry: gent	15-Aug-98	60	Dc1/12r	88
Talbot, James	Dublin, Templeoge	gentry: esquire	17-Feb-75	200	B.L. 19, 844 f. 52	3176
Talbot, James	Dublin, Templeoge	gentry: esquire	17-Feb-75	200	Dc3/164v	2623
Talbot, James	Dublin, Templeoge	gentry: esq, s/h of				
		Sir Henry	31-May-65	200	Dc3/7	2235

Standard	County	Occupation	Date	Amount	MS No	Ident No
Talbot, James	Dublin, Templeoge	gentry: esquire	27-Feb-75	400	B.L. 19, 844 f. 54	3178
Talbot, James	Dublin, Templeoge	gentry: esquire	25-Nov-70	300	Dc3/131v	2503
Talbot, James	Dublin, Templeoge	gentry: son/heir of Henry	15-Dec-65	440	Dc3/17	2260
Talbot, James	Dublin, Templeoge	gentry: esquire	27-Feb-75	400	Dc3/165v	2626
Talbot, James	Dublin, Templeoge	gentry: son/heir of Henry	17-Dec-63	360	B.L. 15, 635 f. 124a	3476
Talbot, James	Dublin, Templeoge	gentry: esquire	18-Nov-71	200	B.L. 15, 636 f. 101a	3796
Talbot, James	Dublin, Templeoge	gentry: esquire	03-Dec-81	2000	B.L. 15, 637 f. 53	3941
Talbot, James	Dublin, Templeoge	gentry: son/heir of Henry	15-Dec-65	440	B.L. 15, 635 f. 161a	3538
Talbot, John	Dublin, Cromlin	gentry: gent	06-Apr-01	100	Dc1/30r	201
Talbot, John	Meath, Agher	gentry: esquire	13-Dec-28	400	Dc2/122v	1571
Talbot, John	Meath, Aherske	gentry: gent	29-Apr-15	240	Dc1/136v	847
Talbot, John	Meath, Agher	gentry: gent	20-Jun-29	120	Dc2/134r	1627
Talbot, John	Meath, Robtston	gentry: gent	08-Jun-27	300	Dc2/94r	1438
Talbot, John	Meath, Roberstowne	gentry: gent	26-Jun-28	200	Dc2/111v	1520
Talbot, John	Meath, Agherskeath	gentry: gent	15-Nov-34	300	Dc2/221v	1991
Talbot, John	Meath, Agher	gentry: gent	10-Dec-14	110	Dc1/133v	830
Talbot, John	Dublin, Cromlen	gentry: gent	10-Mar-07	100	Dc1/57v	458
Talbot, John	Meath, Agher	gentry: gent	07-May-13	140	Dc1/120v	748
Talbot, John	Meath, Robertstowne	gentry: gent	02-Jun-30	1000	Dc2/148v	1692
Talbot, John	Dublin, Tymologe	gentry: gent	08-Feb-23	150	Dc2/44v	1137
Talbot, John	Meath, Robertstowne	gentry: gent	20-Jun-29	120	Dc2/134r	1627
Talbot, John	Dublin, Mallahide	gentry: esquire	28-Aug-63	600	B.L. 15, 635 f. 123a	3474
Talbot, Peter	Wicklow, Rathdowne	gentry: gent	28-May-14	400	Dc1/129v	806
Talbot, Richard	Meath, Knockmark	gentry: gent	27-Mar-01	160	Dc1/29v	197
Talbot, Richard	Dublin, Malahide	gentry: esquire	06-Jun-78	1000	B.L. 19, 844 f. 168	3299
Talbot, Richard	Dublin, Mallahide	gentry: esquire	06-Jun-78	1000	Dc3/189v	2717
Talbot, Richard	Dublin, the city	gentry: esquire	19-Apr-66	1000	Dc3/27	2283
Talbot, Richard	Dublin	merchant	06-Jul-97	84	Dc1/6r	44
Talbot, Richard	Meath, Knockmark late of Agher	gentry: gent	01-Dec-00	500	Dc1/27r	180
Talbot, Richard	Meath, Knockmark	gentry: gent	20-Mar-01	100	Dc1/29v	198
Talbot, Richard	Meath, Agherneskine	gentry: gent	12-May-97	200	Dc1/3v	25
Talbot, Richard	Meath, Hilton	gentry: gent	15-Nov-34	300	Dc2/221v	1991
Talbot, Richard	Meath, Hilton	gentry: son/heir of John	20-Jun-29	120	Dc2/134r	1627
Talbot, Richard	Dublin, the city	gentry: esquire	10-May-67	500	Dc3/60	2354
Talbot, Richard	England, Westminster	soldier: colonel	18-Oct-63	1600	B.L. 15, 635 f. 124	3475
Talbot, Richard	Dublin, Mallahide	gentry: gent	05-Oct-63	150	B.L. 15, 635 f. 121a	3470
Talbot, Richard	Dublin, the city	gentry: esquire	10-May-67	500	B.L. 15, 635 f. 192	3594
Talbot, Robert	Wicklow, Castletalbott	gentry: knight and baronet	04-Dec-35	200	Dc2/241r	2078
Talbot, Robert	Kildare, Cortowne	gentry: baronet	31-May-70	2000	Dc3/120	2480
Talbot, Robert	Kildare, Caretowne	gentry: knight and baronet	15-Dec-65	440	Dc3/17	2260

Standard	County	Occupation	Date	Amount	MS No	Ident No
Talbot, Robert	Dublin, Templeoge	gentry: gent	28-Nov-07	52	Dc1/80r	495
Talbot, Robert	Kildare, Caretowne	gentry: knight and baronet	18-Nov-65	300	Dc3/15	2256
Talbot, Robert	Kildare, Caretowne	gentry: baronet	25-May-66	400	Dc3/29	2289
Talbot, Robert	Kildare, Caretowne	gentry: baronet	08-Feb-66	1200	Dc3/21	2269
Talbot, Robert	Kildare, Cartewise?	gentry: baronet	31-May-70	2000	B.L. 15, 636 f. 63	3729
Talbot, Robert	Kildare, Caretowne	gentry: baronet	08-Feb-66	1200	B.L. 15, 635 f. 169	3549
Talbot, Robert	Kildare, Caretowne	gentry: baronet	15-Dec-65	440	B.L. 15, 635 f. 161a	3538
Talbot, Walter	Cavan, Balleconen	gentry: esquire	10-Dec-14	110	Dc1/133v	830
Talbot, Walter	Cavan, Bellaconnill	gentry: gent	29-Apr-15	240	Dc1/136v	847
Talbot, William	Meath, Robtston	gentry: gent	15-Aug-98	60	Dc1/12r	88
Talbot, William	Louth, Haggardstowne	gentry: esquire	08-Feb-66	1200	Dc3/21	2269
Talbot, William	Louth, Haggartstowne	gentry: esquire	18-Nov-65	300	Dc3/15	2256
Talbot, William	Meath, Robtston	gentry: gent	04-Feb-01	200	Dc1/28v	191
Talbot, William	Louth, Haggerstowne	gentry: esquire	25-May-66	400	Dc3/29	2289
Talbot, William	Dublin, Kylmanagh	gentry: gent	06-Mar-01	60	Dc1/29r	193
Talbot, William	Meath, Robertstown	gentry: gent	03-Mar-98	300	Dc1/10v	75
Talbot, William	Meath, Robtston	gentry: gent	08-Feb-00	200	Dc1/21r	142
Talbot, William	Louth, Haggardstowne	gentry: esquire	08-Feb-66	1200	B.L. 15, 635 f. 169	3549
Tankard, George	Dublin, Ffoxstowne	gentry: gent	10-Mar-35	600	Dc2/230v	2027
Tankard, Patrick	Dublin, Knockan	gentry: gent	10-Mar-35	600	Dc2/230v	2027
Tarleton, Edward	Donegal, Lifford	gentry: esquire	13-Feb-33	100	Dc2/191r	1868
Tarleton, Edward	Tyrone, Drummore	gentry: esquire	26-Feb-34	200	Dc2/207v	1935
Tate, Christopher	Louth, Braganstowne	gentry: esquire	07-Jun-30	300	Dc2/149r	1694
Tate, John	Louth, Braganstowne	gentry: esquire	15-Feb-33	400	Dc2/191v	1869
Tate, Peter	Louth, Hareston	gentry: gent	06-Feb-06	100	Dc1/65r	393
Tate, William	Louth, Hareston	gentry: knight	06-Feb-06	100	Dc1/65r	393
Taylor, Brockhill	Cavan, Ballyhaies	gentry: esquire	16-May-33	400	Dc2/193v	1877
Taylor, Brockhill	Cavan, Ballyhais	gentry: esquire	24-May-33	400	Dc2/194v	1881
Taylor, Brockhill	Cavan, Ballyhais	gentry: esquire	11-May-32	200	Dc2/180r	1824
Taylor, George	Dublin, Swords	gentry: gent	10-Mar-98	800	Dc1/10v	77
Taylor, John	Cavan, Ballyhais	gentry: esquire	28-Sep-19	400	Dc2/25v	1003
Taylor, John	Dublin, Swords	gentry: gent	30-Mar-67	200	Dc3/58	2349
Taylor, John	Dublin, Swords?	gentry: son/heir of Michael	26-Sep-31	600	Dc2/168r	1777
Taylor, John	Dublin, Swords	gentry: gent	30-Mar-67	200	B.L. 15, 635 f. 191	3592
Taylor, Michael	Dublin, Swords	gentry: gent	26-Sep-31	600	Dc2/168r	1777
Taylor, Michael	Dublin, Swords	gentry: gent	20-Jun-31	300	Dc2/165v	1765
Taylor, William	Dublin, the city	trade: brewer	08-May-66	1000	Dc3/28	2285
Taylor, William	Dublin, the city	trade: brewer	08-May-66	1000	B.L. 15, 635 f. 173	3555
Teeling, Richard	Meath, Mulleagh	gentry: gent	07-May-36	40	Dc2/249v	2116
Tellier, Nicholas	Dublin, the city	merchant	13-Mar-32	122	Dc2/177v	1814
Terry, Arthur	Donegal, Moyris	gentry: gent	06-Mar-32	500	Dc2/177v	1813
Terry, David	Cork, the city	gentry: gent	25-Nov-12	105	Dc1/116v	725
Terry, David	Cork, Glankittane	gentry: gent	12-Feb-69	800	Dc3/90	2425

Standard	County	Occupation	Date	Amount	MS No	Ident No
Terry, David	Cork, Glancullanne	gentry: gent	03-Jun-67	583	B.L. 15, 635 f. 195	3600
Terry, David	Cork, Glancullanne	gentry: gent	14-Nov-65	400	B.L. 15, 635 f. 162	3539
Terry, David	Cork, Glankittan	gentry: gent	12-Feb-69	800	B.L. 15, 636 f. 28	3674
Thimblebee, William	Meath, Trym	gentry: gent	08-Jun-26	200	Dc2/79r	1373
Thomas, Maurice	Tipperary, Nenagh	gentry: gent	20-Aug-59	528	B.L. 15, 635 f. 52	3355
Thomson, John	Dublin, the city	gentry: gent	13-Sep-72	450	Dc3/149r	2562
Thomson, John	Dublin, the city	gentry: gent	01-Apr-71	200	Dc3/137v	2521
Thomson, Luke	Dublin, the city	merchant	28-Apr-60	110	B.L. 15, 635 f. 58	3367
Thomson, Ralph		gentry: esquire	30-Jun-97	140	Dc1/5v	38
Thornhill, Robert	Wexford, Carrickclough	gentry: esquire	31-May-58	2000	B.L. 15, 635 f. 29a	3314
Thornhill, Robert	Wexford, Clough	gentry: esquire	13-Feb-58	200	B.L. 19, 843 f. 204a	3116
Thunder, Alexander	Dublin, Colcott	gentry: gent	11-May-35	120	Dc2/235r	2047
Thunder, Alexander	Dublin, Colcott	gentry: gent	07-Apr-36	110	Dc2/249r	2112
Thunder, Alexander	Dublin, Coldcott	gentry: gent	01-Jun-29	100	Dc2/130v	1612
Thunder, John	Louth, Drogheda	gentry: gent	06-Jul-99	40	Dc1/17v	120
Tichborne, Henry	Louth, Bewly	gentry: knight	07-Mar-59	600	B.L. 15, 635 f. 39a	3333
Tichborne, Henry	Dublin, Dunsoghlin	gentry: knight	19-Oct-59	1000	B.L. 15, 635 f. 53	3357
Tichborne, William	Dublin, Dunsoghlin	gentry: s./heir of Sir Henry	19-Oct-59	1000	B.L. 15, 635 f. 53	3357
Tipper, Edmund	Kildare, Tipperston	gentry: gent	07-Dec-05	500	Dc1/63v	385
Tipper, Patrick	Kildare, Tipperston	gentry: gent	07-Dec-05	500	Dc1/63v	385
Tobin, James	Tipperary, Heathstowne	gentry: gent	13-Jun-39	240	B.L. 19, 843 f. 7a	2733
Tobin, John	Tipperary, Killahy	gentry: esquire	05-Dec-17	300	Dc2/12v	929
Tobin, John	Tipperary, Killahie		17-Jun-26	400	Dc2/78r	1374
Todd, Nicholas	Antrim, Carrickfergus	gentry: gent	03-Dec-24	1000	Dc2/59r	1249
Tomlins, Edward	Dublin, the city	gentry: esquire	05-Nov-58	800	B.L. 15, 635 f. 37a	3329
Toogood, George	Tipperary, Collinare	gentry: gent	22-Jun-68	440	Dc3/79	2406
Toogood, George	Tipperary, Collenure	gentry: gent	22-Jun-68	440	B.L. 15, 635 f. 221	3647
Toogood, Sampson	Kilkenny, Tybraghny	gentry: esquire	17-Dec-66	320	Dc3/48	2326
Toogood, Sampson	Kilkenny, Tybraghney	gentry: esquire	01-Aug-64	400	B.L. 15, 635 f. 141a	3502
Toogood, Sampson	Kilkenny, Tibraghny	gentry: esquire	17-Dec-66	320	B.L. 15, 635 f. 189a	3589
Toole, Cahir	Wicklow, Kilmachnocke	gentry: gent	24-Nov-18	120	Dc2/18r	959
Toole, Charles	Wicklow, Kilmekenocke	gentry: gent	19-Jun-35	300	Dc2/237r	2057
Toole, James	Wicklow, Kilcrony?	gentry: gent	24-Nov-18	120	Dc2/18r	959
Toole, Luke	Wicklow, Castlekeavan	gentry: gent	12-May-23	350	Dc2/46v	1154
Toole, Luke	Wicklow, Castlekevin	gentry: esquire	14-Feb-23	240	Dc2/45r	1141
Toole, Luke	Wicklow, Castlekeaven	gentry: esquire	15-Jun-24	240	Dc2/56r	1223
Toole, Luke	Wicklow, Castlekeaven	gentry: gent	25-May-22	600	Dc2/40r	1107
Toole, Luke	Wicklow, Castlekearvyn?	gentry: esquire	01-May-22	350	Dc2/39v	1102
Toole, Luke	Wicklow, Castlekevin	gentry: gent	25-Jun-19	300	Dc2/24r	994
Toole, Luke	Wicklow, Castlekevin	gentry: gent	30-Jun-19	100	Dc2/24v	996
Toole, Peter	Waterford, Aghanboy, Lismore	gentry: gent	22-Nov-39	200	B.L. 19, 843 f. 48a	2815
Topham, John	Dublin, the city	prof: doctor of law	01-May-78	1350	B.L. 15, 637 f. 30	3901
Topham, Thomas	Dublin, the city	prof: doctor of law	01-May-78	1350	Dc3/188v	2711

Standard	County	Occupation	Date	Amount	MS No	Ident No
Touchet, George	England, Somerset, Stowe	peer:				
		baron Audley of Stowe	21-Nov-07	300	Dc1/79ar	492
Touchet, George	England, Somerset, Stowe	peer:				
		baron Audley of Stove	23-Nov-07	600	Dc1/79av	493
Touchet, George	England, Somerset, Stowe	peer:				
		baron Audley of Stowe	31-May-06	1200	Dc1/69r	417
Townley, Henry	Louth, Aclare	gentry: esquire	29-May-74	800	Dc3/161v	2610
Townsend, Brian	Cork, Dunbeacon	gentry: gent	18-Jan-77	1760	B.L. 19, 844 f. 136	3266
Townsend, Brian	Cork, Dunbeacon	gentry: gent	18-Jan-77	880	B.L. 19, 844 f. 130	3260
Townsend, Brian	Cork, Madame	gentry: esquire	02-Nov-83	330	B.L. 15, 637 f. 85	4001
Townsend, Brian	Cork, Downbeacan,					
	WestCarbery	gentry: gent	29-Oct-79	800	B.L. 15, 637 f. 27	3895
Townsend, Brian	Cork, WestCarbery,					
	Dunbeacan	gentry: gent	29-Oct-79	1600	B.L. 15, 637 f. 36	3911
Townsend, Brian	Cork, Downbeacan,					
	WestCarbury	gentry: gent	29-Oct-79	1600	B.L. 15, 637 f. 30a	3902
Townsend, Richard	Cork, Castletowne	gentry: esquire	18-Jan-77	880	B.L. 19, 844 f. 130	3260
Townsend, Richard	Cork, Castletown	gentry: esquire	18-Jan-77	1760	B.L. 19, 844 f. 136	3266
Townsend, Richard	Cork, Castletowne/					
	W. Carbery	gentry: esquire	05-Dec-66	1600	Dc3/44	2322
Townsend, Richard	Cork, Castletowne, Carbery	gentry: esquire	25-Jun-83	800	B.L. 15, 637 f. 79a	3992
Townsend, Richard	Cork, WestCarbery,					
	Castletowne	gentry: esquire	29-Oct-79	1600	B.L. 15, 637 f. 36	3911
Townsend, Richard	Cork, Castletowne, Carbery	gentry: esquire	25-Jun-83	800	B.L. 15, 637 f. 79	3991
Townsend, Richard	Cork, Castletowne,					
	WestCarbery	gentry: esquire	29-Oct-79	800	B.L. 15, 637 f. 27	3895
Townsend, Richard	Cork, Castletowne,					
	WestCarbury	gentry: gent	29-Oct-79	1600	B.L. 15, 637 f. 30a	3902
Tracey, Edmund	Leitrim, Aghederrard	gentry: gent	03-Dec-36	600	Dc2/258v	2161
Tracey, William	Kildare, the Naace	merchant	03-Mar-05	110	Dc1/57r	350
Travers, John	Louth, Drogheda	merchant	27-Jan-36	160	B.L. 19, 843 f. 72a	2864
Travers, Patrick	Dublin, Shanchyll	gentry: gent	02-Dec-00	500	Dc1/27r	181
Travers, Patrick	Dublin, the Newton	gentry: gent	28-May-14	400	Dc1/129v	806
Travers, Richard	Cork, Ballynamony	gentry: esquire	05-Aug-75	660	B.L. 19, 844 f. 70	3198
Travers, Richard	Cork, Ballynomoney	gentry: esquire	01-Jul-67	200	B.L. 15, 635 f. 200	3609
Travers, Richard	Cork, Ballynamony	gentry: esquire	15-Jan-80	480	B.L. 15, 637 f. 26a	3894
Travers, Richard	Cork, Ballymoney	gentry: esquire	19-Nov-84	424	B.L. 15, 637 f. 95	4019
Travers, Robert	Meath, Trym	gentry: esquire	08-Feb-19	200	Dc2/20v	972
Travers, Robert	Cork, Ballymoney	gentry: gent, son/heir of				
		Richard	19-Nov-84	424	B.L. 15, 637 f. 95	4019
Travers, Walter	Dublin, Ballachitery	gentry: gent	18-Nov-08	120	Dc1/84v	526
Treherne, Samuel	Antrim, Carrickfergus		13-Mar-71	88	B.L. 15, 636 f. 82	3764
Trench, John	Carlow, Orchard	gentry: esquire	23-Nov-77	1600	B.L. 19, 844 f. 142a	3273
Tuite, Andrew	Westmeath, Monneley	gentry: son/heir of				
		Theobald	04-Jun-27	200	Dc2/93r	1435

Standard	County	Occupation	Date	Amount	MS No	Ident No
Tuite, Balthazar	Westmeath, Shannagh	gentry: gent	07-Oct-70	200	B.L. 15, 636 f. 75a	3753
Tuite, Bathazar	Westmeath, Shanagh	gentry: gent	07-Oct-70	200	Dc3/127	2495
Tuite, Edmund	Westmeath, Tuytston	gentry: knight	04-Dec-19	600	Dc2/27r	1010
Tuite, Edmund	Westmeath, Tuitston	gentry: knight	31-May-25	200	Dc2/64v	1285
Tuite, Edmund	Westmeath, Tuitston	gentry: knight	30-Jun-26	200	Dc2/80r	1379
Tuite, Edmund	Westmeath, Tuytetowne	gentry: gent	08-May-15	60	Dc1/137r	849
Tuite, Edmund	Westmeath, Tutestowne	gentry: knight	04-Dec-28	400	Dc2/120v	1564
Tuite, Edmund	Westmeath, Tuytston	gentry: esquire	19-Nov-09	60	Dc1/92r	578
Tuite, Edmund	Westmeath, Tuitstown	gentry: knight	19-May-21	400	Dc2/35v	1072
Tuite, Henry	Westmeath, Shanagh	gentry: baronet	07-Oct-70	200	Dc3/127	2495
Tuite, Henry	Westmeath, Shannagh	gentry: baronet	07-Oct-70	200	B.L. 15, 636 f. 75a	3753
Tuite, James	Dublin, the city	gentry: gent	22-Jul-41	200	B.L. 19, 843 f. 105a	2930
Tuite, James	Dublin, the city .	gentry: gent	07-Aug-39	100	B.L. 19, 843 f. 55	2828
Tuite, Oliver	Westmeath, the Sennogh	gentry: esquire	17-Feb-09	300	Dc1/87v	546
Tuite, Oliver	Westmeath, the Sonnagh	gentry: esquire	28-Nov-08	500	Dc1/85r	531
Tuite, Oliver	Westmeath, the Sonnagh	gentry: esquire	08-Feb-17	300	Dc2/4v	891
Tuite, Theobald	Westmeath, Monneley	gentry: gent	04-Jun-27	200	Dc2/93r	1435
Tuite, Theobald	Westmeath, Monylea	gentry: gent	17-Sep-12	500	Dc1/115v	717
Tuite, Tibbot	Westmeath, Moneleigh	gentry: gent	10-Jun-29	50	Dc2/131r	1614
Tuite, Tibbot	Westmeath, Moneleye	gentry: gent	20-Jun-07	80	Dc1/78v	481
Tuite, Walter	Westmeath, Cullanhue	gentry: gent	08-Dec-57	106	B.L. 19, 843 f. 203	3112
Tuite, William	Dublin, the city	merchant	04-Dec-19	600	Dc2/27r	1010
Turner, Samuel	Dublin	trade: gardiner	21-Apr-27	60	Dc2/90r	1424
Turner, Thomas	Dublin	merchant	14-Jul-23	400	Dc2/49v	1176
Turry, Dominic	Cork, the city		02-Dec-30	200	Dc2/157r	1731
Tweedy, Patrick	Dublin, the city	gentry: gent	13-Jan-68	120	Dc3/71	2385
Tweedy, Patrick	Dublin, the city	gentry: gent	13-Jan-68	120	B.L. 15, 635 f. 212	3629
Tyne, Richard	Dublin, the city	gentry: esquire	09-Nov-77	500	Dc3/183v	2696
Tynte, Henry	Cork, Ballycreghane	gentry: esquire	01-Feb-84	836	B.L. 15, 637 f. 86	4003
Tynte, Mabel	Cork, Ballycreghane	gentry: widow	01-Feb-84	836	B.L. 15, 637 f. 86	4003
Tyres, John	Louth, Atherdee	merchant	20-Oct-71	60	B.L. 15, 636 f. 91a	3782
Tyrrell, Christopher	Westmeath, Bolybracke	gentry: esquire	13-May-25	400	Dc2/63v	1279
Tyrrell, Christopher	Westmeath, Bolleebrack	gentry: esquire	19-Jul-27	200	Dc2/97r	1452
Tyrrell, Edward	Westmeath, Lyn	gentry: esquire	17-Dec-74	1100	Dc3/164r	2620
Tyrrell, Edward	Westmeath, Lynn	gentry: esquire	17-Dec-74	1100	B.L. 19, 844 f. 47	3170
Tyrrell, Edward	Westmeath, Lynn	gentry: esquire	28-Jan-78	1800	B.L. 19, 844 f. 149	3280
Tyrrell, Edward	Westmeath, Lynn	gentry: esquire	28-Jan-78	1800	Dc3/184v	2701
Tyrrell, Edward	Westmeath, Symonston	gentry: gent	23-May-26	200	Dc2/78r	1367
Tyrrell, Garret	Westmeath, Rainguill	gentry: esquire, son of James	13-May-25	400	Dc2/63v	1279
Tyrrell, Gerald	Westmeath, Castlelost	gentry: esquire	16-Jun-29	120	Dc2/132v	1619
Tyrrell, Gerald	Westmeath, the Pace	gentry: esquire	09-Dec-18	1000	Dc2/19r	964
Tyrrell, Gerald	Westmeath, Castlelast	gentry: esquire	20-May-31	2000	Dc2/163r	1756
Tyrrell, Gerlad	Westmeath, the Pace	gentry: esquire	20-Nov-16	300	Dc2/2r	878
Tyrrell, James	Westmeath, the Pace	gentry: esquire	20-May-12	200	Dc1/114r	706

Standard	County	Occupation	Date	Amount	MS No	Ident No
Tyrrell, James	Westmeath, Castelos	gentry: gent	17-Jul-99	110	Dc1/17v	121
Tyrrell, James	Westmeath, the pace	gentry: esquire	11-Feb-14	200	Dc1/126v	785
Tyrrell, John			14-Jul-66	200	Dc3/33	2294
Tyrrell, John			14-Jul-66	100	Dc3/33	2295
Tyrrell, John			14-Jul-66	200	Dc3/33	2296
Tyrrell, Maurice	King's Co., Bracklone	gentry: gent	12-Dec-29	400	Dc2/140r	1654
Tyrrell, Maurice	Westmeath, Pierstowne	gentry: gent	16-May-36	600	Dc2/251r	2121
Tyrrell, Maurice	King's Co., Brackline	gentry: gent	07-Apr-36	2000	Dc2/248v	2111
Tyrrell, Maurice	King's Co., Brackland	gentry: gent	23-May-26	200	Dc2/78r	1367
Tyrrell, Philip	Westmeath, Rathcam	gentry: gent	16-May-36	600	Dc2/251r	2121
Tyrrell, Raymond	Westmeath, Portloman	gentry: son/heir of William	20-Jun-15	60	Dc1/138v	860
Tyrrell, Redmond	Westmeath, Kilbride	gentry: son/heir of Richard	20-Nov-26	200	Dc2/83v	1397
Tyrrell, Richard	Westmeath, Newcastle	gentry: esquire	20-May-31	2000	Dc2/163r	1756
Tyrrell, Richard	Westmeath, Clonmoile	gentry: esquire	11-Feb-14	200	Dc1/126v	785
Tyrrell, Richard	Westmeath, Symonston	gentry: gent	13-Nov-14	120	Dc1/132r	822
Tyrrell, Richard	Westmeath, Newcastle	gentry: esquire	25-Apr-27	500	Dc2/91r	1426
Tyrrell, Richard	King's Co., Coulchill	gentry: esquire	16-May-36	600	Dc2/251r	2122
Tyrrell, Richard	Westmeath, Kilbride	gentry: gent	20-Nov-26	200	Dc2/83v	1397
Tyrrell, Richard	Louth, Drogheda	merchant	26-Aug-72	120	B.L. 15, 636 f. 124	3828
Tyrrell, Thomas	Roscommon, Lisgrechan	gentry: esquire	04-Dec-57	120	B.L. 19, 843 f. 201a	3109
Tyrrell, Thomas	Westmeath?, Newcastle?	gentry: son/heir of Richard	25-Apr-27	500	Dc2/91r	1426
Tyrrell, Thomas	Westmeath, Newcastle	gentry: gent	20-Feb-40	100	B.L. 19, 843 f. 44	2806
Tyrrell, Thomas	Westmeath, Robinson	gentry: esquire	15-Apr-36	1400	Dc2/249r	2114
Tyrrell, Thomas	Westmeath, Newcastle	gentry: son/heir of Richard	16-May-36	600	Dc2/251r	2122
Tyrrell, Thomas	Westmeath?, Rathcame	other: son/heir of Richard	03-Feb-30	200	Dc2/141r	1661
Tyrrell, Thomas	Westmeath, Rathcame	gentry: gent	20-May-31	2000	Dc2/163r	1756
Tyrrell, Thomas	Westmeath, Robinson	gentry: esquire	03-Mar-54	200	B.L. 19, 843 f. 136a	2987
Tyrrell, Walter	Westmeath, Kilbride	gentry: gent	03-Mar-54	200	B.L. 19, 843 f. 136a	2987
Tyrrell, William	Westmeath, Portloman	gentry: gent	20-Jun-15	60	Dc1/138v	860
Uniacke, Thomas	Cork, Barnigihy	gentry: esquire	07-Feb-79	2000	B.L. 15, 637 f. 16	3875
Ussher, Alice	Dublin, the city	other: widow	22-May-75	190	Dc3/168r	2637
Ussher, Alice	Dublin, the city	other: widow	10-Nov-73	480	B.L. 19, 844 f. 16	3134
Ussher, Alice	Dublin, the city	other: widow	22-May-75	190	B.L. 19, 844 f. 63	3191
Ussher, Eales	Dublin, the city	other: widow	10-Nov-73	480	Dc3/158ar	2594
Ussher, George	Dublin	merchant	18-Apr-00	200	Dc1/23r	154
Ussher, George	Dublin, the city	merchant	06-Sep-42	200	B.L. 19, 843 f. 109	2937
Ussher, George	Dublin, the city	merchant	07-Dec-38	660	B.L. 19, 843 f. 3	2725
Ussher, James	Meath	prof: bishop of Meath	10-Jun-23	400	Dc2/48r	1164
Ussher, Jocelin	Meath, Balsowne		01-Dec-40	1500	B.L. 19, 843 f. 76	2871

Standard	County	Occupation	Date	Amount	MS No	Ident No
Ussher, Jocelin	Meath, Balsowne?	gentry: son/heir of Mark	05-Jul-30	200	Dc2/154r	1715
Ussher, Jocelin	Meath, Balsowne		12-Jul-33	600	Dc2/197v	1894
Ussher, Jocelin	Meath?, Balsown?	gentry: son of Mark	11-Feb-25	200	Dc2/61v	1265
Ussher, John	Louth, Baltra	gentry: esquire	26-Aug-23	300	Dc2/50r	1180
Ussher, John	Dublin		30-Jun-97	400	Dc1/5v	41
Ussher, John	Louth, Baltra	gentry: esquire	13-Aug-23	150	Dc2/50v	1178
Ussher, Lawrence	Dublin	merchant	03-Mar-99	300	Dc1/16r	109
Ussher, Mark	Meath, Balsowne	gentry: esquire	13-May-29	400	Dc2/128v	1603
Ussher, Mark	Meath, Balstowne	gentry: esquire	19-Jul-25	80	Dc2/68v	1311
Ussher, Mark	Meath, Balsowne	gentry: esquire	15-Dec-28	200	Dc2/123r	1573
Ussher, Mark	Meath, Balsowne?	gentry: esquire	07-Nov-17	200	Dc2/10v	918
Ussher, Mark	Meath, Balsowne	gentry: esquire	05-Jul-30	200	Dc2/154r	1715
Ussher, Mark	Meath, Balsown	gentry: esquire	11-Feb-25	200	Dc2/61v	1265
Ussher, Nathaniel	Meath, Balsowne	gentry: gent	12-Jul-33	600	Dc2/197v	1894
Ussher, Patrick	Dublin, the city	gentry: gent	22-May-75	190	Dc3/168r	2637
Ussher, Patrick	Dublin, the city	gentry: gent	10-Nov-73	480	B.L. 19, 844 f. 16	3134
Ussher, Patrick	Dublin, the city	gentry: gent	10-Nov-73	480	Dc3/158ar	2594
Ussher, Patrick	Dublin, the city	gentry: gent	22-May-75	190	B.L. 19, 844 f. 63	3191
Ussher, Robert	Dublin	merchant	03-Mar-99	300	Dc1/16r	109
Ussher, William	Dublin, the city	gentry: knight	21-May-59	400	B.L. 15, 635 f. 49	3349
Valayer, Melchior	Dublin	trade: beer brewer	13-Mar-33	400	Dc2/192v	1874
Vaughan, Owen	Mayo, Carrowmore	gentry: esquire	23-Dec-65	600	Dc3/18	2264
Vaughan, Owen	Mayo, Carrowmore	gentry: esquire	22-Mar-66	600	Dc3/26	2281
Vaughan, Thomas	Cork, Youghall		10-Feb-57	500	B.L. 15, 635 f. 181	3572
Velden, Christopher	Dublin, the city	gentry: gent	05-Sep-34	200	Dc2/218v	1978
Veldon, Thomas	Meath, Raffine	gentry: gent	26-Nov-24	200	Dc2/59r	1248
Verdon, Christopher	Louth, Kiltalleghe	gentry: gent	19-Jun-05	70	Dc1/60r	366
Verdon, John	Louth, Clonmore	gentry: esquire	10-Feb-29	240	Dc2/124r	1580
Vincent, Thomas	Dublin, Iristowne	gentry: esquire	06-Aug-63	5000	B.L. 15, 635 f. 110a	3451
Virgin, Arthur	Cork, the city	trade: upholster	12-Dec-71	1000	B.L. 15, 636 f. 97a	3791
Wacklie, James	King's Co., Culcore	gentry: gent	04-Feb-26	200	Dc2/73r	1338
Wadding, Paul	Waterford, Towregarre	gentry: gent	23-Nov-30	220	Dc2/156v	1727
Wadding, Richard	Waterford	gentry: gent	18-Nov-02	200	Dc1/40v	262
Wadding, Thomas	Waterford, Duagh	gentry: esquire	16-Apr-40	1400	B.L. 19, 843 f. 65a	2850
Waddington, Henry	Galway, Clistoken	gentry: knight	12-Dec-74	1300	B.L. 19, 844 f. 58a	3183
Waddington, Henry	Galway, Clistoken	gentry: knight	12-Dec-74	1300	Dc3/163v	2619
Waddington, Henry	Galway, Clostrkin	gentry: knight	22-Jun-65	560	Dc3/11	2246
Waddington, Henry	Galway, Clostakin	gentry: knight	22-Jun-65	560	B.L. 15, 636 f. 85a	3771
Waddington, John	Wexford, Newborough	gentry: gent	02-Jun-36	600	Dc2/253r	2133
Waddington, Ralph	Wexford, St. Johns	gentry: esquire	04-Feb-54	2000	B.L. 19, 843 f. 136	2986
Waddington, Ralph	Wexford, St. John's	gentry: esquire	02-Jun-36	600	Dc2/253r	2133
Wafer, John	Meath, Granston	gentry: gent	22-May-06	200	Dc1/68v	414

Standard	County	Occupation	Date	Amount	MS No	Ident No
Wakley, Garret	Meath, the Navan	gentry: son/heir of Gerrot	17-May-09	400	Dc1/89r	555
Wakley, Garret	Meath, the Navan	gentry: gent	17-May-09	400	Dc1/89r	555
Wakley, Gerard	Meath?, the Navan?	gentry: son of Thomas	13-May-08	400	Dc1/83r	515
Wakley, Thomas	Meath, the Navan	gentry: gent	13-May-08	400	Dc1/83r	515
Wakley, Thomas	King's Co., Ballyburlie	gentry: esquire	01-Feb-33	600	Dc2/190v	1866
Wakley, Thomas	King's Co., Ballebeilee	gentry: gent	04-Feb-26	200	Dc2/73r	1338
Wale, Edmund	Carlow, Orghlin	gentry: gent	15-Dec-25	320	Dc2/72r	1332
Wale, Gerald	Kildare, Ffrumpleston?	gentry: gent	13-Nov-24	100	Dc2/58v	1242
Wale, Gerald	Kildare, Frompolston	gentry: gent	11-Aug-14	240	Dc1/131v	817
Wale, Gerrot	Kildare, Phrumpleston	gentry: gent	31-Jan-25	100	Dc2/61r	1259
Walkden, Isaac	Tipperary, Ardmale	gentry: esquire	08-Nov-78	1000	B.L. 19, 844 f. 170	3301
Walker, John	Kerry, Clonelashin	gentry: gent	07-Apr-77	120	B.L. 19, 844 f. 121	3250
Walker, Nicholas	Kildare, Athy	gentry: gent	10-Nov-18	200	Dc2/17r	953
Walker, William	Wexford, Balleteage	gentry: esquire	14-Aug-80	200	B.L. 15, 637 f. 37a	3913
Walker, William	Wexford, Bally Teige	gentry: esquire	22-Nov-81	250	B.L. 15, 637 f. 52a	3940
Wall, Ulick	Carlow, Ballineskill	gentry: gent	04-Jul-64	500	B.L. 15, 635 f. 172	3553
Wall, William	Cork, Cooleclogher	gentry: gent	29-Aug-73	1200	B.L. 19, 844 f. 17	3135
Wallis, Ralph	Dublin, the city	gentry: esquire	22-Jul-65	120	Dc3/12	2247
Wallis, Ralph	Dublin, the city	gentry: esquire	03-Nov-54	400	B.L. 19, 843 f. 146	3006
Wallis, Ralph	Dublin, the city	gentry: esquire	18-Jun-67	300	Dc3/63	2362
Wallis, Ralph	Dublin, the city	gentry: esquire	03-Apr-57	140	B.L. 19, 843 f. 191a	3090
Wallis, Ralph	Dublin, the city	gentry: esquire	18-Jun-67	300	B.L. 15, 635 f. 196a	3603
Wallplate, Nathaniel	King's Co., Castletowne	gentry: gent	09-Jan-62	500	B.L. 15, 635 f. 90a	3417
Walsh, Ardal	Kilkenny, Woollensgrandge	gentry: gent	05-Dec-17	300	Dc2/12v	929
Walsh, David	Tipperary, Ballinuohire?	gentry: esquire	21-Nov-28	200	Dc2/116v	1544
Walsh, Edmund	Kilkenny, Ballinlough	gentry: gent	28-Jun-28	200	Dc2/111v	1521
Walsh, George	Antrim, Carrickfergus	trade: leather worker	29-Jan-72	137	B.L. 15, 636 f. 98	3792
Walsh, George	Antrim, Carrickfergus	trade: leather worker	29-Jan-72	273	B.L. 15, 636 f. 108a	3808
Walsh, Gerald	Kilkenny, the city	gentry: gent	28-Jun-28	200	Dc2/111v	1521
Walsh, Henry	Dublin, Ballawly	gentry: son/heir of James	15-Jul-25	400	Dc2/68v	1310
Walsh, Henry	Waterford	merchant	28-Nov-03	515	Dc1/50r	320
Walsh, Henry	Dublin?, Balleawlie?	gentry: son/heir of James	18-Nov-24	400	Dc2/58v	1244
Walsh, James	Dublin, Ballyawly	gentry: gent	13-May-20	1000	Dc2/30r	1029
Walsh, James	Dublin, Balleawlie	gentry: gent	18-Nov-24	400	Dc2/58v	1244
Walsh, James	Dublin, Ballawly	gentry: gent	01-May-22	350	Dc2/39v	1102
Walsh, James	Dublin, Connogh?	gentry: esquire	09-May-29	400	Dc2/128r	1602
Walsh, James	Dublin, Balleawlw	gentry: gent	12-May-23	350	Dc2/46v	1154
Walsh, James	Tipperary, Ballygurtean	gentry: gent	30-Apr-72	400	Dc3/145v	2551
Walsh, James	Dublin, Ballawly	gentry: gent	15-Jul-25	400	Dc2/68v	1310
Walsh, James	Waterford, Insula	gentry: esquire	21-Apr-40	2000	B.L. 19, 843 f. 66	2851
Walsh, James	Dublin, Connogh	gentry: esquire	22-Jun-26	1000	Dc2/79v	1377
Walsh, James	Tipperary, Ballygurteen	gentry: gent	30-Apr-72	400	B.L. 15, 636 f. 105a	3802
Walsh, James	Dublin, Ballawny	gentry: gent	15-Jun-18	200	Dc2/15r	943

Standard	County	Occupation	Date	Amount	MS No	Ident No
Walsh, John	Kildare, ?	gentry: son/heir of Pierce	19-May-17	600	Dc2/6v	900
Walsh, John	Dublin, Kilgobban	gentry: s/heir of John	08-Feb-09	90	Dc1/87r	544
Walsh, John	Dublin?, Kilgobban?	gentry: son/heir of Pierce	17-Jun-23	100	Dc2/48r	1165
Walsh, John	Dublin, Kilgobban?	gentry: son/heir of Pierce	12-Jun-32	1400	Dc2/182v	1834
Walsh, John	Dublin, Kilgoban	gentry: son/heir of Pierce	18-Sep-11	110	Dc1/106v	663
Walsh, John	Limerick, the abbey of Ownhie	gentry: esquire	20-Jul-24	800	Dc2/57v	1234
Walsh, John	Wicklow, Killincarricke	gentry: gent	07-Jul-32	1000	Dc2/184v	1842
Walsh, John	Dublin	merchant	03-Feb-98	7	Dc1/9v	67
Walsh, John	Dublin, Kilgobban	gentry: son/heir of Pierce	17-Nov-31	1000	Dc2/170v	1786
Walsh, John	Dublin, Kilgobban	gentry: son/heir of Pierce	12-Jun-19	1000	Dc2/23v	992
Walsh, John	Wicklow, Killencarge	gentry: gent	06-May-37	800	Dc2/262r	2177
Walsh, Nicholas	Kilkenny, Clonmore	gentry: knight	15-Dec-28	520	Dc2/122v	1572
Walsh, Nicholas	Waterford, Ballykerroge	gentry: knight	13-Mar-35	400	Dc2/230v	2028
Walsh, Nicholas	Kilkenny, Clonmore	gentry: knight	21-Nov-28	200	Dc2/116v	1544
Walsh, Oliver	Dublin, the city	gentry: gent	06-Feb-55	1000	B.L. 19, 843 f. 156	3026
Walsh, Patrick	Limerick, Cappenewike	gentry: esquire	26-Jun-41	2400	B.L. 19, 843 f. 103	2925
Walsh, Peter	Kildare, Mevalle	gentry: gent	17-Jul-99	110	Dc1/17v	121
Walsh, Pierce	Dublin, Kilgobban	gentry: gent	17-Nov-31	1000	Dc2/170v	1786
Walsh, Pierce	Dublin, Kilgobben	gentry: gent	16-Nov-02	40	Dc1/40r	260
Walsh, Pierce	Dublin, Kilgoban	gentry: gent	18-Sep-11	110	Dc1/106v	663
Walsh, Pierce	Dublin, Kilgobban	gentry: gent	08-Feb-09	90	Dc1/87r	544
Walsh, Pierce	Dublin, Kilgobban	gentry: gent	19-May-17	600	Dc2/6v	900
Walsh, Pierce	Dublin, Kilgobban	gentry: gent	17-Jun-23	100	Dc2/48r	1165
Walsh, Pierce	Dublin, Kilgobban	gentry: gent	12-Jun-32	1400	Dc2/182v	1834
Walsh, Pierce	Dublin, Kilgobban	gentry: gent	12-Jun-19	1000	Dc2/23v	992
Walsh, Richard	Dublin, Kilmainhame	farmer: yeoman	20-Dec-03	300	Dc1/51r	327
Walsh, Richard			20-Dec-02	60	Dc1/43r	274
Walsh, Robert	Dublin, Threecastles	gentry: gent	14-Mar-00	50	Dc1/22r	147
Walsh, Theobald	?, Killencarye		10-Feb-97		Dc1/1v	6
Walsh, William	Wexford	gentry: gent	02-Jun-06	60	Dc1/69v	419
Walsh, William	Queen's Co., Ballybrittas	merchant	14-Mar-68	60	Dc3/74	2392
Ward, Arthur	Dublin, the city	gentry: esquire	29-May-74	800	Dc3/161v	2610
Ward, Peter	Dublin, the city	trade: brewer	26-Aug-59	420	B.L. 15, 635 f. 51	3353
Ware, John	Meath, Castletowne Moylagh	gentry: esquire	15-Jul-41	240	B.L. 19, 843 f. 107a	2934
Ware, John?	Meath, Castleton Moylaghe	gentry: esquire	15-Sep-03	1000	Dc1/49r	316
Ware, Peter	Limerick, the city	gentry: gent	18-Apr-77	300	B.L. 19, 844 f. 139	3269
Warnford, Robert	Queen's Co., Clarehill	gentry: esquire	05-Oct-81	600	B.L. 15, 637 f. 50a	3937

Standard	County	Occupation	Date	Amount	MS No	Ident No
Warnford, Robert	Queen's Co., Clarehill	gentry: esquire	05-Oct-81	700	B.L. 15, 637 f. 50a	3938
Warren, Abel	Kilkenny, The Lodge	gentry: esquire	08-Feb-67	300	Dc3/52	2336
Warren, Abel	Kilkenny, Lalodge	gentry: esquire	08-Feb-67	300	B.L. 15, 635 f. 201	3611
Warren, Abel	Kilkenny, Ballinlodge	gentry: esquire	15-Feb-61	720	B.L. 15, 635 f. 62a	3376
Warren, George	Louth, Warrenston	gentry: gent	29-Nov-21	160	Dc2/37r	1082
Warren, Henry	Kildare, Grangbegg	gentry: esquire	06-Feb-55	2000	B.L. 19, 843 f. 156a	3027
Warren, Henry	Dublin, Lessenshale	gentry: knight	12-Jan-01	160	Dc1/27v	184
Warren, Henry	Kildare, Granbegg	gentry: esquire	06-Feb-55	1000	B.L. 19, 843 f. 156	3026
Warren, Henry	King's Co., Ballibrittain	gentry: knight	26-Apr-27	2000	Dc2/91r	1427
Warren, Henry	Queen's Co., Warinston	gentry: knight	27-Nov-17	2000	Dc2/11v	923
Warren, Henry	Kildare, Grangebegg	gentry: esquire	16-Dec-57	200	B.L. 19, 843 f. 202a	3111
Warren, Henry	King's Co., Ballebritten	gentry: knight	10-Nov-23	600	Dc2/51r	1185
Warren, Henry	King's Co., Ballibrittaine	gentry: knight	03-Feb-05	60	Dc1/55v	344
Warren, Nicholas	Dublin, Harieston	farmer: yeoman	25-Jun-14	400	Dc1/130v	810
Warren, Nicholas	Dublin, Sillocke	gentry: gent	05-May-32	100	Dc2/179r	1819
Warren, William	Kildare, Granbegg	gentry: gent, son/heir of Henry	06-Feb-55	1000	B.L. 19, 843 f. 156	3026
Warren, William	Dublin, the city	merchant	05-May-32	100	Dc2/179r	1819
Warren, William	Dublin, Dromcondraghe	gentry: esquire	06-Jul-97	84	Dc1/6r	43
Warren, William	Kildare, Grangebegg	gentry: son/heir of Henry	16-Dec-57	200	B.L. 19, 843 f. 202a	3111
Warren, William	Kildare, Grangbegg	gentry: gent, son/heir of Henry	06-Feb-55	2000	B.L. 19, 843 f. 156a	3027
Warter, Edward	Limerick, Bilboe	gentry: esquire	07-Oct-82	640	B.L. 15, 637 f. 65	3964
Warter, Gamaliel	Limerick, Dullan Castle	gentry: esquire	19-Dec-57	400	B.L. 19, 843 f. 204	3114
Warter, Gamaliel	Limerick, Dullan Castle?	gentry: esquire	04-Dec-55	600	B.L. 19, 843 f. 206a	3119
Warter, Gamaliel	Tipperary, [Pallatine] Cullen	gentry: esquire	23-Jul-72	1600	Dc3/148v	2560
Waterhouse, Charles	Fermanagh, Castlewaterhouse	gentry: esquire	09-Aug-36	400	Dc2/255r	2146
Waterhouse, Charles	Fermanagh, Rouskie	gentry: gent	09-Aug-36	400	Dc2/255r	2146
Waterhouse, Charles	Cavan, Belterbett	gentry: esquire	22-Nov-31	264	Dc2/172r	1792
Waterhouse, Charles	Fermanagh, Castlewaterhouse	gentry: gent	17-Jul-39	400	B.L. 19, 843 f. 22	2762
Waterhouse, Charles	Fermanagh, Castlewaterhouse	gentry: gent	19-Feb-41	400	B.L. 19, 843 f. 86	2891
Waterhouse, Thomas	Dublin, the city		05-May-56	200	B.L. 19, 843 f. 179a	3065
Waterhouse, Thomas	Dublin, the city		13-Feb-60	200	B.L. 15, 635 f. 57	3365
Waterhouse, Thomas	Dublin, the city		13-Feb-60	200	B.L. 15, 635 f. 57a	3366
Waters, George	Cork, Whiddey	gentry: esquire	18-Dec-67	340	Dc3/71	2384
Waters, George	Cork, Whiddey	gentry: esquire	18-Dec-67	340	B.L. 15, 635 f. 211a	3628
Watkins, Christopher	Wicklow, the town	merchant	31-Dec-59	500	B.L. 15, 635 f. 138a	3498
Watson, Thomas	Carlow, Hacketston	gentry: gent	17-Nov-40	1200	B.L. 19, 843 f. 73	2865
Weaver, John	Queen's Co., Ballymaddock	gentry: esquire	10-Oct-70	2000	Dc3/127	2496

Standard	County	Occupation	Date	Amount	MS No	Ident No
Weaver, John	King's Co., Ballymony	gentry: esquire	06-Dec-60	3000	B.L. 15, 635 f. 60a	3372
Weaver, John	Queen's Co., Ballymadock	gentry: esquire	10-Oct-70	2000	B.L. 15, 636 f. 71a	3745
Webb, Thomas	Dublin	gentry: esquire	27-Apr-22	167	Dc2/39r	1101
Weeks, Mark	Cork, Kilbolane	gentry: gent	13-Aug-80	1000	B.L. 15, 637 f. 38a	3915
Weeks, Nicholas	Limerick, Glanogra	gentry: gent	16-Dec-73	2000	B.L. 19, 844 f. 18	3136
Weeks, Sabina	Limerick, Glanogra	other: widow	16-Dec-73	2000	B.L. 19, 844 f. 18	3136
Weldon, Robert	Kildare, Tullogory	gentry: esquire	05-Mar-29	1000	Dc2/125v	1590
Weldon, Walter	Queen's Co., Rahin	gentry: esquire	09-Dec-85	1000	B.L. 15, 637 f. 102	4032
Wellesley, Edward	Kildare, Allasti	gentry: gent	29-Jan-11	150	Dc1/102r	638
Wellesley, James	Kildare, Corugh	gentry: esq, bar of the Corugh	26-Jul-37	1200	Dc2/270r	2211
Wellesley, James	Kildare, Bellatoer	gentry: esq als b. Narraghmore	08-Dec-40	1000	B.L. 19, 843 f. 76a	2872
Wellesley, James	Kildare, Blakhall	gentry: son/heir of Richard	11-Aug-14	240	Dc1/131v	817
Wellesley, Richard	Kildare, Blakhall	gentry: gent	11-Aug-14	240	Dc1/131v	817
Wentworth, William	Meath, Lough Gore	gentry: gent	16-Jan-23	200	Dc2/44r	1135
Wesley, Edmund	Kildare, Alasty	gentry: gent	19-Jun-07	40	Dc1/78v	479
Wesley, Edward	Kildare, Allasty	gentry: gent	07-Dec-19	120	Dc2/27r	1012
Wesley, Edward	Kildare, Alastie	gentry: gent	15-Apr-08	40	Dc1/81v	505
Wesley, Gerald	Meath, the Dengan	gentry: esquire	14-Jun-02	1000	Dc1/38r	247
Wesley, Gerald	Meath, Dongan	gentry: esquire	29-Jan-80	400	B.L. 15, 637 f. 25	3891
Wesley, Gerald	Meath, Dongan	gentry: esquire	11-Feb-82	400	B.L. 15, 637 f. 55	3945
Wesley, Gerald	Meath, Dongan	gentry: esquire	07-Sep-63	200	B.L. 15, 635 f. 117	3464
Wesley, James	Kildare, Bareston	gentry: son/heir of Richard	25-May-12	80	Dc1/114r	708
Wesley, Joseph	Kildare, Painstowne	gentry: gent	20-Feb-36	200	Dc2/245r	2096
Wesley, Maurice	Meath, Walterston	gentry: gent	17-May-32	200	Dc2/181r	1828
Wesley, Richard	Kildare, Blackhale	gentry: gent	28-Apr-02	200	Dc1/37v	244
Wesley, Richard	Kildare, Bareston	gentry: gent	25-May-12	80	Dc1/114r	708
Wesley, Valentine	Meath, Dengan	gentry: esquire	28-Jun-31	2000	Dc2/165v	1766
Wesley, Valentine	Meath, Dingin	gentry: esquire	30-Jun-37	400	Dc2/266v	2195
Wesley, Valentine	Meath, Dengan	gentry: esquire	14-Jul-23	800	Dc2/49v	1175
Wesley, Valentine	Meath, the Dengen	gentry: esquire	12-Feb-30	300	Dc2/142r	1665
Wesley, Valentine	Meath, the Dingen	gentry: esquire	20-Feb-36	200	Dc2/245r	2096
Wesley, Valentine	Meath, Dengen	gentry: esquire	15-Jul-41	240	B.L. 19, 843 f. 107a	2934
Wesley, Valentine	Meath, Dengen	gentry: esquire	17-Nov-40	600	B.L. 19, 843 f. 89a	2898
Wesley, William	Meath, Dingin?	gentry: son/heir of Valentine	30-Jun-37	400	Dc2/266v	2195
West, Roger	Down, Ballydogan	gentry: esquire	13-Oct-70	1600	Dc3/128	2497
Weston, Christopher	Dublin, the city	merchant	24-Apr-29	200	Dc2/127v	1598
Weston, John	Dublin, the city	merchant	19-Nov-28	200	Dc2/118v	1555
Weston, John	Dublin, the city	merchant	16-Jul-28	300	Dc2/113r	1528
Weston, John	Dublin, the city	merchant	03-Jan-31	160	Dc2/158v	1736
Weston, John	Dublin	merchant	12-Dec-27	220	Dc2/102r	1475

Standard	County	Occupation	Date	Amount	MS No	Ident No
Weston, John	Dublin, the city	merchant	24-Apr-29	200	Dc2/127v	1598
Weston, John	Dublin, the city	merchant	10-Apr-20	500	Dc2/29v	1026
Weston, Nathaniel	Limerick, the city	gentry: gent	15-Aug-76	140	B.L. 19, 844 f. 107	3234
Weston, Nicholas	Dublin		08-Mar-05	1700	Dc1/57r	351
Weston, Nicholas	Dublin		03-Apr-06	1000	Dc1/66r	400
Weston, Richard	Louth, Dundalk	merchant	24-Nov-00	100	Dc1/26v	179
Weston, Thomas	Dublin, the city	gentry: gent	27-Jul-41	200	B.L. 19, 843 f. 106a	2932
Weston, William	Dublin, the city	merchant	18-May-25	80	Dc2/63v	1280
Weston, William	Dublin	merchant	10-Feb-29	300	Dc2/124v	1582
Weymes, Henry	Kilkenny, Dainsfort	gentry: esquire	18-Nov-72	6000	Dc3/149r	2563
Weymes, James	Dublin	gentry: knight	06-Aug-72	400	Dc3/149r	2561
Weymes, James	Dublin, the city	gentry: knight	06-Aug-72	400	B.L. 15, 636 f. 119a	3826
Weymes, Patrick	Kilkenny, Donfart	gentry: esquire	06-Jun-40	4000	B.L. 19, 843 f. 56a	2831
Whalley, Henry	Galway, Athenree	gentry: esquire	19-May-60	500	B.L. 15, 635 f. 58a	3368
Whalley, John	Galway, Athenry	gentry: esquire	18-Jul-70	2048	Dc3/123	2487
Whalley, John	Galway, Loghreagh	gentry: gent	19-May-60	500	B.L. 15, 635 f. 58a	3368
Whalley, John	Galway, Atherny	gentry: esquire	18-Jul-70	2048	B.L. 15, 636 f. 68	3738
Wheeler, Jonah	Queen's Co., Grenon	gentry: esquire	17-Dec-79	1000	B.L. 15, 637 f. 23	3887
White, Arthur	Dublin	gentry: esquire	26-Feb-41	1600	B.L. 19, 843 f. 87	2893
White, Charles	Kildare, Leixlip	gentry: gent	15-Nov-52	494	B.L. 19, 843 f. 127a	2973
White, Christopher	Dublin, the city	gentry: gent	15-May-83	264	B.L. 15, 637 f. 71	3975
White, James	Dublin, the Warde	gentry: gent	23-Feb-26	200	Dc2/74v	1347
White, James	Dublin, the Warde	gentry: gent	26-Jul-26	200	Dc2/82r	1389
White, James	Dublin, the Warde	gentry: gent	12-Mar-31	500	Dc2/161r	1747
White, James	Dublin, the Warde	gentry: gent	27-Jan-27	200	Dc2/87v	1415
White, James	Louth, Balregan	gentry: gent	14-Jun-30	200	Dc2/151r	1702
White, James	Dublin, the warde	gentry: gent	12-May-30	800	Dc2/147r	1687
White, James	Dublin, the Warde?	gentry: gent	02-Oct-27	200	Dc2/99r	1460
White, John	Down, Duffrin	gentry: esquire	15-Jan-06	1000	Dc1/64v	389
White, John	Kildare, Sherlockstowne	gentry: gent	06-Jul-12	700	Dc1/115r	715
White, John	Kildare, Sherlockston	gentry: gent	07-May-97	40	Dc1/3v	21
White, Nathaniel	Dublin, the city	trade: butcher	13-Dec-66	280	Dc3/48	2325
White, Nicholas	Kildare, Leixlipp	gentry: esquire	26-Jun-54	655	B.L. 19, 843 f. 142	2998
White, Nicholas	Dublin	gentry: gent	27-Jan-27	200	Dc2/87v	1415
White, Nicholas	Dublin	gentry: esquire	26-Feb-41	1600	B.L. 19, 843 f. 87	2893
White, Nicholas	Kildare, Leixlipp	gentry: knight	26-Jun-54	655	B.L. 19, 843 f. 142	2998
White, Nicholas	Dublin? Kildare Leixlippe	gentry: esquire	11-Apr-06	400	Dc1/66v	401
White, Nicholas	Louth, Marshallrath	gentry: gent	14-Apr-19	300	Dc2/21v	980
White, Nicholas	Down, Duffrin	gentry: son/heir of John	15-Jan-06	1000	Dc1/64v	389
White, Nicholas	Dublin	gentry: gent	08-Aug-29	400	Dc2/135v	1633
White, Nicholas	Kildare, Leixlipp	gentry: knight	01-Jul-53	400	B.L. 19, 843 f. 140a	2995
White, Nicholas	Kildare, Leixlip	gentry: esquire	15-Nov-52	494	B.L. 19, 843 f. 127a	2973
White, Nicholas	Kildare, Leixlipp	gentry: esquire	01-Jul-53	400	B.L. 19, 843 f. 140a	2995
White, Nicholas	Dublin, the Warde	gentry: gent	23-Feb-26	200	Dc2/74v	1347
White, Nicholas	Kildare, Leixlip	gentry: knight	15-Nov-52	494	B.L. 19, 843 f. 127a	2973

Standard	County	Occupation	Date	Amount	MS No	Ident No
White, Nicholas	Kildare, Leixlipp	gentry: esquire	01-Jul-61	600	B.L. 15, 635 f. 74a	3391
White, Nicholas	Kildare, Leixlipp	gentry: esquire	13-Jul-61	1400	B.L. 15, 635 f. 77	3395
White, Nicholas	Kildare, Leixlipp	gentry: esquire	08-Aug-63	1000	B.L. 15, 635 f. 116	3462
White, Nicholas	Dublin, the Warde	gentry: gent	23-Feb-26	200	Dc2/74v	1347
White, Peter	Waterford, Dongarvan		22-Nov-06	24	Dc1/71lv	435
White, Richard	Louth, Richardstowne	gentry: gent	08-Oct-29	200	Dc2/136v	1639
White, Richard	Dublin	gentry: gent	26-Jul-26	200	Dc2/82r	1389
White, Richard	Dublin, the city	gentry: gent	02-Oct-27	200	Dc2/99r	1460
White, Stephen	Louth, Drogheda	merchant	19-Jun-21	200	Dc2/35v	1073
White, Thomas	Dublin	trade: baker	14-Jul-00	40	Dc1/25r	168
White, Thomas	Cavan, Terrells Bawne	gentry: esquire	15-Feb-56	300	B.L. 19, 843 f. 166a	3047
White, Thomas	Dublin, the city	merchant	06-Feb-24	200	Dc2/53r	1200
White, Thomas	Dublin, the city	trade: baker	14-Feb-23	300	Dc2/45r	1140
White, Thomas	Dublin	merchant	20-Jan-13	1000	Dc1/117v	731
White, Walter	Kildare, Richardstowne	gentry: gent	07-Dec-58	108	B.L. 15, 635 f. 35	3324
White, Walter	Kildare, Pitchfordstowne	gentry: esquire	02-Oct-74	400	Dc3/162v	2616
White, Walter	Kildare, Pitchfortstowne	gentry: esquire	17-Jun-62	800	B.L. 15, 635 f. 92a	3419
White, Walter	Kildare, Puchfordstowne	gentry: esquire	17-Jun-61	320	B.L. 15, 635 f. 81	3401
Whitney, Henry	Queen's Co., Syan als. Shean	gentry: gent	21-May-39	1000	B.L. 19, 843 f. 35	2788
Whitney, Robert	Queen's Co., Sheane	gentry: gent	23-May-09	400	Dc1/89v	558
Whitty, Richard	Wexford, Ballytenge	gentry: gent	03-Jul-01	600	Dc1/33r	218
Wickham, Christopher	Queen's Co., Talbotston		01-Feb-25	200	Dc2/61r	1260
Wickham, Christopher	Wicklow, Talbotston	gentry: gent	13-Nov-24	200	Dc2/58v	1243
Wickham, Christopher	Dublin, Hylton	gentry: gent	18-Jun-00	1000	Dc1/24r	162
Wickham, Christopher	Wicklow, Talbotstowne	gentry: esquire	20-Nov-29	400	Dc1/138v	1646
Wickham, Christopher	Wicklow, Talbotstowne	gentry: gent	03-Dec-14	200	Dc1/133r	828
Wickham, John	Dublin, Glasnevin	gentry: gent	03-Dec-14	200	Dc1/133r	828
Wickham, Peter	Wicklow, Kilneclonagh	gentry: esquire	20-Nov-29	400	Dc1/138v	1646
Wickham, Peter	Wicklow, Kilneclonagh	gentry: gent	13-Nov-24	200	Dc2/58v	1243
Wickham, Peter	Wicklow, Kilneclonagh	gentry: esquire	04-May-30	200	Dc2/145r	1679
Wilder, Mathew	Longford, Clayduffe	gentry: gent	18-Feb-69	460	Dc3/91	2426
Wilder, Mathew	Longford, Clayduffe, bar.Shrow	gentry: gent	18-Feb-69	460	B.L. 15, 636 f. 43	3699
Williams, Abigail	Dublin, parish of St. Audoens	other: widow	28-Jul-68	100	Dc3/82	2409
Williams, Abigail	Dublin, St. Anthony's Parish	other: widow	28-Jul-68	100	B.L. 15, 635 f. 225	3655
Williams, Richard	Limerick, Dromin	gentry: gent	23-Jan-79	420	B.L. 15, 637 f. 17	3877
Williams, Thomas	Dublin, Gallanston	gentry: knight	01-Oct-16	100	Dc2/1v	874
Willoughby, Francis	Dublin, the city	gentry: esquire	13-May-76	100	Dc3/173v	2655
Willoughby, Francis	Dublin, the city	gentry: esquire	20-Mar-55	210	B.L. 19, 843 f. 155	3024
Willoughby, Francis	Dublin, the city	gentry: esquire	13-May-76	100	B.L. 19, 844 f. 102	3229
Willoughby, Francis	Dublin, Dunbrow	gentry: esquire	11-May-64	280	B.L. 15, 635 f. 133	3491

Standard	County	Occupation	Date	Amount	MS No	Ident No
Wilson, John	Donegal, Killianurre	gentry:				
		knight and baronet	07-May-32	280	Dc2/179v	1821
Wilson, Rowland	Westmeath, Stonehall	gentry: esquire	10-Feb-76	500	B.L. 19, 844 f. 90	3217
Wilson, Rowland	Westmeath, Stonehall	gentry: esquire	10-Feb-76	500	Dc3/172r	2649
Wilson, Rowland	Westmeath, Stonehall	gentry: esquire	22-May-75	400	B.L. 19, 844 f. 67	3195
Wilson, Rowland	Westmeath, Stonehall	gentry: esquire	22-May-75	400	Dc3/168r	2636
Wilson, Rowland	Westmeath, Stonehall	gentry: esquire	11-Feb-76	420	Dc3/172r	2650
Wilson, Rowland	Westmeath, Stonehall	gentry: esquire	20-Feb-75	420	B.L. 15, 637 f. 91	4011
Wilson, Samuel	Dublin, the city	gentry: gent	18-Jun-67	300	Dc3/63	2362
Wilson, Samuel	Dublin, the city	gentry: gent	18-Jun-67	300	B.L. 15, 635 f. 196a	3603
Winckworth, John	Wexford, Maudlins	gentry: esquire	18-Jul-83	400	B.L. 15, 637 f. 81a	3995
Windsor, William	Londonderry, Ballidermott?	gentry: knight	13-Jul-26	600	Dc2/81r	1385
Windsor, William	Londonderry, Ballidermott	gentry: knight	13-Aug-27	1800	Dc2/98r	1456
Wingfield, Edward	Wicklow, Powerscourte	gentry: knight	11-Aug-37	1200	Dc2/270r	2213
Wingfield, Edward	Wicklow, Powerscourte	gentry: knight	20-Nov-37	600	Dc2/271v	2218
Wingfield, Thomas	Dublin	gentry: gent	18-Jun-00	440	Dc1/24v	163
Wingfield, Thomas	Dublin	gentry: gent	18-Jun-99	400	Dc1/17r	114
Withington, John	Dublin, the city	trade: ironmonger	28-Jun-76	1200	Dc3/179r	2672
Wogan, John	Dublin, the city	gentry: gent	15-Jul-41	240	B.L. 19, 843 f. 107a	2934
Wogan, John	Dublin, Balroddiry	farmer: yeoman	10-Jun-98	40	Dc1/11r	80
Wogan, Nicholas	Kildare, Racoffe	gentry: gent	23-Jun-00	100	Dc1/24v	166
Wogan, Robert	Dublin, Balrothery	farmer: yeoman	09-Aug-97	52	Dc1/6r	45
Wogan, Robert	Dublin, Balroddiry	farmer	10-Jun-98	40	Dc1/11r	80
Wogan, Thomas	Kildare, Newhall	gentry: gent	16-Aug-98	200	Dc1/12r	87
Wogan, Thomas	Kildare, Newhale	gentry: gent	07-Dec-05	500	Dc1/63v	385
Wogan, Thomas	Kildare, Newhall	gentry: gent	12-Aug-98	1000	Dc1/12r	86
Wogan, Thomas	Kildare, Newhale	gentry: gent	09-Jun-08	100	Dc1/83v	518
Wogan, William	Kildare, Rathcoffy	gentry: esquire	23-Apr-11	500	Dc1/103v	647
Wogan, William	Kildare, the Donuigh?	gentry: gent	01-Feb-06	130	Dc1/65r	391
Wolfe, Patrick	Limerick, the city	merchant: s of Stephen,				
		merch	30-Jan-41	300	B.L. 19, 843 f. 86a	2892
Wolverston, Christopher	Dublin, Raboe	gentry: gent	29-Jun-29	2000	Dc2/134v	1629
Wolverston, Christopher	Dublin, Raboe	gentry: gent	06-Mar-27	400	Dc2/89r	1419
Wolverston, Christopher	Dublin, Raboe	gentry: gent	23-Nov-29	400	Dc2/138r	1644
Wolverston, Christopher	Dublin	merchant	11-Feb-14	200	Dc1/126v	784
Wolverston, George	Dublin, Stalorgan	gentry: son/heir of				
		William	29-Jun-29	2000	Dc2/134v	1629
Wolverston, George	Dublin, Stalorgan	gentry: son/heir of				
		William	23-Nov-29	400	Dc2/138r	1644
Wolverston, James	Dublin, Stellorgan	gentry: gent	30-Oct-04	1000	Dc1/53v	336
Wolverston, John	Wicklow, Newcastell	gentry: esquire	06-Mar-27	400	Dc2/89r	1419
Wolverston, John	Wicklow, Wickloe	gentry: esquire	11-Feb-14	200	Dc1/126v	784
Wolverston, John	Wicklow, Newcastle	gentry: gent	30-Jun-19	500	Dc2/24v	995
Wolverston, John	Wicklow, Wickloe	gentry: esquire	28-Sep-16	80	Dc2/1v	873

Standard	County	Occupation	Date	Amount	MS No	Ident No
Wolverston, Richard	Dublin, Stalorgan	gentry: son, 2nd of William	23-Nov-29	400	Dc2/138r	1644
Wolverston, Robert	Dublin, Stillargan	gentry: esquire	17-Feb-74	400	Dc3/160r	2603
Wolverston, Robert	Wicklow, Rathbran	gentry: gent	28-Sep-16	80	Dc2/1v	873
Wolverston, Robert	Dublin, Stillargan	gentry: esquire	17-Feb-74	400	B.L. 19, 844 f.19	3137
Wolverston, William	King's Co., Moyelly, Kilcoursy	gentry: gent	12-May-81	800	B.L. 15, 637 f. 51	3939
Wolverston, William	Dublin, Raboe	gentry: esquire	11-Feb-14	200	Dc1/126v	784
Wolverston, William	Dublin, Rabocke	gentry: gent	27-Nov-17	200	Dc2/12r	925
Wolverston, William	Dublin, Roboe	gentry: gent	30-Jun-19	500	Dc2/24v	995
Wolverston, William	Dublin, Stalorgan	gentry: gent	29-Jun-29	2000	Dc2/134v	1629
Wolverston, William	Dublin, Stalorgan	gentry: gent	23-Nov-29	400	Dc2/138r	1644
Wood, George	Sligo, Killarragh	gentry: esquire	20-Feb-36	200	Dc2/245v	2097
Woodley, Anthony	Cork, Garteene, Kinalineky	gentry: gent	20-Oct-81	300	B.L. 15, 637 f. 81	3994
Woodward, Henry	Dublin, the city	trade: leather-dresser	22-Dec-34	1000	Dc2/228r	2017
Woodward, Richard	Dublin	farmer: yeoman	01-Apr-41	800	B.L. 19, 843 f. 87a	2894
Worrall, Robert	Dublin, Balrothery		14-Dec-34	120	Dc2/219v	1982
Worth, Edward		prof: bishop of Killaloe	18-Jul-61	1248	B.L. 15, 635 f. 77a	3396
Worth, William	Cork, the city	gentry: esquire	30-Dec-71	600	Dc3/143r	2541
Worth, William	Cork, the city	gentry: esquire	30-Dec-71	600	B.L. 15, 636 f. 94	3786
Wotton, Francis	Monaghan, Monnaghan	gentry: gent	29-Nov-31	400	Dc2/173r	1796
Wotton, Peter	Louth, Petru	gentry: gent	31-Jan-83	160	B.L. 15, 637 f. 68a	3970
Wotton, Peter	Louth, Drogheda	gentry: gent	26-Apr-82	210	B.L. 15, 637 f. 56	3947
Wotton, Walter	Dublin, Balrotheny	farmer	28-Jun-10	230	Dc1/98v	619
Wragg, Jeffrey	Louth, Drogheda	merchant	25-Aug-25	40	Dc2/69r	1312
Wybrants, Peter	Dublin, the city		14-Mar-66	400	Dc3/26	2280
Wybrants, Peter	Dublin, the city		14-Mar-67	1320	Dc3/57	2346
Wybrants, Peter	Dublin, the city		14-Mar-66	400	B.L. 15, 635 f. 166	3545
Wybrants, Peter	Dublin, the city	gentry: esquire	26-Aug-59	420	B.L. 15, 635 f. 51	3353
Wybrants, Peter	Dublin, the city		14-Mar-67	1320	B.L. 15, 635 f. 203a	3616
Wynne, John	Louth, Rathesker	gentry: gent	20-Jan-82	700	B.L. 15, 637 f. 54a	3944
Yeeden, Thomas	Roscommon, Boyle	gentry: gent	06-Apr-77	640	B.L. 19, 844 f. 124	3253
Yeeden, Thomas	Roscommon, Boyle	gentry: gent	06-Apr-77	640	Dc3/182v	2688
Young, George	Dublin, the city	merchant	09-Dec-19	200	Dc2/27v	1013
Young, James	Dublin, the city	gentry: gent	09-Dec-19	200	Dc2/27v	1013
Young, Joseph	Dublin, the city	gentry: gent	16-Feb-58	40	B.L. 15, 635 f. 25a	3308

MAYORS AND CONSTABLES OF THE STAPLE
Compiled by Jane Ohlmeyer and Éamonn Ó Ciardha

Every year the brethren of individual staple towns selected a mayor and two constables of the staple. In Dublin this election took place on St. Paul's Day (25 January); in Waterford on the Monday 'after the visitation of the Blessed Virgin' (31 May); in Carrickfergus on the first Monday after midsummer (24 June); in Wexford 'on the feast of St Michael Archangel' (29 September); and in Youghal on 'the feast of SS [All Saints]' (1 November).[1] Occasionally—when an official was absent, died or refused to take the oath of supremacy—an election took place at other times. Thus in November 1605 when John Elliott, mayor of the Dublin staple, and one of his constables, Nicholas Stephins, refused to take the oath of supremacy they were immediately replaced.[2] When one of the constables of the Dublin staple, Richard Brine, died in October 1617 a replacement was quickly nominated.[3] Sir John Tottie's continued absence from Dublin in 1675 meant that 'no statute staple could be acknowledged' and so 'the wardens and brethren of the staple' elected Sir Joshua Allen as mayor in his place.[4] When Allen wanted to travel to England on business John Desmynieres, a former mayor of the staple, was appointed as his replacement.[5]

On taking up office, the mayor and constables of the staple agreed to enforce the observance of the Ordinance of the Staple. The mayor of the Dublin staple swore to serve 'the Brethren of the said staple without doing them extortion, . . . minister Justice to all folks as well to rich as poor, . . . truly and uprightly observe support and maintain the laws statutes and ordinances of the staple in all points. . . [and] suffer no person to violate or break them'.[6] These staple officials enjoyed considerable legal powers especially with regard to the regulation of trade and to the recovery of debt. In theory they were supposed to limit their services to merchants and brethren of the staple but in practice they took recognizances for debt which did not concern trade and involved individuals who were not members of the staple, or even merchants.[7]

---

[1] In many instances the charter granted by James VI and I to an individual town specified the date of the election and this usually coincided with municipal elections.

[2] ID 379.

[3] ID 913

[4] ID 2638.

[5] ID 2721.

[6] The oath taken by the mayor of the Dublin staple is transcribed in full in Appendix III. Oaths for the provincial staples do not appear to have survived.

[7] See Chapter 1 for details.

The power wielded by staple officials was enhanced by the close relationship they enjoyed with municipal government. The charters granted to a number of towns by James VI and I specifically insisted that the mayor of the town should become mayor of the staple for one year.[8] Thus of the 100 men who served as mayor of the Dublin staple between 1598 and 1687, the vast majority had enjoyed the mayoralty of the city the previous year. Though rarely consecutively, the same man regularly became mayor of the Dublin staple on more than one occasion (seven held it twice, two held it three times, three held it four times, and two held it five times). Despite a relative dearth of evidence, the provincial staples appear to have operated on a similar basis to the Dublin one. For example, the names of 25 mayors of the Carrickfergus staple, between 1639-82, are known; all had served as mayor of the town before becoming mayor of the staple. Five individuals enjoyed the office twice (often consecutively) and one three times (between 1671 and 1677).

The mayors and constables of the staple formed the elite of municipal society and were invariably knights, aldermen, esquires, merchants and occasionally prominent tradesmen. In the cases of Carrickfergus and Wexford the majority of the mayors of the staple described themselves as 'esquires'. Elsewhere aldermen and merchants predominated. For instance of the 35 mayors of the Cork staple 17 were aldermen, 14 merchants and 4 esquires. Similar trends emerge for the Dublin staple. The status of 52 of the 100 mayors is known: 29 were aldermen, 11 were merchants, 8 were merchant/aldermen, 2 were knights and one was an apothecary.

Clerks of the staple were also elected but they held their office for considerable periods of time. For example, in August 1611 Thady Duffe, clerk of the Tholsell, became clerk of the Dublin staple 'during the natural life of the said Thadee'.[9] Francis Roch enjoyed the clerkship of the Cork staple between 1620 and 1635 and was replaced by Robert Coppinger who held the post until 1640. After the restoration Jonathan Perry served as clerk of the Cork staple for over twenty years (between 1664-86); while Daniel Hignet was clerk of the Limerick staple between 1673 and 1682.

The task of appointing these staple officials fell to the brethren of the staple—a carefully selected body of 26 men.[10] On becoming a brother (a privilege that cost three shillings), these men, usually aldermen, merchants,

[8] See, for example, Samuel M'Skimin, *The History and Antiquities of the County of the Town of Carrickfergus* (Belfast, 1823), p. 201. In Dublin the mayor of the staple then became the treasurer of the city, W.G. Strickland, 'The Ancient Official Seals of the City of Dublin' in *Journal of the Royal Society of Antiquaries* 53 (1923), p. 128. In many instances sheriffs of individual towns also went on to become constables of the staple.

[9] See ID 58. In January 1625 Sir Thady Duffe knight, clerk of the Tholsell, replaced Walter Enos as clerk of the staple (ID 1257).

[10] The Charters issued by James VI and I to the staple towns included a list of staple brethren. For Youghal see R. Caulfield, ed., *The Council of the Corporation of Youghal* (Guildford, Surrey, 1878), p. xxxii. For Limerick see Robert Herbert, 'The trade guilds of Limerick' in *North Munster Antiquarian Journal* 2: 3 (spring, 1941), p. 124. I am grateful to Larry Walsh for bringing this reference to my attention.

or 'esquires', swore to 'be present at the election of the mayor and constables', to submit to the jurisdiction of the mayors, and to maintain the laws
and customs of the staple in an honest manner.[11] Since no one could be
elected a member of the staple brethren unless he enjoyed the freedom of
the city, it became an additional and, presumably, coveted privilege. Thus,
as in England, membership of the staple remained the preserve 'of an inner
ring of important citizens' and it is unusual to find a leading patrician who
did not hold some sort of staple office at some point in his career.[12] In
particular the mayors of the staple appear to have enjoyed enormous
political clout within municipal government. Little wonder in October 1646
that the parliamentary military commander, Lord Inchiquin, urged Thomas
Stoute, mayor of the Youghal staple, to use his political influence to ensure
'that places of eminency and trust [on the corporation] be exercised by
persons of the best ability and integrity'.[13] Certainly after the Restoration
the mayors of the Youghal staple sat as members of the court of common
council and played a key role in governing the town.

Understandably staple officials regularly took advantage of their
favoured position to lend—and occasionally borrow—money. For example,
between 1598 and 1687, of the 100 mayors of the Dublin staple 32 appear
in the database as creditors, 12 as both creditors and debtors, and 8 as
debtors. For instance, the Dublin alderman, Gerald Young, who served as
mayor of the city between 1599 and 1600 and mayor of the staple the
following year, lent a total of £3172 on bond on the Dublin staple between
February 1597 and May 1612. Young's 36 creditors included 21 gentlemen,
11 farmers, 2 merchants, a barber and a tanner who hailed largely from
Counties Dublin and Meath and his native Kildare.[14] The lending habits of
the Dublin alderman Richard Tighe, who served as mayor of the Dublin
staple on five occasions (1652-4, 1655-6, and 1660-2), proved more
extensive still. Between February 1656 and October 1670 he lent £14,374
on bond to 22 individuals (15 landed gentlemen, 3 tradesmen, 2 knights,
an alderman, and one merchant) who originated largely from Dublin and
the Pale.[15] It seems likely that these two patricians were investing the profits
from their municipal office by lending on the staple. No doubt further
research will show the extent to which this municipal oligarchy used the
staple as a means of enriching themselves (through moneylending) and
extending their landed estates.[16]

---

[11] For the oath taken by the brethren of the Dublin staple see Appendix III. The
brethren of the Bristol staple swore a similar oath, see Rich, ed., *The Staple Court*, pp. 58-9.
The names of the 'brothers' admitted to the Dublin staple between have survived, see
Appendix II.

[12] E. E. Rich, 'The Mayors of the Staples' in *Cambridge Historical Journal* 4:2 (1933), p. 131
and *The Staple Court*, p. 59.

[13] Caulfield, ed., *Council book of Youghal*, p. 257.

[14] For details see note 85 below.

[15] For details see note 151 below.

[16] Discussed in Chapter 1.

The following list of mayors and constables of the staple towns has been compiled from a variety of sources:[17]

British Library Chancery Volumes:
In every transaction recorded in Chancery, whatever the staple, the names of the mayors and constables of the staples were given. These names have been extracted and listed below, together with the day, month and year of the transaction.

Dublin Staple Volumes:
The names of the mayors, constables and usually clerks of the staple, together with the names of the brethren, were recorded in the Dublin staple books and have been included in the database. They have been assigned an identity number and the names of the officials elected have been entered in the 'text' field. They are listed below and prefixed with an asterisk.[18]

Published Local and Corporation Histories:
The names of the mayors and, where known, constables of the provincial staples have been gleaned from a variety of local and municipal histories (indicated in the notes). They are listed here under the year during which they served as staple officials.

All of the names listed here have been checked in the database. If the individual appears as a creditor the identification number was entered in ordinary case (ID 1234). Italics have been used to indicate a debtor (*ID 4567*). No attempt has been made to modernise or standardise surnames.

Mayor of the staple = first name listed
Constables of the staple = second and third names listed
Clerk of the staple = always indicated

---

[17] Éamonn Ó Ciardha compiled the original list.

[18] A fourth staple book (Dc 4), not included in the database, has also survived for the years 1713-1753. This recorded the minutes of the annual meetings of the mayor, constables and brethren of the staple for the election of the mayor and constables for the forthcoming year.

CARRICKFERGUS:[19]
CARRICKFERGUS 10 Aug 1639
Richard Spearepoint[20]
Clement Bashford
William Cathcart

CARRICKFERGUS 7 Apr 1655
Roger Lyndon[21]
John Bullworthy
John Hall

CARRICKFERGUS 2 Jan 1655/6
Roger Lyndon[22]
John Birtt
Peter Taylor

CARRICKFERGUS 1 May 1657
John Bullworthy[23]
Thomas Dobbin
Robert Witter

CARRICKFERGUS 5 Feb 1657/8
John Bullworthy the elder[24]
William Dobbing
Thomas Griffith

CARRICKFERGUS 8 Apr 1663
John Dallway[25]
Richard Johnston
William Thomson

CARRICKFERGUS 21 June 1664
James Dobbin[26]
Richard Johnson
William Thomson

CARRICKFERGUS 21 Mar 1664/5
Hercules Davies[27]
William Thompson
Jasper Harper

CARRICKFERGUS 2 Nov 1665
Hercules Davies[28]
Jasper Harper
Richard Pendleton

CARRICKFERGUS 12 Oct 1666
Anthony Hall[29]
John Magee
Cornelius Basford

CARRICKFERGUS 13 June 1668
William Dobbin[30]
Richard Wesbrooke
Henry Bur[nes]

CARRICKFERGUS 10 Oct 1668
Edmund Davies[31]
Ezekel Davies
Richard Pendleton

---

[19] The mayors and sheriffs of the city are printed in full in M'Skimin, *The History and Antiquities of the County of the Town of Carrickfergus*, pp. 320-29.

[20] Mayor of Carrickfergus in 1636 and 1637, *ibid.*, p. 323.

[21] Mayor of Carrickfergus in 1653, *ibid.*, p. 324.

[22] Mayor of Carrickfergus in 1653, *ibid.*, p. 324.

[23] Mayor of Carrickfergus in 1654 and 1655, *ibid.*, p. 324.

[24] Mayor of Carrickfergus in 1654 and 1655, *ibid.*, p. 324

[25] Mayor of Carrickfergus in 1660 and 1661, *ibid.*, p. 325.

[26] Mayor of Carrickfergus in 1662, *ibid.*, p. 325.

[27] Mayor of Carrickfergus in 1663, *ibid.*, p. 325.

[28] Mayor of Carrickfergus in 1663, *ibid.*, p. 325.

[29] Mayor of Carrickfergus in 1665, *ibid.*, p. 325.

[30] Mayor of Carrickfergus in 1666, *ibid.*, p. 326.

[31] Mayor of Carrickfergus in 1667, *ibid.*, p. 326.

CARRICKFERGUS 8 Oct 1669
Robert Walsh, esquire[32]
William Hildisch
Samuel Treherne

CARRICKFERGUS 13 Mar 1670/1
Edmond Davies, esquire[33]
Richard Johnson
Henry Burnes

CARRICKFERGUS 3 Nov 1671
Anthony Horseman, esquire[34]
John Stubbs
John Henderson

CARRICKFERGUS 28 Oct 1672
Richard Dobb, esquire[35]
Simon Richardson
William Bennit/Bennet

CARRICKFERGUS 3 Apr 1674
Henry Davies, esquire[36]
Thomas McManus, esquire
John Smith

CARRICKFERGUS 12 Dec 1674
Henry Davies, esquire[37]
James McCullogh
John Davies

CARRICKFERGUS 30 Nov 1675
Anthony Horsman, esquire[38]

George Walsh
Edward Hall

CARRICKFERGUS 20 Apr 1677
Anthony Horsman, esquire[39]
Thomas Harper
Adam Dennison

CARRICKFERGUS 29 Mar 1678
John Byrt, esquire[40]
John Smyth
John Tyso/Tiso

CARRICKFERGUS 5 Apr 1679
Solomon Faith, esquire[41]
James McCullogh
William Dawson

CARRICKFERGUS 27 Nov 1679
Ezekiel Davys, esquire[42]
Robert Willims
Cornelius Bashford

CARRICKFERGUS 29 Dec 1680
Hercules Davys esquire[43]
Richard Pendleton
John Magee

CARRICKFERGUS 27 Mar 1682
Henry Clements, esquire[44]
Andrew Clements
John Byet

[32] Mayor of Carrickfergus in 1668, *ibid.*, p. 326.

[33] Mayor of Carrickfergus in 1667, *ibid.*, p. 326. ID 3808. Appears in the database as a 'merchant'.

[34] Mayor of Carrickfergus in 1669, *ibid.*, p. 326.

[35] Mayor of Carrickfergus in 1671, *ibid.*, p. 326. *ID 3521, 3565, 3884.*

[36] Mayor of Carrickfergus in 1672, *ibid.*, p. 327.

[37] Mayor of Carrickfergus in 1672, *ibid.*, p. 327.

[38] Deputy mayor of Carrickfergus in 1673 and 1674, *ibid.*, p. 328.

[39] *Ibid.*

[40] Mayor of Carrickfergus in 1675 and 1676, *ibid.*, p. 328.

[41] Mayor of Carrickfergus in 1677, *ibid.*, p. 328.

[42] Mayor of Carrickfergus in 1678, *ibid.*, p. 328.

[43] Mayor of Carrickfergus in 1680, *ibid.*, p. 328.

[44] Mayor of Carrickfergus in 1677, *ibid.*, p. 328.

CORK:[45]
CORK 23 Oct 1618
David Tirrie-Ffitzstephen[46]
Peter Gould
Phillip Gould

CORK 16 Aug 1620
William Skiddie, alderman
Patrick Roch-Ffitzmorris
Patrick Roch-Ffitzjames
Francis Roch, clerk of the staple

CORK 17 Mar 1620/1
David Tirry FitzDavid, alderman[47]
John Roch
Edmund Martell

CORK Apr 1628
Henry Goo?, esquire
Stephan Meagh
John Meade

CORK 27 Apr 1630
Edmund Martell, alderman
David Meagh
Stephan Martell
Francis Roch, clerk of staple

CORK 3 Dec 1635
Edmund Tyrrie, alderman
Edward Roch-ffitzmorris
Maurice Roch-fitzjames
Francis Roch, clerk of staple

CORK 23 July 1636
William Roch, alderman[48]

Michael Lavall
John Roch
Robert Coppinger, clerk of staple

CORK 10 Dec 1636
Richard Roch, alderman
Maurice Roch
Thomas Ffitzjohn Gerrald

CORK 24 May 1637
Thomas Martell, alderman[49]
William Fitzjohn Gerald
William Roch

CORK 21 Feb 1638/9
Robert Meagh[50]
James Fitzjohn Gerald
Robert Coppinger, clerk of staple

CORK 1 Apr 1639
Robert Meaghe, alderman[51]
Nicholas Skiddie
James Fitzgerrald
Robert Coppinger, clerk of staple

CORK 6 Aug 1640
Sir John Coppinger
Patrick Arthure
William Verdon
Robert Coppinger, clerk of staple

CORK 25 Oct 1640
Robert Meaghe, alderman[52]
Nicholas Skiddie
James Ffitzgerrald
Robert Coppinger, clerk of staple

---

[45] The election of staple officials has not been recorded in the council book of the corporation of the city. For a list of mayors of the city—not the staple—see Richard Caulfied, ed., *The Council Book of the Corporation of the City of Cork from 1609 to 1643 and from 1690 to 1800* (Guildford, Surrey, 1876), pp. 1166-1177.

[46] *ID 725.*

[47] BL., Add MSS 47,035 f. 127.

[48] *ID 2770, 2911.*

[49] Mayor of Cork in 1635, *ibid.,* p. 1173.

[50] Mayor of Cork in 1636, *ibid.,* p. 1173.

[51] Mayor of Cork in 1636, *ibid.,* p. 1173.

[52] Mayor of Cork in 1636, *ibid.,* p. 1173.

CORK 16 Nov 1640
Andrew Skiddie, alderman
John Roch
Adam Gould
Robert Coppinger, clerk of staple

CORK 16 May 1657
Christopher Oliver, alderman[53]
William Hull
Richard Covett

CORK 3 May 1659
William Hodder, alderman[54]
Christopher Rye
Noblet Dunscomb

CORK 29 Mar 1659/60
William Hodder[55]
Noblett Dunscombes, merchant
William Meeter, clerk of staple

CORK 14 Nov 1662
Walter Cooper, alderman[56]
Simon Everson
John Nevingham

CORK 7 Apr 1664
Richard Bassett, alderman[57]
Thomas Walker
George Capell
Jonathan Perrie, clerk of staple

CORK 23 Jan 1664/5
Noblett Dunscombe, merchant[58]

Thomas Furren, merchant
Richard Harvey, merchant

CORK 14 Nov 1665
Thomas Farren, merchant[59]
Mathew Deane, merchant?
Thomas Cooke, merchant

CORK 25 Aug 1666
Thomas Farren, merchant
Thomas Cooke
Jonathan Perry, clerk of staple

CORK 14 Nov 1666
Christopher Rye, merchant[60]
Timothy Tuckey junior
John Hawkins, merchant
Jonathan Perrye, clerk

CORK 25 Aug 1667
Christopher Oliver, alderman
William Hull, merchant
Richard Lovett, merchant

CORK 18 Jan 1667/8
John Newnham, merchant[61]
Thomas Wills, merchant
Thomas Mills, merchant

CORK 12 Jan 1668/9
George Wright, merchant
William Alwin junior, merchant
William Smith, merchant
Jonathan Perry, clerk of staple

---

[53] ID 3573.
[54] Mayor of Cork in 1657, *ibid.*, p. 1174. ID 3485.
[55] *Ibid.*
[56] Mayor of Cork in 1661, *ibid.*, p. 1174.
[57] Mayor of Cork in 1664, *ibid.*, p. 1174.
[58] Mayor of Cork in 1665, *ibid.*, p. 1174. ID 4023.
[59] Mayor of Cork in 1666, *ibid.*, p. 1174.
[60] Mayor of Cork in 1667-8, *ibid.*, p. 1174. ID 3245.
[61] Mayor of Cork in 1671, *ibid.*, p. 1174. ID 3230, 3627, 3675, 3686.

CORK 20 Jan 1669/70
James Finch[62]
Walter Lane
Patrick Ronayne/Ronane
Jonathan Perry, clerk of staple

CORK 4 Nov 1670
Robert Fletcher, merchant
John Flynne
Thomas Kitchingman
Jonathan Perry, clerk of staple

CORK 17 Nov 1671
John Hawkens, merchant[63]
Benjamin Adams, merchant
William Field, merchant
Jonathan Perry, clerk of the staple

CORK 29 Oct 1672, 7 Nov 1672
Timothy Tuckey, merchant[64]
William Hull
John Bayly
Jonathan Perrie, clerk of staple

CORK 16 Dec 1673
Thomas Kitchingman, merchant[65]
James French, merchant?
John Wright, merchant

CORK 12 Apr 1675
William Field, merchant[66]
Edward Swabie, merchant?
Jonathan Perry, merchant

CORK 13 Nov 1675
Christopher Rye[67]
Robert Rogers
Walter Lane
Jonathan Perrie, clerk of staple

CORK 18 Jan 1676/7
Matthew Deane, alderman[68]
Christopher Crofts/Cross
William Howell/Hovell
Jonathan Perrie, clerk of staple

CORK 9 Mar 1677/8
William Alwin junior, merchant[69]
Jonathan Perry, merchant?
John Wright, merchant
Jonathan Perrie, clerk of staple

CORK 2 Nov 1678
Thomas Wills, merchant
Jonathan Perry
Richard Harvey
Jonathan Perrie, clerk of staple

CORK 29 Nov 1679
John Wright, merchant[70]
Jonathan Perry, merchant?
Patrick Ronaine, merchant
Jonathan Perrie, clerk of staple

CORK 10 Feb 1680/1
Robert Rogers[71]
Jonathan Perrie
Patrick Ronaine

---

[62] Mayor in 1670, *ibid.*, p. 1174.
[63] Mayor of Cork in 1672, *ibid.*, p. 1174.
[64] Mayor of Cork in 1677, *ibid.*, p. 1175.
[65] Mayor of Cork in 1678, *ibid.*, p. 1175.
[66] Mayor of Cork in 1676, *ibid.*, p. 1174.
[67] ID 3245.
[68] ID 3304, 3870, 4025, 4049 and *3981*.
[69] Mayor of Cork in 1681, *ibid.*, p. 1175.
[70] Mayor of Cork in 1683, *ibid.*, p. 1175.
[71] Mayor of Cork in 1680, *ibid.*, p. 1175.

CORK 17 Mar 1681/2
William Alwin, esquire[72]
Jonathan Perrie, merchant
John Baylie, merchant
Jonathan Perrie, clerk of staple

CORK 21 Mar 1682/3
Richard Covet, esquire[73]
Patrick Ronaine, merchant
Richard Harvey, merchant

CORK 5 Nov 1683
Christopher Rye, alderman
Jonathan Perrie, merchant?
Walter Lane, merchant
Jonathan Perrie, clerk of staple

CORK 20 Oct 1681
Robert Rogers, alderman[74]
Jonathan Perrie, merchant?
Patrick Ronaine, merchant
Jonathan Perrie, clerk of staple

CORK 19 Nov 1684
John Bayly, alderman[75]
Edward Hoare
John Bayly junior, merchant
Jonathan Perrie, clerk of staple

CORK 20 Jan 1683/4
Christopher Rye, alderman
Jonathan Perrie
Walter Lane, merchant

CORK 10 Apr 1686
Christopher Crofts, esquire[76]
Daniel Crone, merchant?
Jonathan Perry, merchant
Jonathan Perrie, clerk of staple

CORK 19 Feb 1686/7
Edward Hoare, esquire[77]
Jonathan Perrie, merchant?
John Champion, merchant
Henry Luther, merchant

CORK 1693
Christopher Rye, alderman
Jonathan Perrie, merchant?
Walter Lane, merchant

DUBLIN:[78]
DUBLIN *25 Jan 1597/8
Michael Chamberlen[79]
John Shelton
Alexander Palles[80]

---

[72] Mayor of Cork in 1681, *ibid.,* p. 1175.

[73] Mayor of Cork in 1682, *ibid.,* p. 1175.

[74] Mayor of Cork in 1680, *ibid.,* p. 1175.

[75] Mayor of Cork in 1679, *ibid.,* p. 1175. ID 3696.

[76] Mayor of Cork in 1685, *ibid.,* p. 1175.

[77] Mayor of Cork in 1686, *ibid.,* p. 1175. ID 4015, 4016.

[78] This list has been extensively referenced against J.T. Gilbert's, *Calendar of ancient Records of Dublin in possession of the municipal corporation* (17 vols., Dublin, 1889-1916) and C. Lennon, *The Lords of Dublin in the age of the Reformation* (Dublin, 1989). The names of the mayors of Dublin have been taken from T. W. Moody, F. X. Martin and F. J. Byrne, eds., *A New History of Ireland,* vol. ix, *Maps, genealogies, lists* (Oxford, 1984), pp. 555-7. For a list of the mayors of the Dublin staple 1530-1555 see *Anc. Rec. Dub.,* I, 395-7, 400, 402-3, 405, 408-9, 411, 423, 426, 429, 433, 437.

[79] Mayor of Dublin, 1596-7. ID 5, 256, 313, 326, 438, 569, 572 and *324, 423, 457, 460, 573, 664.*

[80] Shelton and Palles were sheriffs of the city of Dublin in 1596, *Anc. Rec. Dub.,* II, 294; also see Lennon, *Lords,* pp. 238, 270, 262. On 20 November John Shelton was elected mayor but he refused to swear the Oath of Supremacy and so Robert Ball was elected, *Anc. Rec. Dub.,* II, 430.

DUBLIN *25 Jan 1598/9
Nicholas Weston[81]
Robert Panting
John Goodwing[82]

DUBLIN *25 Jan 1599/1600
James Bellew[83]
John Bryse
Edmond Pursell[84]

DUBLIN *25 Jan 1600/1
Gerrott Yong, alderman[85]
John Arthur
John Cusacke[86]

DUBLIN *25 Jan 1601/2
Nicholas Quinn

Robert Ball
Thomas Byshop[87]

DUBLIN *25 Jan 1602/3
Mathew Handcocke[88]
Robert Kennedy
William Turnor[89]

DUBLIN *25 Jan 1603/4
Sir John Terrell[90]
Nicholas Stephens
Peter Dermot[91]

DUBLIN *25 Jan 1604/5
John Elliote[92]
James Tirrell
Richard Stephens[93]

[81] Mayor of Dublin, 1597-8. ID 90, 233 and *ID 179, 400.*

[82] In 1597 Robert Panting was a sheriff of the city of Dublin, Thomas Buyshope was another sheriff until September 1597 when John Goudinge replaced him, *Anc. Rec. Dub.*, II, 308; Lennon, *Lords,* pp. 232, 275, 262, 255.

[83] Mayor of Dublin, 1598-9. ID 196.

[84] In 1598, John Bryse was sheriff of the city of Dublin. Thomas Eustace was the other sheriff but was then dismissed and Edmund Pursell elected in his place, *Anc. Rec. Dub.*, II, 318, 320. In 1607 Pursell refused to become mayor and was discharged as an alderman and from having freedom of the city and was fined £200. He was readmitted the following year, *ibid.*, p. 491. See also Lennon, *Lords,* pp. 231, 234, 264.

[85] Mayor of Dublin, 1599-1600. ID 3, 20, 74, 116, 147, 157, 160, 161, 166, 170, 171, 254, 260, 271, 292, 294, 421, 437, 459, 479, 494, 497, 505, 507, 523, 524, 527, 597, 619, 645, 660, 708.

[86] Arthur and Cusacke were listed as sheriffs of the city of Dublin in 1599, *Anc. Rec. Dub.*, II, 329. See also Lennon, Lords, pp. 276, 225, 240, 276.

[87] Ball and Buyshope were sheriffs of the city of Dublin, *Anc. Rec. Dub.*, II, 348; Lennon, *Lords,* pp. 227, 232.

[88] Mayor of Dublin, 1601-2. ID 98, 519 and *661.*

[89] In 1601 Kennedy and Turnor were sheriffs of the city of Dublin, *Anc. Rec. Dub.*, II, 375, 405; Lennon, *Lords,* pp. 257, 227, 232.

[90] Mayor of Dublin, 1602-3. ID 51.

[91] In 1602 Richard Barry and John Bennes were listed as sheriffs of the city of Dublin, by December Nicholas Stephins and Peter Dermod were sheriffs, *Anc. Rec. Dub.*, II, 385, 398; Lennon, *Lords,* p. 272.

[92] Mayor of Dublin, 1604. ID 283.

[93] James Tirrell was sheriff of Dublin in 1603, the other sheriff was Thomas Carole, *An. Rec. Dub.*, II, 407; Lennon, *Lords,* pp. 232, 242, 246. By November 1605 John Elliot (Ellyotte) and Richard Stephins had been replaced by Ball (as mayor of the staple) and Thomas Bishop and Richard Bellew as constables.

DUBLIN *25 Jan 1605/6
Robert Ball[94]
Thomas Buyshoppe
Richard Barry[95]

DUBLIN *25 Jan 1606/7
John Bryne
John Bennes
Richard Browne[96]

DUBLIN *25 Jan 1607/8
John Bryne
Lawrence White
Nicholas Stephins[97]

DUBLIN *25 Jan 1608/9
Thomas Plonnket[98]
Thomas Dromgoule
Robert Malpas[99]

DUBLIN *25 Jan 1609/10
John Cusacke[100]
George Devinish
Thomas Allen[101]

DUBLIN *25 Jan 1610/11
Robert Kenedy[102]
William Preston
Thomas Longe[103]

DUBLIN *25 Jan 1611/2
Richard Barry[104]
Nicholas Stephines
Edward Ball[105]

DUBLIN *25 Jan 1612/3
Thomas Bysshoppe[106]
William Turnor
Nicholas Stephins

[94] Mayor of Dublin, 1604-5. ID 646, 718, 866 and *278, 865.*

[95] On 20 November John Shelton was elected mayor but he refused to swear the Oath of Supremacy and so Robert Ball was elected, *Anc. Rec. Dub.,* II, 430. Richard Barry was sheriff of Dublin in 1604, the other sheriff was Edmond Malone (p. 421); also see Lennon, *Lords,* pp. 227, 232, 230.

[96] John Bennes was sheriff of the city of Dublin in 1605, James Tailor was the other sheriff. Richard Browne is also listed as a sheriff, *Anc. Rec. Dub.,* II, 442, 454; see also Lennon, *Lords,* p. 232, 234, 235.

[97] *An. Rec. Dub.,* II, 460.

[98] Mayor of Dublin 1606-7. ID 315, 318, 326, 442, 461, 471, 474, 533, 864, 869, 888, 898, 922, 952, 973, 1023, 1054, 1058, 1091, 1208, 1237, 1362, 1366, 1390 and *243, 324, 506, 534, 1027, 1127.*

[99] In 1607 Thomas Dromgoule, haberdasher, was sheriff of the city of Dublin, the other sheriff was James Bee, *Anc. Rec. Dub.,* II, 478, 488. Robert Mapas refused to stand as sheriff and John Dowdie was elected instead (pp. 461-2); also see Lennon, *Lords,* p. 263.

[100] Mayor of Dublin, 1608-9. ID 47, 149, 290, 291, 338, 373, 393, 464, 529, 598, 667, 759 and *574, 772, 973.*

[101] *An. Rec. Dub.,* II, 499, 503. Thomas Allen was sheriff of the city of Dublin in 1608, the other sheriff was Patrick Crolye, shoemaker. Robert Eustace, baker (p. 503), replaced Crolye; also see Lennon, *Lords,* pp. 240, 245, 225.

[102] In August 1611 Sir John Terrell was elected mayor. Lennon, *Lords,* p. 272. ID 72, 85, 187, 239, 333, 440, 509, 726, 1041, 1316, 1997, 2822, 2824 and *1129.*

[103] William Preston and Thomas Longe were sheriffs in 1609, *An. Rec. Dub.,* II, 524, 518, 524; also see Lennon, *Lords,* p. 259.

[104] Mayor of Dublin, 1610-11. ID 819, 935, 990, 1008, 1216, 1296, 1434, 1518, 1711, 1715.

[105] *Anc. Rec. Dub.,* II, 533; Lennon, *Lords,* pp. 230, 225.

[106] Mayor of Dublin, 1611-12. ID 516, 581, 587. See *Anc. Rec. Dub.,* III, 8 and Lennon, *Lords,* p. 230.

DUBLIN *25 Jan 1613/4
Thomas Carroll, alderman[107]
Patrick Mapas
Christopher Colman[108]

DUBLIN *25 Jan 1614/5
Richard Forster[109]
Thady Duffe
Nicholas Lynehanne[110]

DUBLIN *25 Jan 1616/7
Richard Browne[111]
Richard Byrne
Patrick George

DUBLIN *25 Jan 1617/8
John Bennes[112]
Nicholas Kelly
Edward Gough?

DUBLIN *25 Jan 1618/9
Sir James Carroll[113]
Nicholas Kelly
William Bushopp[114]

DUBLIN *25 Jan 1619/20
John Lany[115]

Walter Ussher
Nicholas Kennis?

DUBLIN *25 Jan 1620/1
Richard Forster[116]
Walter Ussher[117]
Edward Arthure

DUBLIN *25 Jan 1621/22
Robert Ball[118]
Edward Jones
Edward Arthore

DUBLIN *25 Jan 1622/3
Edward Ball[119]
Christopher Forster
Christopher Handcock

DUBLIN *25 Jan 1623/4
Richard Nuggett[120]
Thomas White
Christopher White

DUBLIN *25 Jan 1624/5
Sir Thadee Duffe[121]
George Jones
Christopher Wolferston

---

[107] Mayor of Dublin, 1612-13. ID 177, 452, 488, 611, 764, 765. See Lennon, *Lords,* p. 237.

[108] *Anc. Rec. Dub.,* III, 38.

[109] Mayor of Dublin, 1613-14. ID 522 and *271, 1453.*

[110] For Richard Forster and Mr Thady Duffe, see Lennon, *Lords,* pp. 252, 246.

[111] Mayor of Dublin, 1614-16. ID 282. See Lennon, *Lords,* p. 235

[112] Mayor of Dublin, 1616-17. ID 192, 387, 794 and *843, 1203, 1371, 1847.* See Lennon, *Lords,* p. 232.

[113] Mayor of Dublin, 1617-18.

[114] For Sir James Carroll and William Bushopp, see Lennon, *Lords,* pp. 237, 233.

[115] Mayor of Dublin, 1618-19.

[116] Mayor of Dublin, 1619-20. See Lennon, *Lords,* p. 252.

[117] *Ibid.,* p. 81.

[118] *Ibid.,* p. 227. ID 283, 1715. Richard Browne was mayor of Dublin, 1620-21.

[119] Mayor of Dublin, 1621-2. ID 249, 594, 763. Lennon, *Lords,* p. 225

[120] Richard Wiggett was mayor of Dublin, 1622-3.

[121] Mayor of Dublin, 1623-4. ID 536, 653, 664, 665, 673, 700, 799, 1181, 1359, 1421, 1576,

DUBLIN *25 Jan 1625/6
Sir William Bushopp[122]
George Jones
William Weston

DUBLIN *25 Jan 1626/7
William Turnor[123]
Christopher Whyt
Nicholas Kenny

DUBLIN *25 Jan 1627/8
Walter Usher[124]
Robert Arthore
Francis Dowde

DUBLIN *25 Jan 1628/9
Edward Jans[125]
Michael Browne
Thomas Shelton

DUBLIN *25 Jan 1629/30
Robert Bennett[126]
William Bagott
James Bellew

DUBLIN *25 Jan 1630/1
Sir Christopher Forster[127]
Charles Forster
William Bagotte

DUBLIN *25 Jan 1631/2
Thomas Evans[128]
Sankey Sulliard
John Ffleming

DUBLIN *25 Jan 1632/3
George Jones[129]
Mathew Tirrell
John Stanley

DUBLIN *25 Jan 1633/4
Edward Arthoure[130]
David Begg
Walter Kennedie

DUBLIN *25 Jan 1634/5, 12 May 1635
Edward Jans[131]
Thomas Wakfield
Christopher Brine, Brice

DUBLIN *25 Jan 1635/6, 1 June 1636
Robert Arthur[132]
John Gibson
Edward Branigan/ Branngan?

DUBLIN *25 Jan 1636/7
Christopher White[133]
John Carberie
William Purcell

1615, 1627, 1629, 1643, 1644 and *956*.

[122] Mayor of Dublin, 1624-5. ID 769, 915, 1105, 1110, 1111, 1113.

[123] ID 1191, 1547, 1656.

[124] ID 634, 985, 986, 1105, 1110, 1111, 1113, 1164, 1599, 1819. Thomas Evans was mayor of Dublin, 1601-2.

[125] Mayor of Dublin, 1627-8. ID 1379, 1488, 1796, 2150, 2168 and *1372*.

[126] Mayor of Dublin, 1628-9. ID 1884.

[127] Mayor of Dublin, 1629-30.

[128] Mayor of Dublin, 1630-1.

[129] Mayor of Dublin, 1631-2. ID 949, 1119 and *866, 948*.

[130] ID 852, 881, 865, 1240, 1380, 1381, 1655, 1668, 2081 and *1536*. Robert Bennett was mayor of Dublin, 1632-3.

[131] ID 1379, 1488, 1796, 2150, 2168 and *1372*. Robert Dixon was mayor of Dublin, 1633-4.

[132] ID 1144, 1182, 1255, 1289, 1297, 1317, 1322, 1347, 1388, 1405, 1415, 1447, 1732, 1798, 1842, 1923, 1924, 1980, 1985, 2065, 2205, 2206. Sir James Carroll was mayor of Dublin, 1634-5.

DUBLIN 17 Nov 1638
Sir Christopher Forster[134]
Thomas Arthur
Sankey Sulliard

DUBLIN 21 May 1639
James Watson[135]
Thomas Aryhur
Sankey Sullyard

DUBLIN July 1639
Robert Arthur[136]
John Gibson
Edward Brangen

DUBLIN 16 Oct 1639
James Watson[137]
William Arthure
Sankey Sulliard

DUBLIN 20 Feb 1639/40
James Watson[138]
Andrew Clearke
Sankey Sullyard

DUBLIN 9 Feb 1640/1
Charles Forster[139]
Edward Lake
Richard Barnewall

DUBLIN 15 July 1642
Sir Christopher Forster[140]
Sankey Sullyard
John Fleminge

DUBLIN 25 Apr 1643
Sir Christopher Forster[141]
Nicholas Stephens
William Purcell

DUBLIN 12 Mar 1643/4
Walter Kennedy[142]
John Pue
Christopher Brice

DUBLIN 5 May 1645
David Begg[143]
John Miller
Nicholas Stephens

DUBLIN 17 Aug 1646
Andrew Clarke[144]
John Brice
Maurice Pue

DUBLIN 11 June 1647
William Smith[145]
Edward Hughes
John Collins

---

[133] Sir Christopher Forster was mayor of Dublin, 1635-7.

[134] Mayor of Dublin, 1635-7 and 1638-9.

[135] Mayor of Dublin, 1637-8. ID 1806, 2017.

[136] Mayor of Dublin, 1608-9. ID 47, 149, 290, 291, 338, 373, 393, 464, 529, 598, 667, 759 and *574, 772, 973.*

[137] Mayor of Dublin, 1637-8. ID 1806, 2017.

[138] Mayor of Dublin, 1637-8. ID 1806, 2017.

[139] Mayor of Dublin, 1639-40.

[140] Mayor of Dublin, 1638-9.

[141] Mayor of Dublin, 1638-9.

[142] *ID 1129.* Thomas Wakefield, mayor of Dublin, 1640-2.

[143] ID 1762, 1871, 1874, 2049, 2071, 2073, 2088, 2093.

[144] ID 1174, 1218, 1226, 1263, 1376.

[145] Mayor of Dublin, 1642-7. *ID 2607, 2694, 3272, 3306.*

DUBLIN 12 Oct 1648
William Smyth[146]
John Flemminge
Maurice Pue

DUBLIN 28 Apr 1649
William Bladen[147]
Sankey Syliard
John Collins

DUBLIN 18 Apr 1650
John Pue, alderman[148]
Maurice Pue
Peter Wybrants

DUBLIN 10 Oct 1651
Sankey Sullyard[149]
John Weston
Mark Quinne

DUBLIN 15 Nov 1652
Raphael Hunt[150]
George Gilbert
Richard Cooke

DUBLIN 8 Feb 1652/3
Richard Tighe[151]
Ridgely Hatfield
Richard Heyden

DUBLIN 16 Feb 1653/4
Richard Tighe[152]
Robert Mills
John Cranwell

DUBLIN 27 Apr 1654
William Bladen[153]
Robert Mills
John Cranwell

DUBLIN 2 Jan 1654/5
William Bladen[154]
Robert Mills
John Cranwell

DUBLIN 27 Jan 1654/5
John Preston[155]
Tobias Cramer/Creamer
John Betson

DUBLIN 6 Aug 1655
Richard Tighe[156]
Tobias Cramer
John Betson

DUBLIN 26 Feb 1655/6
Thomas Hooke[157]
John Disminieres
Owen Jones

---

[146] Mayor of Dublin, 1642-7. *ID 2607, 2694, 3272, 3306.*

[147] Mayor of Dublin, 1647-8.

[148] Mayor of Dublin, 1648-9.

[149] Mayor of Dublin, 1650.

[150] Mayor of Dublin, 1650-1. ID 3041.

[151] Mayor of Dublin, 1651-2. ID 2240, 2241, 2260, 2269, 2496, 3072, 3073, 3372, 3373, 3421, 3459, 3460, 3461, 3483, 3496, 3526, 3527, 3538, 3549, 3745.

[152] *Ibid.*

[153] Mayor of Dublin, 1647-8.

[154] *Ibid.*

[155] Mayor of Dublin, 1653-4. ID 3014, 3087, 3094, 3407.

[156] Mayor of Dublin, 1651-2. ID 2240, 2241, 2260, 2269, 2496, 3072, 3073, 3372, 3373, 3421, 3459, 3460, 3461, 3483, 3496, 3526, 3527, 3538, 3549, 3745.

[157] Mayor of Dublin, 1654-5. ID 3434.

DUBLIN 21 Feb 1656/7, 13 Dec 1657
William Smyth[158]
Mathew French
John Serrant/Sergeant

DUBLIN 22 Feb 1657/8, 24 Mar 1657/8
Ridgley Hatfield[159]
Richard Phillipps
Henry Bollard/Pollard?

DUBLIN 7 Feb 1658/9
Thomas Waterhouse[160]
John Forrest
Samuel Salte/onstall

DUBLIN 13 Feb 1659/60
Peter Wybrants[161]
Richard Cooke
John Eastwood

DUBLIN 11 Sept 1660
Ridgley Hatfield[162]
Richard Eastwood
John Eastwood

DUBLIN 15 Feb 1660/1
Richard Tighe[163]
Enoch Reader
Obediah Bradshawe

DUBLIN 9 Jan 1661/2
Richard Tighe[164]
Enoch Reader
Obediah Bradshaw

DUBLIN 17 June 1662
Sir Hubart Adryan Verneer[165]
Thomas Howard
Obediah Bradshaw

DUBLIN 21 Feb 1662/3
Sir George Gilbert[166]
George Hewlett
William Whitshed

DUBLIN 25 Jan 1663/4
John Cranwell, esquire[167]
Christopher Bennett
Elia Best

DUBLIN *25 Jan 1664/5
William Smith, alderman[168]
John Totty, alderman
William Brookes, alderman

DUBLIN *25 Jan 1665/6
William Smith, alderman[169]
Joshua Allen, alderman
Francis Brewester, alderman

---

[158] Mayor of Dublin, 1642-7. *ID 2694, 3272, 3306.*

[159] Mayor of Dublin, 1656-7. ID 2960.

[160] Mayor of Dublin, 1657-8. ID 3476 and *3065, 3365, 3366.*

[161] Mayor of Dublin, 1658-9. ID 3029 and *2280, 2346, 3353, 3545, 3616.*

[162] Mayor of Dublin, 1656-7. ID 2960.

[163] Mayor of Dublin, 1651-52, 1655-6. ID 2240, 2241, 2260, 2269, 2496, 3072, 3073, 3372, 3373, 3421, 3459, 3460, 3461, 3483, 3496, 3526, 3527, 3538, 3549, 3745.

[164] Mayor of Dublin, 1651-52, 1655-6. ID 2240, 2241, 2260, 2269, 2496, 3072, 3073, 3372, 3373, 3421, 3459, 3460, 3461, 3483, 3496, 3526, 3527, 3538, 3549, 3745.

[165] Mayor of Dublin, 1660-1.

[166] Mayor of Dublin, 1661-2. *ID 3351, 3352, 3365, 3366.*

[167] Mayor of Dublin, 1662-3.

[168] Mayor of Dublin, 1642-7 and 1663-5. *ID 2607, 2694, 3272, 3306.*

[169] Mayor of Dublin, 1642-7 and 1663-5. I*D 2607, 2694, 3272, 3306.*

DUBLIN 24 Sept 1666
William Smith, alderman[170]
Joshua Allen
John Totty

DUBLIN *25 Jan 1666/7
Sir Daniel Bellingham[171]
Christopher Lovett
Rice Phillipps

DUBLIN 16 May 1668
John Desmynieres[172]
Philip Castlton
Warner Weston[173]

DUBLIN 10 Dec 1668
John Desmynieres[174]
Phillip Castleton
Obediah Bradshaw

DUBLIN *25 Jan 1668/9
Mark Quinn[175]
George Stoughton
Simon Carrick

DUBLIN *25 Jan 1669/70
John Forrest, alderman[176]
William Harvey
Giles Mee

DUBLIN 23 Feb 1669/70
John Forrest[177]
William Harrys/Harris
Giles Mee

DUBLIN 7 Oct 1670
Sir George Gilbert[178]
William Harrys
Giles Mee

DUBLIN *25 Jan 1670/1
Lewis Desmynieres[179]
Walter Mottly
Nathaniel Phillpott

DUBLIN *25 Jan 1671/2
John Totty, alderman[180]
William Gressingham
John Dutton

DUBLIN *25 Jan 1672/3, 4 Feb
   1672/3
Sir John Tottie[181]
Walter Harris
Philip Danncey?

DUBLIN *25 Jan 1673/4
Sir John Tottie[182]
Henry Ashton
Richard Warren

[170] Mayor of Dublin, 1642-7 and 1663-5. *ID 2607, 2694, 3272, 3306.*

[171] Mayor of Dublin, 1665-6. *ID 2253.*

[172] Mayor of Dublin, 1666-7. ID 2522, 3758.

[173] 10 November 1668 Obadia Bradshaw, merchant, replaced Weston as a constable of the staple.

[174] Mayor of Dublin, 1666-7. ID 2522, 3758.

[175] Mayor of Dublin, 1667-8. ID 2280, 2287, 3098, 3099, 3523, 3545, 3551.

[176] Mayor of Dublin, 1668-9. ID 3082.

[177] Mayor of Dublin, 1668-9. ID 3082.

[178] Mayor of Dublin, 1661-2. *ID 3351, 3352, 3365, 3366.*

[179] Mayor of Dublin, 1669-70.

[180] Mayor of Dublin, 1671-2.

[181] Mayor of Dublin, 1671-2.

[182] Mayor of Dublin, 1671-2.

DUBLIN 9 Mar 1674/5
Sir John Tottie[183]
Humphrey Jervis
William Eager

DUBLIN 22 May 1675
Sir John Tottie[184]
Humphrey Jervis
William Sands

DUBLIN 29 Sept 1675
Sir Joshua Allen[185]
William Sands
William Eager

DUBLIN 4 Feb 1675/6
Sir Joshua Allen[186]
John Castleton
George Kenedy

DUBLIN *25 Jan 1676/7
Sir Joshua Allen[187]
John Knox, alderman
George Blackill?

DUBLIN 5 Jan 1677/8
Sir George Gilbert[188]
William Harrys
Giles Mee

DUBLIN *25 Jan 1677/8
Christopher Lovett, alderman[189]
William Watt
Benjamin Leadbetter

DUBLIN 5 June 1678
Sir Joshua Allen[190]
William Watt
Benjamin Leadbetter

DUBLIN 29 Nov 1678
John Desmynieres[191]
William Watt
Benjamin Leadbetter

DUBLIN 29 Jan 1678/9
John Smith, alderman[192]
William Story
William Billington

DUBLIN 29 Jan 1679/80
Peter Ward, alderman[193]
Henry Rowlands/Rowlandson
Edward Page

DUBLIN 28 Jan 1681/2
John Eastwood, alderman[194]
James Cottingham
Michael Mitchell

---

[183] Mayor of Dublin, 1671-2.

[184] When Sir John Tottie absented himself from the city he was replaced with Sir Joshua Allen.

[185] Mayor of Dublin 1673-4. ID 2369, 2473, 3619, 3719.

[186] Mayor of Dublin 1673-4. ID 2369, 2473, 3619, 3719.

[187] Mayor of Dublin 1673-4. ID 2369, 2473, 3619, 3719.

[188] Mayor of Dublin, 1661-2. *ID 3351, 3352, 3365, 3366.*

[189] Christopher Lovett, mayor of Dublin 1676-7, requested that he be replaced before completing his term and Sir Joshua Allen became mayor of the staple. For Lovett see ID 2495, 2573, 3753, 3829 and *2617, 3160.*

[190] Mayor of Dublin 1673-4. ID 2369, 2473, 3619, 3719.

[191] Mayor of Dublin, 1666-7. ID 2522, 3758.

[192] Mayor of Dublin, 1677-8.

[193] Mayor of Dublin, 1678-9. *ID 3353.*

[194] Mayor of Dublin, 1679-80.

DUBLIN 11 Feb 1681/2
Luke Lowther, alderman[195]
Edward Rose
William Gibbons

DUBLIN 5 Feb 1682/3
Enoch Reader, alderman[196]
Thom Litchfield
Edmond Kelly

DUBLIN 21 Feb 1683/4
Sir Humphrey Jervis[197]
William Litchfield
William Haynes

DUBLIN 12 Nov 1684
Sir Humphrey Jervis[198]
William Hanes/Haines
Edward Haines

DUBLIN 28 May 1685
John Castleton, alderman[199]
Edward Haines
Thomas Goold

DUBLIN 5 Feb 1685/6
Sir Abel Ram[200]
Thomas Quin
Andrew Brice

DUBLIN 15 June 1687
Sir John Knox[201]
Samuel Walton
Richard Lord

DROGHEDA:
DROGHEDA 20 July 1636
William Hamlyn[202]
James Dromgoole
Gerald Tyrrell

DROGHEDA 16 June 1638
John Jeeve
Stephan Dowding
George Garnett

DROGHEDA 19 Mar 1638/9, 7
   Dec 1638/9
Christopher Bath[203]
James Penteny
Christopher Malone

DROGHEDA 30 Aug 1639
Christopher Bath, alderman[204]
James Pentenie
Christopher Malone

DROGHEDA 18 Apr 1640
William Hamlin[205]
Nicholas Cuny
Peter Walsh

---

[195] Mayor of Dublin, 1680-1.

[196] Mayor of Dublin, 1670-1. ID 2583, 3370, 3371, 3589, 3850 and *3898*.

[197] Mayor of Dublin, 1681-2. ID 3808 and *2684, 3257*.

[198] Mayor of Dublin, 1681-2. ID 3808 and *2684, 3257*.

[199] Mayor of Dublin, 1686-7. ID 2630, 2643, 2709, 2713, 3181, 3208, 3283, 3284, 3903, 3958, 3973, 3996, 4006, 4018.

[200] Mayor of Dublin, 1684-5. ID 3272.

[201] Mayor of Dublin, 1685-6.

[202] *ID 2941*, 2946.

[203] *ID 1032, 1033*.

[204] *Ibid.*

[205] *ID 2941, 2946*.

DROGHEDA 5 Apr 1641
Barnaby Bellings, alderman[206]
Richard Mortimer
Thomas Stoker

DROGHEDA 27 Mar 1644
Thomas Delahoid[207]
George Pippard
Roger Bellings

DROGHEDA 1649
Nicholas Simpson, alderman
Thomas Stoker
David Sheaperde[208]

DROGHEDA 1657
Thomas Dickson
Gabriel Meade
Francis Poole[209]

DROGHEDA 1658
Thomas Stoker, esquire
Joseph Whirlowe
Edward Nicholls[210]

DROGHEDA 1659
Samuel Stanbridge, alderman
Ferdinand Rosse
Richard Jackson[211]

DROGHEDA 1660
Edward Martin, esquire
John Tempest
Thomas Leigh[212]

DROGHEDA 1661
Jonas Ellwood, esquire
Richard Orson
John Hardwicke[213]

DROGHEDA 1662
John Jeeve, alderman
John Stoker
Thomas Newton[214]

DROGHEDA 1663
John Metcalfe, alderman
Alexander Boddington
John Watkins[215]

DROGHEDA 1665
John Towers, alderman[216]

DROGHEDA 1666
Joseph Whorley, alderman
Edward Bythall
John Killough[217]

---

[206] ID 1342.
[207] ID 2900.
[208] Listed as mayor and constables of the staple in T. Gogarty, ed, *Council Book of Drogheda 1649-1734* (Dundalk, 1988), pp. 24-5. The word Coroner seems to be used synonymously with constable.
[209] Listed as mayor and constables of the staple in *ibid.*, pp. 49-50. Thomas Dickson was described as 'late mayor' of the city.
[210] Listed as mayor and constables of the staple in *ibid.*, p. 58.
[211] Listed as mayor and constables of the staple in *ibid.*, p. 71.
[212] Listed as mayor and constables of the staple in *ibid.*, p. 81.
[213] Listed as mayor and constables of the staple in *ibid.*, p.90.
[214] Listed as mayor and constables of the staple in *ibid.*, p. 100.
[215] Listed as mayor and constables of the staple in *ibid.*, p. 106.
[216] Listed as mayor and constables of the staple in *ibid.*, p. 126.
[217] Listed as mayor and constables of the staple in *ibid.*, p. 134.

DROGHEDA 1667
Gabriel Meade, alderman
Edmond Graves, merchant
David Doran[218]

DROGHEDA 1668
Samuel Osborne, alderman[219]
Edward Singleton
Thomas Powell[220]

DROGHEDA 17 May 1670
Thomas Leigh[221]
Edward Shingleton
Thomas Ouldam[222]

DROGHEDA 19 Apr 1671
John Stoker, esquire
Thomas Willis
Thomas Smallpage[223]

DROGHEDA 20 Oct 1671
Robert Ford[224]
Bartholomew Doyle
William Robinson[225]

DROGHEDA 30 Jan 1672/3
Sir James Graham
Jerome Cheevers
John Carter[226]

DROGHEDA 14 Feb 1673/4
Jonas Ellwood
Richard Jackson
Richard Blumfield[227]

DROGHEDA 27 Apr 1675
Edward Nicholls, esquire
Richard Lloyd
Henry Watkins[228]

DROGHEDA 7 March 1675/6
Thomas Newton,
    alderman/esquire
John Sandeford
William Barron[229]

DROGHEDA 4 Mar 1677/8
George Richardson, alderman
Thomas Percivall, alderman, one of
    the constables
John Barry[230]

DROGHEDA 2 Jan 1677/8
Edward Singleton, esquire[231]
Johan Osborne
Bartholomew Doyle[232]

---

[218] Listed as mayor and constables of the staple in *ibid.*, p. 138.
[219] ID 3143.
[220] Listed as mayor and constables of the staple in *ibid.*, p. 142.
[221] ID 3424 and *2530*.
[222] Listed as mayor and constables of the staple on 15 October 1669 in *ibid.*, p. 147. Edward Singleton was town treasurer.
[223] Listed as mayor and constables of the staple in *ibid.*, p. 150.
[224] ID 3824.
[225] Listed as mayor and constables of the staple in *ibid.*, p. 154.
[226] Listed as mayor and constables of the staple in *ibid.*, p. 158.
[227] Listed as mayor and constables of the staple in *ibid.*, p. 160.
[228] Listed as mayor and constables of the staple in *ibid.*, p. 164.
[229] Listed as mayor and constables of the staple in *ibid.*, p. 167.
[230] Listed as mayor and constables of the staple in *ibid.*, p. 171.
[231] ID 2548, 3807.
[232] Listed as mayor and constables of the staple in *ibid.*, p. 177.

DROGHEDA 16 Jan 1678/9
John Tomlinson, esquire[233]
William Elwood
Thomas Newton[234]

DROGHEDA 16 June 1680
Richard Jackson, esquire
James Vanbobbart
Robert Hardiman[235]

DROGHEDA 22 Aug 1681
John Sandiford, esquire
Henry Nicholls
James Vanbobbart[236]

DROGHEDA 20 Jan 1681/2
Thomas Percivall, esquire
William Forde
Richard Griffith[237]

DROGHEDA 24 Oct 1682
John Osborne, esquire
William Stoker
Edward Cheshire[238]

DROGHEDA 9 July 1684
William Elwood, esquire
Thomas Shephard
Richard Griffith[239]

DROGHEDA 1684
Henry Nicholls, alderman
John Siddell
Gilbert Lucus[240]

DROGHEDA 1685
George Richardson, alderman
Charles Isaack
James Fairbrother[241]

DROGHEDA 1686
John Sandiford
John Good
John Curtis[242]

DROGHEDA 1687
William Barron
Ignatius Fleming
Bartholomew Doyle[243]

DROGHEDA 1688
Christopher Pippard-Fitz-Ignatius,
    alderman[244]
Christopher Dowdall, alderman
James Kelshey

DROGHEDA 1690
Edward Singleton, alderman
William Newton
Charles Issack[245]

---

[233] ID 2423, 3149, 3219, 3678, 3798, 3799, 3800, 3814, 3815, 3828, 3851, 3936, 3947, 3963, 3970, 3988.

[234] Listed as mayor and constables of the staple in *ibid.*, p. 182.

[235] Listed as mayor and constables of the staple in *ibid.*, p. 187.

[236] Listed as mayor and constables of the staple in *ibid.*, p. 191. Paul Eaton was listed as constable.

[237] Listed as mayor and constables of the staple in *ibid.*, p. 194.

[238] Listed as mayor and constables of the staple in *ibid.*, p. 199.

[239] Listed as mayor and constables of the staple in *ibid.*, p. 204.

[240] Listed as mayor and constables of the staple in *ibid.*, p. 208.

[241] Listed as mayor and constables of the staple in *ibid.*, p. 212. By July 1686 Gilbert Lucas and John Liddle were the constables.

[242] Listed as mayor and constables of the staple in *ibid.*, p. 215.

[243] Listed as mayor and constables of the staple in *ibid.*, pp. 220-1.

[244] *ID 3867.*

[245] Listed as mayor and constables of the staple in *ibid.*, p. 237.

GALWAY:[246]
GALWAY, 1612[247]
Richard Martin, mayor of staple

GALWAY, 1615[248]
Nicholas Darcy, mayor of staple

GALWAY, 1615 and 1616[249]
Andrew Lynch, mayor of staple

GALWAY, 1623[250]
Patrick Martin, mayor of staple

GALWAY, 1624[251]
Marcus Oge French, mayor of staple

GALWAY, 1625[252]
Robert Blake, mayor of staple

GALWAY, 1626[253]
Thomas Lynch, mayor of staple

GALWAY, 1627[254]
James Lynch, mayor of staple

GALWAY, 1630[255]
Nicholas? Lynch, mayor of staple

GALWAY, 1632[256]
Geoffrey Martin, mayor of staple

GALWAY, 1633[257]
George Martin, mayor of staple

GALWAY, 1634[258]
Patrick French, mayor of staple

GALWAY, 1635[259]
Dominick Browne, mayor of staple

GALWAY, 1636[260]
Nicholas Lynch, mayor of staple

GALWAY, 1637[261]
Anthony Lynch, mayor of staple

GALWAY, 1638[262]
Thomas Blake, mayor of staple

[246] James Hardiman Library, Galway, Minute books of the Corporation of the town of Galway (Liber A). For a transcription see J. T. Gilbert, *Historical Manuscripts Commission. Tenth Report. Appendix* V, pp. 380-520. I am grateful to Marie Boran for providing me with this information.

[247] ID 2181, 2928.

[248] Minute books of the Corporation of the town of Galway (Liber A)., Darcy was mayor of the city in 1614.

[249] *Ibid.*, Lynch was mayor of the city in 1620.

[250] *Ibid.*, Martin was mayor of the city in 1622.

[251] *Ibid.*, French was mayor of the city in 1623.

[252] *Ibid.*, Blake was mayor of the city in 1624. ID 371, 439, 582, 591, 758, 813, 849, 851.

[253] *Ibid.*, Lynch was mayor of the city in 1625.

[254] *Ibid.*, Lynch was mayor of the city in 1626.

[255] *Ibid.*, Lynch was mayor of the city in 1629.

[256] *Ibid.*

[257] *Ibid.*, Martin was mayor of the city in 1632.

[258] *Ibid.*, French was mayor of the city in 1633. ID 680.

[259] *Ibid.*, Browne was mayor of the city in 1634.

[260] *Ibid.*, Lynch was mayor of the city in 1635.

[261] *Ibid.*, Lynch was mayor of the city in 1636.

[262] *Ibid.*, Blake was mayor of the city in 1637.

GALWAY, 1639[263]
Robucke Lynch, mayor of staple

GALWAY, 1640[264]
John Bodkin, mayor of staple

GALWAY, 1641[265]
Francis Blake, mayor of staple

GALWAY, 1643[266]
Richard Martin, mayor of staple

GALWAY, 1644[267]
Valentine Blake, mayor of staple

GALWAY, 1646[268]
Edmond Kirwan, mayor of staple

GALWAY, 1648[269]
Walter Browne, mayor of staple

GALWAY, 1649[270]
Walter Blake, mayor of staple

GALWAY, 1650[271]
Thomas Lynch, mayor of staple

GALWAY, 1651[272]
Richard Kirwan
Thomas Lynch
Arthur Lynch

GALWAY 12 Mar 1654/5
Martin Lynch, alderman
Nicholas French
Arthur Lynch[273]

GALWAY, 1655[274]
Peter Stubbard, mayor

GALWAY 21 Mar 1659/60
Peter Stubbs, esquire
John May
Richard Ormsbey[275]

GALWAY, 1661[276]
John Morgan
George Morgan
John Dod

GALWAY 27 Apr 1664?
Edward Eyre, alderman
John Barrett
Richard Walcott[277]

[263] *Ibid.*, Lynch was mayor of the city in 1638.

[264] *Ibid.*, Bodkin was mayor of the city in 1639. ID *3713*.

[265] *Ibid.*, Blake was mayor of the city in 1640.

[266] *Ibid.*, Martin was mayor of the city in 1642.

[267] *Ibid.*, Blake was mayor of the city in 1643. ID 1325, 1761.

[268] *Ibid.*, Kirwan was mayor of the city in 1645.

[269] *Ibid.*

[270] *Ibid.*, Blake was mayor of the city in 1648.

[271] *Ibid.*, Lynch was mayor of the city in 1649.

[272] *Ibid.*

[273] French was listed as a sheriff of the city in 1653 and Lynch-Fitzanthony as mayor of the city in 1653, J. Hardiman, *History* (Dublin, 1820; reprinted, 1958), p. 223.

[274] Minute books of the Corporation of the town of Galway (Liber A), Stubbard was mayor of the city in 1654.

[275] Colonel Peter Stubbers was mayor of the city in 1654. John May was mayor in 1670, Hardiman, *Galway* p. 225. Richard Ormsby was sheriff in 1658 and mayor in 1671, *ibid.*, pp. 224-5.

[276] Minute books of the Corporation of the town of Galway (Liber A), Morgan was mayor of the city in 1660.

[277] Edward Eyre was mayor of the city in 1663, Barrett and Walcott were sheriffs in 1663. Eyre was M.P. for Galway in 1661, Hardiman, *Galway*, pp. 238, 224.

GALWAY, 1665[278]
John Morgan, mayor
William Heninge
Thomas Semper

GALWAY, 1666[279]
John Spencer
Robert Warner
George Younge

GALWAY 29 Jan 1667
John Spencer, esquire
George Davison
William Jackson[280]

GALWAY, 1668
James Berry
George Davison

GALWAY, 1669[281]
John Spencer
John Jull?
Robert Warner

GALWAY 30 Oct 1670[282]
John Peters
William Hardiman
John Barrett

GALWAY 3 Sept 1674
Gregory Constable
Thomas Andrewes
William? Hill[283]

GALWAY, 1687[284]
Thomas Stanton, mayor

KILKENNY:
KILKENNY 30 Apr 1639
Nicholas Knarisborough, esquire
John Archer
Robert Tobin

KILKENNY 7 Nov 1639
George Shee
John Donogho
Michael Langton

KILKENNY 2 Oct 1640
Michael Archer[285]
William Randall
Nicholas Archer

KILKENNY 22 May 1662
John Tooner, esquire
Thomas Chapmen, one of the
    constables

LIMERICK:[286]
LIMERICK 5 Feb 1638/9
James Stretch
John Fox
Nicholas Fox

---

[278] Minute books of the Corporation of the town of Galway (Liber A), Morgan was mayor of the city in 1664 and 1660.

[279] *Ibid.*, Spencer was mayor of the city in 1665 and 1666.

[280] Colonel John Spence was mayor of the city 1666-68. Davidson and Jackson were constables in 1666, Hardiman, *Galway*, p. 224

[281] Minute books of the Corporation of the town of Galway (Liber A), Spencer was mayor of the city in 1665, 1666 and 1668.

[282] John Peters was mayor of the city in 1669 and Hardiman was sheriff in 1669, Hardiman, *Galway*, pp. 224-5.

[283] Constable was mayor of the city in 1671 and 1673, Andrews and Hill were sheriffs in 1672, Hardiman, *Galway*, p. 225.

[284] Minute books of the Corporation of the town of Galway (Liber A).

[285] ID 955.

[286] For a full listing of mayors and sheriffs see Maurice Lenihan, *Limerick its history and antiquities* (Dublin, 1866), pp. 700-5.

LIMERICK 9 Nov 1639
Andrew Creagh
David White
William Stretch

LIMERICK 10 Nov 1640
Andrew Creagh
John Comyn
Henry Casie

LIMERICK 9 Nov 1641
James Lylles
David Roch
James Hackett

LIMERICK 9 Aug 1660
William Yarwell[287]
Christopher Key[e]s
Robert Pas[s]ey

LIMERICK 25 Oct 1661
Thomas Miller, esquire[288]
Henry Pryce
Robert Shule

LIMERICK 8 Oct 1666
Sir Ralph Wilson[289]
Samuel Foxon
Joshua Lynch

LIMERICK 5 June 1667
Sir William King[290]
Henry Price
John Symes
George Roch, clerk of staple

LIMERICK 26 July 1669
Edward Warr, esquire

John Bucknor
Anthony Bartlett

LIMERICK 16 Jan 1672/3
Robert Shute, esquire
Francis Whitamore
Thomas Bennis
Daniel Hignet, clerk of staple

LIMERICK 17 Jan 1673/4
John Bourne, esquire
Daniel Hignet
John Harte
Daniel Hignet, clerk of staple

LIMERICK 30 July 1675
John Bourne
Daniel Hignet
John Hart
Daniel Hignet, clerk of staple

LIMERICK 30 Nov 1676
William Yorke, esquire[291]
Robert Higgins
Thomas Rosse
Daniel Hignet, clerk of staple

LIMERICK 6 Sept 1678
Edward Clarke, esquire[292]
Robert Smith, esquire
William Craven, esquire
Daniel Hignet, clerk of staple

LIMERICK 7 Oct 1682
Edward Wight, esquire
Richard Lylles, esquire
William Rule, esquire
Daniel Hignet, clerk of staple

---

[287] Mayor of Limerick in 1658, *ibid.,* p. 703.

[288] Mayor of Limerick in 1660, *ibid.*

[289] Mayor of Limerick in 1663 and 1664, *ibid.*

[290] Mayor of Limerick in 1665, *ibid.* ID 3409.

[291] Mayor of Limerick in 1673, 1674 and 1678, *ibid.,* pp. 703-4. ID 3147.

[292] Mayor of Limerick in 1675, *ibid.,* p. 703.

LIMERICK 13 Aug 1685
John Craven, esquire
Nathaniel Webb
Thomas Flexen

LONDONDERRY:
LONDONDERRY 13 Feb 1685/6
Samuel Norman, esquire
Andrew Conningham

SLIGO:
SLIGO 26 Jan 1632/3
Sir Roger Jones[293]
John Fowlowe, merchant
James French, merchant

SLIGO 11 July 1638
John Murtagh, gent
Andrew Creane, esquire
James French, merchant

SLIGO 22 June 1639
John Murtagh, gent
Roebuck Creane, merchant
John Fowlowe

SLIGO 1 July 1640
James French, esquire[294]
Robin Creane
John Fowlowe, merchant

WATERFORD:[295]
WATERFORD 26 Oct 1630[296]
William Dobin, esquire
John Fagan
William Cleere

WATERFORD 10 Mar 1635/6[297]
John Skiddy
William Lincoln
Gerrot Lincoln
John Lee, clerk of the staple

WATERFORD 5 Mar 1638/9[298]
Nicholas Wise, esquire
John Blewet
John Morgan

WATERFORD 16 Apr 1640[299]
Robert Lumbard, esquire
Lucas White
John Fitzgerald
Paul Ailward, deputy clerk of the
    staple
John Ailwarde, clerk of the staple

WATERFORD 4 Aug 1641[300]
Mathew Grant, esquire
Mathew Porter
Henry White

---

[293] ID 1204, 1510.

[294] ID 2737, 2738.

[295] For a complete listing of the mayors, bailiffs and sheriffs of the city 1377-1745 see Charles Smith, *The Antient and present state of the county and city of Waterford* (Dublin, 1846), pp. 159-66.

[296] In 1629 Dobbin was the mayor of the city; Fagan and Cleere were the sheriffs, *ibid.*, p. 163.

[297] In 1635 Skiddy was the mayor of the city; William and Garret Lincoln were the sheriffs, *ibid.*, p. 164.

[298] In 1638 Wise was the mayor of the city; Blewet and Girke Morgan were the sheriffs, *ibid.*, p. 164.

[299] In 1639 Lumbard was the mayor of the city; White and FitzGerald were the sheriffs, *ibid.*, p. 164.

[300] In 1640 Grant was the mayor of the city; White and Porter were the sheriffs, *ibid.*, p. 164.

WATERFORD 1 Oct 1670[301]
William Hurst?
Francis Knowles
William Joy[302]

WATERFORD 2 Oct 1671
Thomas Bolton[303]

WEXFORD:
WEXFORD 1609[304]
John Brown
Richard Stafford
Stephen Codd

WEXFORD 26 Sept 1674
Francis Harvey, esquire
Thomas Scott
John Nixon

WEXFORD 27 Aug 1680
James Roe, esquire
Mathew Kinselagh

WEXFORD 11 Dec 1680
John Rigbie, esquire
Gerald Curcy, gent
William Mercer, gent

WEXFORD 18 July 1683
John Slegge?, esquire
Nicholas Harley

WEXFORD 25 Mar 1684
Abraham Bates, esquire
Thomas Rabi/Raby
William Gregg

WEXFORD 1687[305]
Anthony Talbot
Matthew Kinsellagh
Morgan Byrne

YOUGHAL:
YOUGHAL 1618[306]
Nicholas Galwan
Walter Unet
William Llewellen

YOUGHAL 14 Mar 1639[307]
William Gough, alderman
John Hassard, one of the consta-
   bles
Dom. Forresste, deputy clerk

---

[301] In 1670 Hurst was the mayor of the city; Knowles and Joy were the sheriffs, *ibid.*, p. 164.

[302] S. Pender (ed.), *Council Books of the Corporation of Waterford* (Irish Manuscripts Commission, Dublin, 1964), p. 76. Only the names of the sheriffs are given.

[303] Pender, *Waterford*, p. 87. The names of the sheriffs were not given but were probably Joseph Ivie and William Lamb, see Smith, *Waterford*, p. 164.

[304] Charter granted to Wexford in 1609 reprinted in P. H. Hore, *History of town and county of Wexford* (6 vols., London, 1900), I, 216.

[305] *Ibid.*, p. 378.

[306] R. Caulfield, ed., *The Council Book of the Corporation of Youghal* (Guilford Surrey, 1878), p. xxxii reprints the patent making Youghal a staple town. The names of the mayors and burgesses for the years 1610-1659, 1666-1687, and 1690-1800 are recorded in full (pp. 617-24). The names of staple officials are recorded from 1667. Invariably the mayor of the corporation became mayor of the staple and after 1666 sat as a member of the court of common council.

[307] Mayor of Youghal in 1638-9; bailiffs were John Hassard and John Bluett, Caulfied, *Youghal*, p. 193.

YOUGHAL 7 Jan 1640/1[308]
Maurice Uniake, alderman
William Lewes
Nicholas Nagle
Michael Forest, deputy clerk

YOUGHAL 1646[309]
Thomas Stoute, mayor of staple

YOUGHAL 10 Feb 1657/8[310]
John Farthing, alderman
Peter Godwyn, one of the
    constables
Andrew Wandrick, recorder
Patrick Harper, deputy clerk

YOUGHAL 6 Mar 1660/1[311]
Thomas Warren, alderman
Abraham Vaughan, one of the
    constables
Patrick Harper, clerk of the staple

YOUGHAL 5 Jan 1664/5
John Lanyer
John Deacon
William Norman

YOUGHAL 1666[312]
Thomas Baker, mayor of staple

YOUGHAL 16 Dec 1667
John Luther, alderman[313]
Samuel Haymons
Thomas Hilgrove

YOUGHAL 1668
John Deacon, mayor of staple[314]

YOUGHAL 1670
John Farthing, mayor of staple[315]

YOUGHAL 1671
Samuel Hayman, mayor of staple[316]

YOUGHAL 17 May 1674
Edward Laundy[317]
Barry Bryant, one of the
    constables
John Houghton, clerk of staple

YOUGHAL 3 Nov 1674
Mathew Spencer[318]
Richard Laundy, one of the
    constables

YOUGHAL 1675
Edward Perry, mayor of staple[319]

---

[308] Mayor of Youghal in 1639-40; bailiffs were William Lewis, Nicholas Nogle, and Thomas Vaughan, *ibid.*, p. 195.

[309] In a letter from Inchiquin, dated 6 October 1646, *ibid.*, p. 257.

[310] Mayor of Youghal in 1656-7; bailiffs were John Stout and Peter Goodwin, *ibid.*, p. 303.

[311] The council minutes recording the election of corporation officials are missing for the years 1659-1660.

[312] He served as a member of the court of common council held on 23 October 1666, *ibid.*, p. 314.

[313] He served as a member of the court of common 1667-8, *ibid.*, pp. 318-22.

[314] He served as a member of the court of common council 1668-9, *ibid.*, pp. 323-5.

[315] He served as a member of the court of common council 1670-1, *ibid.*, pp. 332-7.

[316] He served as a member of the court of common council 1671-2, *ibid.*, pp. 336-8.

[317] Mayor of Youghal 1672-3, *ibid.*, p. 339; served as a member of the court of common council, 1673-4. ID 3875.

[318] Mayor of Youghal 1673-4, *ibid.*, pp. 339-44; served as a member of the court of common council, 1674-5.

[319] He served as a member of the court of common council 1675-6, *ibid.*, pp. 348-50.

YOUGHAL 6 Feb 1676/7
John Atkin, esquire[320]
William Palmer, one of the
    constables

YOUGHAL 9 July 1678
Nicholas Lucas, alderman[321]
Peter Hopkins, one of the
    constables
John Emerey, clerk of the staple

YOUGHAL 7 Feb 1678/9
John Morrick, alderman[322]
Edward Crockford
Jonah Clove

YOUGHAL 5 Sept 1680
Edward Laundy, alderman[323]
Richard Paradice
Robert Ball

YOUGHAL 5 June 1683[324]
John Luthar, alderman

Jasper Lucas, merchant
Edward Nicholas, merchant

YOUGHAL 24 Oct 1683
Edward Laundy[325]
John FitzGerrald, one of the
    constables

YOUGHAL 1 Feb 1683/4
Jonas Clove, alderman[326]
John Scamaden, merchant?
Thomas Vaughan merchant

YOUGHAL 1684-85
Richard Paradice, mayor of
    staple[327]

YOUGHAL 21 Sept 1686
Edward Crockford, alderman[328]
John Cook, merchant?
Henry Luther

YOUGHAL 1690-91
Edward Perry, mayor of staple[329]

---

[320] He served as a member of the court of common council 1675 and again 1676-7, *ibid.*, pp. 347-8, 350-1.

[321] Mayor of Youghal 1675-6, *ibid.*, p. 350; served as a member of the court of common council, 1677-8. ID 4003.

[322] Mayor of Youghal 1677-8, *ibid.*, p. 351; served as a member of the court of common council, 1678-9.

[323] Mayor of Youghal 1679-80, *ibid.*, p. 353; served as a member of the court of common council, 1680-1.

[324] Luther served as a member of the common council. On 2 January 1682[-3] the council ordered that Luther 'Jasper Lucas and Edward Nicholas, constables of the staple, be saved harmless for disposing of (for the use of the Corporation) the wreck brandy found in the liberties in March, 1681, when they were mayor and baylives', *ibid.*, p. 357.

[325] Mayor of Youghal 1672-3, *ibid.*, p. 339; served as a member of the court of common council, 1673-4. ID 3875.

[326] Mayor of Youghal 1682-3, *ibid.*, p. 360; served as a member of the court of common council, 1683-4.

[327] Mayor of Youghal 1683-4; he served as a member of the court of common council 1684-5, *ibid.*, pp. 364-5. The minute of 10 October 1685 indicated that stones the mayor of the staple had provided for the building of a key 'on the south side of the fort' (p. 366) were to be used instead to build stables.

[328] Mayor of Youghal 1684-5, *ibid.*, p. 367; served as a member of the court of common council, 1685-6.

[329] *Ibid.*, p. 382.

YOUGHAL 1691-92
Francis Baker, mayor of staple[330]

YOUGHAL 1694-95
Thomas Walter, mayor of staple[331]

YOUGHAL 1695-96
Jasper Lucas, mayor of staple[332]

YOUGHAL 1696-97
Edward Nicholas, mayor of staple[333]

YOUGHAL 1698-99
John Cooke, mayor of staple[334]

YOUGHAL 1703-4
Thomas Croker, mayor of staple[335]

YOUGHAL 1710-11
Richard Giles, mayor of staple[336]

YOUGHAL 1711-12
Benjamin Murdock, mayor of staple[337]

YOUGHAL 1716-17
Gregory Salter, mayor of staple[338]

[330] *Ibid.*, p. 389.
[331] *Ibid.*, p. 393.
[332] *Ibid.*, p. 393.
[333] *Ibid.*, p. 395.
[334] *Ibid.*, p. 398.
[335] *Ibid.*, p. 399.
[336] *Ibid.*, p. 400.
[337] *Ibid.*, p. 401.
[338] *Ibid.*, p. 408.

BRETHREN OF THE DUBLIN STAPLE
Transcribed by Bridget McCormack

The task of appointing the staple officials fell to the brethren of the staple—a carefully selected body of 26 men. On becoming a brother (a privilege that cost three shillings), these men, usually aldermen, merchants, or esquires, swore to 'be present at the election of the mayor and constables', to submit to the jurisdiction of the mayors, and to maintain the laws and customs of the staple in an honest manner.[1] No one could be elected a member of the staple brethren unless he enjoyed the freedom of the city. Thus freedom of the staple became an additional and presumably coveted privilege and the mayors, constables and brethren of the staple formed a municipal oligarchy with staple offices circulating amongst comparatively few men.

Lengthy lists of the brethren of the Dublin staple (1616-37 and 1664-1674) were recorded in the second and third Dublin staple books. These lists and annotations have been transcribed in full below. No attempt has been made to modernise or standardise the spelling.

The brethren of the Dublin staple (1616-37 and 1664-1674):

[Dc 2 f. 285r]
The names of those that weare admitted bretherin of the staple the first of August 1616. Mr Michaell Chamberlayne, mayor of the staple, Mr Thady Duffe and Richard Brice constables.
James Bellew sworne and hathe paid iii s
William Floode sworne and hathe paid iii s
Richard Archbold sworne and hathe paid iii s
John Borran sworne and hathe paid iii s

The names of those that weare admitted bretherin of the staple 14 January 1616/7.
Fraunces Dowde sworne and hathe paid iii s
Robart Barnewall sworne and hathe paid iii s
George Tayellor sworne and hathe paid iii s
Thomas Shelton sworne and hathe paid iii s
Mr Richard Broune, alderman sworne and hathe paid iii s
Edward Tankard sworne and hathe paid iii s

---

[1] For the oath see Appendix III. The brethren of the Bristol staple swore a similar oath, see Rich, ed., *The Staple Court*, pp. 58-9.

[Dc 2 f. 284r]
The names of those that weare admitted brethren of the staple from July 1617. Mr Richard Forester maior... Mr Thady Duffe and Mr Patricke Gough constables.
Gerald Leach sworne and hathe paid 3s
Thomas Whitt the younger .....
Sir James Carroll, knight.....
Marten Forster......

[Dc 2 f. 283r]
The names of those that weare admitted brethren of the stappell from July 1618. Mr John Bennes maior... Mr Edward Gough and Mr Nicholas Kelley constables....
Edward Borran sworne and hath paid 3s
Thomas Clerk ....
Michaell Latten....
Thomas Lallor....
Edmund Woolff....

11 December 1618
Thomas Preston sworne and hath pd 3s and interest on.

18 January 1618/9
Thomas Chalenor sworne and hath paid 3s
James Byrn....
Ric. Savadg....

19 January 1618/9
Wm Weston......
Walter Fleming....
Patt Helun......
George Porter.....
Patt Doyn.....

[Dc 2/282v]
The names of those that weare admitted brethren of the staple. Sir James Carroll myere, Mr William Byshoppe and Mr Kelley constables.
Mr John Laney sworn and hath paid 3s
Walter Floode......

[Dc 2/282r]
The names of those that weare admitted brethren of the staple 5 Marche 1619/20. Mr Johne Laney mayor of the stapple, Mr Walter Usher and Mr Nicholas Keney constables.
Christopher Whitte sworn and hath paid 3s Irish
Walter Doyne...

Edward Fitzwilliames....
Johne Chamberlyne....
Nicholas Barrey....
Walter Chowsack[Cusacke]....
Robart Talouer [Taylor], the younger....
Thomas Fleminge.....
James Newgent.....
Nicholas Leous [Lewis].....
Edward Rolleick...

The names of those that weare admitted Brethren of the staple. Mr Edward Ball the maior, Xpofer Forster and Xpofer Handcocke being constables.
Mr Richard Wiggett alderman was sworne brother of ye same staple 9 Jan 1623/4 and paid a fine 3s
Allander Usher sworne and hath paid 3s Ir
Nicholas Skarly.......
Richard Rich......
Mary Fitzwilliams......

[Dc 2/281v]
Such as were sworne bretherne of the staple in maioralty of Mr Richard Wiggett, Mr Thomas Whyte and Mr Xpofer Whyte being constables.

19 July 1624
Adam Talbott, merchant, sworne and paid for a fine 3s ster

13 Oct 1624
Thomas Watherby, merchant, sworne and paid 3s ster
Mr George Jones was sworne and paid 3s ster
John Chivers merchant paid 3s ster

22 January 1625/6: Before Sir Tha: Duffe maior, Geo: Jones and Xpo: [Wolverston]
William Purssell sworne 3s st
John Jurdanne was sworn 3s st
John Quine was sworn 3s and 7s 6d for in trust on seven shillings & 6 pence

14 October 1626: Sir William Bushoppe maior of staple, Mr Geordge Johnes and Mr Willm Weston constables
William Higgine sworne 3s st
Geordge Russell 3s st
Walter Kennedie 3s st

15 January 1626/7
Mr Robart Arthor, shirife, admitted 3s st
Mr Walter Condran admitted 3s st

Mr William Waring admitted 3s st
Mr Christopher Ffild admitted 3s
David Begge admitted 3s
Adam Behan admitted 6s.8d and 3s [In margin] not paid yet
Edmond Hues admitted 5s and 3s

[Dc 2 f. 278r]
Willm Turnor maior stapill. Christopher Whitt and Nicholas Keninge constabilles 1627
Edmond Barnewall was grantyd to be a brother of the stapell the 17 of July 1626 and not sworne till nowe the 12 of September 1627 and so sworne and admyttyd brother of the stapill and payed 3s.

[Dc 2 f. 276r]
the 24 day of January 1627/8
Mr William Turnor maior of the staple, Christopher Whitt and Nicholas Kenne constables, thes brethren following weare admitted and sworne the daie aforesaid.
Paull Tornor—and hath paid 3s Ir
Bartholme Hall admitted and hath paid 3s ir
James Relie ......3s Ir

the 20 of January 1628/9
Mr Walter Usher maior of the staple, Mr Robert Arthoure and Mr Frauncis Dowde constables thes brethren foll: weare admitted and sworne the daie aforesaid.
Richard Gouldinge sworne and paid 3s st
Davide Bourcke ......3s st
Mr Robarte Bennett maior ....3s st

the 20 Aprill 1629
Mr Edward Jans maior of the staple, Mr Michaell Browne and Mr Thomas Shelton constables theise brethren following weare admitted and sworn.
James Fitzgerrald sworn and paied 3s st
Richard Barnewall ..... 3s st

[Dc 2 f. 275v]
Richard Dowde ......
Jaques Chrainne

[Dc 2 f. 274r]
The 24 January 1631/2
Sir Christopher Forster maior of the staple, Mr Charles Forster and Mr Willm Baggote constables theise bretherin followinge weare admitted and sworn the daye aforesaid.
Peter Quyn sworne and paid 3s st
Mr Sanckie Sylliard ......

[Dc 2 f. 273v]
24 Aprill 1632
The names of suche of the brethren as weare sworn to the staple in
Alderman Thome Evans yeare, Mr Sanckie Sylliard and Mr John Fleming
constables.
Imprimis Geordge Proudfoote sworne and paied 3s
Richard Barnewalle the younger ......
Christopher Turnor ......

Oct 1632
James Moore admitted, sworne and paied 3s
William Preston sworn and paied 3s
Geordg Plunckett ......
Richard Bennett ....

[Dc 2 f. 273r]
12 January 1632/3
The names of such of the brethrein as weare sworn to the staple in
Alderman Geordge Johns yeare beinge chosen in steed of Alderman
Thomas Evans deceased. Mr Sanckie Sylliard and Mr John Fleming consta-
bles.
Imprimis Thomas Nugent sworn and paid 3s
Richard Fleming .....
Patricke Reade .....
John Carbree ....
Mr Mathewe Terrell ......
Mr John Stanlie ....

21 October 1633
The names of suche of the brethren as weare sworn in alderman Johns
yeare to the staple, Mr Mathew Tyrrell and Mr Johne Stanly constables.
Mr Thomas Wackfield sworn and paied 3s
Robarte Lallor .....

23 January 1634/5
The names of suche of the brethren as weare sworn in alderman Edward
Arthure his yeare to the stapell. Mr Walter Kenedy and Mr Davie Begge
constables.
Patricke Jordan sworn and paid 3s

[Dc 2 f. 272v]
25 January 1637/8
The right hon[orable] James Wattsonn maior of this cittie admitted and
sworn a brother of the staple, and hathe paied 3s.

[Dc 3/App I]

Memorand that upon 25 January 1664/5 Thomas Johnson was admitted a brother of the staple paying 3 shillings fine.

[Same format for the following individuals]

Robert Mead

George Surdevill

Paul Delasaule

Barnard Vizard?

Francis Brewster

William Fullam

William Crosse

Thomas Whitmore

Edward Page

Henry Warren

Nathaniell Phillpott

George Stoughton

Christopher Lovett

Peter Ashenhurst

[Dc 3/App II]

25 Jan 1664/5 cont.

Henry Orsen

James Lees

Mr Richard Lawrence

Mr Timothy Grother

25 Jan 1665/6: These whose names heerafter follow were admitted brethern of the staple of the citty of Dublin for their fines of 3s apeece.

George Fisher obyt

William Eager

Walter Harris

George Nangle

Richard Houghton

25 Jan 1666/7 ...

Henry Aston

William Brookeing

John Cannon

Phillip Castleton

Robt Seacom

Walter Motley

John Fletcher

Thomas Eeely

John Elwood

25 Jan 1668/9
Mr William Gressingham
Mr John Linaker
Mr Giles Mee
Mr Thomas Huchinson
Mr Henry Aston
Mr Richard Warren
Mr Walter Hyde
Mr Thomas Goold
Mr Arthur Eccles
Mr Ralph Moxon
Mr Michaell Chreshan

[Dc 3/App III]

Noia fratr staple de civit Dublin hodie vivenc vigint
[blank]

[Dc 3/App V]

Noia fratr staple de civit Dublin hodie Vivenc vicesimo quarto die January
1669/70
Alderman

1656	Lewis Desmyniere Lord Mayor [Lord mayor is crossed out]
1626[sic]	Walter Kennedy mort. [crossed out]
	John Carbery mort. [crossed out]
1642	Wm Smith
1648	Mark Quine mort [crossed out]
	John Preston
	Peter Wybrant
1649	John Desmynieres
1650	Ridgley Hatfield mort. [crossed out]
1651	Ald Tigh mort [crossed out]
	Geo Gilbert
	Rich Croke obyt Jan 1670 [crossed out]
1652	John Cramorell
1655	Tho Hooke mort
	Daniell Hutchinson mort [crossed out]
	Chris Bennett
1656	John Forrest
1657	Enoch Reader
1659	Robt Deey
1660	Sir Daniell Bellingham mort [crossed out]
	Josua Allen
1663	John Totty
	Francis Brewster
	Christo Lovett

Thomas Jones
John Smith
Abell Ram

Sherriffes Peeres
1641   Lawrence Allen
1651   Mathew French
           Tho Springham obyt 23 Jan 1671 [crossed out]
           Samuell Saltonstall obyt 1671 [crossed out]
1653   Tobias Creamer
1656   Mynard Christian
           John Smith
           Richard Phillipps
1660   Elias Best
           William Brookes
1664   Robt Mead
           Geo Sardefield obyt 1670 [crossed out]
1666   Phillipp Castleton
           William Gressingham

[Dc 3/ App VI]
           John Linacre
           Giles Mee

[Dc 3/App VII]
Brethern of the staple elected and sworne
25 Jan 1623/4   Arlander Usher mort [crossed out]
1625   John Jordan mort [crossed out]
1641   William Martin
           James Cleere
           Oliver Barnewall
1651   Bice Phillipps
           John Eastwood
1656   John S:geant
           Jeromy Berstow
           Obadin Bradshaw obyt 1669 [crossed out]
           Simon Carrick
           Andrew Lloyd
           Charles Andrews mort
           John Dutton mort
1660   William Harris
           Samuell Dowty
           James Nowland
           Henry Reynolds
           John Kilburne

	Geo Stoughton
	Josua Rowlandson mort [crossed out]
1664	Thomas Johnson
	Paul Delasaule
	Barnard Vizard?
	William Fullam
	Thom Whitmore
	Edw Page
	Henry Warren
	Nath Phillpott
	Henry Orsen
	James Lees
	Rich Lawrence
1665	George Fisher mort
	William Eager
	Walter Harris
	Geo Nangle
1666	Richard Houghton
	William Brookeing
	Geo Kenedy
	John Cannon
	Robt Seacom
	Walter Motley
	John Fletcher
	John Elwood
1668	Tho Hutchinson
	Henry Aston

[Dc 3/App VIII]

	Richard Warren
	Walter Hyde
	Thomas Goold
	Arthur Eccles
	Ralph Moxon
	Michaell Chrishan
1669	John Howard
	Jonathan Northeast
	Samuel Cuthbert
	Gerrard Colley
	Robert Juce
	Thomas Speght
1670	Wm Haines mer
	Isaack Gill mer
	Charles Byrne mer
	Thomas Edwards mer

John Quelch mer
Henry Rowlandson mer
John Coyne mer
Richard Hanway mer
Rich Woodfall mer
Rich Huish obyt [crossed out]
1671 Philip Dauncey
William Taylor
Joseph Hawknall
Thomas Gernon
Mathew Bowen [crossed out]
George Fletcher
Nicholas Nolan
William Smith
Henry Stephens
Thomas Howard
1672 Thomas Clinton
Thomas Newton
Edward Robinson
Peter Ormsby
John Castleton
Patrick Redmond
1673 Rich Ward
John Knox
David Johnston [crossed out]
Richard Greenwood mer
1674 Sir Wm Davys knt
Wm Kenedy
Harbert Caine
Edw Bellew
Wm Sands
Frauncis Worrall
Nicholas White
Belew Dempsy
Peter Caine
Thomas Litchfield
Walter Prendergast
Isaack Ambros
Wm Fisher
Josua Huntington

STAPLE BONDS AND INDENTURES OF DEFEAZANCE
AND OATHS TAKEN BY
OFFICIALS OF THE DUBLIN STAPLE

Transcribed by Bridget McCormack and Éamonn Ó Ciardha

The mayors of the staple were empowered to take recognizances of debt incurred on the staple. The clerk of the staple then recorded these transactions in a register. These recognizances, known as statutes staple, were a form of registered bond by which the debtor(s) entered into a recognizance to pay the creditor(s) a fixed sum, at a given time, together with interest at 10%. The amount of the bond was not a record of the actual loan but security for the loan and was usually double the amount of the loan. These formulaic entries were recorded in English and the information they contain remains remarkably consistent between entries. For examples see Section A 1-4 (below). Increasingly indentures of defeazance, outlining a repayment schedule or the lands that secured the bond, accompanied these statutes staple and were also recorded by the clerk of the staple. For examples see Section B 1 (below).

Though they rarely survive, the debtor would also have entered into a recognizance for the outstanding amount. The mayor of the staple and one of the staple constables would have signed this recognizance and attached the seal of the staple (see Plate 1). These were usually in Latin and for an example, with an English translation, see Section C 1 (below). An indenture of defeazance, in English, usually accompanied the recognizance outlining a repayment schedule and the lands that secured the bond. For an example see Section C 2 (below).

If a debtor defaulted on repayment and he lived within the jurisdiction of the staple town, the mayor had the power to imprison him or to take possession of his moveable goods and his lands and to use them to repay the creditor. However in many cases, especially if the debtor lived outside the jurisdiction of the staple, the clerk of the recognizances certified the debt in the Court of Chancery. These entries were generally in Latin. For English examples see Section D 1-2 (below). The Chancery volumes often include lengthy memoranda and indentures of defeazance, in English, which outlined a repayment timetable and occasionally indicated why an individual wanted to borrow money in the first place. For examples see Section E 1-3 (below).

For a transcript of the oath taken by the mayor and constable of the Dublin staple see Section F 1 (below). For a transcript of the oath taken by the brethren of the Dublin staple see Section F 2 (below).

The Irish Statute Staple Books

SECTION A: Examples of statute staple bonds recorded on the Dublin Staple:[1]

A 1. During the reign of Elizabeth I[2]

Memorandum that the xxix March 1597 and in the xxxix year of the reign of our sovereigne Lady Queen Elizabeth Richard Boyle of Dublin gent did acknowledge make seal and deliver before the mayor and constables a bond of the staple of the sum of £150 current money of England unto Patrick Crosby of Mareborrugh in the Queen's Co. gent to be paid at his will and pleasure, the bond bereth date the day and year aforesaid.

A 2. During the reign of James VI and I[3]

Memorandum that the xxiiii day of December Anno Dm. 1603 and in the first year of the reign of our sovereigne lord King James I John King and John Binglie of Dublin gent did acknowledge make seal and deliver before the said maior and constables one bond of the staple of the number of twelve thousand ounces of good and pure silver plate or mettaill unto Sir James Dillon of Moymot knight to be paid at his will and pleasure the said bond bereth date the day and year aforesaid.

A 3. During the reign of Charles I[4]

Memorandum that the 24th day November 1627 and in the third year of the reign of our sovrign lord King Charles Patrick Comin of Ardnekelly in the county of Clare gent James Comin of Downebegg in the same county gent Tyrlagh O'Brien of Tullamore in the said county gent and Charles O'Connor of Laughcloven in the said county gent joyntly and severally did acknowledge make seal and deliver before the said maior and constables of the staple one bond of the staple of the sum of £100 ster currt money of and in England unto . . .William Creagh of Limbrick gent his executors or assignes at his or their will and pleasure as by the said bond of the staple bearing date which? their presence may appear.

A 4. During the reign of Charles II[5]

Memorandum that upon eight day of Ffeb in the year of our lord God one thousand six hundred and sixty six Abell Warren de Le Lodge in the county of Kilkenny esqr came before the said maior and constables and did acknowledge one bond of the staple of the sum of three hundred pounds good and lawful money of and in England unto Garrett Gold of Knockraghy in the county of Cork gent to be paid to the said Garrett Gold his executors administrators or assignes at his or their will and pleasure.

---

[1] Éamonn Ó Ciardha transcribed Sections A, B, D, and E.

[2] Dc 1 f. 3r (ID 17).

[3] Dc 1 f. 50v (ID 325).

[4] Dc 2 f. 100r (ID 1465).

[5] Dc 3 f. 52 (ID 2336).

SECTION B: Example of an indenture of defeazance recorded on the Dublin Staple:

B 1. Indenture of defeazance between Henry Martin (debtor) and James Nowland (creditor), 31 January 1667

Defeazance on this statute is that if the said Henry Martin his heires executors or administrators doe well and truly satisfy content and pay or cause to be well and truly satisfied contented and paid unto the said James Newland his executors administrators or assignes the sum £10 ster att or upon the 1st Aug next ennsueing the like sum of £10 ster at or upon the 1 Feb the next following and the sum of £210 sterling good and lawful money of and in England upon the 1st day of August which shall be in the year 1668 for and to the only...use and behalf of Thomas Whitchett and Samuell Whitchett sonnes of the said William Whitchett and Hester Whitchett then the said bond of the staple to be void otherwise otherwise to stand in full force and effect in lawe.[6]

SECTION C: Example of the staple bond and defeazance in possession of the debtor[7]

C 1. Bond, or recognizance, of the staple

Noverint vniversi per presentes me Johannem Gybbons de Clondalkan in comitatu Dublinensi generosum recognoscere coram Edmondo Devnish maiore Stapule ciuitatis Dubliniæ Nichola Barran et Waltero Galtrom constabulariis eiusdem Stapule teneri et per presentes firmiter obligari ffrauncisco Taylor de Dublinia, alderman, in quadringenti libris currente monete Anglie pro lanis corriis et plumbis ab eodem ffrauncisco Taylor emptis et receptis, Solvendum eidem fffauncisco, executoribus vel assignatis suis ad voluntates suas. Ad quam quidem solucionem bene et fideliter faciendam obligo me heredes executores et assignatos meos ac omnia bona et catalla mea mobilia et immobilia viua et mortua tam presencia quam futura vbicumque fuerent inventa terrae tenementa et hereditamenta mea in pena Statute Stapule predictae et in articulis in predicto Statuto expressis iuxta vim formam et effectum Statute Stapule predictae in hac parte editum et provisum. In cuius rei testimonium tam sigillum officii Stapule predictae ad meum rogatum quam sigillum meum presentibus sunt appensa. Datum xv die marcii anno domini 1591 et anno regni domine Regine nostrae Elizabeth que nunc est xxxiiii°.

John Gybbons is X marcke.

(*Seal of John Gybbons*)   (*Seal the Staple*)

---

[6] Dc 3 f. 51 (ID 2334).

[7] The transcription and translation of C1 and the transcription of C2 have been taken from W. G. Strickland, 'The Ancient Official Seals of the City of Dublin' in *Journal of the Royal Society of Antiquaries*, 53: 2 (1923), pp. 129-131. The original deeds do not appear to have survived.

The contractions in the original have been expanded. The following is a translation:-

Know all (people) by (these) presents that I John Gybbons of Clondalkan in the County of Dublin gentleman recognise before Edmond Devenish, mayor or the Staple of the City of Dublin Nichaolas Barran and Walter Goltrom constables of the said Staple, that I am held and by (these) presents firmly bound to Francis Taylor of Dublin, alderman, in four hundred pounds current money of England for wool, leather and lead bought and received from the said Francis Taylor to be paid the said Francis, his executors or assigns at their pleasure, to the making which payment well and faithfully I bind myself my heirs executors and assigns and all my goods and chattels moveable and immoveable, living and dead, as well present as to come wherever they may be found, my lands, tenements and hereditaments under pain of the Statute of the Staple aforesaid and in the articles in the said Statute expressed according to the force form and effect of the said Statute of the Staple aforesaid in this behalf published and provided. In witness whereof as well the seal of the office of the Staple aforesaid at my request as also my seal are appended to (these) presents. Given the 15th day of March in the year of the Lord 1591 and in the thirty-fourth year of the reign of our lady Queen Elizabeth who now is.

John Gybbons his marcke.

C 2. The indenture of defeazance accompanying the staple bond

This Indenture of defeasance made the fiften day of Marche in the year of our lord god 1591 and in the thirti and foure yeare of the Raigne of our soveraigne Ladye Qwene Elizabeth Betwixt ffrauncis Taylor of Dublin merchaunte on the one partye & John Gibbons of Clondollkan in the countie of Dubline gentl. on the other partie, Witnessthe that wheare the saide John his heyres ex. And assig. standethe bounde to the said ffrauncis by a staple bond in the som of foure hundrethe pounds ster. currante mony of England taken & acknowledged before Edmond Dewnysh mayor of the staple, Nicholas Barrane and Walter Galtrem constables of the same staple, bearing date with these presents- Nevertheless hit ys covenanted graunted & agreed betwixt the saide ffrauncis and the said John, that yf the said John, his heires feoffes grauntors recoverers or assignes that are or shalbe, from tyme to tyme, & all & every psone or psons, seysed or to be seased of the saide John is lands tenementts or heareditamentts, In the cittie of dublin or liberties thereof, to the vse of the saied John & his heires or to the vse of his heires in taile generall or speaciall, do & shall make, cause or pcure to be made, & suffer to be made to the saied ffrauncis his heyres or assignes, or to such as the saied ffrauncis his heyres or assig' shall nominate or apoint to the vse of the saied ffrauncis & his heires a goode pfitt suere & indefeasible estate in lawe, by fine, feoffment recovery or otherwyse, of a howse in the highstreate of Dublin with the aportenauncs, bondinge to the ram lane alias picotts lane. In the pishe of St Audeons within the said cittie aforsaid, And yf also the saied ffrauncis according to the estate aforesaide, & accordinge the true meaninge of this bargaine shall Quietlie hold, have & enjoye the saied howse wth the aportinauncs, Immediatlie after the recoverie therof from such as detainethe the same, from the saide John & his heyres, that then wthowt delay the saide John his heyres feoffes & assignes shall make an Assured estate In fee simple to the vse of the saide ffrauncis his heyres and assignes for eaver, & the said Johne his heyres ex', & assign' shall at the wyll and pleasure of the saied ffrauncis his heyres and assignes psecute and comence such accions or accions suit or suits, in any her maties courtts, for the recovery of the said howse wth the apurtenauncs from tyme to tyme, and at all tymes so ofte as the learned counsell of the saiede ffrauncis his heares or assig' shall devise or advise at the pper costs and chardgs of the saied ffrauncis & his assignes, Also if the saide John do vpon his corporall othe vpon the evangelist deliver to the saied ffrauncis his heires or assignes, for his better securitye all such evidences scripts and muniments that now he hathe conserning the pmisses in his possesion or that eny tyme heare after shall come to his possesion or costodie, & Also yf that he the saide John his feoffes or assignes hathe not passed before the date of these psents over his or theire right tittlle state or vse in the pmisses or in eny pte or pcell therof, to eny psone or psons whatsoever by any conveyance or assuraunce in lawe, And also yf he the saiede John his heires feoffes or assignes do not pmitte or do eny acte or acts to the delay or hendrence of the recoverye of the pmisses That then the saide bond of the Staple to be voide Other wyse to stand & remaine in full force and effect in lawe. In wittnesse whereof the pties aforesaid have to these psents Interchangablye sett theyr hands & sealls the day and year first abowe written.

John gibbons X is marcke.

The deed has the following Endorsement:

P'sent at the ensealinge and deliverie herof by the wthin named John Gibbons, vnto the wthin mencioned ffrauncis tailor, and when the said John did sweare vpon the holie evangelist to deliver vnto the saide ffrauncis all the evidencs that nove he hath conserning the wthin mencioned land and also to deliuer all such evidences censerning the pmisses vnto the siad ffrauncis as at eny tym here after shall com to his possession or costody, and to do such othor things as by his othe wthin mencioned, he is to do and obsarue, the psons whose names ensueth.

Edmond Dewnys maior stap'll

Nicho' Barraun, constabll ye stabl'

Willm Goughe present

SECTION D: Examples of statute staple bonds certified into Court of Chancery:

D 1. Staple bond certified into the Court of Chancery, 26 June 1656

Be it know unto all men by these presente that I Phillipp Fferneley of the city of Dublin esqur. have acknowledged before Thomas Hooke maior of the staple of the city of Dublin, John Desminieers and Owen Jones constables of the sd staple to bee bound and by the statute of the staple firmly obliged unto Thomas Jones of the foresaid city of Dublin esqr. in the sum of six hundred pounds sterl for wooll hides and leade bought and received from the said Thomas Jones, to be paid unto the said Thomas Jones, his executors or assignes at his or their will and pleasure. To the wch. payment well and truly to be made I doe bind mee my heires executors and administrators and all my goods and chattells, moveable and unnmovable, liveing and dead, as well present as to come wheresoever they shall be found, my lands tenements and hereditaments, in the penalty of the said statute of the staple and in the articles of the said statute of the staple expressed, according to the forme force and effect of the said statute in that case made and provided. In witness whereof as well the seal of the office of the staple aforesaid, at my request as mine own are to these present affixed. Dated this day of June in the year of

Phil. Ferneley

Entred the 26 June 1656.[8]

D 2. Staple bond certified into the Court of Chancery, 26 August 1676

Be it known unto all men by these prsents that I Gerrald Ffay of Dernegarah in the county of Westmeath esqre. have acknowledged before Sir Joshua Allen knt. mayor of ye staple of ye city of Dublin John Castleton esqre. and George Kenedy merchant constables of the sd staple to bee bound and by ye statute of the staple firmly obliged unto Richard Ward of the city of Dublin merchant in the sum of three hundred fifty seven pounds six shills. for wooll hides and lead bought and reced. from the said Richard Ward to bee paid unto the sd Richard Ward his exrs. adms. and asignes att his or their will and pleasure To the payment well and truly to be made and done I bind me for the whole my heyres, exrs admrs all my goods and chattles moveable and immoveable living and dead as well present as to come wherever they shall be found, my lands tenemts and hereditamts whatsoever in ye penalty of ye said statute according to ye force, forme and effect of ye said statute of ye staple in that case made and provided. IN WITTNESSE whereof as well the seal of the office of the staple aforesaid at my request as my own seale are to these psents affixed DATED the ffifteenth day of July in the twenty-eight year of the reign of our soveraigne lord Charles the second by the grace of God of England

---

[8] BL, 19,843 f. 175 (ID 3061).

Scotland Ffrance and Ireland King Defender of the faith and in the year of our lord God One thousand six hundred and seventy six

Gerrald Ffay

Signed sealed and ded. in the presence of us Phil. Croft
Wm. Hough [his marke]
Anthony Harrison
Intr 26 die. Augti. Ano. Dm. 1676.[9]

SECTION E: Examples of indentures of defeazance recorded in the Court of Chancery:

E 1. Indenture of defeazance between Sir Lucas Dillon (debtor) and John Boswell (creditor), 4 August 1653

This indenture of defeazance made the fowrth day of August in the yeare of our Lord God one thousand six hundred and fifty three. Between John Boswell of Donecoghy in the County of Sligoe esquire of the one parte, And Sr. Lucas Dillon of Loghlynn in the County of Roscommon Knt. of the other parte. Wittnesseth that whereas the said Sir Lucas Dillon hath acknowledged sealed and delivered before Richard Tigh maior of the staple of the city of Dublin Ridgley Hattfeild and Richard Heyden constables of the said staple one bond of the staple of the sum of ffower hundred fforty and eight pounds sterling unto the said John Boswell his executors or assignes at his, or their will pleasure, as by the said bond of the staple bearing date with these presents., more at large appeareth. It is nevertheless covenanted, graunted, condiscended, and agreed upon by and between the said pties. And the condition of the said bond of the staple is such that if the said Sir Lucas Dillon, his executors administrators or assignes doe, and shall well and truely content satisfie and pay, or cause to be paid unto the said John Boswell his executors, administrators or assignes, at once whole and entire payment the inst and full sum of two hundred and twenty four and fourteen shillings sterl, at by or before the three and twentieth day of Sept next and immediately ensuing the date hereof without fraud suite or coven That then the said bond of the staple to be voide otherwise to stand and remaine on full force and effect in lawe. In wittness whereof the pties aforesaid have to these presents. . . interchangeably their hands and seales the day and year . . . above written.

Lucas Dillon

The defezance above mentioned was entered 13 Jan 1653/4
Signed, sealed and delivered in the presence of
R. Tigh maior
Richard Heyden
William Clife constables[10]

---

[9] BL, 19,844 f. 105 (ID 3232). For the original transaction on the Dublin staple, see ID 2673.
[10] BL, 19, 843 f. 134a (ID 2983).

E 2. Indenture of defeazance between Sir Maurice Eustace (debtor) and Dame Elizabeth Purbeck (creditor), 9 April 1663

This indenture made the 9th of Aprill in the year of our Lord God one thousand and six hundred and sixty three in the fifteenth yeare of the reign of our soveraigne Lord Charles the second by the grace of God of England, Scotland Ffrance and Ireland Kinge Defender of the Faith between the Rt. Honble Lady Elizabeth Viscountess Purbecke of the one part and the Right Honble Sir Mawrice Eustace Kt. Lord Chancellor of Ireland of the other part, Witneseth that Whereas the said Sr Mawrice Eustace by one writing of Recognizance bearing date wth these prsents made according to the statute provided and sett forth for the recovery of debt sealed taken and acknowledged before Sir George Gilbert Kt. mayor of the staple of the city of Dublin, George Hewlett and William Whitshed constables of the said staple is and standeth bound unto the said Elizabeth Viscountesse in the full and just sume of six hundred pounds sterling of current and lawful money of England to be paid to the said Elizabeth Viscountess Purbeck her executors, administrators or assignes at her and their will and pleasure as by the same being thereunto had it doth and may more at large appeare. Neverthelesse it is concluded covenanted and agreed upon by and betweene the said partys to the presents and the said Elizabeth Viscountesse Purbecke is contented and pleased and doth for us her heires executors and administrators covenant grant to and with the said Sr Mawrice Eustace his executors administrators and asignes in mannor and form following That is that if the said Sr Mawrice Eustace his heires and administrators doe and shall well and truely observe performe fullfill pay and keep all and singular the covenants grannts articles, provisoes, payments and agreements wch on the part and behalfe of himself the said Sr Mawrice Eustace his heires executors and administrators and every of them or ought to be observed, performed, fulfilled paid and kept contained and specified in one paire of indentures bearing even date wth these presents made or expressed to bee made between the said Sr Mawrice Eustace of the one part, and the said Elizabeth Viscountess Purbecke of the other part in all thinges according to the tennor effect and true intentions and meaninge of the said indenture that then and in such case the said writing of Recognizance of six hundred pounds shall be utterly voyd, frustrate and of none effect to all intents and purposes as if the same had never been made. In wittnesse whereof the said party to these presents have hereunto interchangably sett their hands and seales dated the day and year first above written

Signed sealed and delivered in the presence of us

      George Gilbert mayor staple
      William Whitshed
      Ant. Morgan constables of the staple

Int 9 May 1663[11]

---

[11] BL, 15, 635 f. 103 (ID 3440).

E 3. Acknowledgment by Martha Delaney that an outstanding debt has been paid, 29 October 1705

To Edward Richardson esqr. one of the six clkes. of the high court of chancery in Ireland or to any of the said six clkes of the sd court of chancery.

Whereas Daniell Byrne late of the citty of Dublin taylor deced. and Sr Gregory Byrne Barrt. son of the said Daniell did on or about the 10th day of July wch. was in the year 1674 enter into and acknowledge one bond of the staple of the penalty of four hundred and eighty pounds ster before John Tottie Knt. then mayor of the staple of the citty of Dublin and Henry Aston and Richard Warren constable of ye said staple whereby then ye said Daniell and Sr Gregory bound themselves their exrs. admrs. joyntly and severally and their and every of their lands and tennets. goods and chattles for ye true paymt. of two hundred and forty pounds sterling unto Gideon Delanne late of the city of Dublin gent deced. wch. bond or statute staple was according to the statute in that behalfe duely entered and enrolled wth the clke of ye recognizances and statute staple in the said high court of chancery as by ye inrollment or record thereof may att large app. and Whereas part of the estate of Walter Byrne esqr. grandson of the said Daniell and son of John Byrne esqr. deced. hath been extended for ye said debt by meanes whereof the sd debt and all interest due for ye same and all costs and charges relateing thereto have been fully satisfied and paid. KNOW all men by these prtents. yt I Martha Delaune of ye city of Dublin wid. ye surviving exr. of the said Gideon Delaune do acknowledge that full satisfaction and payment is made of all the said debt interest cost and charges and therefore I the said Martha do by these prsents. fully and irrevocably impower ye said Edwr. Richardson or any other of ye six clkes of the said High Court of chancery to acknowledge satisfaion. of the said debt bond or statute staple upon ye inrollment of record thereof and for you or any of you so seeing this shall be your sufficient warrant and discharge irrevocable. Wittness my hand and seal the 29 Oct 1705 in ye 4th year of the reign of our soveraigne Lady Queen Anne.

Martha Delanne

Wittness present
Wm Purefoy
James Brown[12]

---

[12] B.L. 19, 844 f. 30a (ID 3153).

SECTION F: Oaths taken by officials of the Dublin staple:[13]

F 1. Oath taken by the mayor and constables of the Dublin staple[14]
14 February 1554: Anno Regnoru Phill et Mariæ primo et secundo

The oath of the maior and constables of the staple given by
Mr Bartholome Ball, maior

You shall swere that you shall well and truelie serve your soveraigne Lord the king and our soveraigne Lady the Queene, in the office of maior and constables of the staple of this Cittie of Dublin, as long as you shall abide in the office aforesaid, and well and truelie you shall demeane the Brethren of the said staple without doeing them extortion, yee shall minister Justice to all ffolks as well to ritch as poore, you shall [d]espuit noe mans right contrary to the lawes and ordinances of the staple, yee shall truely and uprightlie observe support and mentain the lawes statutes and ordinances of the staple in all points, you shall suffer noe person to violat or breake them to your knowledge and power, yee shall not conceale any thinge wrought to the contrary of ye same ordinances. Theis and all other things appertaining to the office of maior and constables of the staple, yee shall rightlie and justlie execut and doe to your power, soe God you helpe and all saints and by that Booke.

The maior and constables of the staple have for every obligation of one hundred pounds or under for every pound a halfepenny and of every obligation above a hundred for every pound a farthen.

F 2. Oath taken by the Brethren of the Dublin staple[15]

The oath of a brother of the staple

You shall sweare on that booke that you shall truly and rightly observe, support and maintaine the Lawes statutes and ordinances of the staple in this citty of Dublin in all points. You shall suffer noe person to violate or breake them to your knowledge and power. You shall not conceale any thing wrought to the contrary of the said staple and duly attend the summons of the maior and constables of the said staple for the time being alsoe you shall not absent yourselfe on St Paules Day but be present at the election of the maior and constables (if you have not a lawfull excuse) Theis and all other lawfull points belonging to a brother of the staple you shall observe to your power so God you helpe and by the contents of that booke.[16]

---

[13] Transcribed by Bridget McCormack.

[14] Dc2/281r. This oath is also contained in front of Dc3 but the reference to the Lady Queen is omitted, and the words 'and all saints' have been struck out.

[15] Dc3 Oaths.

[16] The brethren of the Bristol staple swore a similar oath, see Rich, ed., *The Staple Court*, pp. 58-9.

Clerk of the Recognizance of the staple[17]

'The oath that I took when I entred upon the execution of the clke and decrees office. As followeth vizt:

You shall swear by the holy evangelist well and truly to execute the office of the clke of the decrees of recognizance of his majties his high court of chancery in Ireland according to the best of yr skill and knowledge. And soe help you god. . .'

[17] In the front of BL, Add MSS 19,843.

APPENDIX IV:

REGULATION OF TRADE
Transcribed by Bridget McCormack and Éamonn Ó Ciardha

The Irish staple, which dated from the thirteenth century, was initially established to regulate the trade of basic, or staple, goods such as wool and hides which could only be sold to foreign merchants in designated 'staple' towns—originally Dublin, Waterford, Cork and Drogheda. Throughout the seventeenth century the staple towns—which expanded to include Carrickfergus, Derry, Galway, Kilkenny, Limerick, New Ross, Sligo, Wexford, and Youghal—continued to do this. However only details concerning the regulation of trade for the Dublin staple appear to have survived. All three Dublin staple volumes contain permits to ship staple goods, especially wool and salt hides (Section A below); lists of customs dues (Section B below); and disciplinary hearings of merchants and aldermen, who had infringed staple regulations (Section C below). With the exception of Dc1, where this information appears throughout the volume, this was recorded at the back of the volume and is reproduced here as it appears in the original volumes.

SECTION A: Permits issued by the staple:[1]

[Dc 1 f. 35v (ID 233)]
'The entry of the 'Constane of Kerlade' of Skotland. . . under god John Tenant the 28 January 1601/2. Permit John Kill and John Tyrell alderman [sic] to lode abord the sayd shipp one laste and four diker salt hydes'. 'Permit Robt Kyle skotcshman to lod. . . the 'Constante for Kerkade' the number of one laste and four diker hyde boght of Mr John Tyrell alderman the 28 Jan 1601/2.' 'Permit Thomas Plunkett of Dublin merchant to lode abode ? Under god ? & laste of salted hyde 30 Jan 1601/2.' 'Permit John Tyrell ald to lod aborde the 'Speedwell of Dublin' 30 dikers salted hyds & 9 dikers dry hides 1 Fe 1601/2.' 'Permit Thomas Banth of Carlingford to load aborde the 'Crostant of Kircade' one laste of salted hides boght of Mr Panting and one last of salted hides boght of Pa: Clensher? ? Of Feb 1601/2.' '[Permit] Thomas Dilen Dub merchant, aborde 'the town of Dur', 4 March 1601/2, 2 last salted hyde.' '[Permit] Thomas Walsh of Waterford, aborde 'Abot of Fethon', 3 last salt hides 11 March 1601/2. Salt hides abord 'Abot of Waterford' 2 last & diker salt.' '[Permit] John Rath aborde ? 8 diker salt hyde 11 March 1601/2.' '[Permit] John Babtyst abord 'Lavanter of Turnes' in Bryttan 4 last dry hyde.' In the margin are the following: 'George Roch aborde the 'Mary of Carnarvan' 6 ?.' 'Peter Ges? Of Flathers aborde 'Nightingall of Flughens' 9 dikers salt hy[de]s boght of

[1] Transcribed by Éamonn Ó Ciardha.

Ja: Tyrell.' 'Tho Plunkett the 'Johnas of Weixford' v last salf hyde & I last dry hyed 9 August 1602.' '26 August 1602 Mr Chamberlen aborde barke 'Balenger of Croseke' 4 last of salt & dry hydes'.

[Dc 1 f. 44r (ID 281)]

'Permit Denis Daniell of Crosswick to load aborde the 'Denis of Crossick' aforesaid ten dicker of sault hides the 14 Feb 1602/3.'

[Dc 1 f. 45v (ID 290)]

'Permit James Jans alderman merchant of the staple to loade aborde the 'Angell of Dublin' 24 dicker salt hides the 12th Aprill 1603.' 'Permit Nicholas Queatrod merchant of the staple to loade aborde the said shipp.'

[Dc 1 f. 47ar (ID 306)]

'Permit Christopher Colman merchant of the staple to loade aborde the 'Dennis of Croswick' 8 dicker salt the 19 of July 1603.'

[Dc 1 f. 48r (ID 310)]

'Permit John Donndee merchant of the staple to loade aborde the 'Perrot of Crosswick' 12 dicker sault hides, the 6th Aug 1603'.

[Dc 1 f. 48r (ID 312)]

'Permit James Terrell merchant of the staple to loade aborde the good shipp the '? Of Burnt Island' in Scotland 2 last decker? Of salt hides 27 Aug 1603.' 'Permit Nicholas Queatrod merchant . . . 2 last decker salt hides 26 Aug.' 'Permit Nicholas Queatrod merchant..'Sonday of Fetherd' 3 last decker salt hides 30 Aug 1603.'

[Dc 1 f. 52r (ID 330)]

'Permit John Governe of St Analose to lode abord the 'Danyell' of that town 5 last salt hydes 23 Feb 1603/4.'

[Dc 2 f. 284r]

The 14 Aprill 1627
Richard Quyne of Dublin marchant and also stapler dothe enter xi fardelles of shipp[sheep] skeynes in the unitt/vuitt of Forbey—3d.
Willm Husone mason bound for Fynpolle and ped for entry.

[Dc 2 f. 282v]

24th daye January 1627
Mr Richard Quyne stapler entered 19 fardelles of the shep skeynes abord the benet of Forinbey for Chester Watter pd. 3d.

[Dc 2 f. 274r]

Goods entered before Sir Christopher Forster maior of the staple, Charles Forster and Wm Baggot constables of the same staple this 11 Feb 1630.

Permitt Geo: Fletcher to loade aborde Edward Warninghams shipp six fardelles of sheepe fell and one bagg of woole which weare bought of James Bellew and Henry Orphy merchants this 11 of February 1630.

Permit Robert Morgen to loade abourde the good barke called the 'Blessing of Corke', 4 baraylls of tallow, 2 packs of yarne, 6 barraylls of beek, 1200 of flocks for that he hath payd uppon his submission five shillings English dated the 25 Aprill 1631.

Permit Ralphe Whitaker to load aboorde the 'Elizabeth of Lerpole' 500 stons of woole and 500 waight of locks for that he hath pd uppon his submission 5/8.

[Dc 2 f. 273v]
Permitt Geordge Proudfoote to enter aboorde the 'Ann of Elinor' and the 'Abraham of Elinore' the number of 60 packe of woole and flocke als locke.

SECTION B: Customs dues:[2]

[Dc 2 f. 277v]
Customes due to this cittie by act of parliament made the elevent yeere of the reigne of Queene Elizabeth in the 10 Chapter for thes goods following that shall be transport by stranger[s] [In margin] See Boulton in his Irish Statutes.

for each 1lb of beefe casked or unkasked	1d st
for each stone of woole and flocks	4s st
for each 1lb of yarne flax or wool yarne	8d st
for each sheep fell, got fell, caulf fell	3d st
for each read deere fell	20d st
for each fallow deare fell	18d st
for each stone of tallow	18d st
for each pound of wax	3d st
for each pound of butter	3d st
and for eche dicker of cow hyd tanyd or untanyd	——

SECTION C: Disciplinary hearings:

[Dc 2 f. 287r]
Staple the jurie for Mr Charles Forster
John Jurdan
Edmond Hughes
Xpofer Fyelds
Bartholme Halle
Peeter Quynn

[2]Bridget McCormack transcribed Sections B and C.

Richard Barnewalle, Sir
Edward Delamare
Edmond Hamlinge
Geordge Taylor
Robart Barnewalle
Arlander Usher
Edmond Ffyanne
Stephine Usher
Stephine Whitt
Peeter Foorde
James Doyne
The 12 Aprill 1640: The Jurie above named are for ther default and noe attendance fyned by the maior and constables in 40 sh apece.

[Dc 2 f. 280r]
Nomina Iur ad inquirend pro dno: rege in Cur: stapulæ Civitat Dublin.
John Moore merchant
Thomas Shelton, merchant
Thomas Wetherby, merchant
Xpofer Brice, merchant
Wm Baggott, merchant
Nicholas Lewes, merchant
James Nugent, merchant
James Bellew, merchant
Walter Doyne, merchant
Edmont Fyan, merchant
John Begg, merchant
James Byrne, merchant
Peter Drew, merchant
Edwd: Fitzwilliams, merchant

Inquisitio capta apud Theolonin civitat Dublin infra Com: civitat Dublin et franches eiusd in Cur stapulæ dict civitat fecund cons: eiusd civitat Coran Thadeo Duffe milite Maiore stapulæ Civitat Dublin Georgio Jones et Xpofero Wolferston Constabular eiusd stapulæ die Joins vizt. xxvii die Octobr A. dni: 1625. A[nno] qd regni regis Caroli primo. Per sacramt: probor et legal: homin: suprascriptor stapule predict.

Qui Iurat dic supersacramt: suid qd omes: subsequentes occupauer mrchandiz stapulæ et qd no sunt m'cat stapulæ nec aliquis eor est m'cat stapulæ, ac transgress sunt et contrabetuer statut et ordinat stapule predict in ea parte eddit et provis.

[Compt—in margin] Peter Wibrand of St Patricks street neere Dublin for buying of hides and other staple wares, not being free of the said staple and within the said staple by way of merchandizing transporting the same into parts beyond seas contrary etc and for not serving the same to the said maior and constables nor entring them.

Xpr Bure of the same for the like.

John Johnson als Hubbart for the like

Jaques Caymans for the like

Leonard deLoge for the like

Thomas Ellis for the like

Peter Bodwyn for the like

Henry Lemon for the like

Quyntin Brocke for the like

John Crafford for the like

John Greames for the like

[Dc 2 f. 279v]

Thomas Blieth for the like

Allexander Lesty for the like

John Kitt & Wm Kitt of Glostershire for the like

John Callard for the like

James Watson for the like

Phillipp Watson for the like

Wm Higgin for the like [In margin] poinse in gra £3

Robt Lalor for the like [In margin] sub. se. fined 10s

John Jordan for the like [In margin] Fined £3st

Thomas Geegin for the like

Martin Marty for the like

James Fyan for the like

Richard Ball for the like

Wm Locke for the like

Rich: Roch for the like [In margin] disch: for he is abrothe

Thomas Hamlin for the like

Edmond Hoare for the like

Garrott Neaell for the like

Robt Plunckett for the like

George Dowdall for the like

James Archbold for the like

Christop: Ffield for the like

James Fitzgerrald for the like

Symon Orpy for the like

Keadagh Mageoghegan for the like [In margin] fined 10s

Thomas Dillon for the like

Robart Dillon for the like

Dorby Sheman, tanner, for buying hids and other staple ware or being free stapler.

John Dillon for the like

Pierce Boe for the like

John Quyrke, weaver, for the like

Rose Magabe, glover, for the like
Robt Sherlocke of the Naas for the like
Wm Kelly of the same for the like
Thomas Sherlocke of the same for the like
Thomas Enos of the same for the like
Morrish Enos of the same for the like
Patricke Kena of the same for the like
James Connor of the same for the like
Walter Ash and Wm Kena of the same of the like.

[Dc 2 f. 279r]
Patrick Begg of the Navan for the like.
John Begg of the same for the like
Hugh Kent ......
George Cusake ....
George Travers .....
Wm Reyly
Edmond Maning .....
James Maning .....
Christopher Maning ....
Peter Tyrrell of Athboy for the like
Thomas Tyrrell of the same for the like
Phillip Duffe ....
Richard Browne ....
Richard Lalour ....
Thomas Groghegan ....
Thomas Begg .....
James Malone of Trim for the like
John Malone ....
James Gorry.....
John Nugent......
Henry Stafford of Mullengare for the like
John Rilling of the same of the like
Richard Nelan ....
James Nolan
Wm Mortemer
Dionis Carnan
Nicholas Casy
Wm Chamberline
Thomas Chamberline
Dionis Genner
Morgan Hughes
Morish Moghan
Tho: Nealan and Nich: Nealan
Edward Bettit
James Crisell

[Dc 2 f. 278v]
Nicholas Tyrrell and Lawrence Fraine of Killoken for the like
Patrick Meagh of Wickloe for the like
Henry Fitzgerrald
Edward Arthor
John Joyce
Peter Whyte
Wm Kelly of Luske for the like
Owin Duffe of Rathouth for the like
Michaell Hollywood
Patricke Murcho
Teige O'Ruoirke
Hugh Birond
Clement Owins of Kilcott for the like
Symon Owins
John Kelly
Ambrose White
Stephen Whyte
Edmond Chamberline of the same for the like
Robt Whyte of Lucan for the like
Abraham Euer, glover, of Dublin for the like
Stephen Cooke of the same for the like
Wm Scott .....
Bartholme Jry...

28 March 1627
Willm Turnor maior of the stapill, Nicholas Keynge and Xpofer Whit
constables of the same did cause Thome Borane sargant of the mace to
areste 11 packes of shypes sheynes lodyd at the krane at Dublin bound for
Chester with Randall Morgane of Chester who bought the same of Larance
Usher and James Bedlow marchants of Dublin contrary to the lawes of the
stapill and statuts, they the byeres did sybmytt and ped a fyne.

[Dc 2 f. 278r]
About the 10 August 1627
James Watterstone, lether dreser and a freemane of Dublin, haveing
sodene for dying above xxiii bags wolle beinge a stapler thes goods was
arestyd by Thome Borane one of the Watter balef for the mayor and
constables of the staple and he submyttyd and ped a good fyne for his
wronge doinge.

A merchant of Brystowl was also then arestyd for xii bages of wolle bound
for Brystowl beene at new crane and he submyttyd and ped a fyne to the
maior and constalbes of the sayd stapill.

Mr Dyott: of Londone for the caringe of shepp fell and wolle for sall for
and bought som of brothers fro[m] Gallwaye and of the stapelers ther and
submyttyd ther and ped a small fyne, the said month of August 1627.

12 September 1627
James Euer, Skottsmarchant beinge questyonyd for shep fell wolle and
lamb fell submyttyd and ped for his intrudinge on the stapill

[Dc 2 f. 277v]
About the 2 October 1627: Thomas Turnor of St Patricke street beinge
arestyd of his goods by Thome Borane sargant of the mace by derectyon of
the mayor and constabilles of the stapill for fifty bages of wolle he
compleyened to the Lord Depty: the Depty compellyd the wolle to passe in
regard of this liscence given Turnor for the same and left the stapill to take
their Remeyd at Comon lawe: and would not have his lycence contradictyd
in saying wolle or any other prohibitt wares the they were stapill wares.

[Dc 2 f. 277r]
A true and infallible president for indicements heanceforth generallie for
to bee observed: sett downe and obtained by the right honble Sir Richard
Bolton Lo: Chiefe Baron his ma:ties seargeant and other learned consellors
at lawe.

Inquisitio capta apud theolonu civit Dublin et infra Comit civit Dublin et
franches eiusdem In Curia stapl dict civit iuxta consuetudinem eiusdem
civit coram Gulielmo Turnor maior stapul dict civit Christpohero Whitt et
Nicholas Kennyn constabl eiusdem stapulæ. Die 15 Marty Anno regni dmi
regis Caroli secundo Per sacramento proborum et legalium hominum dicta
stapulæ.

Qui Iurati dicunt super sacramentu suu quod Petrus Weybran alias
Peterson de St Patricis iuxta Dublin, 13 die Aprilis Anno regis Domini
nostri regis Caroli Angliæ, Scotiæ, Fraunciæ, et Hiberniæ secundo apud
Dublin in portu civit Dublin infra Comit civit. Dublin et infra stapulam
eiusdem civit per viam merchandiz: onerauit in quadam Naui/Navi viginti
Decades alias Anglice dickars corior: salsorum valor £40 ster eademq: Coria
die et anno dict transportauit in transmarinas partes contra forma statuti in
huiusmodi casu provis et ulterius dicunt quod dict Petrus Weybran alias
Peterson in tempore transportationis dict coriora non fuit mercat. stapl
dict et Ulterius dicunt qd. dictus Petrus Weybran non monstrauit dict coria
nec eorum aliqd. dicto. maiori aut constapl nec eorum alicui nec aliquam
Intraconem fecit de predictis corys in stapula præfat nec aliquam licentiam
habuit de prefat maiori aut constabl aut de eorum aliquo ad mercandum
aut ad transportandum dicta Coria aut eoru aliqd. Et super hoc preceptum
fuit per perfat maior et constabl. dict. stapl. vice-comiti civitat Dublin
predictæ quod.

Peter Weybran alias Peterson hath transported such a day of the month
such a year soe many dickers of hides, in such a ship as doth appeare by the
certificat out of his maties custome hous. [Initialled] P.T.

[Dc 2 f. 275r]

Inquisico Capt apud theolon civitat Dublin et infra com civitat Dublin, et franches eiusd in cur staple dict civit iuxta consuetud eiusd civit cora Edwardo Jans maior stapul dict civitat, Miche Browne, et Thoma Shelton constabul euisd stapul nono die Marty An: regni dni regis Caroli quarto. Per sacrament probor et leglium ho:ium dcæ stapulæ.

Qui Iurat dic sup. Sacrament suu qd Petrus Weybrand als Peterson de St Patricio iuxta Dublin 19 February A: regni Dni nostri Regis Caroli Angl, Scot, Franc, et Hibnie quarto apud Dublin, in portu Civitat Dublin infra Com civitat Dublin, et infra stapul eiusd civit per viam merchaniz onerauit in quadam naui sexcent coria bouile[?] salsa valor centu, et quinquagint libr sterl ead Coria die, et A: dict transportauit in transmarinas ptes contra form statut in huiusmod casu provis. Et ulter dic qd. dict Petrus Weybrand non monstrauit dict coria nec eor aliquod dicto maior, aut constabul, nec eor alicui nec aliqua Intraconem fec de pred. Corys in stapul predict nec aliqua licentia habuit de prefat maior aut constabul, aut de eor aliquo ad mcand aut ad transportand dict Coria, aut eor aliquid. Et super hoc precept fuit per prefat maior, et constabul dict staple vic com civit Dublin pred qd.

[Dc 2 f. 274v]

The said jury doe present Daniel Weybrand of the same for that he the 30 day of January 1628 laded 24 barrelles of tallow and transported them beyond the seas.

The said jury doe present John Hunte of St Patricke Streete for that hee the 30 day of January 1628 laided 500 hides and transported them beyond the seas.

The said jury doe present Phillip Watson of the same for that hee the 30 day of January 1628 laded 30 sackes of woole and flockes and transported them beyond the seas.

SELECT BIBLIOGRAPHY

Manuscript sources:

Ireland:
Dublin City Archives
Dc1 - Register of Staple Staple, February 1597-June 1630
Dc2 - Register of Staple Staple, August 1615-December 1666
Dc3 - Register of Staple Staple, January 1665-June1678
Dc4 - Minute Book, 1713-1753

National Archives
C.3471 - Legal proceedings involving the Colvill family
D. 15,237-D.15,248 - Colvill Family Papers
NA 2/446/5/137-138 - Equity Exchequer Orders, 1604-73
RC 6/1-6/2 - Transcripts of the Chancery Decree Books

National Library of Ireland
Ormond Deeds (typed listings shelved in the Manuscript Reading Room)
MS 6,240 - General rental for Boyle estate, 1639-40
MS 6,897-6,900 - Boyle estate rentals, 1626-1645

England:
British Library
Additional MSS 15,635 - Original register of statutes staple in the office of the clerk of the recognizance of the Court of Chancery in Dublin, November 1641-December 1668
Additional MSS 15,636 - Original register of statutes staple in the office of the clerk of the recognizance of the Court of Chancery in Dublin, May 1659-March 1674
Additional MSS 15,637 - Original register of statutes staple in the office of the clerk of the recognizance of the Court of Chancery in Dublin, January 1671-June 1687
Additional MSS 19,843 - Register of the statute staple of different Irish cities kept by the clerk of the recognizance of the Court of Chancery in Dublin, October 1618-March 1679
Additional MSS 19,844 - Register of the statute staple of different Irish cities kept by the clerk of the recognizance of the Court of Chancery in Dublin, May 1668-November 1678
Additional MSS 46,920-46,951, 46,960, 47,035, 47,038 - Percival Estate Papers

Primary sources:
'A supplement to the London inhabitants list of 1695 compiled by staff at Guildhall Library' in *Guildhall Studies in London History*, 11:2 (1976)

Ainsworth, John, 'Some abstracts of Chancery suits relating to Ireland' in *Journal of the Royal Society of Antiquaries of Ireland*, 9 (1939)

An index to Griffith's Valuation which is now available on CD ROM (Baltimore, 1998)

Blake Butler, T., 'Chancery Bills 1610-1634' in *Journal of the Butler Society*, 3 (1991)

Bolton, Richard, *The statutes of Ireland . . .* (Dublin, 1621)

Calendar of state papers, domestic series

Calendar of state papers relating to Ireland

Caulfield, Richard, ed., *The Council of the Corporation of Youghal* (Guildford, Surrey, 1878)

—, *The Council Book of the Corporation of the city of Cork* (Guildford, Surrey, 1876)

General Alphabetical Index to the Townlands and Towns, parishes, and baronies of Ireland (Dublin, 1861; reprinted Baltimore Maryland, 1984)

Gilbert, J. T., *Historical Manuscripts Commission. Tenth Report. Appendix V*

Gilbert, J. T., ed., *Calendar of the ancient records of Dublin . . .* (17 vols., Dublin, 1889-1916)

Gillespie, Raymond, ed., *Settlement and Survival on an Ulster estate. The Brownlow Leasebook 1667-1711* (Belfast, 1988)

Goblet, Y. M., ed., *Index of Parishes and Townlands of Ireland from seventeenth century Maps* (Irish Manuscripts Commission, 1932)

Gogarty, T., ed., *Council book of the corporation of Drogheda* (Dundalk, 1988)

Griffith, M. C., ed., *Irish Patent Rolls of James I* (Irish Manuscripts Commission, Dublin, 1966)

Grosart, A. B., ed., *Lismore papers* (5 vols., np, 1886)

Hickson, Mary, ed., *Selections from Old Kerry Records* (2 vols., London, 1872 and 1874)

Historical Manuscripts Commission. Report on the Manuscripts of the Earl of Egmont (2 vols., London, 1905)

Larkin, James F., and Hughes, Paul L., eds., *Stuart Royal Proclamations* vol. 1 *Royal Proclamations of King James I 1603-1625* (London, 1973)

Journals of the [Irish] House of Commons 1613-1661 vol. 1 (Dublin, 1763)

Journals of the [Irish] House of Lords 1634-1698 vol. 1 (Dublin, 1779)

Morrin, James, ed., *Calendar of the Patent and Close Rolls of Chancery. . . of the reign of Charles I* (London, 1863)

Pender, Seamus, ed., *A census of Ireland circa 1659* (Irish Manuscripts Commission, 1939)

— *Council books of the Corporation of Waterford 1662-1700* (Irish Manuscripts Commission, Dublin, 1964)

Petty, Sir William, *The Political Anatomy of Ireland*, ed., John Donovan (Shannon, 1970)

Rich, E. E., ed., *The Ordinance book of the merchants of the staple* (Cambridge, 1937)

— *The Staple Court Books of Bristol* (Bristol Record Society, vol. 5, Bristol, 1934)

Tallon, Geraldine, 'Act of Settlement 1662. Court of Claims' (Irish Manuscripts Commission, forthcoming)

The Statutes at Large from Magna Carta to the end of the last Parliament, 1761 (8 vols., London, 1763)

Young, Robert M., ed., *Historical Notices of Old Belfast and its vicinity* (Belfast, 1896)

— *The Town book of the corporation of Belfast 1613-1816* (Belfast, 1892)

Secondary sources:

Agnew, Jean, *Belfast Merchant Families in the Seventeenth Century* (Dublin, 1996)

Allen, Robert, 'The price of freehold land and the interest rate in the 17th and 18th centuries' in *Economic History Review*, 2nd series, 41:1 (1988)

Anderson, B. L., 'Money and the structure of credit in the eighteenth century' in *Business History* 12 (1970)

Andrews, J. H., '"More suitable to the English tongue": the cartography of Celtic placenames' in *Ulster Local Studies*, 14:2 (1992)

Armstrong, E. C. R., *Irish seal-matrices and seals* (Dublin, 1913)

Arnold, L. J., 'Valentine Greatrakes: a seventeenth-century 'touch doctor'' in *Eire-Ireland* 11:1 (1976)

Ashton, T. S., *An economic history of England: the eighteenth century* (London, 1955)

Baker, J. H., *An introduction to English legal history* (London, 1979)

Ball, F. E., *History of the County of Dublin in four parts* (Dublin, 1902)

Barnard, T. C., 'Lawyers and the law in later seventeenth-century Ireland' in *Irish Historical Studies*, 28: 111 (1993), pp. 256-82.

Beavan, E., *The Aldermen of the city of London* (2 vols., London, 1913)

Benn, George, *A History of the town of Belfast* (London, 1877)

Brady, Ciaran and Gillespie, Raymond eds., *Natives and Newcomers* (Dublin, 1986)

Brown, J. J., 'The social, political and economic influence of the Edinburgh merchant elite 1600-1638' (unpublished Ph.D. thesis, Edinburgh, 1985)

Brown, James, 'Merchant princes and mercantile investment in early seventeenth century Scotland' in M. Lynch, ed., *The early modern town in Scotland* (Wolfeboro, New Hampshire, 1987)

Burke, John, ed., *Jowitt's Dictionary of English Law* (London, 1977)

Canny, Nicholas, 'What really happened in 1641' in Jane Ohlmeyer, ed., *Ireland from independence to occupation, 1641-1660* (Cambridge, 1995)

— 'The 1641 Depositions as a source for the writing of Social History: County Cork as a Case Study' in Patrick O'Flanagan and Cornelius G. Buttimer, eds., *Cork. History and Society* (Dublin, 1993)

Casway, Jerrold, 'Two Phelim O'Neills' in *Seanchas Ardmhacha*, XI, no. 2 (1985)

Cheney, C. R., ed., *Handbook of dates* (London, 1978)

G. E. C[okayne], *Complete peerage of England, Scotland, Ireland, Great Britain and the United Kingdom* (8 vols., London, 1887-98; revised edn., 14 vols., 1910-59)

Cotton, Henry, *Fastic ecclesiae Hibernicae: the succession of the prelates and members of the ecclesiastical bodies in Ireland* (6 vols., Dublin, 1845-78).

Cregan, Donal, 'Irish Catholic admissions to the English Inns of Court, 1558-1625' in *Irish Jurist* (summer, 1970)

—— 'Irish Recusant lawyers in politics in the reign of James I' in *Irish Jurist* (winter, 1970)

Cullen, Louis, *An economic history of Ireland since 1660* (London, 1972)

D'Alton, John, *The History of Drogheda* (2 vols in 1, Dublin, 1863)

—— *The History of the County of Dublin* (Dublin, 1838)

The Dictionary of National Biography

R. Dudley Edwards, 'The beginnings of municipal government in Dublin' in *Dublin Historical Record* 1 (1938-9)

Floud, Roderick, *An introduction to quantative methods for historians* (London, 1973)

Fryde, E. B., Greenway, D. E., Porter, S. and Roy, I., eds., *The Handbook of British Chronology* (3rd edn., London, 1986)

Gay Davies, Margaret, 'Country gentry and payments to London 1650-1714' in *Economic History Review* 24:1 (1971)

Gibson, A. J. S. and Smout, T. C., eds., *Prices, food and wages in Scotland 1550-1780* (Cambridge, 1995)

Gillespie, Raymond, *Thomas Howell and his friends: Serving Christ Church Cathedral, Dublin, 1570-1700* (Dublin, 1997)

—— 'The Irish Economy at War' in Ohlmeyer, ed., *Ireland*, pp. 165-6.

—— 'The murder of Arthur Champion and the 1641 rising in Fermanagh' in *Clogher Record* 14 (1993)

—— *The Transformation of the Irish Economy 1550-1700* (Dundalk, 1991)

—— 'Peter French's petition for an Irish mint' in *Irish Historical Studies*, 25: 100 (1987)

Hardiman, J., *The History of the Town and County of Galway* (Galway, 1958)

Hardy Ivamy, E. R., ed., *Mozley and Whiteley's Law Dictionary* (London, 1988)

Harvey, Charles and Press, Jon, *Databases in Historical Research* (London, 1996)

Healy, William, *History and Antiquities of Kilkenny* (Kilkenny, 1893)

Herbert, Robert, 'The trade guilds of Limerick' in *North Munster Antiquarian Journal* 2: 3 (spring, 1941)

Holdsworth, W. S., *A History of English Law* (17 vols., 2nd edn, London, 1965)

Hore, P. H., *History of town and county of Wexford* (6 vols., London, 1900-1911)

Jones, W. J., *The Elizabethan Court of Chancery* (Oxford, 1967)

Kerridge, E., *Trade and banking in early modern England* (Manchester, 1988)

Kew, J. E., 'Mortgages in mid-Tudor Devonshire' in *Transactions of the Devonshire Association* 99 (1967)

Latham, R. E., *Revised medieval Latin word list from British and Irish sources* (Oxford, 1965)

Lenihan, Maurice, *Limerick its history and antiquities* (Dublin, 1866)

Lennon, Colm, *The Lords of Dublin in the Age of Reformation* (Dublin, 1989)

Lodge, J., *The peerage of Ireland; or a genealogical history of the present nobility of that kingdom. . .* (4 vols., Dublin, 1754).

MacCarthy-Morrogh, Michael, 'Credit and Remittance: Monetary Problems in early seventeenth-century Munster' in *Irish Economic and Social History* 14 (1987)

Macinnes, Allan I., Clanship, *Commerce and the house of Stuart, 1603-1788* (Edinburgh, 1996).

MacNiven, Duncan, 'Merchant and trader in early seventeenth century Aberdeen' (unpublished M.Litt thesis, Aberdeen, 1977)

McGrath, Bríd, 'A biographical dictionary of the Irish House of Commons 1640-1641' (Trinity College Dublin, Ph.D. Thesis, 1998)

—, 'The membership of the Irish House of Commons 1613-1615' (Trinity College Dublin, M. Litt. Thesis, 1986)

M'Skimin, Samuel, T*he History and Antiquities of the County of the Town of Carrickfergus* (Belfast, 1823)

Moody, T. W. and Vaughan, W. E., eds., *A New History of Ireland* vol iv. *Eighteenth-Century Ireland 1691-1800* (Oxford, 1986)

Moody, T. W., Martin, F. X., and Byrne, F. J., eds., *A New History of Ireland*, vol. ix, *Maps, genealogies, lists* (Oxford, 1984)

Muldrew, Craig, 'The culture of reconciliation: community and the settlement of economic disputes in early modern England' in *Historical Journal* 39:4 (1996)

—, 'Credit and the courts: debt litigation in a seventeenth century urban community' in *Economic History Review* 46: 1 (1993)

O'Brien, George, *The Economic History of Ireland in the eighteenth century* (London, 1918, reprinted, Philadelphia, 1977)

—, *The Economic History of Ireland in the seventeenth century* (London, 1919, reprinted, Clifton, NJ, 1972)

— 'The Irish Staple Organization in the Reign of James I' in *Economic History* 1 (1926-9)

O'Hart, J., *Irish and Anglo-Irish gentry when Cromwell came to Ireland* (Dublin, 1884; later edn 1892)

Ohlmeyer, Jane, *Civil War and Restoration in the Three Stuart Kingdoms* (Cambridge, 1993)

O'Rorke, T., *The History of Sligo: Town and County* (2 vols., Dublin, 1890)

O'Sullivan, M. D., *Old Galway* (Cambridge, 1942; reprinted, 1982)

O'Sullivan, William, *The Economic History of Cork City* (Cork, 1937)

Rich, E. E., 'The Mayors of the Staples' in *Cambridge Historical Journal* 4:2 (1933)

— and Wilson, C. H., ed., *The Cambridge Economic History of Europe* vol 5 *The Economic organization of early modern Europe* (Cambridge, 1977)

Richards, R. B., 'The Pioneers of banking in England' in *Economic History* 1:4 (1929)

Ryan, James G. ed., *Irish Church Records. Their history, availability and use in family and local history research* (Dublin, 1992)

Smith, Charles, *The Antient and present state of the county and city of Waterford* (Dublin, 1846)

Smout, T. C., 'The Glasgow merchant community in the seventeenth century' in *Scottish Historical Review* 48 (1968)

Strickland, W. G., 'The Ancient Official Seals of the City of Dublin' in *The Journal of the Royal Society of Antiquaries* 53 (1923)

Styles, J., 'Our traitorous money makers' in J. Brewer and J. Styles, eds., *An ungovernable people: the English and their law* (New Brunswick, NJ, 1980)

Townend, Peter, ed., *Burke's Peerage, Baronetage and Knightage* (2 vols., London, 1970)

Trevor-Roper, H. R., 'The Elizabethan Aristocracy' in *Economic History Review*, 2nd series, 3:3 (1951)

Walton, Julian C., 'The freemen of Waterford, 1542-1650' in *The Irish Genealogist* 5:5 (1978)

Webb, John J., *Municipal government in Ireland* (Dublin, 1918)

Wrigley, E. A., ed., *Identifying people in the past* (London, 1973)

—, *An introduction to English historical demography from the sixteenth to the nineteenth century* (London, 1966)